Presented
to

_____

by

_____

on

_____

The Amplified Bible

Containing the
AMPLIFIED NEW TESTAMENT

ZONDERVAN PUBLISHING HOUSE
GRAND RAPIDS, MICHIGAN

Library of Congress Catalog Card Number 87–50612
Published by Zondervan Publishing House
Grand Rapids, Michigan 49530, U.S.A.
http://www.zondervan.com
Printed in the United States of America
All rights reserved

97 98 99 00 01 02 15 14 13 12 11

In 1958 The Lockman Foundation and Zondervan Publishing House issued the first edition of The Amplified New Testament after more than 20,000 hours of research and prayerful study. Some four years later the first of two Old Testament volumes appeared (The Amplified Old Testament, Part Two—Job to Malachi), followed in 1964 by the publication of The Amplified Old Testament, Part One—Genesis to Esther. The next year (1965) The Amplified Bible came out in one volume.

The purpose of all the characters in the story of the making of The Amplified Bible is still relevant today: to communicate the Word of God to people and to exalt Jesus Christ. This has been the fourfold aim of The Lockman Foundation from the beginning:

1. These publications shall be true to the original Hebrew, Aramaic and Greek.
2. They shall be grammatically correct.
3. They shall be understandable to the masses.
4. They shall give the Lord Jesus Christ His proper place, the place which the Word gives Him.

From the days of John Wycliffe (1329-1384) and the first English Bible to the present, translators have worked diligently on English versions designed to faithfully present the Scriptures in contemporary language. The Amplified Bible is not an attempt to duplicate what has already been achieved, nor is it intended to be a substitute for other translations. Its genius lies in its rigorous attempt to go beyond the traditional "word-for-word" concept of translation to bring out the richness of the Hebrew and Greek languages. In a sense, the creative use of amplification merely helps the reader comprehend what the Hebrew and Greek listener instinctively understood (as a matter of course).

Take as an example the Greek word *pisteuo*, which the vast majority of versions render "believe." That simple translation, however, hardly does justice to the many meanings contained in the Greek *pisteuo*: "to adhere to, cleave to; to trust, to have faith in; to rely on, to depend on." Consequently, the reader gains understanding through the use of amplification, as in John 11:25: "Jesus said to her, I am [Myself] the Resurrection and the Life. Whoever believes in (adheres to, trusts in, and relies on) Me, although he may die, yet he shall live."

INTRODUCTION

TO THE
AMPLIFIED
BIBLE

About The Amplified Bible

The story of The Amplified Bible is a remarkable story of faith, hope, and love. It's the story of a woman, a foundation, a committee, and a publisher. Commitment, energy, enthusiasm, giftedness—these are the words that paint the picture, the picture of the making of a translation.

Frances Siewert (Litt. B., B.D., M.A., Litt. D.) was a woman with an intense dedication to the study of the Bible. It was Mrs. Siewert (1881-1967) who laid the foundation of The Amplified Bible, devoting her life to a familiarity with the Bible, with the Hebrew and Greek languages, and with the cultural and archaeological background of Biblical times, which would result in the publication of this unique translation.

Every vision needs visionaries willing to follow the cause. The story of this dream is no different. Mrs. Siewert's vision was seen by a California non-profit foundation called The Lockman Foundation, made up of Christian men and women who through their commitment, their expertise, and their financial support undergirded Mrs. Siewert's monumental translation project. The Lockman Foundation's purpose remains today what it was then: to promote Bible translation, Christian evangelism, education, and benevolence.

Commitment, energy, enthusiasm, giftedness—the things visions are made of—describes the efforts of the committee appointed by The Lockman Foundation to carefully review the impressive work of Mrs. Siewert. This Editorial Board, made up of dedicated people, lent credibility and organization to this unprecedented attempt to bring out the richness of the Hebrew and Greek languages within the English text itself.

One chapter yet remained to bring the vision into reality. A publishing house in Grand Rapids, Michigan, on its way to becoming a major religious publishing firm, seized the opportunity to participate in a project which all visionaries involved strongly believed would be used by God to change lives. The Zondervan Publishing House joined the team, and the dream became reality with the publication of The Amplified New Testament in 1958, followed by the two-volume Amplified Old Testament in 1962 and 1964, and the one-volume Amplified Bible in 1965.

Features of The Amplified New Testament

The Amplified New Testament features the text of The Amplified New Testament, with explanatory footnotes; a reference system contained within the text; and a comprehensive bibliography of original sources cited in the footnotes.

THE TEXT OF THE AMPLIFIED NEW TESTAMENT

The text of The Amplified New Testament is easy to understand, and is made even easier to understand by the inclusion of informative footnotes which often alert readers to different textual readings and give insight into

Greek grammar and translation. Numerous Bible translations are among the
sources cited in the footnotes, as well as some of the greatest lexicographers
of all time and some of the best of Bible commentators.

To help readers achieve the greatest possible clarity and understanding in
their reading of the text of The Amplified New Testament, some explanation
of the various markings within the text is necessary:

Parentheses ( ) signify additional phases of meaning included in the original
word, phrase, or clause of the original language.

Brackets [ ] contain justified clarifying words or comments not actually
expressed in the immediate original text, as well as definitions of Greek
names.

Italics point out:
1. certain familiar passages now recognized as not adequately supported
   by the original manuscripts. This is the primary use of italics in the
   New Testament, so that, upon encountering italics, the reader is
   alerted to a matter of textual readings. Often these will be
   accompanied by a footnote. See as an example Matthew 16:2-3.
2. conjunctions such as "and," "or," and the like, not in the original text,
   but used to connect additional English words indicated in the same
   original word. In this use, the reader, upon encountering a conjunction
   in italics, is alerted to the addition of an amplified word or phrase.
   See as an example Acts 24:3.

Capitals are used:
1. in names and personal pronouns referring to the Deity. See as an
   example 1 Peter 2:6.
2. in proper names of persons, places, specific feasts, topographical
   names, personifications, and the like. See as an example John 7:2.

Abbreviations may on occasion be encountered in either the text or in the
footnotes:
cf. compare, confer
ch., chs. chapter, chapters
e.g. for example
etc. and so on
i.e. that is
v., vv. verse, verses
ff. following
ft. foot
c. about
KJV King James Version
RV Revised Version
ASV American Standard Version

THE REFERENCE SYSTEM

The reference system of The Amplified New Testament is contained
within the text. The Scripture references are placed within brackets at the end
of a verse, and are intended to cover any part of the preceding verse to which
they apply. If a verse contains more than one Scripture reference, the list of
references is in Biblical order.

THE BIBLIOGRAPHY

A comprehensive, though not exhaustive, bibliography of original sources cited in the footnotes is included in the back of the Bible. The bibliography lists basic information such as author or editor/editors, book or periodical title, publisher (and location of publisher), and date of publication. For more information on the bibliography, see the introduction to the bibliography.

TABLE OF CONTENTS

The New Testament

The New
Testament

THE GOSPEL ACCORDING TO
MATTHEW

CHAPTER 1

THE BOOK of the ancestry (gene-alogy) of Jesus Christ (the Messiah, the Anointed), the son (descendant) of David, the son (descendant) of Abraham. [Ps. 132:11; Isa. 11:1.]

2 Abraham was the father of Isaac, Isaac the father of Jacob, Jacob the father of Judah and his brothers,

3 Judah the father of Perez and Zerah, whose mother was Tamar, Perez the father of Hezron, Hezron the father of Aram,

4 Aram the father of Aminadab, Aminadab the father of Nahshon, Nahshon the father of Salmon,

5 Salmon the father of Boaz, whose mother was Rahab, Boaz the father of Obed, whose mother was Ruth, Obed the father of Jesse,

6 Jesse the father of King David, King David the father of Solomon, whose mother had been the wife of Uriah, [Ruth 4:18–22; I Chron. 2:13–15.]

7 Solomon the father of Rehoboam, Rehoboam the father of Abijah, Abijah the father of Asa,

8 Asa the father of Jehoshaphat, Jehoshaphat the father of Joram [Jehoram], Joram the father of Uzziah,

9 Uzziah the father of Jotham, Jotham the father of Ahaz, Ahaz the father of Hezekiah,

10 Hezekiah the father of Manasseh, Manasseh the father of Amon, Amon the father of Josiah,

11 And Josiah became the father of Jeconiah [also called C

hoiachin] and his brothers about the time of the removal (deportation) to Babylon. [II Kings 24:14; I Chron. 3:15, 16.]

12 After the exile to Babylon, Jeconiah became the father of Shealtiel [Salathiel], Shealtiel the father of Zerubbabel,

13 Zerubbabel the father of Ahiud, Ahiud the father of Eliakim, Eliakim the father of Azor,

14 Azor the father of Sadoc, Sadoc the father of Achim, Achim the father of Eliud,

15 Eliud the father of Eleazar, Eleazar the father of Matthan, Matthan the father of Jacob,

16 Jacob the father of Joseph, the husband of Mary, of whom was born Jesus, Who is called the Christ.

17 So all the generations from Abraham to David are fourteen, from David to the Babylonian exile (deportation) fourteen generations, from the Babylonian exile to the Christ fourteen generations.

18 Now the birth of Jesus Christ took place under these circumstances: When His mother Mary had been promised in marriage to Joseph, before they came together, she was found to be pregnant [through the power] of the Holy Spirit.

19 And her [promised] husband Joseph, being an upright man and not willing to expose her publicly and disgrace her, decided to repudiate and dismiss (divorce) her quietly and secretly.

But as he was thinking this over, behold, an angel of the Lord appeared to him in a dream, saying, Joseph, descendant of David, do not be afraid to take Mary [as] your wife, for that which is conceived in her is of (from, out of) the Holy Spirit.

21 She will bear a Son, and you shall call His name Jesus [the Greek form of the Hebrew Joshua, which means Savior], for He will save His people from their sins [that is, prevent them from ªfailing and missing the true end and scope of life, which is God].

22 All this took place that it might be fulfilled which the Lord had spoken through the prophet,

23 Behold, the virgin shall become pregnant and give birth to a Son, and they shall call His name Emmanuel —which, when translated, means, God with us. [Isa. 7:14.]

24 When Joseph, being aroused from his sleep, did as the angel of the Lord had commanded him: he took [her to his side as] his wife.

25 But he had no union with her as her husband until she had borne *her firstborn* Son; and he called His name Jesus.

CHAPTER 2

N OW WHEN Jesus was born in Bethlehem of Judea in the days of Herod the king, behold, wise men [astrologers] from the east came to Jerusalem, asking,

2 Where is He Who has been born King of the Jews? For we have seen His star in the east ᵇat its rising and have come to worship Him. [Num. ▪▪ 17; Jer. 23:5; Zech. 9:9.]

he wasⁿ Herod the king heard this, the whole ᵗᵘⁱbed *and* troubled, and 4 So he calⁿ▪▪lem with him.

priests and learned men (scribes) of the people and ᶜanxiously asked them where the Christ was to be born.

5 They replied to him, In Bethlehem of Judea, for so it is written by the prophet:

6 And you Bethlehem, in the land of Judah, you are not in any way least *or* insignificant among the ᵈchief cities of Judah; for from you shall come a Ruler (ᵉLeader) Who will govern *and* ᶠshepherd My people Israel. [Mic. 5:2.]

7 Then Herod sent for the wise men [astrologers] secretly, and ᶠaccurately to the last point ascertained from them the time of the appearing of the star [that is, ʰhow long the star had made itself visible since its rising in the east].

8 Then he sent them to Bethlehem, saying, Go and search for the Child carefully *and* diligently, and when you have found ᵍHim, bring me word, that I too may come and worship Him.

9 When they had listened to the king, they went their way, and behold, the star which had been seen in the east ᵇin its rising went before them until it came and stood over the place where the young Child was.

10 When they saw the star, they were thrilled with ecstatic joy.

11 And on going into the house, they saw the Child with Mary His mother, and they fell down and worshiped Him. Then opening their treasure bags, they presented to Him gifts—gold and frankincense and myrrh.

12 And ᶠreceiving an answer to their asking, they were divinely instructed *and* warned in a dream not

a Marvin Vincent, *Word Studies*.
Williams, *The New Testament*
Greek-English Lexicon of the ▪▪
Vocabulary of the Greek Testame.▪▪▪
what He is, the spotless Son of God, ▪▪▪

b Alternate translation.   c Charles B.
▪▪▪ *New Testament.*   d Joseph Henry Thayer, *A*
▪▪ the Language of the People.   e James Hope Moulton and George Milligan, *The*
▪▪cent, *Word Studies.*   g Capitalized because of
▪▪ay have thought He was.

to go back to Herod; so they departed to their own country by a different way.

13 Now after they had gone, behold, an angel of the Lord appeared to Joseph in a dream and said, Get up! [hTenderly] take *unto you* the young Child and His mother and flee to Egypt; and remain there till I tell you [otherwise], for Herod intends to search for the Child in order to destroy Him.

14 And having risen, he took the Child and His mother by night and withdrew to Eygpt

15 And remained there until Herod's death. This was to fulfill what the Lord had spoken by the prophet, Out of Egypt have I called My Son. [Hos. 11:1.]

16 Then Herod, when he realized that he had been misled by the wise men, was furiously enraged, and he sent and put to death all the male children in Bethlehem and in all that territory who were two years old and under, reckoning according to the date which he had investigated diligently *and* had learned exactly from the wise men.

17 Then was fulfilled what was spoken by the prophet Jeremiah:

18 A voice was heard in Ramah, wailing and loud lamentation, Rachel weeping for her children; she refused to be comforted, because they were no more. [Jer. 31:15.]

19 But when Herod died, behold, an angel of the Lord appeared in a dream to Joseph in Egypt

20 And said, Rise, [htenderly] take *unto you* the Child and His mother and go to the land of Israel, for those who sought the Child's life are dead.

21 Then he awoke and arose and [htenderly] took the Child and His mother and came into the land of Israel.

22 But because he heard that Archelaus was ruling over Judea in the place of his father Herod, he was afraid to go there. And being divinely warned in a dream, he withdrew to the region of Galilee.

23 He went and dwelt in a town called Nazareth, so that what was spoken through the prophets might be fulfilled: He shall be called a Nazarene [Branch, Separated One]. [Isa. 11:1.]

CHAPTER 3

IN THOSE days there appeared John the Baptist, preaching in the Wilderness (Desert) of Judea

2 And saying, Repent (ithink differently; change your mind, regretting your sins and changing your conduct), for the kingdom of heaven is at hand.

3 This is he who was mentioned by the prophet Isaiah when he said, The voice of one crying in the wilderness [shouting in the desert], Prepare the road for the Lord, make His highways straight (level, jdirect). [Isa. 40:3.]

4 This *same* John's garments were made of camel's hair, and he wore a leather girdle about his waist; and his food was locusts and wild honey. [Lev. 11:22; II Kings 1:8; Zech. 13:4.]

5 Then Jerusalem and all Judea and all the country round about the Jordan went out to him;

6 And they were baptized in the Jordan by him, confessing their sins.

7 But when he saw many of the Pharisees and Sadducees coming for baptism, he said to them, You brood of vipers! Who warned you to flee *and* escape from the wrath *and* indig-

h Charles B. Williams, *The New Testament: A Translation.* Abbott-Smith, *Manual Greek Lexicon of the New Testament.*   i Marvin Vincent, *Word Studies.*   j G.

nation [of God against disobedience] that is coming?

8 Bring forth fruit that is consistent with repentance [let your lives prove your change of heart];

9 And do not presume to say to yourselves, We have Abraham for our forefather; for I tell you, God is able to raise up descendants for Abraham from these stones!

10 And already the ax is lying at the root of the trees; every tree therefore that does not bear good fruit is cut down and thrown into the fire.

11 I indeed baptize you [k]in (with) water [l]because of repentance [that is, because of your [m]changing your minds for the better, heartily amending your ways, with abhorrence of your past sins]. But He Who is coming after me is mightier than I, Whose sandals I am not worthy or fit to take off or carry; He will baptize you with the Holy Spirit and with fire.

12 His winnowing fan (shovel, fork) is in His hand, and He will thoroughly clear out and clean His threshing floor and gather and store His wheat in His barn, but the chaff He will burn up with fire that cannot be put out.

13 Then Jesus came from Galilee to the Jordan to John to be baptized by him.

14 But John [n]protested strenuously, having in mind to prevent Him, saying, It is I who have need to be baptized by You, and do You come to me?

15 But Jesus replied to him, [m]Permit it just now; for this is the fitting way for [both of] us to fulfill all righteousness [that is, to [m]perform completely whatever is right]. Then he permitted Him.

16 And when Jesus was baptized, He went up at once out of the water; and behold, the heavens were opened, and he [John] saw the Spirit of God descending like a dove and alighting on Him.

17 And behold, a voice from heaven said, This is My Son, My Beloved, in Whom I delight! [Ps. 2:7; Isa. 42:1.]

CHAPTER 4

THEN JESUS was led (guided) by the [Holy] Spirit into the wilderness (desert) to be tempted (tested and tried) by the devil.

2 And He went without food for forty days and forty nights, and later He was hungry. [Exod. 34:28; I Kings 19:8.]

3 And the tempter came and said to Him, If You are God's Son, command these stones to be made [o]loaves of] bread.

4 But He replied, It has been written, Man shall not live and be upheld and sustained by bread alone, but by every word that comes forth from the mouth of God. [Deut. 8:3.]

5 Then the devil took Him into the holy city and placed Him on [p]a turret (pinnacle, [q]gable) of the temple [r]sanctuary. [Neh. 11:1; Dan. 9:24.]

6 And he said to Him, If You are the Son of God, throw Yourself down; for it is written, He will give His angels charge over you, and they will bear you up on their hands, lest you strike your foot against a stone. [Ps. 91:11, 12.]

7 Jesus said to him, [n]On the other

k En, the preposition used here, is translated both "in" and "with" in the Greek lexicons and concordances generally. The King James Version (the Authorized Version) gives preference to "with," putting "in" in the margin; the American Standard Version gives preference to "in," putting "with" in the margin. Many modern versions choose one or the other about equally.　l Charles B. Williams, The New Testament: A Translation.　m Joseph Thayer, A Greek-English Lexicon.　n Marvin Vincent, Word Studies. o John Wycliffe, The Wycliffe Bible.　p G. Abbott-Smith, Manual Greek Lexicon.　q James Moulton and George Milligan, The Vocabulary.　r Richard Trench, Synonyms of the New Testament.

hand, it is written also, You shall not tempt, *test thoroughly, *or *try exceedingly the Lord your God. [Deut. 6:16.]

8 Again, the devil took Him up on a very high mountain and showed Him all the kingdoms of the world and the glory (the splendor, magnificence, preeminence, and excellence) of them.

9 And he said to Him, These things, all taken together, I will give You, if You will prostrate Yourself before me and do homage *and worship me.

10 Then Jesus said to him, Begone, Satan! For it has been written, You shall worship the Lord your God, and Him alone shall you serve. [Deut. 6:13.]

11 Then the devil departed from Him, and behold, angels came and ministered to Him.

12 Now when Jesus heard that John had been arrested *and put in prison, He withdrew into Galilee.

13 And leaving Nazareth, He went *and dwelt in Capernaum by the sea, in the country of Zebulun and Naphtali—

14 That what was spoken by the prophet Isaiah might be brought to pass:

15 The land of Zebulun and the land of Naphtali, in the *way to the sea, beyond the Jordan, Galilee of the Gentiles [of the *peoples who are not of Israel]— [Isa. 9:1–2.]

16 The people who sat *(dwelt enveloped) in darkness have seen a great Light, and for those who sat in the land and shadow of death Light has dawned.

17 From that time Jesus began to preach, *crying out, Repent (*change your mind for the better, heartily amend your ways, with abhorrence of your past sins), for the kingdom of heaven is at hand.

18 As He was walking by the Sea of Galilee, He noticed two brothers, Simon who is called Peter and Andrew his brother, throwing a dragnet into the sea, for they were fishermen.

19 And He said to them, Come *after Me [as disciples—letting Me be your Guide], follow Me, and I will make you fishers of men!

20 At once they left their nets and *became His disciples [sided with His party and followed Him].

21 And going on further from there He noticed two other brothers, James son of Zebedee and his brother John, in the boat with their father Zebedee, mending their nets *and putting them right; and He called them.

22 At once they left the boat and their father and *joined Jesus as disciples [sided with His party and followed Him].

23 And He went about all Galilee, teaching in their synagogues and preaching the good news (Gospel) of the kingdom, and healing every disease and every weakness *and infirmity among the people.

24 So the report of Him spread throughout all Syria, and they brought Him all who were sick, those afflicted with various diseases and torments, those under the power of demons, and epileptics, and paralyzed people, and He healed them.

25 And great crowds joined *and accompanied Him about, coming from Galilee and Decapolis [the district of the ten cities east of the Sea of Galilee] and Jerusalem and Judea and from the other [the east] side of the Jordan.

s Joseph Thayer, *A Greek-English Lexicon.*   t Robert Young, *Analytical Concordance to the Bible.*   u Hermann Cremer, *Biblico-Theological Lexicon of New Testament Greek.*   v John Wycliffe, *The Wycliffe Bible.*   w Marvin Vincent, *Word Studies.*

CHAPTER 5

S EEING THE crowds, He went
up on the mountain; and when
He was seated, His disciples came to
Him.

2 Then He opened His mouth and
taught them, saying:

3 Blessed (happy, ˣto be envied,
and ʸspiritually prosperous—ᶻwith
life-joy and satisfaction in God's favor and salvation, regardless of their
outward conditions) are the poor in
spirit (the humble, who rate themselves insignificant), for theirs is the
kingdom of heaven!

4 Blessed *and* enviably happy
[with a ᶻhappiness produced by the
experience of God's favor and especially conditioned by the revelation
of His matchless grace] are those
who mourn, for they shall be comforted! [Isa. 61:2.]

5 Blessed (happy, blithesome, joyous, ʸspiritually prosperous—ᶻwith
life-joy and satisfaction in God's favor and salvation, regardless of their
outward conditions) are the meek
(the mild, patient, long-suffering), for
they shall inherit the earth! [Ps.
37:11.]

6 Blessed *and* fortunate *and* happy
and ʸspiritually prosperous (in that
state in which the born-again child of
God ᶻenjoys His favor and salvation)
are those who hunger and thirst for
righteousness (uprightness and right
standing with God), for they shall be
ʸcompletely satisfied! [Isa. 55:1, 2.]

7 Blessed (happy, ˣto be envied,
and ʸspiritually prosperous—ᶻwith
life-joy and satisfaction in God's favor and salvation, regardless of their
outward conditions) are the merciful,
for they shall obtain mercy!

8 Blessed (happy, ᵃenviably fortunate, and ʸspiritually prosperous—

possessing the ᶻhappiness produced
by the experience of God's favor and
especially conditioned by the revelation of His grace, regardless of their
outward conditions) are the pure in
heart, for they shall see God! [Ps.
24:3, 4.]

9 Blessed (enjoying ᵃenviable happiness, ʸspiritually prosperous—
ᶻwith life-joy and satisfaction in
God's favor and salvation, regardless
of their outward conditions) are the
makers *and* ᵇmaintainers of peace,
for they shall be called the sons of
God!

10 Blessed *and* happy *and* ᵃenviably fortunate *and* ʸspiritually prosperous ᶻ(in the state in which the
born-again child of God enjoys and
finds satisfaction in God's favor and
salvation, regardless of his outward
conditions) are those who are persecuted for righteousness' sake (for being and doing right), for theirs is the
kingdom of heaven!

11 Blessed (happy, ˣto be envied,
and ʸspiritually prosperous—ᶻwith
life-joy and satisfaction in God's favor and salvation, regardless of your
outward conditions) are you when
people revile you and persecute you
and say all kinds of evil things against
you falsely on My account.

12 Be glad *and* supremely joyful,
for your reward in heaven is great
(strong and intense), for in this same
way people persecuted the prophets
who were before you. [II Chron.
36:16.]

13 You are the salt of the earth, but
if salt has lost its taste (its strength,
its quality), how can its saltness be
restored? It is not good for anything
any longer but to be thrown out and
trodden underfoot by men.

14 You are the light of the world. A
city set on a hill cannot be hidden.

x Alexander Souter, *Pocket Lexicon of the Greek New Testament.*   y Marvin Vincent, *Word Studies.*
z Hermann Cremer, *Biblico-Theological Lexicon.*   a Alexander Souter, *Pocket Lexicon.*   b William
Tyndale, *The Tyndale Bible.*

15 Nor do men light a lamp and put it under a peck measure, but on a lampstand, and it gives light to all in the house.

16 Let your light so shine before men that they may see your cmoral excellence *and* your praiseworthy, noble, *and* good deeds and crecognize *and* honor *and* praise *and* glorify your Father Who is in heaven.

17 Do not think that I have come to do away with *or* dundo the Law or the Prophets; I have come not to do away with *or* undo but to complete *and* fulfill them.

18 For truly I tell you, until the sky and earth pass away *and* perish, not one smallest letter nor one little hook [identifying certain Hebrew letters] will pass from the Law until all things [it foreshadows] are accomplished.

19 Whoever then breaks *or* does away with *or* relaxes one of the least *important* of these commandments and teaches men so shall be called least *important* in the kingdom of heaven, but he who practices them and teaches others to do so shall be called great in the kingdom of heaven.

20 For I tell you, unless your righteousness (your uprightness and your right standing with God) is more than that of the scribes and Pharisees, you will never enter the kingdom of heaven.

21 You have heard that it was said to the men of old, You shall not kill, and whoever kills shall be cliable to *and* unable to escape the punishment imposed by the court. [Exod. 20:13; Deut. 5:17; 16:18.]

22 But I say to you that everyone who continues to be fangry with his brother *or* harbors malice (enmity of heart) against him shall be cliable to *and* unable to escape the punishment imposed by the court; and whoever speaks contemptuously *and* insultingly to his brother shall be cliable to *and* unable to escape the punishment imposed by the Sanhedrin, and whoever says, You ecursed fool! [You empty-headed idiot]! shall be cliable to *and* unable to escape the hell (Gehenna) of fire.

23 So if when you are offering your gift at the altar you there remember that your brother has any [grievance] against you,

24 Leave your gift at the altar and go. First make peace with your brother, and then come back *and* present your gift.

25 Come to terms quickly with your accuser while you are on the way traveling with him, lest your accuser hand you over to the judge, and the judge to the guard, and you be put in prison.

26 Truly I say to you, you will not be released until you have paid the last fraction of a penny.

27 You have heard that it was said, You shall not commit adultery. [Exod. 20:14; Deut. 5:18.]

28 But I say to you that everyone who so much as looks at a woman with evil desire for her has already committed adultery with her in his heart.

29 If your right eye serves as a trap to ensnare you *or* is an occasion for you to stumble *and* sin, pluck it out and throw it away. It is better that you lose one of your members than that your whole body be cast into hell (Gehenna).

30 And if your right hand serves as a trap to ensnare you *or* is an occasion for you to stumble *and* sin, cut it off and cast it from you. It is better that you lose one of your members

c Hermann Cremer, *Biblico-Theological Lexicon*.   d John Wycliffe, *The Wycliffe Bible*.   e Joseph Thayer, *A Greek-English Lexicon*.   f Some manuscripts insert here: "without cause."   g Charles B. Williams, *The New Testament: A Translation*.

than that your entire body should be cast into hell (Gehenna).

31 It has also been said, Whoever divorces his wife must give her a certificate of divorce.

32 But I tell you, Whoever dismisses *and* repudiates *and* divorces his wife, except on the grounds of unfaithfulness (sexual immorality), causes her to commit adultery, and whoever marries a woman who has been divorced commits adultery. [Deut. 24:1–4.]

33 Again, you have heard that it was said to the men of old, You shall not swear falsely, but you shall perform your oaths to the Lord [as a religious duty].

34 But I tell you, Do not bind yourselves by an oath at all: either by heaven, for it is the throne of God;

35 Or by the earth, for it is the footstool of His feet; or by Jerusalem, for it is the city of the Great King. [Ps. 48:2; Isa. 66:1.]

36 And do not swear by your head, for you are not able to make a single hair white or black.

37 Let your Yes be simply Yes, and your No be simply No; anything more than that comes from the evil one. [Lev. 19:12; Num. 30:2; Deut. 23:21.]

38 You have heard that it was said, An eye for an eye, and a tooth for a tooth. [Exod. 21:24; Lev. 24:20; Deut. 19:21.]

39 But I say to you, Do not resist the evil man [who injures you]; but if anyone strikes you on the right jaw *or* cheek, turn to him the other one too.

40 And if anyone wants to sue you and take your undershirt (tunic), let him have your coat also.

41 And if anyone forces you to go one mile, go with him two [miles].

42 Give to him who keeps on begging from you, and do not turn away from him who would borrow [*h*at interest] from you. [Deut. 15:8; Prov. 24:29.]

43 You have heard that it was said, You shall love your neighbor and hate your enemy; [Lev. 19:18; Ps. 139:21, 22.]

44 But I tell you, Love your enemies and pray for those who persecute you, [Prov. 25:21, 22.]

45 To show that you are the children of your Father Who is in heaven; for He makes His sun rise on the wicked and on the good, and makes the rain fall upon the upright and the wrongdoers [alike].

46 For if you love those who love you, what reward can you have? Do not even the tax collectors do that?

47 And if you greet only your brethren, what more than others are you doing? Do not even the Gentiles (the heathen) do that?

48 You, therefore, must be perfect [growing into complete *j*maturity of godliness in mind and character, *i*having reached the proper height of virtue and integrity], as your heavenly Father is perfect. [Lev. 19:2, 18.]

CHAPTER 6

TAKE CARE not to do your good deeds publicly *or* before men, in order to be seen by them; otherwise you will have no reward [*h*reserved for and awaiting you] with *and* from your Father Who is in heaven.

2 Thus, whenever you give to the poor, do not blow a trumpet before you, as the hypocrites in the synagogues and in the streets like to do, that they may be *k*recognized *and* honored *and* praised by men. Truly I tell you, they have their reward *h*in full already.

3 But when you give to charity, do

h Marvin Vincent, *Word Studies. Word Studies in the New Testament.* i Joseph Thayer, *A Greek-English Lexicon.* j Kenneth Wuest. k Hermann Cremer, *Biblico-Theological Lexicon.*

not let your left hand know what your right hand is doing,

4 So that your deeds of charity may be in secret; and your Father Who sees in secret will reward you *openly*.

5 Also when you pray, you must not be like the hypocrites, for they love to pray standing in the synagogues and on the corners of the streets, that they may be seen by people. Truly I tell you, they have their reward [i]in full already.

6 But when you pray, go into your [most] private room, and, closing the door, pray to your Father, Who is in secret; and your Father, Who sees in secret, will reward you *in the open*.

7 And when you pray, do not heap up phrases (multiply words, repeating the same ones over and over) as the Gentiles do, for they think they will be heard for their much speaking. [I Kings 18:25–29.]

8 Do not be like them, for your Father knows what you need before you ask Him.

9 Pray, therefore, like this: Our Father Who is in heaven, hallowed (kept holy) be Your name.

10 Your kingdom come, Your will be done on earth as it is in heaven.

11 Give us this day our daily bread.

12 And forgive us our debts, as we also have forgiven (m[left, remitted, and let go of the debts, and have [n]given up resentment against) our debtors.

13 And lead (bring) us not into temptation, but deliver us from the evil one. *For Yours is the kingdom and the power and the glory forever. Amen.*

14 For if you forgive people their trespasses [their [l]reckless and willful sins, [m]leaving them, letting them go,

and [n]giving up resentment], your heavenly Father will also forgive you.

15 But if you do not forgive others their trespasses [their [l]reckless and willful sins, [m]leaving them, letting them go, and [n]giving up resentment], neither will your Father forgive you your trespasses.

16 And whenever you are fasting, do not look gloomy *and* [o]sour *and* [p]dreary like the hypocrites, for they put on a dismal countenance, that their fasting may be apparent to *and* seen by men. Truly I say to you, they have their reward [i]in full already. [Isa. 58:5.]

17 But when you fast, perfume your head and wash your face,

18 So that your fasting may not be noticed by men but by your Father, Who sees in secret; and your Father, Who sees in secret, will reward you *in the open*.

19 Do not [q]gather *and* heap up *and* store up for yourselves treasures on earth, where moth and rust *and* worm consume *and* destroy, and where thieves break through and steal.

20 But [q]gather *and* heap up *and* store for yourselves treasures in heaven, where neither moth nor rust *nor* worm consume *and* destroy, and where thieves do not break through and steal;

21 For where your treasure is, there will your heart be also.

22 The eye is the lamp of the body. So if your eye is sound, your entire body will be full of light.

23 But if your eye is unsound, your whole body will be full of darkness. If then the very light in you [your [r]con-

---

[i] Marvin Vincent, *Word Studies*.　[m] James Moulton and George Milligan, *The Vocabulary*.　[n] *Webster's New International Dictionary* offers this phrase as a definition of the word "forgive."　[o] Martin Luther, cited by Marvin Vincent, *Word Studies*.　[p] Richard Trench, *Synonyms of the New Testament*.　[q] Joseph Thayer, *A Greek-English Lexicon*.　[r] Hermann Cremer, *Biblico-Theological Lexicon*.

science] is darkened, how dense is that darkness!

24 No one can serve two masters; for either he will hate the one and love the other, or he will stand by *and* be devoted to the one and despise and be sagainst the other. You cannot serve God and mammon (tdeceitful riches, money, possessions, or uwhatever is trusted in).

25 Therefore I tell you, stop being vperpetually uneasy (anxious and worried) about your life, what you shall eat *or what you shall drink;* or about your body, what you shall put on. Is not life greater [in quality] than food, and the body [far above and more excellent] than clothing?

26 Look at the birds of the air; they neither sow nor reap nor gather into barns, and yet your heavenly Father keeps feeding them. Are you not worth much more than they?

27 And who of you by worrying *and* being anxious can add one unit of measure (cubit) to his stature *or* to the wspan of his life? [Ps. 39:5–7.]

28 And why should you be anxious about clothes? Consider the lilies of the field *and* ulearn thoroughly how they grow; they neither toil nor spin.

29 Yet I tell you, even Solomon in all his umagnificence (excellence, dignity, and grace) was not arrayed like one of these. [I Kings 10:4–7.]

30 But if God so clothes the grass of the field, which today is alive *and* green and tomorrow is tossed into the furnace, will He not much more surely clothe you, O you of little faith?

31 Therefore do not worry *and* be anxious, saying, What are we going to have to eat? or, What are we going

to have to drink? or, What are we going to have to wear?

32 For the Gentiles (heathen) wish for *and* crave *and* diligently seek all these things, and your heavenly Father knows well that you need them all.

33 But seek (uaim at and strive after) first of all His kingdom and His righteousness (xHis way of doing and being right), and then all these things utaken together will be given you besides.

34 So do not worry *or* be anxious about tomorrow, for tomorrow will have worries *and* anxieties of its own. Sufficient for each day is its own trouble.

CHAPTER 7

DO NOT judge *and* criticize *and* condemn others, so that you may not be judged *and* criticized *and* condemned yourselves.

2 For just as you judge *and* criticize *and* condemn others, you will be judged *and* criticized *and* condemned, and in accordance with the measure you [use to] deal out to others, it will be dealt out again to you.

3 Why do you sstare from without at the yvery small particle that is in your brother's eye but do not become aware of *and* consider the beam zof timber that is in your own eye?

4 Or how can you say to your brother, Let me get the tiny particle out of your eye, when there is the beam zof timber in your own eye?

5 You hypocrite, first get the beam of timber out of your own eye, and then you will see clearly to take the tiny particle out of your brother's eye.

s Marvin Vincent, *Word Studies.*　　t Hermann Cremer, *Biblico-Theological Lexicon.*　　u Joseph Thayer, *A Greek-English Lexicon.*　　v Kenneth Wuest, *Word Studies.*　　w Alexander Souter, *Pocket Lexicon:* the word translated "cubit" is used as a measurement of time, as well as a measurement of length. x Charles B. Williams, *The New Testament: A Translation.*　　y James Moulton and George Milligan, *The Vocabulary.*　　z G. Abbott-Smith, *Manual Greek Lexicon.*

6 Do not give that which is holy (the sacred thing) to the dogs, and do not throw your pearls before hogs, lest they trample upon them with their feet and turn *and* tear you in pieces.

7 [a]Keep on asking and it will be given you; [a]keep on seeking and you will find; [a]keep on knocking [reverently] and [the door] will be opened to you.

8 For everyone who keeps on asking receives; and he who keeps on seeking finds; and to him who keeps on knocking, [the door] will be opened.

9 Or what man is there of you, if his son asks him for a loaf of bread, will hand him a stone?

10 Or if he asks for a fish, will hand him a serpent?

11 If you then, evil as you are, know how to give good *and* [b]advantageous gifts to your children, how much more will your Father Who is in heaven [perfect as He is] give good *and* [b]advantageous things to those who [a]keep on asking Him!

12 So then, whatever you desire that others would do to *and* for you, even so do also to *and* for them, for this is (sums up) the Law and the Prophets.

13 Enter through the narrow gate; for wide is the gate and spacious *and* broad is the way that leads away to destruction, and many are those who are entering through it.

14 But the gate is narrow (contracted [c]by pressure) and the way is straitened *and* compressed that leads away to life, and few are those who find it. [Deut. 30:19; Jer. 21:8.]

15 Beware of false prophets, who come to you dressed as sheep, but inside they are devouring wolves. [Ezek. 22:27.]

16 You will [d]fully recognize them by their fruits. Do people pick grapes from thorns, or figs from thistles?

17 Even so, every healthy (sound) tree bears good fruit [[b]worthy of admiration], but the sickly (decaying, worthless) tree bears bad (worthless) fruit.

18 A good (healthy) tree cannot bear bad (worthless) fruit, nor can a bad (diseased) tree bear [b]excellent fruit [worthy of admiration].

19 Every tree that does not bear good fruit is cut down and cast into the fire.

20 Therefore, you will [d]fully know them by their fruits.

21 Not everyone who says to Me, Lord, Lord, will enter the kingdom of heaven, but he who does the will of My Father Who is in heaven.

22 Many will say to Me on that day, Lord, Lord, have we not prophesied in Your name and driven out demons in Your name and done many mighty works in Your name?

23 And then I will say to them openly (publicly), I never knew you; depart from Me, you who act wickedly [disregarding My commands]. [Ps. 6:8.]

24 So everyone who hears these words of Mine and acts upon them [obeying them] will be like a [e]sensible (prudent, practical, wise) man who built his house upon the rock.

25 And the rain fell and the floods came and the winds blew and beat against that house; yet it did not fall, because it had been founded on the rock.

26 And everyone who hears these words of Mine and does not do them will be like a stupid (foolish) man who built his house upon the sand.

27 And the rain fell and the floods came and the winds blew and beat

---

a Kenneth Wuest, *Word Studies.* **b** Hermann Cremer, *Biblico-Theological Lexicon.* **c** Alexander Souter, *Pocket Lexicon.* **d** Marvin Vincent, *Word Studies.* **e** G. Abbott-Smith, *Manual Greek Lexicon.*

against that house, and it fell—and great *and* complete was the fall of it.

28 When Jesus had finished these sayings [the Sermon on the Mount], the crowds were astonished *and* overwhelmed with bewildered wonder at His teaching,

29 For He was teaching as One Who had [and was] authority, and not as [did] the scribes.

CHAPTER 8

WHEN JESUS came down from the mountain, great throngs followed Him.

2 And behold, a leper came up to Him and, prostrating himself, worshiped Him, saying, Lord, if You are willing, You are able to [f]cleanse me by curing me.

3 And He reached out His hand and touched him, saying, I am willing; be cleansed [by being cured. And instantly his leprosy was cured *and* cleansed.

4 And Jesus said to him, See that you tell nothing about this to anyone; but go, show yourself to the priest and present the offering that Moses commanded, for a testimony [to your healing] *and* as an evidence to the people. [Lev. 14:2.]

5 As Jesus went into Capernaum, a centurion came up to Him, begging Him,

6 And saying, Lord, my servant boy is lying at the house paralyzed *and* [f]distressed with intense pains.

7 And Jesus said to him, I will come and restore him.

8 But the centurion replied to Him, Lord, I am not worthy *or* fit to have You come under my roof; but only speak the word, and my servant boy will be cured.

9 For I also am a man subject to

authority, with soldiers subject to me. And I say to one, Go, and he goes; and to another, Come, and he comes; and to my slave, Do this, and he does it.

10 When Jesus heard him, He marveled and said to those who followed Him [[who adhered steadfastly to Him, conforming to His example in living and, if need be, in dying also], I tell you truly, I have not found so much faith as this [g]with anyone, even in Israel.

11 I tell you, many will come from east and west, and will sit at table with Abraham, Isaac, and Jacob in the kingdom of heaven,

12 While the sons *and* heirs of the kingdom will be driven out into the darkness outside, where there will be weeping and grinding of teeth. [Ps. 107:2, 3; Isa. 49:12; 59:19; Mal. 1:11.]

13 Then to the centurion Jesus said, Go; it shall be done for you as you have believed. And the servant boy was restored to health at that very [h]moment.

14 And when Jesus went into Peter's house, He saw his mother-in-law lying ill with a fever.

15 He touched her hand and the fever left her; and she got up and began waiting on Him.

16 When evening came, they brought to Him many who were [f]under the power of demons, and He drove out the spirits with a word and restored to health all who were sick.

17 And thus He fulfilled what was spoken by the prophet Isaiah, He Himself took [[in order to carry away] our weaknesses *and* infirmities and bore [away our diseases. [Isa. 53:4.]

18 Now Jesus, when He saw the great throngs around Him, gave or-

---

f Joseph Thayer, *A Greek-English Lexicon.* g Some manuscripts add "with anyone." h James Moulton and George Milligan, *The Vocabulary.* i G. Abbott-Smith, *Manual Greek Lexicon;* George Ricker Berry, *Greek-English New Testament Lexicon;* Alexander Souter, *Pocket Lexicon;* Joseph Thayer, *A Greek-English Lexicon;* W.J. Hickie, *Greek-English Lexicon.*

ders to cross to the other side [of the lake].

19 And a scribe came up and said to Him, Master, I will accompany You wherever You go.

20 And Jesus replied to him, Foxes have holes and the birds of the air have lodging places, but the Son of Man has nowhere to lay His head.

21 Another of the disciples said to Him, Lord, let me first go and bury [¹care for till death] my father.

22 But Jesus said to him, Follow Me, and leave the dead [ᵏin sin] to bury their own dead.

23 And after He got into the boat, His disciples followed Him.

24 And ʲsuddenly, behold, there arose a violent storm on the sea, so that the boat was being covered up by the waves; but He was sleeping.

25 And they went and awakened Him, saying, Lord, rescue and preserve us! We are perishing!

26 And He said to them, Why are you timid and afraid, O you of little faith? Then He got up and rebuked the winds and the sea, and there was a great and wonderful calm (ᵐa perfect peaceableness).

27 And the men were stunned with bewildered wonder and marveled, saying, What kind of Man is this, that even the winds and the sea obey Him!

28 And when He arrived at the other side in the country of the Gadarenes, two men under the control of demons went to meet Him, coming out of the tombs, so fierce and savage that no one was able to pass that way.

29 And behold, they shrieked and screamed, What have You to do with us, Jesus, Son of God? Have You come to torment us before the ap-

pointed time? [Judg. 11:12; II Sam. 16:10.]

30 Now at some distance from there a drove of many hogs was grazing.

31 And the demons begged Him, If You drive us out, send us into the drove of hogs.

32 And He said to them, Begone! So they came out and went into the hogs, and behold, the whole drove rushed down the steep bank into the sea and died in the water.

33 The herdsmen fled and went into the town and reported everything, including what had happened to the men under the power of demons.

34 And behold, the whole town went out to meet Jesus; and as soon as they saw Him, they begged Him to depart from their locality.

CHAPTER 9

AND JESUS, getting into a boat, crossed to the other side and came to His own town [Capernaum].

2 And behold, they brought to Him a man paralyzed and prostrated by illness, lying on a sleeping pad; and when Jesus saw their faith, He said to the paralyzed man, Take courage, son; your sins are forgiven and the ⁿpenalty remitted.

3 And behold, some of the scribes said to themselves, This man blasphemes [He claims the rights and prerogatives of God]!

4 But Jesus, knowing (ᵒseeing) their thoughts, said, Why do you think evil and harbor ⁿmalice in your hearts?

5 For which is easier: to say, Your sins are forgiven and the ⁿpenalty remitted, or to say, Get up and walk?

6 But in order that you may know

ʲ Many commentators interpret it thus.　　ᵏ Albert Barnes, *Notes on the New Testament*.　　ˡ Marvin Vincent, *Word Studies*.　　ᵐ John Wycliffe, *The Wycliffe Bible*.　　ⁿ Joseph Thayer, *A Greek-English Lexicon*.　　ᵒ Many manuscripts so read.

that the Son of Man has authority on earth to forgive sins *and* premit the penalty, He then said to the paralyzed man, Get up! Pick up your sleeping pad and go to your own house.

7 And he got up and went away to his own house.

8 When the crowds saw it, they were struck with fear *and* awe; and they qrecognized God *and* praised *and* thanked Him, Who had given such power *and* authority to men.

9 As Jesus passed on from there, He saw a man named Matthew sitting at the tax collector's office; and He said to him, pBe My disciple [side with My party and follow Me]. And he rose and followed Him.

10 And as Jesus reclined at table in the house, behold, many tax collectors and r[especially wicked] sinners came and sat (reclined) with Him and His disciples.

11 And when the Pharisees saw this, they said to His disciples, Why does your Master eat with tax collectors and those [preeminently] sinful?

12 But when Jesus heard it, He replied, Those who are strong *and* well (healthy) have no need of a physician, but those who are weak *and* sick.

13 Go and learn what this means: I desire mercy [that is, preadiness to help those in trouble] and not sacrifice *and* sacrificial victims. For I came not to call *and* invite [to repentance] the righteous (those who are upright and in right standing with God), but sinners (the erring ones and all those not free from sin). [Hos. 6:6.]

14 Then the disciples of John came to Jesus, inquiring, Why is it that we and the Pharisees fast soften, [that is, abstain from food and drink as a religious exercise], but Your disciples do not fast?

15 And Jesus replied to them, Can the wedding guests mourn while the bridegroom is still with them? The days will come when the bridegroom is taken away from them, and then they will fast.

16 And no one puts a piece of cloth that has not been shrunk on an old garment, for such a patch tears away from the garment and a worse rent (tear) is made.

17 Neither is new wine put in old wineskins; for if it is, the skins burst and are ptorn in pieces, and the wine is spilled and the skins are ruined. But new wine is put into fresh wineskins, and so both are preserved.

18 While He was talking this way to them, behold, a ruler entered and, kneeling down, worshiped Him, saying, My daughter has just snow died; but come and lay Your hand on her, and she will come to life.

19 And Jesus got up and accompanied him, with His disciples.

20 And behold, a woman who had suffered from a flow of blood for twelve years came up behind Him and touched the fringe of His garment; [Matt. 14:36.]

21 For she kept saying to herself, If I only touch His garment, I shall be restored to health.

22 Jesus turned around and, seeing her, He said, Take courage, daughter! Your faith has made you well. And at once the woman was restored to health.

23 And when Jesus came to the ruler's house and saw the flute players and the crowd making an uproar *and* din,

24 He said, Go away; for the girl is not dead but sleeping. And they laughed *and* jeered at Him.

---

p Joseph Thayer, *A Greek-English Lexicon.* Abbott-Smith, *Manual Greek Lexicon.* Studies.   q Hermann Cremer, *Biblico-Theological Lexicon.*   r G. s Many manuscripts so read.   t Marvin Vincent, *Word Studies.*

25 But when the crowd had been ordered to go outside, He went in and took her by the hand, and the girl arose.

26 And the news about this spread through all that district.

27 As Jesus passed on from there, two blind men followed Him, shouting loudly, Have pity *and* mercy on us, Son of David!

28 When He reached the house and went in, the blind men came to Him, and Jesus said to them, Do you believe that I am able to do this? They said to Him, Yes, Lord.

29 Then He touched their eyes, saying, According to your faith *and* trust *and* reliance [on the power invested in Me] be it done to you;

30 And their eyes were opened. And Jesus earnestly *and* sternly charged them, See that you let no one know about this.

31 But they went off and blazed *and* spread His fame abroad throughout that whole district.

32 And while they were going away, behold, a dumb man under the power of a demon was brought to Jesus.

33 And when the demon was driven out, the dumb man spoke; and the crowds were stunned with bewildered wonder, saying, Never before has anything like this been seen in Israel.

34 But the Pharisees said, He drives out demons through *and* with the help of the prince of demons.

35 And Jesus went about all the cities and villages, teaching in their synagogues and proclaiming the good news (the Gospel) of the kingdom and curing all kinds of disease and every weakness *and* infirmity.

36 When He saw the throngs, He was moved with pity *and* sympathy for them, because they were bewil-

dered (harassed and distressed and dejected and helpless), like sheep without a shepherd. [Zech. 10:2.]

37 Then He said to His disciples, The harvest is indeed plentiful, but the laborers are few.

38 So pray to the Lord of the harvest to [a]force out *and* thrust laborers into His harvest.

CHAPTER 10

AND JESUS summoned to Him His twelve disciples and gave them power *and* authority over unclean spirits, to drive them out, and to cure all kinds of disease and all kinds of weakness *and* infirmity.

2 Now these are the names of the twelve apostles (special messengers): first, Simon, who is called Peter, and Andrew his brother; James son of Zebedee, and John his brother;

3 Philip and Bartholomew [Nathaniel]; Thomas and Matthew the tax collector; James son of Alphaeus, and Thaddaeus [Judas, not Iscariot].

4 Simon the Cananaean, and Judas Iscariot, who also betrayed Him.

5 Jesus sent out these twelve, charging them, Go nowhere among the Gentiles and do not go into any town of the Samaritans;

6 But go rather to the lost sheep of the house of Israel.

7 And as you go, preach, saying, The kingdom of heaven is at hand!

8 Cure the sick, raise the dead, cleanse the lepers, drive out demons. Freely (without pay) you have received, freely (without charge) give.

9 Take no gold nor silver nor [even] copper money in your purses (belts);

10 And do not take a provision bag *or* a [v]wallet for a collection bag for your journey, nor two undergar-

u Marvin Vincent, *Word Studies.*   v James Moulton and George Milligan, *The Vocabulary.*

ments, nor sandals, nor a staff; for the workman deserves his support (his living, his food).

11 And into whatever town or village you go, inquire who in it is deserving, and stay there [at his house] until you leave [that vicinity].

12 As you go into the house, give your greetings *and* wish it well.

13 Then if indeed that house is deserving, let come upon it your peace [that is, ^wfreedom from all the distresses that are experienced as the result of sin]. But if it is not deserving, let your peace return to you.

14 And whoever will not receive *and* accept *and* welcome you nor listen to your message, as you leave that house or town, shake the dust [of it] from your feet.

15 Truly I tell you, it shall be more tolerable on the day of judgment for the land of Sodom and Gomorrah than for that town.

16 Behold, I am sending you out like sheep in the midst of wolves; be ^xwary *and* wise as serpents, and be innocent (harmless, guileless, and ^ywithout falsity) as doves. [Gen. 3:1.]

17 Be on guard against men [whose ^wway or nature is to act in opposition to God]; for they will deliver you up to councils and flog you in their synagogues,

18 And you will be brought before governors and kings for My sake, as a witness to bear testimony before them and to the Gentiles (the nations).

19 But when they deliver you up, do not be anxious about how *or* what you are to speak; for what you are to say will be given you in that very hour *and* ^zmoment,

20 For it is not you who are speaking, but the Spirit of your Father speaking through you.

21 Brother will deliver up brother to death, and the father his child; and children will take a stand against their parents and will have them put to death.

22 And you will be hated by all for My name's sake, but he who perseveres *and* endures to the end will be saved [^afrom spiritual disease and death in the world to come].

23 When they persecute you in one town [that is, pursue you in a manner that would injure you and cause you to suffer because of your belief], flee to another town; for truly I tell you, you will not have gone through all the towns of Israel before ^bthe Son of Man comes.

24 A disciple is not above his teacher, nor is a servant *or* slave above his master.

25 It is sufficient for the disciple to be like his teacher, and the servant *or* slave like his master. If they have called the Master of the house Beelzebub [^cmaster of the dwelling], how much more will they speak evil of those of His household. [II Kings 1:2.]

26 So have no fear of them; for nothing is concealed that will not be revealed, or kept secret that will not become known.

27 What I say to you in the dark, tell in the light; and what you hear whispered in the ear, proclaim upon the housetops.

28 And do not be afraid of those who kill the body but cannot kill the soul; but rather be afraid of Him who can destroy both soul and body in hell (Gehenna).

---

w Hermann Cremer, *Biblico-Theological Lexicon*. Luther, cited by Marvin Vincent, *Word Studies*.
a G. Abbott-Smith, *Manual Greek Lexicon*.

x John Wycliffe, *The Wycliffe Bible*.   y Martin
z James Moulton and George Milligan, *The Vocabulary*.
b Believed by many to mean the coming of the Holy Spirit at Pentecost. Other commentators observe that the saying seems to teach that the Gospel will continue to be preached to the Jews until Christ's second coming.   c John D. Davis, *A Dictionary of the Bible*.

29 Are not two ᵈlittle sparrows sold for a penny? And yet not one of them will fall to the ground without your Father's leave (consent) and notice.

30 But even the very hairs of your head are all numbered.

31 Fear not, then; you are of more value than many sparrows.

32 Therefore, everyone who acknowledges Me before men and confesses Me [out of a state of oneness with Me], I will also acknowledge him before My Father Who is in heaven, and ᵈconfess [that I am abiding in] him.

33 But whoever denies and disowns Me before men, I also will deny and disown him before My Father Who is in heaven.

34 Do not think that I have come to bring peace upon the earth; I have not come to bring peace, but a sword.

35 For I have come to part asunder a man from his father, and a daughter from her mother, and a ᵈnewly married wife from her mother-in-law—

36 And a man's foes will be they of his own household [Mic. 7:6.]

37 He who loves [and ᵉtakes more pleasure in] father or mother more than [in] Me is not worthy of Me; and he who loves [and takes more pleasure in] son or daughter more than [in] Me is not worthy of Me,

38 And he who does not take up his cross and follow Me [ᶠcleave steadfastly to Me, conforming wholly to My example in living and, if need be, in dying also] is not worthy of Me.

39 Whoever finds his [ᵉlower] life will lose it [the higher life], and whoever loses his [lower] life on My account will find it [the higher life].

40 He who receives and welcomes and accepts you receives and welcomes and accepts Me, and he who receives and welcomes and accepts Me receives and welcomes and accepts Him Who sent Me.

41 He who receives and welcomes and accepts a prophet because he is a prophet shall receive a prophet's reward, and he who receives and welcomes and accepts a righteous man because he is a righteous man shall receive a righteous man's reward.

42 And whoever gives to one of these little ones [in rank or influence] even a cup of cold water because he is My disciple, surely I declare to you, he shall not lose his reward.

CHAPTER 11

WHEN JESUS had finished His charge to His twelve disciples, He left there to teach and to preach in their [Galilean] cities.

2 Now when John in prison heard about the activities of Christ, he sent a message by his disciples

3 And asked Him, Are You the One Who was to come, or should we keep on expecting a different one? [Gen. 49:10; Num. 24:17.]

4 And Jesus replied to them, Go and report to John what you hear and see:

5 The blind receive their sight and the lame walk, lepers are cleansed (by healing) and the deaf hear, the dead are raised up and the poor have good news (the Gospel) preached to them. [Isa. 35:5, 6; 61:1.]

6 And blessed (happy, fortunate, and ᵍto be envied) is he who takes no offense at Me and finds no cause for stumbling in or through Me and is not hindered from seeing the Truth.

7 Then as these men went their way, Jesus began to speak to the crowds about John: What did you go out in the wilderness (desert) to see? A reed swayed by the wind?

8 What did you go out to see then?

---

d Marvin Vincent, *Word Studies.*   e Kenneth Wuest, *Word Studies.*   f Joseph Thayer, *A Greek-English Lexicon.*   g Alexander Souter, *Pocket Lexicon.*

A man clothed in soft garments? Behold, those who wear soft clothing are in the houses of kings.

9 But what did you go out to see? A prophet? Yes, I tell you, and one [hout of the common, more eminent, more remarkable, and] hsuperior to a prophet.

10 This is the one of whom it is written, Behold, I send My messenger ahead of You, who shall make ready Your way before You. [Mal. 3:1.]

11 Truly I tell you, among those born of women there has not risen anyone greater than John the Baptist; yet he who is least in the kingdom of heaven is greater than he.

12 And from the days of John the Baptist until the present time, the kingdom of heaven has endured violent assault, and violent men seize it by force [as a precious prize—a ishare in the heavenly kingdom is sought with most ardent zeal and intense exertion]

13 For all the Prophets and the Law prophesied up until John.

14 And if you are willing to receive and accept it, John himself is Elijah who was to come [before the kingdom]. [Mal. 4:5.]

15 He who has ears to hear, let him be listening and let him consider and hperceive and comprehend by hearing.

16 But to what shall I liken this generation? It is like little children sitting in the marketplaces who call to their playmates,

17 We piped to you [playing wedding], and you did not dance; we wailed dirges [playing funeral], and you did not mourn and beat your breasts and weep aloud.

18 For John came neither eating nor drinking [with others], and they say, He has a demon!

19 The Son of Man came eating and drinking [with others], and they say, Behold, a glutton and a wine drinker, a friend of tax collectors and [hespecially wicked] sinners! Yet wisdom is justified and vindicated by what she does (her deeds) and by jher children.

20 Then He began to censure and reproach the cities in which most of His mighty works had been performed, because they did not repent [and their hearts were not changed].

21 Woe to you, Chorazin! Woe to you, Bethsaida! For if the mighty works done in you had been done in Tyre and Sidon, they would long ago have repented in sackcloth and ashes [and their hearts would have been changed].

22 I tell you [further], it shall be more endurable for Tyre and Sidon on the day of judgment than for you.

23 And you, Capernaum, are you to be lifted up to heaven? You shall be brought down to Hades [the region of the dead]! For if the mighty works done in you had been done in Sodom, it would have continued until today.

24 But I tell you, it shall be more endurable for the land of Sodom on the day of judgment than for you.

25 At that time Jesus began to say, I thank You, Father, Lord of heaven and earth [and iI acknowledge openly and joyfully to Your honor], that You have hidden these things from the wise and clever and learned, and revealed them to babies [to the ichildish, untaught, and unskilled].

26 Yes, Father, [I praise You that] such was Your gracious will and good pleasure.

27 All things have been entrusted

h G. Abbott-Smith, *Manual Greek Lexicon.*   i Joseph Thayer, *A Greek-English Lexicon.*   j Many manuscripts read "children" here, as in Luke 7:35.

and delivered to Me by My Father; and no one ᵏfully knows *and* ˡaccurately understands the Son except the Father, and no one ᵏfully knows *and* ˡaccurately understands the Father except the Son and anyone to whom the Son ˡdeliberately wills to make Him known.

28 Come to Me, all you who labor and are heavy-laden *and* overburdened, and I will cause you to rest. [I will ᵐease and relieve and ʳrefresh ˡyour souls.]

29 Take My yoke upon you and learn of Me, for I am gentle (meek) and humble (lowly) in heart, and you will find rest (ᵒrelief and ease and refreshment and ʳrecreation and blessed quiet) for your souls. [Jer. 6:16.]

30 For My yoke is wholesome (useful, ᵖgood—not harsh, hard, sharp, or pressing, but comfortable, gracious, and pleasant), and My burden is light *and* easy to be borne.

CHAPTER 12

AT THAT ᵏparticular time Jesus went through the fields of standing grain on the Sabbath; and His disciples were hungry, and they began to pick off the spikes of grain and to eat. [Deut. 23:25.]

2 And when the Pharisees saw it, they said to Him, See there! Your disciples are doing what is unlawful *and* not permitted on the Sabbath.

3 He said to them, Have you not even read what David did when he was hungry, and those who accompanied him—[Lev. 24:9; I Sam. 21:1–6.]

4 How he went into the house of God and ate the loaves of the showbread—which was not lawful for him to eat, nor for the men who accompa-

nied him, but for the priests only?

5 Or have you never read in the Law that on the Sabbath the priests in the temple violate the sanctity of the Sabbath [breaking it] and yet are guiltless? [Num. 28:9, 10.]

6 But I tell you, Something greater *and* ˡmore exalted *and* more majestic than the temple is here!

7 And if you had only known what this saying means, I desire mercy [readiness to help, to spare, to forgive] rather than sacrifice *and* sacrificial victims, you would not have condemned the guiltless. [Hos. 6:6; Matt. 9:13.]

8 For the Son of Man is Lord [even] of the Sabbath.

9 And going on from there, He went into their synagogue.

10 And behold, a man was there with one withered hand. And they said to Him, Is it lawful *or* allowable to cure people on the Sabbath days? —that they might accuse Him.

11 But He said to them, What man is there among you, if he has only one sheep and it falls into a pit *or* ditch on the Sabbath, will not take hold of it and lift it out?

12 How much better *and* of more value is a man than a sheep! So it is lawful *and* allowable to do good on the Sabbath days.

13 Then He said to the man, Reach out your hand. And the man reached it out and it was restored, as sound as the other one.

14 But the Pharisees went out and held a consultation against Him, how they might do away with Him.

15 But being aware of this, Jesus went away from there. And many people ˡjoined *and* accompanied Him, and He cured all of them,

16 And strictly charged them *and*

ᵏ Marvin Vincent, *Word Studies*.　ˡ Joseph Thayer, *A Greek-English Lexicon*.　ᵐ William Tyndale, *The Tyndale Bible*.　ⁿ John Wycliffe, *The Wycliffe Bible*.　ᵒ Alexander Souter, *Pocket Lexicon*.　ᵖ James Moulton and George Milligan, *The Vocabulary*.

sharply warned them not to make Him [q]publicly known.

17 This was in fulfillment of what was spoken by the prophet Isaiah,

18 Behold, My Servant Whom I have chosen, My Beloved in and with Whom My soul is well pleased and [q]has found its delight. I will put My Spirit upon Him, and He shall proclaim and [q]show forth justice to the nations.

19 He will not strive or wrangle or cry out loudly; nor will anyone hear His voice in the streets;

20 A bruised reed He will not break, and a smoldering (dimly burning) wick He will not quench, till He brings [r]justice and a just cause to victory.

21 And in and on His name will the Gentiles (the [s]peoples outside of Israel) set their hopes. [Isa. 42:1–4.]

22 Then a blind and dumb man under the power of a demon was brought to Jesus, and He cured him, so that the blind and dumb man both spoke and saw.

23 And all the [crowds of] people were stunned with bewildered wonder and said, This cannot be the Son of David, can it?

24 But the Pharisees, hearing it, said, This [t]Man drives out demons only by and with the help of Beelzebub, the prince of demons.

25 And knowing their thoughts, He said to them, Any kingdom that is divided against itself is being brought to desolation and laid waste, and no city or house divided against itself will last or continue to stand.

26 And if Satan drives out Satan, he has become divided against himself and disunified; how then will his kingdom last or continue to stand?

27 And if I drive out the demons by [help of] Beelzebub, by whose [help] do your sons drive them out? [q]For this reason they shall be your judges.

28 But if it is by the Spirit of God that I drive out the demons, then the kingdom of God has come upon you [[u]before you expected it].

29 Or how can a person go into a strong man's house and carry off his goods (the entire equipment of his house) without first binding the strong man? Then indeed he may plunder his house.

30 He who is not with Me [definitely [r]on My side] is against Me, and he who does not [definitely] gather with Me and for [r]My side scatters.

31 Therefore I tell you, every sin and blasphemy (every evil, abusive, [v]injurious speaking, or indignity against sacred things) can be forgiven men, but blasphemy against the [Holy] Spirit shall not and [v]cannot be forgiven.

32 And whoever speaks a word against the Son of Man will be forgiven, but whoever speaks against the Spirit, the Holy One, will not be forgiven, either in this world and age or in the world and age to come.

33 Either make the tree sound (healthy and good), and its fruit sound (healthy and good), or make the tree rotten (diseased and bad), and its fruit rotten (diseased and bad); for the tree is known and recognized and judged by its fruit.

34 You offspring of vipers! How can you speak good things when you are evil (wicked)? For out of the fullness (the overflow, the [w]superabundance) of the heart the mouth speaks.

35 The good man from his inner good treasure [u]flings forth good things, and the evil man out of his

q John Darby, The New Testament, a New Translation.   r Joseph Thayer, A Greek-English Lexicon.
s Hermann Cremer, Biblico-Theological Lexicon.   t Capitalized because of what He is, the spotless Son
of God, not what the speakers may have thought He was.   u Marvin Vincent, Word Studies.
v Charles B. Williams, The New Testament: A Translation.   w Alexander Souter, Pocket Lexicon.

inner evil storehouse ˣflings forth evil things.

36 But I tell you, on the day of judgment men will have to give account for every ˣidle (inoperative, nonworking) word they speak.

37 For by your words you will be justified *and* acquitted, and by your words you will be condemned *and* sentenced.

38 Then some of the scribes and Pharisees said to Him, Teacher, we desire to see a sign *or* miracle from You [proving that You are what You claim to be].

39 But He replied to them, An evil and adulterous generation (a generation ˣmorally unfaithful to God) seeks *and* demands a sign; but no sign shall be given to it except the sign of the prophet Jonah.

40 For even as Jonah was three days and three nights in the belly of the sea monster, so will the Son of Man be three days and three nights in the heart of the earth. [Jonah 1:17.]

41 The men of Nineveh will stand up at the judgment with this generation and condemn it; for they repented at the preaching of Jonah, and behold, Someone more *and* greater than Jonah is here! [Jonah 3:5.]

42 The queen of the South will stand up at the judgment with this generation and condemn it; for she came from the ends of the earth to listen to the wisdom of Solomon, and behold, Someone more *and* greater than Solomon is here. [I Kings 10:1; II Chron. 9:1.]

43 But when the unclean spirit has gone out of a man, it roams through dry [arid] places in search of rest, but it does not find any.

44 Then it says, I will go back to my house from which I came out. And when it arrives, it finds the place unoccupied, swept, put in order, *and* decorated.

45 Then it goes and brings with it seven other spirits more wicked than itself, and they go in and make their home there. And the last condition of that man becomes worse than the first. So also shall it be with this wicked generation.

46 Jesus was still speaking to the people when behold, His mother and brothers stood outside, seeking to speak to Him.

47 ʸ*Someone said to Him, Listen! Your mother and Your brothers are standing outside, seeking to speak to You.*

48 But He replied to the man who told Him, Who is My mother, and who are My brothers?

49 And stretching out His hand toward [not only the twelve disciples but all] ᶻHis adherents, He said, Here are My mother and My brothers.

50 For whoever does the will of My Father in heaven is My brother and sister and mother!

CHAPTER 13

THAT SAME day Jesus went out of the house and was sitting beside the sea.

2 But such great crowds gathered about Him that He got into a boat and remained sitting there, while all the throng stood on the shore.

3 And He told them many things in parables (stories by way of illustration and comparison), saying, A sower went out to sow.

4 And as he sowed, some seeds fell by the roadside, and the birds came and ate them up.

5 Other seeds fell on rocky ground, where they had not much soil; and at once they sprang up, because they had no depth of soil.

x Marvin Vincent, *Word Studies.*   y Some manuscripts omit verse 47.   z Hermann Cremer, *Biblico-Theological Lexicon.*

6 But when the sun rose, they were scorched, and because they had no root, they dried up *and* withered away.

7 Other seeds fell among thorns, and the thorns grew up and choked them out.

8 Other seeds fell on good soil, and yielded grain—some a hundred times as much as was sown, some sixty times as much, and some thirty.

9 He who has ears [to hear], let him be listening *and* let him ªconsider *and* ᵇperceive *and* comprehend by hearing.

10 Then the disciples came to Him and said, Why do You speak to them in parables?

11 And He replied to them, To you it has been given to know the secrets *and* mysteries of the kingdom of heaven, but to them it has not been given.

12 For whoever has [spiritual knowledge], to him will more be given *and* he will ªbe furnished richly so that he will have abundance; but from him who has not, even what he has will be taken away.

13 This is the reason that I speak to them in parables: because ªhaving the power of seeing, they do not see; and ªhaving the power of hearing, they do not hear, nor do they grasp *and* understand.

14 In them indeed is ᶜthe process of fulfillment of the prophecy of Isaiah, which says: You shall indeed hear *and* hear but never grasp *and* understand; and you shall indeed look *and* look but never see *and* perceive.

15 For this nation's heart has grown gross (fat and dull), and their ears heavy *and* difficult of hearing, and their eyes they have tightly closed, lest they see *and* perceive with their eyes, and hear *and* com-

prehend the sense with their ears, and grasp *and* understand with their heart, and turn *and* I should heal them. [Isa. 6:9, 10.]

16 But blessed (happy, fortunate, and ᵈto be envied) are your eyes because they do see, and your ears because they do hear.

17 Truly I tell you, many prophets and righteous men [men who were upright and in right standing with God] yearned to see what you see, and did not see it, and to hear what you hear, and did not hear it.

18 Listen then to the [meaning of the] parable of the sower:

19 ᶜWhile anyone is hearing the Word of the kingdom and does not grasp *and* comprehend it, the evil one comes and snatches away what was sown in his heart. This is what was sown along the roadside.

20 As for what was sown on thin (rocky) soil, this is he who hears the Word and at once welcomes *and* accepts it with joy;

21 Yet it has no real root in him, but is temporary (inconstant, ᵉlasts but a little while); and when affliction *or* trouble *or* persecution comes on account of the Word, at once he is caused to stumble [he is repelled and ªbegins to distrust and desert Him Whom he ought to trust and obey] *and* he falls away.

22 As for what was sown among thorns, this is he who hears the Word, but the cares of the world and the pleasure *and* delight *and* glamour *and* deceitfulness of riches choke *and* suffocate the Word, and it yields no fruit.

23 As for what was sown on good soil, this is he who hears the Word and grasps *and* comprehends it; he indeed bears fruit and yields in one case a hundred times as much as was

a Joseph Thayer, *A Greek-English Lexicon.*   b G. Abbott-Smith, *Manual Greek Lexicon.*   c Marvin Vincent, *Word Studies.*   d Alexander Souter, *Pocket Lexicon.*   e John Wycliffe, *The Wycliffe Bible.*

sown, in another sixty times as much, and in another thirty.

24 Another parable He set forth before them, saying, The kingdom of heaven is like a man who sowed good seed in his field.

25 But while he was sleeping, his enemy came and sowed also darnel (weeds resembling wheat) among the wheat, and went on his way.

26 So when the plants sprouted and formed grain, the darnel (weeds) appeared also.

27 And the servants of the owner came to him and said, Sir, did you not sow good seed in your field? Then how does it have darnel shoots in it?

28 He replied to them, An enemy has done this. The servants said to him, Then do you want us to go and weed them out?

29 But he said, No, lest in gathering the wild wheat (weeds resembling wheat), you root up the [true] wheat along with it.

30 Let them grow together until the harvest; and at harvest time I will say to the reapers, Gather the darnel first and bind it in bundles to be burned, but gather the wheat into my granary.

31 Another story by way of comparison He set forth before them, saying, The kingdom of heaven is like a grain of mustard seed, which a man took and sowed in his field.

32 Of all the seeds it is the smallest, but when it has grown it is the largest of the garden herbs and becomes a tree, so that the birds of the air come and find shelter in its branches.

33 He told them another parable: The kingdom of heaven is like leaven (ᶠsour dough) which a woman took and covered over in three measures of meal *or* flour till all of it was leavened. [Gen. 18:6.]

34 These things ᵍall taken together Jesus said to the crowds in parables; indeed, without a parable He said nothing to them.

35 This was in fulfillment of what was spoken by the prophet: I will open My mouth in parables; I will utter things that have been hidden since the foundation of the world. [Ps. 78:2.]

36 Then He left the throngs and went into the house. And His disciples came to Him saying, Explain to us the parable of the darnel in the field.

37 He answered, He Who sows the good seed is the Son of Man.

38 The field is the world, and the good seed means the children of the kingdom; the darnel is the children of the evil one,

39 And the enemy who sowed it is the devil. The harvest is the close *and* consummation of the age, and the reapers are angels.

40 Just as the darnel (the weeds, the wild wheat) is gathered and burned with fire, so it will be at the close of the age.

41 The Son of Man will send forth His angels, and they will gather out of His kingdom all causes of offense [ᵍpersons by whom others are drawn into error or sin] and all who do iniquity *and* act wickedly,

42 And will cast them into the furnace of fire; there will be weeping *and* wailing and grinding of teeth.

43 Then will the righteous (those who are upright and in right standing with God) shine forth like the sun in the kingdom of their Father. Let him who has ears [to hear] be listening, *and* let him ᵍconsider *and* perceive *and* understand by hearing. [Dan. 12:3.]

44 The kingdom of heaven is like ᵍsomething precious buried in a field,

f John Wycliffe, *The Wycliffe Bible*.   g Joseph Thayer, *A Greek-English Lexicon*.

which a man found and hid again;
then in his joy he goes and sells all he
has and buys that field.

45 Again the kingdom of heaven is
like a man who is a dealer in search of
fine *and* [h]precious pearls,

46 Who, on finding a single pearl of
great price, went and sold all he had
and bought it.

47 Again, the kingdom of heaven is
like a [j]dragnet which was cast into
the sea and gathered in fish of every
sort.

48 When it was full, men dragged it
up on the beach, and sat down and
sorted out the good fish into baskets,
but the worthless ones they threw
away.

49 So it will be at the close *and*
consummation of the age. The angels
will go forth and separate the wicked
from the righteous (those who are upright and in right standing with God)

50 And cast them [the wicked] into
the furnace of fire; there will be
weeping *and* wailing and grinding of
teeth.

51 Have you understood [h]all these
things [parables] taken together?
They said to Him, Yes, *Lord.*

52 He said to them, Therefore every [h]teacher *and* interpreter of the
Sacred Writings who has been instructed *and* trained for the
kingdom of heaven and has [i]become
a disciple is like a householder who
brings forth out of his storehouse
treasure that is new and [treasure
that is] old [the fresh as well as the
familiar].

53 When Jesus had finished these
parables (these comparisons), He left
there.

54 And coming to His own country
[Nazareth], He taught in their synagogue so that they were amazed with
bewildered wonder, and said, Where

did this [j]Man get this wisdom and
these miraculous powers?

55 Is not this the carpenter's Son?
Is not His mother called Mary? And
are not His brothers James and Joseph and Simon and Judas?

56 And do not all His sisters live
here among us? Where then did this
Man get all this?

57 And they took offense at Him
[they were repelled and hindered
from acknowledging His authority,
and caused to stumble]. But Jesus
said to them, A prophet is not without honor except in his own country
and in his own house.

58 And He did not do many works
of power there, because of their unbelief (their lack of faith [i]in the divine
mission of Jesus).

CHAPTER 14

AT THAT time Herod the governor
heard the reports about Jesus,

2 And he said to his attendants,
This is John the Baptist; He has been
raised from the dead, and that is why
the powers [i]of performing miracles
are at work in Him.

3 For Herod had arrested John and
bound him and put him in prison [to
[k]stow him out of the way] on account
and for the sake of Herodias, his
brother Philip's wife,

4 For John had said to him, It is not
lawful *or* right for you to have her.
[Lev. 18:16; 20:21.]

5 Although he wished to have him
put to death, he was afraid of the
people, for they regarded John as a
prophet.

6 But when Herod's birthday
came, the daughter of Herodias
danced in the midst [before the com-
pany] and pleased *and* fascinated
Herod,

7 And so he promised with an oath

h Joseph Thayer, *A Greek-English Lexicon.* i Marvin Vincent, *Word Studies.* j See footnote on Matt. 2:8. k G. Abbott-Smith, *Manual Greek Lexicon.*

to give her whatever she might ask.

8 And she, being put forward *and* prompted by her mother, said, Give me the head of John the Baptist right here on a ¹platter.

9 And the king was distressed *and* sorry, but because of his oaths and his guests, he ordered it to be given her;

10 He sent and had John beheaded in the prison.

11 And his head was brought in on a ¹platter and given ᵐto the little maid, and she brought it to her mother.

12 And John's disciples came and took up the body and buried it. Then they went and told Jesus.

13 When Jesus heard it, He withdrew from there privately in a boat to a solitary place. But when the crowds heard of it, they followed Him [by land] on foot from the towns.

14 When He went ashore and saw a great throng of people, He had compassion (pity and deep sympathy) for them and cured their sick.

15 When evening came, the disciples came to Him and said, This is a remote *and* barren place, and the day is now over; send the throngs away into the villages to buy food for themselves.

16 Jesus said, They do not need to go away; you give them something to eat.

17 They said to Him, We have nothing here but five loaves and two fish.

18 He said, Bring them here to Me.

19 Then He ordered the crowds to recline on the grass; and He took the five loaves and the two fish, and, looking up to heaven, He gave thanks *and* blessed and broke the loaves and handed the pieces to the disciples, and the disciples gave them to the people.

20 And they all ate and were satisfied. And they picked up twelve [ⁿsmall hand] baskets full of the broken pieces left over.

21 And those who ate were about 5,000 men, not including women and children.

22 Then He directed the disciples to get into the boat and go before Him to the other side, while He sent away the crowds.

23 And after He had dismissed the multitudes, He went up into the hills by Himself to pray. When it was evening, He was still there alone.

24 But the boat was by this time out on the sea, *many furlongs* [a furlong is one-eighth of a mile] *distant from the land*, beaten and tossed by the waves, for the wind was against them.

25 And in the fourth watch [between 3:00—6:00 a.m.] of the night, Jesus came to them, walking on the sea.

26 And when the disciples saw Him walking on the sea, they were terrified and said, It is a ghost! And they screamed out with fright.

27 But instantly He spoke to them, saying, Take courage! I AM! Stop being afraid! [Exod. 3:14.]

28 And Peter answered Him, Lord, if it is You, command me to come to You on the water.

29 He said, Come! So Peter got out of the boat and walked on the water, and he came toward Jesus.

30 But when he perceived *and* felt the strong wind, he was frightened, and as he began to sink, he cried out, Lord, save me [from death]!

31 Instantly Jesus reached out His hand and caught *and* held him, say-

---

l William Tyndale, *The Tyndale Bible*.   m Martin Luther, cited by Marvin Vincent, *Word Studies*.
n Marvin Vincent, *Word Studies*. But according to James Moulton and George Milligan, *The Vocabulary*, the term refers to the type of material of which the basket is constructed (perhaps a wicker basket) and not necessarily the size of the basket.

ing to him, O you of little faith, why did you doubt?

32 And when they got into the boat, the wind ceased.

33 And those in the boat knelt and worshiped Him, saying, Truly You are the Son of God!

34 And when they had crossed over to the other side, they went ashore at Gennesaret.

35 And when the men of that place recognized Him, they sent around into all the surrounding country and brought to Him all who were sick

36 And begged Him to let them merely touch the fringe of His garment; and as many as touched it were perfectly restored. [Matt. 9:20.]

CHAPTER 15

THEN FROM Jerusalem came scribes and Pharisees and said,

2 Why do Your disciples transgress and violate the rules handed down by the elders of the past? For they do not practice [ceremonially] washing their hands before they eat.

3 He replied to them, And why also do you transgress and violate the commandment of God for the sake of the rules handed down to you by your forefathers (the elders)?

4 For God commanded, Honor your father and your mother, and, He who curses or reviles or speaks evil of or abuses or treats improperly his father or mother, let him surely come to his end by death. [Exod. 20:12; 21:17; Lev. 20:9; Deut. 5:16.]

5 But you say, If anyone tells his father or mother, What you would have gained from me [that is, the money and whatever I have that might be used for helping you] is already dedicated and as a gift to God, then he is exempt and no longer under ob-

ligation to honor and help his father or his mother.

6 So for the sake of your tradition (the rules handed down by your forefathers), you have set aside the Word of God [depriving it of force and authority and making it of no effect].

7 You pretenders (hypocrites)! Admirably and truly did Isaiah prophesy of you when he said:

8 These people draw near Me with their mouths and honor Me with their lips, but their hearts hold off and are far away from Me.

9 Uselessly do they worship Me, for they teach as doctrines the commands of men. [Isa. 29:13.]

10 And Jesus called the people to Him and said to them, Listen and grasp and comprehend this:

11 It is not what goes into the mouth of a man that makes him unclean and defiled, but what comes out of the mouth; this makes a man unclean and defiles [him].

12 Then the disciples came and said to Him, Do You know that the Pharisees were displeased and offended and indignant when they heard this saying?

13 He answered, Every plant which My heavenly Father has not planted will be torn up by the roots. [Isa. 60:21.]

14 Let them alone and disregard them; they are blind guides and teachers. And if a blind man leads a blind man, both will fall into a ditch.

15 But Peter said to Him, Explain this °proverb (this ᵖmaxim) to us.

16 And He said, Are you also even yet dull and ignorant [without understanding and ᑫunable to put things together]?

17 Do you not see and understand that whatever goes into the mouth passes into the ʳabdomen and so

o G. Abbott-Smith, *Manual Greek Lexicon.*
q Hermann Cremer, *Biblico-Theological Lexicon. Vocabulary.*

p Joseph Thayer, *A Greek-English Lexicon.*
r James Moulton and George Milligan, *The*

passes on into the place where discharges are deposited?

18 But whatever comes out of the mouth comes from the heart, and this is what makes a man unclean *and* defiles [him].

19 For out of the heart come evil thoughts (reasonings and disputings and designs) such as murder, adultery, sexual vice, theft, false witnessing, slander, *and* irreverent speech.

20 These are what make a man unclean *and* defile [him]; but eating with unwashed hands does not make him unclean *or* defile [him].

21 And going away from there, Jesus withdrew to the district of Tyre and Sidon.

22 And behold, a woman who was a Canaanite from that district came out and, with a [loud, troublesomely urgent] cry, begged, Have mercy on me, O Lord, Son of David! My daughter is miserably *and* distressingly *and* cruelly possessed by a demon!

23 But He did not answer her a word. And His disciples came and implored Him, saying, Send her away, for she is crying out after us.

24 He answered, I was sent only to the lost sheep of the house of Israel.

25 But she came and, kneeling, worshiped Him and kept praying, Lord, help me!

26 And He answered, It is not right (proper, becoming, or fair) to take the children's bread and throw it to the ˢlittle dogs.

27 She said, Yes, Lord, yet even the little pups (ᵗlittle whelps) eat the crumbs that fall from their [young] masters' table.

28 Then Jesus answered her, O woman, great is your faith! Be it done for you as you wish. And her daughter was cured from that ᵘmoment.

29 And Jesus went on from there and passed along the shore of the Sea of Galilee. Then He went up into the hills and kept sitting there.

30 And a great multitude came to Him, bringing with them the lame, the maimed, the blind, the dumb, and many others, and they put them down at His feet; and He cured them,

31 So that the crowd was amazed when they saw the dumb speaking, the maimed made whole, the lame walking, and the blind seeing; and they ᵛrecognized *and* praised *and* thanked *and* glorified the God of Israel.

32 Then Jesus called His disciples to Him and said, I have pity *and* sympathy *and* am deeply moved for the crowd, because they have been with Me now three days and they have nothing [at all left] to eat; and I am not willing to send them away hungry, lest they faint *or* become exhausted on the way.

33 And the disciples said to Him, Where are we to get bread sufficient to feed so great a crowd in this isolated *and* desert place?

34 And Jesus asked them, How many loaves of bread do you have? They replied, Seven, and a few small fish.

35 And ordering the crowd to recline on the ground,

36 He took the seven loaves and the fish, and when He had given thanks, He broke them and gave them to the disciples, and the disciples gave them to the people.

37 And they all ate and were satisfied. And they gathered up seven [ᵂlarge provision] baskets full of the broken pieces that were left over.

38 Those who ate were 4,000 men, not including the women and the children.

---

s Marvin Vincent, *Word Studies.*   t John Wycliffe, *The Wycliffe Bible.*   u James Moulton and George Milligan, *The Vocabulary.*   v Hermann Cremer, *Biblico-Theological Lexicon.*   w Marvin Vincent, *Word Studies.* See also footnote on Matt. 14:20.

39 Then He dismissed the crowds, got into the boat, and went to the district of Magadan.

CHAPTER 16

NOW THE Pharisees and Sadducees came up to Jesus, and they asked Him to show them a sign (spectacular miracle) from heaven [attesting His divine authority].

2 He replied to them, *When it is evening you say, It will be fair weather, for the sky is red,*

3 *And in the morning, It will be stormy today, for the sky is red and has a gloomy and threatening look. You know how to interpret the appearance of the sky, but you cannot interpret the signs of the times.*

4 A wicked and morally unfaithful generation craves a sign, but no sign shall be given to it except the sign of *the prophet* Jonah. Then He left them and went away. [Jonah 3:4, 5.]

5 When the disciples reached the other side of the sea, they found that they had forgotten to bring any bread.

6 Jesus said to them, Be careful *and* on your guard against the leaven (ferment) of the Pharisees and Sadducees.

7 And they reasoned among themselves about it, saying, *It is* because we did not bring any bread.

8 But Jesus, aware of this, asked, Why are you discussing among yourselves the fact that you have no bread? O you [men, how little trust you have in Me, how] little faith!

9 Do you not yet discern (perceive and understand)? Do you not remember the five loaves of the five thousand, and how many [ysmall hand] baskets you gathered?

10 Nor the seven loaves for the four thousand, and how many [zlarge provision] baskets you took up?

11 How is it that you fail to understand that I was not talking to you about bread? But beware of the leaven (ferment) of the Pharisees and Sadducees.

12 Then they discerned that He did not tell them to beware of the leaven of bread, but of the teaching of the Pharisees and Sadducees.

13 Now when Jesus went into the region of Caesarea Philippi, He asked His disciples, Who do people say that the Son of Man is?

14 And they answered, Some say John the Baptist; others say Elijah; and others Jeremiah or one of the prophets.

15 He said to them, But who do you [yourselves] say that I am?

16 Simon Peter replied, You are the Christ, the Son of the living God.

17 Then Jesus answered him, Blessed (happy, fortunate, and ato be envied) are you, Simon Bar-Jonah. For flesh and blood [men] have not revealed this to you, but My Father Who is in heaven.

18 And I tell you, you are bPeter [Greek, *Petros*—a large piece of rock], and on this rock [Greek, *petra*—a chuge rock like Gibraltar] I will build My church, and the gates of Hades (the powers of the dinfernal region) shall enot overpower it [or be strong to its detriment or hold out against it].

19 I will give you the keys of the kingdom of heaven; and whatever you bind (declare to be improper and

---

x Some manuscripts do not have the rest of verse 2 and all of verse 3.   y Marvin Vincent, *Word Studies.* See also footnote on Matt. 14:20.   z Marvin Vincent, *Word Studies.* See also footnote on Matt. 14:20. a Alexander Souter, *Pocket Lexicon.*   b The rock on which the church is built is traditionally interpreted as either Peter's inspired confession of faith in Jesus as the Messiah, or it may be Peter himself (see Eph. 2:20).   c Kenneth Wuest, *Word Studies.*   d Kenneth Wuest, *Word Studies.*   e Joseph Thayer, *A Greek-English Lexicon.*

unlawful) on earth ᶠmust be what is already bound in heaven; and whatever you loose (declare lawful) on earth ᶠmust be what is already loosed in heaven. [Isa. 22:22.]

20 Then He sternly *and* strictly charged *and* warned the disciples to tell no one that He was *Jesus* the Christ.

21 From that time forth Jesus began [clearly] to show His disciples that He must go to Jerusalem and suffer many things at the hands of the elders and the high priests and scribes, and be killed, and on the third day be raised ᶠfrom death.

22 Then Peter took Him aside ʰto speak to Him privately and began to reprove and ᶦcharge Him sharply, saying, God forbid, Lord! This must never happen to You!

23 But Jesus turned ʰaway from Peter and said to him, Get behind Me, Satan! You are in My way [an offense and a hindrance and a snare to Me]; for you are ʰminding what partakes not of the nature *and* quality of God, but of men.

24 Then Jesus said to His disciples, If anyone desires to be My disciple, let him deny himself [disregard, lose sight of, and forget himself and his own interests] and take up his cross and follow Me [ᶜcleave steadfastly to Me, conform wholly to My example in living and, if need be, in dying, also].

25 For whoever is bent on saving his [temporal] life [his comfort and security here] shall lose it [eternal life]; and whoever loses his life [his comfort and security here] for My sake shall find it [life everlasting].

26 For what will it profit a man if he gains the whole world and forfeits his life [his blessed ᶦlife in the kingdom of God]? Or what would a man give as an exchange for his [blessed] ᶦlife [in the kingdom of God]?

27 For the Son of Man is going to come in the glory (majesty, splendor) of His Father with His angels, and then He will render account *and* reward every man in accordance with what he has done.

28 Truly I tell you, there are some standing here who will not taste death before they see the Son of Man coming in (into) His kingdom.

CHAPTER 17

AND SIX days after this, Jesus took with Him Peter and James and John his brother, and led them up on a high mountain by themselves.

2 And His appearance underwent a change in their presence; and His face shone ᵍclear and bright like the sun, and His clothing became as white as light.

3 And behold, there appeared to them Moses and Elijah, who kept talking with Him.

4 Then Peter began to speak and said to Jesus, Lord, it is good *and* delightful that we are here; if You approve, I will put up three booths here—one for You and one for Moses and one for Elijah.

5 While he was still speaking, behold, a shining cloud [ᶦcomposed of light] overshadowed them, and a voice from the cloud said, This is My Son, My Beloved, with Whom I am [and ʲhave always been] delighted. Listen to Him! [Ps. 2:7; Isa. 42:1.]

6 When the disciples heard it, they fell on their faces and were ᶦseized with alarm *and* struck with fear.

7 But Jesus came and touched them and said, Get up, and do not be afraid.

f Charles B. Williams, *The New Testament: A Translation*: "The perfect passive participle, here referring to a state of having been already forbidden [or permitted]."   g Hermann Cremer, *Biblico-Theological Lexicon.*   h Marvin Vincent, *Word Studies.*   i Joseph Thayer, *A Greek-English Lexicon.*   j Charles B. Williams, *The New Testament: A Translation*: "suggested by the aorist (past) tense."

8 And when they raised their eyes, they saw no one but Jesus only.

9 And as they were going down the mountain, Jesus cautioned *and* commanded them, Do not mention to anyone what you have seen, until the Son of Man has been raised from the dead.

10 The disciples asked Him, Then why do the scribes say that Elijah must come first?

11 He replied, Elijah does come and will get everything restored *and* ready.

12 But I tell you that Elijah has come already, and they did not know *or* recognize him, but did to him as they liked. So also the Son of Man is going to be treated *and* suffer at their hands.

13 Then the disciples understood that He spoke to them about John the Baptist. [Mal. 4:5.]

14 And when they approached the multitude, a man came up to Him, kneeling before Him and saying,

15 Lord, do pity *and* have mercy on my son, for he has epilepsy (is [k]moonstruck) and he suffers terribly; for frequently he falls into the fire and many times into the water.

16 And I brought him to Your disciples, and they were not able to cure him.

17 And Jesus answered, O you unbelieving ([l]warped, wayward, rebellious) and [m]thoroughly perverse generation! How long am I to remain with you? How long am I to bear with you? Bring him here to Me.

18 And Jesus rebuked the demon, and it came out of him, and the boy was cured instantly.

19 Then the disciples came to Jesus and asked privately, Why could we not drive it out?

20 He said to them, Because of the littleness of your faith [that is, your lack of [n]firmly relying trust]. For truly I say to you, if you have faith [[o]that is living] like a grain of mustard seed, you can say to this mountain, Move from here to yonder place, and it will move; and nothing will be impossible to you.

21 [p]*But this kind does not go out except by prayer and fasting.*

22 When they were going about here and there in Galilee, Jesus said to them, The Son of Man is going to be turned over into the hands of men.

23 And they will kill Him, and He will be raised [to life] again on the third day. And they were deeply *and* exceedingly grieved *and* distressed.

24 When they arrived in Capernaum, the collectors of the half shekel [the temple tax] went up to Peter and said, Does not your Teacher pay the half shekel? [Exod. 30:13; 38:26.]

25 He answered, Yes. And when he came home, Jesus spoke to him [about it] first, saying, What do you think, Simon? From whom do earthly rulers collect duties *or* tribute—from their own sons or from others [q]not of their own family?

26 And when Peter said, From other people [q]not of their own family, Jesus said to him, Then the sons are exempt.

27 However, in order not to give offense *and* cause them to stumble [that is, to cause them [q]to judge unfavorably and unjustly] go down to the sea and throw in a hook. Take the first fish that comes up, and when you open its mouth you will find there a shekel. Take it and give it to them to pay the temple tax for Me and for yourself.

k Joseph Thayer, *A Greek-English Lexicon*: "Epilepsy is supposed to return and increase with the increase of the moon." **l** Marvin Vincent, *Word Studies*. **m** Literally, "throughout" *(dia)*. **n** Hermann Cremer, *Biblico-Theological Lexicon*. **o** Charles B. Williams, *The New Testament: A Translation*. **p** Some manuscripts do not contain this verse. **q** Joseph Thayer, *A Greek-English Lexicon*.

CHAPTER 18

AT THAT time the disciples came up and asked Jesus, Who then is [really] the greatest in the kingdom of heaven?

2 And He called a little child to Himself and put him in the midst of them,

3 And said, Truly I say to you, unless you repent (change, turn about) and become like little children [trusting, lowly, loving, forgiving], you can never enter the kingdom of heaven [at all].

4 Whoever will humble himself therefore and become like this little child [trusting, lowly, loving, forgiving] is greatest in the kingdom of heaven.

5 And whoever receives *and* accepts *and* welcomes one little child like this for My sake and in My name receives *and* accepts *and* welcomes Me.

6 But whoever causes one of these little ones who believe in *and* [r]acknowledge *and* cleave to Me to stumble and sin [that is, who entices him or hinders him in right conduct or thought], it would be better ([s]more expedient and profitable or advantageous) for him to have a great millstone fastened around his neck and to be sunk in the depth of the sea.

7 Woe to the world for such temptations to sin *and* influences to do wrong! It is necessary that temptations come, but woe to the person on whose account *or* by whom the temptation comes!

8 And if your hand *or* your foot causes you to stumble *and* sin, cut it off and throw it away from you; it is better (more profitable and wholesome) for you to enter life maimed *or* lame than to have two hands or two

feet and be thrown into everlasting fire.

9 And if your eye causes you to stumble *and* sin, pluck it out and throw it away from you; it is better (more profitable and wholesome) for you to enter life with only one eye than to have two eyes and be thrown into the hell (Gehenna) of fire.

10 Beware that you do not despise *or* feel scornful toward *or* think little of one of these little ones, for I tell you that in heaven their angels always are in the presence of *and* look upon the face of My Father Who is in heaven.

11 [t]*For the Son of man came to save [*from the penalty of eternal death] that which was lost.*

12 What do you think? If a man has a hundred sheep, and one of them has gone astray *and* gets lost, will he not leave the ninety-nine on the mountain and go in search of the one that is lost?

13 And if it should be that he finds it, truly I say to you, he rejoices more over it than over the ninety-nine that did not get lost.

14 Just so it is not the will of My Father Who is in heaven that one of these little ones should be lost *and* perish.

15 If your brother wrongs you, go and show him his fault, between you and him privately. If he listens to you, you have won back your brother.

16 But if he does not listen, take along with you one or two others, so that every word may be confirmed *and* upheld by the testimony of two or three witnesses.

17 If he pays no attention to them [refusing to listen and obey], tell it to the church; and if he refuses to listen even to the church, let him be to you

r Hermann Cremer, *Biblico-Theological Lexicon.*   s G. Abbott-Smith, *Manual Greek Lexicon.*
t Many manuscripts do not contain this verse.

as a pagan and a tax collector. [Lev. 19:17; Deut. 19:15.]

18 Truly I tell you, whatever you forbid *and* declare to be improper and unlawful on earth must be ᵘwhat is already forbidden in heaven, and whatever you permit *and* declare proper and lawful on earth must be ᵘwhat is already permitted in heaven.

19 Again I tell you, if two of you on earth agree (harmonize together, make a symphony together) about whatever [anything and ᵛeverything] they may ask, it will come to pass *and* be done for them by My Father in heaven.

20 For wherever two or three are gathered (drawn together as My followers) in (into) My name, there I AM in the midst of them. [Exod. 3:14.]

21 Then Peter came up to Him and said, Lord, how many times may my brother sin against me and I forgive him *and* ᵂlet it go? [As many as] up to seven times?

22 Jesus answered him, I tell you, not up to seven times, but seventy times seven! [Gen. 4:24.]

23 Therefore the kingdom of heaven is like a human king who wished to settle accounts with his attendants.

24 When he began the accounting, one was brought to him who owed him 10,000 talents [probably about $10,000,000],

25 And because he could not pay, his master ordered him to be sold, with his wife and his children and everything that he possessed, and payment to be made.

26 So the attendant fell on his knees, begging him, Have patience with me and I will pay you everything.

27 And his master's heart was moved with compassion, and he re-leased him and forgave him [cancelling] the debt.

28 But that same attendant, as he went out, found one of his fellow attendants who owed him a hundred denarii [about twenty dollars]; and he caught him by the throat and said, Pay what you owe!

29 So his fellow attendant fell down and begged him earnestly, Give me time, and I will pay you *all*!

30 But he was unwilling, and he went out and had him put in prison till he should pay the debt.

31 When his fellow attendants saw what had happened, they were greatly distressed, and they went and told everything that had taken place to their master.

32 Then his master called him and said to him, You contemptible *and* wicked attendant! I forgave *and* cancelled all that [great] debt of yours because you begged me to.

33 And should you not have had pity *and* mercy on your fellow attendant, as I had pity *and* mercy on you?

34 And in wrath his master turned him over to the torturers (the jailers), till he should pay all that he owed.

35 So also My heavenly Father will deal with every one of you if you do not freely forgive your brother from your heart *his* offenses.

CHAPTER 19

N OW WHEN Jesus had finished saying these things, He left Galilee and went into the part of Judea that is beyond the Jordan;

2 And great throngs accompanied Him, and He cured them there.

3 And Pharisees came to Him and put Him to the test by asking, Is it lawful *and* right to dismiss *and* repudiate *and* divorce one's wife for any *and* ˣevery cause?

u See footnote on Matt. 16:19.   v John Wycliffe, *The Wycliffe Bible.*   w Joseph Thayer, *A Greek-English Lexicon.*   x Marvin Vincent, *Word Studies.*

4 He replied, Have you never read that He Who made them from the beginning made them male and female,

5 And said, For this reason a man shall leave his father and mother and shall be united firmly (joined inseparably) to his wife, and the two shall become one flesh? [Gen. 1:27; 2:24.]

6 So they are no longer two, but one flesh. What therefore God has joined together, let not man put asunder (separate)

7 They said to Him, Why then did Moses command [us] to give a certificate of divorce and thus to dismiss *and* repudiate a wife? [Deut. 24:1-4.]

8 He said to them, Because of the hardness (stubbornness and perversity) of your hearts Moses permitted you to dismiss *and* repudiate *and* divorce your wives; but from the beginning it has not been ʸso [ordained].

9 I say to you: whoever dismisses (repudiates, divorces) his wife, except for unchastity, and marries another commits adultery, ᶻ*and he who marries a divorced woman commits adultery.*

10 The disciples said to Him, If the case of a man with his wife is like this, it is neither profitable *nor* advisable to marry.

11 But He said to them, Not all men can accept this saying, but it is for those to whom [the capacity to receive] it has been given.

12 For there are eunuchs who have been born incapable of marriage; and there are eunuchs who have been made so by men; and there are eunuchs who have made themselves incapable of marriage for the sake of the kingdom of heaven. Let him who is able to accept this accept it.

13 Then little children were brought to Jesus, that He might put His hands on them and pray; but the disciples rebuked those who brought them.

14 But He said, Leave the children alone! Allow the little ones to come to Me, and do not forbid *or* restrain *or* hinder them, for of such [as these] is the kingdom of heaven *composed.*

15 And He put His hands upon them, and then went on His way.

16 And behold, there came a man up to Him, saying, Teacher, what excellent *and* perfectly *and* essentially good deed must I do to possess eternal life? [Lev. 18:5.]

17 And He said to him, Why do you ask Me about the perfectly *and* essentially good? There is only One Who is good [perfectly and essentially]—God, If you would enter into the Life, you must continually keep the commandments.

18 He said to Him, What ᵃsort of commandments? [Or, which ones?] And Jesus answered, You shall not kill, You shall not commit adultery, You shall not steal, You shall not bear false witness, [Exod. 20:12-16; Deut. 5:16-20.]

19 Honor your father and your mother, and, You shall love your neighbor as [you do] yourself. [Lev. 19:18; Matt. 22:39.]

20 The young man said, I have observed all these *from my youth;* what still do I lack?

21 Jesus answered him, If you would be perfect [that is, ᵇhave that spiritual maturity which accompanies self-sacrificing character], go and sell what you have and give to the poor, and you will have riches in heaven; and come, ʸbe My disciple [side with My party and follow Me].

22 But when the young man heard this, he went away sad (grieved and

y Joseph Thayer, *A Greek-English Lexicon.*   z Some manuscripts do not contain this phrase.   a Charles B. Williams, *The New Testament: A Translation:* "Interrogative of quality."   b Kenneth Wuest, *Word Studies.*

in much distress), for he had great possessions.

23 And Jesus said to His disciples, Truly I say to you, it will be difficult for a rich man to get into the kingdom of heaven.

24 Again I tell you, it is easier for a camel to go through the eye of a needle than for a rich man to go into the kingdom of heaven.

25 When the disciples heard this, they were utterly puzzled (astonished, bewildered), saying, Who then can be saved [cfrom eternal death]?

26 But Jesus looked at them and said, With men this is impossible, but all things are possible with God. [Gen. 18:14; Job 42:2.]

27 Then Peter answered Him, saying, Behold, we have left [our] all and have become dYour disciples [sided with Your party and followed You]. What then shall we receive?

28 Jesus said to them, Truly I say to you, in the new age (the eMessianic rebirth of the world), when the Son of Man shall sit down on the throne of His glory, you who have [become My disciples, sided with My party and] followed Me will also sit on twelve thrones and judge the twelve tribes of Israel.

29 And anyone and everyone who has left houses or brothers or sisters or father or mother or children or lands for My name's sake will receive fmany [even a hundred] times more and will inherit eternal life.

30 But many who [now] are first will be last [then], and many who [now] are last will be first [then].

CHAPTER 20

FOR THE kingdom of heaven is like the owner of an estate who went out in the morning galong with the dawn to hire workmen for his vineyard.

2 After agreeing with the laborers for a denarius a day, he sent them into his vineyard.

3 And going out about the third hour (nine o'clock), he saw others standing idle in the marketplace;

4 And he said to them, You go also into the vineyard, and whatever is right I will pay you. And they went.

5 He went out again about the sixth hour (noon), and the ninth hour (three o'clock) he did the same.

6 And about the eleventh hour (five o'clock) he went out and found still others standing around, and said to them, Why do you stand here idle all day?

7 They answered him, Because nobody has hired us. He told them, You go out into the vineyard also hand you will get whatever is just and fair.

8 When evening came, the owner of the vineyard said to his manager, Call the workmen and pay them their wages, beginning with the last and ending with the first. [Lev. 19:13; Deut. 24:15.]

9 And those who had been hired at the eleventh hour (five o'clock) came and received a denarius each.

10 Now when the first came, they supposed they would get more, but each of them also received a denarius.

11 And when they received it, they grumbled at the owner of the estate,

12 Saying, These [men] who came last worked no more than an hour, and yet you have made them rank with us who have borne the burden and the gscorching heat of the day.

13 But he answered one of them, Friend, I am doing you no injustice. Did you not agree with me for a denarius?

---

c Hermann Cremer, *Biblico-Theological Lexicon.*   d Joseph Thayer, *A Greek-English Lexicon.*
e James Moulton and George Milligan, *The Vocabulary.*   f Some manuscripts read "manifold."
g Marvin Vincent, *Word Studies.*   h Some manuscripts do not contain this phrase.

14 Take what belongs to you and go. I choose to give to this man hired last the same as I give to you.

15 Am I not permitted to do what I choose with what is mine? [Or do you begrudge my being generous?] Is your eye evil because I am good?

16 So those who [now] are last will be first [then], and those who [now] are first will be last [then]. *For many are called, but few chosen.

17 And as Jesus was going up to Jerusalem, He took the twelve disciples aside along the way and said to them,

18 Behold, we are going up to Jerusalem, and the Son of Man will be handed over to the chief priests and scribes; and they will sentence Him to death

19 And deliver Him over to the Gentiles to be mocked and whipped and crucified, and He will be raised [to life] on the third day.

20 Then the mother of Zebedee's children came up to Him with her sons and, kneeling, worshiped Him and asked a favor of Him.

21 And He asked her, What do you wish? She answered Him, Give orders that these two sons of mine may sit, one at Your right hand and one at Your left in Your kingdom.

22 But Jesus replied, You do not realize what you are asking. Are you able to drink the cup that I am about to drink *and to be baptized with the baptism with which I am baptized? They answered, We are able.

23 He said to them, You will drink My cup, but seats at My right hand and at My left are not Mine to give, but they are for those for whom they have been ʲordained *and prepared by My Father.

24 But when the ten [other disciples] heard this, they were indignant at the two brothers.

25 And Jesus called them to Him and said, You know that the rulers of the Gentiles lord it over them, and their great men hold them in subjection [tyrannizing over them].

26 Not so shall it be among you; but whoever wishes to be great among you must be your servant,

27 And whoever desires to be first among you must be your slave—

28 Just as the Son of Man came not to be waited on but to serve, and to give His life as a ransom for many [the price paid to set them free].

29 And as they were going out of Jericho, a great throng accompanied Him.

30 And behold, two blind men were sitting by the roadside, and when they heard that Jesus was passing by, they cried out, Lord, have pity *and mercy on us, [You] Son of David!

31 The crowds reproved them and told them to keep still; but they cried out all the more, Lord, have pity *and mercy on us, [You] Son of David!

32 And Jesus stopped and called them, and asked, What do you want Me to do for you?

33 They answered Him, Lord, we want our eyes to be opened!

34 And Jesus, in pity, touched their eyes; and instantly they received their sight and followed Him.

CHAPTER 21

AND WHEN they came near Jerusalem and had reached Bethphage at the Mount of Olives, Jesus sent two disciples on ahead,

2 Saying to them, Go into the village that is opposite you, and at once you will find a donkey tied, and a colt with her; untie [them] and bring [them] to Me.

3 If anyone says anything to you, you shall reply, The Lord needs

---

ⁱ Some manuscripts do not contain this phrase.   ʲ Joseph Thayer, *A Greek-English Lexicon.*

them, and he will let them go without delay.

4 This happened that what was spoken by the prophet might be fulfilled, saying,

5 Say to the Daughter of Zion [inhabitants of Jerusalem], Behold, your King is coming to you, lowly and riding on a donkey, and on a colt, the foal of a donkey [a beast of burden]. [Isa. 62:11; Zech. 9:9.]

6 Then the disciples went and did as Jesus had directed them.

7 They brought the donkey and the colt and laid their coats upon them, and He seated Himself on them [the clothing].

8 And most of the crowd kept spreading their garments on the road, and others kept cutting branches from the trees and scattering them on the road.

9 And the crowds that went ahead of Him and those that followed Him kept shouting, Hosanna (kO be propitious, graciously inclined) to the Son of David, [kthe Messiah]! Blessed (praised, glorified) is He Who comes in the name of the Lord! Hosanna (O be favorably disposed) in the highest [heaven]! [Ps. 118:26.]

10 And when He entered Jerusalem, all the city became agitated and l[trembling with excitement] said, Who is mThis?

11 And the crowds replied, This is the prophet Jesus from Nazareth of Galilee.

12 And Jesus went into the temple (nwhole temple enclosure) and drove out all who bought and sold in the ksacred place, and He turned over the ofour-footed tables of the money changers and the chairs of those who sold doves.

13 He said to them, The Scripture says, My house shall be called a house of prayer; but you have made it a den of robbers. [Isa. 56:7; Jer. 7:11.]

14 And the blind and the lame came to Him in the nporches and courts of the temple, and He cured them.

15 But when the chief priests and the scribes saw the wonderful things that He did and the boys and the girls and the pyouths and the maidens crying out in the nporches and courts of the temple, Hosanna (O be propitious, graciously inclined) to the Son of David! they were indignant.

16 And they said to Him, Do You hear what these are saying? And Jesus replied to them, Yes; have you never read, Out of the mouths of babes and unweaned infants You have made (provided) perfect praise? [Ps. 8:2.]

17 And leaving them, He departed from the city and went out to Bethany and lodged there.

18 In the early dawn the next morning, as He was coming back to the city, He was hungry.

19 And as He saw lone single leafy fig tree kabove the roadside, He went to it but He found nothing but leaves on it [qseeing that in the fig tree the fruit appears at the same time as the leaves]. And He said to it, Never again shall fruit grow on you! And the fig tree withered up at once.

20 When the disciples saw it, they marveled greatly and asked, How is it that the fig tree has withered away all at once?

21 And Jesus answered them, Truly I say to you, if you have faith (a rfirm relying trust) and do not doubt,

k Joseph Thayer, *A Greek-English Lexicon.* l Literal meaning. m Capitalized because of what He is, the spotless Son of God, not what the speakers may have thought He was. n Richard Trench, *Synonyms of the New Testament.* o James Moulton and George Milligan, *The Vocabulary.* p G. Abbott-Smith, *Manual Greek Lexicon.* q James Orr et al., eds., *International Standard Bible Encyclopedia.* r Hermann Cremer, *Biblico-Theological Lexicon.*

you will not only do what has been done to the fig tree, but even if you say to this mountain, Be taken up and cast into the sea, it will be done.

22 And whatever you ask for in prayer, having faith *and* [really] believing, you will receive.

23 And when He entered the sacred *enclosure* of the temple, the chief priests and elders of the people came up to Him as He was teaching and said, By what *power of authority arc You doing these things, and who gave You this power of authority?

24 Jesus answered them, I also will ask you a question, and if you give Me the answer, then I also will tell you by what *power of authority I do these things.

25 The baptism of John—from where was it? From heaven or from men? And they reasoned *and* argued with one another, If we say, From heaven, *He will ask us, Why then did you not believe him?

26 But if we say, From men—we are afraid of *and* must reckon with the multitude, for they all regard John as a prophet.

27 So they answered Jesus, We do not know. And He said to them, Neither will I tell you by what *power of authority I do these things.

28 What do you think? There was a man who had two sons. He came to the first and said, Son, go and work today in the vineyard.

29 And he answered, I will not; but afterward he changed his mind and went.

30 Then the man came to the second and said the same [thing]. And he replied, I will [go], sir; but he did not go.

31 Which of the two did the will of the father? They replied, The first one. Jesus said to them, Truly I tell you, the tax collectors and the harlots will get into the kingdom of heaven before you.

32 For John came to you walking in the way of an upright man in right standing with God, and you did not believe him, but the tax collectors and the harlots did believe him; and you, even when you saw that, did not afterward change your minds and believe him [adhere to, trust in, and rely on what he told you].

33 Listen to another parable: There was a master of a house who planted a vineyard and put a hedge around it and dug a wine vat in it and built a watchtower. Then he let it out [for rent] to tenants and went into another country.

34 When the fruit season drew near, he sent his servants to the tenants to get his [share of the] fruit.

35 But the tenants took his servants and beat one, killed another, and stoned another.

36 Again he sent other servants, more than the first time, and they treated them the same way.

37 Finally he sent his own son to them, saying, They will respect *and* give heed to my son.

38 But when the tenants saw the son, they said to themselves, This is the heir; come on, let us kill him and have his inheritance.

39 And they took him and threw him out of the vineyard and killed him.

40 Now when the owner of the vineyard comes back, what will he do to those tenants?

41 They said to Him, He will put those wretches to a miserable death and rent the vineyard to other tenants *of such a character that they

---

s Richard Trench, *Synonyms of the New Testament.*   t Joseph Thayer, *A Greek-English Lexicon.*
u Capitalized because of what He is, the spotless Son of God, not what the speakers may have thought He was.
v Marvin Vincent, *Word Studies.*

will give him the fruits promptly in their season. [Isa. 5:1–7.]

42 Jesus asked them, Have you never read in the Scriptures: The very Stone which the builders rejected *and* threw away has become the Cornerstone; this is the Lord's doing, and it is marvelous in our eyes? [Ps. 118:22, 23.]

43 I tell you, for this reason the kingdom of God will be taken away from you and given to a people who will produce the fruits of it.

44 *ʷAnd whoever falls on this Stone will be broken to pieces, but he on whom It falls will be crushed to powder [and It will ˣwinnow him, ʸscattering him like dust].* [Isa. 8:14; Dan. 2:34, 35.]

45 And when the chief priests and the Pharisees heard His parables (comparisons, stories used to illustrate and explain), they perceived that He was talking about them.

46 And although they were trying to arrest Him, they feared the throngs because they regarded Him as a prophet.

CHAPTER 22

AND AGAIN Jesus spoke to them in parables (comparisons, stories used to illustrate and explain), saying,

2 The kingdom of heaven is like a king who gave a wedding banquet for his son

3 And sent his servants to summon those who had been invited to the wedding banquet, but they refused to come.

4 Again he sent other servants, saying, Tell those who are invited, Behold, I have prepared my banquet; my bullocks and my fat calves are killed, and everything is prepared; come to the wedding feast.

5 But they were not concerned *and* paid no attention [they ignored and made light of the summons, treating it with contempt] and they went away—one to his farm, another to his business,

6 While the others seized his servants, treated them shamefully, and put them to death.

7 [Hearing this] the king was infuriated; and he sent his soldiers and put those murderers to death and burned their city.

8 Then he said to his servants, The wedding [feast] is prepared, but those invited were not worthy.

9 So go to the thoroughfares where they leave the city [where the main roads and those from the country end] and invite to the wedding feast as many as you find.

10 And those servants went out on the crossroads and got together as many as they found, both bad and good, so [the room in which] the wedding feast [was held] was filled with guests.

11 But when the king came in to view the guests, he looked intently at a man there who had on no wedding garment.

12 And he said, Friend, how did you come in here without putting on the [appropriate] wedding garment? And he was speechless (ᶻmuzzled, gagged).

13 Then the king said to the attendants, Tie him hand and foot, and throw him into the darkness outside; there will be weeping and grinding of teeth.

14 For many are called (invited and summoned), but few are chosen.

15 Then the Pharisees went and consulted *and* plotted together how they might entangle Jesus in His talk.

16 And they sent their disciples to

ʷ Some manuscripts do not contain verse 44. ˣ Joseph Thayer, *A Greek-English Lexicon.* ʸ Marvin Vincent, *Word Studies.* ᶻ Literal translation.

Him along with the Herodians, saying, Teacher, we know that You are [a]sincere *and* what You profess to be and that You teach the way of God truthfully, regardless of consequences *and* being afraid of no man; for You are impartial *and* do not regard either the person *or* the position of anyone.

17 Tell us then what You think about this: Is it lawful to pay tribute [levied on individuals and to be paid yearly] to Caesar or not?

18 But Jesus, aware of their malicious plot, asked, Why do you put Me to the test *and* try to entrap Me, you pretenders (hypocrites)?

19 Show me the money *used* for the tribute. And they brought Him a denarius.

20 And Jesus said to them, Whose likeness and title are these?

21 They said, Caesar's. Then He said to them, Pay therefore to Caesar the things that are due to Caesar, and pay to God the things that are due to God.

22 When they heard it they were amazed *and* marveled; and they left Him and departed.

23 The same day some Sadducees, who say that there is no resurrection [of the dead], came to Him and they asked Him a question,

24 Saying, Teacher, Moses said, If a man dies, leaving no children, his brother shall marry the widow and raise up a family for his brother. [Deut. 25:5.]

25 Now there were seven brothers among us; the first married and died, and, having no children, left his wife to his brother.

26 The second also died childless, and the third, down to the seventh.

27 Last of all, the woman died also.

28 Now, in the resurrection, to which of the seven will she be wife? For they all had her.

29 But Jesus replied to them, You are wrong because you know neither the Scriptures nor God's power.

30 For in the resurrected state neither do [men] marry nor are [women] given in marriage, but they are like the angels in heaven.

31 But as to the resurrection of the dead—have you never read what was said to you by God,

32 I am the God of Abraham, and the God of Isaac, and the God of Jacob? He is not the God of the dead but of the living! [Exod. 3:6.]

33 And when the throng heard it, they were astonished *and* filled with [b]glad] amazement at His teaching.

34 Now when the Pharisees heard that He had silenced ([c]muzzled) the Sadducees, they gathered together.

35 And one of their number, a lawyer, asked Him a question to test Him.

36 Teacher, which [d]kind of commandment is great and important (the principal kind) in the Law? [Some commandments are light—which are heavy?]

37 And He replied to him, You shall love the Lord your God with all your heart and with all your soul and with all your mind (intellect). [Deut. 6:5.]

38 This is the great (most important, principal) and first commandment.

39 And a second is like it: You shall love your neighbor as [you do] yourself. [Lev. 19:18.]

40 These two commandments [b]sum up *and* upon them depend all the Law and the Prophets.

41 Now while the Pharisees were still assembled there, Jesus asked them a question,

---

a Hermann Cremer, *Biblico-Theological Lexicon.*   b Joseph Thayer, *A Greek-English Lexicon.*
c Literal translation.   d Marvin Vincent, *Word Studies.*

42 Saying, What do you think of the Christ? Whose Son is He? They said to Him, The Son of David.

43 He said to them, How is it then that David, under the influence of the [Holy] Spirit, calls Him Lord, saying,

44 The Lord said to My Lord, Sit at My right hand until I put Your enemies under Your feet? [Ps. 110:1.]

45 If then David thus calls Him Lord, how is He his Son?

46 And no one was able to answer Him a word, nor from that day did anyone venture *or* dare to question Him.

CHAPTER 23

THEN JESUS said to the multitudes and to His disciples,

2 The scribes and Pharisees sit on Moses' seat [of authority].

3 So observe and practice all they tell you; but do not do what they do, for they preach, but do not practice.

4 They lie up heavy loads, *hard to bear*, and place them on men's shoulders, but they themselves will not lift a finger to help bear them.

5 They do all their works to be seen of men; for they make wide their phylacteries (°small cases enclosing certain Scripture passages, worn during prayer on the left arm and forehead) and make long their fringes [worn by all male Israelites, according to the command]. [Exod. 13:9; Num. 15:38; Deut. 6:8.]

6 And they ʳtake pleasure in *and* [thus] love the place of honor at feasts and the best seats in the synagogues,

7 And to be greeted with honor in the marketplaces and to have people call them rabbi.

8 But you are not to be called rabbi (teacher), for you have one Teacher and you are all brothers.

9 And do not call anyone [in the church] on earth father, for you have one Father, Who is in heaven.

10 And you must not be called masters (leaders), for you have one Master (Leader), the Christ.

11 He who is greatest among you shall be your servant.

12 Whoever exalts himself [ᵍwith haughtiness and empty pride] shall be humbled (brought low), and whoever humbles himself [whoever has a modest opinion of himself and behaves accordingly] shall be ᵍraised to honor.

13 But woe to you, scribes and Pharisees, pretenders (hypocrites)! For you shut the kingdom of heaven in men's faces; for you neither enter yourselves, nor do you allow those who are about to go in to do so.

14 ʰ*Woe to you, scribes and Pharisees, pretenders (hypocrites)! For you swallow up widows' houses and for a pretense to cover it up make long prayers; therefore you will receive the greater condemnation and the heavier sentence.*

15 Woe to you, scribes and Pharisees, pretenders (hypocrites)! For you travel over sea and land to make a single proselyte, and when he becomes one [a proselyte], you make him doubly as much a child of hell (Gehenna) as you are.

16 Woe to you, blind guides, who say, If anyone swears by the ⁱsanctuary of the temple, it is nothing; but if anyone swears by the gold of the ⁱsanctuary, he is a debtor [bound by his oath].

17 You blind fools! For which is greater: the gold, or the ⁱsanctuary of the temple that has made the gold sacred? [Exod. 30:29.]

e John D. Davis, *A Dictionary of the Bible.*   f Kenneth Wuest, *Word Studies.*   g Joseph Thayer, *A Greek-English Lexicon.*   h Some manuscripts do not contain verse 14.   i Richard Trench, *Synonyms of the New Testament.*

18 You say too, Whoever swears by the altar is not duty bound; but whoever swears by the offering on the altar, his oath is binding.

19 You blind men! Which is greater: the gift, or the altar which makes the gift sacred?

20 So whoever swears by the altar swears by it and by everything on it.

21 And he who swears by the ʲsanctuary of the temple swears by it and by Him Who dwells in it. [I Kings 8:13; Ps. 26:8.]

22 And whoever swears by heaven swears by the throne of God and by Him Who sits upon it.

23 Woe to you, scribes and Pharisees, pretenders (hypocrites)! For you give a tenth of your mint and dill and cummin, and have neglected *and* omitted the weightier (more important) matters of the Law—right *and* justice and mercy and fidelity. These you ought [particularly] to have done, without neglecting the others.

24 You blind guides, filtering out a ᵏcamel! [Lev. 27:30; Mic. 6:8.]

25 Woe to you, scribes and Pharisees, pretenders (hypocrites)! For you clean the outside of the cup and of the plate, but within they are full of extortion (prey, spoil, plunder) and grasping self-indulgence.

26 You blind Pharisee! First clean the inside of the cup and of the plate, so that the outside may be clean also.

27 Woe to you, scribes and Pharisees, pretenders (hypocrites)! For you are like tombs that have been whitewashed, which look beautiful on the outside but inside are full of dead men's bones and everything impure.

28 Just so, you also outwardly seem to people to be just *and* upright but inside you are full of pretense and lawlessness *and* iniquity. [Ps. 5:9.]

29 Woe to you, scribes and Pharisees, pretenders (hypocrites)! For you build tombs for the prophets and decorate the monuments of the righteous,

30 Saying, If we had lived in the days of our forefathers, we would not have aided them in shedding the blood of the prophets.

31 Thus you are testifying against yourselves that you are the descendants of those who murdered the prophets.

32 Fill up, then, the measure of your fathers' sins to the brim [so ˡthat nothing may be wanting to a full measure].

33 You serpents! You spawn of vipers! How can you escape the ˡpenalty to be suffered in hell (Gehenna)?

34 Because of this, take notice: I am sending you prophets and wise men (interpreters and teachers) and scribes (men learned in the Mosaic Law and the Prophets); some of them you will kill, even crucify, and some you will flog in your synagogues and pursue *and* persecute from town to town,

35 So that upon your heads may come all the blood of the righteous (ᵐthose who correspond to the divine standard of right) shed on earth, from the blood of the righteous Abel to the blood of Zechariah son of Barachiah, whom you murdered between the sanctuary and the altar [of burnt offering]. [Gen. 4:8; II Chron. 24:21.]

36 Truly I declare to you, all these [ˡevil, calamitous times] will come upon this generation. [II Chron. 36:15, 16.]

37 O Jerusalem, Jerusalem, murdering the prophets and stoning those who are sent to you! How often would I have gathered your children

---

j Richard Trench, *Synonyms of the New Testament.* unclean animals, whereas the gnat was the smallest of unclean animals.   k The camel was also unclean, one of the largest of unclean animals (Lev. 11:4).   l Joseph Thayer, *A Greek-English Lexicon.*   m G. Abbott-Smith, *Manual Greek Lexicon.*

together as a mother fowl gathers her brood under her wings, and you refused!

38 Behold, your house is forsaken and desolate (abandoned and left destitute of God's help). [I Kings 9:7; Jer. 22:5.]

39 For I declare to you, you will not see Me again until you say, Blessed (magnified in worship, adored, and exalted) is He Who comes in the name of the Lord! [Ps. 118:26.]

CHAPTER 24

JESUS DEPARTED from the temple [n]area and was going on His way when His disciples came up to Him to call His attention to the buildings of the temple *and* point them out to Him.

2 But He answered them, Do you see all these? Truly I tell you, there will not be left here one stone upon another that will not be thrown down.

3 While He was seated on the Mount of Olives, the disciples came to Him privately and said, Tell us, when will this take place, and what will be the sign of Your coming *and* of the end (the completion, the consummation) of the age?

4 Jesus answered them, Be careful that no one misleads you [deceiving you and leading you into error].

5 For many will come in (on the strength of) My name [[o]appropriating the name which belongs to Me], saying, I am the Christ (the Messiah), and they will lead many astray.

6 And you will hear of wars and rumors of wars; see that you are not frightened *or* troubled, for this must take place, but the end is not yet.

7 For nation will rise against nation, and kingdom against kingdom,

and there will be famines and earthquakes in place after place;

8 All this is but the beginning [the early pains] of the [p]birth pangs [of the [o]intolerable anguish].

9 Then they will hand you over to suffer affliction *and* tribulation and put you to death, and you will be hated by all nations for My name's sake.

10 And then many will be offended *and* repelled *and* will [o]begin to distrust *and* desert [Him Whom they ought to trust and obey] *and* will stumble and fall away and betray one another *and* pursue one another with hatred.

11 And many false prophets will rise up and deceive *and* lead many into error.

12 And the love of [q]the great body of people will grow cold because of the multiplied lawlessness *and* iniquity,

13 But he who endures to the end will be saved.

14 And this good news of the kingdom (the Gospel) will be preached throughout the whole world as a testimony to all the nations, and then will come the end.

15 So when you see the appalling sacrilege [the abomination that astonishes and makes desolate], spoken of by the prophet Daniel, standing in the Holy Place—let the reader take notice *and* [o]ponder *and* consider *and* heed [this]—[Dan. 9:27; 11:31; 12:11.]

16 Then let those who are in Judea flee to the mountains;

17 Let him who is on the housetop not come down *and* go into the house to take anything;

18 And let him who is in the field not turn back to get his overcoat.

19 And alas for the women who are

n Richard Trench, *Synonyms of the New Testament.*   o Joseph Thayer, *A Greek-English Lexicon.*
p Literal translation.   q Marvin Vincent. *Word Studies.*

pregnant and for those who have nursing babies in those days!

20 Pray that your flight may not be in winter or on a Sabbath.

21 For then there will be great tribulation (affliction, distress, and oppression) such as has not been from the beginning of the world until now —no, and never will be [again]. [Dan. 12:1; Joel 2:2.]

22 And if those days had not been shortened, no human being would endure *and* survive, but for the sake of the elect (God's chosen ones) those days will be shortened.

23 If anyone says to you then, Behold, here is the Christ (the Messiah)! or, There He is! do not believe it.

24 For false Christs and false prophets will arise, and they will show great signs and wonders so as to deceive *and* lead astray, if possible, even the elect (God's chosen ones).

25 See, I have warned you beforehand.

26 So if they say to you, Behold, He is in the wilderness (desert)—do not go out there; if they tell you, Behold, He is in the secret places *or* inner rooms—do not believe it.

27 For just as the lightning flashes from the east and shines *and* [is seen as far as the west, so will the coming of the Son of Man be.

28 Wherever there is a fallen body (a corpse), there the vultures (or eagles) will flock together. [Job 39:30.]

29 Immediately after the tribulation of those days the sun will be darkened, and the moon will not shed its light, and the stars will fall from the sky, and the powers of the heavens will be shaken. [Isa. 13:10; 34:4; Joel 2:10, 11; Zeph. 1:15.]

30 Then the sign of the Son of Man will appear in the sky, and then all the tribes of the earth will mourn *and* [beat their breasts *and* lament in anguish, and they will see the Son of Man coming on the clouds of heaven with power and great glory [in brilliancy and splendor]. [Dan. 7:13; Rev. 1:7.]

31 And He will send out His angels with a loud trumpet call, and they will gather His elect (His chosen ones) from the four winds, [even] from one end of the [universe to the other. [Isa. 27:13; Zech. 9:14.]

32 From the fig tree learn this lesson: as soon as its [young shoots become soft and tender and it puts out its leaves, you know [of a surety that summer is near.

33 So also when you see these signs, [all taken together, coming to pass, you may know [of a surety that He is near, at the very doors.

34 Truly I tell you, this generation ([the whole multitude of people living at the same time, [in a definite, [given period) will not pass away till all these things [taken together take place.

35 [Sky and earth will pass away, but My words will not pass away.

36 But of that [exact] day and hour no one knows, not even the angels of heaven, nor the Son, but only the Father.

37 As were the days of Noah, so will be the coming of the Son of Man.

38 For just as in those days before the flood they were eating and drinking, [men] marrying and [women] being given in marriage, until the [very] day when Noah went into the ark,

39 And they did not know *or* understand until the flood came and swept them all away—so will be the coming of the Son of Man. [Gen. 6:5–8; 7:6–24.]

r Marvin Vincent, *Word Studies.*   s G. Abbott-Smith, *Manual Greek Lexicon.*   t Joseph Thayer, *A Greek-English Lexicon.*   u Hermann Cremer, *Biblico-Theological Lexicon.*   v James Moulton and George Milligan, *The Vocabulary.*

40 At that time two men will be in the field; one will be taken and one will be left.

41 Two women will be grinding at the hand mill; one will be taken and one will be left.

42 Watch therefore [ʷgive strict attention, be cautious and active], for you do not know in what kind of a day [ˣwhether a near or remote one] your Lord is coming.

43 But understand this: had the householder known in what [part of the night, whether in a ˣnight or a morning] watch the thief was coming, he would have watched and would not have allowed his house to be ʸundermined *and* broken into.

44 You also must be ready therefore, for the Son of Man is coming at an hour when you do not expect Him.

45 Who then is the faithful, thoughtful, *and* wise servant, whom his master has put in charge of his household to give to the others the food *and* supplies at the proper time?

46 Blessed (happy, fortunate, and ᶻto be envied) is that servant whom, when his master comes, he will find so doing.

47 I solemnly declare to you, he will set him over all his possessions.

48 But if that servant is wicked and says to himself, My master is delayed *and* is going to be gone a long time,

49 And begins to beat his fellow servants and to eat and drink with the drunken,

50 The master of that servant will come on a day when he does not expect him and at an hour of which he is not aware,

51 And will punish him [ʷcut him up by scourging] and put him with the pretenders (hypocrites); there will be weeping and grinding of teeth.

CHAPTER 25

THEN THE kingdom of heaven shall be likened to ten virgins who took their lamps and went to meet the bridegroom.

2 Five of them were foolish (thoughtless, without forethought) and five were wise (sensible, intelligent, and prudent).

3 For when the foolish took their lamps, they did not take any [extra] oil with them;

4 But the wise took flasks of oil along with them [also] with their lamps.

5 While the bridegroom lingered *and* was slow in coming, they all began nodding their heads, and they fell asleep.

6 But at midnight there was a shout, Behold, the bridegroom! Go out to meet him!

7 Then all those virgins got up and put their own lamps in order.

8 And the foolish said to the wise, Give us some of your oil, for our lamps are going out.

9 But the wise replied, There will not be enough for us and for you; go instead to the dealers and buy for yourselves.

10 But while they were going away to buy, the bridegroom came, and those who were prepared went in with him to the marriage feast; and the door was shut.

11 Later the other virgins also came and said, Lord, Lord, open [the door] to us!

12 But He replied, I solemnly declare to you, I do not know you [I am not acquainted with you].

13 Watch therefore [give strict attention and be cautious and active], for you know neither the day nor the hour *when the Son of Man will come.*

14 For it is like a man who was

w Joseph Thayer, *A Greek-English Lexicon.*   x Marvin Vincent, *Word Studies.*   y John Wycliffe, *The Wycliffe Bible.*   z Alexander Souter, *Pocket Lexicon.*

about to take a long journey, and he called his servants together and entrusted them with his property.

15 To one he gave five talents [probably about $5,000], to another two, to another one—to each in proportion to his own [a]personal ability. Then he departed and left the country.

16 He who had received the five talents went at once and traded with them, and he gained five talents more.

17 And likewise he who had received the two talents—he also gained two talents more.

18 But he who had received the one talent went and dug a hole in the ground and hid his master's money.

19 Now after a long time the master of those servants returned and settled accounts with them.

20 And he who had received the five talents came and brought him five more, saying, Master, you entrusted to me five talents; see, here I have gained five talents more.

21 His master said to him, Well done, you upright (honorable, [b]admirable) and faithful servant! You have been faithful and trustworthy over a little; I will put you in charge of much. Enter into and share the joy (the delight, the [c]blessedness) which your master enjoys.

22 And he also who had the two talents came forward, saying, Master, you entrusted two talents to me; here I have gained two talents more.

23 His master said to him, Well done, you upright (honorable, [b]admirable) and faithful servant! You have been faithful and trustworthy over a little; I will put you in charge of much. Enter into and share the joy (the delight, the [c]blessedness) which your master enjoys.

24 He who had received one talent also came forward, saying, Master, I knew you to be a harsh and hard man, reaping where you did not sow, and gathering where you had not winnowed [the grain].

25 So I was afraid, and I went and hid your talent in the ground. Here you have what is your own.

26 But his master answered him, You wicked and lazy and idle servant! Did you indeed know that I reap where I have not sowed and gather [grain] where I have not winnowed?

27 Then you should have invested my money with the bankers, and at my coming I would have received what was my own with interest.

28 So take the talent away from him and give it to the one who has the ten talents.

29 For to everyone who has will more be given, and he will be [c]furnished richly so that he will have an abundance; but from the one who does not have, even what he does have will be taken away.

30 And throw the good-for-nothing servant into the outer darkness; there will be weeping and grinding of teeth.

31 When the Son of Man comes in His glory (His majesty and splendor), and all the holy angels with Him, then He will sit on the throne of His glory.

32 All nations will be gathered before Him, and He will separate them [the people] from one another as a shepherd separates his sheep from the goats; [Ezek. 34:17.]

33 And He will cause the sheep to stand at His right hand, but the goats at His left.

34 Then the King will say to those at His right hand, Come, you blessed

a Marvin Vincent, *Word Studies.*   b Hermann Cremer, *Biblico-Theological Lexicon.*   c Joseph Thayer, *A Greek-English Lexicon.*

of My Father [you dfavored of God and appointed to eternal salvation], inherit (receive as your own) the kingdom prepared for you from the foundation of the world.

35 For I was hungry and you gave Me food, I was thirsty and you gave Me something to drink, I was a stranger and you ebrought Me together with yourselves and welcomed and entertained and flodged Me,

36 I was naked and you clothed Me, I was sick and you visited Me gwith help and ministering care, I was in prison and you came to see Me. [Isa. 58:7.]

37 Then the just and upright will answer Him, Lord, when did we see You hungry and gave You food, or thirsty and gave You something to drink?

38 And when did we see You a stranger and welcomed and entertained You, or naked and clothed You?

39 And when did we see You sick or in prison and came to visit You?

40 And the King will reply to them, Truly I tell you, in so far as you did it for one of the least [din the estimation of men] of these My brethren, you did it for Me. [Prov. 19:17.]

41 Then He will say to those at His left hand, Begone from Me, you cursed, into the eternal fire prepared for the devil and his angels!

42 For I was hungry and you gave Me no food, I was thirsty and you gave Me nothing to drink,

43 I was a stranger and you did not welcome Me and entertain Me, I was naked and you did not clothe Me, I was sick and in prison and you did not visit Me gwith help and ministering care.

44 Then they also [in their turn] will answer, Lord, when did we see

You hungry or thirsty or a stranger or naked or sick or in prison, and did not minister to You?

45 And He will reply to them, Solemnly I declare to you, in so far as you failed to do it for the least [din the estimation of men] of these, you failed to do it for Me. [Prov. 14:31; 17:5.]

46 Then they will go away into eternal punishment, but those who are just and upright and in right standing with God into eternal life. [Dan. 12:2.]

CHAPTER 26

WHEN JESUS had ended this discourse, He said to His disciples,

2 You know that the Passover is in two days—and the Son of Man will be delivered up dtreacherously to be crucified.

3 Then the chief priests and the elders of the people gathered in the [hopen] court of the palace of the high priest, whose name was Caiaphas,

4 And consulted together in order to arrest Jesus by stratagem secretly and put Him to death.

5 But they said, It must not be during the Feast, for fear that there will be a riot among the people.

6 Now when Jesus came back to Bethany and was in the house of Simon the leper,

7 A woman came up to Him with an alabaster flask of very precious perfume, and she poured it on His head as He reclined at table.

8 And when the disciples saw it, they were indignant, saying, For what purpose is all this waste?

9 For this perfume might have been sold for a large sum and the money given to the poor.

10 But Jesus, fully aware of this,

d Joseph Thayer, A Greek-English Lexicon. Bible.   e Literal meaning.   f William Tyndale, The Tyndale
g Kenneth Wuest, Word Studies.   h Marvin Vincent, Word Studies.

said to them, Why do you bother the woman? She has done a noble (praiseworthy and beautiful) thing to Me.

11 For you always have the poor among you, but you will not always have Me. [Deut. 15:11.]

12 In pouring this perfume on My body she has done something to prepare Me for My burial.

13 Truly I tell you, wherever this good news (the Gospel) is preached in the whole world, what this woman has done will be told also, in memory of her.

14 Then one of the Twelve [apostles], who was called Judas Iscariot, went to the chief priests

15 And said, What are you willing to give me if I hand Him over to you? And they weighed out for and paid to him thirty pieces of silver [about twenty-one dollars and sixty cents]. [Exod. 21:32; Zech. 11:12.]

16 And from that moment he sought a fitting opportunity to betray Him.

17 Now on the first day of Unleavened Bread [Passover week], the disciples came to Jesus and said to Him, Where do You wish us to prepare for You to eat the Passover supper?

18 He said, Go into the city to a certain man and say to him, The Master says: My time is near; I will keep the Passover at your house with My disciples.

19 And accordingly the disciples did as Jesus had directed them, and they made ready the Passover supper. [Deut. 16:5-8.]

20 When it was evening, He was reclining at table with the twelve disciples.

21 And as they were eating, He said, Solemnly I say to you, one of you will betray Me!

22 They were exceedingly pained and distressed and deeply hurt and sorrowful and began to say to Him one after another, Surely it cannot be I, Lord, can it?

23 He replied, He who has [just] dipped his hand in the same dish with Me will betray Me!

24 The Son of Man is going just as it is written of Him; but woe to that man by whom the Son of Man is betrayed! It would have been better (more profitable and wholesome) for that man if he had never been born! [Ps. 41:9.]

25 Judas, the betrayer, said, Surely it is not I, is it, Master? He said to him, You have stated [the fact].

26 Now as they were eating, Jesus took bread and, ipraising God, gave thanks and asked Him to bless it to their use, and when He had broken it, He gave it to the disciples and said, Take, eat; this is My body.

27 And He took a cup, and when He had given thanks, He gave it to them, saying, Drink of it, all of you;

28 For this is My blood of the new covenant, which [jratifies the agreement and] is being poured out for many for the forgiveness of sins. [Exod. 24:6-8.]

29 I say to you, I shall not drink again of this fruit of the vine until that day when I drink it with you new and jof superior quality in My Father's kingdom.

30 And when they had sung a hymn, they went out to the Mount of Olives.

31 Then Jesus said to them, You will all be offended and stumble and fall away because of Me this night [distrusting and deserting Me], for it is written, I will strike the Shepherd, and the sheep of the flock will be scattered. [Zech. 13:7.]

32 But after I am raised up [to life

---

i Marvin Vincent, *Word Studies*.   j Joseph Thayer, *A Greek-English Lexicon*.

again], I will go ahead of you to Galilee.

33 Peter declared to Him, Though they all are offended *and* stumble *and* fall away because of You [and distrust and desert You], I will never do so.

34 Jesus said to him, Solemnly I declare to you, this very night, before a [k]single rooster crows, you will deny *and* disown Me three times.

35 Peter said to Him, Even if I must die with You, I will not deny *or* disown You! And all the disciples said the same thing.

36 Then Jesus went with them to a place called Gethsemane, and He told His disciples, Sit down here while I go over yonder and pray.

37 And taking with Him Peter and the two sons of Zebedee, He began to [k]show grief *and* distress of mind and was [l]deeply depressed.

38 Then He said to them, My soul is very sad *and* deeply grieved, so that [m]I am almost dying of sorrow. Stay here and keep awake *and* keep watch with Me.

39 And going a little farther, He threw Himself upon the ground on His face and prayed saying, My Father, if it is possible, let this cup pass away from Me; nevertheless, not what I will [not what I desire], but as You will *and* desire.

40 And He came to the disciples and found them sleeping, and He said to Peter, What! Are you so utterly unable to stay awake *and* keep watch with Me for one hour?

41 All of you must keep awake (give strict attention, be cautious and active) *and* watch and pray, that you may not come into temptation. The spirit indeed is willing, but the flesh is weak.

42 Again a second time He went away and prayed, My Father, if this cannot pass by unless I drink it, Your will be done.

43 And again He came and found them sleeping, for their eyes were weighed down with sleep.

44 So, leaving them again, He went away and prayed for the third time, using the same words.

45 Then He returned to the disciples and said to them, Are you still sleeping and taking your rest? Behold, the hour is at hand, and the Son of Man is betrayed into the hands of [n]especially wicked sinners [[o]whose way or nature it is to act in opposition to God].

46 Get up, let us be going! See, My betrayer is at hand!

47 As He was still speaking, Judas, one of the Twelve [apostles], came up, and with him a great crowd with swords and clubs, from the chief priests and elders of the people.

48 Now the betrayer had given them a sign, saying, The One I shall kiss is the Man; seize Him.

49 And he came up to Jesus at once and said, Hail (greetings, good health to You, long life to You), Master! And he [p]embraced Him and kissed Him [q]with [pretended] warmth and devotion.

50 Jesus said to him, Friend, for what are you here? Then they came up and laid hands on Jesus and arrested Him.

51 And behold, one of those who were with Jesus reached out his hand and drew his sword and, striking the body servant of the high priest, cut off his ear.

52 Then Jesus said to him, Put your sword back into its place, for all who

---

k Marvin Vincent, *Word Studies.*   l George R. Berry, *Greek-English New Testament Lexicon.*
m Joseph Thayer, *A Greek-English Lexicon.*   n G. Abbott-Smith, *Manual Greek Lexicon.*
o Hermann Cremer, *Biblico-Theological Lexicon.*   p H.A.W. Meyer, *Critical and Exegetical Handbook to the Gospel of Matthew.*   q Kenneth Wuest, *Word Studies.*

draw the sword will die by the sword. [Gen. 9:6.]

53 Do you suppose that I cannot appeal to My Father, and He will immediately provide Me with more than twelve legions [[r]more than 80,000] of angels?

54 But how then would the Scriptures be fulfilled, that it must come about this way?

55 At that moment Jesus said to the crowds, Have you come out with swords and clubs as [you would] against a robber to capture Me? Day after day I was [s]accustomed to sit in the [t]porches *and* courts of the temple teaching, and you did not arrest Me.

56 But all this has taken place in order that the Scriptures of the prophets might be fulfilled. Then all the disciples deserted Him and, fleeing, escaped.

57 But those who had seized Jesus took Him away to Caiaphas, the high priest, where the scribes and the elders had assembled.

58 But Peter followed Him at a distance, as far as the courtyard of the high priest's home; he even went inside and sat with the guards to see the end.

59 Now the chief priests and the whole council (the Sanhedrin) sought to get false witnesses to testify against Jesus, so that they might put Him to death;

60 But they found none, though many witnesses came forward [to testify]. At last two men came forward

61 And testified, This [u]Fellow said, I am able to tear down the [t]sanctuary of the temple of God and to build it up again in three days.

62 And the high priest stood up and said, Have You no answer to make? What about this that these men testify against You?

63 But Jesus kept silent. And the high priest said to Him, [s]I call upon you to swear by the living God, and tell us whether you are the Christ, the Son of God.

64 Jesus said to him, [s]You have stated [the fact]. More than that, I tell you: You will in the future see the Son of Man seated at the right hand of [r]the Almighty and coming on the clouds of the sky. [Ps. 110:1; Dan. 7:13.]

65 Then the high priest tore his clothes and exclaimed, He has uttered blasphemy! What need have we of further evidence? You have now heard His blasphemy. [Lev. 24:16; Num. 14:6.]

66 What do you think now? They answered, He deserves to be put to death.

67 Then they spat in His face and struck Him with their fists; and some [r]slapped Him in the face, [Isa. 50:6.]

68 Saying, Prophesy to us, You Christ (the Messiah)! Who was it that struck You?

69 Now Peter was sitting outside in the courtyard, and [s]one maid came up to him and said, You were also with Jesus the Galilean!

70 But he denied it [v]falsely before them all, saying, I do not know what you mean.

71 And when he had gone out to the porch, another maid saw him, and she said to the bystanders, This fellow was with Jesus the Nazarene!

72 And again he denied it and [v]disowned Him with an oath, saying, I do not know the Man!

73 After a little while, the bystanders came up and said to Peter, You certainly are one of them too, for even your accent betrays you.

r Joseph Thayer, *A Greek-English Lexicon*. s Marvin Vincent, *Word Studies*. t Richard Trench, *Synonyms of the New Testament*. u Capitalized because of what He is, the spotless Son of God, not what the speakers may have thought He was. v Hermann Cremer, *Biblico-Theological Lexicon*.

74 Then Peter began to invoke a curse on himself and to swear, I do not even know the Man! And at that moment a rooster crowed.

75 And Peter remembered Jesus' words, when He had said, Before a *single rooster crows, you will deny *and* disown Me three times. And he went outside and wept bitterly.

CHAPTER 27

WHEN IT was morning, all the chief priests and the elders of the ˙ people held a consultation against Jesus to put Him to death;

2 And they bound Him and led Him away and handed Him over to Pilate the governor.

3 When Judas, His betrayer, saw that [Jesus] was condemned, [Judas was ˣafflicted in mind and troubled for his former folly; and] with remorse [with little more than a selfish dread of the consequences] he brought back the thirty pieces of silver to the chief priests and the elders, [Exod. 21:32.]

4 Saying, I have sinned in betraying innocent blood. They replied, What is that to us? See to that yourself.

5 And casting the pieces of silver [forward] into the [Holy Place of the ʸsanctuary of the] temple, he departed; and he went off and hanged himself.

6 But the chief priests, picking up the pieces of silver, said, It is not legal to put these in the [consecrated] treasury, for it is the price of blood.

7 So after consultation they bought with them [the pieces of silver] the potter's field [as a place] in which to bury strangers.

8 Therefore that piece of ground has been called the Field of Blood to the present day.

9 Then were fulfilled the words spoken by Jeremiah the prophet when he said, And they took the thirty pieces of silver, the price of Him on Whom a price had been set by some of the sons of Israel, [Zech. 11:12, 13.]

10 And they gave them for the potter's field, as the Lord directed me.

11 Now Jesus stood before the governor [Pilate], and the governor asked Him, Are you the King of the Jews? Jesus said to him, You have stated [the fact].

12 But when the charges were made against Him by the chief priests and elders, He made no answer. [Isa. 53:7.]

13 Then Pilate said to Him, Do You not hear how many *and* how serious are the things they are testifying against You?

14 But He made no reply to him, not even to a single accusation, so that the governor marveled greatly.

15 Now at the Feast [of the Passover] the governor was in the habit of setting free for the people any one prisoner whom they chose.

16 And at that time they had a notorious prisoner whose name was Barabbas.

17 So when they had assembled for this purpose, Pilate said to them, Whom do you want me to set free for you, Barabbas, or Jesus Who is called Christ?

18 For he knew that it was because of envy that they had handed Him over to him.

19 Also, while he was seated on the judgment bench, his wife sent him a message, saying, Have nothing to do with that just *and* upright Man, for I have had a painful experience today in a dream because of Him.

20 But the chief priests and the el-

---

w Marvin Vincent, *Word Studies*.   x Jeremy Taylor and Aristotle, cited by Richard Trench, *Synonyms of the New Testament*.   y Richard Trench, *Synonyms of the New Testament*.

ders prevailed on the people to ask for Barabbas, and put Jesus to death.

21 Again the governor said to them, Which of the two do you wish me to release for you? And they said, Barabbas!

22 Pilate said to them, Then what shall I do with Jesus Who is called Christ?

23 They all replied, Let Him be crucified! And he said, Why? What has He done that is evil? But they shouted all the louder, Let Him be crucified!

24 So when Pilate saw that he was getting nowhere, but rather that a riot was about to break out, he took water and washed his hands in the presence of the crowd, saying, I am not guilty of nor responsible for this zrighteous Man's blood; see to it yourselves. [Deut. 21:6–9; Ps. 26:6.]

25 And all the people answered, Let His blood be on us and on our children! [Josh. 2:19.]

26 So he set free for them Barabbas; and he [had] Jesus whipped, and delivered Him up to be crucified.

27 Then the governor's soldiers took Jesus into the palace, and they gathered the whole battalion about Him.

28 And they stripped off His clothes and put a scarlet robe (agarment of dignity and office worn by Roman officers of rank) upon Him,

29 And, weaving a crown of thorns, they put it on His head and put a reed (staff) in His right hand. And kneeling before Him, they made sport of Him, saying, Hail (greetings, good health to You, long life to You), King of the Jews!

30 And they spat on Him, and took the reed (staff) and struck Him on the head.

31 And when they finished making sport of Him, they stripped Him of the robe and put His own garments on Him and led Him away to be crucified.

32 As they were marching forth, they came upon a man of Cyrene named Simon; this man they forced to carry the cross of Jesus.

33 And when they came to a place called Golgotha [Latin: Calvary], which means The Place of a Skull,

34 They offered Him wine mingled with gall to drink; but when He tasted it, He refused to drink it.

35 And when they had crucified Him, they divided and distributed His garments [among them] by casting lots bso that the prophet's saying was fulfilled, They parted My garments among them and over My apparel they cast lots. [Ps. 22:18.]

36 Then they sat down there and kept watch over Him.

37 And over His head they put the accusation against Him (cthe cause of His death), which read, This is Jesus, the King of the Jews.

38 At the same time two robbers were crucified with Him, one on the right hand and one on the left.

39 And those who passed by spoke reproachfully and abusively and jeered at Him, wagging their heads, [Ps. 22:7, 8; 109:25.]

40 And they said, You Who would tear down the asanctuary of the temple and rebuild it in three days, rescue Yourself dfrom death. If You are the Son of God, come down from the cross.

41 In the same way the chief priests, with the scribes and elders, made sport of Him, saying,

42 He rescued others dfrom death; Himself He cannot rescue dfrom death. He is the King of Israel? Let Him come down from the cross now,

z Some manuscripts so read.   a Richard Trench, Synonyms of the New Testament.   b Many manuscripts do not contain this part of verse 35.   c William Tyndale, The Tyndale Bible.   d Hermann Cremer, Biblico-Theological Lexicon.

and we will believe in and eacknowledge and cleave to Him.

43 He trusts in God; let God deliver Him now if He cares for Him and will have Him, for He said, I am the Son of God.

44 And the robbers who were crucified with Him also abused and reproached and made sport of Him in the same way.

45 Now from the sixth hour (noon) there was darkness over all the land until the ninth hour (three o'clock).

46 And about the ninth hour (three o'clock) Jesus cried with a loud voice, Eli, Eli, lama sabachthani?—that is, My God, My God, why have You abandoned Me [leaving Me fhelpless, forsaking and failing Me in My need]? [Ps. 22:1.]

47 And some of the bystanders, when they heard it, said, This Man is calling for Elijah!

48 And one of them immediately ran and took a sponge, soaked it with vinegar (a sour wine), and put it on a reed (staff), and was gabout to give it to Him to drink. [Ps. 69:21.]

49 But the others said, Wait! Let us see whether Elijah will come to save Him gfrom death.

50 And Jesus cried again with a loud voice and gave up His spirit.

51 And at once the curtain of the hsanctuary of the temple was torn in two from top to bottom; the earth shook and the rocks were split. [Exod. 26:31–35.]

52 The tombs were opened and many bodies of the saints who had fallen asleep cin death were raised [to life];

53 And coming out of the tombs after His resurrection, they went into the holy city and appeared to many people.

54 When the centurion and those who were with him keeping watch over Jesus observed the earthquake and all that was happening, they were terribly frightened and filled with awe, and said, Truly this was God's Son!

55 There were also numerous women there, looking on from a distance, who were of those who had accompanied Jesus from Galilee, ministering to Him.

56 Among them were Mary of Magdala, and Mary the mother of James and Joseph, and the mother of Zebedee's sons.

57 When it was evening, there came a rich man from Arimathea, named Joseph, who also was a disciple of Jesus.

58 He went to Pilate and asked for the body of Jesus, and Pilate ordered that it be given to him.

59 And Joseph took the body and irolled it up in a clean linen cloth jused for swathing dead bodies

60 And laid it in his own fresh (eundefiled) tomb, which he had hewn in the rock; and he rolled a big boulder over the door of the tomb and went away.

61 And Mary of Magdala and the other Mary kept sitting there opposite the tomb.

62 The next day, that is, the day after the day of Preparation [for the Sabbath], the chief priests and the Pharisees assembled before Pilate

63 And said, Sir, we have just remembered how that evagabond Imposter said while He was still alive, After three days I will rise again.

64 Therefore give an order to have the tomb made secure and safeguarded until the third day, for fear that His disciples will come and steal Him away and tell the people that He has risen from the dead, and the last de-

e Hermann Cremer, *Biblico-Theological Lexicon.*   f Kenneth Wuest, *Word Studies.*   g Marvin
Vincent, *Word Studies.*   h Richard Trench, *Synonyms of the New Testament.*   i Robert Young,
Analytical Concordance.   j James Moulton and George Milligan, *The Vocabulary.*

ception *and* fraud will be worse than the first.

65 Pilate said to them, You have a guard [of soldiers; take them and] go, make it as secure as you can.

66 So they went off and made the tomb secure by sealing the boulder, a guard of soldiers being with them *and* remaining to watch.

CHAPTER 28

NOW AFTER the Sabbath, near dawn of the first day of the week, Mary of Magdala and the other Mary went to take a look at the tomb.

2 And behold, there was a great earthquake, for an angel of the Lord descended from heaven and came and rolled the boulder back and sat upon it.

3 His appearance was like lightning, and his garments as white as snow.

4 And those keeping guard were so frightened at the sight of him that they were agitated *and* they trembled and became like dead men.

5 But the angel said to the women, Do not be alarmed *and* frightened, for I know that you are looking for Jesus, Who was crucified.

6 He is not here; He has risen, as He said [He would do]. Come, see the place where He lay.

7 Then go quickly and tell His disciples, He has risen from the dead, and behold, He is going before you to Galilee; there you will see Him. Behold, I have told you.

8 So they left the tomb hastily with fear and great joy and ran to tell the disciples.

9 And *as they went,* behold, Jesus met them and said, Hail (greetings)! And they went up to Him and clasped His feet and worshiped Him.

10 Then Jesus said to them, Do not be alarmed *and* afraid; go and tell My brethren to go into Galilee, and there they will see Me.

11 While they were on their way, behold, some of the guards went into the city and reported to the chief priests everything that had occurred.

12 And when they [the chief priests] had gathered with the elders and had consulted together, they gave a sufficient sum of money to the soldiers,

13 And said, Tell people, His disciples came at night and stole Him away while we were sleeping.

14 And if the governor hears of it, we will appease him and make you safe *and* free from trouble *and* care.

15 So they took the money and did as they were instructed; and this story has been current among the Jews to the present day.

16 Now the eleven disciples went to Galilee, to the mountain to which Jesus had directed *and* made appointment with them.

17 And when they saw Him, they fell down and worshiped Him; but some doubted.

18 Jesus approached and, [k]breaking the silence, said to them, All authority (all power of rule) in heaven and on earth has been given to Me.

19 Go then and make disciples of all the nations, baptizing them [k]into the name of the Father and of the Son and of the Holy Spirit,

20 Teaching them to observe everything that I have commanded you, and behold, I am with you [l]all the days ([m]perpetually, uniformly, and on every occasion), to the [very] close *and* consummation of the age. [n]*Amen (so let it be).*

---

k Marvin Vincent, *Word Studies.* l John Wycliffe, *The Wycliffe Bible.* m *Webster's New International Dictionary* offers this phrase as a definition of "always." n Some manuscripts do not contain this ending.

THE GOSPEL ACCORDING TO
MARK

CHAPTER 1

THE BEGINNING [of the facts] of the good news (the Gospel) of Jesus Christ, ᵃ*the Son of God.*

2 ᵇJust as it is written in the prophet Isaiah: Behold, I send My messenger before Your face, who will make ready Your way—[Mal. 3:1.]

3 A voice of one crying in the wilderness [shouting in the desert], Prepare the way of the Lord, make His ᶜbeaten tracks straight (level and passable)! [Isa. 40:3.]

4 John the Baptist appeared in the wilderness (desert), preaching a baptism [ᵈobligating] repentance (ᵉa change of one's mind for the better, heartily amending one's ways, with abhorrence of his past sins) in order ᶠto obtain forgiveness of *and* release from sins.

5 And there kept going out to him [continuously] all the country of Judea and all the inhabitants of Jerusalem; and they were baptized by him in the river Jordan, ᵈas they were confessing their sins.

6 And John wore clothing woven of camel's hair and had a leather girdle around his loins and ate locusts and wild honey.

7 And he preached, saying, After me comes He Who is stronger (more powerful and more valiant) than I, the strap of Whose sandals I am not worthy *or* fit to stoop down and unloose.

8 I have baptized you with water, but He will baptize you with the Holy Spirit.

9 In those days Jesus came from Nazareth of Galilee and was baptized by John in the Jordan.

10 And when He came up out of the water, at once he [John] saw the heavens torn open and the [Holy] Spirit like a dove coming down [ᵈto enter] ᵍinto Him. [John 1:32.]

11 And there came a voice ᵇout from within heaven, You are My Beloved Son; in You I am well pleased. [Ps. 2:7; Isa. 42:1.]

12 Immediately the [Holy] Spirit [from within] drove Him out into the wilderness (desert),

13 And He stayed in the wilderness (desert) forty days, being tempted [all the while] by Satan; and He was with the wild beasts, and the angels ministered to Him [continually].

14 Now after John was arrested *and* put in prison, Jesus came into Galilee, preaching the good news (the Gospel) of *the kingdom of* God,

15 And saying, The [appointed period of] time is fulfilled (completed), and the kingdom of God is at hand; repent (ʰhave a change of mind which issues in regret for past sins and in change of conduct for the better) and

---

a Some manuscripts do not contain this phrase.   **b** Kenneth Wuest, *Word Studies in the Greek New Testament.*   **c** James Moulton and George Milligan, *The Vocabulary of the Greek Testament.*   **d** Kenneth Wuest, *Word Studies.*   **e** Joseph Thayer, *A Greek-English Lexicon of the New Testament.*   **f** Charles B. Williams, *The New Testament: A Translation in the Language of the People.*   **g** Literal translation of *eis.*   **h** Marvin Vincent, *Word Studies in the New Testament.*

believe (trust in, rely on, and adhere to) the good news (the Gospel).

16 And passing along the shore of the Sea of Galilee, He saw Simon [Peter] and Andrew the brother of Simon casting a net [to and fro] in the sea, for they were fishermen.

17 And Jesus said to them, Come after Me *and* ᶦbe My disciples, and I will make you to become fishers of men.

18 And at once they left their nets and [ᶦyielding up all claim to them] followed [with] Him [ᶦjoining Him as disciples and siding with His party].

19 He went on a little farther and saw James the *son* of Zebedee, and John his brother, who were in [their] boat putting their nets in order.

20 And immediately He called out to them, and [ᶦabandoning all mutual claims] they left their father Zebedee in the boat with the hired men and went off after Him [ᶦto be His disciples, side with His party, and follow Him].

21 And they entered into Capernaum, and immediately on the Sabbath He went into the synagogue and began to teach.

22 And they were completely astonished at His teaching, for He was teaching as One Who possessed authority, and not as the scribes.

23 Just at that time there was in their synagogue a man [who was in the power] of an unclean spirit; and now [immediately] he raised a deep *and* terrible cry from the depths of his throat, saying,

24 What have You to do with us, Jesus of Nazareth? Have You come to destroy us? I know who You are —the Holy One of God!

25 And Jesus rebuked him, saying,

Hush up (be muzzled, gagged), and come out of him!

26 And the unclean spirit, throwing the man into convulsions and ᶦscreeching with a loud voice, came out of him.

27 And they were all so amazed *and* ᵏalmost terrified that they kept questioning *and* demanding one of another, saying, What is this? What new (fresh) teaching! With authority He gives orders even to the unclean spirits and they obey Him!

28 And immediately rumors concerning Him spread [everywhere] throughout all the region surrounding Galilee.

29 And at once He left the synagogue and went into the house of Simon [Peter] and Andrew, accompanied by James and John.

30 Now Simon's mother-in-law ᶦhad for some time been lying sick with a fever, and at once they told Him about her.

31 And He went up to her and took her by the hand and raised her up; and the fever left her, and she began to wait on them.

32 Now when it was evening, after the sun had set, they brought to Him all who were sick and those under the power of demons,

33 Until the whole town was gathered together about the door.

34 And He cured many who were afflicted with various diseases; and He drove out many demons, but would not allow the demons to talk because they knew Him [ᵐintuitively].

35 And in the morning, long before daylight, He got up and went out to a ⁿdeserted place, and there He prayed.

36 And Simon [Peter] and those

i Joseph Thayer, *A Greek-English Lexicon*.   j A.T. Robertson, *Word Pictures in the New Testament*.
k Alexander Souter, *Pocket Lexicon of the Greek New Testament*.   l Kenneth Wuest, *Word Studies*.
m Charles B. Williams, *The New Testament: A Translation*.   n James Moulton and George Milligan, *The Vocabulary*.

who were with him followed Him [°pursuing Him eagerly and hunting Him out],

37 And they found Him and said to Him, Everybody is looking for You.

38 And He said to them, Let us be going on into the neighboring country towns, that I may preach there also; for that is why I came out.

39 [So] He went throughout the whole of Galilee, preaching in their synagogues and driving out demons.

40 And a leper came to Him, begging Him on his knees and saying to Him, If You are willing, You are able to make me clean.

41 And being moved with pity *and* sympathy, Jesus reached out His hand and touched him, and said to him, I am willing; be made clean!

42 And at once the leprosy [completely] left him and he was made clean [by being healed].

43 And Jesus charged him sternly (sharply and threateningly, and with earnest admonition) and [acting with deep feeling thrust him forth and] sent him away at once,

44 And said to him, See that you tell nothing [of this] to anyone; but begone, show yourself to the priest, and offer for your purification what Moses commanded, as a proof (an evidence and witness) to the people [that you are really healed]. [Lev. 13:49; 14:2–32.]

45 But he went out and began to talk so freely about it and blaze abroad the news [spreading it everywhere] that [Jesus] could no longer openly go into a town but was outside in [lonely] desert places. But the people kept on coming to Him from [p]all sides *and* every quarter.

CHAPTER 2

AND JESUS having returned to Capernaum, after some days it was rumored about that He was in the house [probably Peter's].

2 And so many people gathered together there that there was no longer room [for them], not even around the door; and He was discussing the Word.

3 Then they came, bringing a paralytic to Him, who had been picked up *and* was being carried by four men.

4 And when they could not get him to a place in front of Jesus because of the throng, they dug through the roof above Him; and when they had [o]scooped out an opening, they let down the [°thickly padded] quilt *or* mat upon which the paralyzed man lay.

5 And when Jesus saw their faith [their confidence in God through Him], He said to the paralyzed man, Son, your sins are forgiven [you] *and* put away [that is, the [q]penalty is remitted, the sense of guilt removed, and you are made upright and in right standing with God].

6 Now some of the scribes were sitting there, holding a dialogue with themselves as they questioned in their hearts,

7 Why does this [r]Man talk like this? He is blaspheming! Who can forgive sins [[q]remove guilt, remit the penalty, and bestow righteousness instead] except God alone?

8 And at once Jesus, becoming fully aware in His spirit that they thus debated within themselves, said to them, Why do you argue (debate, reason) about all this in your hearts?

9 Which is easier: to say to the paralyzed man, Your sins are forgiven *and* [q]put away, or to say, Rise,

o Marvin Vincent, *Word Studies*. p James Moulton and George Milligan, *The Vocabulary*.
q Kenneth Wuest, *Word Studies*. r Capitalized because of what He is, the spotless Son of God, not what the speakers may have thought He was.

take up your sleeping pad *or* mat, and start walking about [and ˢkeep on walking]?

10 But that you may know positively *and* beyond a doubt that the Son of Man has right *and* authority *and* power on earth to forgive sins —He said to the paralyzed man,

11 I say to you, arise, pick up *and* carry your sleeping pad *or* mat, and be going on home.

12 And he arose at once and picked up the sleeping pad *or* mat and went out before them all, so that they were all amazed *and* ᵗrecognized *and* praised *and* thanked God, saying, We have never seen anything like this before!

13 [Jesus] went out again along the seashore; and all the multitude kept gathering about Him, and He kept teaching them.

14 And as He was passing by, He saw Levi (Matthew) son of Alphaeus sitting at the tax office, and He said to him, Follow Me! [Be ᵘjoined to Me as a disciple, side with My party!] And he arose and joined Him as His disciple *and* sided with His party *and* accompanied Him.

15 And as Jesus, together with His disciples, sat at table in his [Levi's] house, many tax collectors and persons [ᵛdefinitely stained] with sin were dining with Him, for there were many who walked the same road (followed) with Him.

16 And the scribes [belonging to the party] of the Pharisees, when they saw that He was eating with [those ᵈdefinitely known to be especially wicked] sinners and tax collectors, said to His disciples, Why does He eat *and* drink with tax collectors and [notorious] sinners?

17 And when Jesus heard it, He said to them, Those who are strong *and* well have no need of a physician, but those who are weak *and* sick; I came not to call the righteous ones *to repentance*, but sinners (the ᵛerring ones and ᵈall those not free from sin).

18 Now John's disciples and the Pharisees were observing a fast; and [some people] came and asked Jesus, Why are John's disciples and the disciples of the Pharisees fasting, but Your disciples are not doing so?

19 Jesus answered them, Can the wedding guests fast (abstain from food and drink) while the bridegroom is with them? As long as they have the bridegroom with them, they cannot fast.

20 But the days will come when the bridegroom will be taken away from them, and then they will fast in that day.

21 No one sews a patch of unshrunken (new) goods on an old garment; if he does, the patch tears away from it, the new from the old, and the rent (tear) becomes bigger *and* worse [than it was before].

22 And no one puts new wine into old wineskins; if he does, the wine will burst the skins, and the wine is lost and the bottles destroyed; but new wine is to be put in new (fresh) wineskins.

23 One Sabbath He was going along beside the fields of standing grain, and as they made their way, His disciples began to ᵛpick off the grains. [Deut. 23:25.]

24 And the Pharisees said to Him, Look! Why are they doing what is not permitted *or* lawful on the Sabbath?

25 And He said to them, Have you never [even] read what David did when he was in need and was hungry, he and those who were accompanying him?—

26 How he went into the house of

God when Abiathar was the high priest, and ate the sacred loaves set forth [before God], which it is not permitted *or* lawful for any but the priests to eat, and [how he] also gave [them] to those who were with him? [I Sam. 21:1–6; II Sam. 8:17.]

27 And Jesus said to them, The Sabbath was made on account *and* for the sake of man, not man for the Sabbath; [Exod. 23:12; Deut. 5:14.]

28 So the Son of Man is Lord even of the Sabbath.

CHAPTER 3

AGAIN JESUS went into a synagogue, and a man was there who had one withered hand [ʷas the result of accident or disease].

2 And [the Pharisees] kept watching Jesus [closely] to see whether He would cure him on the Sabbath, so that they might get a charge to bring against Him [ˣformally].

3 And He said to the man who had the withered hand, Get up [and stand here] in the midst.

4 And He said to them, Is it lawful *and* right on the Sabbath to do good or to do evil, to save life or to take it? But they kept silence.

5 And He glanced around at them with vexation *and* anger, grieved at the hardening of their hearts, and said to the man, Hold out your hand. He held it out, and his hand was [completely] restored.

6 Then the Pharisees went out and immediately held a consultation with the Herodians against Him, how they might [devise some means to] put Him to death.

7 And Jesus retired with His disciples to the lake, and a great throng from Galilee followed Him. Also from Judea

8 And from Jerusalem and Idumea and from beyond the Jordan and from about Tyre and Sidon—a vast multitude, hearing all the many things that He was doing, came to Him.

9 And He told His disciples to have a little boat in [constant] readiness for Him because of the crowd, lest they press hard upon Him *and* crush Him.

10 For He had healed so many that all who had distressing bodily diseases kept falling upon Him *and* pressing upon Him in order that they might touch Him.

11 And the spirits, the unclean ones, ʷas often as they might see Him, fell down before Him and kept screaming out, You are the Son of God!

12 And He charged them strictly *and* severely under penalty again *and* again that they should not make Him known.

13 And He went up on the hillside and called to Him [ˣfor Himself] those whom He wanted *and* chose, and they came to Him.

14 And He appointed twelve to ˣcontinue to be with Him, and that He might send them out to preach [as apostles or special messengers]

15 And to have authority *and* power to *heal the sick and to* drive out demons:

16 [They were] Simon, and He surnamed [him] Peter;

17 James son of Zebedee and John the brother of James, and He surnamed them Boanerges, that is, Sons of Thunder;

18 And Andrew, and Philip, and Bartholomew (Nathaniel), and Matthew, and Thomas, and James son of Alphaeus, and Thaddaeus (Judas, not Iscariot), and Simon the Cananaean [also called Zelotes],

19 And Judas Iscariot, he who betrayed Him.

ʷ Marvin Vincent, *Word Studies.*　　ˣ Kenneth Wuest, *Word Studies.*

20 Then He went to a house [probably Peter's], and a throng came together again, so that Jesus and His disciples could not even take food.

21 And when those ʸwho belonged to Him (ᶻHis kinsmen) heard it, they went out to take Him by force, for they kept saying, He is out of ᵃHis mind (beside Himself, deranged)!

22 And the scribes who came down from Jerusalem said, He is possessed by Beelzebub, and, By [the help of] the prince of demons He is casting out demons.

23 And He summoned them to Him and said to them in parables (illustrations or comparisons put beside truths to explain them), How can Satan drive out Satan?

24 And if a kingdom is divided and rebelling against itself, that kingdom cannot stand.

25 And if a house is divided (split into factions and rebelling) against itself, that house will not be able to last.

26 And if Satan has raised an insurrection against himself and is divided, he cannot stand but is [surely] coming to an end.

27 But no one can go into a strong man's house and ransack his household goods right and left and seize them as plunder unless he first binds the strong man; then indeed he may [thoroughly] plunder his house. [Isa. 49:24, 25.]

28 Truly and solemnly I say to you, all sins will be forgiven the sons of men, and whatever abusive and blasphemous things they utter;

29 But whoever speaks abusively against or maliciously misrepresents the Holy Spirit can never get forgiveness, but is guilty of and is in the grasp of ᶻan everlasting trespass.

30 For they ᵇpersisted in saying, ᵃHe has an unclean spirit.

31 Then His mother and His brothers came and, standing outside, they sent word to Him, calling [for] Him.

32 And a crowd was sitting around Him, and they said to Him, Your mother and Your brothers and Your sisters are outside asking for You.

33 And He replied, Who are My mother and My brothers?

34 And looking around on those who sat in a circle about Him, He said, See! Here are My mother and My brothers;

35 For whoever does the things God wills is My brother and sister and mother!

CHAPTER 4

AGAIN JESUS began to teach beside the lake. And a very great crowd gathered about Him, so that He got into a ship in order to sit in it on the sea, and the whole crowd was at the lakeside on the shore.

2 And He taught them many things in parables (illustrations or comparisons put beside truths to explain them), and in His teaching He said to them:

3 Give attention to this! Behold, a sower went out to sow.

4 And as he was sowing, some seed fell along the path, and the birds came and ate it up.

5 Other seed [of the same kind] fell on ground full of rocks, where it had not much soil; and at once it sprang up, because it had no depth of soil;

6 And when the sun came up, it was scorched, and because it had not taken root, it withered away.

7 Other seed [of the same kind] fell among thorn plants, and the thistles grew and pressed together and utter-

y William Tyndale, *The Tyndale Bible.*   z John Wycliffe, *The Wycliffe Bible.*   a Capitalized for what He is, the spotless Son of God, not what the speakers may have thought He was.   b Marvin Vincent, *Word Studies.*

ly choked *and* suffocated it, and it yielded no grain.

8 And other seed [of the same kind] fell into good (well-adapted) soil and brought forth grain, growing up and increasing, and yielded up to thirty times as much, and sixty times as much, and even a hundred times as much as had been sown.

9 And He said, He who has ears to hear, let him be hearing [and let him ᶜconsider, and comprehend].

10 And as soon as He was alone, those who were around Him, with the Twelve [apostles], began to ask Him about the parables.

11 And He said to them, To you has been entrusted the mystery of the kingdom of God [that is, ᵈthe secret counsels of God which are hidden from the ungodly]; but for those outside [ᵉof our circle] everything becomes a parable,

12 In order that they may [indeed] look *and* look but not see *and* perceive, and may hear *and* hear but not grasp *and* comprehend, ᶠlest haply they should turn again, and it [ᵍtheir willful rejection of the truth] should be forgiven them. [Isa. 6:9, 10; Matt. 13:13–15.]

13 And He said to them, Do you not discern *and* understand this parable? How then is it possible for you to discern *and* understand all the parables?

14 The sower sows the Word.

15 The ones along the path are those who have the Word sown [in their hearts], but when they hear, Satan comes at once and [by force] takes away the message which is sown in them.

16 And in the same way the ones sown upon stony ground are those who, when they hear the Word, at once receive *and* accept *and* welcome it with joy;

17 And they have no real root in themselves, and so they endure for a little while; then when trouble or persecution arises on account of the Word, they immediately are offended (become displeased, indignant, resentful) *and* they stumble *and* fall away.

18 And the ones sown among the thorns are others who hear the Word;

19 Then the cares *and* anxieties of the world *and* distractions of the age, and the pleasure *and* delight *and* false glamour *and* deceitfulness of riches, and the craving *and* passionate desire for other things creep in and choke *and* suffocate the Word, and it becomes fruitless.

20 And those sown on the good (well-adapted) soil are the ones who hear the Word and receive *and* accept *and* welcome it and bear fruit —some thirty times as much as was sown, some sixty times as much, and some [even] a hundred times as much.

21 And He said to them, Is the lamp brought in to be put under a ᵍpeck measure or under a bed, and not [to be put] on the lampstand?

22 [ʰ Things are hidden temporarily only as a means to revelation.] For there is nothing hidden except to be revealed, nor is anything [temporarily] kept secret except in order that it may be made known.

23 If any man has ears to hear, let him be listening *and* let him perceive *and* comprehend.

24 And He said to them, Be careful what you are hearing. The measure ⁱ[of thought and study] you give [to

---

c Joseph Thayer, *A Greek-English Lexicon*.   d Kenneth Wuest, *Word Studies*.   e Marvin Vincent, *Word Studies*.   f A.T. Robertson, *Word Pictures*.   g James Moulton and George Milligan, *The Vocabulary*.   h Henry Swete, *The Gospel According to Saint Mark*; A.T. Robertson, *Word Pictures*; Marvin Vincent, *Word Studies*; and others.   i W. Robertson Nicoll, ed., *The Expositor's Greek New Testament*.

ʲthe truth you hear] will be the measure ᵏ[of virtue and knowledge] that comes back to you—and more [besides] will be given to you *who hear*.

25 For to him who has will more be given; and from him who has nothing, even what he has will be taken away [ˡby force],

26 And He said, The kingdom of God is like a man who scatters seed upon the ground,

27 And then continues sleeping and rising night and day while the seed sprouts and grows *and* ˡincreases— he knows not how.

28 The earth produces [acting] by itself—first the blade, then the ear, then the full grain in the ear.

29 But when the grain is ripe *and* permits, immediately he ᵐsends forth [the reapers] *and* puts in the sickle, because the harvest stands ready.

30 And He said, With what can we compare the kingdom of God, or what parable shall we use to illustrate *and* explain it?

31 It is like a grain of mustard seed, which, when sown upon the ground, is the smallest of all seeds upon the earth;

32 Yet after it is sown, it grows up and becomes the greatest of all garden herbs and puts out large branches, so that the birds of the air are able to make nests *and* dwell in its shade.

33 With many such parables [Jesus] spoke the Word to them, as they were able to hear *and* ˡto comprehend *and* understand.

34 He did not tell them anything without a parable; but privately to His disciples [ⁿthose who were peculiarly His own) He explained everything [fully].

35 On that same day [when] evening had come, He said to them, Let us go over to the other side [of the lake].

36 And leaving the throng, they took Him with them, [just] as He was, in the boat [in which He was sitting]. And other boats were with Him.

37 And a furious storm of wind [ⁿof hurricane proportions] arose, and the waves kept beating into the boat, so that it was already becoming filled.

38 But He [Himself] was in the stern [of the boat], asleep on the [leather] cushion; and they awoke Him and said to Him, Master, do You not care that we are perishing?

39 And He arose and rebuked the wind and said to the sea, Hush now! Be still (muzzled)! And the wind ceased (ᵐsank to rest as if exhausted by its beating) and there was [immediately] a great calm (ᵒa perfect peacefulness).

40 He said to them, Why are you so timid *and* fearful? How is it that you have no faith (no ᵖfirmly relying trust)?

41 And they were filled with great awe *and* ᵐfeared exceedingly and said one to another, Who then is this, that even wind and sea obey Him?

CHAPTER 5

THEY CAME to the other side of the sea to the region of the Gerasenes.

2 And as soon as He got out of the boat, there met Him out of the tombs a man [under the power] of an unclean spirit.

3 This man ⁿcontinually lived among the tombs, and no one could

ʲ James C. Gray and George M. Adams, *Bible Commentary*; Kenneth Wuest, *Word Studies*; Albert Barnes, *Notes on the New Testament*; and others.   ᵏ W. Robertson Nicoll, ed., *The Expositor's Greek New Testament*.   ˡ Joseph Thayer, *A Greek-English Lexicon*.   ᵐ Marvin Vincent, *Word Studies*. ⁿ Kenneth Wuest, *Word Studies*.   ᵒ John Wycliffe, *The Wycliffe Bible*.   ᵖ Hermann Cremer, *Biblico-Theological Lexicon*.

subdue him any more, even with a chain;

4 For he had been bound often with shackles for the feet and ᵈhandcuffs, but the handcuffs of [light] chains he wrenched apart, and the shackles he rubbed *and* ground together *and* broke in pieces; and no one had strength enough to restrain *or* tame him.

5 Night and day among the tombs and on the mountains he was always ᵈshrieking *and* screaming and ʳbeating *and* bruising *and* ᵉcutting himself with stones.

6 And when from a distance he saw Jesus, he ran and fell on his knees before Him in homage.

7 And crying out with a loud voice, he said, What have You to do with me, Jesus, Son of the Most High God? [What is there in common between us?] I ᵗsolemnly implore you by God, do not begin to torment me!

8 For Jesus was commanding, Come out of the man, you unclean spirit!

9 And He asked him, What is your name? He replied, My name is Legion, for we are many.

10 And he kept begging Him urgently not to send them [himself and the other demons] away out of that region.

11 Now a great herd of hogs was grazing there on the hillside.

12 And *the demons* begged Him, saying, Send us to the hogs, that we may go into them!

13 So He gave them permission. And the unclean spirits came out [of the man] and entered into the hogs; and the herd, numbering about 2,000, rushed headlong down the steep slope into the sea and were drowned in the sea.

14 The hog feeders ran away, and told [it] in the town and in the country. And [the people] came to see what it was that had taken place.

15 And they came to Jesus and looked intently *and* searchingly at the man who had been a demoniac, sitting there, clothed and in his right mind, [the same man] who had had the legion [of demons]; and they were ᵠseized with alarm *and* struck with fear.

16 And those who had seen it related in full what had happened to the man possessed by demons and to the hogs.

17 And they began to beg [Jesus] to leave their neighborhood.

18 And when He had stepped into the boat, the man who had been controlled by the unclean spirits kept begging Him that he might be with Him.

19 But Jesus refused to permit him, but said to him, Go home to your own [family and relatives and friends] and bring back word to them of how much the Lord has done for you, and [how He has] had sympathy for you *and* mercy on you.

20 And he departed and began to publicly proclaim in Decapolis [the region of the ten cities] how much Jesus had done for him, and all the people were astonished *and* marveled. [Matt. 4:25.]

21 And when Jesus had recrossed in the boat to the other side, a great throng gathered about Him, and He was at the lakeshore.

22 Then one of the rulers of the synagogue came up, Jairus by name; and seeing Him, he prostrated himself at His feet

23 And begged Him earnestly, saying, My little daughter is at the point

q Joseph Thayer, *A Greek-English Lexicon.*   r James Moulton and George Milligan, *The Vocabulary.*
s G. Abbott-Smith, *Manual Greek Lexicon.*   t Kenneth Wuest, *Word Studies.*

of death. Come and lay Your hands on her, so that she may be healed *and* live.

24 And Jesus went with him; and a great crowd kept following Him and pressed Him u from all sides [so as almost to suffocate Him].

25 And there was a woman who had had a flow of blood for twelve years,

26 And who had endured much v suffering under [the hands of] many physicians and had spent all that she had, and was no better but instead grew worse.

27 She had heard the reports concerning Jesus, and she came up behind Him in the throng and touched His garment,

28 For she kept saying, If I only touch His garments, I shall be restored to health.

29 And immediately her flow of blood was dried up at the source, and [w suddenly] she felt in her body that she was healed of her [u distressing] ailment.

30 And Jesus, recognizing in Himself that the power proceeding from Him had gone forth, turned around immediately in the crowd and said, Who touched My clothes?

31 And the disciples kept saying to Him, You see the crowd pressing hard around You u from all sides, and You ask, Who touched Me?

32 Still He kept looking around to see her who had done it.

33 But the woman, knowing what had been done for her, though alarmed *and* frightened and trembling, fell down before Him and told Him the whole truth.

34 And He said to her, Daughter, your faith (your u trust and confidence in Me, springing from faith in God) has restored you to health. Go

in w (into) peace and be continually healed *and* freed from your [u distressing bodily] disease.

35 While He was still speaking, there came some from the ruler's house, who said [to Jairus], Your daughter has died. Why bother *and* distress the Teacher any further?

36 x *Overhearing* but ignoring what they said, Jesus said to the ruler of the synagogue, Do not be seized with alarm *and* struck with fear; only keep on believing.

37 And He permitted no one to accompany Him except Peter and James and John the brother of James.

38 When they arrived at the house of the ruler of the synagogue, He w looked [carefully and with understanding] at [the] tumult and *the people* weeping and wailing loudly.

39 And when He had gone in, He said to them, Why do you make an uproar and weep? The little girl is not dead but is sleeping.

40 And they laughed *and* v jeered at Him. But He put them all out, and, taking the child's father and mother and those who were with Him, He went in where the little girl was *lying*.

41 Gripping her [firmly] by the hand, He said to her, Talitha cumi— which translated is, Little girl, I say to you, arise [u from the sleep of death]!

42 And instantly the girl got up and started walking around—for she was twelve years old. And they were utterly astonished *and* overcome with amazement.

43 And He strictly commanded *and* warned them that no one should know this, and He [u expressly] told them to give her [something] to eat.

u Joseph Thayer, *A Greek-English Lexicon*. *Word Studies*.   v Marvin Vincent, *Word Studies*.   w Kenneth Wuest, *Word Studies*.   x Some manuscripts so read.   y G. Abbott-Smith, *Manual Greek Lexicon*.

CHAPTER 6

JESUS WENT away from there and came to His [own] country and hometown [Nazareth], and His disciples followed [with] Him.

2 And on the Sabbath He began to teach in the synagogue; and many who listened to Him were utterly astonished, saying, Where did this [z]Man acquire all this? What is the wisdom [the broad and full intelligence which has been] given to Him? What mighty works and exhibitions of power are wrought by His hands!

3 Is not this the Carpenter, the son of Mary and the brother of James and Joses and Judas and Simon? And are not His sisters here among us? And they took offense at Him and [a]were hurt [that is, they [b]disapproved of Him, and it hindered them from acknowledging His authority] and they were caused to stumble and fall.

4 But Jesus said to them, A prophet is not without honor (deference, reverence) except in his [own] country and among [his] relatives and in his [own] house.

5 And He was not able to do [b]even one work of power there, except that He laid His hands on a few sickly people [and] cured them.

6 And He marveled because of their unbelief (their lack of faith in Him). And He went about among the surrounding villages and continued teaching.

7 And He called to Him the Twelve [apostles] and began to send them out [as His ambassadors] two by two and gave them authority and power over the unclean spirits.

8 He charged them to take nothing for their journey except a walking stick—no bread, [c]no wallet for a col-

lection bag, no money in their belts (girdles, purses).

9 But to go with sandals on their feet and not to put on two tunics (undergarments).

10 And He told them, Wherever you go into a house, stay there until you leave that place.

11 And if any community will not receive and accept and welcome you, and they refuse to listen to you, when you depart, shake off the dust that is on your feet, for a testimony against them. [d]Truly I tell you, it will be more tolerable for Sodom and Gomorrah in the judgment day than for that town.

12 So they went out and preached that men should repent [[e]that they should change their minds for the better and heartily amend their ways, with abhorrence of their past sins].

13 And they drove out many unclean spirits and anointed with oil many who were sick and cured them.

14 King Herod heard of it, for [Jesus'] name had become well known. [f]He and they [of his court] said, John the Baptist has been raised from the dead; that is why these mighty powers [[g]of performing miracles] are at work in Him.

15 [But] others kept saying, It is Elijah! And others said, It is a prophet, like one of the prophets [of old].

16 But when Herod heard [of it], he said, [[h]This very] John, whom I beheaded, has been raised [from the dead].

17 For [this] Herod himself had sent and seized John and bound him in prison for the sake of Herodias, his brother Philip's wife, because he [Herod] had married her.

18 For John had told Herod, It is

z Capitalized because of what He is, the spotless Son of God, not what the speakers may have thought He was.   a William Tyndale, *The Tyndale Bible*.   b Kenneth Wuest, *Word Studies*.   c James Moulton and George Milligan, *The Vocabulary*.   d Some manuscripts do not contain the last section of verse 11.   e Joseph Thayer, *A Greek-English Lexicon*.   f Some ancient manuscripts read "he," while others read "they."   g G. Abbott-Smith, *Manual Greek Lexicon*.   h Marvin Vincent, *Word Studies*.

not lawful *and* you have no right to have your brother's wife.

19 And Herodias was angry (enraged) with him *and* held a grudge against him and wanted to kill him; but she could not,

20 For Herod had [¹a reverential] fear of John, knowing that he was a righteous and holy man, and [continually] kept him safe [³under guard]. When he heard [John speak], he was much perplexed; and [yet] he heard him gladly.

21 But an opportune time came [for Herodias] when Herod on his birthday gave a banquet for his nobles and the high military commanders and chief men of Galilee.

22 For when the daughter ᵏof Herodias herself came in and danced, she pleased *and* ᵏfascinated Herod and his guests; and the king said to the girl, Ask me for whatever you desire, and I will give it to you.

23 And he put himself under oath to her, Whatever you ask me, I will give it to you, even to the half of my kingdom. [Esth. 5:3, 6.]

24 Then she left the room and said to her mother, What shall I ask for [myself]? And she replied, The head of John the Baptist!

25 And she rushed back instantly to the king and requested, saying, I wish you to give me right now the head of John the Baptist on a platter.

26 And the king was deeply pained *and* grieved *and* exceedingly sorry, but because of his oaths and his guests, he did not want to slight her [by breaking faith with her].

27 And immediately the king sent off one [of the soldiers] of his bodyguard and gave him orders to bring [John's] head. He went and beheaded him in the prison

28 And brought his head on a plat-

ter and handed it to the girl, and the girl gave it to her mother.

29 When his disciples learned of it, they came and took [John's] body and laid it in a tomb.

30 The apostles [sent out as missionaries] came back *and* gathered together to Jesus, and told Him all that they had done and taught.

31 And He said to them, [ᵏAs for you] come away by yourselves to a deserted place, and rest a while—for many were [continually] coming and going, and they had not even leisure enough to eat.

32 And they went away in a boat to a solitary place by themselves.

33 Now many [people] saw them going and recognized them, and they ran there on foot from all the surrounding towns, and they got there ahead [of those in the boat].

34 As Jesus landed, He saw a great crowd waiting, and He was moved with compassion for them, because they were like sheep without a shepherd; and He began to teach them many things.

35 And when ᵏthe day was already far gone, His disciples came to Him and said, This is a desolate *and* isolated place, and the hour is now late.

36 Send the crowds away to go into the country and villages round about and buy themselves something to eat.

37 But He replied to them, Give them something to eat yourselves. And they said to Him, Shall we go and buy 200 ¹denarii [about forty dollars] worth of bread and give it to them to eat? [II Kings 4:42–44.]

38 And He said to them, How many loaves do you have? Go and see. And when they [had looked and] knew, they said, Five [loaves] and two fish.

i G. Abbott-Smith, *Manual Greek Lexicon*.   j Marvin Vincent, *Word Studies*.   k Kenneth Wuest, *Word Studies*.   l The usual pay for a day's work was one denarius.

39 Then He commanded the people all to recline on the green grass by companies.

40 So they threw themselves down in ranks of hundreds and fifties [with the [m]regularity of an arrangement of beds of herbs, looking [n]like so many garden plots].

41 And taking the five loaves and two fish, He looked up to heaven and, praising God, gave thanks and broke the loaves and kept on giving them to the disciples to set before the people; and He [also] divided the two fish among [them] all.

42 And they all ate and were satisfied.

43 And they took up twelve [[o]small hand] baskets full of broken pieces [from the loaves] and of the fish.

44 And those who ate the loaves were 5,000 men.

45 And at once He insisted that the disciples get into the boat and go ahead of Him to the other side to Bethsaida, while He was sending the throng away.

46 And after He had taken leave of them, He went off into the hills to pray.

47 Now when evening had come, the boat was out in the middle of the lake, and He was by Himself on the land.

48 And having seen that they were troubled *and* tormented in [their] rowing, for the wind was against them, about the fourth watch of the night [between 3:00–6:00 a.m.] He came to them, walking [directly] on the sea. And He acted as if He meant to pass by them,

49 But when they saw Him walking on the sea they thought it was a ghost, and [p]raised a [deep, throaty] shriek of terror.

50 For they all saw Him and were agitated (troubled and filled with fear and dread). But immediately He talked with them and said, Take heart! I AM! Stop being alarmed *and* afraid. [Exod. 3:14.]

51 And He went up into the boat with them, and the wind ceased ([q]sank to rest as if exhausted by its own beating). And they were astonished exceedingly [beyond measure],

52 For they failed to consider *or* understand [the teaching and meaning of the miracle of] the loaves; [in fact] their hearts had [p]grown callous [had become dull and had [p]lost the power of understanding].

53 And when they had crossed over, they reached the land of Gennesaret and [p]came to [anchor at] the shore.

54 As soon as they got out of the boat, [the people] recognized Him,

55 And they ran about the whole countryside, and began to carry around sick people on their sleeping pads *or* mats to any place where they heard that He was.

56 And wherever He came into villages or cities or the country, they would lay the sick in the marketplaces and beg Him that they might touch even the fringe of His outer garment, and as many as touched Him were restored to health.

CHAPTER 7

NOW THERE gathered together to [Jesus] the Pharisees and some of the scribes who had come from Jerusalem,

2 For they had seen that some of His disciples ate with [r]common hands, that is, unwashed [with hands defiled and unhallowed, because

m James Moulton and George Milligan, *The Vocabulary*. **n** Richard Trench, *Notes on the Miracles of our Lord*. **o** Marvin Vincent, *Word Studies*. See also footnote on Matt. 14:20. **p** Joseph Thayer, *A Greek-English Lexicon*. **q** Marvin Vincent, *Word Studies*. **r** William Tyndale, *The Tyndale Bible*.

they had not given them a ˢceremonial washing]—

3 For the Pharisees and all of the Jews do not eat unless [merely for ceremonial reasons] they wash their hands [diligently ᵘup to the elbow] with clenched fist, adhering [carefully and faithfully] to the tradition of [practices and customs handed down to them by] their forefathers [to be observed].

4 And [when they come] from the marketplace, they do not eat unless they purify themselves; and there are many other traditions [oral, man-made laws handed down to them, which they observe faithfully and diligently, such as] the washing of cups and wooden pitchers and wide-mouthed jugs and utensils of copper and ᵘbeds—

5 And the Pharisees and scribes kept asking [Jesus], Why do Your disciples not order their way of living according to the tradition handed down by the forefathers [to be observed], but eat with hands unwashed *and* ceremonially not purified?

6 But He said to them, Excellently *and* truly [ᵛso that there will be no room for blame] did Isaiah prophesy of you, the pretenders *and* hypocrites, as it stands written: These people [constantly] honor Me with their lips, but their hearts hold off *and* are far distant from Me.

7 In vain (fruitlessly and without profit) do they worship Me, ordering *and* teaching [to be obeyed] as doctrines the commandments *and* precepts of men. [Isa. 29:13.]

8 You disregard *and* give up *and* ask to depart from you the commandment of God and cling to the tradition of men [keeping it carefully and faithfully].

9 And He said to them, You have a fine way of rejecting [thus thwarting and nullifying and doing away with] the commandment of God in order to keep your tradition (your own human regulations)!

10 For Moses said, Honor (revere with tenderness of feeling and deference) your father and your mother, and, He who curses *or* reviles *or* speaks evil of *or* abuses *or* treats improperly his father or mother, let him surely die. [Exod. 20:12; 21:17; Lev. 20:9; Deut. 5:16.]

11 But [as for you] you say, A man is exempt if he tells [his] father or [his] mother, What you would otherwise have gained from me [everything I have that would have been of use to you] is Corban, that is, is a gift [already given as an offering to God],

12 Then you no longer are permitting him to do anything for [his] father or mother [but are letting him off from helping them].

13 Thus you are nullifying *and* making void *and* of no effect [the authority of] the Word of God through your tradition, which you [in turn] hand on. And many things of this kind you are doing.

14 And He called the people to [Him] again and said to them, Listen to Me, all of you, and understand [what I say].

15 There is not [even] one thing outside a man which by going into him can pollute *and* defile him; but the things which come out of a man are what defile him *and* make him unhallowed *and* unclean.

16 ʷ*If any man has ears to hear, let him be listening [and let him* ᵗ*perceive and comprehend by hearing].*

s Charles B. Williams, *The New Testament: A Translation.*   t G. Abbott-Smith, *Manual Greek Lexicon.*
u James Moulton and George Milligan, *The Vocabulary* and Robert Young, *Analytical Concordance* agree with most lexicons in reading "beds" here. Some manuscripts end verse 4 after "utensils of copper."
v Joseph Thayer, *A Greek-English Lexicon.*   w Many manuscripts do not contain this verse.

17 And when He had left the crowd and had gone into the house, His disciples began asking Him about the parable.

18 And He said to them, Then are you also unintelligent *and* dull *and* without understanding? Do you not discern *and* see that whatever goes into a man from the outside cannot make him unhallowed *or* unclean,

19 Since it does not reach *and* enter his heart but [only his] digestive tract, and so passes on [into the place designed to receive waste]? Thus He was making *and* declaring all foods [ceremonially] clean [that is, ˣabolishing the ceremonial distinctions of the Levitical Law].

20 And He said, What comes out of a man is what makes a man unclean *and* renders [him] unhallowed.

21 For from within, [that is] out of the hearts of men, come base *and* wicked thoughts, sexual immorality, stealing, murder, adultery,

22 Coveting (a greedy desire to have more wealth), dangerous *and* destructive wickedness, deceit; ʸunrestrained (indecent) conduct; an evil eye (envy), slander (evil speaking, malicious misrepresentation, abusiveness), pride (ᶻthe sin of an uplifted heart against God and man), foolishness (folly, lack of sense, recklessness, thoughtlessness).

23 All these evil [purposes and desires] come from within, and they make the man unclean *and* render him unhallowed.

24 And Jesus arose and went away from there to the region of Tyre *and* Sidon. And He went into a house and did not want anyone to know [that He was there]; but it was not possible for Him to be hidden [from public notice].

25 Instead, at once, a woman whose little daughter had (was under the control of) an unclean spirit heard about Him and came and flung herself down at His feet.

26 Now the woman was a Greek (Gentile), a Syrophoenician by nationality. And she kept begging Him to drive the demon out of her little daughter.

27 And He said to her, First let the children be fed, for it is not becoming *or* proper *or* right to take the children's bread and throw it to the [little house] dogs.

28 But she answered Him, Yes, Lord, yet even the small pups under the table eat the little children's scraps of food.

29 And He said to her, Because of this saying, you may go your way; the demon has gone out of your daughter [permanently].

30 And she went home and found the child thrown on the couch, and the demon departed.

31 Soon after this, Jesus, coming back from the region of Tyre, passed through Sidon on to the Sea of Galilee, through the region of Decapolis [the ten cities].

32 And they brought to Him a man who was deaf and had difficulty in speaking, and they begged Jesus to place His hand upon him.

33 And taking him aside from the crowd [privately], He thrust His fingers into the man's ears and spat and touched his tongue;

34 And looking up to heaven, He sighed as He said, Ephphatha, which means, Be opened!

35 And his ears were opened, his tongue was loosed, and he began to speak distinctly *and* as he should.

36 And Jesus [ªin His own interest]

---

x W. Robertson Nicoll, ed., *The Expositor's Greek New Testament*. **y** Alexander Souter, *Pocket Lexicon of the Greek New Testament*. **z** Marvin Vincent, *Word Studies*. **a** Kenneth Wuest, *Word Studies*: The Greek uses the middle voice here to show that the charge is given with the speaker's personal interest in view.

admonished *and* ordered them sternly *and* expressly to tell no one; but the more He commanded them, the more zealously they proclaimed it.

37 And they were overwhelmingly astonished, saying, He has done everything excellently (commendably and nobly)! He even makes the deaf to hear and the dumb to speak!

CHAPTER 8

IN THOSE days when [again] an immense crowd had gathered and they had nothing to eat, Jesus called His disciples to Him and told them,

2 I have pity *and* sympathy for the people *and* My heart goes out to them, for they have been with Me now three days and have nothing [left] to eat;

3 And if I send them away to their homes hungry, they will be feeble through exhaustion *and* faint along the road; and some of them have come a long way.

4 And His disciples replied to Him, How can anyone fill *and* satisfy [these people] with loaves of bread here in [this] desolate *and* uninhabited region?

5 And He asked them, How many loaves have you? They said, Seven.

6 And He commanded the multitude to recline upon the ground, and He [then] took the seven loaves [of bread] and, having given thanks, He broke them and kept on giving them to His disciples to put before [the people], and they placed them before the crowd.

7 And they had a few small fish; and when He had [b]praised God *and* given thanks *and* asked Him to bless them [to their use], He ordered that these also should be set before [them].

8 And they ate and were satisfied;

and they took up seven [c]large provision] baskets full of the broken pieces left over.

9 And there were about 4,000 people. And He dismissed them,

10 And at once He got into the boat with His disciples and went to the district of Dalmanutha (or Magdala).

11 The Pharisees came and began to argue with *and* question Him, demanding from Him a sign (an attesting miracle from heaven) [maliciously] to test Him.

12 And He groaned *and* sighed deeply in His spirit and said, Why does this generation demand a sign? Positively I say to you, no sign shall be given this generation.

13 And He went away *and* left them and, getting into the boat again, He departed to the other side.

14 Now they had [d]completely]forgotten to bring bread, and they had only one loaf with them in the boat.

15 And Jesus [repeatedly and expressly] charged *and* admonished them, saying, Look out; keep on your guard *and* beware of the leaven of the Pharisees and the leaven of Herod [e]*and the Herodians*.

16 And they discussed it *and* reasoned with one another, It is because we have no bread.

17 And being aware [of it], Jesus said to them, Why are you reasoning *and* saying it is because you have no bread? Do you not yet discern or understand? Are your hearts in [a settled state of] hardness? [Isa. 6:9, 10; Jer. 5:21.]

18 Having eyes, do you not see [with them], and having ears, do you not hear *and* perceive *and* understand the sense of what is said? And do you not remember?

19 When I broke the five loaves for

b Joseph Thayer, *A Greek-English Lexicon.* 14:20.   d Kenneth Wuest, *Word Studies.*

c Marvin Vincent, *Word Studies.* See also footnote on Matt.

e Some ancient manuscripts add "and the Herodians."

the 5,000, how many [fsmall hand] baskets full of broken pieces did you take up? They said to Him, Twelve.

20 And [when I broke] the seven loaves for the 4,000, how many [glarge provision] baskets full of broken pieces did you take up? And they said to Him, Seven.

21 And He gkept repeating, Do you not yet understand?

22 And they came to Bethsaida. And [people] brought to Him a blind man and begged Him to touch him.

23 And He hcaught the blind man by the hand and led him out of the village; and when He had spit on his eyes and put His hands upon him, He asked him, Do you [gpossibly] see anything?

24 And he looked up and said, I see people, but [they look] like trees, walking.

25 Then He put His hands on his eyes again; and the man looked intently [that is, fixed his eyes on definite objects], and he was restored and saw everything distinctly [even what was iat a distance].

26 And He sent him away to his house, telling [him], Do not [even] enter the village jor tell anyone there.

27 And Jesus went on with His disciples to the villages of Caesarea Philippi; and on the way He asked His disciples, Who do people say that I am?

28 And they answered [Him], John the Baptist; and others [say], Elijah; but others, one of the prophets.

29 And He asked them, But who do you yourselves say that I am? Peter replied to Him, You are the Christ (the Messiah, the Anointed One).

30 And He charged them sharply to tell no one about Him.

31 And He began to teach them that the Son of Man must of necessity suffer many things and be tested *and* disapproved *and* rejected by the elders and the chief priests and the scribes, and be put to death, and after three days rise again [kfrom death].

32 And He said this freely (frankly, plainly, and explicitly), making it unmistakable). And Peter took Him iby the hand *and* led Him aside and then [facing Him] began to rebuke Him.

33 But turning around [His back to Peter] and seeing His disciples, He rebuked Peter, saying, Get behind Me, Satan! For you do not have a mind iintent on promoting what God wills, but what pleases men [you are not on God's side, but that of men].

34 And Jesus called [to Him] the throng with His disciples and said to them, If anyone intends to come after Me, let him deny himself [forget, ignore, disown, and ilose sight of himself and his own interests] and take up his cross, and [ijoining Me as a disciple and siding with My party] follow lwith Me [continually, cleaving steadfastly to Me].

35 For whoever wants to save his [mhigher, spiritual, eternal] life, will lose it [the mlower, natural, temporal life iwhich is lived only on earth]; and whoever gives up his life [which is lived only on earth] for My sake and the Gospel's will save it [his mhigher, spiritual life iin the eternal kingdom of God].

36 For what does it profit a man to gain the whole world, and forfeit his life [iin the eternal kingdom of God]?

37 For what can a man give as an exchange (ka compensation, a ransom, in return) for his [blessed] life [iin the eternal kingdom of God]?

f Marvin Vincent, *Word Studies*. See also footnote on Matt. 14:20.   g W. Robertson Nicoll, ed., *The Expositor's Greek New Testament*.   h William Tyndale, *The Tyndale Bible*.   i Joseph Thayer, *A Greek-English Lexicon*.   j Some manuscripts add this phrase.   k Hermann Cremer, *Biblico-Theological Lexicon*.   l Kenneth Wuest, *Word Studies*.   m Robert Jamieson, A.R. Fausett and David Brown, *A Commentary on the Old and New Testaments*.

38 For whoever [n]is ashamed [here and now] of Me and My words in this adulterous (unfaithful) and [preeminently] sinful generation, of him will the Son of Man also be ashamed when He comes in the glory [splendor and majesty] of His Father with the holy angels.

CHAPTER 9

AND JESUS said to them, Truly *and* solemnly I say to you, there are some standing here who will in no way taste death before they see the kingdom of God come in [its] power.

2 Six days after this, Jesus took with Him Peter and James and John and led them up on a high mountain apart by themselves. And He was transfigured before them *and* became resplendent with divine brightness.

3 And His garments became glistening, intensely white, as no fuller (cloth dresser, launderer) on earth could bleach them.

4 And Elijah appeared [there] to them, accompanied by Moses, and they were [o]holding [a protracted] conversation with Jesus.

5 And [p]Peter took up the conversation, saying, Master, it is good *and* suitable *and* beautiful for us to be here. Let us make three booths (tents)—one for You and one for Moses and one for Elijah.

6 For he did not [really] know what to say, for they were in a violent fright ([q]aghast with dread).

7 And a cloud threw a shadow upon them, and a voice came out of the cloud, saying, This is My Son, the [[q]most dearworthy] Beloved One. Be [o]constantly listening to *and* obeying Him!

8 And looking around, they suddenly no longer saw anyone with them except Jesus only.

9 And as they were coming back down the mountain, He admonished *and* [r]expressly ordered them to tell no one what they had seen until the Son of Man should rise from among the dead.

10 So they carefully *and* faithfully kept the matter to themselves, questioning *and* disputing with one another about what rising from among the dead meant.

11 And they asked Him, Why do the scribes say that it is necessary for Elijah to come first? [Mal. 4:5, 6.]

12 And He said to them, Elijah, it is true, does come first to restore all things *and* [s]set them to rights. And how is it written of the Son of Man that He will suffer many things *and* be utterly despised *and* be treated with contempt *and* rejected? [Isa. 53:3.]

13 But I tell you that Elijah has already come, and [people] did to him whatever they desired, as it is written of him.

14 And when they came to the [nine] disciples, they saw a great crowd around them and scribes questioning *and* disputing with them.

15 And immediately all the crowd, when they saw Jesus [[r]returning from the holy mount, His face and person yet glistening], they were greatly amazed and ran up to Him [and] greeted Him.

16 And He asked them, About what are you questioning *and* discussing with them?

17 And one of the throng replied to Him, Teacher, I brought my son to You, for he has a dumb spirit.

18 And wherever it lays hold of him [so as to make it its own], it

---

n A.T. Robertson, *Word Pictures.*   o Kenneth Wuest, *Word Studies.*   p H.A.A. Kennedy, *Sources of New Testament Greek.*   q John Wycliffe, *The Wycliffe Bible.*   r G. Abbott-Smith, *Manual Greek Lexicon.*   s Matthew Henry, *Commentary on the Holy Bible.*   t Richard Trench, *Notes on the Miracles.*

dashes him down *and* convulses him, and he foams [at the mouth] and grinds his teeth, *and* he [u"falls into a motionless stupor and] is wasting away. And I asked Your disciples to drive it out, and they were not able [to do it].

19 And He answered them, O unbelieving generation [without any faith]! How long ushall I [have to do] with you? How long am I to bear with you? Bring him to Me.

20 So they brought [the boy] to Him, and when the spirit saw Him, at once it completely convulsed the boy, and he fell to the ground and kept rolling about, foaming [at the mouth].

21 And [Jesus] asked his father, How long has he had this? And he answered, From the time he was a little boy.

22 And it has often thrown him both into fire and into water, intending to kill him. But if You can do anything, do have pity on us and help us.

23 And Jesus said, [You say to Me], If You can do anything? [Why,] all things can be (are possible) to him who believes!

24 At once the father of the boy gave [an veager, wpiercing, inarticulate] cry *with tears,* and he said, Lord, I believe! [Constantly] help my xweakness of faith!

25 But when Jesus noticed that a crowd [of people] came running together, He rebuked the unclean spirit, saying to it, You dumb and deaf spirit, I charge you to come out of him and never go into him again.

26 And after giving a [hoarse, clamoring, fear-stricken] shriek of anguish and convulsing him terribly, it came out; and the boy lay [pale and motionless] like a corpse, so that many of them said, He is dead.

27 But Jesus took [ua strong grip of] his hand and began lifting him up, and he stood.

28 And when He had gone indoors, His disciples asked Him privately, Why could not we drive it out?

29 And He replied to them, This kind cannot be driven out by anything but prayer y*and fasting.*

30 They went on from there and passed along through Galilee. And He did not wish to have anyone know it,

31 For He was [engaged for the time being in] teaching His disciples. He said to them, The Son of Man is being delivered into the hands of men, and they will put Him to death; and when He has been killed, after three days He will rise [zfrom death].

32 But they did not comprehend what He was saying, and they were afraid to ask Him [what this statement meant].

33 And they arrived at Capernaum; and when [they were] in the house, He asked them, What were you discussing *and* arguing about on the road?

34 But they kept still, for on the road they had discussed *and* disputed with one another as to who was the greatest.

35 And He sat down and called the Twelve [apostles], and He said to them, If anyone desires to be first, he must be last of all, and servant of all.

36 And He took a little child and put him in the center of their group; and taking him in [His] arms, He said to them,

37 Whoever in My name *and* for My sake accepts *and* receives *and* welcomes one such child also accepts *and* receives *and* welcomes

u Kenneth Wuest, *Word Studies.*   v W. Robertson Nicoll, ed., *The Expositor's Greek New Testament.*
w Henry Swete, *The Gospel According to Saint Mark.*   x Joseph Thayer, *A Greek-English Lexicon.*
y Some manuscripts add "and fasting."   z Hermann Cremer, *Biblico-Theological Lexicon.*

Me; and whoever so receives Me receives not only Me but Him Who sent Me.

38 John said to Him, Teacher, we saw a man who does not follow along with us driving out demons in Your name, and we forbade him to do it, because he [a]is not one of our band [of Your disciples].

39 But Jesus said, Do not restrain *or* hinder *or* forbid him; for no one who does a mighty work in My name will soon afterward be able to speak evil of Me.

40 For he who is not against us is for us. [Num. 11:27–29.]

41 For I tell you truly, whoever gives you a cup of water to drink because you belong to *and* bear the name of Christ will by no means fail to get his reward.

42 And whoever causes one of these little ones (these believers) who [b]acknowledge *and* cleave to Me to stumble *and* sin, it would be better (more profitable and wholesome) for him if a [huge] millstone were hung about his neck, and he were thrown into the sea.

43 And if your hand puts a stumbling block before you *and* causes you to sin, cut it off! It is more profitable *and* wholesome for you to go into life [[c]that is really worthwhile] maimed than with two hands to go to hell (Gehenna), into the fire that cannot be put out. [d]

45 And if your foot is a cause of stumbling *and* sin to you, cut it off! It is more profitable *and* wholesome for you to enter into life [that is really worthwhile] cripp[led] with two feet, to be c[ast int] [Gehenna][e].

47 And i[   ]

stumble *and* sin, pluck it out! It is more profitable *and* wholesome for you to enter the kingdom of God with one eye than with two eyes to be thrown into hell (Gehenna).

48 Where their worm [[f]which preys on the inhabitants and is a symbol of the wounds inflicted on the man himself by his sins] does not die, and the fire is not put out. [Isa. 66.24.]

49 For everyone shall be salted with fire.

50 Salt is good (beneficial), but if salt has lost its saltness, how will you restore [the saltness to] it? Have salt within yourselves, and be at peace *and* live in harmony with one another.

CHAPTER 10

AND [Jesus] left there [Capernaum] and went to the region of Judea and beyond [east of] the Jordan; and crowds [constantly] gathered around Him again, and as was His custom, He began to teach them again.

2 And some Pharisees came up, and, in order to test Him *and* try to find a weakness in Him, asked, Is it lawful for a man to [a]dismiss *and* repudiate *and* divorce his wife?

3 He answered them, What did Moses command you?

4 They replied, Moses allowed a man to write a bill of di[vorce]...

[overlapping torn paper fragments with partially visible text:]

...because put her aw[ay]... your con-
...this ...precept in
...the call of
...the beginning of cre...

remer, *Biblico-Theological Lexicon*...
are identical with verse 48, are not found in
according to Saint Mark.
[f] Ezra Palmer Gould, cited by A.T.
[g] Henry Swete, The...

[a] Joseph Th...
[c] Kenneth...
the be...
Rob[ert]...
G[   ]

...Sain[t]...
...ek New Testament Lexicon, Word...
...cording to Saint Mark.

ation God made them male and female. [Gen. 1:27; 5:2.]

7 For this reason a man shall leave
[behind] his father and his mother
[h]and be [i]joined to his wife and cleave
closely to her permanently,

8 And the two shall become one
flesh, so that they are no longer two,
but one flesh. [Gen. 2:24.]

9 What therefore God has united
(joined together), let not man separate or divide.

10 And indoors the disciples questioned Him again about this subject.

11 And He said to them, Whoever
[j]dismisses (repudiates and divorces)
his wife and marries another commits adultery against her;

12 And if a woman dismisses
(repudiates and divorces) her husband and marries another, she commits adultery.

13 And they kept bringing young
children to Him that He might touch
them, and the disciples were reprov-
ing them [for it].

14 But when Jesus saw [it], He was
indignant and [k]pained and said to
them, Allow the children to come to
Me—do not forbid or prevent or hinder them—for to such belongs the
kingdom of God.

15 Truly I tell you, whoever does
not receive and accept and welcome
the kingdom of God like a little child
[l]does] positively shall not enter it at
all.

16 And He took them [the children
up] in His arms and [m]fer[vent]l blessing, placing
His journl blessing
before Him]

[You are [n]essentially and perfectly
[o]morally] good, what must I do to
inherit eternal life [that is, [n]to partake
of eternal salvation in the Messiah's
kingdom]?

18 And Jesus said to him, Why do
you call Me [[n]essentially and perfectly [o]morally] good? There is no one
[[n]essentially and perfectly [o]morally]
good—except God alone.

19 You know the commandments:
Do not kill, do not commit adultery,
do not steal, do not bear false witness, do not defraud, honor your father and mother. [Exod. 20:12–16;
Deut. 5:16–20.]

20 And he replied to Him, Teacher, I have carefully guarded and observed all these and taken care not to
violate them from my boyhood.

21 And Jesus, looking upon him,
loved him, and He said to him, You
lack one thing; go and sell all you
have and give [the money] to the
poor, and you will have treasure in
heaven; and come [and] accompany
Me [[p]walking the same road that I
walk].

22 At that saying the man's countenance fell and was gloomy, and he
went away grieved and sorrowing,
for he was holding great possessions.

23 And Jesus looked around and
said to His disciples, With what difficulty will those who possess wealth
and [q]keep on holding it enter the
kingdom of God!

24 And the disciples were amazed
and bewildered and perplexed at His
words. But Jesus said to them again,
Children, how hard it is [r]for those
who trust (place their confidence,
their sense of safety) in riches to enter the kingdom of God!

h Some manuscripts. i Heb...
Vocabulary. I W. Robe...g out on
Pictures. j Greek New Testament...
Greek Biblico-Theological Lexicon...nelt
manuscripts do not contain this...

j James Moulton and George Milligan, The
...Mark. k A.T. Robertson, Word
...nent. m Henry Alford, The
o Hermann Cremer,
...Studies. r Some

25 It is easier for a camel to go through the eye of a needle than for a rich man to enter the kingdom of God.

26 And they were shocked *and* exceedingly astonished, and said to Him *and* [s]to one another, Then who can be saved?

27 Jesus glanced around at them and said, With men [it is] impossible, but not with God; for all things are possible with God.

28 Peter started to say to Him. Behold, we have [t]yielded up *and* abandoned everything [once and for all and [u]joined You as Your disciples, siding with Your party] and accompanied You [[v]walking the same road that You walk].

29 Jesus said, Truly I tell you, there is no one who has given up *and* left house or brothers or sisters or mother or father or children or lands for My sake and for the Gospel's

30 Who will not receive a hundred times as much now in this time— houses and brothers and sisters and mothers and children and lands, with persecutions—and in the age to come, eternal life.

31 But many [who are now] first will be last [then], and many [who are now] last will be first [then].

32 They were on the way going up to Jerusalem, and Jesus was walking on in front of them; and they were bewildered *and* perplexed *and* greatly astonished, and those [who were still] following were seized with alarm *and* were afraid. And He took the Twelve [apostles] again and began to tell them what was about to happen to Him,

33 [Saying], Behold, we are going up to Jerusalem, and the Son of Man will be turned over to the chief priests and the scribes; and they will condemn *and* sentence Him to death and turn Him over to the Gentiles.

34 And they will mock Him and spit on Him, and whip Him and put Him to death; but after three days He will rise again [[w]from death].

35 And James and John, the sons of Zebedee, approached Him and said to Him, Teacher, we desire You to do for us whatever we ask of You.

36 And He replied to them, What do you desire Me to do for you?

37 And they said to Him, Grant that we may sit, one at Your right hand and one at [Your] left hand, in Your glory (Your majesty and splendor).

38 But Jesus said to them, You do not know what you are asking. Are you able to drink the cup that I drink or be baptized with the baptism [of affliction] with which I am baptized?

39 And they replied to Him, We are able. And Jesus told them, The cup that I drink you will drink, and you will be baptized with the baptism with which I am baptized,

40 But to sit at My right hand or at My left hand is not Mine to give; but [it will be given to those] for whom it is ordained *and* prepared.

41 And when the other ten [apostles] heard it, they began to be indignant with James and John.

42 But Jesus called them to [Him] and said to them, You know that those who are recognized as governing *and* are supposed to rule the Gentiles (the nations) lord it over them [ruling with absolute power, holding them in subjection], and their great men exercise authority *and* dominion over them.

43 But this is not to be so among you; instead, whoever desires to be great among you must be your servant,

---

s Many ancient manuscripts add "to one another." Thayer, *A Greek-English Lexicon.*   t Kenneth Wuest, *Word Studies.*   u Joseph   v Literal translation.   w Hermann Cremer, *Biblico-Theolog[ical] Lexicon.*

44 And whoever wishes to be most important *and* first in rank among you must be slave of all.

45 For even the Son of Man came not to have service rendered to Him, but to serve, and to give His life as a ransom for [ˣinstead of] many.

46 Then they came to Jericho. And as He was leaving Jericho with His disciples and a great crowd, Bartimaeus, a blind beggar, a son of Timaeus, was sitting by the roadside.

47 And when he heard that it was Jesus of Nazareth, he began to shout, saying, Jesus, Son of David, have pity *and* mercy on me [ʸnow]!

48 And many ᶻseverely censured *and* reproved him, telling him to keep still, but he kept on shouting out all the more, You Son of David, have pity *and* mercy on me [now]!

49 And Jesus stopped and said, Call him. And they called the blind man, telling him, Take courage! Get up! He is calling you.

50 And throwing off his outer garment, he leaped up and came to Jesus.

51 And Jesus said to him, What do you want Me to do for you? And the blind man said to Him, Master, let me receive my sight.

52 And Jesus said to him, Go your way; your faith has healed you. And at once he received his sight and accompanied Jesus on the road. [Isa. 42:6, 7.]

CHAPTER 11

WHEN THEY were getting near to Jerusalem, to Bethphage and Bethany at the Mount of Olives, He sent ahead two of His disciples

2 And instructed them, Go into the village in front of you, and as soon as you enter it, you will find a colt tied,

which has never been ridden by anyone; unfasten it and bring it [here].

3 If anyone asks you, Why are you doing this? answer, The Lord needs it, and He will send it back here presently.

4 So they went away and found a colt tied at the door out in the [winding] open street, and they loosed it.

5 And some who were standing there said to them, What are you doing, untying the colt?

6 And they replied as Jesus had directed them, and they allowed them to go.

7 And they brought the colt to Jesus and threw their outer garments upon it, and He sat on it.

8 And many [of the people] spread their garments on the road, and others [scattered a layer of] leafy branches which they had cut from the fields.

9 And those who went before and those who followed cried out [ᵃwith a cry of happiness], Hosanna! [Be graciously inclined and propitious to Him!] Praised *and* blessed is He Who comes in the name of the Lord! [Ps. 118:26.]

10 Praised *and* blessed *in the name of the Lord* is the coming kingdom of our father David! Hosanna (O save us) in the highest [heaven]!

11 And Jesus went into Jerusalem and entered the temple [ᵇenclosure]; and when He had looked around, surveying *and* observing everything, as it was already late, He went out to Bethany together with the Twelve [apostles].

12 On the day following, when they had come away from Bethany, He was hungry.

13 And seeing in the distance a fig tree [covered] with leaves, He went to see if He could find any [fruit] on it

x Marvin Vincent, *Word Studies*.   **y** Kenneth Wuest, *Word Studies*: The Greek aorist (past tense) imperative.   **z** Joseph Thayer, *A Greek-English Lexicon*.   **a** Alexander Souter, *Pocket Lexicon*.   **b** Richard Trench, *Synonyms of the New Testament*.

[cfor in the fig tree the fruit appears at the same time as the leaves]. But when He came up to it, He found nothing but leaves, for the fig season had not yet come.

14 And He said to it, No one ever again shall eat fruit from you. And His disciples were listening [to what He said].

15 And they came to Jerusalem. And He went into the temple [area, the dporches and courts] and began to drive out those who sold and bought in the temple area, and He overturned the [cfour-footed] tables of the money changers and the seats of those who dealt in doves;

16 And He would not permit anyone to carry any household equipment through the temple enclosure [thus making the temple area a short-cut traffic lane].

17 And He taught and said to them, Is it not written, My house shall be called a house of prayer for all the nations? But you have turned it into a den of robbers. [Isa. 56:7; Jer. 7:11.]

18 And the chief priests and the scribes heard [of this] and kept seeking some way to destroy Him, for they feared Him, because the entire multitude was struck with astonishment at His teaching.

19 And when evening came on, *He and fHis disciples*, as accustomed, went out of the city.

20 In the morning, when they were passing along, they noticed that the fig tree was withered [completely] away to its roots.

21 And Peter remembered and said to Him, Master, look! The fig tree which You doomed has withered away!

22 And Jesus, replying, said to them, Have faith in God [constantly].

23 Truly I tell you, whoever says to this mountain, Be lifted up and thrown into the sea! and does not doubt at all in his heart but believes that what he says will take place, it will be done for him.

24 For this reason I am telling you, whatever you ask for in prayer, believe (trust and be confident) that it is granted to you, and you will [get it].

25 And whenever you stand praying, if you have anything against anyone, forgive him *and* elet it drop (leave it, let it go), in order that your Father Who is in heaven may also forgive you your [own] failings *and* shortcomings *and* let them drop.

26 gBut if you do not forgive, neither will your Father in heaven forgive your failings and shortcomings.

27 And they came again to Jerusalem. And when Jesus was walking about in the [dcourts and porches of the] temple, the chief priests and the scribes and the elders came to Him,

28 And they kept saying to Him, By what [sort of] authority are You doing these things, or who gave You this authority to do them?

29 Jesus told them, I will ask you a question. Answer Me, and then I will tell you by what [sort of] authority I do these things.

30 Was the baptism of John from heaven or from men? Answer Me.

31 And they reasoned *and* argued with one another, If we say, From heaven, He will say, Why then did you not believe him?

32 But [on the other hand] can we say, From men? For they were afraid of the people, because everybody considered *and* held John actually to be a prophet.

33 So they replied to Jesus, We do not know. And Jesus said to them, Neither am I going to tell you what

c James Orr et al., eds., *The International Standard Bible Encyclopedia.* d Richard Trench, *Synonyms of the New Testament.* e James Moulton and George Milligan, *The Vocabulary.* f Some manuscripts read "they." g Some manuscripts do not contain verse 26.

[sort of] authority I have for doing these things.

CHAPTER 12

AND [Jesus] started to speak to them in parables [with comparisons and illustrations]. A man planted a vineyard and put a hedge around it and dug a pit for the winepress and built a tower and let it out [for rent] to vinedressers and went into another country.

2 When the season came, he sent a bond servant to the tenants to collect from them some of the fruit of the vineyard.

3 But they took him and beat him and sent him away without anything.

4 Again he sent to them another bond servant, and they *stoned him and* wounded him in the head and treated him shamefully [sending him away with insults].

5 And he sent another, and that one they killed; then many others—some they beat, and some they put to death.

6 He had still one left [to send], a beloved son; last of all he sent him to them, saying, They will respect my son.

7 But those tenants said to one another, Here is the heir; come on, let us put him to death, and [then] the inheritance will be ours.

8 And they took him and killed him, and threw [his body] outside the vineyard.

9 Now what will the owner of the vineyard do? He will come and destroy the tenants, and give the vineyard to others.

10 Have you not even read this [passage of] Scripture: The very Stone which [hafter putting It to the test] the builders rejected has be-

come the Head of the corner [Cornerstone];

11 This is from the Lord *and* is His doing, and it is marvelous in our eyes? [Ps. 118:22, 23.]

12 And they were trying to get hold of Him, but they were afraid of the people, for they knew that He spoke this parable with reference to and against them. So they left Him and departed. [Isa. 5:1–7.]

13 But they sent some of the Pharisees and of the Herodians to Him for the purpose of entrapping Him in His speech.

14 And they came up and said to Him, Teacher, we know that You are isincere *and* what You profess to be, that You cannot lie, *and* that You have no personal bias for anyone; for You are not influenced by partiality *and* have no jregard for anyone's external condition *or* position, but in [and on the basis of] truth You teach the way of God. Is it lawful (permissible and right) to give tribute (jpoll taxes) to Caesar or not?

15 Should we pay [them] or should we not pay [them]? But knowing their hypocrisy, He asked them, Why do you put Me to the test? Bring Me a coin (a denarius), so I may see it.

16 And they brought [Him one]. Then He asked them, Whose image (picture) is this? And whose superscription (htitle)? They said to Him, Caesar's.

17 Jesus said to them, Pay to Caesar the things that are Caesar's and to kGod the things that are God's. And they hstood marveling *and* greatly amazed at Him.

18 And [some] Sadducees came to Him, [of that party] who say there is no resurrection, and they asked Him a question, saying,

---

h Kenneth Wuest, *Word Studies.* Thayer, *A Greek-English Lexicon.*

i Hermann Cremer, *Biblico-Theological Lexicon.*

k A rebuke of emperor worship.

j Joseph

19 Teacher, Moses gave us [a law] that if a man's brother died, leaving a wife but no child, the man must marry the widow and raise up offspring for his brother. [Deut. 25:5.]

20 Now there were seven brothers; the first one took a wife and died, leaving no children.

21 And the second [brother] married her, and died, leaving no children; and the third did the same;

22 And all seven, leaving no children. Last of all, the woman died also.

23 Now in the resurrection, whose wife will she be? For the seven were married to her.

24 Jesus said to them, Is not this where you wander out of the way and go wrong, because you know neither the Scriptures nor the power of God?

25 For when they arise from among the dead, [men] do not marry nor are [women] given in marriage, but are like the angels in heaven.

26 But concerning the dead being raised—have you not read in the book of Moses, [in the passage] about the [burning] bush, how God said to him, I am the God of Abraham and the God of Isaac and the God of Jacob? [Exod. 3:2–6.]

27 He is not the God of [the] dead, but of [the] living! You are very wrong.

28 Then one of the scribes came up and listened to them disputing with one another, and, noticing that Jesus answered them fitly *and* admirably, he asked Him, Which commandment is first *and* most important of all [¹in its nature]?

29 Jesus answered, The first *and* principal *one of all commands* is: Hear, O Israel, The Lord our God is one Lord;

30 And you shall love the Lord your God ¹out of *and* with your whole heart and out of *and* with all your soul (your ᵐlife) and out of *and* with all your mind (with ¹your faculty of thought and your moral understanding) and out of *and* with all your strength. ⁿ*This is the first and principal commandment.* [Deut. 6:4, 5.]

31 The second *is like it and* is this, You shall love your neighbor as yourself. There is no other commandment greater than these. [Lev. 19:18.]

32 And the scribe said to Him, Excellently *and* fitly *and* admirably answered, Teacher! You have said truly that He is One, and there is no other but Him;

33 And to love Him out of *and* with all the heart and with all the understanding [with the ¹faculty of quick apprehension and intelligence and keenness of discernment] and with all the strength, and to love one's neighbor as oneself, is much more than all the whole burnt offerings and sacrifices. [I Sam. 15:22; Hos. 6:6; Mic. 6:6 8; Heb. 10:8.]

34 And when Jesus saw that he answered intelligently (discreetly and ¹having his wits about him), He said to him, You are not far from the kingdom of God. And after that no one ventured *or* dared to ask Him any further question.

35 And as Jesus taught in [a ᵒporch or court of] the temple, He said, How can the scribes say that the Christ is David's Son?

36 David himself, [inspired] in the Holy Spirit, declared, The Lord said to my Lord, Sit at My right hand until I make Your enemies [a footstool] under Your feet. [Ps. 110:1.]

37 David himself calls Him Lord; so how can it be that He is his Son? Now the great mass of the people

---

l Marvin Vincent, *Word Studies.*   m Hermann Cremer, *A Biblico-Theological Lexicon.*   n Some manuscripts do not contain this part of verse 30.   o Richard Trench, *Synonyms of the New Testament.*

heard [Jesus] gladly [listening to Him with delight].

38 And in [the course of] His teaching, He said, Beware of the scribes, who like to go around in long robes and [to get] greetings in the marketplaces [public forums],

39 And [have] the front seats in the synagogues and the [p]chief couches (places of honor) at feasts,

40 Who devour widows' houses and to cover it up make long prayers. They will receive the heavier [sentence of] condemnation.

41 And He sat down opposite the treasury and saw how the crowd was casting money into the treasury. Many rich [people] were throwing in large sums.

42 And a widow who was poverty-stricken came and put in two copper mites [the smallest of coins], which together make [q]half of a cent.

43 And He called His disciples [to Him] and said to them, Truly *and* surely I tell you, this widow, [she who is] poverty-stricken, has put in more than all those contributing to the treasury.

44 For they all threw in out of their abundance; but she, out of her deep poverty, has put in everything that she had—[even] all she had on which to live.

CHAPTER 13

AND AS [Jesus] was coming out of the temple [[p]area], one of His disciples said to Him, Look, Teacher! Notice the sort *and* quality of these stones and buildings!

2 And Jesus replied to him, You see these great buildings? There will not be left here one stone upon another that will not be loosened *and* torn down.

3 And as He sat on the Mount of Olives opposite the temple [[p]enclosure], Peter and James and John and Andrew asked Him privately,

4 Tell us when is this to take place and what will be the sign when these things, all [of them], are about to be accomplished?

5 And Jesus began to tell them, Be careful *and* watchful that no one misleads you [about it].

6 Many will come in [[r]appropriating to themselves] the name [of Messiah] which belongs to Me [[s]basing their claims on the use of My name], saying, I am [He]! And they will mislead many.

7 And when you hear of wars and rumors of wars, do not get alarmed (troubled and frightened); it is necessary [that these things] take place, but the end is not yet.

8 For nation will rise against nation, and kingdom against kingdom. There will be earthquakes in various places; there will be famines *and calamities*. This is but the beginning of the [r]intolerable anguish *and* suffering [only the first of the [t]birth pangs].

9 But look to yourselves; for they will turn you over to councils, and you will be beaten in the synagogues, and you will stand before governors and kings for My sake as a testimony to them.

10 And the good news (the Gospel) must first be preached to all nations.

11 Now when they take you [to court] and put you under arrest, do not be anxious beforehand about what you are to say [u]*nor* [*even*] *meditate about it;* but say whatever is given you in that hour *and* at [v]the moment, for it is not you who will be speaking, but the Holy Spirit.

12 And brother will hand over brother to death, and the father his

p Richard Trench, *Synonyms of the New Testament*. **q** John D. Davis, *A Dictionary of the Bible*.
r Joseph Thayer, *A Greek-English Lexicon*. **s** Marvin Vincent, *Word Studies*. **t** Literal meaning.
u Most manuscripts do not contain this phrase. **v** James Moulton and George Milligan, *The Vocabulary*.

child; and children will take a stand against their parents and [have] them put to death.

13 And you will be hated *and* detested by everybody for My name's sake, but he who patiently perseveres *and* endures to the end will be saved (ʷmade a partaker of the salvation by Christ, and delivered ʷfrom spiritual death).

14 But when you see the abomination of desolation *mentioned by Daniel the prophet* standing where it ought not to be—[and] let the one who reads take notice *and* consider *and* understand *and* heed [this]— then let those who are in Judea flee to the mountains. [Dan. 9:27; 11:31; 12:11.]

15 Let him who is on the housetop not go down *into the house* nor go inside to take anything out of his house;

16 And let him who is in the field not turn back again to get his mantle (cloak).

17 And alas for those who are pregnant and for those who have nursing babies in those days!

18 Pray that it may not occur in winter,

19 For at that time there will be such affliction (oppression and tribulation) as has not been from the beginning of the creation which God created until this particular time— and ˣpositively never will be [again].

20 And unless the Lord had shortened the days, no human being would be saved (rescued); but for the sake of the elect, His chosen ones (those whom He ʸpicked out for Himself), He has shortened the days. [Dan. 12:1.]

21 And then if anyone says to you, See, here is the Christ! or, Look, there He is! do not believe it.

22 False Christs (Messiahs) and false prophets will arise and show signs and [work] miracles to deceive *and* lead astray, if possible, even the elect (those God has chosen out for Himself).

23 But look to yourselves *and* be on your guard; I have told you everything beforehand.

24 But in those days, after [the affliction and oppression and distress of] that tribulation, the sun will be darkened, and the moon will not give its light; [Isa. 13:10.]

25 And the stars will be falling from the sky, and the powers in the heavens will be shaken. [Isa. 34:4.]

26 And then they will see the Son of Man coming in clouds with great (kingly) power and glory (majesty and splendor). [Dan. 7:13, 14.]

27 And then He will send out the angels and will gather together His elect (those He has ʸpicked out for Himself) from the four winds, from the farthest bounds of the earth to the farthest bounds of heaven.

28 Now learn a lesson from the fig tree: as soon as its branch becomes tender and it puts forth its leaves, you recognize *and* know that summer is near.

29 So also, when you see these things happening, you may recognize *and* know that He is near, at [the very] door.

30 Surely I say to you, this generation (ᶻthe whole multitude of people living at that one time) positively will not perish *or* pass away before all these things take place.

31 Heaven and earth will perish *and* pass away, but My words will not perish *or* pass away.

32 But of that day or that hour not a [single] person knows, not even the

w Joseph Thayer, *A Greek-English Lexicon*.   x Kenneth Wuest, *Word Studies*.   y G. Abbott-Smith, *Manual Greek Lexicon*.   z Hermann Cremer, *Biblico-Theological Lexicon*; Joseph Thayer, *A Greek-English Lexicon*; and G. Abbott-Smith, *Manual Greek Lexicon*.

angels in heaven, nor the Son, but only the Father.

33 Be on your guard [constantly alert], and watch [a]*and pray;* for you do not know when the time will come.

34 It is like a man [[b]already] going on a journey; when he leaves home, he puts his servants in charge, each with his particular task, and he gives orders to the doorkeeper to be constantly alert *and* on the watch.

35 Therefore watch (give strict attention, be cautious and alert), for you do not know when the Master of the house is coming—in the evening, or at midnight, or at cockcrowing, or in the morning—

36 [Watch, I say] lest He come suddenly *and* unexpectedly and find you asleep.

37 And what I say to you I say to everybody: Watch (give strict attention, be cautious, active, and alert)!

CHAPTER 14

IT WAS now two days before the Passover and the Feast of Unleavened Bread, and the chief priests and the scribes were all the while seeking to arrest [Jesus] by secrecy *and* deceit and put [Him] to death,

2 For they kept saying, It must not be during the Feast, for fear that there might be a riot of the people.

3 And while He was in Bethany, [a guest] in the house of Simon the leper, as He was reclining [at table], a woman came with an alabaster jar of ointment ([c]*perfume) of pure nard, very costly *and* precious; and she broke the jar and poured [the perfume] over His head.

4 But there were some who were moved with indignation and said to themselves, To what purpose was the ointment ([c]*perfume) thus wasted?

5 For it was possible to have sold this [perfume] for more than 300 denarii [a laboring man's wages for a year] and to have given [the money] to the poor. And they censured *and* reproved her.

6 But Jesus said, Let her alone; why are you troubling her? She has done a good *and* beautiful thing to Me [praiseworthy and noble].

7 For you always have the poor with you, and whenever you wish you can do good to them; but you will not always have Me. [Deut. 15:11.]

8 She has done what she could; she came beforehand to anoint My body for the burial.

9 And surely I tell you, wherever the good news (the Gospel) is proclaimed in the entire world, what she has done will be told in memory of her.

10 Then Judas Iscariot, who was one of the Twelve [apostles], went off to the chief priests in order to betray *and* hand Him over to them.

11 And when they heard it, they rejoiced *and* were delighted, and they promised to give him money. And he [busying himself continually] sought an opportunity to betray Him.

12 On the first day [of the Feast] of Unleavened Bread, when [as was customary] they killed the Passover lamb, [Jesus'] disciples said to Him, Where do You wish us to go [and] prepare the Passover [supper] for You to eat?

13 And He sent two of His disciples and said to them, Go into the city, and a man carrying an [earthen] jar *or* pitcher of water will meet you; follow him.

14 And whatever [house] he enters, say to the master of the house,

---

a Some manuscripts add "and pray."   b John Wycliffe, *The Wycliffe Bible;* William Tyndale, *The Tyndale Bible.*   c James Moulton and George Milligan, *The Vocabulary.*

The Teacher says: Where is My guest room, where I may eat the Passover [supper] with My disciples?

15 And he will [himself] show you a large upper room, furnished [with carpets and with dining couches properly spread] and ready; there prepare for us.

16 Then the disciples set out and came to the city and found [everything] just as He had told them; and they prepared the Passover.

17 And when it was evening, He came with the Twelve [apostles].

18 And while they were at the table eating, Jesus said, Surely I say to you, one of you will betray Me, [one] who is eating [here] with Me. [Ps. 41:9.]

19 And they began to show that they were sad and hurt, and to say to Him one after another, Is it I? or, It is not I, is it?

20 He replied to them, It is one of the Twelve [apostles], one who is dipping [bread] into the [same deep] dish with Me.

21 For the Son of Man is going as it stands written concerning Him; but woe to that man by whom the Son of Man is betrayed! It would have been good (profitable and wholesome) for that man if he had never been born. [Ps. 41:9.]

22 And while they were eating, He took a loaf [of bread], praised God and gave thanks and asked Him to bless it to their use. [Then] He broke [it] and gave to them and said, Take. Eat. This is My body.

23 He also took a cup [of the juice of grapes], and when He had given thanks, He gave [it] to them, and they all drank of it.

24 And He said to them, This is My blood [which ratifies] the new covenant, [the blood] which is being poured out for (on account of) many. [Exod. 24:8.]

25 Solemnly and surely I tell you, I shall not again drink of the fruit of the vine till that day when I drink it dof a new and a higher quality in God's kingdom.

26 And when they had sung a hymn, they went out to the Mount of Olives.

27 And Jesus said to them, You will all fall away this night [that is, you will be caused to stumble and will begin to distrust and desert Me], for it stands written, I will strike the Shepherd, and the sheep will be scattered. [Zech. 13:7.]

28 But after I am raised [to life], I will go before you into Galilee.

29 But Peter said to Him, Even if they all fall away and are caused to stumble and distrust and desert You, yet I will not [do so]!

30 And Jesus said to him, Truly I tell you, this very night, before a cock crows twice, you will utterly deny Me [disclaiming all connection with Me] three times.

31 But [Peter] said more vehemently and repeatedly, [Even] if it should be necessary for me to die with You, I will not deny or disown You! And they all kept saying the same thing.

32 Then they went to a place called Gethsemane, and He said to His disciples, Sit down here while I pray.

33 And He took with Him Peter and James and John, and began to be estruck with terror and amazement and deeply troubled and depressed.

34 And He said to them, My soul is exceedingly sad (overwhelmed with grief) so that it almost kills Me! Remain here and keep awake and be watching.

35 And going a little farther, He fell on the ground and kept praying that if

d Marvin Vincent, *Word Studies.*   e Joseph Thayer, *A Greek-English Lexicon.*

it were possible the [fatal] hour might pass from Him.

36 And He was saying, Abba, [which means] Father, everything is possible for You. Take away this cup from Me; yet not what I will, but what You [will].

37 And He came back and found them sleeping, and He said to Peter, Simon, are you asleep? Have you not the strength to keep awake *and* watch [with Me for] one hour?

38 Keep awake *and* watch and pray [constantly], that you may not enter into temptation; the spirit indeed is willing, but the flesh is weak.

39 He went away again and prayed, saying the same words.

40 And again He came back and found them sleeping, for their eyes were very heavy; and they did not know what answer to give Him.

41 And He came back a third time and said to them, Are you still sleeping and resting? It is enough [of that]! The hour has come. The Son of Man is betrayed into the hands of sinful men (men *g*whose way or nature is to act in opposition to God).

42 Get up, let us be going! See, My betrayer is at hand!

43 And at once, while He was still speaking, Judas came, one of the Twelve [apostles], and with him a crowd of men with swords and clubs, [who came] from the chief priests and the scribes and the elders [of the Sanhedrin].

44 Now the betrayer had given them a signal, saying, The One I shall kiss is [the Man]; seize Him and lead [Him] away safely [so as to prevent His escape].

45 And when he came, he went up to Jesus immediately and said, Master! *Master!* and he *h*embraced Him *and* kissed Him fervently.

46 And they threw their hands on Him and arrested Him.

47 But one of the bystanders drew his sword and struck the bond servant of the high priest and cut off his ear.

48 And Jesus said to them, Have you come out with swords and clubs as [you would] against a robber to capture Me?

49 I was with you daily in the temple [*i*porches and courts] teaching, and you did not seize Me; but [this has happened] that the Scriptures might be fulfilled.

50 Then [His disciples], forsaking Him, fled, all [of them].

51 And a young man was following Him, with nothing but a linen cloth (*j*sheet) thrown about [his] naked [body]; and they laid hold of him,

52 But, leaving behind the linen cloth (*j*sheet), he fled from them naked.

53 And they led Jesus away to the high priest, and all the chief priests and the elders and the scribes were gathered together.

54 And Peter followed Him at a distance, even right into the courtyard of the high priest. And he was sitting [*k*in the firelight] with the guards and warming himself at the fire.

55 Now the chief priests and the entire council (the Sanhedrin) were constantly seeking [to get] testimony against Jesus with a view to condemning Him *and* putting Him to death, but they did not find any.

56 For many were repeatedly bearing false witness against Him, but their testimonies did not agree.

57 And some stood up and were bearing false witness against Him, saying,

58 We heard Him say, I will de-

f Joseph Thayer, *A Greek-English Lexicon.*   g Hermann Cremer, *Biblico-Theological Lexicon.* h H.A.W. Meyer, *Critical and Exegetical Handbook to the Gospel of Mark.*   i Richard Trench, *Synonyms of the New Testament.*   j Alexander Souter, *Pocket Lexicon.*   k Marvin Vincent, *Word Studies.*

stroy this temple (sanctuary) which is made with hands, and in three days I will build another, made without hands.

59 Still not even [in this] did their testimony agree.

60 And the high priest stood up in the midst and asked Jesus, Have You not even one answer to make? What [about this which] these [men] are testifying against You?

61 But He kept still and did not answer at all. Again the high priest asked Him, Are You the Christ (the Messiah, the Anointed One), the Son of the Blessed?

62 And Jesus said, I AM; and you will [all] see the Son of Man seated at the right hand of Power ([the Almighty) and coming on the clouds of heaven. [Ps. 110:1; Dan. 7:13.]

63 Then the high priest tore his garments and said, What need have we for more witnesses? [Num. 14:6.]

64 You have heard His blasphemy. What is your decision? And they all condemned Him as being guilty *and* deserving of death. [Lev. 24:16.]

65 And some of them began to spit on Him and to blindfold Him and to strike Him with their fists, saying to Him, Prophesy! And the guards received Him with blows *and* by slapping Him.

66 While Peter was down below in the courtyard, one of the [serving] maids of the high priest came;

67 And when she saw Peter warming himself, she gazed intently at him and said, You were with Jesus of Nazareth too.

68 But he denied it ᵐfalsely *and* disowned Him, saying, I neither know nor understand what you say. Then he went outside [the courtyard and

was] into the ⁿvestibule. ᵒ*And a cock crowed.*

69 And the maidservant saw him, and began again to say to the bystanders, This [man] is [one] of them.

70 But again he denied it ᵖfalsely *and* disowned Him. And after a short while, again the bystanders said to Peter, ᵐReally, you are one of them, for you are a Galilean ᵖ*and your dialect shows it.*

71 Then he commenced invoking a curse on himself [should he not be telling the truth] and swearing, I do not know the Man about Whom you are talking!

72 And at once for the second time a cock crowed. And Peter remembered how Jesus said to him, Before a cock crows twice, you will ᵍutterly deny Me [disclaiming all connection with Me] three times. And ᵍhaving put his thought upon it [and remembering], he broke down *and* wept aloud *and* ˡlamented.

CHAPTER 15

AND IMMEDIATELY when it was morning, the chief priests, with the elders and the scribes and the whole council, held a consultation; and when they had bound Jesus, they took Him away [¹violently] and handed Him over to Pilate. [Isa. 53:8.]

2 And Pilate inquired of Him, Are You the King of the Jews? And He replied, It is as you say.

3 And the chief priests kept accusing Him of many things.

4 And Pilate again asked Him, Have ʳYou no answer to make? See how many charges they are bringing against You!

5 But Jesus made no further an-

---

l Joseph Thayer, *A Greek-English Lexicon.*   m Hermann Cremer, *Biblico-Theological Lexicon.*   n Marvin Vincent, *Word Studies.*   o Some manuscripts add this sentence.   p Some manuscripts contain this phrase instead.   q Kenneth Wuest, *Word Studies.*   r Capitalized because of what He is, the spotless Son of God, not what the speaker may have thought He was.

swer at all, so that Pilate wondered *and* marveled. [Isa. 53:7.]

6 Now at the Feast he [was accustomed to] set free for them any one prisoner whom they requested.

7 And among the rioters in the prison who had committed murder in the insurrection there was a man named Barabbas.

8 And the throng came up and began asking Pilate to do as he usually did for them.

9 And he replied to them, Do you wish me to set free for you the King of the Jews?

10 For he was aware that it was [ˢbecause they were prompted] by envy that the chief priests had delivered Him up.

11 But the chief priests stirred up the crowd to get him to release for them Barabbas instead.

12 And again Pilate said to them, Then what shall I do with the Man Whom you call the King of the Jews?

13 And they shouted back again, Crucify Him!

14 But Pilate said to them, Why? What has He done that is evil? But they shouted with all their might all the more, Crucify Him [ᵗat once]!

15 So Pilate, wishing to satisfy the crowd, set Barabbas free for them; and after having Jesus whipped, he handed [Him] over to be crucified. [Isa. 53:5.]

16 Then the soldiers led Him away to the courtyard inside the palace, that is, the Praetorium, and they called the entire detachment of soldiers together.

17 And they dressed Him in [a] purple [robe], and, weaving together a crown of thorns, they placed it on Him.

18 And they began to salute Him, Hail (greetings, good health to You,

long life to You), King of the Jews!

19 And they struck His head with a staff made of a [bamboo-like] reed and spat on Him and kept bowing their knees in homage to Him. [Isa. 50:6.]

20 And when they had [finished] making sport of Him, they took the purple [robe] off of Him and put His own clothes on Him. And they led Him out [of the city] to crucify Him.

21 And they forced a passerby, Simon of Cyrene, the father of Alexander and Rufus, who was coming in from the field (country), to carry His cross.

22 And they led Him to Golgotha [Latin: Calvary], meaning The Place of a Skull.

23 And they [attempted to] give Him wine mingled with myrrh, but He would not take it.

24 And they crucified Him; and they divided His garments *and* distributed them among themselves, throwing lots for them to decide who should take what. [Ps. 22:18.]

25 And it was the third hour (about nine o'clock in the morning) when they crucified Him. [Ps. 22:14–16.]

26 And the inscription of the accusation against Him was written above, The King of the Jews.

27 And with Him they crucified two robbers, one on [His] right hand and one on His left.

28 ᵘ*And the Scripture was fulfilled which says, He was counted among the transgressors.* [Isa. 53:12.]

29 And those who passed by kept reviling Him and reproaching Him abusively in harsh *and* insolent language, wagging their heads and saying, Aha! You Who would destroy the temple and build it in three days,

30 Now rescue ᵛYourself [ʷfrom death], coming down from the cross!

---

s Joseph Thayer, *A Greek-English Lexicon.*   t Kenneth Wuest, *Word Studies.*   u Many manuscripts do not contain this verse.   v Capitalized because of what He is, the spotless Son of God, not what the speakers may have thought He was.   w Hermann Cremer, *Biblico-Theological Lexicon.*

31 So also the chief priests, with the scribes, made sport of Him to one another, saying, He rescued others [*from death]; Himself He is unable to rescue. [Ps. 22:7, 8.]

32 Let the Christ (the Messiah), the King of Israel, come down now from the cross, that we may see [it] and trust in *and* rely on Him *and* adhere to Him! Those who were crucified with Him also reviled *and* reproached Him [speaking abusively, harshly, and insolently].

33 And when the sixth hour (about midday) had come, there was darkness over the whole land until the ninth hour (about three o'clock).

34 And at the ninth hour Jesus cried with a loud voice, Eloi, Eloi, lama sabachthani?—which means, My God, My God, why have You forsaken Me [*deserting Me and leaving Me helpless and abandoned]? [Ps. 22:1.]

35 And some of those standing by, [and] hearing it, said, See! He is calling Elijah!

36 And one man ran, and, filling a sponge with vinegar (a *mixture of sour wine and water], put it on a staff made of a [bamboo-like] reed and gave it to Him to drink, saying, Hold off! Let us see whether Elijah [does] come to take Him down. [Ps. 69:21.]

37 And Jesus uttered a loud cry, and breathed out His life.

38 And the curtain [of the Holy of Holies] of the temple was torn in two from top to bottom.

39 And when the centurion who stood facing Him saw Him expire this way, he said, *Really, this Man was God's Son!

40 Now some women were there also, looking on from a distance, among whom were Mary Magdalene, and Mary the mother of James the younger and of Joses, and Salome,

41 Who, when [Jesus] was in Galilee, were in the habit of accompanying and ministering to Him; and [there were] also many other [women] who had come up with Him to Jerusalem.

42 As evening had already come, since it was the day of Preparation, that is, [the day] before the Sabbath, [Deut. 21:22, 23.]

43 Joseph, he of Arimathea, noble *and* honorable in rank *and* a respected member of the council (Sanhedrin), who was himself waiting for the kingdom of God, daring the consequences, took courage *and* ventured to go to Pilate and asked for the body of Jesus.

44 But Pilate wondered whether He was dead so soon, and, having called the centurion, he asked him whether [Jesus] was already dead.

45 And when he learned from the centurion [that He was indeed dead], he gave the body to Joseph.

46 And Joseph bought a [fine] linen cloth [*for swathing dead bodies], and, taking Him down from the cross, he *rolled Him up in the [fine] linen cloth and placed Him in a tomb which had been hewn out of a rock. Then he rolled a [very large] stone against the door of the tomb. [Isa. 53:9; Matt. 16:4.]

47 And Mary Magdalene and Mary [the mother] of Joses were [*attentively] observing where He was laid.

CHAPTER 16

AND WHEN the Sabbath was past [that is, after the sun had set], Mary Magdalene, and Mary [the

x Hermann Cremer, *Biblico-Theological Lexicon.*
z James Moulton and George Milligan, *The Vocabulary.*
b Marvin Vincent, *Word Studies.*
y Joseph Thayer, *A Greek-English Lexicon.*
a Robert Young, *Analytical Concordance.*

mother] of James, and Salome purchased sweet-smelling spices, so that they might go and anoint [Jesus' body],

2 And very early on the first day of the week they came to the tomb; [by then] the sun had risen.

3 And they said to one another, Who will roll back the stone for us out of [the groove across the floor at] the door of the tomb?

4 And when they looked up, they [distinctly] saw that the stone was already rolled back, for it was very large.

5 And going into the tomb, they saw a young man sitting [there] on the right [side], clothed in a [ᶜlong, stately, sweeping] robe of white, and they were utterly amazed and struck with terror.

6 And he said to them, Do not be amazed and terrified; you are looking for Jesus of Nazareth, Who was crucified. He has risen; He is not here. See the place where they laid Him. [Ps. 16:10.]

7 But be going; tell the disciples and Peter, He goes before you into Galilee; you will see Him there, [just] as He told you. [Mark 14:28.]

8 Then they went out [and] fled from the tomb, for trembling and bewilderment and consternation had seized them. And they said nothing about it to anyone, for they were held by alarm and fear.

9 ᵈNow Jesus, having risen [ᵉfrom death] early on the first day of the week, appeared first to Mary Magdalene, from whom He had driven out seven demons.

10 She went and reported it to those who had been with Him, as they grieved and wept.

11 And when they heard that He

was alive and that she had seen Him, they did not believe it.

12 After this, He appeared in a different form to two of them as they were walking [along the way] into the country.

13 And they returned [to Jerusalem] and told the others, but they did not believe them either.

14 Afterward He appeared to the Eleven [apostles themselves] as they reclined at table; and He reproved and reproached them for their unbelief (their lack of faith) and their hardness of heart, because they had refused to believe those who had seen Him and looked at Him attentively after He had risen [ᵉfrom death].

15 And He said to them, Go into all the world and preach and publish openly the good news (the Gospel) to every creature [of the whole ᶠhuman race].

16 He who believes [who adheres to and trusts in and relies on the Gospel and Him Whom it sets forth] and is baptized will be saved [ᵉfrom the penalty of eternal death]; but he who does not believe [who does not adhere to and trust in and rely on the Gospel and Him Whom it sets forth] will be condemned.

17 And these attesting signs will accompany those who believe: in My name they will drive out demons; they will speak in new languages;

18 They will pick up serpents; and [even] if they drink anything deadly, it will not hurt them; they will lay their hands on the sick, and they will get well.

19 So then the Lord Jesus, after He had spoken to them, was taken up into heaven and He sat down at the right hand of God. [Ps. 110:1.]

20 And they went out and preached everywhere, while the

c Richard Trench, *Synonyms of the New Testament.*
verses 9-20.   e Hermann Cremer, *Biblico-Theological Lexicon.*
Lexicon.
d Some of the earliest manuscripts do not contain
f Joseph Thayer, *A Greek-English*

Lord kept working with them and confirming the message by the attesting signs *and* miracles that closely accompanied [it]. Amen (so be it).

THE GOSPEL ACCORDING TO
LUKE

CHAPTER 1

SINCE [ᵍas is well known] many have undertaken to put in order *and* draw up a [ᵍthorough] narrative of the surely established deeds which have been accomplished *and* fulfilled ᵇin *and* among us,

2 Exactly as they were handed down to us by those who from the [ᵍofficial] beginning [of Jesus' ministry] were eyewitnesses and ministers of the Word [that is, of ᶦthe doctrine concerning the attainment through Christ of salvation in the kingdom of God],

3 It seemed good *and* desirable to me, [and so I have determined] also after ʲhaving searched out diligently *and* followed all things closely *and* traced accurately the course from the highest to the minutest detail from the very first, to write an orderly account for you, most excellent Theophilus, [Acts 1:1.]

4 [My purpose is] that you may know the full truth *and* understand with certainty *and* security against error the accounts (histories) *and* doctrines of the faith of which you have been informed *and* in which you have been ᵉorally instructed.

5 In the days when Herod was king of Judea there was a certain priest whose name was Zachariah, ᵍof the daily service (the division) of Abia; and his wife was also a descendant of

Aaron, and her name was Elizabeth.

6 And they both were righteous in the sight of God, walking blamelessly in all the commandments and requirements of the Lord.

7 But they had no child, for Elizabeth was barren; and both were ʰfar advanced in years.

8 Now while on duty, serving as priest before God in the order of his division,

9 As was the custom of the priesthood, it fell to him by lot to enter [the ᵏsanctuary of] the temple of the Lord and burn incense. [Exod. 30:7.]

10 And all the throng of people were praying outside [in the court] at the hour of incense [burning].

11 And there appeared to him an angel of the Lord, standing at the right side of the altar of incense.

12 And when Zachariah saw him, he was troubled, and fear took possession of him.

13 But the angel said to him, Do not be afraid, Zachariah, because your petition ʲwas heard, and your wife Elizabeth will bear you a son, and you must call his name John [God is favorable].

14 And you shall have joy and exultant delight, and many will rejoice over his birth,

15 For he will be great *and* distinguished in the sight of the Lord. And he must drink no wine nor strong

---

g Marvin Vincent, *Word Studies in the New Testament.*   h John Wycliffe, *The Wycliffe Bible.*
i Joseph Thayer, *A Greek-English Lexicon of the New Testament.*   j William Tyndale, *The Tyndale Bible.*
k Richard Trench, *Synonyms of the New Testament.*

drink, and he will be filled with *and* controlled by the Holy Spirit even [1]in *and* from his mother's womb. [Num. 6:3.]

16 And he will turn back *and* cause to return many of the sons of Israel to the Lord their God,

17 And he will [himself] go before Him in the spirit and power of Elijah, to turn back the hearts of the fathers to the children, and the disobedient *and* incredulous *and* unpersuadable to the wisdom of the upright [which is [m]the knowledge and holy love of the will of God]—in order to make ready for the Lord a people [perfectly] prepared [in spirit, [n]adjusted and disposed and placed in the right moral state]. [Isa. 40:3; Mal. 4:5, 6.]

18 And Zachariah said to the angel, By what shall I know *and* be sure of this? For I am an old man, and my wife is well advanced in years.

19 And the angel replied to him, I am Gabriel. I stand in the [very] presence of God, and I have been sent to talk to you and to bring you this good news. [Dan. 8:16; 9:21.]

20 Now behold, you will be *and* [n]will continue to be silent and not able to speak till the day when these things take place, because you have not believed what I told you; but my words are [o]of a kind which will be fulfilled in the appointed *and* proper time.

21 Now the people kept waiting for Zachariah, and they wondered at his delaying [so long] in the [o]sanctuary.

22 But when he did come out, he was unable to speak to them; and they [n]clearly] perceived that he had seen a vision in the [o]sanctuary; and he kept making signs to them, still he remained dumb.

23 And when his time of perform-

ing priestly functions was ended, he returned to his [own] house.

24 Now after this his wife Elizabeth became pregnant, and for five months she secluded herself [o]entirely, saying, [I have hid myself]

25 [n]Because thus the Lord has dealt with me in the days when He deigned to look on me to take away my reproach among men. [Gen. 30:23; Isa. 4:1.]

26 Now in the sixth month [after that], the angel Gabriel was sent from God to a town of Galilee named Nazareth,

27 To a girl never having been married *and* a [p]virgin engaged to be married to a man whose name was Joseph, a descendant of the house of David; and the virgin's name was Mary.

28 And he came to her and said, Hail, O favored one [[e]endued with grace]! The Lord is with you! [r]*Blessed (favored of God) are you before all other women!*

29 But *when she saw him,* she was greatly troubled *and* disturbed *and* confused at what he said and kept revolving in her mind what such a greeting might mean.

30 And the angel said to her, Do not be afraid, Mary, for you have found grace ([n]free, spontaneous, absolute favor and loving-kindness) with God.

31 And listen! You will become pregnant and will give birth to a Son, and you shall call His name Jesus.

32 He will be great (eminent) and will be called the Son of the Most High; and the Lord God will give to Him the throne of His forefather David,

33 And He will reign over the house of Jacob throughout the ages;

---

l William Tyndale, *The Tyndale Bible.*　m Joseph Thayer, *A Greek-English Lexicon.*　n Marvin Vincent, *Word Studies.*　o Richard Trench, *Synonyms of the New Testament.*　p This Greek word *parthenos* (virgin) is used in Isa. 7:14 in *The Septuagint,* the Greek Old Testament translation which Jesus read and quoted.　q Literal translation.　r Some manuscripts do not contain this phrase.

and of His reign there will be no end. [Isa. 9:6, 7; Dan. 2:44.]

34 And Mary said to the angel, How can this be, since I have no [intimacy with any man as a] husband?

35 Then the angel said to her, The Holy Spirit will come upon you, and the power of the Most High will overshadow you [like a shining cloud]; and so the holy (pure, sinless) Thing (Offspring) which shall be born of *you* will be called the Son of God. [Exod. 40:34; Isa. 7:14.]

36 And listen! Your relative Elizabeth in her old age has also conceived a son, and this is now the sixth month with her who was called barren.

37 For with God nothing is ever impossible *and* no word from God shall be without power *or* impossible of fulfillment.

38 Then Mary said, Behold, I am the handmaiden of the Lord; let it be done to me according to what you have said. And the angel left her.

39 And at that time Mary arose and went with haste into the hill country to a town of Judah,

40 And she went to the house of Zachariah and, entering it, saluted Elizabeth.

41 And it occurred that when Elizabeth heard Mary's greeting, the baby leaped in her womb, and Elizabeth was filled with *and* controlled by the Holy Spirit.

42 And she cried out with a loud cry, and then exclaimed, Blessed (favored of God) above all other women are you! And blessed (favored of God) is the Fruit of your womb!

43 And how [have I deserved that this honor should] be granted to me, that the mother of my Lord should come to me?

44 For behold, the instant the sound of your salutation reached my ears, the baby in my womb leaped for joy.

45 And blessed (happy, [s]to be envied) is she who believed that there would be a fulfillment of the things that were spoken to her from the Lord.

46 And Mary said, My soul magnifies *and* extols the Lord,

47 And my spirit rejoices in God my Savior,

48 For He has looked upon the low station *and* humiliation of His handmaiden. For behold, from now on all generations [of all ages] will call me blessed *and* declare me happy *and* [t]to be envied!

49 For He Who is almighty has done great things for me—and holy is His name [to be venerated in His purity, majesty and glory]!

50 And His mercy (His compassion and kindness toward the miscrable and afflicted) is on those who fear Him with godly reverence, from generation to generation *and* age to age. [Ps. 103:17.]

51 He has shown strength *and* [u]made might with His arm; He has scattered the proud *and* haughty in *and* by the imagination *and* purpose *and* designs of their hearts.

52 He has put down the mighty from their thrones and exalted those of low degree.

53 He has filled *and* satisfied the hungry with good things, and the rich He has sent away empty-handed [without a gift].

54 He has laid hold on His servant Israel [to help him, to espouse his cause], in remembrance of His mercy,

55 Even as He promised to our forefathers, to Abraham and to his descendants forever. [Gen. 17:7;

---

s Alexander Souter, *Pocket Lexicon of the Greek New Testament.*   t Alexander Souter, *Pocket Lexicon.*
u John Wycliffe, *The Wycliffe Bible.*

18:18; 22:17; I Sam. 2:1–10; Mic. 7:20.]

56 And Mary remained with her [Elizabeth] for about three months and [then] returned to her [own] home.

57 Now the time that Elizabeth should be delivered came, and she gave birth to a son.

58 And her neighbors and relatives heard that the Lord had shown great mercy on her, and they rejoiced with her.

59 And it occurred that on the eighth day, when they came to circumcise the child, they were intending to call him Zachariah after his father, [Gen. 17:12; Lev. 12:3.]

60 But his mother answered, Not so! But he shall be called John.

61 And they said to her, None of your relatives is called by that name.

62 And they inquired with signs to his father [as to] what he wanted to have him called.

63 Then Zachariah asked for a writing tablet and wrote, His name is John. And they were all astonished.

64 And at once his mouth was opened and his tongue loosed, and he began to speak, blessing and praising and thanking God.

65 And awe and reverential fear came on all their neighbors; and all these things were discussed throughout the hill country of Judea.

66 And all who heard them laid them up in their hearts, saying, Whatever will this little boy be then? For the hand of the Lord was [ᵛso evidently] with him [protecting and aiding him].

67 Now Zachariah his father was filled with and controlled by the Holy Spirit and prophesied, saying,

68 Blessed (praised and extolled and thanked) be the Lord, the God of Israel, because He has come and brought deliverance and redemption to His people!

69 And He has raised up a Horn of salvation [a mighty and valiant Helper, the Author of salvation] for us in the house of David His servant—

70 This is as He promised by the mouth of His holy prophets from the most ancient times [in the memory of man]—

71 That we should have deliverance and be saved from our enemies and from the hand of all who detest and pursue us with hatred;

72 To make true and show the mercy and compassion and kindness [promised] to our forefathers and to remember and carry out His holy covenant [to bless, which is ʷall the more sacred because it is made by God Himself],

73 That covenant He sealed by oath to our forefather Abraham:

74 To grant us that we, being delivered from the hand of our foes, might serve Him fearlessly

75 In holiness (divine consecration) and righteousness [in accordance with the everlasting principles of right] within His presence all the days of our lives.

76 And you, little one, shall be called a prophet of the Most High; for you shall go on before the face of the Lord to make ready His ways, [Isa. 40:3; Mal. 4:5.]

77 To bring and give the knowledge of salvation to His people in the forgiveness and remission of their sins,

78 Because of and through the heart of tender mercy and lovingkindness of our God, a Light from on high will dawn upon us and visit [us] [Mal. 4:2.]

79 To shine upon and give light to those who sit in darkness and in the shadow of death, to direct and guide

v Albert Barnes, Notes on the New Testament.   w Joseph Thayer, A Greek-English Lexicon.

our feet in a straight line into the way of peace. [Isa. 9:2.]

80 And the little boy grew and became strong in spirit; and he was in the deserts (wilderness) until the day of his appearing to Israel [the commencement of his public ministry].

CHAPTER 2

IN THOSE days it occurred that a decree went out from Caesar Augustus that the whole xRoman empire should be registered.

2 This was the first enrollment, and it was made when Quirinius was governor of Syria.

3 And all the people were going to be registered, each to his own city or town.

4 And Joseph also went up from Galilee from the town of Nazareth to Judea, to the town of David, which is called Bethlehem, because he was of the house and family of David,

5 To be enrolled with Mary, his espoused (ymarried) wife, who was about to become a mother. [Matt. 1:18–25.]

6 And while they were there, the time came for her delivery,

7 And she gave birth to her Son, her Firstborn; and she wrapped Him in swaddling clothes and laid Him in a manger, because there was no room or place for them in the inn.

8 And in that vicinity there were shepherds living [out under the open sky] in the field, watching [in shifts] over their flock by night.

9 And behold, an angel of the Lord stood by them, and the glory of the Lord flashed and shone all about them, and they were terribly frightened.

10 But the angel said to them, Do not be afraid; for behold, I bring you good news of a great joy which will come to all the people.

11 For to you is born this day in the town of David a Savior, Who is Christ (the Messiah) the Lord! [Mic. 5:2.]

12 And this will be a sign for you [by which you will recognize Him]: you will find [zafter searching] a Baby wrapped in swaddling clothes and lying in a manger. [I Sam. 2:34; II Kings 19:29; Isa. 7:14.]

13 Then suddenly there appeared with the angel an army of the troops of heaven (aa heavenly knighthood), praising God and saying,

14 Glory to God in the highest [heaven], and on earth peace among men with whom He is well pleased [bmen of goodwill, of His favor].

15 When the angels went away from them into heaven, the shepherds said one to another, Let us go over to Bethlehem and see this thing (ysaying) that has come to pass, which the Lord has made known to us.

16 So they went with haste and [zby searching] found Mary and Joseph, and the Baby lying in a manger.

17 And when they saw it, they made known what had been told them concerning this Child.

18 And all who heard it were astounded and marveled at what the shepherds told them.

19 But Mary was keeping ywithin herself all these things (ysayings), weighing and pondering them in her heart.

20 And the shepherds returned, glorifying and praising God for all the things they had heard and seen, just as it had been told them.

21 And at the end of eight days, when [the Baby] was to be circumcised, He was called Jesus, the name

x George R. Berry. Greek-English New Testament Lexicon.   y Marvin Vincent, Word Studies. z Joseph Thayer, A Greek-English Lexicon.   a John Wycliffe, The Wycliffe Bible.   b John Wycliffe, The Wycliffe Bible.

given by the angel before He was conceived in the womb.

22 And when the time for their purification [the mother's purification and the Baby's dedication] came according to the Law of Moses, they brought Him up to Jerusalem to present Him to the Lord—[Lev. 12:1–4.]

23 As it is written in the Law of the Lord, Every [firstborn] male that opens the womb shall be set apart and dedicated and called holy to the Lord—[Exod. 13:1, 2, 12; Num. 8:17.]

24 And [they came also] to offer a sacrifice according to what is said in the Law of the Lord: a pair of turtledoves or two young pigeons. [Lev. 12:6–8.]

25 Now there was a man in Jerusalem whose name was Simeon, and this man was righteous and devout [cautiously and carefully observing the divine Law], and looking for the Consolation of Israel; and the Holy Spirit was upon him.

26 And it had been divinely revealed (communicated) to him by the Holy Spirit that he would not see death before he had seen the Lord's Christ (the Messiah, the Anointed One).

27 And prompted by the [Holy] Spirit, he came into the temple [cenclosure]; and when the parents brought in the little child Jesus to do for Him what was customary according to the Law,

28 [Simeon] took Him up in his arms and praised and thanked God and said,

29 And now, Lord, You are releasing Your servant to depart (leave this world) in peace, according to Your word.

30 For with my [own] eyes I have seen Your Salvation, [Isa. 52:10.]

31 Which You have ordained and prepared before (in the presence of) all peoples,

32 A Light for drevelation to the Gentiles [to disclose what was before unknown] and [to bring] praise and honor and glory to Your people Israel. [Isa. 42:6; 49:6.]

33 And His [legal] father and [His] mother were marveling at what was said about Him.

34 And Simeon blessed them and said to Mary His mother, Behold, this Child is appointed and destined for the fall and rising of many in Israel, and for a sign that is spoken against—[Isa. 8:14, 15.]

35 And a sword will pierce through your own soul also—that the secret thoughts and purposes of many hearts may be brought out and disclosed.

36 And there was also a prophetess, Anna, the daughter of Phanuel, of the tribe of Asher. She was very old, having lived with her husband seven years from her maidenhood, [Josh. 19:24.]

37 And as a widow even for eighty-four years. She did not go out from the temple cenclosure, but was worshiping night and day with fasting and prayer.

38 And she too came up at that same hour, and she returned thanks to God and talked of [Jesus] to all who were looking for the redemption (deliverance) of Jerusalem.

39 And when they had done everything according to the Law of the Lord, they went back into Galilee to their own town, Nazareth.

40 And the Child grew and became strong in spirit, filled with wisdom; and the grace (favor and spiritual blessing) of God was upon Him. [Judg. 13:24; I Sam. 2:26.]

41 Now His parents went to Jeru-

c Richard Trench, *Synonyms of the New Testament.*   d Marvin Vincent, *Word Studies.*

salem every year to the Passover Feast. [Deut. 16:1–8; Exod. 23:15.]

42 And when He was twelve years [old], they went up, as was their custom.

43 And when the Feast was ended, as they were returning, the boy Jesus remained behind in Jerusalem. Now His parents did not know this,

44 But, supposing Him to be in the caravan, they traveled on a day's journey; and [then] they sought Him [diligently, looking up and down for Him] among their kinsfolk and acquaintances.

45 And when they failed to find Him, they went back to Jerusalem, looking for Him [up and down] all the way.

46 After three days they found Him [came upon Him] in the e[court of the] temple, sitting among the teachers, listening to them and asking them questions.

47 And all who heard Him were astonished and overwhelmed with bewildered wonder at His intelligence and understanding and His replies.

48 And when they [Joseph and Mary] saw Him, they were amazed; and His mother said to Him, Child, why have You treated us like this? Here Your father and I have been anxiously looking for You [distressed and tormented]?

49 And He said to them, How is it that you had to look for Me? Did you not see and know that it is necessary [as a duty] for Me f to be in My Father's house and [occupied] about My Father's business?

50 But they did not comprehend what He was saying to them.

51 And He went down with them and came to Nazareth and was [habitually] obedient to them; and his

mother kept and closely and persistently guarded all these things in her heart.

52 And Jesus increased in wisdom (in broad and full understanding) and in stature and years, and in favor with God and man.

CHAPTER 3

IN THE fifteenth year of Tiberius Caesar's reign—when Pontius Pilate was governor of Judea, and Herod was tetrarch of Galilee, and his brother Philip tetrarch of the region of Ituraea and Trachonitis, and Lysanias tetrarch of Abilene—

2 In the high priesthood of Annas and Caiaphas, the Word of God [ªconcerning the attainment through Christ of salvation in the kingdom of God] came to John son of Zachariah in the wilderness (desert).

3 And he went into all the country round about the Jordan, preaching a baptism of repentance (ªof hearty amending of their ways, with abhorrence of past wrongdoing) unto the forgiveness of sin.

4 As it is written in the book of the words of Isaiah the prophet, The voice of one crying in the wilderness [shouting in the desert]: Prepare the way of the Lord, make His beaten paths straight.

5 Every valley and ravine shall be filled up, and every mountain and hill shall be leveled; and the crooked places shall be made straight, and the rough roads shall be made smooth;

6 And all mankind shall see (behold and ªunderstand and at last acknowledge) the salvation of God (the deliverance from eternal death ªdecreed by God). [Isa. 40:3–5.]

7 So he said to the crowds who came out to be baptized by him, You

e Richard Trench, *Synonyms of the New Testament.*   f Literally, "in the things of My Father."
g Joseph Thayer, *A Greek-English Lexicon.*   h James Gray and George Adams, *Bible Commentary.*

offspring of vipers! Who [i]secretly warned you to flee from the coming wrath?

8 Bear fruits that are deserving and consistent with [your] repentance [that is, [j]conduct worthy of a heart changed, a heart abhorring sin]. And do not begin to say to yourselves, We have Abraham as our father; for I tell you that God is able from these stones to raise up descendants for Abraham.

9 Even now the ax is laid to the root of the trees, so that every tree that does not bear good fruit is cut down and cast into the fire.

10 And the multitudes asked him, Then what shall we do?

11 And he replied to them, He who has two tunics (undergarments), let him share with him who has none; and he who has food, let him do it the same way.

12 Even tax collectors came to be baptized, and they said to him, Teacher, what shall we do?

13 And he said to them, Exact and collect no more than the fixed amount appointed you.

14 Those serving as soldiers also asked him, And we, what shall we do? And he replied to them, Never demand or enforce [k]by terrifying people or by accusing wrongfully, and always be satisfied with your rations (supplies) and with your allowance (wages).

15 As the people were in suspense and waiting expectantly, and everybody reasoned and questioned in their hearts concerning John, whether he perhaps might be the Christ (the Messiah, the Anointed One),

16 John answered them all by saying, I baptize you with water; but He Who is mightier than I is coming, the strap of Whose sandals I am not fit to unfasten. He will baptize you with the Holy Spirit and with fire.

17 His winnowing shovel (fork) is in His hand to thoroughly clear and cleanse His [threshing] floor and to gather the wheat and store it in His granary, but the chaff He will burn with fire that cannot be extinguished.

18 So with many other [various] appeals and admonitions he preached the good news (the Gospel) to the people.

19 But Herod the tetrarch, who had been [repeatedly] told about his fault and reproved with rebuke [k]producing conviction by [John] for [having] Herodias, his brother's wife, and for all the wicked things that Herod had done,

20 Added this to them all—that he shut up John in prison.

21 Now when all the people were baptized, and when Jesus also had been baptized, and [while He was still] praying, the [visible] heaven was opened

22 And the Holy Spirit descended upon Him in bodily form like a dove, and a voice came from heaven, saying, You are My Son, My Beloved! In You I am well pleased and find delight! [Ps. 2:7; Isa. 42:1.]

23 Jesus Himself, when He began [His ministry], was about thirty years of age, being the Son, as was supposed, of Joseph, the son of Heli,

24 The son of Matthat, the son of Levi, the son of Melchi, the son of Jannai, the son of Joseph,

25 The son of Mattathias, the son of Amos, the son of Nahum, the son of Esli, the son of Naggai,

26 The son of Maath, the son of Mattathias, the son of Semein, the son of Josech, the son of Joda,

27 The son of Joanan, the son of Rhesa, the son of Zerubbabel, the son of Shealtiel, the son of Neri,

---

i Literal translation.   j Joseph Thayer, *A Greek-English Lexicon*.   k Marvin Vincent, *Word Studies*.

28 The son of Melchi, the son of Addi, the son of Cosam, the son of Elmadam, the son of Er,

29 The son of Jesus, the son of Eliezer, the son of Jorim, the son of Matthat, the son of Levi,

30 The son of Simeon, the son of Judah, the son of Joseph, the son of Jonam, the son of Eliakim,

31 The son of Melea, the son of Menna, the son of Mattatha, the son of Nathan, the son of David,

32 The son of Jesse, the son of Obed, the son of Boaz, the son of Salmon (Sala), the son of Nahshon,

33 The son of Aminadab, the son of Admin, the son of Arni, the son of Hezron, the son of Perez, the son of Judah,

34 The son of Jacob, the son of Isaac, the son of Abraham, the son of Terah, the son of Nahor,

35 The son of Serug, the son of Reu, the son of Peleg, the son of Eber, the son of Shelah,

36 The son of Cainan, the son of Arphaxad, the son of Shem, the son of Noah, the son of Lamech,

37 The son of Methuselah, the son of Enoch, the son of Jared, the son of Mahalaleel, the son of Cainan,

38 The son of Enos, the son of Seth, the son of Adam, the son of God. [Gen. 5:3–32; 11:10–26; Ruth 4:18–22; I Chron. 1:1–4, 24–28; 2:1–15.]

CHAPTER 4

THEN JESUS, full of and controlled by the Holy Spirit, returned from the Jordan and was led in [by] the [Holy] Spirit

2 For (during) forty days in the wilderness (desert), where He was tempted ([1]tried, tested exceedingly) by the devil. And He ate nothing during those days, and when they were completed, He was hungry. [Deut. 9:9; I Kings 19:8.]

3 Then the devil said to Him, If You are the Son of God, order this stone to turn into a loaf [of bread].

4 And Jesus replied to him, It is written, Man shall not live and be sustained by (on) bread alone [m]but by every word and expression of God. [Deut. 8:3.]

5 Then the devil took Him up to a high mountain and showed Him all the kingdoms of the habitable world in a moment of time [[n]in the twinkling of an eye].

6 And he said to Him, To You I will give all this power and authority and their glory (all their magnificence, excellence, preeminence, dignity, and grace), for it has been turned over to me, and I give it to whomever I will.

7 Therefore if You will do homage to and worship me [[o]just once], it shall all be Yours.

8 And Jesus replied to him, [m]Get behind Me, Satan! It is written, You shall do homage to and worship the Lord your God, and Him only shall you serve. [Deut. 6:13; 10:20.]

9 Then he took Him to Jerusalem and set Him on [p]a gable of the temple, and said to Him, If You are the Son of God, cast Yourself down from here;

10 For it is written, He will give His angels charge over you to guard and watch over you closely and carefully;

11 And on their hands they will bear you up, lest you strike your foot against a stone. [Ps. 91:11, 12.]

12 And Jesus replied to him, [The Scripture] says, You shall not tempt

---

[l] Robert Young, *Analytical Concordance to the Bible.* [n] William Tyndale, *The Tyndale Bible.* [o] Charles B. Williams, *The New Testament: A Translation in the Language of the People:* "expressed by the Greek aorist tense." [m] Some manuscripts add this phrase. [p] James Moulton and George Milligan, *The Vocabulary of the Greek Testament.*

(try, ᵠtest exceedingly) the Lord your God. [Deut. 6:16.]

13 And when the devil had ended every [the complete cycle of] temptation, he [temporarily] left Him [that is, ʳstood off from Him] until another more opportune and favorable time.

14 Then Jesus went back full of and under the power of the [Holy] Spirit into Galilee, and the fame of Him spread through the whole region round about.

15 And He Himself conducted [ˢa course of] teaching in their synagogues, being ᵗrecognized and honored and praised by all.

16 So He came to Nazareth, [ᵘthat Nazareth] where He had been brought up, and He entered the synagogue, as was His custom on the Sabbath day. And He stood up to read.

17 And there was handed to Him [the roll of] the book of the prophet Isaiah. He opened (unrolled) the book and found the place where it was written, [Isa. 61:1, 2.]

18 The Spirit of the Lord [is] upon Me, because He has anointed Me [the Anointed One, the Messiah] to preach the good news (the Gospel) to the poor; He has sent Me to announce release to the captives and recovery of sight to the blind, to send forth as delivered those who are oppressed [who are downtrodden, bruised, crushed, and broken down by calamity],

19 To proclaim the accepted and acceptable year of the Lord [the day ᵛwhen salvation and the free favors of God profusely abound. [Isa. 61:1, 2.]

20 Then He rolled up the book and gave it back to the attendant and sat down; and the eyes of all in the synagogue were gazing [attentively] at Him.

21 And He began to speak to them: Today this Scripture has been fulfilled ᵛwhile you are present and hearing.

22 And all spoke well of Him and marveled at the words of grace that came forth from His mouth; and they said, Is not this Joseph's ʷSon?

23 So He said to them, You will doubtless quote to Me this proverb: Physician, heal Yourself! What we have learned by hearsay that You did in Capernaum, do here also in Your [own] town.

24 Then He said, Solemnly I say to you, no prophet is acceptable and welcome in his [own] town (country).

25 But in truth I tell you, there were many widows in Israel in the days of Elijah, when the heavens were closed up for three years and six months, so that there came a great famine over all the land;

26 And yet Elijah was not sent to a single one of them, but only to Zarephath in the country of Sidon, to a woman who was a widow. [I Kings 17:1, 8–16; 18:1.]

27 And there were many lepers in Israel in the time of Elisha the prophet, and yet not one of them was cleansed [by being healed]—but only Naaman the Syrian. [II Kings 5:1–14.]

28 When they heard these things, all the people in the synagogue were filled with rage.

29 And rising up, they pushed and drove Him out of the town, and, [laying hold of Him] they led Him to the [projecting] upper part of the hill on which their town was built, that they

---

q Robert Young. *Analytical Concordance.*   r Kenneth Wuest, *Word Studies in the Greek New Testament.*   s Marvin Vincent, *Word Studies:* in Greek imperfect tense.   t Hermann Cremer, *Biblico-Theological Lexicon of New Testament Greek.*   u James Moulton and George Milligan, *The Vocabulary of the Greek Testament.*   v Joseph Thayer, *A Greek-English Lexicon.*   w Capitalized because of what He is, the spotless Son of God, not what the speakers may have thought He was.

might hurl Him headlong down [over the cliff].

30 But passing through their midst, He went on His way.

31 And He descended to Capernaum, a town of Galilee, and there He continued to teach the people on the Sabbath days.

32 And they were amazed at His teaching, for His word was with authority *and* ability *and* weight *and* power.

33 Now in the synagogue there was a man who was possessed by the foul spirit of a demon; and he cried out with a loud (deep, terrible) cry,

34 Ah, *'let us alone!* What have You to do with us [What have 'we in common], Jesus of Nazareth? Have You come to destroy us? I know Who You are—the Holy One of God!

35 But Jesus rebuked him, saying, Be silent (muzzled, gagged), and come out of him! And when the demon had thrown the man down in their midst, he came out of him without injuring him in any ²possible way.

36 And they were all amazed and said to one another, What kind of talk is this? For with authority and power He commands the foul spirits and they come out!

37 And a rumor about Him spread into every place in the surrounding country.

38 Then He arose and left the synagogue and went into Simon's (Peter's) house. Now Simon's mother-in-law was suffering in the grip of a burning fever, and they pleaded with Him for her.

39 And standing over her, He rebuked the fever, and it left her; and immediately she got up and began waiting on them.

40 Now at the setting of the sun [indicating the end of the Sabbath],

all those who had any [who were] sick with various diseases brought them to Him, and He laid His hands upon every one of them and cured them.

41 And demons even came out of many people, screaming *and* crying out, You are the Son of God! But He rebuked them and would not permit them to speak, because they knew that He was the Christ (the Messiah).

42 And when daybreak came, He left [Peter's house] and went into an isolated [desert] place. And the people looked for Him until they came up to Him and tried to prevent Him from leaving them.

43 But He said to them, I must preach the good news (the Gospel) of the kingdom of God to the other cities [and towns] also, for I was sent for this [purpose].

44 And He continued to preach in the synagogues of Galilee.

CHAPTER 5

NOW IT occurred that while the people pressed upon Jesus to hear the message of God, He was standing by the Lake of Gennesaret (Sea of Galilee).

2 And He saw two boats drawn up by the lake, but the fishermen had gone down from them and were washing their nets.

3 And getting into one of the boats, [the one] that belonged to Simon (Peter), He requested him to draw away a little from the shore. Then He sat down and continued to teach the crowd [of people] from the boat.

4 When He had stopped speaking, He said to Simon (Peter), Put out into the deep [water], and lower your nets for a haul.

5 And Simon (Peter) answered, Master, we toiled all night [ªexhaust-

ingly] and caught nothing [in our nets]. But [b]on the ground of Your word, I will lower the nets [again].

6 And when they had done this, they caught a great number of fish; and as their nets were [c]at the point of] breaking,

7 They signaled to their partners in the other boat to come and take hold with them. And they came and filled both the boats, so that they began to sink.

8 But when Simon Peter saw this, he fell down at Jesus' knees, saying, Depart from me, for I am a sinful man, O Lord.

9 For he was gripped with bewildering amazement [allied to terror], and all who were with him, at the haul of fish which they had made;

10 And so also were James and John, the sons of Zebedee, who were partners with Simon (Peter). And Jesus said to Simon, Have no fear; from now on you will be catching men!

11 But after they had run their boats on shore, they left everything and [d]joined Him as His disciples and sided with His party and accompanied Him.

12 While He was in one of the towns, there came a man full of (covered with) leprosy; and when he saw Jesus, he fell on his face and implored Him, saying, Lord, if You are willing, You are able to cure me and make me clean.

13 And [Jesus] reached out His hand and touched him, saying, I am willing; be cleansed! And immediately the leprosy left him.

14 And [Jesus] charged him to tell no one [bthat he might chance to meet], [e]until [He said] you go and show yourself to the priest, and make an offering for your purification, as

Moses commanded, for a testimony and proof to the people, that they may have evidence [of your healing]. [Lev. 13:49; 14:2–32.]

15 But so much the more the news spread abroad concerning Him, and great crowds kept coming together to hear [Him] and to be healed by Him of their infirmities.

16 But He Himself withdrew [in retirement] to the wilderness (desert) and prayed.

17 One of those days, as He was teaching, there were Pharisees and teachers of the Law sitting by, who had come from every village and town of Galilee and Judea and from Jerusalem. And the power of the Lord was [present] with Him to heal [f]them.

18 And behold, some men were bringing on a stretcher a man who was paralyzed, and they tried to carry him in and lay him before [Jesus].

19 But finding no way to bring him in because of the crowd, they went up on the roof and lowered him with his stretcher through the tiles into the midst, in front of Jesus.

20 And when He saw [their confidence in Him, springing from] their faith, He said, Man, your sins are forgiven you!

21 And the scribes and the Pharisees began to reason and question and argue, saying, Who is this [Man] Who speaks blasphemies? Who can forgive sins but God alone?

22 But Jesus, knowing their thoughts and questionings, answered them, Why do you question in your hearts?

23 Which is easier: to say, Your sins are forgiven you, or to say, Arise and walk [about]?

24 But that you may know that the Son of Man has the [dpower of] au-

---

b Marvin Vincent, *Word Studies*.   c Richard Trench, *Synonyms of the New Testament*.   d Joseph
Thayer, *A Greek-English Lexicon*.   e Richard Trench, *Notes on the Miracles of our Lord*.   f Some
ancient manuscripts so read.

thority *and* right on earth to forgive sins, He said to the paralyzed man, I say to you, arise, pick up your litter (stretcher), and go to your own house!

25 And instantly [the man] stood up before them and picked up what he had been lying on and went away to his house, ^grecognizing *and* praising *and* thanking God.

26 And overwhelming astonishment *and* ecstasy seized them all, and they ^grecognized *and* praised *and* thanked God; and they were filled with *and* controlled by reverential fear and kept saying, We have seen wonderful *and* strange *and* incredible *and* unthinkable things today!

27 And after this, Jesus went out and looked [attentively] at a tax collector named Levi sitting at the tax office; and He said to him, ^hJoin Me as a disciple *and* side with My party *and* accompany Me.

28 And he forsook everything and got up and followed Him [becoming His disciple and siding with His party].

29 And Levi (Matthew) made a great banquet for Him in his own house, and there was a large company of tax collectors and others who were reclining [at the table] with them.

30 Now the Pharisees and their scribes were grumbling against Jesus' disciples, saying, Why are you eating and drinking with tax collectors and [preeminently] sinful people?

31 And Jesus replied to them, It is not those who are healthy who need a physician, but those who are sick.

32 I have not come to arouse *and* invite *and* call the righteous, but ⁱthe erring ones (^hthose not free from sin)

to repentance [^hto change their minds for the better and heartily to amend their ways, with abhorrence of their past sins].

33 Then they said to Him, The disciples of John practice fasting often and offer up prayers of [special] petition, and so do [the disciples] of the Pharisees also, but Yours eat and drink.

34 And Jesus said to them, Can you make the wedding guests fast as long as the bridegroom is with them?

35 But the days will come when the bridegroom will be taken from them; and then they will fast in those days.

36 He told them a ^jproverb also: No one puts a patch from a new garment on an old garment; if he does, he will both tear the new one, and the patch from the new [one] will not match the old [garment].

37 And no one pours new wine into old wineskins; if he does, the fresh wine will burst the skins and it will be spilled and the skins will be ruined (destroyed).

38 But new wine must be put into fresh wineskins.

39 And no one after drinking old wine immediately desires new wine, for he says, The old is good *or* ^kbetter.

CHAPTER 6

ONE SABBATH while Jesus was passing through the fields of standing grain, it occurred that His disciples picked some of the spikes and ate [of the grain], rubbing it out in their hands. [Deut. 23:25.]

2 But some of the Pharisees asked them, Why are you doing what is not permitted to be done on the Sabbath days? [Exod. 20:10; 23:12; Deut. 5:14.]

---

g Hermann Cremer, *Biblico-Theological Lexicon.*   **h** Joseph Thayer, *A Greek-English Lexicon.*   **i** Robert Young, *Analytical Concordance.*   **j** G. Abbott-Smith, *Manual Greek Lexicon of the New Testament.*   **k** Many ancient manuscripts read "better."

3 And Jesus replied to them, saying, Have you never so much as read what David did when he was hungry, he and those who were with him?—[I Sam. 21:1–6.]

4 How he went into the house of God and took and ate the [sacred] loaves of the showbread, which it is not permitted for any except only the priests to eat, and also gave to those [who were] with him? [Lev. 24:9.]

5 And He said to them, The Son of Man is Lord even of the Sabbath.

6 And it occurred on another Sabbath that when He went into the synagogue and taught, a man was present whose right hand was withered.

7 And the scribes and the Pharisees kept watching Jesus to see whether He would [actually] heal on the Sabbath, in order that they might get [some ground for] accusation against Him.

8 But He was aware all along of their thoughts, and He said to the man with the withered hand, Come and stand here in the midst. And he arose and stood there.

9 Then Jesus said to them, I ask you, is it lawful and right on the Sabbath to do good [¹so that someone derives advantage from it] or to do evil, to save a life [and ᵐmake a soul safe] or to destroy it?

10 Then He glanced around at them all and said to the man, Stretch out your hand! And he did so, and his hand was fully restored ⁿlike the other one.

11 But they were filled with lack of understanding and senseless rage and discussed (consulted) with one another what they might do to Jesus.

12 Now in those days it occurred that He went up into a mountain to pray, and spent the whole night in prayer to God.

13 And when it was day, He summoned His disciples and selected from them twelve, whom He named apostles (special messengers):

14 They were Simon, whom He named Peter, and his brother Andrew; and James and John; and Philip and Bartholomew;

15 And Matthew and Thomas; and James son of Alphaeus, and Simon who was called the Zealot,

16 And Judas son of James, and Judas Iscariot, who became a traitor (a treacherous, basely faithless person).

17 And Jesus came down with them and took His stand on a level spot, with a great crowd of His disciples and a vast throng of people from all over Judea and Jerusalem and the seacoast of Tyre and Sidon, who came to listen to Him and to be cured of their diseases—

18 Even those who were disturbed and troubled with unclean spirits, and they were being healed [also].

19 And all the multitude were seeking to touch Him, for healing power was all the while going forth from Him and curing them all [ᵒsaving them from severe illnesses or calamities].

20 And solemnly lifting up His eyes on His disciples, He said: Blessed (happy—¹with life-joy and satisfaction in God's favor and salvation, apart from your outward condition—and ᵖto be envied) are you poor and ᑫlowly and afflicted (destitute of wealth, influence, position, and honor), for the kingdom of God is yours!

21 Blessed (happy—¹with life-joy and satisfaction in God's favor and salvation, apart from your outward condition—and ᵖto be envied) are

l Hermann Cremer, Biblico-Theological Lexicon. manuscripts add this phrase. o Marvin Vincent, Word Studies. Lexicon. q Joseph Thayer, A Greek-English Lexicon. m John Wycliffe, The Wycliffe Bible. n Some p Alexander Souter, Pocket

you who hunger *and* seek with eager desire now, for you shall be filled *and* completely satisfied! Blessed (happy—[r]with life-joy and satisfaction in God's favor and salvation, apart from your outward condition—and [s]to be envied) are you who weep *and* sob now, for you shall laugh!

22 Blessed (happy—[r]with life-joy and satisfaction in God's favor and salvation, apart from your outward condition—and [s]to be envied) are you when people despise (hate) you, and when they exclude *and* excommunicate you [as disreputable] and revile *and* denounce you and defame *and* cast out *and* spurn your name as evil (wicked) on account of the Son of Man.

23 Rejoice *and* be glad at such a time and exult *and* leap for joy, for behold, your reward is rich *and* great *and* strong *and* intense *and* abundant in heaven; for even so their forefathers treated the prophets.

24 But woe to (alas for) you who are rich ([t]abounding in material resources), for you already are receiving your consolation (the solace and sense of strengthening and cheer that come from prosperity) *and* have taken and enjoyed your comfort in full [having nothing left to be awarded you].

25 Woe to (alas for) you who are full now (completely filled, luxuriously gorged and satiated), for you shall hunger *and* suffer want! Woe to (alas for) you who laugh now, for you shall mourn and weep *and* wail!

26 Woe to (alas for) you when everyone speaks fairly *and* handsomely of you *and* praises you, for even so their forefathers did to the false prophets.

27 But I say to you who are listening now to Me: [u]in order to heed, make it a practice to] love your enemies, treat well (do good to, act nobly toward) those who detest you *and* pursue you with hatred,

28 Invoke blessings upon *and* pray for the happiness of those who curse you, implore God's blessing (favor) upon those who abuse you [who revile, reproach, disparage, and highhandedly misuse you].

29 To the one who strikes you on the [j]jaw *or* cheek, offer the other [j]jaw *or* cheek also; and from him who takes away your outer garment, do not withhold your undergarment as well.

30 Give away to everyone who begs of you [who is [i]in want of necessities], and of him who takes away from you your goods, do not demand *or* require them back again.

31 And as you would like *and* desire that men would do to you, do exactly so to them.

32 If you [merely] love those who love you, what [u]quality of credit *and* thanks is that to you? For even [v]the [very] sinners love their lovers (those who love them).

33 And if you are kind *and* good *and* do favors to *and* benefit those who are kind *and* good *and* do favors to *and* benefit you, what [u]quality of credit *and* thanks is that to you? For even [v]the preeminently sinful do the same.

34 And if you lend money [u]at interest to those from whom you hope to receive, what [u]quality of credit *and* thanks is that to you? Even notorious sinners lend money [u]at interest to sinners, so as to recover as much again.

35 But love your enemies and be kind *and* do good [doing favors [r]so that someone derives benefit from them] and lend, expecting *and* hoping for nothing in return *but* [u]con-

r Hermann Cremer, *Biblico-Theological Lexicon.*   s Alexander Souter, *Pocket Lexicon.*   t Joseph Thayer, *A Greek-English Lexicon.*   u Marvin Vincent, *Word Studies.*   v William Tyndale, *The Tyndale Bible.*

sidering nothing as lost *and* despairing of no one; and then your recompense (your reward) will be great (rich, strong, intense, and abundant), and you will be sons of the Most High, for He is kind *and* charitable *and* good to the ungrateful *and* the selfish and wicked.

36 So be merciful (sympathetic, tender, responsive, and compassionate) even as your Father is [all these].

37 Judge not [neither pronouncing judgment nor subjecting to censure], and you will not be judged; do not condemn *and* pronounce guilty, and you will not be condemned *and* pronounced guilty; acquit *and* forgive *and* *release (give up resentment, let it drop), and you will be acquitted *and* forgiven *and* *released.

38 Give, and [gifts] will be given to you; good measure, pressed down, shaken together, and running over, will they pour *y*into [the pouch formed by] the bosom [of your robe and used as a bag]. For with the measure you deal out [with the measure you use when you confer benefits on others], it will be measured back to you.

39 He further told them *z*a proverb: Can a blind [man] guide *and* direct a blind [man]? Will they not both stumble into a ditch *or* a *a*hole in the ground?

40 A pupil is not superior to his teacher, but everyone [when he is] completely trained (readjusted, restored, set to rights, and perfected) will be like his teacher.

41 Why do you see the speck that is in your brother's eye but do not notice *or* consider the beam [of timber] that is in your own eye?

42 Or how can you say to your brother, Brother, allow me to take out the speck that is in your eye,

when you yourself do not see the beam that is in your own eye? You actor (pretender, hypocrite)! First take the beam out of your own eye, and then you will see clearly to take out the speck that is in your brother's eye.

43 For there is no good (healthy) tree that bears decayed (worthless, stale) fruit, nor on the other hand does a decayed (worthless, sickly) tree bear good fruit.

44 For each tree is known *and* identified by its own fruit; for figs are not gathered from thornbushes, nor is a cluster of grapes picked from a bramblebush.

45 The upright (honorable, intrinsically good) man out of the good treasure [stored] in his heart produces what is upright (honorable and intrinsically good), and the evil man out of the evil storehouse brings forth that which is depraved (wicked and intrinsically evil); for out of the abundance (overflow) of the heart his mouth speaks.

46 Why do you call Me, Lord, Lord, and do not [practice] what I tell you?

47 For everyone who comes to Me and listens to My words [in order to heed their teaching] and does them, I will show you what he is like:

48 He is like a man building a house, who dug and went down deep and laid a foundation upon the rock; and when a flood arose, the torrent broke against that house and could not shake *or* move it, because it had been securely built *or* *b*founded on a rock.

49 But he who merely hears and does not practice doing My words is like a man who built a house on the ground without a foundation, against which the torrent burst, and immedi-

---

w Literal translation.   x Literal meaning.   y Marvin Vincent, *Word Studies*.   z G. Abbott-Smith, *Manual Greek Lexicon*.   a Alexander Souter, *Pocket Lexicon*.   b Some manuscripts so read.

ately it collapsed *and* fell, and the breaking *and* ruin of that house was great.

CHAPTER 7

AFTER JESUS had finished all that He had to say in the hearing of the people [on the mountain], He entered Capernaum

2 Now a centurion had a bond servant who was held in honor *and* highly valued by him, who was sick and at the point of death.

3 And when the centurion heard of Jesus, he sent some Jewish elders to Him, requesting Him to come and make his bond servant well.

4 And when they reached Jesus, they begged Him earnestly, saying, He is worthy that You should do this for him,

5 For he loves our nation and he built us our synagogue [at his own expense].

6 And Jesus went with them. But when He was not far from the house, the centurion sent [some] friends to Him, saying, Lord, do not trouble [Yourself], for I am not csufficiently worthy to have You come under my roof;

7 Neither did I consider myself worthy to come to You. But [just] speak a word, and my servant boy will be healed.

8 For I also am a man [daily] subject to authority, with soldiers under me. And I say to one, Go, and he goes; and to another, Come, and he comes; and to my bond servant, Do this, and he does it.

9 Now when Jesus heard this, He marveled at him, and He turned and said to the crowd that followed Him, I tell you, not even in [all] Israel have I found such great faith [as this].

10 And when the messengers who had been sent returned to the house, they found the bond servant dwho had been ill quite well again.

11 eSoon afterward, Jesus went to a town called Nain, and His disciples and a great throng accompanied Him.

12 [Just] as He drew near the gate of the town, behold, a man who had died was being carried out—the only son of his mother, and she was a widow; and a large gathering from the town was accompanying her.

13 And when the Lord saw her, He had compassion on her and said to her, Do not weep.

14 And He went forward and touched the funeral bier, and the pallbearers stood still. And He said, Young man, I say to you, arise [ffrom death]!

15 And the man [who was] dead sat up and began to speak. And [Jesus] gave him [back] to his mother.

16 Profound *and* reverent fear seized them all, and they began gto recognize God *and* praise *and* give thanks, saying, A great hProphet has appeared among us! And God has visited His people [in order to help and care for and provide for them]!

17 And this report concerning [Jesus] spread through the whole of Judea and all the country round about. [I Kings 17:17–24; II Kings 4:32–37.]

18 And John's disciples brought him [who was now in prison] word of all these things.

19 And John summoned to him a certain two of his disciples and sent them to the Lord, saying, Are You He Who is to come, or shall we [continue to] look for another?

20 So the men came to Jesus and

---

c Literal translation: "sufficient." manuscripts read "the next day." Thayer, *A Greek-English Lexicon*. what the speakers may have thought He was.

d Some manuscripts add this phrase. e Many ancient f Hermann Cremer, *Biblico-Theological Lexicon*. g Joseph h Capitalized because of what He is, the spotless Son of God, not

said, John the Baptist sent us to You to ask, Are You the One Who is to come, or shall we [continue to] look for another?

21 In that very hour Jesus was healing many [people] of sicknesses and distressing bodily plagues and evil spirits, and to many who were blind He gave ['a free, gracious, joy-giving gift of] sight.

22 So He replied to them, Go and tell John what you have seen and heard: the blind receive their sight, the lame walk, the lepers are cleansed, the deaf hear, the dead are raised up, and the poor have the good news (the Gospel) preached to them. [Isa. 29:18, 19; 35:5, 6; 61:1.]

23 And blessed (happy—ʲwith life-joy and satisfaction in God's favor and salvation, apart from outward conditions—and ᵏto be envied) is he who takes no offense in Me *and* who is not hurt *or* resentful *or* annoyed *or* repelled *or* made to stumble ['whatever may occur].

24 And the messengers of John having departed, Jesus began to speak to the crowds about John: What did you go out into the desert to gaze on? A reed shaken *and* swayed by the wind?

25 Then what did you go out to see? A man dressed up in soft garments? Behold, those who wear fine apparel and live in luxury are in the courts *or* palaces of kings.

26 What then did you go out to see? A prophet (a forthteller)? Yes, I tell you, and far more than a prophet.

27 This is the one of whom it is written, Behold, I send My messenger before Your face, who shall make ready Your way before You. [Mal. 3:1.]

28 I tell you, among those born of women there is no one greater than

John; but 'he that is inferior [to the other citizens] in the kingdom of God is greater [in incomparable privilege] than he.

29 And all the people who heard Him, even the tax collectors, acknowledged the justice of God [in ˡcalling them to repentance and in pronouncing future wrath on the impenitent], being baptized with the baptism of John.

30 But the Pharisees and the lawyers [of the Mosaic Law] annulled *and* rejected *and* brought to nothing God's purpose concerning themselves, by [refusing and] not being baptized by John.

31 So to what shall I compare the men of this generation? And what are they like?

32 They are like little children sitting in the marketplace, calling to one another and saying, We piped to you [playing wedding], and you did not dance; we sang dirges *and* wailed [playing funeral], and you did not weep.

33 For John the Baptist has come neither eating bread nor drinking wine, and you say, He has a demon.

34 The Son of Man has come eating and drinking, and you say, Behold, a Man Who is a glutton and a wine drinker, a friend of tax collectors and notorious sinners.

35 Yet wisdom is vindicated (ᵐshown to be true and divine) by all her children [ᵐby their life, character, and deeds].

36 One of the Pharisees asked Jesus to dine with him, and He went into the Pharisee's house and reclined at table.

37 And behold, a woman of the town who was 'an especially wicked sinner, when she learned that He was reclining at table in the Pharisee's

i Marvin Vincent, *Word Studies.*   j Hermann Cremer, *Biblico-Theological Lexicon.*   k Alexander Souter, *Pocket Lexicon.*   l Joseph Thayer, *A Greek-English Lexicon.*   m Albert Barnes, *Notes on the New Testament.*

house, brought an alabaster flask of ointment (perfume).

38 And standing behind Him at His feet weeping, she began to wet His feet with [her] tears; and she wiped them with the hair of her head and kissed His feet [affectionately] and anointed them with the ointment (perfume).

39 Now when the Pharisee who had invited Him saw it, he said to himself, If this Man were a prophet, He would surely know who and what sort of woman this is who is touching Him—for she is a notorious sinner (a social outcast, devoted to sin).

40 And Jesus, replying, said to him, Simon, I have something to say to you. And he answered, Teacher, say it.

41 A certain lender of money [at interest] had two debtors: one owed him five hundred denarii, and the other fifty.

42 When they had no means of paying, he freely forgave them both. Now which of them will love him more?

43 Simon answered, The one, I take it, for whom he forgave *and* cancelled more. And Jesus said to him, You have decided correctly.

44 Then turning toward the woman, He said to Simon, Do you see this woman? When I came into your house, you gave Me no water for My feet, but she has wet My feet with her tears and wiped them with her hair.

45 You gave Me no kiss, but she from the moment I came in has not ceased [[n]intermittently] to kiss My feet tenderly *and* caressingly.

46 You did not anoint My head with [o][cheap, ordinary] oil, but she has anointed My feet with [o][costly, rare] perfume.

47 Therefore I tell you, her sins, many [as they are], are forgiven her —because she has loved much. But he who is forgiven little loves little.

48 And He said to her, Your sins are forgiven!

49 Then those who were at table with Him began to say among themselves, Who is this Who even forgives sins?

50 But Jesus said to the woman, Your faith has saved you; go (enter) [n]into peace [[o]in freedom from all the distresses that are experienced as the result of sin].

CHAPTER 8

SOON AFTERWARD, [Jesus] went on through towns and villages, preaching and bringing the good news (the Gospel) of the kingdom of God. And the Twelve [apostles] were with Him,

2 And also some women who had been cured of evil spirits and diseases: Mary, called Magdalene, from whom seven demons had been expelled,

3 And Joanna, the wife of Chuza, Herod's household manager; and Susanna; and many others, who ministered to *and* provided for [p]Him and them out of their property *and* personal belongings.

4 And when a very great throng was gathering together and people from town after town kept coming to Jesus, He said in a parable:

5 A sower went out to sow seed; and as he sowed, some fell along the traveled path and was trodden underfoot, and the birds of the air ate it up.

6 And some [seed] fell on the rock, and as soon as it sprouted, it withered away because it had no moisture.

7 And other [seed] fell in the midst

n Marvin Vincent, *Word Studies.* o Hermann Cremer, *Biblico-Theological Lexicon.* p Some ancient manuscripts read "Him" instead of "them."

of the thorns, and the thorns grew up with it and choked it [off].

8 And some seed fell into good soil, and grew up and yielded a crop a hundred times [as great]. As He said these things, He called out, He who has ears to hear, let him be listening *and* let him qconsider *and* understand by hearing!

9 And when His disciples asked Him the meaning of this parable,

10 He said to them, To you it has been given to [come progressively to] know (to recognize and understand more strongly and clearly) the mysteries *and* secrets of the kingdom of God, but for others they are in parables, so that, [though] looking, they may not see; and hearing, they may not comprehend. [Isa. 6:9, 10; Jer. 5:21; Ezek. 12:2.]

11 Now the meaning of the parable is this: The seed is the Word of God.

12 Those along the traveled road are the people who have heard; then the devil comes and carries away the message out of their hearts, that they may not believe (qacknowledge Me as their Savior and devote themselves to Me) and be saved [here and hereafter].

13 And those upon the rock [are the people] who, when they hear [the Word], receive *and* welcome it with joy; but these have no root. They believe for a while, and in time of trial *and* temptation fall away (withdraw and stand aloof).

14 And as for what fell among the thorns, these are [the people] who hear, but as they go on their way they are choked *and* suffocated with the anxieties *and* cares and riches and pleasures of life, and their fruit does not ripen (come to maturity and perfection).

15 But as for that [seed] in the good soil, these are [the people] who, hearing the Word, hold it fast in a just (rnoble, virtuous) and worthy heart, and steadily bring forth fruit with patience.

16 No one after he has lighted a lamp covers it with a vessel or puts it under a [dining table] couch; but he puts it on a lampstand, that those who come in may see the light.

17 For there is nothing hidden that shall not be disclosed, nor anything secret that shall not be known and come out into the open.

18 Be careful therefore how you listen. For to him who has [spiritual knowledge] will more be given; and from him who does not have [spiritual knowledge], even what he thinks *and* sguesses *and* tsupposes that he has will be taken away.

19 Then Jesus' mother and His brothers came along toward Him, but they could not get to Him because of the crowd.

20 And it was told Him, Your mother and Your brothers are standing outside, desiring to have an interview with You.

21 But He answered them, My mother and My brothers are those who listen to the Word of God and do it!

22 One of those days He and His disciples got into a boat, and He said to them, Let us go across to the other side of the lake. So they put out to sea.

23 But as they were sailing, He fell off to sleep. And a uwhirlwind revolving from below upwards swept down on the lake, and the boat was filling with water, and they were in great danger.

24 And the disciples came and woke Him, saying, Master, Master, we are perishing! And He, being

q Joseph Thayer, *A Greek-English Lexicon*.   r Marvin Vincent, *Word Studies*.   s John Wycliffe, *The Wycliffe Bible*.   t William Tyndale, *The Tyndale Bible*.   u J.H. Heinrich Schmidt, cited by Joseph Thayer, *A Greek-English Lexicon*.

thoroughly awakened, ʸcensured *and* ʷblamed *and* rebuked the wind and the raging waves; and they ceased, and there came a calm.

25 And He said to them, [Why are you so fearful?] Where is your faith (your trust, your confidence in Me —in My veracity and My integrity)? And they were seized with alarm *and* profound *and* reverent dread, and they marveled, saying to one another, Who then is this, that He commands even wind and sea, and they obey Him?

26 Then they came to the country of the Gerasenes, which is opposite Galilee.

27 Now when Jesus stepped out on land, there met Him a certain man out of the town who had [was possessed by] demons. For a long time he had worn no clothes, and he lived not in a house but in the tombs.

28 And when he saw Jesus, he raised a deep (terrible) cry [from the depths of his throat] and fell down before Him [in terror] and shouted loudly, What have You [to do] with me, Jesus, Son of the Most High God? [*What have we in common?]* I beg You, do not torment me!

29 For Jesus was already commanding the unclean spirit to come out of the man. For many times it had snatched *and* held him; he was kept under guard and bound with chains and fetters, but he would break the bonds and be driven by the demon into the wilderness (desert).

30 Jesus then asked him, What is your name? And he answered, Legion; for many demons had entered him.

31 And they begged [Jesus] not to command them to depart into the Abyss (bottomless pit). [Rev. 9:1.]

32 Now a great herd of swine was there feeding on the hillside; and [the demons] begged Him to give them leave to enter these. And He allowed them [to do so].

33 Then the demons came out of the man and entered into the swine, and the herd rushed down the steep cliff into the lake and were drowned.

34 When the herdsmen saw what had happened, they ran away and told it in the town and in the country.

35 And [people] went out to see what had occurred, and they came to Jesus and found the man from whom the demons had gone out, sitting at the feet of Jesus, clothed and in his right (sound) mind; and they were seized with alarm *and* fear.

36 And those [also] who had seen it told them how he who had been possessed with demons was restored [to health].

37 Then all the people of the country surrounding the Gerasenes' district asked [Jesus] to depart from them, for they were possessed *and* suffering with dread *and* terror; so He entered a boat and returned [to the west side of the Sea of Galilee].

38 But the man from whom the demons had gone out kept begging *and* ˣpraying that he might accompany Him *and* be with Him, but [Jesus] sent him away, saying,

39 Return to your home, and recount [the story] of how many *and* great things God has done for you. And [the man] departed, proclaiming throughout the whole city how much Jesus had done for him.

40 Now when Jesus came back [to Galilee], the crowd received *and* welcomed Him gladly, for they were all waiting *and* looking for Him.

41 And there came a man named Jairus, who had [for a ʸlong time] been a director of the synagogue; and

v James Moulton and George Milligan, *The Vocabulary.*   w John Wycliffe, *The Wycliffe Bible.*   x Marvin Vincent, *Word Studies.*   y Charles B. Williams, *The New Testament: A Translation:* "The Greek imperfect tense expresses this idea of duration."

falling at the feet of Jesus, he begged Him to come to his house,

42 For he had an only daughter, about twelve years of age, and she was dying. As [Jesus] went, the people pressed together around Him [almost suffocating Him].

43 And a woman who had suffered from a flow of blood for twelve years ²and had spent all her living upon physicians, and could not be healed by anyone,

44 Came up behind Him and touched the fringe of His garment, and immediately her flow of blood ceased.

45 And Jesus said, Who is it who touched Me? When all were denying it, Peter ªand those who were with him said, Master, the multitudes surround You and press You on every side!

46 But Jesus said, Someone did touch Me; for I perceived that [healing] power has gone forth from Me.

47 And when the woman saw that she had not escaped notice, she came up trembling, and, falling down before Him, she declared in the presence of all the people for what reason she had touched Him and how she had been instantly cured.

48 And He said to her, Daughter, your faith (your confidence and trust in Me) has made you well! Go (enter) ᵇinto peace (ᶜuntroubled, undisturbed well-being).

49 While He was still speaking, a man from the house of the director of the synagogue came and said [to Jairus], Your daughter is dead; do not ᵇweary and trouble the Teacher any further.

50 But Jesus, on hearing this, answered him, Do not be seized with alarm or struck with fear; simply believe [ᵈin Me as able to do this], and she shall be made well.

51 And when He came to the house, He permitted no one to enter with Him except Peter and John and James, and the girl's father and mother.

52 And all were weeping for and bewailing her; but He said, Do not weep, for she is not dead but sleeping.

53 And they laughed Him to scorn, knowing full well that she was dead.

54 And grasping her hand, He called, saying, Child, arise [ᵈfrom the sleep of death]!

55 And her spirit returned [ᵉfrom death], and she arose immediately; and He directed that she should be given something to eat.

56 And her parents were amazed, but He charged them to tell no one what had occurred.

CHAPTER 9

THEN JESUS called together the Twelve [apostles] and gave them power and authority over all demons, and to cure diseases,

2 And He sent them out to announce and preach the kingdom of God and to bring healing.

3 And He said to them, Do not take anything for your journey—neither walking stick, nor ᵉwallet [for a collection bag], nor food of any kind, nor money, and do not have two undergarments (tunics).

4 And whatever house you enter, stay there until you go away [from that place].

5 And wherever they do not receive and accept and welcome you, when you leave that town shake off [even] the dust from your feet, as a testimony against them.

---

z Many manuscripts add this phrase.   a Some manuscripts add this phrase.   b Richard Trench, Synonyms of the New Testament.   c Hermann Cremer, Biblico-Theological Lexicon.   d Joseph Thayer, A Greek-English Lexicon.   e James Moulton and George Milligan, The Vocabulary.

6 And departing, they went about from village to village, preaching the Gospel and restoring the afflicted to health everywhere.

7 Now Herod the tetrarch heard of all that was being done by [Jesus], and he was [thoroughly] perplexed and troubled, because it was said by some that John [the Baptist] had been raised from the dead,

8 And by others that Elijah had appeared, and by others that one of the prophets of old had come back to life.

9 But Herod said, John I beheaded; but Who is this about Whom I [learn] such things by hearsay? And he sought to see Him.

10 Upon their return, the apostles reported to Jesus all that they had done. And He took them [along with Him] and withdrew into privacy near a town called Bethsaida.

11 But when the crowds learned of it, [they] followed Him; and He welcomed them and talked to them about the kingdom of God, and healed those who needed restoration to health.

12 Now the day began to decline, and the Twelve came and said to Him, Dismiss the crowds and send them away, so that they may go to the neighboring hamlets and villages and the surrounding country and find lodging and get a [supply of provisions, for we are here in an uninhabited (barren, solitary) place.

13 But He said to them, You [yourselves] give them [food] to eat. They said, We have no more than five loaves and two fish—unless we are to go and buy food for all this crowd, [II Kings 4:42–44.]

14 For there were about 5,000 men. And [Jesus] said to His disciples, Have them [sit down] reclining in table groups (companies) of about fifty each.

15 And they did so, and made them all recline.

16 And taking the five loaves and the two fish, He looked up to heaven and [praising God] gave thanks and asked Him to bless them [to their use]. Then He broke them and gave them to the disciples to place before the multitude.

17 And all the people ate and were satisfied. And they gathered up what remained over—twelve [*small hand] baskets of broken pieces.

18 Now it occurred that as Jesus was praying privately, the disciples were with Him, and He asked them, Who do men say that I am?

19 And they answered, John the Baptist; but some say, Elijah; and others, that one of the ancient prophets has come back to life.

20 And He said to them, But who do you [yourselves] say that I am? And Peter replied, The Christ of God!

21 But He strictly charged and sharply commanded them [*under penalty] to tell this to no one [no one, *whoever he might be],

22 Saying, The Son of Man must suffer many things and be [*deliberately] disapproved and repudiated and rejected on the part of the elders and chief priests and scribes, and be put to death and on the third day be raised [again].

23 And He said to all, If any person wills to come after Me, let him deny himself [*disown himself, *forget, lose sight of himself and his own interests, *refuse and give up himself] and take up his cross daily and follow Me [*cleave steadfastly to Me, conform wholly to My example in living and, if need be, in dying also).

f Marvin Vincent, *Word Studies.*   g Marvin Vincent, *Word Studies.* See also footnote on Matt. 14:20.
h James Moulton and George Milligan, *The Vocabulary.*   i Joseph Thayer, *A Greek-English Lexicon.*
j Hermann Cremer, *Biblico-Theological Lexicon.*

24 For whoever would preserve his life *and* save it will lose *and* destroy it, but whoever loses his life for My sake, he will preserve *and* save it [*k*from the penalty of eternal death].

25 For what does it profit a man, if he gains the whole world and ruins or forfeits (loses) himself?

26 Because whoever is ashamed of Me and of My teachings, of him will the Son of Man be ashamed when He comes in the [*l*threefold] glory (the splendor and majesty) of Himself and of the Father and of the holy angels.

27 However I tell you truly, there are some of those standing here who will not taste death before they see the kingdom of God.

28 Now about eight days after these teachings, Jesus took with Him Peter and John and James and went up on the mountain to pray.

29 And as He was praying, the appearance of His countenance became altered (different), and His raiment became dazzling white [*l*flashing with the brilliance of lightning].

30 And behold, two men were conversing with Him—Moses and Elijah,

31 Who appeared in splendor *and* majesty *and* brightness and were speaking of His exit [from life], which He was about to bring to realization at Jerusalem.

32 Now Peter and those with him were weighed down with sleep, but when they fully awoke, they saw His glory (splendor and majesty and brightness) and the two men who stood with Him.

33 And it occurred as the men were parting from Him that Peter said to Jesus, Master, it is delightful *and* good that we are here; and let us construct three booths *or* huts—one for You and one for Moses and one for

Elijah! not noticing *or* knowing what he was saying.

34 But even as he was saying this, a cloud came and began to overshadow them, and they were seized with alarm *and* struck with fear as they entered into the cloud.

35 Then there came a voice out of the cloud, saying, This is My Son, My Chosen One *or* *m*My Beloved; listen to *and* yield to *and* obey Him!

36 And when the voice had died away, Jesus was found there alone. And they kept still, and told no one at that time any of these things that they had seen.

37 Now it occurred the next day, when they had come down from the mountain, that a great multitude met Him.

38 And behold, a man from the crowd shouted out, Master, I implore You to look at my son, for he is my only child;

39 And behold, a spirit seizes him and suddenly he cries out; it convulses him so that he foams at the mouth; and he is sorely shattered, and it will scarcely leave him.

40 And I implored Your disciples to drive it out, but they could not.

41 Jesus answered, O [faithless ones] unbelieving *and* without trust in God, a perverse (*n*wayward, *o*crooked and *l*warped) generation! Until when *and* how long am I to be with you and bear with you? Bring your son here [to Me].

42 And even while he was coming, the demon threw him down and [completely] convulsed him. But Jesus censured *and* severely rebuked the unclean spirit and healed the child and restored him to his father.

43 And all were astounded at the evidence of God's mighty power *and* His majesty and magnificence. But

k Hermann Cremer, *Biblico-Theological Lexicon*. ancient manuscripts so read. n John Wycliffe, *The Wycliffe Bible*.

l Marvin Vincent, *Word Studies*. m Many o William Tyndale, *The Tyndale Bible*.

[while] they were all marveling at everything Jesus was doing, He said to His disciples,

44 Let these words sink into your ears: the Son of Man is about to be delivered into the hands of men [[p]whose conduct is opposed to God].

45 However, they did not comprehend this saying; and it was kept hidden from them, so that they should not grasp it *and* understand, and they were afraid to ask Him about the statement.

46 But a controversy arose among them as to which of them might be the greatest [surpassing the others in excellence, worth, and authority].

47 But Jesus, as He perceived the thoughts of their hearts, took a little child and put him at His side

48 And told them, Whoever receives *and* accepts *and* welcomes this child in My name *and* for My sake receives *and* accepts *and* welcomes Me; and whoever so receives Me so also receives Him Who sent Me; for he who is least *and* lowliest among you all—he is [the one who is truly] great.

49 John said, Master, we saw a man driving out demons in Your name and we commanded him to stop it, for he does not follow along with us.

50 But Jesus told him, Do not forbid [such people]; for whoever is not against you is for you.

51 Now when the time was almost come for Jesus to be received up [to heaven], He steadfastly *and* determinedly set His face to go to Jerusalem.

52 And He sent messengers before Him; and they reached and entered a Samaritan village to make [things] ready for Him;

53 But [the people] would not welcome *or* receive *or* accept Him, because His face was [set as if He was] going to Jerusalem.

54 And when His disciples James and John observed this, they said, Lord, do You wish us to command fire to come down from heaven and consume them, [q]*even as Elijah did*? [II Kings 1:9–16.]

55 But He turned and rebuked *and* severely censured them. [r]*He said, You do not know of what sort of spirit you are,*

56 *For the Son of Man did not come to destroy men's lives, but to save them* [p]*[from the penalty of eternal death]*. And they journeyed on to another village.

57 And it occurred that as they were going along the road, a man said to Him, *Lord,* I will follow You wherever You go.

58 And Jesus told him, Foxes have lurking holes and the birds of the air have roosts *and* nests, but the Son of Man has no place to lay His head.

59 And He said to another, [s]Become My disciple, side with My party, and accompany Me! But he replied, *Lord,* permit me first to go and bury ([t]await the death of) my father.

60 But Jesus said to him, Allow the dead to bury their own dead; but as for you, go *and* publish abroad [u]throughout all regions the kingdom of God.

61 Another also said, I will follow You, Lord, *and* become Your disciple *and* side with Your party; but let me first say good-bye to those at my home.

62 Jesus said to him, No one who puts his hand to the plow and looks back [to the things behind] is fit for the kingdom of God.

p Hermann Cremer, *Biblico-Theological Lexicon.* **q** Some manuscripts add this phrase. **r** Some manuscripts add this to verse 55 and continue into verse 56. **s** Joseph Thayer, *A Greek-English Lexicon.* **t** Many commentators interpret it thus. **u** Marvin Vincent, *Word Studies.*

CHAPTER 10

NOW AFTER this the Lord chose *and* appointed seventy others and sent them out ahead of Him, two by two, into every town and place where He Himself was about to come (visit).

2 And He said to them, The harvest indeed is abundant ᵛ[there is much ripe grain], but the farmhands are few. Pray therefore the Lord of the harvest to send out laborers into His harvest.

3 Go your way; behold, I send you out like lambs into the midst of wolves.

4 Carry no purse, no provisions bag, no [change of] sandals; refrain from [retarding your journey by] saluting *and* wishing anyone well along the way.

5 Whatever house you enter, first say, Peace be to this household! [ʷFreedom from all the distresses that result from sin be with this family].

6 And if anyone [worthy] of peace *and* blessedness is there, the peace *and* blessedness you wish shall come upon him; but if not, it shall come back to you.

7 And stay on in the same house, eating and drinking what they provide, for the laborer is worthy of his wages. Do not keep moving from house to house.

8 Whenever you go into a town and they receive *and* accept *and* welcome you, eat what is set before you;

9 And heal the sick in it and say to them, The kingdom of God has come close to you.

10 But whenever you go into a town and they do not receive *and* accept *and* welcome you, go out into its streets and say,

11 Even the dust of your town that clings to our feet we are wiping off against you; yet know *and* understand this: the kingdom of God has come near *you.*

12 I tell you, it shall be more tolerable in that day for Sodom than for that town. [Gen. 19:24–28.]

13 Woe to you, Chorazin! Woe to you, Bethsaida! For if the mighty miracles performed in you had been performed in Tyre and Sidon, they would have repented long ago, sitting in sackcloth and ashes.

14 However, it shall be more tolerable in the judgment for Tyre and Sidon than for you.

15 And you, Capernaum, will you be exalted unto heaven? You shall be brought down to Hades (the regions of the dead).

16 He who hears *and* heeds you [disciples] hears *and* heeds Me; and he who slights *and* rejects you slights *and* rejects Me; and he who slights *and* rejects Me slights *and* rejects Him who sent Me.

17 The seventy returned with joy, saying, Lord, even the demons are subject to us in Your name!

18 And He said to them, I saw Satan falling like a lightning [flash] from heaven.

19 Behold! I have given you authority *and* power to trample upon serpents and scorpions, and [physical and mental strength and ability] over all the power that the enemy [possesses]; and nothing shall in any way harm you.

20 Nevertheless, do not rejoice at this, that the spirits are subject to you, but rejoice that your names are enrolled in heaven. [Exod. 32:32; Ps. 69:28; Dan. 12:1.]

21 In that same hour He rejoiced *and* gloried in the Holy Spirit and said, I thank You, Father, Lord of heaven and earth, that You have concealed these things [relating to salva-

v John Wycliffe, *The Wycliffe Bible.*   w Hermann Cremer, *Biblico-Theological Lexicon.*

tion] from the wise and understanding *and* learned, and revealed them to babes (the childish, unskilled, and untaught). Yes, Father, for such was Your gracious ˣwill *and* choice *and* good pleasure.

22 All things have been given over into My power by My Father; and no one knows Who the Son is except the Father, or Who the Father is except the Son and anyone to whom the Son may choose to reveal *and* make Him known.

23 Then turning to His disciples, He said privately, Blessed (happy, ʸto be envied) are those whose eyes see what you see!

24 For I tell you that many prophets and kings longed to see what you see and they did not see it, and to hear what you heard and they did not hear it.

25 And then a certain lawyer arose to try (test, tempt) Him, saying, Teacher, what am I to do to inherit everlasting life [that is, to partake of eternal salvation in the Messiah's kingdom]?

26 Jesus said to him, What is written in the Law? How do you read it?

27 And he replied, You must love the Lord your God with all your heart and with all your soul and with all your strength and with all your mind; and your neighbor as yourself. [Lev. 19:18; Deut. 6:5.]

28 And Jesus said to him, You have answered correctly; do this, and you will live [enjoy active, blessed, endless life in the kingdom of God].

29 And he, ᶻdetermined to acquit himself of reproach, said to Jesus, And who is my neighbor?

30 Jesus, ᶻtaking him up, replied, A certain man was going from Jerusalem down to Jericho, and he fell among robbers, who stripped him of his clothes and belongings and beat him and went their way, [ᶻunconcernedly] leaving him half dead, as it happened.

31 Now by ᶻcoincidence a certain priest was going down along that road, and when he saw him, he passed by on the other side.

32 A Levite likewise came down to the place and saw him, and passed by on the other side [of the road].

33 But a certain Samaritan, as he traveled along, came down to where he was; and when he saw him, he was moved with pity *and* sympathy [for him],

34 And went to him and dressed his wounds, pouring on [them] oil and wine. Then he set him on his own beast and brought him to an inn and took care of him.

35 And the next day he took out two denarii [two day's wages] and gave [them] to the innkeeper, saying, Take care of him; and whatever more you spend, I [myself] will repay you when I return.

36 Which of these three do you think proved himself a neighbor to him who fell among the robbers?

37 He answered, The one who showed pity *and* mercy to him. And Jesus said to him, Go and do likewise.

38 Now while they were on their way, it occurred that Jesus entered a certain village, and a woman named Martha received *and* welcomed Him into her house.

39 And she had a sister named Mary, who seated herself at the Lord's feet and was listening to His teaching.

40 But Martha [overly occupied and too busy] was distracted with much serving; and she came up to

x Joseph Thayer, *A Greek-English Lexicon.*   y Alexander Souter, *Pocket Lexicon.*   z Marvin Vincent, *Word Studies.*

Him and said, Lord, is it nothing to You that my sister has left me to serve alone? Tell her then to help me [to lend a hand and do her part along with me]!

41 But the Lord replied to her by saying, Martha, Martha, you are anxious and troubled about many things;

42 There is need of only one *or but [a]a few things*. Mary has chosen the good portion [[b]that which is to her advantage], which shall not be taken away from her.

CHAPTER 11

THEN HE was praying in a certain place; and when He stopped, one of His disciples said to Him, Lord, teach us to pray, [just] as John taught his disciples.

2 And He said to them, When you pray, say: *Our* Father *Who is in heaven*, hallowed be Your name, Your kingdom come. *Your will be done [held holy and revered] on earth as it is in heaven.*

3 Give us daily our bread [[c]food for the morrow].

4 And forgive us our sins, for we ourselves also forgive everyone who is indebted to us [who has offended us or done us wrong]. And bring us not into temptation *but rescue us from evil.*

5 And He said to them, Which of you who has a friend will go to him at midnight and will say to him, Friend, lend me three loaves [of bread],

6 For a friend of mine who is on a journey has just come, and I have nothing to put before him;

7 And he from within will answer, Do not disturb me; the door is now closed, and my children are with me

in bed; I cannot get up and supply you [with anything]?

8 I tell you, although he will not get up and supply him anything because he is his friend, yet because of his shameless persistence *and* insistence he will get up and give him as much as he needs.

9 So I say to you, Ask *and* [d]keep on asking and it shall be given you; seek *and* [d]keep on seeking and you shall find; knock *and* [d]keep on knocking and the door shall be opened to you.

10 For everyone who asks *and* [d]keeps on asking receives; and he who seeks *and* [d]keeps on seeking finds; and to him who knocks *and* [d]keeps on knocking, the door shall be opened.

11 What father among you, if his son asks for *[e]a loaf of bread, will give him a stone; or if he asks for* a fish, will instead of a fish give him a serpent?

12 Or if he asks for an egg, will give him a scorpion?

13 If you then, evil as you are, know how to give good gifts [gifts [b]that are to their advantage] to your children, how much more will your heavenly Father give the Holy Spirit to those who ask *and* [d]continue to ask Him!

14 Now Jesus was driving out a demon that was dumb; and it occurred that when the demon had gone out, the dumb man spoke. And the crowds marveled.

15 But some of them said, He drives out demons [because He is in league with and] by Beelzebub, the prince of demons,

16 While others, to try *and* test *and* tempt Him, demanded a sign of Him from heaven.

---

a Some ancient manuscripts read "a few things," while others read "only one," and still others read "a few and only one."   b Hermann Cremer, *Biblico-Theological Lexicon.*   c James Moulton and George Milligan, *The Vocabulary.*   d Charles B. Williams, *The New Testament: A Translation:* The idea of continuing or repeated action is often carried by the present imperative and present participles in Greek.   e Some manuscripts contain this portion within verse 11.

17 But He, [well] aware of their intent *and* purpose, said to them, Every kingdom split up against itself is doomed *and* brought to desolation, and so house falls upon house. [The disunited household will collapse.]

18 And if Satan also is divided against himself, how will his kingdom last? For you say that I expel demons with the help of *and* by Beelzebub.

19 Now if I expel demons with the help of *and* by Beelzebub, with whose help *and* by whom do your sons drive them out? Therefore they shall be your judges.

20 But if I drive out the demons by the finger of God, then the kingdom of God has [already] come upon you.

21 When the strong man, fully armed, [°from his courtyard] guards his own dwelling, his belongings are undisturbed [his property is at peace and is secure].

22 But when one stronger than he attacks him and conquers him, he robs him of his whole armor on which he had relied and divides up *and* distributes all his goods as plunder (spoil).

23 He who is not with Me [siding and believing with Me] is against Me, and he who does not gather with Me [engage in My interest], scatters.

24 When the unclean spirit has gone out of a person, it roams through waterless places in search [of a place] of rest (release, refreshment, ease); and finding none it says, I will go back to my house from which I came.

25 And when it arrives, it finds [the place] swept *and* put in order and furnished *and* decorated.

26 And it goes and brings other spirits, seven [of them], more evil than itself, and they enter in, settle down, *and* dwell there; and the last state of that person is worse than the first.

27 Now it occurred that as He was saying these things, a certain woman in the crowd raised her voice and said to Him, Blessed (happy and °to be envied) is the womb that bore You and the breasts that You sucked!

28 But He said, Blessed (happy and °to be envied) rather are those who hear the Word of God and obey *and* practice it!

29 Now as the crowds were [increasingly] thronging Him, He began to say, This present generation is a wicked one; it seeks *and* demands a sign (miracle), but no sign shall be given to it except the sign of Jonah [the prophet]. [Jonah 1:17; Matt. 12:40.]

30 For [just] as Jonah became a sign to the people of Nineveh, so will also the Son of Man be [a sign] to this age *and* generation. [Jonah 3:4–10.]

31 The queen of the South will arise in the judgment with the people of this age *and* generation and condemn them; for she came from the ends of the [inhabited] earth to listen to the wisdom of Solomon, and notice, °here is more than Solomon. [I Kings 10:1–13; II Chron. 9:1–12.]

32 The men of Nineveh will appear as witnesses at the judgment with this generation and will condemn it; for they repented at the preaching of Jonah, and behold, °here is more than Jonah. [Jonah 3:4–10.]

33 No one after lighting a lamp puts it in a cellar *or* crypt or under a bushel measure, but on a lampstand, that those who are coming in may see the light.

34 Your eye is the lamp of your body; when your eye (°your conscience) is sound *and* fulfilling its of-

---

f Marvin Vincent, *Word Studies.*   g Alexander Souter, *Pocket Lexicon.*   h John Wycliffe, *The Wycliffe Bible.*   i Hermann Cremer, *Biblico-Theological Lexicon.*

fice, your whole body is full of light; but when it is not sound *and* is not fulfilling its office, your body is full of darkness.

35 Be careful, therefore, that the light that is in you is not darkness.

36 If then your entire body is illuminated, having no part dark, it will be wholly bright [with light], as when a lamp with its bright rays gives you light.

37 Now while Jesus was speaking, a Pharisee invited Him to take dinner with him, so He entered and reclined at table.

38 The Pharisee noticed and was astonished [to see] that Jesus did not first wash before dinner.

39 But the Lord said to him, Now you Pharisees cleanse the outside of the cup and of the plate, but inside you yourselves are full of greed *and* robbery *and* extortion and malice *and* wickedness.

40 You senseless (foolish, stupid) ones [acting without reflection or intelligence]! Did not He Who made the outside make the inside also?

41 But [dedicate your inner self and] give as donations to the poor of those things which are within [of inward righteousness] and behold, everything is purified *and* clean for you.

42 But woe to you, Pharisees! For you tithe mint and rue and every [little] herb, but disregard *and* neglect justice and the love of God. These you ought to have done without leaving the others undone. [Lev. 27:30; Mic. 6:8.]

43 Woe to you, Pharisees! For you love the best seats in the synagogues and [you love] to be greeted *and* bowed down to in the [public] marketplaces.

44 Woe to you! For you are like graves which are not marked *or* seen,

and men walk over them without being aware of it [and are ceremonially defiled].

45 One of the experts in the [Mosaic] Law answered Him, Teacher, in saying this, You reproach *and* outrage *and* affront even us!

46 But He said, Woe to you, the lawyers, also! For you load men with oppressive burdens hard to bear, and you do not personally [even ʲgently] touch the burdens with one of your fingers.

47 Woe to you! For you are ᵏrebuilding *and* repairing the tombs of the prophets, whom your fathers killed (destroyed).

48 So you bear witness and give your full approval *and* consent to the deeds of your fathers; for they actually killed them, and you rebuild *and* repair monuments to them.

49 For this reason also the wisdom of God said, I will send them prophets and apostles, [some] of whom they will put to death and persecute,

50 So that the blood of all the prophets shed from the foundation of the world may be charged against *and* required of this age *and* generation,

51 From the blood of Abel to the blood of Zechariah, who was slain between the altar and the sanctuary. Yes, I tell you, it shall be charged against *and* required of this age *and* generation. [Gen. 4:8; II Chron. 24:20, 21; Zech. 1:1.]

52 Woe to you, lawyers (experts in the Mosaic Law)! For you have taken away the key to knowledge; you did not go in yourselves, and you hindered *and* prevented those who were entering.

53 As He left there, the scribes and the Pharisees [followed Him closely, and they] began ᵏto be enraged with *and* set themselves violently against

j Marvin Vincent, *Word Studies*.   k Joseph Thayer, *A Greek-English Lexicon*.

Him and to draw Him out *and* provoke Him to speak of many things.

54 Secretly watching *and* plotting *and* lying in wait for Him, to seize upon something He might say [that they might accuse Him].

CHAPTER 12

IN THE meanwhile, when so many thousands of the people had gathered that they were trampling on one another, Jesus commenced by saying primarily to His disciples, Be on your guard against the leaven (ferment) of the Pharisees, which is hypocrisy [producing unrest and violent agitation].

2 Nothing is [so closely] covered up that it will not be revealed, or hidden that it will not be known.

3 Whatever you have spoken in the darkness shall be heard *and* listened to in the light, and what you have whispered in [people's] ears and behind closed doors will be proclaimed upon the housetops.

4 I tell you, My friends, do not dread *and* be afraid of those who kill the body and after that have nothing more that they can do.

5 But I will warn you whom you should fear: fear Him Who, after killing, has power to hurl into hell (Gehenna); yes, I say to you, fear Him!

6 Are not five sparrows sold for two pennies? And [yet] not one of them is forgotten *or* uncared for in the presence of God.

7 But [even] the very hairs of your head are all numbered. Do not be struck with fear *or* seized with alarm; you are of greater worth than many [flocks] of sparrows.

8 And I tell you, Whoever declares openly [speaking out freely] *and* confesses that he is My worshiper and acknowledges Me before men, the Son of Man also will declare *and* confess *and* acknowledge him before the angels of God.

9 But he who disowns *and* denies *and* rejects *and* refuses to acknowledge Me before men will be disowned *and* denied *and* rejected *and* refused acknowledgement in the presence of the angels of God.

10 And everyone who makes a statement *or* speaks a word against the Son of Man, it will be forgiven him; but he who blasphemes against the Holy Spirit [that is, whoever [1]intentionally comes short of the reverence due the Holy Spirit], it will not be forgiven him [for him there is no forgiveness].

11 And when they bring you before the synagogues and the magistrates and the authorities, do not be anxious [beforehand] how you shall reply in defense or what you are to say.

12 For the Holy Spirit will teach you in that very hour *and* [m]moment what [you] ought to say.

13 Someone from the crowd said to Him, Master, order my brother to divide the inheritance *and* share it with me.

14 But He told him, Man, who has appointed Me a judge or umpire *and* divider over you?

15 And He said to them, Guard yourselves and keep free from all covetousness (the immoderate desire for wealth, the greedy longing to have more); for a man's life does not consist in *and* is not derived from possessing [n]overflowing abundance *or* that which is [o]over and above his needs.

16 Then He told them a parable, saying, The land of a rich man was fertile *and* yielded plentifully.

17 And he considered *and* debated

l Joseph Thayer, *A Greek-English Lexicon.*   m James Moulton and George Milligan, *The Vocabulary.*   n Alexander Souter, *Pocket Lexicon.*   o G. Abbott-Smith, *Manual Greek Lexicon.*

within himself, What shall I do? I have no place [in which] to gather together my harvest.

18 And he said, I will do this: I will pull down my storehouses and build larger ones, and there I will store all [p]my grain *or produce* and my goods.

19 And I will say to my soul, Soul, you have many good things laid up, [enough] for many years. Take your ease; eat, drink, *and* enjoy yourself merrily.

20 But God said to him, You fool! This very night [q]they [the messengers of God] will demand your soul of you; and all the things that you have prepared, whose will they be? [Job 27:8; Jer. 17:11.]

21 So it is with the one who continues to lay up *and* hoard possessions for himself and is not rich [in his relation] to God [this is how he fares].

22 And [Jesus] said to His disciples, Therefore I tell you, do not be anxious *and* troubled [with cares] about your life, as to what you will [have to] eat; or about your body, as to what you will [have to] wear.

23 For life is more than food, and the body [more] than clothes.

24 Observe *and* consider the ravens; for they neither sow nor reap, they have neither storehouse nor barn; and [yet] God feeds them. Of how much more worth are you than the birds!

25 And which of you by being overly anxious *and* troubled with cares can add a [r]cubit to his stature *or* a moment [unit] of time to his [r]age [the length of his life]?

26 If then you are not able to do such a little thing as that, why are you anxious *and* troubled with cares about the rest?

27 Consider the lilies, how they grow. They neither [wearily] toil nor spin *nor* [s]*weave;* yet I tell you, even Solomon in all his glory (his splendor and magnificence) was not arrayed like one of these. [I Kings 10:4–7.]

28 But if God so clothes the grass in the field, which is alive today, and tomorrow is thrown into the furnace, how much more will He clothe you, O you [people] of little faith?

29 And you, do not seek [by meditating and reasoning to inquire into] what you are to eat and what you are to drink; nor be of anxious (troubled) mind [[t]unsettled, excited, worried, and [u]in suspense];

30 For all the pagan world is [greedily] seeking these things, and your Father knows that you need them.

31 Only aim at *and* strive for *and* seek His kingdom, and all these things shall be supplied to you also.

32 Do not be seized with alarm *and* struck with fear, little flock, for it is your Father's good pleasure to give you the kingdom!

33 Sell what you possess and give donations to the poor; provide yourselves with purses *and* handbags that do not grow old, an unfailing *and* inexhaustible treasure in the heavens, where no thief comes near and no moth destroys.

34 For where your treasure is, there will your heart be also.

35 Keep your loins girded and your lamps burning,

36 And be like men who are waiting for their master to return home from the marriage feast, so that when he returns from the wedding and comes and knocks, they may open to him immediately.

37 Blessed (happy, fortunate, and

p Some ancient manuscripts read "grain;" some read "produce" or "fruits." **q** Marvin Vincent, *Word Studies*: "The indefiniteness is impressive." **r** G. Abbott-Smith, *Manual Greek Lexicon*: "A stage of growth, whether measured by age or stature." **s** Some ancient manuscripts read "weave." **t** Marvin Vincent, *Word Studies*. **u** G. Abbott-Smith, *Manual Greek Lexicon*.

ᵛto be envied) are those servants whom the master finds awake and alert and watching when he comes. Truly I say to you, he will gird himself and have them recline at table and will come and serve them!

38 If he comes in the second watch (before midnight) or the third watch (after midnight), and finds them so, blessed (happy, fortunate, and ᵛto be envied) are those servants!

39 But of this be assured: if the householder had known at what time the burglar was coming, he would have been awake and alert and watching and would not have permitted his house to be dug through and broken into.

40 You also must be ready, for the Son of Man is coming at an hour and a ʷmoment when you do not anticipate it.

41 Peter said, Lord, are You telling this parable for us, or for all alike?

42 And the Lord said, Who then is that faithful steward, the wise man whom his master will set over those in his household service to supply them their allowance of food at the appointed time?

43 Blessed (happy and ᵛto be envied) is that servant whom his master finds so doing when he arrives.

44 Truly I tell you, he will set him in charge over all his possessions.

45 But if that servant says in his heart, My master is late in coming, and begins to strike the menservants and the maids and to eat and drink and get drunk,

46 The master of that servant will come on a day when he does not expect him and at an hour of which he does not know, and will punish him and cut him off and assign his lot with ˣthe unfaithful.

47 And that servant who knew his master's will but did not get ready or act as he would wish him to act shall be beaten with many [lashes].

48 But he who did not know and did things worthy of a beating shall be beaten with few [lashes]. For everyone to whom much is given, of him shall much be required; and of him to whom men entrust much, they will require and demand all the more. [Num. 15:29, 30; Deut. 25:2, 3.]

49 I have come to cast fire upon the earth, and how I wish that it were already kindled!

50 I have a baptism with which to be baptized, and how greatly and sorely I am urged on (impelled, ˣconstrained) until it is accomplished!

51 Do you suppose that I have come to give peace upon earth? No, I say to you, but rather division;

52 For from now on in one house there will be five divided [among themselves], three against two and two against three.

53 They will be divided, father against son and son against father, mother against daughter and daughter against mother, mother-in-law against her daughter-in-law and daughter-in-law against her mother-in-law. [Mic. 7:6.]

54 He also said to the crowds of people, When you see a cloud rising in the west, at once you say, It is going to rain! And so it does.

55 And when [you see that] a south wind is blowing, you say, There will be severe heat! And it occurs.

56 You playactors (hypocrites)! You know how [intelligently] to discern and interpret and ˣprove the looks of the earth and sky; but how is it that you do not know how to discern and interpret and apply the proof to this present time?

57 And why do you not judge what

v Alexander Souter, *Pocket Lexicon*.   w James Moulton and George Milligan, *The Vocabulary*.   x John Wycliffe, *The Wycliffe Bible*.

is just *and* personally decide what is right?

58 Then as you go with your accuser before a magistrate, on the way make a diligent effort to settle *and* be quit (free) of him, lest he drag you to the judge, and the judge turn you over to the officer, and the officer put you in prison.

59 I tell you, you will never get out until you have paid the very last [fraction of a] cent.

CHAPTER 13

JUST AT that time there [arrived] some people who informed Jesus about the Galileans whose blood Pilate had mixed with their sacrifices.

2 And He replied by saying to them, Do you think that these Galileans were greater sinners than all the other Galileans because they have suffered in this way?

3 I tell you, No; but unless you repent (ʸchange your mind for the better and heartily amend your ways, with abhorrence of your past sins), you will all likewise perish *and* be lost ᶻeternally.

4 Or those eighteen on whom the tower in Siloam fell and killed them —do you think that they were more guilty offenders (debtors) than all the others who dwelt in Jerusalem?

5 I tell you, No; but unless you repent (ʸchange your mind for the better and heartily amend your ways, with abhorrence of your past sins), you will all likewise perish *and* be lost ᶻeternally.

6 And He told them this parable: A certain man had a fig tree, planted in his vineyard, and he came looking for fruit on it, but did not find [any].

7 So he said to the vinedresser, See here! For these three years I have come looking for fruit on this fig tree and I find none. Cut it down! Why should it continue also to use up the ground [to ᵃdeplete the soil, intercept the sun, and take up room]?

8 But he replied to him, Leave it alone, sir, [just] this one more year, till I dig around it and put manure [on the soil].

9 Then perhaps it will bear fruit after this; but if not, you can cut it down *and* out.

10 Now Jesus was teaching in one of the synagogues on the Sabbath.

11 And there was a woman there who for eighteen years had had an ᵇinfirmity caused by a spirit (ᶜa demon of sickness). She was ʸbent completely forward and utterly unable to straighten herself up *or* to ᵈlook upward.

12 And when Jesus saw her, He called [her to Him] and said to her, Woman, you are released from your infirmity!

13 Then He laid [His] hands on her, and instantly she was made straight, and she ᵃrecognized *and* thanked *and* praised God.

14 But the ᵈleader of the synagogue, indignant because Jesus had healed on the Sabbath, said to the crowd, There are six days on which work ought to be done; so come on those days and be cured, and not on the Sabbath day..[Exod. 20:9, 10.]

15 But the Lord replied to him, saying, You playactors (hypocrites)! Does not each one of you on the Sabbath loose his ox or his donkey from the stall and lead it out to water it?

16 And ought not this woman, a daughter of Abraham, whom Satan has kept bound for eighteen years, be

y Joseph Thayer, *A Greek-English Lexicon. Commentary on the Old and New Testaments.*   z Robert Jamieson, A.R. Fausett and David Brown, *A Johann Bengel,* cited by Marvin Vincent, *Word Studies.*   b Marvin Vincent, *Word Studies.*   c Hermann Cremer, *Biblico-Theological Lexicon.*   d Alexander Souter, *Pocket Lexicon.*

loosed from this bond on the Sabbath day?

17 Even as He said this, all His opponents were put to shame, and all the people were rejoicing over all the glorious things that were being done by Him.

18 This led Him to say, What is the kingdom of God like? And to what shall I compare it?

19 It is like a grain of mustard seed, which a man took and planted in his own garden; and it grew and became a tree, and the wild birds 'found shelter *and* roosted *and* nested in its branches.

20 And again He said, To what shall I liken the kingdom of God?

21 It is like leaven which a woman took and hid in three measures of wheat flour *or* meal until it was all leavened (fermented).

22 [Jesus] journeyed on through towns and villages, teaching, and making His way toward Jerusalem.

23 And someone asked Him, Lord, will only a few be saved (rescued, delivered from the penalties of the last judgment, and made partakers of the salvation by Christ)? And He said to them,

24 Strive to enter by the narrow door [force yourselves through it], for many, I tell you, will try to enter and will not be able.

25 When once the Master of the house gets up and closes the door, and you begin to stand outside and to knock at the door [again and again], saying, Lord, open to us! He will answer you, I do not know where [ᶠwhat household—certainly not Mine] you come from.

26 Then you will begin to say, We ate and drank in Your presence, and You taught in our streets.

27 But He will say, I tell you, I do not know where [ᶠwhat household—certainly not Mine] you come from; depart from Me, all you wrongdoers!

28 There will be weeping and grinding of teeth when you see Abraham and Isaac and Jacob and all the prophets in the kingdom of God, but you yourselves being cast forth (banished, driven away).

29 And [people] will come from east and west, and from north and south, and sit down (feast at table) in the kingdom of God.

30 And behold, there are some [now] last who will be first [then], and there are some [now] first who will be last [then].

31 At that very hour some Pharisees came up and said to Him, Go away from here, for Herod is determined to kill You.

32 And He said to them, Go and tell that fox [sly and crafty, skulking and cowardly], Behold, I drive out demons and perform healings today and tomorrow, and on the third day I finish (complete) My course.

33 Nevertheless, I must continue on My way today and tomorrow and the day after that—for it will never do for a prophet to be destroyed away from Jerusalem!

34 O Jerusalem, Jerusalem, you who continue to kill the prophets and to stone those who are sent to you! How often I have desired *and* yearned to gather your children together [around Me], as a hen [gathers] her young under her wings, but you would not!

35 Behold, your house is forsaken (abandoned, left to you destitute of God's help)! And I tell you, you will not see Me again until the time comes when you shall say, Blessed (to be celebrated with praises) is He Who comes in the name of the Lord! [Ps. 118:26; Jer. 22:5.]

e James Moulton and George Milligan, *The Vocabulary.*   f Marvin Vincent, *Word Studies.*

CHAPTER 14

IT OCCURRED one Sabbath, when [Jesus] went for a meal at the house of one of the ruling Pharisees, that they were [engaged in] watching Him [closely].

2 And behold, [just] in front of Him there was a man who had dropsy.

3 And Jesus asked the lawyers and the Pharisees, Is it lawful and right to cure on the Sabbath or not?

4 But they kept silent. Then He took hold [of the man] and cured him and ᵍsent him away.

5 And He said to them, Which of you, having a son ʰor a donkey or an ox that has fallen into a well, will not at once pull him out on the Sabbath day?

6 And they were unable to reply to this.

7 Now He told a parable to those who were invited, [when] He noticed how they were selecting the places of honor, saying to them,

8 When you are invited by anyone to a marriage feast, do not recline on the chief seat [in the place of honor], lest a more distinguished person than you has been invited by him, [Prov. 25:6, 7.]

9 And he who invited both of you will come to you and say, Let this man have the place [you have taken]. Then, with humiliation and a guilty sense of impropriety, you will begin to take the lowest place.

10 But when you are invited, go and recline in the lowest place, so that when your host comes in, he may say to you, Friend, go up higher! Then you will be honored in the presence of all who sit [at table] with you.

11 For everyone who exalts himself will be humbled (ranked below others who are honored or rewarded), and he who humbles himself (keeps a modest opinion of himself and behaves accordingly) will be exalted (elevated in rank).

12 Jesus also said to the man who had invited Him, When you give a dinner or a supper, do not invite your friends or your brothers or your relatives or your wealthy neighbors, lest perhaps they also invite you in return, and so you are paid back.

13 But when you give a banquet or a reception, invite the poor, the disabled, the lame, and the blind.

14 Then you will be blessed (happy, fortunate, and ⁱto be envied), because they have no way of repaying you, and you will be recompensed at the resurrection of the just (upright).

15 When one of those who reclined [at the table] with Him heard this, he said to Him, Blessed (happy, fortunate, and ⁱto be envied) is he who shall eat bread in the kingdom of God!

16 But Jesus said to him, A man was once giving a great supper and invited many;

17 And at the hour for the supper he sent his servant to say to those who had been invited, Come, for all is now ready.

18 But they all alike began to make excuses and to beg off. The first said to him, I have bought a piece of land, and I have to go out and see it; I beg you, have me excused.

19 And another said, I have bought five yoke of oxen, and I am going to examine and ʲput my approval on them; I beg you, have me excused.

20 And another said, I have married a wife, and because of this I am unable to come. [Deut. 24:5.]

21 So the servant came and reported these [answers] to his master. Then the master of the house said in wrath to his servant, Go quickly into

g Joseph Thayer, A Greek-English Lexicon.   h Many ancient manuscripts so read.   i Alexander Souter, Pocket Lexicon.   j Kenneth Wuest, Word Studies.

the ᵏgreat streets and the small streets of the city and bring in here the poor and the disabled and the blind and the lame.

22 And the servant [returning] said, Sir, what you have commanded me to do has been done, and yet there is room.

23 Then the master said to the servant, Go out into the highways and hedges and urge *and* constrain [them] to yield *and* come in, so that my house may be filled.

24 For I tell you, not one of those who were invited shall taste my supper.

25 Now huge crowds were going along with [Jesus], and He turned and said to them,

26 If anyone comes to Me and does not hate his [own] father and mother [ᶦin the sense of indifference to or relative disregard for them in comparison with his attitude toward God] and [likewise] his wife and children and brothers and sisters—[yes] and even his own life also—he cannot be My disciple.

27 Whoever does not persevere *and* carry his own cross and come after (follow) Me cannot be My disciple.

28 For which of you, wishing to build a ᵐfarm building, does not first sit down and calculate the cost [to see] whether he has sufficient means to finish it?

29 Otherwise, when he has laid the foundation and is unable to complete [the building], all who see it will begin to mock *and* jeer at him,

30 Saying, This man began to build and was not able (ⁿworth enough) to finish.

31 Or what king, going out to engage in conflict with another king, will not first sit down and consider

and take counsel whether he is able with ten thousand [men] to meet him who comes against him with twenty thousand?

32 And if he cannot [do so], when the other king is still a great way off, he sends an envoy and asks the terms of peace.

33 So then, any of you who does not forsake (renounce, surrender claim to, give up, ⁿsay good-bye to) all that he has cannot be My disciple.

34 Salt is good [an excellent thing], but if salt has lost its strength *and* has become saltless (insipid, flat), how shall its saltness be restored?

35 It is fit neither for the land nor for the manure heap; men throw it away. He who has ears to hear, let him listen *and* consider *and* comprehend by hearing!

CHAPTER 15

NOW THE tax collectors and [notorious and ᵒespecially wicked] sinners were all coming near to [Jesus] to listen to Him.

2 And the Pharisees and the scribes kept muttering *and* indignantly complaining, saying, This man accepts *and* receives *and* welcomes [ᵒpreeminently wicked] sinners and eats with them.

3 So He told them this parable:

4 What man of you, if he has a hundred sheep and should lose one of them, does not leave the ninety-nine in the wilderness (desert) and go after the one that is lost until he finds it?

5 And when he has found it, he lays it on his [own] shoulders, rejoicing.

6 And when he gets home, he summons together [his] friends and [his] neighbors, saying to them, Rejoice with me, because I have found my sheep which was lost.

k John Wycliffe, *The Wycliffe Bible.*
and George Milligan, *The Vocabulary.*
Greek-English Lexicon.

l G. Abbott-Smith, *Manual Greek Lexicon.*
n Marvin Vincent, *Word Studies.*

m James Moulton
o Joseph Thayer, A

7 Thus, I tell you, there will be more joy in heaven over one [ᵖespecially] wicked person who repents (ᵖchanges his mind, abhorring his errors and misdeeds, and determines to enter upon a better course of life) than over ninety-nine righteous persons who have no need of repentance.

8 Or what woman, having ten [silver] drachmas [each equal to a day's wages], if she loses one coin, does not light a lamp and sweep the house and look carefully and diligently until she finds it?

9 And when she has found it, she summons her [women] friends and neighbors, saying, Rejoice with me, for I have found the silver coin which I had lost.

10 Even so, I tell you, there is joy among and in the presence of the angels of God over one [ᵖespecially] wicked person who repents (ᵖchanges his mind for the better, heartily amending his ways, with abhorrence of his past sins).

11 And He said, There was a certain man who had two sons;

12 And the younger of them said to his father, Father, give me the part of the property that falls [to me]. And he divided the estate between them. [Deut. 21:15–17.]

13 And not many days after that, the younger son gathered up all that he had, and journeyed into a distant country, and there he wasted his fortune in reckless and loose [from restraint] living.

14 And when he had spent all he had, a ᑫmighty famine came upon that country, and he began to fall behind and be in want.

15 So he went and forced (glued) himself upon one of the citizens of

that country, who sent him into his fields to feed hogs.

16 And he would gladly have fed on and ʳfilled his belly with the ˢcarob pods that the hogs were eating, but [they could not satisfy his hunger and] nobody gave him anything [better]. [Jer. 30:14.]

17 Then when he came to himself, he said, How many hired servants of my father have enough food, and [even food] to spare, but I am perishing (dying) here of hunger!

18 I will get up and go to my father, and I will say to him, Father, I have sinned against heaven and in your sight.

19 I am no longer worthy to be called your son; [just] make me like one of your hired servants.

20 So he got up and came to his [own] father. But while he was still a long way off, his father saw him and was moved with pity and tenderness [for him]; and he ran and embraced him and kissed him [ˢfervently].

21 And the son said to him, Father, I have sinned against heaven and in your sight; I am no longer worthy to be called your son [I no longer deserve to be recognized as a son of yours]!

22 But the father said to his bond servants, Bring quickly the best robe (the festive robe of honor) and put it on him; and give him a ring for his hand and sandals for his feet. [Gen. 41:42; Zech. 3:4.]

23 And bring out ˢthat [wheat-fattened calf and kill it; and let us ᵗrevel and feast and be happy and make merry,

24 Because this my son was dead and is alive again; he was lost and is found! And they began to ᵗrevel and feast and make merry.

25 But his older son was in the

---

p Joseph Thayer, *A Greek-English Lexicon.*   q G. Abbott-Smith, *Manual Greek Lexicon.*   r Many ancient manuscripts so read.   s William Tyndale, *The Tyndale Bible.*   t Alexander Souter, *Pocket Lexicon.*

field; and as he returned and came near the house, he heard music and dancing.

26 And having called one of the servant [boys] to him, he began to ask what this meant.

27 And he said to him, Your brother has come, and your father has killed [u]that [wheat-]fattened calf, because he has received him back safe and well.

28 But [the elder brother] was angry [with deep-seated wrath] and resolved not to go in. Then his father came out and began to plead with him,

29 But he answered his father, Look! These many years I have served you, and I have never disobeyed your command. Yet you never gave me [so much as] a [little] kid, that I might [v]revel *and* feast *and* be happy *and* make merry with my friends;

30 But when this son of yours arrived, who has devoured your estate with immoral women, you have killed for him [u]that [wheat-]fattened calf!

31 And the father said to him, Son, you are always with me, and all that is mine is yours.

32 But it was fitting to make merry, to [v]revel *and* feast and rejoice, for this brother of yours was dead and is alive again! He was lost and is found!

CHAPTER 16

ALSO [Jesus] said to the disciples, There was a certain rich man who had a [w]manager of his estate, and accusations [against this man] were brought to him, that he was squandering his [master's] possessions.

2 And he called him and said to him, What is this that I hear about you? Turn in the account of your management [of my affairs], for you can be [my] manager no longer.

3 And the manager of the estate said to himself, What shall I do, seeing that my master is taking the management away from me? I am not able to dig, and I am ashamed to beg.

4 I have come to know what I will do, so that they [my master's debtors] may accept *and* welcome me into their houses when I am put out of the management.

5 So he summoned his master's debtors one by one, and he said to the first, How much do you owe my master?

6 He said, A hundred measures [about 900 gallons] of oil. And he said to him, Take back your written acknowledgement of [x]obligation, and sit down quickly and write fifty [about 450 gallons].

7 After that he said to another, And how much do you owe? He said, A hundred measures [about 900 bushels] of wheat. He said to him, Take back your written acknowledgement of [y]obligation, and write eighty [about 700 bushels].

8 And [his] master praised the dishonest (unjust) manager for acting [z]shrewdly *and* [y]prudently; for the sons of this age are shrewder *and* more prudent *and* wiser in [[a]relation to] their own generation [to their own age and [u]kind] than are the sons of light.

9 And I tell you, make friends for yourselves by means of unrighteous mammon ([y]deceitful riches, money, possessions), so that when it fails, they [those you have favored] may receive *and* welcome you into the everlasting habitations (dwellings).

10 He who is faithful in a very little [thing] is faithful also in much, and he

u William Tyndale, *The Tyndale Bible.*   v Alexander Souter, *Pocket Lexicon.*   w James Moulton and George Milligan, *The Vocabulary.*   x John Wycliffe, *The Wycliffe Bible.*   y John Wycliffe, *The Wycliffe Bible.*   z Marvin Vincent, *Word Studies.*   a Marvin Vincent, *Word Studies.*

who is dishonest *and* unjust in a very little [thing] is dishonest *and* unjust also in much.

11 Therefore if you have not been faithful in the [case of] unrighteous mammon ([b]deceitful riches, money, possessions), who will entrust to you the true riches?

12 And if you have not proved faithful in that which belongs to another [whether God or man], who will give you that which is your own [that is, [c]the true riches]?

13 No servant is able to serve two masters; for either he will hate the one and love the other, or he will stand by *and* be devoted to the one and despise the other. You cannot serve God and mammon (riches, or [d]anything in which you trust and on which you rely).

14 Now the Pharisees, who were covetous *and* lovers of money, heard all these things [taken together], and they began to sneer at *and* ridicule *and* scoff at Him.

15 But He said to them, You are the ones who declare yourselves just *and* upright before men, but God knows your hearts. For what is exalted *and* highly thought of among men is detestable *and* abhorrent (an abomination) in the sight of God. [I Sam. 16:7; Prov. 21:2.]

16 Until John came, there were the Law and the Prophets; since then the good news (the Gospel) of the kingdom of God is being preached, and everyone strives violently to go in [would force his [e]own way rather than God's way into it].

17 Yet it is easier for heaven and earth to pass away than for one dot of the Law to fail *and* become void.

18 Whoever divorces (dismisses and repudiates) his wife and marries another commits adultery, and he who marries a woman who is divorced from her husband commits adultery.

19 There was a certain rich man who [habitually] clothed himself in purple and fine linen and [f]reveled *and* feasted *and* made merry in splendor every day.

20 And at his gate there [f]was [carelessly] dropped down *and* left a certain [f]utterly destitute man named Lazarus, [reduced to begging alms and] covered with [c]ulcerated] sores.

21 He [eagerly] desired to be satisfied with what fell from the rich man's table; moreover, the dogs even came and licked his sores.

22 And it occurred that the man [reduced to] begging died and was carried by the angels to Abraham's bosom. The rich man also died and was buried.

23 And in Hades (the realm of the dead), being in torment, he lifted up his eyes and saw Abraham far away, and Lazarus in his bosom.

24 And he cried out and said, Father Abraham, have pity *and* mercy on me and send Lazarus to dip the tip of his finger in water and cool my tongue, for I am in anguish in this flame.

25 But Abraham said, Child, remember that you in your lifetime fully received [what is due you in] comforts *and* delights, and Lazarus in like manner the discomforts *and* distresses; but now he is comforted here and you are in anguish.

26 And besides all this, between us and you a great chasm has been fixed, in order that those who want to pass from this [place] to you may not be able, and no one may pass from there to us.

27 And [the man] said, Then, fa-

---

b Alexander Souter, *Pocket Lexicon.*   c Marvin Vincent, *Word Studies.*   d Joseph Thayer, *A Greek-English Lexicon.*   e Gerrit Verkuyl, *The Berkeley Version in Modern English.*   f Marvin Vincent, *Word Studies.*

ther, I beseech you to send him to my father's house—

28 For I have five brothers—so that he may give [solemn] testimony *and* warn them, lest they too come into this place of torment.

29 But Abraham said, They have Moses and the Prophets; let them hear *and* listen to them.

30 But he answered, No, father Abraham, but if someone from the dead goes to them, they will repent (ᵍchange their minds for the better and heartily amend their ways, with abhorrence of their past sins).

31 He said to him, If they do not hear *and* listen to Moses and the Prophets, neither will they be persuaded *and* convinced *and* believe [even] if someone should rise from the dead.

CHAPTER 17

AND [Jesus] said to His disciples, Temptations (snares, traps set to entice to sin) are sure to come, but woe to him by *or* through whom they come!

2 It would be more profitable for him if a millstone were hung around his neck and he were hurled into the sea than that he should cause to sin *or* be a snare to one of these little ones [ʰlowly in rank or influence].

3 ⁱPay attention *and* always be on your guard [looking out for one another]. If your brother sins (misses the mark), solemnly tell him so *and* reprove him, and if he repents (feels sorry for having sinned), forgive him.

4 And even if he sins against you seven times in a day, and turns to you seven times and says, I repent [I am sorry], you must forgive him (give up resentment and consider the offense as recalled and annulled).

5 The apostles said to the Lord,

Increase our faith (that trust and confidence that spring from our belief in God).

6 And the Lord answered, If you had faith (trust and confidence in God) even [so small] like a grain of mustard seed, you could say to this mulberry tree, Be pulled up by the roots, and be planted in the sea, and it would obey you.

7 Will any man of you who has a servant plowing or tending sheep say to him when he has come in from the field, Come at once and take your place at the table?

8 Will he not instead tell him, Get my supper ready and gird yourself and serve me while I eat and drink; then afterward you yourself shall eat and drink?

9 Is he grateful *and* does he praise the servant because he did what he was ordered to do?

10 Even so on your part, when you have done everything that was assigned *and* commanded you, say, We are unworthy servants [possessing no merit, for we have not gone beyond our obligation]; we have [merely] done what was our duty to do.

11 As He went on His way to Jerusalem, it occurred that [Jesus] was passing [along the border] between Samaria and Galilee.

12 And as He was going into one village, He was met by ten lepers, who stood at a distance.

13 And they raised up their voices and called, Jesus, Master, take pity *and* have mercy on us!

14 And when He saw them, He said to them, Go [at once] and show yourselves to the priests. And as they went, they were cured *and* made clean. [Lev. 14:2–32.]

15 Then one of them, upon seeing that he was cured, turned back, ʲrec-

---

ognizing *and* thanking *and* praising God with a loud voice;

16 And he fell prostrate at Jesus' feet, thanking Him [over and over]. And he was a Samaritan.

17 Then Jesus asked, Were not [all] ten cleansed? Where are the nine?

18 Was there no one found to return and to ᵏrecognize *and* give thanks *and* praise to God except this alien?

19 And He said to him, Get up and go on your way. Your faith (your trust and confidence that spring from your belief in God) has restored you to health.

20 Asked by the Pharisees when the kingdom of God would come, He replied to them by saying, The kingdom of God does not come with signs to be observed *or* with visible display,

21 Nor will people say, Look! Here [it is]! or, See, [it is] there! For behold, the kingdom of God is within you [in your hearts] *and* among you [surrounding you].

22 And He said to the disciples, The time is coming when you will long to see [even] one of the days of the Son of Man, and you will not see [it].

23 And they will say to you, Look! [He is] there! or, Look! [He is] here! But do not go out or follow [them].

24 For like the lightning, that flashes and lights up the sky from one end to the other, so will the Son of Man be in His [own] day.

25 But first He must suffer many things and be disapproved *and* repudiated *and* rejected by this age and generation.

26 And [just] as it was in the days of Noah, so will it be in the time of the Son of Man.

27 [People] ate, they drank, they married, they were given in marriage, right up to the day when Noah went into the ark, and the flood came and destroyed them all. [Gen. 6:5–8; 7:6–24.]

28 So also [it was the same] as it was in the days of Lot. [People] ate, they drank, they bought, they sold, they planted, they built;

29 But on the [very] day that Lot went out of Sodom, it rained fire and brimstone from heaven and destroyed [them] all.

30 That is the way it will be on the day that the Son of Man is revealed. [Gen. 18:20–33; 19:24, 25.]

31 On that day let him who is on the housetop, with his belongings in the house, not come down [and go inside] to carry them away; and likewise let him who is in the field not turn back.

32 Remember Lot's wife! [Gen. 19:26.]

33 Whoever tries to preserve his life will lose it, but whoever loses his life will preserve and ᶦquicken it.

34 I tell you, in that night there will be two men in one bed; one will be taken and the other will be left.

35 There will be two women grinding together; one will be taken and the other will be left.

36 ᵐ*Two men will be in the field; one will be taken and the other will be left.*

37 Then they asked Him, Where, Lord? He said to them, Wherever the dead body is, there will the vultures *or* eagles be gathered together.

CHAPTER 18

ALSO [Jesus] told them a parable to the effect that they ought always to pray and not to ⁿturn coward (faint, lose heart, and give up).

---

k Hermann Cremer, *Biblico-Theological Lexicon.* manuscripts do not contain this verse.   l John Wycliffe, *The Wycliffe Bible.*   m Many   n Marvin Vincent, *Word Studies.*

2 He said, In a certain city there was a judge who neither reverenced *and* feared God nor respected *or* considered man.

3 And there was a widow in that city who kept coming to him and saying, Protect *and* defend *and* give me justice against my adversary.

4 And for a time he would not; but later he said to himself, Though I have neither reverence *or* fear for God nor respect *or* consideration for man,

5 Yet because this widow continues to bother me, I will defend *and* protect *and* avenge her, lest she give me ºintolerable annoyance *and* wear me out by her continual coming *or* Pat the last she come and rail on me *or* ªassault me *or* ʳstrangle me.

6 Then the Lord said, Listen to what the unjust judge says!

7 And will not [our just] God defend *and* protect *and* avenge His elect (His chosen ones), who cry to Him day and night? Will He ºdefer them *and* ªdelay help on their behalf?

8 I tell you, He will defend *and* protect *and* avenge them speedily. However, when the Son of Man comes, will He find [ªpersistence in] faith on the earth?

9 He also told this parable to some people who trusted in themselves *and* were confident that they were righteous [that they were upright and in right standing with God] and scorned *and* made nothing of all the rest of men:

10 Two men went up into the temple [ˢenclosure] to pray, the one a Pharisee and the other a tax collector.

11 The Pharisee ªtook his stand ostentatiously and began to pray thus before *and* with himself: God, I

thank You that I am not like the rest of men—extortioners (robbers), swindlers [unrighteous in heart and life], adulterers—or even like this tax collector here.

12 I fast twice a week; I give tithes of all that I gain.

13 But the tax collector, [merely] standing at a distance, would not even lift up his eyes to heaven, but kept striking his breast, saying, O God, be favorable (be gracious, be merciful) to me, the ºespecially wicked sinner that I am!

14 I tell you, this man went down to his home justified (forgiven and made upright and in right standing with God), rather than the other man; for everyone who exalts himself will be humbled, but he who humbles himself will be exalted.

15 Now they were also bringing [even] babies to Him that He might touch them, and when the disciples noticed it, they reproved them.

16 But Jesus called them [ᵗthe parents] to Him, saying, Allow the little children to come to Me, and do not hinder them, for to such [as these] belongs the kingdom of God.

17 Truly I say to you, whoever does not accept *and* receive *and* welcome the kingdom of God like a little child [does] shall not in any way enter it [at all].

18 And a certain ruler asked Him, Good Teacher [You who are ºessentially and perfectly ªmorally good], what shall I do to inherit eternal life [to partake of eternal salvation in the Messiah's kingdom]?

19 Jesus said to him, Why do you call Me [ºessentially and perfectly ªmorally] good? No one is [ºessentially and perfectly ªmorally] good—except God only.

o Joseph Thayer, *A Greek-English Lexicon*.   p William Tyndale, *The Tyndale Bible*.   q Marvin Vincent, *Word Studies*.   r John Wycliffe, *The Wycliffe Bible*.   s Richard Trench, *Synonyms of the New Testament*.   t Matthew Henry, *Commentary on the Holy Bible*.   u Hermann Cremer, *Biblico-Theological Lexicon*.

20 You know the commandments: Do not commit adultery, do not kill, do not steal, do not witness falsely, honor your father and your mother. [Exod. 20:12–16; Deut. 5:16–20.]

21 And he replied, All these I have kept from my youth.

22 And when Jesus heard it, He said to him, One thing you still lack. Sell everything that you have and ᵛdivide [the money] among the poor, and you will have [rich] treasure in heaven; and come back [and] follow Me [become My disciple, join My party, and accompany Me].

23 But when he heard this, he became distressed and very sorrowful, for he was rich—exceedingly so.

24 Jesus, observing him, said, How difficult it is for those who have wealth to enter the kingdom of God!

25 For it is easier for a camel to enter through a needle's eye than [for] a rich man to enter the kingdom of God.

26 And those who heard it said, Then who can be saved?

27 But He said, What is impossible with men is possible with God. [Gen. 18:14; Jer. 32:17.]

28 And Peter said, See, we have left our own [things—home, family, and business] and have followed You.

29 And He said to them, I say to you truly, there is no one who has left house or wife or brothers or parents or children for the sake of the kingdom of God

30 Who will not receive in return many times more in this world and, in the coming age, eternal life.

31 Then taking the Twelve [apostles] aside, He said to them, Listen! We are going up to Jerusalem, and all things that are written about the Son of Man through and by the prophets will be fulfilled. [Isa. 53:1–12.]

32 For He will be handed over to the Gentiles and will be made sport of and scoffed and jeered at and insulted and spit upon. [Isa. 50:6.]

33 They will flog Him and kill Him; and on the third day He will rise again. [Ps. 16:10.]

34 But they understood nothing of these things; His words were a mystery and hidden from them, and they did not comprehend what He was telling them.

35 As He came near to Jericho, it occurred that a blind man was sitting by the roadside begging.

36 And hearing a crowd going by, he asked what it meant.

37 They told him, Jesus of Nazareth is passing by.

38 And he shouted, saying, Jesus, Son of David, take pity and have mercy on me!

39 But those who were in front reproved him, telling him to keep quiet; yet he ʷscreamed and shrieked so much the more, Son of David, take pity and have mercy on me!

40 Then Jesus stood still and ordered that he be led to Him; and when he came near, Jesus asked him,

41 What do you want Me to do for you? He said, Lord, let me receive my sight!

42 And Jesus said to him, Receive your sight! Your faith (ˣyour trust and confidence that spring from your faith in God) has healed you.

43 And instantly he received his sight and began to follow Jesus, ˣrecognizing, praising, and honoring God; and all the people, when they saw it, praised God.

---

v Joseph Thayer, *A Greek-English Lexicon.*   w Marvin Vincent, *Word Studies.*   x Hermann Cremer, *Biblico-Theological Lexicon.*

CHAPTER 19

AND [Jesus] entered Jericho and was passing through it.

2 And there was a man called Zacchaeus, a chief tax collector, and [he was] rich.

3 And he was trying to see Jesus, which One He was, but he could not on account of the crowd, because he was small in stature.

4 So he ran on ahead and climbed up in a sycamore tree in order to see Him, for He was about to pass that way.

5 And when Jesus reached the place, He looked up and said to him, Zacchaeus, hurry and come down; for I must stay at your house today.

6 So he hurried and came down, and he received *and* welcomed Him joyfully.

7 And when the people saw it, they all ymuttered among themselves *and* indignantly complained, He has gone in to be the guest of *and* lodge with a man who is devoted to sin *and* preeminently a sinner.

8 So then Zacchaeus stood up and solemnly declared to the Lord, See, Lord, the half of my goods I [now] give [by way of restoration] to the poor, and if I have cheated anyone out of anything, I [now] restore four times as much. [Exod. 22:1; Lev. 6:5; Num. 5:6, 7.]

9 And Jesus said to him, Today is [zMessianic and spiritual] salvation come to [all the members of] this household, since Zacchaeus too is a [real spiritual] son of Abraham;

10 For the Son of Man came to seek and to save that which was lost.

11 Now as they were listening to these things, He proceeded to tell a parable, because He was approaching Jerusalem and because they thought that the kingdom of God was going to be brought to light *and* shown forth immediately.

12 He therefore said, A certain nobleman went into a distant country to obtain for himself a kingdom and then to return.

13 Calling ten of his [own] bond servants, he gave them ten minas [each equal to about one hundred days' wages or nearly twenty dollars] and said to them, aBuy *and* sell with these bwhile I go *and* then return.

14 But his citizens detested him and sent an embassy after him to say, We do not want this man to become ruler over us.

15 When he returned after having received the kingdom, he ordered these bond servants to whom he had given the money to be called to him, that he might know how much each one had made by abuying *and* selling.

16 The first one came before him, and he said, Lord, your mina has made ten [additional] minas.

17 And he said to him, Well done, excellent bond servant! Because you have been faithful *and* trustworthy in a very little [thing], you shall have authority over ten cities.

18 The second one also came and said, Lord, your mina has made five more minas.

19 And he said also to him, And you will take charge over five cities.

20 Then another came and said, Lord, here is your mina, which I have kept laid up in a zhandkerchief.

21 For I was [constantly] afraid of you, because you are a stern (hard, severe) man; you pick up what you did not lay down, and you reap what you did not sow.

22 He said to the servant, I will judge *and* condemn you out of your own mouth, you wicked slave! You knew [did you] that I was a stern

---

y G. Abbott-Smith, *Manual Greek Lexicon.*   z James Moulton and George Milligan, *The Vocabulary.*
a William Tyndale, *The Tyndale Bible.*   b Marvin Vincent, *Word Studies.*

(hard, severe) man, picking up what I did not lay down, and reaping what I did not sow?

23 Then why did you not put my money in a bank, so that on my return, I might have collected it with interest?

24 And he said to the bystanders, Take the mina away from him and give it to him who has the ten minas.

25 And they said to him, Lord, he has ten minas [already]!

26 And [said Jesus,] I tell you that to everyone who gets and has will more be given, but from the man who does not get and does not have, even what he has will be taken away.

27 [The indignant king ended by saying] But as for these enemies of mine who did not want me to reign over them—bring them here and cslaughter them in my presence!

28 And after saying these things, Jesus went on ahead of them, going up to Jerusalem.

29 When He came near Bethphage and Bethany at the mount called [the Mount of] Olives, He sent two of His disciples,

30 Telling [them], Go into the village yonder; there, as you go in, you will find a donkey's colt tied, on which no man has ever yet sat. Loose it and bring [it here].

31 If anybody asks you, Why are you untying [it]? you shall say this: Because the Lord has need of it.

32 So those who were sent went away and found it [just] as He had told them.

33 And as they were loosening the colt, its owners said to them, Why are you untying the colt?

34 And they said, The Lord has need of it.

35 And they brought it to Jesus; then they threw their garments over the colt and set Jesus upon it. [Zech. 9:9.]

36 And as He rode along, the people kept spreading their garments on the road. [II Kings 9:13.]

37 As He was approaching [the city], at the descent of the Mount of Olives, the whole crowd of the disciples began to rejoice and to praise God [extolling Him exultantly and] loudly for all the mighty miracles and works of power that they had witnessed,

38 Crying, Blessed (celebrated with praises) is the King Who comes in the name of the Lord! Peace in heaven [dfreedom there from all the distresses that are experienced as the result of sin] and glory (majesty and splendor) in the highest [heaven]! [Ps. 118:26.]

39 And some of the Pharisees from the throng said to Jesus, Teacher, reprove Your disciples!

40 He replied, I tell you that if these keep silent, the very stones will cry out. [Hab. 2:11.]

41 And as He approached, He saw the city, and He wept [caudibly] over it,

42 Exclaiming, Would that you had known personally, even at least in this your day, the things that make for peace (for dfreedom from all the distresses that are experienced as the result of sin and upon which your peace—your esecurity, safety, prosperity, and happiness— depends)! But now they are hidden from your eyes.

43 For a time is coming upon you when your enemies will throw up a cbank [with pointed stakes] about you and surround you and shut you in on every side. [Isa. 29:3; Jer. 6:6; Ezek. 4:2.]

44 And they will dash you down to

c Marvin Vincent, Word Studies.   d Hermann Cremer, Biblico-Theological Lexicon.   e Joseph Thayer, A Greek-English Lexicon.

the ground, you [Jerusalem] and your children within you; and they will not leave in you one stone upon another, [all] because you did not come progressively to recognize *and* know *and* understand [from observation and experience] the time of your visitation [that is, when God was visiting you, the time [f]in which God showed Himself gracious toward you and offered you salvation through Christ].

45 Then He went into the temple [[g]enclosure] and began to drive out those who were selling,

46 Telling them, It is written, My house shall be a house of prayer; but you have made it a [h]cave of robbers. [Isa. 56:7; Jer. 7:11.]

47 And He continued to teach day after day in the temple [[g]porches and courts]. The chief priests and scribes and the leading men of the people were seeking to put Him to death,

48 But they did not discover anything they could do, for all the people hung upon His words *and* [i]stuck by Him.

CHAPTER 20

ONE DAY as Jesus was instructing the people in the temple [[g]porches] and preaching the good news (the Gospel), the chief priests and the scribes came up with the elders (members of the Sanhedrin)

2 And said to Him, Tell us by what [sort of] authority You are doing these things? Or who is it who gave You this authority?

3 He replied to them, I will also ask you a question. Now answer Me:

4 Was the baptism of John from heaven, or from men?

5 And they argued *and* discussed [it] *and* reasoned together [j]with

themselves, saying, If we reply, From heaven, He will say, Why then did you not believe him?

6 But if we answer, From men, all the people will stone us [j]to death, for they are [j]long since firmly convinced that John was a prophet.

7 So they replied that they did not know from where it came.

8 Then Jesus said to them, Neither will I tell you by what authority I do these things.

9 Then He began to relate to the people this parable ([f]this story to figuratively portray what He had to say): A man planted a vineyard and leased it to some vinedressers and went into another country for a long stay. [Isa. 5:1–7.]

10 When the [right] season came, he sent a bond servant to the tenants, that they might give him [his part] of the fruit of the vineyard; but the tenants beat ([h]thrashed) him and sent him away empty-handed.

11 And he sent still another servant; him they also beat ([h]thrashed) and dishonored *and* insulted him [k]disgracefully and sent him away empty-handed.

12 And he sent yet a third; this one they wounded and threw out [of the vineyard].

13 Then the owner of the vineyard said, What shall I do? I will send my beloved son; it is [j]probable that they will respect him.

14 But when the tenants saw him, they argued among themselves, saying, This is the heir; let us kill him, so that the inheritance may be ours.

15 So they drove him out of the vineyard and killed him. What then will the owner of the vineyard do to them?

16 He will come and [[f]utterly] put an end to those tenants and will give

---

f Joseph Thayer, *A Greek-English Lexicon.*   g Richard Trench, *Synonyms of the New Testament.*
h James Moulton and George Milligan, *The Vocabulary.*   i William Tyndale, *The Tyndale Bible.*
j Marvin Vincent, *Word Studies.*   k Alexander Souter, *Pocket Lexicon.*

the vineyard to others. When they [the chief priests and the scribes and the elders] heard this, they said, May it never be!

17 But [Jesus] looked at them and said, What then is [the meaning of] this that is written: The [very] Stone which the builders rejected has become the chief Stone of the corner [Cornerstone]? [Ps. 118:22, 23.]

18 Everyone who falls on that Stone will be broken [in pieces]; but upon whomever it falls, It will crush him [winnow him and [1]scatter him as dust]. [Isa. 8:14, 15; Dan. 2:34, 35.]

19 The scribes and the chief priests desired *and* tried to find a way to arrest Him at that very hour, but they were afraid of the people; for they discerned that He had related this parable against them.

20 So they watched [for an opportunity to ensnare] Him, and sent spies who pretended to be upright (honest and sincere), that they might lay hold of something He might say, so as to turn Him over to the control and authority of the governor.

21 They asked Him, Teacher, we know that You speak and teach what is right, and that You show no partiality to anyone but teach the way of God honestly *and* in truth.

22 Is it lawful for us to give tribute to Caesar or not?

23 But He recognized *and* understood their cunning *and* [m]unscrupulousness and said to them,

24 Show Me a denarius (a coin)! Whose image and inscription does it have? They answered, Caesar's.

25 He said to them, Then render to Caesar the things that are Caesar's, [n]and to God the things that are God's.

26 So they could not in the presence of the people take hold of anything He said to turn it against Him; but marveling at His reply, they were silent.

27 Also there came to Him some Sadducees, those who say that there is no resurrection.

28 And they asked Him a question, saying, Teacher, Moses wrote for us [a law] that if a man's brother dies, leaving a wife and no children, the man shall take the woman and raise up offspring for his brother. [Deut. 25:5, 6.]

29 Now there were seven brothers; and the first took a wife and died without [having any] children.

30 And the second

31 And then the third took her, and in like manner all seven, and they died, leaving no children.

32 Last of all, the woman died also.

33 Now in the resurrection whose wife will the woman be? For the seven married her.

34 And Jesus said to them, The people of this world *and* present age marry and are given in marriage;

35 But those who are considered worthy to gain that other world *and* that future age and to attain to the resurrection from the dead neither marry nor are given in marriage;

36 For they cannot die again, but they are [o]angel-like *and* [p]equal to angels. And being sons of *and* [q]sharers in the resurrection, they are sons of God.

37 But that the dead are raised [[e]from death]—even Moses made known *and* showed in the passage concerning the [burning] bush, where he calls the Lord, The God of Abraham, the God of Isaac, and the God of Jacob. [Exod. 3:6.]

38 Now He is not the God of the dead, but of the living, for to Him all men are alive [whether in the body or

l James Moulton and George Milligan, *The Vocabulary*.   m Marvin Vincent, *Word Studies*.   n A rebuke of emperor worship.   o Hermann Cremer, *Biblico-Theological Lexicon*.   p G. Abbott-Smith, *Manual Greek Lexicon*.   q Joseph Thayer, *A Greek-English Lexicon*.

out of it] *and* they are alive [not dead] unto Him [in definite relationship to Him].

39 And some of the scribes replied, Teacher, you have spoken well *and* expertly [ʳso that there is no room for blame].

40 For they did not dare to question Him further.

41 But He asked them, How can people say that the Christ (the Messiah, the Anointed One) is David's Son?

42 For David himself says in [the] Book of Psalms, The Lord said to my Lord, Sit at My right hand

43 Until I make Your enemies a footstool for Your feet. [Ps. 110:1.]

44 So David calls Him Lord; how then is He his Son?

45 And with all the people listening, He said to His disciples,

46 Beware of the scribes, who like to walk about in long robes and love to be saluted [with honor] in places where people congregate and love the front *and* best seats in the synagogues and places of distinction at feasts,

47 Who make away with *and* devour widows' houses, and [to cover it up] with pretense make long prayers. They will receive the greater condemnation (the heavier sentence, the severer punishment).

CHAPTER 21

LOOKING UP, [Jesus] saw the rich people putting their gifts into the treasury.

2 And He saw also a poor widow putting in two mites (copper coins).

3 And He said, Truly I say to you, this poor widow has put in more than all of them;

4 For they all gave out of their abundance (their surplus); but she

has contributed out of her lack *and* her want, putting in all that she had on which to live.

5 And as some were saying of the temple that it was decorated with handsome (shapely and magnificent) stones and consecrated offerings [ʳlaid up to be kept], He said,

6 As for all this that you [thoughtfully] look at, the time will come when there shall not be left here one stone upon another that will not be thrown down.

7 And they asked Him, Teacher, when will this happen? And what sign will there be when this is about to occur?

8 And He said, Be on your guard *and* be careful that you are not led astray; for many will come in My name [ʳappropriating to themselves the name Messiah which belongs to Me], saying, I am He! and, The time is at hand! Do not go out after them.

9 And when you hear of wars and insurrections (disturbances, disorder, and confusion), do not become alarmed *and* panic-stricken *and* terrified; for all this must take place first, but the end will not [come] immediately.

10 Then He told them, Nation will rise against nation, and kingdom against kingdom. [II Chron. 15:6; Isa. 19:2.]

11 There will be mighty *and* violent earthquakes, and in various places famines and pestilences (plagues: ˢmalignant and contagious or infectious epidemic diseases which are deadly and devastating); and there will be sights of terror and great signs from heaven.

12 But previous to all this, they will lay their hands on you and persecute you, turning you over to the synagogues and prisons, and you will be

---

r Joseph Thayer, *A Greek-English Lexicon.*   s *Webster's New International Dictionary* offers this phrase
as a definition of "plague" and "pestilence."

led away before kings and governors for My name's sake.

13 This will be a time (an opportunity) for you to bear testimony.

14 Resolve and settle it in your minds not to meditate and prepare beforehand how you are to make your defense and how you will answer.

15 For I [Myself] will give you a mouth and such utterance and wisdom that all of your foes combined will be unable to stand against or refute.

16 You will be delivered up and betrayed even by parents and brothers and relatives and friends, and [some] of you they will put to death.

17 And you will be hated (despised) by everyone because [you bear] My name and for its sake.

18 But not a hair of your head shall perish. [I Sam. 14:45.]

19 By your steadfastness and patient endurance you 'shall win the ᵘtrue life of your souls.

20 But when you see Jerusalem surrounded by armies, then know and understand that its desolation has come near.

21 Then let those who are in Judea flee to the mountains, and let those who are inside [the city] get out of it, and let not those who are out in the country come into it;

22 For those are days of vengeance [of rendering full justice or satisfaction], that all things that are written may be fulfilled.

23 Alas for those who are pregnant and for those who have babies which they are nursing in those days! For great misery and anguish and distress shall be upon the land and indignation and punishment and retribution upon this people.

24 They will fall by ᵛthe mouth and the edge of the sword and will be led away as captives to and among all nations; and Jerusalem will be trodden down by the Gentiles until the times of the Gentiles are fulfilled (completed). [Isa. 63:18; Dan. 8:13.]

25 And there will be signs in the sun and moon and stars; and upon the earth [there will be] distress (trouble and anguish) of nations in bewilderment and perplexity [ᵂwithout resources, left wanting, embarrassed, in doubt, not knowing which way to turn] at the roaring (ᵗthe echo) of the tossing of the sea, [Isa. 13:10; Joel 2:10; Zeph. 1:15.]

26 Men swooning away or expiring with fear and dread and apprehension and expectation of the things that are coming on the world; for the [very] powers of the heavens will be shaken and ᵘcaused to totter.

27 And then they will see the Son of Man coming in a cloud with great (transcendent and overwhelming) power and [all His kingly] glory (majesty and splendor). [Dan. 7:13, 14.]

28 Now when these things begin to occur, look up and lift up your heads, because your redemption (deliverance) is drawing near.

29 And He told them a parable: Look at the fig tree and all the trees;

30 When they put forth their buds and come out in leaf, you see for yourselves and perceive and know that summer is already near.

31 Even so, when you see these things taking place, understand and know that the kingdom of God is at hand.

32 Truly I tell you, this generation (ᵂthose living at that definite period of time) will not perish and pass away until all has taken place.

33 The ˣsky and the earth (ᵘthe uni-

t Marvin Vincent, *Word Studies.*   u Joseph Thayer, *A Greek-English Lexicon.*   v John Wycliffe, *The Wycliffe Bible.*   w Hermann Cremer, *Biblico-Theological Lexicon.*   x James Moulton and George Milligan, *The Vocabulary.*

verse, the world) will pass away, but My words will not pass away,

34 But take heed to yourselves *and* be on your guard, lest your hearts be overburdened *and* depressed (weighed down) with the ʸgiddiness *and* headache *and* ᶻnausea of self-indulgence, drunkenness, and worldly worries *and* cares pertaining to [the ᵃbusiness of] this life, and [lest] that day come upon you suddenly like a trap *or* a noose;

35 For it will come upon all who live upon the face of the entire earth.

36 Keep awake then *and* watch at all times [be discreet, attentive, and ready], praying that you may have the full strength *and* ability *and* be accounted worthy to escape all these things [taken together] that will take place, and to stand in the presence of the Son of Man.

37 Now in the daytime Jesus was teaching in [ᵇthe porches and courts of] the temple, but at night He would go out and stay on the mount called Olivet.

38 And early in the morning all the people came to Him in the temple [ᵇporches or courts] to listen to Him.

CHAPTER 22

NOW THE Festival of Unleavened Bread was drawing near, which is called the Passover.

2 And the chief priests and the scribes were seeking how to do away with [Jesus], for they feared the people.

3 But [then] Satan entered into Judas, called Iscariot, who was one of the Twelve [apostles].

4 And he went away and discussed with the chief priests and captains how he might betray Him *and* deliver Him up to them,

5 And they were delighted and pledged [themselves] to give him money.

6 So he agreed [to this], and sought an opportunity to betray Him to them [without an uprising] in the absence of the throng.

7 Then came the day of Unleavened Bread on which the Passover [lamb] had to be slain. [Exod. 12:18–20; Deut. 16:5–8.]

8 So Jesus sent Peter and John, saying, Go and prepare for us the Passover meal, that we may eat it.

9 They said to Him, Where do You want us to prepare [it]?

10 He said to them, Behold, when you have gone into the city, a man carrying an earthen jug *or* pitcher of water will meet you; follow him into the house which he enters,

11 And say to the master of the house, The Teacher asks you, Where is the guest room, where I may eat the Passover [meal] with My disciples?

12 And he will show you a large room upstairs, furnished [with carpets and with couches properly spread]; there make [your] preparations.

13 And they went and found it [just] as He had said to them; and they made ready the Passover [supper].

14 And when the hour came, [Jesus] reclined at table, and the apostles with Him.

15 And He said to them, I have earnestly *and* intensely desired to eat this Passover with you before I suffer;

16 For I say to you, I shall eat it no more until it is fulfilled in the kingdom of God.

17 And He took a cup, and when He had given thanks, He said, Take

---

y Joseph Thayer, *A Greek-English Lexicon.*   z G. Abbott-Smith, *Manual Greek Lexicon.*   a John Wycliffe, *The Wycliffe Bible.*   b Richard Trench, *Synonyms of the New Testament.*

this and divide *and* distribute it among yourselves;

18 For I say to you that from now on I shall not drink of the fruit of the vine at all until the kingdom of God comes.

19 Then He took a loaf [of bread], and when He had given thanks, He broke [it] and gave it to them saying, This is My body which is given for you; do this in remembrance of Me.

20 And in like manner, He took the cup after supper, saying, This cup is the new testament *or* covenant [ratified] in My blood, which is shed (poured out) for you.

21 But, behold, the hand of him who cis now engaged in betraying Me is with Me on the table. [Ps. 41:9.]

22 For the Son of Man is going as it has been determined *and* appointed, but woe to that man by whom He is betrayed *and* delivered up!

23 And they began to inquire among themselves which of them it was who was about to do this. [Ps. 41:9.]

24 Now can eager contention arose among them [as to] which of them was considered *and* reputed to be the greatest.

25 But Jesus said to them, The kings of the Gentiles dare deified by them *and* exercise lordship [druling as emperor-gods] over them; and those in authority over them are called benefactors *and* well-doers.

26 But this is not to be so with you; on the contrary, let him who is the greatest among you become like the youngest, and him who is the chief *and* leader like one who serves.

27 For who is the greater, the one who reclines at table (the master), or the one who serves? Is it not the one who reclines at table? But I am in your midst as One Who serves.

28 And you are those who have remained [throughout] *and* persevered with Me in My trials;

29 And as My Father has appointed a kingdom *and* conferred it on Me, so do I confer on you [the privilege and decree],

30 That you may eat and drink at My table in My kingdom and sit on thrones, judging the twelve tribes of Israel.

31 Simon, Simon (Peter), listen! Satan ehas asked excessively that [all of] you be given up to him [out of the power and keeping of God], that he might sift [all of] you like grain, [Job 1:6–12; Amos 9:9.]

32 But I have prayed especially for you [Peter], that your [own] faith may not fail; and when you yourself have turned again, strengthen *and* establish your brethren.

33 And [Simon Peter] said to Him, Lord, I am ready to go with You both to prison and to death.

34 But Jesus said, I tell you, Peter, before a [single] cock shall crow this day, you will three times [utterly] deny that you know Me.

35 And He said to them, When I sent you out with no purse or [provision] bag or sandals, did you lack anything? They answered, Nothing!

36 Then He said to them, But now let him who has a purse take it, and also [his provision] bag; and let him who has no sword sell his mantle and buy a sword.

37 For I tell you that this Scripture must yet be fulfilled in Me: And He was counted *and* classed among the wicked (the outlaws, the criminals); for what is written about Me has its fulfillment [has reached its end and is finally settled]. [Isa. 53:12.]

38 And they said, Look, Lord!

---

c Marvin Vincent, *Word Studies*.   d Kenneth Wuest, *Word Studies*.   e Joseph Thayer, *A Greek-English Lexicon*.

Here are two swords. And He said to them, It is enough.

39 And He came out and went, as was His habit, to the Mount of Olives, and the disciples also followed Him.

40 And when He came to the place, He said to them, Pray that you may not [at all] enter into temptation.

41 And He withdrew from them about a stone's throw and knelt down and prayed,

42 Saying, Father, if You are willing, remove this cup from Me; yet not My will, but [[f]]always] Yours be done.

43 And there appeared to Him an angel from heaven, strengthening Him in spirit.

44 And being in an agony [of mind], He prayed [all the] more earnestly *and* intently, and His sweat became like great [g]clots of blood dropping down upon the ground.

45 And when He got up from prayer, He came to the disciples and found them sleeping from grief,

46 And He said to them, Why do you sleep? Get up and pray that you may not enter [at all] into temptation.

47 And while He was still speaking, behold, there came a crowd, and the man called Judas, one of the Twelve [apostles], was going before [leading] them. He drew near to Jesus to kiss Him,

48 But Jesus said to him, Judas! Would you betray *and* deliver up the Son of Man with a kiss?

49 And when those who were around Him saw what was about to happen, they said, Lord, shall we strike with the sword?

50 And one of them struck the bond servant of the high priest and cut off his ear, the right one.

51 But Jesus said, Permit [g]them to go so far [as to seize Me]. And He touched the [h]little (insignificant) ear and healed him.

52 Then Jesus said to those who had come out against Him—the chief priests and captains of the temple and elders [of the Sanhedrin]—Have you come out with swords and clubs as [you would] against a robber?

53 When I was with you day after day in the temple [[i]enclosure], you did not stretch forth [your] hands against Me. But this is your hour—and the power [which] darkness [gives you has its way].

54 Then they seized Him and led Him away, bringing Him into the house of the high priest. Peter was following at a distance.

55 And when they had kindled a fire in the middle of the courtyard and were seated together, Peter sat among them.

56 Then a servant girl, seeing him as he sat in the firelight and gazing [intently] at him, said, This man too was with [j]Him.

57 But he denied it and said, Woman, I do not know Him!

58 And a little later someone else saw him and said, You are one of them also. But Peter said, Man, I am not!

59 And when about an hour more had elapsed, still another emphatically insisted, It is the truth that this man also was with Him, for he too is a Galilean!

60 But Peter said, Man, I do not know what you are talking about. And instantly, while he was still speaking, the cock crowed.

61 And the Lord turned and looked at Peter. And Peter recalled the Lord's words, how He had told him,

---

f Charles B. Williams, *The New Testament: A Translation*: "in the Greek present imperative, denoting continued action."   g Marvin Vincent, *Word Studies*.   h John Wycliffe, *The Wycliffe Bible*.
i Richard Trench, *Synonyms of the New Testament*.   j Capitalized because of what He is, the spotless Son of God, not what the speaker may have thought He was.

Before the cock crows today, you will deny Me thrice.

62 And he went out and wept bitterly [that is, with painfully moving grief].

63 Now the men who had Jesus in custody treated Him with contempt and scoffed at and ridiculed Him and beat Him;

64 They blindfolded Him also and asked Him, Prophesy! Who is it that struck kYou?

65 And they said many other evil and slanderous and insulting words against Him, reviling Him.

66 As soon as it was day, the assembly of the elders of the people gathered together, both chief priests and scribes; and they led Him into their council (the Sanhedrin), and they said,

67 If You are the Christ (the Messiah), tell us. But He said to them, If I tell you, you will not believe (trust in, cleave to, and rely on what I say);

68 And if I question you, you will not answer.

69 But hereafter (from this time on), the Son of Man shall be seated at the right hand of the power of God. [Ps. 110:1.]

70 And they all said, You are the Son of God, then? And He said to them, lIt is just as you say; I AM.

71 And they said, What further evidence do we need? For we have heard [it] ourselves from His own mouth!

CHAPTER 23

THEN THE whole assembly of them got up and conducted [Jesus] before Pilate.

2 And they began to accuse Him, asserting, We found this kMan perverting (misleading, corrupting, and turning away) our nation and forbid-

ding to pay tribute to Caesar, saying that He Himself is Christ (the Messiah, the Anointed One), a King!

3 So Pilate asked Him, Are You the King of the Jews? And He answered him, [lIt is just as] you say. [I AM.]

4 And Pilate said to the chief priests and the throngs, I find no guilt or crime in this Man.

5 But they were urgent and emphatic, saying, He stirs up and excites the people, teaching throughout all Judea—from Galilee, where He began, even to this place.

6 Upon hearing this, Pilate asked whether the Man was a Galilean.

7 And when he found out [certainly] that He belonged to Herod's jurisdiction, he sent Him up to Herod [a higher authority], who was also in Jerusalem in those days.

8 Now when Herod saw Jesus, he was exceedingly glad, for he had eagerly desired to see Him for a long time because of what he had heard concerning Him, and he was hoping to witness some sign (some striking evidence or spectacular performance) done by Him.

9 So he asked Him many questions, but He made no reply. [Isa. 53:7.]

10 Meanwhile, the chief priests and the scribes stood by, continuing vehemently and violently to accuse Him.

11 And Herod, with his soldiers, treated Him with contempt and scoffed at and ridiculed Him; then, dressing Him up in bright and gorgeous apparel, he sent Him back to Pilate. [Isa. 53:8.]

12 And that very day Herod and Pilate became friends with each other—[though] they had been at enmity before this.

k Capitalized because of what He is, the spotless Son of God, not what the speaker may have thought He was.
l Joseph Thayer, *A Greek-English Lexicon*.

13 Pilate then called together the chief priests and the rulers and the people.

14 And said to them, You brought this Man before me as One Who was perverting *and* misleading *and* [m]turning away *and* corrupting the people; and behold, after examining Him before you, I have not found any offense (crime or guilt) in this Man in regard to your accusations against Him;

15 No, nor indeed did Herod, for he sent Him back to us; behold, He has done nothing deserving of death.

16 I will therefore chastise Him *and* [m]deliver Him amended (reformed, taught His lesson) and release Him.

17 [n]*For it was necessary for him to release to them one prisoner at the Feast.*

18 But they all together raised a deep cry [from the depths of their throats], saying, Away with this Man! Release to us Barabbas!

19 He was a man who had been thrown into prison for raising a riot in the city, and for murder.

20 Once more Pilate called to them, wishing to release Jesus;

21 But they kept shouting out, Crucify, crucify Him!

22 A third time he said to them, Why? What wrong has He done? I have found [no offense or crime or guilt] in Him nothing deserving of death; I will therefore chastise Him [[o]in order to teach Him better] and release Him.

23 But they were insistent *and* urgent, demanding with loud cries that He should be crucified. And their voices prevailed (accomplished their purpose).

24 And Pilate gave sentence, that what they asked should be done.

25 So he released the man who had been thrown into prison for riot and murder, for whom they continued to ask, but Jesus he delivered up to be done with as they willed.

26 And as they led Him away, they seized one Simon of Cyrene, who was coming in from the country, and laid on him the cross and made him carry it behind Jesus.

27 And there accompanied [Jesus] a great multitude of the people, [including] women who bewailed and lamented Him.

28 But Jesus, turning toward them, said, Daughters of Jerusalem, do not weep for Me, but weep for yourselves and for your children.

29 For behold, the days are coming during which they will say, Blessed (happy, fortunate, and [p]to be envied) are the barren, and the wombs that have not borne, and the breasts that have never nursed [babies]!

30 Then they will begin to say to the mountains, Fall on us! and to the hills, Cover (conceal, hide) us!

31 For if they do these things when the timber is green, what will happen when it is dry?

32 Two others also, who were criminals, were led away to be executed with Him. [Isa. 53:12.]

33 And when they came to the place which is called The Skull [Latin: Calvary; Hebrew: Golgotha], there they crucified Him, and [along with] the criminals, one on the right and one on the left.

34 And Jesus prayed, Father, forgive them, for they know not what they do. And they divided His garments *and* distributed them by casting lots for them. [Ps. 22:18.]

35 Now the people stood by [[o]calmly and leisurely] watching; but the rulers scoffed *and* sneered

---

m John Wycliffe, *The Wycliffe Bible.*　　n Many manuscripts do not contain this verse.　　o Marvin Vincent, *Word Studies.*　　p Alexander Souter, *Pocket Lexicon.*

(ⁿturned up their noses) at Him, saying, He rescued others ['from death]; let Him now rescue Himself, if He is the Christ (the Messiah) of God, His Chosen One!

36 The soldiers also ridiculed *and* made sport of Him, coming up and offering Him vinegar (a sour wine mixed with water) [Ps. 69:21.]

37 And saying, If you are the King of the Jews, save (rescue) Yourself ['from death].

38 For there was also an inscription above Him ˢ*in letters of Greek and Latin and Hebrew*: This is the King of the Jews.

39 One of the criminals who was suspended kept up a railing at Him, saying, Are You not the Christ (the Messiah)? Rescue Yourself and us ['from death]!

40 But the other one reproved him, saying, Do you not even fear God, seeing you yourself are under the same sentence of condemnation *and* suffering the same penalty?

41 And we indeed suffer it justly, receiving the due reward of our actions; but this Man has done nothing out of the way [nothing 'strange or eccentric or perverse or unreasonable].

42 Then he said to Jesus, *Lord*, remember me when You come ᵗin Your kingly glory!

43 And He answered him, Truly I tell you, today you shall be with Me in Paradise.

44 It was now about the sixth hour (midday), and darkness enveloped the whole land *and* earth until the ninth hour (about three o'clock in the afternoon),

45 While the sun's light faded *or* ᵘ*was darkened*; and the curtain [of the Holy of Holies] of the temple was torn in two. [Exod. 26:31–35.]

46 And Jesus, crying out with a loud voice, said, Father, into Your hands I commit My spirit! And with these words, He expired. [Ps. 31:5.]

47 Now the centurion, having seen what had taken place, ᵛrecognized God *and* thanked *and* praised Him, and said, Indeed, without question, this Man was upright (just and innocent)!

48 And all the throngs that had gathered to see this spectacle, when they saw what had taken place, returned to their homes, beating their breasts.

49 And all the acquaintances of [Jesus] and the women who had followed Him from Galilee stood at a distance and watched these things.

50 Now notice, there was a man named Joseph from the Jewish town of Arimathea. He was a member of the council (the Sanhedrin), and a good (upright, ᵗadvantageous) man, and righteous (in right standing with God and man),

51 Who had not agreed with *or* assented to the purpose and action of the others; and he was expecting *and* waiting for the kingdom of God.

52 This man went to Pilate and asked for the body of Jesus.

53 Then he took it down and ᵛrolled it up in a linen cloth ʷfor swathing dead bodies and laid Him in a rock-hewn tomb, where no one had ever yet been laid.

54 It was the day of Preparation [for the Sabbath], and the Sabbath was dawning (approaching).

55 The women who had come with [Jesus] from Galilee followed closely and saw the tomb and how His body was laid.

56 Then they went back and made ready spices and ointments (perfumes). On the Sabbath day they

---

q Literal translation.   r Hermann Cremer, *Biblico-Theological Lexicon.*   s Some manuscripts add this phrase.   t Marvin Vincent, *Word Studies.*   u Many ancient manuscripts so read.   v Robert Young, *Analytical Concordance.*   w James Moulton and George Milligan, *The Vocabulary.*

rested in accordance with the commandment. [Exod. 12:16; 20:10.]

CHAPTER 24

BUT ON the first day of the week, at early dawn, [the women] went to the tomb, taking the spices which they had made ready.

2 And they found the stone rolled back from the tomb,

3 But when they went inside, they did not find the body of the Lord Jesus.

4 And while they were perplexed *and* wondering what to do about this, behold, two men in dazzling raiment suddenly stood beside them.

5 And as [the women] were frightened and were bowing their faces to the ground, the men said to them, Why do you look for the living among [those who are] dead?

6 He is not here, but has risen! Remember how He told you while He was still in Galilee

7 That the Son of Man must be given over into the hands of sinful men (men ˣwhose way or nature is to act in opposition to God) and be crucified and on the third day rise [ʸfrom death]. [Ps. 16:10.]

8 And they remembered His words.

9 And having returned from the tomb, they reported all these things [taken together] to the eleven apostles and to all the rest.

10 Now it was Mary Magdalene and Joanna and Mary the mother of James, and the other women with them, who reported these things to the apostles.

11 But these reports seemed to the men an idle tale (ʸmadness, ᶻfeigned things, ᵃnonsense), and they did not believe the women.

12 But Peter got up and ran to the tomb; and stooping down and looking in, he saw the linen cloths alone by themselves, and he went away, wondering about *and* marveling at what had happened.

13 And behold, that very day two of [the disciples] were going to a village called Emmaus, [which is] about seven miles from Jerusalem.

14 And they were talking with each other about all these things that had occurred.

15 And while they were conversing and discussing together, Jesus Himself caught up with them and was already accompanying them.

16 But their eyes were held, so that they did not recognize Him.

17 And He said to them, What is this discussion that you are exchanging (ᵇthrowing back and forth) between yourselves as you walk along? And they stood still, looking sad *and* downcast.

18 Then one of them, named Cleopas, answered Him, Do you alone dwell as a stranger in Jerusalem and not know the things that have occurred there in these days?

19 And He said to them, What [kind of] things? And they said to Him, About Jesus of Nazareth, Who was a Prophet mighty in work and word before God and all the people—

20 And how our chief priests and rulers gave Him up to be sentenced to death, and crucified Him.

21 But we were hoping that it was He Who would redeem *and* set Israel free. Yes, and besides all this, it is now the third day since these things occurred.

22 And moreover, some women of our company astounded us *and* ᵇdrove us out of our senses. They

---

x Hermann Cremer, *Biblico-Theological Lexicon*.   y John Wycliffe, *The Wycliffe Bible*.   z William Tyndale, *The Tyndale Bible*.   a James Moulton and George Milligan, *The Vocabulary*.   b Literal translation.

were at the tomb early [in the morning]

23 But did not find His body; and they returned saying that they had [even] seen a vision of angels, who said that He was alive!

24 So some of those [who were] with us went to the tomb and they found it just as the women had said, but Him they did not see.

25 And [Jesus] said to them, O foolish ones [sluggish in mind, dull of perception] and slow of heart to believe (adhere to and trust in and rely on) everything that the prophets have spoken!

26 Was it not necessary *and* ᶜessentially fitting that the Christ (the Messiah) should suffer all these things before entering into His glory (His majesty and splendor)?

27 Then beginning with Moses and [throughout] all the Prophets, He went on explaining *and* interpreting to them in all the Scriptures the things concerning *and* referring to Himself.

28 Then they drew near the village to which they were going, and He acted as if He would go further.

29 But they urged *and* insisted, saying to Him, Remain with us, for it is toward evening, and the day is now far spent. So He went in to stay with them.

30 And it occurred that as He reclined at table with them, He took [a loaf of] bread and praised [God] *and* gave thanks *and* asked a blessing, and then broke it and was giving it to them

31 When their eyes were [instantly] opened and they [clearly] recognized Him, and He vanished (ᵈdeparted invisibly).

32 And they said to one another, Were not our hearts greatly moved *and* burning within us while He was talking with us on the road and as He opened *and* explained to us [the sense of] the Scriptures?

33 And rising up that very hour, they went back to Jerusalem, where they found the Eleven [apostles] gathered together and those who were with them,

34 Who said, The Lord really has risen and has appeared to Simon (Peter)!

35 Then they [themselves] ᶜrelated [in full] what had happened on the road, and how He was known *and* recognized by them in the breaking of bread.

36 Now while they were talking about this, Jesus Himself took His stand among them and said to them, Peace (ᵈfreedom from all the distresses that are experienced as the result of sin) be to you!

37 But they were so startled and terrified that they thought they saw a spirit.

38 And He said to them, Why are you disturbed *and* troubled, and why do such doubts *and* questionings arise in your hearts?

39 See My hands and My feet, that it is I Myself! Feel *and* handle Me and see, for a spirit does not have flesh and bones, as you see that I have.

40 And when He had said this, He showed them His hands and His feet.

41 And while [since] they still could not believe it for sheer joy and marveled, He said to them, Have you anything here to eat?

42 They gave Him a piece of broiled fish,

43 And He took [it] and ate [it] before them.

44 Then He said to them, This is what I told you while I was still with you: everything which is written concerning Me in the Law of Moses and

---

c Marvin Vincent, *Word Studies.*   d Hermann Cremer, *Biblico-Theological Lexicon.*

the Prophets and the Psalms must be fulfilled.

45 Then He [thoroughly] opened up their minds to understand the Scriptures,

46 And said to them, Thus it is written that the Christ (the Messiah) should suffer and on the third day rise from (e among) the dead, [Hos. 6:2.]

47 And that repentance [with a view to and as the condition of] forgiveness of sins should be preached in His name to all nations, beginning from Jerusalem.

48 You are witnesses of these things.

49 And behold, I will send forth upon you what My Father has promised; but remain in the city [Jerusalem] until you are clothed with power from on high.

50 Then He conducted them out as far as Bethany and, lifting up His hands, He invoked a blessing on them.

51 And it occurred that while He was blessing them, He parted from them and was taken up into heaven.

52 And they, worshiping Him, went back to Jerusalem with great joy;

53 And they were continually in the temple *celebrating with praises and* blessing *and* extolling God. *Amen (so be it).*

THE GOSPEL ACCORDING TO

JOHN

CHAPTER 1

IN THE beginning [before all time] was the Word ('Christ), and the Word was with God, and the Word was God °Himself. [Isa. 9:6.]

2 He was present originally with God,

3 All things were made *and* came into existence through Him; and without Him was not even one thing made that has come into being.

4 In Him was Life, and the Life was the Light of men.

5 And the Light shines on in the darkness, for the darkness has never overpowered it [put it out or absorbed it or appropriated it, and is unreceptive to it].

6 There came a man sent from God, whose name was John. [Mal. 3:1.]

7 This man came to witness, that he might testify of the Light, that all men might believe in it [adhere to it, trust it, and rely upon it] through him.

8 He was not the Light himself, but came that he might bear witness regarding the Light.

9 There it was—the true Light [was then] coming into the world [the genuine, perfect, steadfast Light] that illumines every person. [Isa. 49:6.]

10 He came into the world, and though the world was made through

e George Ricker Berry, *Greek-English New Testament Lexicon.*   f In John's vision (Rev. 19), he sees Christ returning as Warrior-Messiah-King, and ''the title by which He is called is The Word of God . . . and Lord of lords'' (Rev. 19:13, 16).   g Charles B. Williams, *The New Testament: A Translation in the Language of the People*: ''God'' appears first in the Greek word order in this phrase, denoting emphasis—so ''God Himself.''

Him, the world did not recognize Him [did not know Him].

11 He came to that which belonged to Him [to His own—His domain, creation, things, world], and they who were His own did not receive Him *and* did not welcome Him.

12 But to as many as did receive *and* welcome Him, He gave the authority (power, privilege, right) to become the children of God, that is, to those who believe in (adhere to, trust in, and rely on) His name—[Isa. 56:5.]

13 Who owe their birth neither to hbloods nor to the will of the flesh [that of physical impulse] nor to the will of man [that of a natural father], but to God. [They are born of God!]

14 And the Word (Christ) became flesh (human, incarnate) and tabernacled (fixed His tent of flesh, lived awhile) among us; and we [actually] saw His glory (His honor, His majesty), such glory as an only begotten son receives from his father, full of grace (favor, loving-kindness) and truth. [Isa. 40:5.]

15 John testified about Him and cried out, This was He of Whom I said, He Who comes after me has priority over me, for He was before me. [He takes rank above me, for He existed before I did. He has advanced before me, because He is my Chief.]

16 For out of His fullness (abundance) we have all received [all had a share and we were all supplied with] one grace after another *and* spiritual blessing upon spiritual blessing *and* even favor upon favor *and* gift [heaped] upon gift.

17 For while the Law was given through Moses, grace (iunearned, undeserved favor and spiritual bless-

ing) and truth came through Jesus Christ. [Exod. 20:1.]

18 No man has ever seen God at any time; *the only junique Son, or* kthe only begotten God, Who is in the bosom [in the intimate presence] of the Father, He has declared Him [He has revealed Him and brought Him out where He can be seen; He has interpreted Him and He has made Him known]. [Prov. 8:30.]

19 And this is the testimony of John when the Jews sent priests and Levites to him from Jerusalem to ask him, Who are you?

20 He confessed (admitted the truth) and did not try to conceal it, but acknowledged, I am not the Christ!

21 They asked him, What then? Are you Elijah? And he said, I am not! Are you the Prophet? And he answered, No! [Deut. 18:15, 18; Mal. 4:5.]

22 Then they said to him, Who are you? Tell us, so that we may give an answer to those who sent us. What do you say about yourself?

23 He said, I am the voice of one crying aloud in the wilderness [the voice of one shouting in the desert], Prepare the way of the Lord [level, straighten out, the path of the Lord], as the prophet Isaiah said. [Isa. 40:3.]

24 The messengers had been sent from the Pharisees.

25 And they asked him, Why then are you baptizing if you are not the Christ, nor Elijah, nor the Prophet?

26 John answered them, I [only] baptize lin (with) water. Among you there stands One Whom you do not recognize *and* with Whom you are not acquainted *and* of Whom you know nothing. [Mal. 3:1.]

27 It is He Who, coming after me,

---

h Literal translation. i Richard Trench, *Synonyms of the New Testament.* j James Moulton and George Milligan, *The Vocabulary of the Greek Testament.* k Marvin Vincent, *Word Studies in the New Testament*: This reading is supported by "a great mass of ancient evidence." l The Greek can be translated "with" or "in;" also in verses 31 and 33. The KJV prefers "with," while the ASV prefers "in."

is preferred before me, the string of Whose sandal I am not worthy to unloose.

28 These things occurred in Bethany (Bethabara) across the Jordan [mat the Jordan crossing], where John was then baptizing.

29 The next day John saw Jesus coming to him and said, Look! There is the Lamb of God, Who takes away the sin of the world! [Exod. 12:3; Isa. 53:7.]

30 This is He of Whom I said, After me comes a Man Who has priority over me [Who takes rank above me] because He was before me and existed before I did.

31 And I did not know Him and did not recognize Him [myself]; but it is in order that He should be made manifest and be revealed to Israel [be brought out where we can see Him] that I came baptizing ᶰin (with) water.

32 John gave further evidence, saying, I have seen the Spirit descending as a dove out of heaven, and it dwelt on Him [never to depart].

33 And I did not know Him nor recognize Him, but He Who sent me to baptize ᶰin (with) water said to me, Upon Him Whom you shall see the Spirit descend and remain, that One is He Who baptizes with the Holy Spirit.

34 And I have seen [that happen—I actually did see it] and my testimony is that this is the Son of God!

35 Again the next day John was standing with two of his disciples,

36 And he looked at Jesus as He walked along, and said, Look! There is the Lamb of God!

37 The two disciples heard him say this, and they followed Him.

38 But Jesus turned, and as He saw them following Him, He said to them, What are you looking for? [And what is it you wish?] And they answered Him, Rabbi—which translated is Teacher—where are You staying?

39 He said to them, Come and see. So they went and saw where He was staying, and they remained with Him ᵒthat day. It was then about the tenth hour (about four o'clock in the afternoon).

40 One of the two who heard what John said and followed Jesus was Andrew, Simon Peter's brother.

41 He first sought out and found his own brother Simon and said to him, We have found (discovered) the Messiah!—which translated is the Christ (the Anointed One).

42 Andrew then led (brought) Simon to Jesus. Jesus looked at him and said, You are Simon son of John. You shall be called Cephas—which translated is Peter [Stone].

43 The next day Jesus desired and decided to go into Galilee; and He found Philip and said to him, Join Me as My attendant and follow Me.

44 Now Philip was from Bethsaida, of the same city as Andrew and Peter.

45 Philip sought and found Nathanael and told him, We have found (discovered) the One Moses in the Law and also the Prophets wrote about—Jesus from Nazareth, the [legal] son of Joseph!

46 Nathanael answered him, [Nazareth!] Can anything good come out of Nazareth? Philip replied, Come and see!

47 Jesus saw Nathanael coming toward Him and said concerning him, See! Here is an Israelite indeed [a true descendant of Jacob], in whom

m George M. Lamsa, *The New Testament According to the Ancient Text.*   n See footnote on John 1:26.
o George M. Lamsa, *Gospel Light from the Aramaic:* In accordance with Oriental hospitality, the guests would be invited to remain that night also.

there is no guile *nor* deceit *nor* falsehood *nor* duplicity!

48 Nathanael said to Jesus, How do You know me? [How is it that You know these things about me?] Jesus answered him, Before [ever] Philip called you, when you were still under the fig tree, I saw you.

49 Nathanael answered, Teacher, You are the Son of God! You are the King of Israel!

50 Jesus replied, Because I said to you, I saw you beneath the fig tree, do you believe in *and* rely on *and* trust in Me? You shall see greater things than this!

51 Then He said to him, I assure you, most solemnly I tell you all, you shall see heaven opened, and the angels of God ascending and descending upon the Son of Man! [Gen. 28:12; Dan. 7:13.]

CHAPTER 2

ON THE third day there was a wedding at Cana of Galilee, and the mother of Jesus was there.

2 Jesus also was invited with His disciples to the wedding.

3 And when the wine was all gone, the mother of Jesus said to Him, They have no more wine!

4 Jesus said to her, [[p]Dear] woman, what is that to you and to Me? [What do we have in common? Leave it to Me.] My time (hour to act) has not yet come. [Eccl. 3:1.]

5 His mother said to the servants, Whatever He says to you, do it.

6 Now there were six waterpots of stone standing there, as the Jewish custom of purification (ceremonial washing) demanded, holding twenty to thirty gallons apiece.

7 Jesus said to them, Fill the waterpots with water. So they filled them up to the brim.

8 Then He said to them, Draw some out now and take it to the manager of the feast [to the one presiding, the superintendent of the banquet]. So they took him some.

9 And when the manager tasted the water just now turned into wine, not knowing where it came from—though the servants who had drawn the water knew—he called the bridegroom

10 And said to him, Everyone else serves his best wine first, and when people have drunk freely, then he serves that which is not so good; but you have kept back the good wine until now!

11 This, the first of His signs (miracles, wonderworks), Jesus performed in Cana of Galilee, and manifested His glory [by it He displayed His greatness and His power openly], and His disciples believed in Him [adhered to, trusted in, and relied on Him]. [Deut. 5:24; Ps. 72:19.]

12 After that He went down to Capernaum with His mother and brothers and disciples, and they stayed there only a few days.

13 Now the Passover of the Jews was approaching, so Jesus went up to Jerusalem.

14 There He found in the temple [[q]enclosure] those who were selling oxen and sheep and doves, and the money changers sitting there [also at their stands].

15 And having made a lash (a whip) of cords, He drove them all out of the temple [[q]enclosure]—both the sheep and the oxen—spilling *and* scattering the brokers' money and upsetting *and* tossing around their trays (their stands).

16 Then to those who sold the doves He said, Take these things away (out of here)! Make not My Fa-

p G. Abbott-Smith, *Manual Greek Lexicon of the New Testament*: "a term of respect and endearment."
q Richard Trench, *Synonyms of the New Testament*.

ther's house a house of merchandise (a marketplace, a sales shop)! [Ps. 93:5.]

17 And His disciples remembered that it is written [in the Holy Scriptures], Zeal (the fervor of love) for Your house will eat Me up. [I will be consumed with jealousy for the honor of Your house.] [Ps. 69:9.]

18 Then the Jews retorted, What sign can ʳYou show us, seeing You do these things? [What sign, miracle, token, indication can You give us as evidence that You have authority and are commissioned to act in this way?]

19 Jesus answered them, Destroy (undo) this temple, and in three days I will raise it up again.

20 Then the Jews replied, It took forty-six years to build this temple (sanctuary), and will You raise it up in three days?

21 But He had spoken of the temple which was His body.

22 When therefore He had risen from the dead, His disciples remembered that He said this. And so they believed *and* trusted *and* relied on the Scripture and the word (message) Jesus had spoken. [Ps. 16:10.]

23 But when He was in Jerusalem during the Passover Feast, many believed in His name [identified themselves with His party] after seeing His signs (wonders, miracles) which He was doing.

24 But Jesus [for His part] did not trust Himself to them, because He knew all [men];

25 And He did not need anyone to bear witness concerning man [needed no evidence from anyone about men], for He Himself knew what was in human nature. [He could read men's hearts.] [I Sam. 16:7.]

CHAPTER 3

NOW THERE was a certain man among the Pharisees named Nicodemus, a ruler (a leader, an authority) among the Jews,

2 Who came to Jesus at night and said to Him, Rabbi, we know *and* are certain that You have come from God [as] a Teacher; for no one can do these signs (these wonderworks, these miracles—and produce the proofs) that You do unless God is with him.

3 Jesus answered him, I assure you, most solemnly I tell you, that unless a person is born again (anew, from above), he cannot ever see (know, be acquainted with, and experience) the kingdom of God.

4 Nicodemus said to Him, How can a man be born when he is old? Can he enter his mother's womb again and be born?

5 Jesus answered, I assure you, most solemnly I tell you, unless a man is born of water and [ˢeven] the Spirit, he cannot [ever] enter the kingdom of God. [Ezek. 36:25–27.]

6 What is born of [from] the flesh is flesh [of the physical is physical]; and what is born of the Spirit is spirit.

7 Marvel not [do not be surprised, astonished] at My telling you, You must all be born anew (from above).

8 The wind blows (breathes) where it wills; and though you hear its sound, yet you neither know where it comes from nor where it is going. So it is with everyone who is born of the Spirit.

9 Nicodemus answered by asking, How can all this be possible?

10 Jesus replied, Are you the teacher of Israel, and yet do not know *nor* understand these things? [Are they strange to you?]

11 I assure you, most solemnly I

ʳ Capitalized because of what He is, the spotless Son of God, not what the speaker may have thought He was.
ˢ The Greek "kai" ("and") may be rendered "even."

tell you, We speak only of what we know [we know absolutely what we are talking about]; we have actually seen what we are testifying to [we were eyewitnesses of it]. And still you do not receive our testimony [you reject and refuse our evidence—that of Myself and of all those who are born of the Spirit].

12 If I have told you of things that happen right here on the earth and yet none of you believes Me, how can you believe (trust Me, adhere to Me, rely on Me) if I tell you of heavenly things?

13 And yet no one has ever gone up to heaven, but there is One Who has come down from heaven—the Son of Man [Himself], [t]Who is (dwells, has His home) in heaven.

14 And just as Moses lifted up the serpent in the desert [on a pole], so must [so it is necessary that] the Son of Man be lifted up [on the cross], [Num. 21:9.]

15 In order that everyone who believes in Him [who cleaves to Him, trusts Him, and relies on Him] may [t]not perish, but have eternal life and [actually] live forever!

16 For God so greatly loved and dearly prized the world that He [even] gave up His only begotten ([u]unique) Son, so that whoever believes in (trusts in, clings to, relies on) Him shall not perish (come to destruction, be lost) but have eternal (everlasting) life.

17 For God did not send the Son into the world in order to judge (to reject, to condemn, to pass sentence on) the world, but that the world might find salvation and be made safe and sound through Him.

18 He who believes in Him [who clings to, trusts in, relies on Him] is not judged [he who trusts in Him never comes up for judgment; for him

there is no rejection, no condemnation—he incurs no damnation]; but he who does not believe (cleave to, rely on, trust in Him) is judged already [he has already been convicted and has already received his sentence] because he has not believed in and trusted in the name of the only begotten Son of God. [He is condemned for refusing to let his trust rest in Christ's name.]

19 The [basis of the] judgment (indictment, the test by which men are judged, the ground for the sentence) lies in this: the Light has come into the world, and people have loved the darkness rather than and more than the Light, for their works (deeds) were evil. [Isa. 5:20.]

20 For every wrongdoer hates (loathes, detests) the Light, and will not come out into the Light but shrinks from it, lest his works (his deeds, his activities, his conduct) be exposed and reproved.

21 But he who practices truth [who does what is right] comes out into the Light; so that his works may be plainly shown to be what they are—wrought with God [divinely prompted, done with God's help, in dependence upon Him].

22 After this, Jesus and His disciples went into the land (the countryside) of Judea, where He remained with them, and baptized.

23 But John also was baptizing at Aenon near Salim, for there was an abundance of water there, and the people kept coming and being baptized.

24 For John had not yet been thrown into prison.

25 Therefore there arose a controversy between some of John's disciples and a Jew in regard to purification.

26 So they came to John and re-

---

t Some manuscripts add this phrase.　　u James Moulton and George Milligan, The Vocabulary.

ported to him, Rabbi, the Man Who was with you on the other side of the Jordan [vat the Jordan crossing]— and to Whom you yourself have borne testimony—notice, here He is baptizing too, and everybody is flocking to Him!

27 John answered, A man can receive nothing [he can claim nothing, he can wtake unto himself nothing] except as it has been granted to him from heaven. [A man must be content to receive the gift which is given him from heaven; there is no other source.]

28 You yourselves are my witnesses [you personally bear me out] that I stated, I am not the Christ (the Anointed One, the Messiah), but I have [only] been sent before Him [in advance of Him, to be His appointed forerunner, His messenger, His announcer]. [Mal. 3:1.]

29 He who has the bride is the bridegroom; but the groomsman who stands by and listens to him rejoices greatly and heartily on account of the bridegroom's voice. This then is my pleasure and joy, and it is now complete. [S. of Sol. 5:1.]

30 He must increase, but I must decrease. [He must grow more prominent; I must grow less so.] [Isa. 9:7.]

31 He Who comes from above (heaven) is [far] above all [others]; he who comes from the earth belongs to the earth, and talks the language of earth [his words are from an earthly standpoint]. He Who comes from heaven is [far] above all others [far superior to all others in prominence and in excellence].

32 It is to what He has [actually] seen and heard that He bears testimony, and yet no one accepts His testimony [no one receives His evidence as true].

33 Whoever receives His testimony has set his seal of approval to this: God is true. [That man has definitely certified, acknowledged, declared once and for all, and is himself assured that it is divine truth that God cannot lie].

34 For since He Whom God has sent speaks the words of God [proclaims God's own message], God does not give Him His Spirit sparingly or by measure, but boundless is the gift God makes of His Spirit! [Deut. 18:18.]

35 The Father loves the Son and has given (entrusted, committed) everything into His hand. [Dan. 7:14.]

36 And he who believes in (has faith in, clings to, relies on) the Son has (now possesses) eternal life. But whoever disobeys (is unbelieving toward, refuses to trust in, disregards, is not subject to) the Son will never see (experience) life, but [instead] the wrath of God abides on him. [God's displeasure remains on him; His indignation hangs over him continually.] [Hab. 2:4.]

CHAPTER 4

NOW WHEN the Lord knew (learned, became aware) that the Pharisees had been told that Jesus was winning and baptizing more disciples than John—

2 Though Jesus Himself did not baptize, but His disciples—

3 He left Judea and returned to Galilee.

4 It was necessary for Him to go through Samaria.

5 And in doing so, He arrived at a Samaritan town called Sychar, near the tract of land that Jacob gave to his son Joseph.

6 And Jacob's well was there. So Jesus, tired as He was from His jour-

---

v George M. Lamsa, *The New Testament.*   w Joseph Thayer, *A Greek-English Lexicon of the New Testament.*

ney, sat down [to rest] by the well. It was then about the sixth hour (about noon).

7 Presently, when a woman of Samaria came along to draw water, Jesus said to her, Give Me a drink—

8 For His disciples had gone off into the town to buy food—

9 The Samaritan woman said to Him, How is it that ˣYou, being a Jew, ask me, a Samaritan [and a] woman, for a drink?—For the Jews have nothing to do with the Samaritans—

10 Jesus answered her, If you had only known *and* had recognized God's gift and Who this is that is saying to you, Give Me a drink, you would have asked Him [instead] and He would have given you living water.

11 She said to Him, Sir, You have nothing to draw with [no drawing bucket] and the well is deep; how then can You provide living water? [Where do You get Your living water?]

12 Are You greater than *and* superior to our ancestor Jacob, who gave us this well and who used to drink from it himself, and his sons and his cattle also?

13 Jesus answered her, All who drink of this water will be thirsty again.

14 But whoever takes a drink of the water that I will give him shall never, no never, be thirsty any more. But the water that I will give him shall become a spring of water welling up (flowing, bubbling) [continually] within him unto (into, for) eternal life.

15 The woman said to Him, Sir, give me this water, so that I may never get thirsty nor have to come [continually all the way] here to draw.

16 At this, Jesus said to her, Go,

call your husband and come back here.

17 The woman answered, I have no husband. Jesus said to her, You have spoken truly in saying, I have no husband.

18 For you have had five husbands, and the man you are now living with is not your husband. In this you have spoken truly.

19 The woman said to Him, Sir, I see *and* understand that You are a prophet.

20 Our forefathers worshiped on this mountain, but you [Jews] say that Jerusalem is the place where it is necessary *and* proper to worship.

21 Jesus said to her, Woman, believe Me, a time is coming when you will worship the Father neither [merely] in this mountain nor [merely] in Jerusalem.

22 You [Samaritans] do not know what you are worshiping [you worship what you do not comprehend]. We do know what we are worshiping [we worship what we have knowledge of and understand], for [after all] salvation comes from [among] the Jews.

23 A time will come, however, indeed it is already here, when the true (genuine) worshipers will worship the Father in spirit and in truth (reality); for the Father is seeking just such people as these as His worshipers.

24 God is a Spirit (a spiritual Being) and those who worship Him must worship *Him* in spirit and in truth (reality).

25 The woman said to Him, I know that Messiah is coming, He Who is called the Christ (the Anointed One); and when He arrives, He will tell us everything we need to know *and* make it clear to us.

26 Jesus said to her, I Who now speak with you am He.

ˣ Capitalized because of what He is, the spotless Son of God, not what the speaker may have thought He was.

27 Just then His disciples came and they wondered (were surprised, astonished) to find Him talking with a woman [a married woman]. However, not one of them asked Him, What are You inquiring about? *or* What do You want? or, Why do You speak with her?

28 Then the woman left her water jar and went away to the town. And she began telling the people,

29 Come, see a Man Who has told me everything that I ever did! Can this be [is not this] the Christ? [Must not this be the Messiah, the Anointed One?]

30 So the people left the town and set out to go to Him.

31 Meanwhile, the disciples urged Him saying, Rabbi, eat something.

32 But He assured them, I have food (nourishment) to eat of which you know nothing *and* have no idea.

33 So the disciples said one to another, Has someone brought Him something to eat?

34 Jesus said to them, My food (nourishment) is to do the will (pleasure) of Him Who sent Me and to accomplish *and* completely finish His work.

35 Do you not say, It is still four months until harvest time comes? Look! I tell you, raise your eyes and observe the fields *and* see how they are already white for harvesting.

36 Already the reaper is getting his wages [he who does the cutting now has his reward], for he is gathering fruit (crop) unto life eternal, so that he who does the planting and he who does the reaping may rejoice together.

37 For in this the saying holds true, One sows and another reaps.

38 I sent you to reap a crop for which you have not toiled. Other men have labored and you have stepped in to reap the results of their work.

39 Now numerous Samaritans from that town believed in *and* trusted in Him because of what the woman said when she declared *and* testified, He told me everything that I ever did.

40 So when the Samaritans arrived, they asked Him to remain with them, and He did stay there two days.

41 Then many more believed in *and* adhered to *and* relied on Him because of His personal message [what He Himself said].

42 And they told the woman, Now we no longer believe (trust, have faith) just because of what you said; for we have heard Him ourselves [personally], and we know that He truly is the Savior of the world, *the Christ.*

43 But after these two days Jesus went on from there into Galilee—

44 Although He Himself declared that a prophet has no honor in his own country.

45 However, when He came into Galilee, the Galileans also welcomed Him *and* took Him to their hearts eagerly, for they had seen everything that He did in Jerusalem during the Feast; for they too had attended the Feast.

46 So Jesus came again to Cana of Galilee, where He had turned the water into wine. And there was a certain royal official whose son was lying ill in Capernaum.

47 Having heard that Jesus had come back from Judea into Galilee, he went away to meet Him and began to beg Him to come down and cure his son, for he was lying at the point of death.

48 Then Jesus said to him, Unless you see signs and miracles happen, you [people] never will believe (trust, have faith) at all.

49 The king's officer pleaded with

Him, Sir, do come down at once before my little child is dead!

50 Jesus answered him, Go in peace; your son will live! And the man put his trust in what Jesus said and started home.

51 But even as he was on the road going down, his servants met him and reported, saying, Your son lives!

52 So he asked them at what time he had begun to get better. They said, Yesterday during the seventh hour (about one o'clock in the afternoon) the fever left him.

53 Then the father knew that it was at that very hour when Jesus had said to him, Your son will live. And he and his entire household believed (adhered to, trusted in, and relied on Jesus).

54 This is the second sign (wonderwork, miracle) that Jesus performed after He had come out of Judea into Galilee.

CHAPTER 5

LATER ON there was a Jewish festival (feast) for which Jesus went up to Jerusalem.

2 Now there is in Jerusalem a pool near the Sheep Gate. This pool in the Hebrew is called Bethesda, having five porches (alcoves, colonnades, doorways).

3 In these lay a great number of sick folk—some blind, some crippled, and some paralyzed (shriveled up)—*waitinɡ for the bubbling up of the water.

4 *For an angel of the Lord went down at appointed seasons into the pool and moved and stirred up the water; whoever then first, after the stirring up of the water, stepped in was cured of whatever disease with which he was afflicted.*

5 There was a certain man there who had suffered with a deep-seated *and* lingering disorder for thirty-eight years.

6 When Jesus noticed him lying there [helpless], knowing that he had already been a long time in that condition, He said to him, Do you want to become well? [Are you really in earnest about getting well?]

7 The invalid answered, Sir, I have nobody when the water is moving to put me into the pool; but while I am trying to come [into it] myself, somebody else steps down ahead of me.

8 Jesus said to him, Get up! Pick up your bed (sleeping pad) and walk!

9 Instantly the man became well *and* recovered his strength and picked up his bed and walked. But that happened on the Sabbath.

10 So the Jews kept saying to the man who had been healed, It is the Sabbath, and you have no right to pick up your bed [it is not lawful].

11 He answered them, The ²Man Who healed me *and* gave me back my strength, He Himself said to me, Pick up your bed and walk!

12 They asked him, Who is the Man Who told you, Pick up your bed and walk?

13 Now the invalid who had been healed did not know who it was, for Jesus had quietly gone away [had passed on unnoticed], since there was a crowd in the place.

14 Afterward, when Jesus found him in the temple, He said to him, See, you are well! Stop sinning or something worse may happen to you.

15 The man went away and told the Jews that it was Jesus Who had made him well.

16 For this reason the Jews began to persecute (annoy, torment) Jesus ³*and sought to kill Him,* because He

y Many manuscripts omit the last part of verse 3 and all of verse 4.   z Capitalized because of what He is, the spotless Son of God, not what the speaker may have thought He was.   a Some manuscripts add this phrase.

was doing these things on the Sabbath.

17 But Jesus answered them, My Father has worked [even] until now, [He has never ceased working; He is still working] and I, too, must be at [divine] work.

18 This made the Jews more determined than ever to kill Him [to do away with Him]; because He not only was breaking (weakening, violating) the Sabbath, but He actually was speaking of God as being [in a special sense] His own Father, making Himself equal [putting Himself on a level] with God.

19 So Jesus answered them by saying, I assure you, most solemnly I tell you, the Son is able to do nothing of Himself (of His own accord); but He is able to do only what He sees the Father doing, for whatever the Father does is what the Son does in the same way [in His turn].

20 The Father dearly loves the Son and discloses to (shows) Him everything that He Himself does. And He will disclose to Him (let Him see) greater things yet than these, so that you may marvel and be full of wonder and astonishment.

21 Just as the Father raises up the dead and gives them life [makes them live on], even so the Son also gives life to whomever He wills and is pleased to give it.

22 Even the Father judges no one, for He has given all judgment (the last judgment and the whole business of judging) entirely into the hands of the Son,

23 So that all men may give honor (reverence, homage) to the Son just as they give honor to the Father. [In fact] whoever does not honor the Son does not honor the Father, Who has sent Him.

24 I assure you, most solemnly I

tell you, the person whose ears are open to My words [who listens to My message] and believes and trusts in and clings to and relies on Him Who sent Me has (possesses now) eternal life. And he does not come into judgment [does not incur sentence of judgment, will not come under condemnation], but he has already passed over out of death into life.

25 Believe Me when I assure you, most solemnly I tell you, the time is coming and is here now when the dead shall hear the voice of the Son of God and those who hear it shall live.

26 For even as the Father has life in Himself and is self-existent, so He has given to the Son to have life in Himself and be self-existent.

27 And He has given Him authority and granted Him power to execute (exercise, practice) judgment because He is [b]a Son of man [very man].

28 Do not be surprised and wonder at this, for the time is coming when all those who are in the tombs shall hear His voice,

29 And they shall come out—those who have practiced doing good [will come out] to the resurrection of [new] life, and those who have done evil will be raised for judgment [raised to meet their sentence]. [Dan. 12:2.]

30 I am able to do nothing from Myself [independently, of My own accord—but only as I am taught by God and as I get His orders]. Even as I hear, I judge [I decide as I am bidden to decide. As the voice comes to Me, so I give a decision], and My judgment is right (just, righteous), because I do not seek or consult My own will [I have no desire to do what is pleasing to Myself, My own aim, My own purpose] but only the will

and pleasure of the Father Who sent Me.

31 If I alone testify in My behalf, My testimony is not valid *and* cannot be worth anything.

32 There is Another Who testifies concerning Me, and I know *and* am certain that His evidence on My behalf is true and valid.

33 You yourselves have sent [an inquiry] to John and he has been a witness to the truth.

34 But I do not receive [a mere] human witness [the evidence which I accept on My behalf is not from man]; but I simply mention all these things in order that you may be saved (made and kept safe and sound).

35 John was the lamp that kept on burning and shining [to show you the way], and you were willing for a while to delight (sun) yourselves in his light.

36 But I have as My witness something greater (weightier, higher, better) than that of John; for the works that the Father has appointed Me to accomplish *and* finish, the very same works that I am now doing, are a witness *and* proof that the Father has sent Me.

37 And the Father Who sent Me has Himself testified concerning Me. Not one of you has ever given ear to His voice or seen His form (His face—what He is like). [You have always been deaf to His voice and blind to the vision of Him.]

38 And you have not His word (His thought) living in your hearts, because you do not believe *and* adhere to *and* trust in *and* rely on Him Whom He has sent. [That is why you do not keep His message living in you, because you do not believe in the Messenger Whom He has sent.]

39 You search *and* investigate *and* pore over the Scriptures diligently, because you suppose *and* trust that you have eternal life through them.

And these [very Scriptures] testify about Me!

40 And still you are not willing [but refuse] to come to Me, so that you might have life.

41 I receive not glory from men [I crave no human honor, I look for no mortal fame],

42 But I know you and recognize *and* understand that you have not the love of God in you.

43 I have come in My Father's name *and* with His power, and you do not receive Me [your hearts are not open to Me, you give Me no welcome]; but if another comes in his own name *and* his own power *and* with no other authority but himself, you will receive him *and* give him your approval.

44 How is it possible for you to believe [how can you learn to believe], you who [are content to seek and] receive praise *and* honor *and* glory from one another, and yet do not seek the praise *and* honor *and* glory which come from Him Who alone is God?

45 Put out of your minds the thought *and* do not suppose [as some of you are supposing] that I will accuse you before the Father. There is one who accuses you—it is Moses, the very one on whom you have built your hopes [in whom you trust].

46 For if you believed *and* relied on Moses, you would believe *and* rely on Me, for he wrote about Me [personally].

47 But if you do not believe *and* trust his writings, how then will you believe *and* trust My teachings? [How shall you cleave to and rely on My words?]

CHAPTER 6

AFTER THIS, Jesus went to the farther side of the Sea of Galilee— that is, the Sea of Tiberias.

2 And a great crowd was following Him because they had seen the signs (miracles) which He [continually] performed upon those who were sick.

3 And Jesus walked up the mountainside and sat down there with His disciples.

4 Now the Passover, the feast of the Jews, was approaching.

5 Jesus looked up then, and seeing that a vast multitude was coming toward Him, He said to Philip, Where are we to buy bread, so that all these people may eat?

6 But He said this to prove (test) him, for He well knew what He was about to do.

7 Philip answered Him, Two hundred pennies' (forty dollars) worth of bread is not enough that everyone may receive even a little.

8 Another of His disciples, Andrew, Simon Peter's brother, said to Him,

9 There is a little boy here, who has [with him] five barley loaves, and two small fish; but what are they among so many people?

10 Jesus said, Make all the people recline (sit down). Now the ground (a pasture) was covered with thick grass at the spot, so the men threw themselves down, about 5,000 in number.

11 Jesus took the loaves, and when He had given thanks, He distributed 'to the disciples and the disciples to the reclining people; so also [He did] with the fish, as much as they wanted.

12 When they had all had enough, He said to His disciples, Gather up now the fragments (the broken pieces that are left over), so that nothing may be lost and wasted.

13 So accordingly they gathered

them up, and they filled twelve [dsmall hand] baskets with fragments left over by those who had eaten from the five barley loaves.

14 When the people saw the sign (miracle) that Jesus had performed, they began saying, Surely and beyond a doubt this is the Prophet Who is to come into the world! [Deut. 18:15, 18; John 1:21; Acts 3:22.]

15 Then Jesus, knowing that they meant to come and seize Him that they might make Him king, withdrew again to the hillside by Himself alone.

16 When evening came, His disciples went down to the sea,

17 And they took a boat and were going across the sea to Capernaum. It was now dark, and still Jesus had not [yet] come back to them.

18 Meanwhile, the sea was getting rough and rising high because of a great and violent wind that was blowing.

19 [However] when they had rowed three or four miles, they saw Jesus walking on the sea and approaching the boat. And they were afraid (terrified).

20 But Jesus said to them, It is I; be not afraid! [I AM; stop being frightened!] [Exod. 3:14.]

21 Then they were quite willing and glad for Him to come into the boat. And now the boat went at once to the land they had steered toward. [And immediately they reached the shore toward which they had been slowly making their way.]

22 The next day the crowd [that still remained] standing on the other side of the sea realized that there had been only one small boat there, and that Jesus had not gone into it with His disciples, but that His disciples had gone away by themselves.

---

c Some manuscripts add this phrase. Matt. 14:20.　　d G. Abbott-Smith, *Manual Greek Lexicon*. See also footnote on

23 But now some other boats from Tiberias had come in near the place where they ate the bread after the Lord had given thanks.

24 So the people, finding that neither Jesus nor His disciples were there, themselves got into the small boats and came to Capernaum looking for Jesus.

25 And when they found Him on the other side of the lake, they said to Him, Rabbi! When did You come here?

26 Jesus answered them, I assure you, most solemnly I tell you, you have been searching for Me, not because you saw the miracles *and* signs but because you were fed with the loaves and were filled *and* satisfied.

27 Stop toiling *and* doing *and* producing for the food that perishes *and* decomposes [in the using], but strive *and* work *and* produce rather for the [lasting] food which endures [continually] unto life eternal; the Son of Man will give (furnish) you that, for God the Father has authorized *and* certified Him *and* put His seal of endorsement upon Him.

28 They then said, What are we to do, that we may [habitually] be working the works of God? [What are we to do to carry out what God requires?]

29 Jesus replied, This is the work (service) that God asks of you: that you believe in the One Whom He has sent [that you cleave to, trust, rely on, and have faith in His Messenger].

30 Therefore they said to Him, What sign (miracle, wonderwork) will ᵉYou perform then, so that we may see it and believe *and* rely on *and* adhere to You? What [supernatural] work have You [to show what You can do]?

31 Our forefathers ate the manna in the wilderness; as the Scripture says, He gave them bread out of heaven to eat. [Exod. 16:15; Neh. 9:15; Ps. 78:24.]

32 Jesus then said to them, I assure you, most solemnly I tell you, Moses did not give you the Bread from heaven [what Moses gave you was not the Bread from heaven], but it is My Father Who gives you the true heavenly Bread.

33 For the Bread of God is He Who comes down out of heaven and gives life to the world.

34 Then they said to Him, Lord, give us this bread always (all the time)!

35 Jesus replied, I am the Bread of Life. He who comes to Me will never be hungry, and he who believes in *and* cleaves to *and* trusts in *and* relies on Me will never thirst any more (at any time).

36 But [as] I told you, although you have seen Me, still you do not believe *and* trust *and* have faith.

37 All whom My Father gives (entrusts) to Me will come to Me; and the one who comes to Me I will most certainly not cast out [I will never, no never, reject one of them who comes to Me].

38 For I have come down from heaven not to do My own will *and* purpose but to do the will *and* purpose of Him Who sent Me.

39 And this is the will of Him Who sent Me, that I should not lose any of all that He has given Me, but that I should give new life *and* raise [them all] up at the last day.

40 For this is My Father's will *and* His purpose, that everyone who sees the Son and believes in *and* cleaves to *and* trusts in *and* relies on Him should have eternal life, and I will raise him up [from the dead] at the last day.

41 Now the Jews murmured *and*

e Capitalized because of what He is, the spotless Son of God, not what the speaker may have thought He was.

found fault with *and* grumbled about Jesus because He said, I am [Myself] the Bread that came down from heaven.

42 They kept asking, Is not this Jesus, the †Son of Joseph, Whose father and mother we know? How then can He say, I have come down from heaven?

43 So Jesus answered them, Stop grumbling *and* saying things against Me to one another.

44 No one is able to come to Me unless the Father Who sent Me attracts *and* draws him *and* gives him the desire to come to Me, and [then] I will raise him up [from the dead] at the last day.

45 It is written in [the book of] the Prophets, And they shall all be taught of God [have Him in person for their Teacher]. Everyone who has listened to and learned from the Father comes to Me— [Isa. 54:13.]

46 Which does not imply that anyone has seen the Father [not that anyone has ever seen Him] except He [Who was with the Father] Who comes from God; He [alone] has seen the Father.

47 I assure you, most solemnly I tell you, he who believes *in Me* [who adheres to, trusts in, relies on, and has faith in Me] has (now possesses) eternal life.

48 I am the Bread of Life [that gives life—the Living Bread].

49 Your forefathers ate the manna in the wilderness, and [yet] they died.

50 [But] this is the Bread that comes down from heaven, so that [any]one may eat of it and never die.

51 I [Myself] am this Living Bread that came down from heaven. If anyone eats of this Bread, he will live forever; and also the Bread that I

shall give for the life of the world is My flesh (body).

52 Then the Jews angrily contended with one another, saying, How is He able to give us His flesh to eat?

53 And Jesus said to them, I assure you, most solemnly I tell you, you cannot have any life in you unless you eat the flesh of the Son of Man and drink His blood [unless you appropriate His life and the saving merit of His blood].

54 He who feeds on My flesh and drinks My blood has (possesses now) eternal life, and I will raise him up [from the dead] on the last day.

55 For My flesh is true *and* genuine food, and My blood is true *and* genuine drink.

56 He who feeds on My flesh and drinks My blood dwells continually in Me, and I [in like manner dwell continually] in him.

57 Just as the living Father sent Me and I live by (through, because of) the Father, even so whoever continues to feed on Me [whoever takes Me for his food *and* is nourished by Me] shall [in his turn] live through *and* because of Me.

58 This is the Bread that came down from heaven. It is not like the manna which our forefathers ate, and yet died; he who takes this Bread for his food shall live forever.

59 He said these things in a synagogue while He was teaching at Capernaum.

60 When His disciples heard this, many of them said, This is a hard *and* difficult *and* strange saying (an offensive and unbearable message). Who can stand to hear it? [Who can be expected to listen to such teaching?]

61 But Jesus, knowing within Himself that His disciples were complain-

---

† Capitalized because of what He is, the spotless Son of God, not what the speaker may have thought He was.

ing *and* protesting *and* grumbling about it, said to them: Is this a stumbling block *and* an offense to you? [Does this upset and displease and shock and scandalize you?]

62 What then [will be your reaction] if you should see the Son of Man ascending to [the place] where He was before?

63 It is the Spirit Who gives life [He is the Life-giver]; the flesh conveys no benefit whatever [there is no profit in it]. The words (truths) that I have been speaking to you are spirit and life.

64 But [still] some of you fail to believe *and* trust *and* have faith. For Jesus knew from the first who did not believe *and* had no faith and who would betray Him *and* be false to Him.

65 And He said, This is why I told you that no one can come to Me unless it is granted him [unless he is enabled to do so] by the Father.

66 After this, many of His disciples drew back (returned to their old associations) and no longer accompanied Him.

67 Jesus said to the Twelve, Will you also go away? [And do you too desire to leave Me?]

68 Simon Peter answered, Lord, to whom shall we go? You have the words (the message) of eternal life.

69 And we have learned to believe *and* trust, and [more] we have come to know [surely] that You are *the Holy One of God*, the Christ (the Anointed One), the Son of the living God.

70 Jesus answered them, Did I not choose you, the Twelve? And [yet] one of you is a devil (of the evil one and a false accuser).

71 He was speaking of Judas, the son of Simon Iscariot, for he was

about to betray Him, [although] he was one of the Twelve.

CHAPTER 7

AFTER THIS, Jesus went from place to place in Galilee, for He would not travel in Judea because the Jews were seeking to kill Him.

2 Now the Jewish Feast of Tabernacles was drawing near.

3 So His brothers said to Him, Leave here and go into Judea, so that *g*Your disciples [there] may also see the works that You do. [This is no place for You.]

4 For no one does anything in secret when he wishes to be conspicuous *and* secure publicity. If You [must] do these things [if You must act like this], show Yourself openly *and* make Yourself known to the world!

5 For [even] His brothers did not believe in *or* adhere to *or* trust in *or* rely on Him either.

6 Whereupon Jesus said to them, My time (opportunity) has not come yet; but any time is suitable for you *and* your opportunity is ready any time [is always here].

7 The world cannot [be expected to] hate you, but it does hate Me because I denounce it for its wicked works *and* reveal that its doings are evil.

8 Go to the Feast yourselves. I am not [yet] going up to the Festival, because My time is not ripe. [My term is not yet completed; it is not time for Me to go.]

9 Having said these things to them, He stayed behind in Galilee.

10 But afterward, when His brothers had gone up to the Feast, He went up also, not publicly [not with a caravan], but by Himself quietly *and* as if He did not wish to be observed.

11 Therefore the Jews kept looking

g Capitalized because of what He is, the spotless Son of God, not what the speaker may have thought He was.

for Him at the Feast and asking, Where can He be? [Where is that Fellow?]

12 And there was among the mass of the people much whispered discussion *and* hot disputing about Him. Some were saying, He is good! [He is a good Man!] Others said, No, He misleads *and* deceives the people [gives them false ideas]!

13 But no one dared speak out boldly about Him for fear of [the leaders of] the Jews.

14 When the Feast was already half over, Jesus went up into the temple [bcourt] and began to teach.

15 The Jews were astonished. They said, How is it that this Man has learning [is so versed in the sacred Scriptures and in theology] when He has never studied?

16 Jesus answered them by saying, My teaching is not My own, but His Who sent Me.

17 If any man desires to do His will (God's pleasure), he will know (have the needed illumination to recognize, and can tell for himself) whether the teaching is from God or whether I am speaking from Myself *and* of My own accord *and* on My own authority.

18 He who speaks on his own authority seeks to win honor for himself. [He whose teaching originates with himself seeks his own glory.] But He Who seeks the glory *and* is eager for the honor of Him Who sent Him, He is true; and there is no unrighteousness *or* falsehood *or* deception in Him.

19 Did not Moses give you the Law? And yet not one of you keeps the Law. [If that is the truth] why do you seek to kill Me [for not keeping it]?

20 The crowd answered Him, You are possessed by a demon! [You are raving!] Who seeks to kill You?

21 Jesus answered them, I did one work, and you all are astounded. [John 5:1–9.]

22 Now Moses established circumcision among you—though it did not originate with Moses but with the previous patriarchs—and you circumcise a person [even] on the Sabbath day.

23 If, to avoid breaking the Law of Moses, a person undergoes circumcision on the Sabbath day, have you any cause to be angry with (indignant with, bitter against) Me for making a man's whole body well on the Sabbath?

24 Be honest in your judgment *and* do not decide at a glance (superficially and by appearances); but judge fairly *and* righteously.

25 Then some of the Jerusalem people said, Is not this the Man they seek to kill?

26 And here He is speaking openly, and they say nothing to Him! Can it be possible that the rulers have discovered *and* know that this is truly the Christ?

27 No, we know where this Man comes from; when the Christ arrives, no one is to know from what place He comes.

28 Whereupon Jesus called out as He taught in the temple [bporches], Do you know Me, and do you know where I am from? I have not come on My own authority *and* of My own accord *and* as self-appointed, but the One Who sent Me is true (real, genuine, steadfast); and Him you do not know!

29 I know Him [Myself] because I come from His [very] presence, and it was He [personally] Who sent Me.

30 Therefore they were eager to arrest Him, but no one laid a hand on Him, for His hour (time) had not yet come.

---

h Richard Trench, *Synonyms of the New Testament*.

31 And besides, many of the multitude believed in Him [adhered to Him, trusted in Him, relied on Him]. And they kept saying, When the Christ comes, will He do [can He be expected to do] more miracles *and* produce more proofs *and* signs than what this Man has done?

32 The Pharisees learned how the people were saying these things about Him under their breath; and the chief priests and Pharisees sent attendants (guards) to arrest Him.

33 Therefore Jesus said, For a little while I am [still] with you, and then I go back to Him Who sent Me.

34 You will look for Me, but you will not [be able to] find Me; where I am, you cannot come.

35 Then the Jews said among themselves, Where does this Man intend to go that we shall not find Him? Will He go to the Jews who are scattered in the Dispersion among the Greeks, and teach the Greeks?

36 What does this statement of His mean, You will look for Me and not be able to find Me, and, Where I am, you cannot come?

37 Now on the final and most important day of the Feast, Jesus stood, and He cried in a loud voice, If any man is thirsty, let him come to Me and drink!

38 He who believes in Me [who cleaves to *and* trusts in *and* relies on Me] as the Scripture has said, From his innermost being shall flow [continuously] springs *and* rivers of living water.

39 But He was speaking here of the Spirit, Whom those who believed (trusted, had faith) in Him were afterward to receive. For the [Holy] Spirit had not yet been given, because Jesus was not yet glorified (raised to honor).

40 Listening to those words, some of the multitude said, This is certain-ly *and* beyond doubt the Prophet! [Deut. 18:15, 18; John 1:21; 6:14; Acts 3:22.]

41 Others said, This is the Christ (the Anointed One)! But some said, What? Does the Christ come out of Galilee?

42 Does not the Scripture tell us that the Christ will come from the offspring of David and from Bethlehem, the village where David lived? [Ps. 89:3, 4; Mic. 5:2.]

43 So there arose a division *and* dissension among the people concerning Him.

44 Some of them wanted to arrest Him, but no one [ventured and] laid hands on Him.

45 Meanwhile the attendants (guards) had gone back to the chief priests and Pharisees, who asked them, Why have you not brought Him here with you?

46 The attendants replied, Never has a man talked as this Man talks! [No mere man has ever spoken as He speaks!]

47 The Pharisees said to them, Are you also deluded *and* led astray? [Are you also swept off your feet?]

48 Has any of the authorities or of the Pharisees believed in Him?

49 As for this multitude (rabble) that does not know the Law, they are contemptible *and* doomed *and* accursed!

50 Then Nicodemus, who came to Jesus before at night and was one of them, asked,

51 Does our Law convict a man without giving him a hearing and finding out what he has done?

52 They answered him, Are you too from Galilee? Search [the Scriptures yourself], and you will see that no prophet comes (will rise to prominence) from Galilee.

53 [i]And they went [back], each to his own house.

CHAPTER 8

B UT JESUS went to the Mount of Olives.

2 Early in the morning (at dawn), He came back into the temple [[i]court], and the people came to Him in crowds. He sat down and was teaching them.

3 When the scribes and Pharisees brought a woman who had been caught in adultery. They made her stand in the middle of the court and put the case before Him.

4 Teacher, they said, This woman has been caught in the very act of adultery.

5 Now Moses in the Law commanded us that such [women—offenders] shall be stoned to death. But what do You say [to do with her—what is Your sentence]? [Deut. 22:22–24.]

6 This they said to try (test) Him, hoping they might find a charge on which to accuse Him. But Jesus stooped down and wrote on the ground with His finger.

7 However, when they persisted with their question, He raised Himself up and said, Let him who is without sin among you be the first to throw a stone at her.

8 Then He bent down and went on writing on the ground with His finger.

9 They listened to Him, and then they began going out, conscience-stricken, one by one, from the oldest down to the last one of them, till Jesus was left alone, with the woman standing there before Him in the center of the court.

10 When Jesus raised Himself up, He said to her, Woman, where are your accusers? Has no man condemned you?

11 She answered, No one, Lord! And Jesus said, I do not condemn you either. Go on your way and from now on sin no more.

12 Once more Jesus addressed the crowd. He said, I am the Light of the world. He who follows Me will not be walking in the dark, but will have the Light which is Life.

13 Whereupon the Pharisees told Him, You are testifying on Your own behalf; Your testimony is not valid and is worthless.

14 Jesus answered, Even if I do testify on My own behalf, My testimony is true and reliable and valid, for I know where I came from and where I am going; but you do not know where I come from or where I am going.

15 You [set yourselves up to] judge according to the flesh (by what you see). [You condemn by external, human standards.] I do not [set Myself up to] judge or condemn or sentence anyone.

16 Yet even if I do judge, My judgment is true [My decision is right]; for I am not alone [in making it], but [there are two of Us] I and the Father, Who sent Me.

17 In your [own] Law it is written that the testimony (evidence) of two persons is reliable and valid. [Deut. 19:15.]

18 I am One [of the Two] bearing testimony concerning Myself; and My Father, Who sent Me, He also testifies about Me.

19 Then they said to Him, Where is this [k]Father of Yours? Jesus an-

i John 7:53 to 8:11 is absent from most of the older manuscripts, and those that have it sometimes place it elsewhere. The story may well be authentic. Indeed, Christ's response of compassion and mercy is so much in keeping with His character that we accept it as authentic, and feel that to omit it would be most unfortunate. j Richard Trench, *Synonyms of the New Testament*. k Capitalized because of Who He is, the everlasting Father, not who the speaker may have thought He was.

swered, You know My Father as little as you know Me. If you knew Me, you would know My Father also.

20 Jesus said these things in the treasury while He was teaching in the temple [¹court]; but no one ventured to arrest Him, because His hour had not yet come.

21 Therefore He said again to them, I am going away, and you will be looking for Me, and you will die in (under the curse of) your sin. Where I am going, it is not possible for you to come.

22 At this the Jews began to ask among themselves, Will He kill Himself? Is that why He says, Where I am going, it is not possible for you to come?

23 He said to them, You are from below; I am from above. You are of this world (of this earthly order); I am not of this world.

24 That is why I told you that you will die in (under the curse of) your sins; for if you do not believe that I am He [Whom I claim to be—if you do not adhere to, trust in, and rely on Me], you will die in your sins.

25 Then they said to Him, Who are You anyway? Jesus replied, [Why do I even speak to you!] I am exactly what I have been telling you from the first.

26 I have much to say about you and to judge and condemn. But He Who sent Me is true (reliable), and I tell the world [only] the things that I have heard from Him.

27 They did not perceive (know, understand) that He was speaking to them about the Father.

28 So Jesus added, When you have lifted up the Son of Man [on the cross], you will realize (know, understand) that I am He [for Whom you look] and that I do nothing of Myself (of My own accord or on My own authority), but I say [exactly] what My Father has taught Me.

29 And He Who sent Me is ever with Me; My Father has not left Me alone, for I always do what pleases Him.

30 As He said these things, many believed in Him [trusted, relied on, and adhered to Him].

31 So Jesus said to those Jews who had believed in Him, If you abide in My word [hold fast to My teachings and live in accordance with them], you are truly My disciples.

32 And you will know the Truth, and the Truth will set you free.

33 They answered Him, We are Abraham's offspring (descendants) and have never been in bondage to anybody. What do You mean by saying, You will be set free?

34 Jesus answered them, I assure you, most solemnly I tell you, Whoever commits *and* practices sin is the slave of sin.

35 Now a slave does not remain in a household permanently (forever); the son [of the house] does remain forever.

36 So if the Son liberates you [makes you free men], then you are really *and* unquestionably free.

37 [Yes] I know that you are Abraham's offspring; yet you plan to kill Me, because My word has no entrance (makes no progress, does not find any place) in you.

38 I tell the things which I have seen *and* learned at My Father's side, and your actions also reflect what you have heard *and* learned from your father.

39 They retorted, Abraham is our father. Jesus said, If you were [truly] Abraham's children, then you would do the works of Abraham [follow his example, do as Abraham did].

40 But now [instead] you are want-

l Richard Trench, *Synonyms of the New Testament.*

ing *and* seeking to kill Me, a Man Who has told you the truth which I have heard from God. This is not the way Abraham acted.

41 You are doing the works of your [own] father. They said to Him, We are not illegitimate children *and* born out of fornication; we have one Father, even God.

42 Jesus said to them, If God were your Father, you would love Me *and* respect Me *and* welcome Me gladly, for I proceeded (came forth) from God [out of His very presence]. I did not even come on My own authority *or* of My own accord (as self-appointed); but He sent Me.

43 Why do you misunderstand what I say? It is because you are unable to hear what I am saying. [You cannot bear to listen to My message; your ears are shut to My teaching.]

44 You are of your father, the devil, and it is your will to practice the lusts *and* gratify the desires [which are characteristic] of your father. He was a murderer from the beginning and does not stand in the truth, because there is no truth in him. When he speaks a falsehood, he speaks what is natural to him, for he is a liar [himself] and the father of lies *and* of all that is false.

45 But because I speak the truth, you do not believe Me [do not trust Me, do not rely on Me, or adhere to Me].

46 Who of you convicts Me of wrongdoing *or* finds Me guilty of sin? Then if I speak truth, why do you not believe Me [trust Me, rely on, and adhere to Me]?

47 Whoever is of God listens to God. [Those who belong to God hear the words of God.] This is the reason that you do not listen [to those words, to Me]: because you do not

belong to God *and* are not of God *or* in harmony with Him.

48 The Jews answered Him, Are we not right when we say You are a Samaritan and that You have a demon [that You are under the power of an evil spirit]?

49 Jesus answered, I am not possessed by a demon. On the contrary, I honor *and* reverence My Father and you dishonor (despise, vilify, and scorn) Me.

50 However, I am not in search of honor for Myself. [I do not seek and am not aiming for My own glory.] There is One Who [looks after that; He] seeks [My glory], and He is the Judge.

51 I assure you, most solemnly I tell you, if anyone observes My teaching [lives in accordance with My message, keeps My word], he will by no means ever see *and* experience death.

52 The Jews said to Him, Now we know that You are under the power of a demon (ᵐinsane). Abraham died, and also the prophets, yet You say, If a man keeps My word, he will never taste of death into all eternity.

53 Are You greater than our father Abraham? He died, and all the prophets died! Who do You make Yourself out to be?

54 Jesus answered, If I were to glorify Myself (magnify, praise, and honor Myself), I would have no real glory, for My glory would be nothing *and* worthless. [My honor must come to Me from My Father.] It is My Father Who glorifies Me [Who extols Me, magnifies, and praises Me], of Whom you say that He is your God.

55 Yet you do not know Him *or* recognize Him *and* are not acquainted with Him, but I know Him. If I should say that I do not know Him, I

ᵐ Joseph Thayer, *A Greek-English Lexicon.*

would be a liar like you. But I know Him and keep His word [obey His teachings, am faithful to His message].

56 Your forefather Abraham was extremely happy at the hope *and* prospect of seeing My day (My incarnation); and he did see it and was delighted. [Heb. 11:13.]

57 Then the Jews said to Him, You are not yet fifty years old, and have You seen Abraham?

58 Jesus replied, I assure you, most solemnly I tell you, before Abraham was born, I AM. [Exod. 3:14.]

59 So they took up stones to throw at Him, but Jesus, by mixing with the crowd, concealed Himself and went out of the temple [ⁿenclosure].

CHAPTER 9

AS HE passed along, He noticed a man blind from his birth.

2 His disciples asked Him, Rabbi, who sinned, this man or his parents, that he should be born blind?

3 Jesus answered, It was not that this man or his parents sinned, but he was born blind in order that the workings of God should be manifested (displayed and illustrated) in him.

4 We must work the works of Him Who sent Me *and* be busy with His business while it is daylight; night is coming on, when no man can work.

5 As long as I am in the world, I am the world's Light.

6 When He had said this, He spat on the ground and made clay (mud) with His saliva, and He spread it [as ointment] on the man's eyes.

7 And He said to him, Go, wash in the Pool of Siloam—which means Sent. So he went and washed, and came back seeing.

8 When the neighbors and those who used to know him by sight as a beggar saw him, they said, Is not this the man who used to sit and beg?

9 Some said, It is he. Others said, No, but he looks very much like him. But he said, Yes, I am the man.

10 So they said to him, How were your eyes opened?

11 He replied, The Man called Jesus made mud and smeared it on my eyes and said to me, Go to Siloam and wash. So I went and washed, and I obtained my sight!

12 They asked him, Where is He? He said, I do not know.

13 Then they conducted to the Pharisees the man who had formerly been blind.

14 Now it was on the Sabbath day that Jesus mixed the mud and opened the man's eyes.

15 So now again the Pharisees asked him how he received his sight. And he said to them, He smeared mud on my eyes, and I washed, and now I see.

16 Then some of the Pharisees said, This Man [Jesus] is not from God, because He does not observe the Sabbath. But others said, How can a man who is a sinner (a bad man) do such signs *and* miracles? So there was a difference of opinion among them.

17 Accordingly they said to the blind man again, What do you say about Him, seeing that He opened your eyes? And he said, He is [He must be] a prophet!

18 However, the Jews did not believe that he had [really] been blind and that he had received his sight until they called (summoned) the parents of the man.

19 They asked them, Is this your son, whom you reported as having been born blind? How then does he see now?

ⁿ Richard Trench, *Synonyms of the New Testament.*

20 His parents answered, We know that this is our son, and that he was born blind.

21 But as to how he can now see, we do not know; or who has opened his eyes, we do not know. He is of age. Ask him; let him speak for himself and give his own account of it.

22 His parents said this because they feared [the leaders of] the Jews; for the Jews had already agreed that if anyone should acknowledge Jesus to be the Christ, he should be expelled and excluded from the synagogue.

23 On that account his parents said, He is of age; ask him.

24 So the second time they summoned the man who had been born blind, and said to him, Now give God the glory (praise). This °Fellow we know is only a sinner (a wicked person).

25 Then he answered, I do not know whether He is a sinner and wicked or not. But one thing I do know, that whereas I was blind before, now I see.

26 So they said to him, What did He [actually] do to you? How did He open your eyes?

27 He answered, I already told you and you would not listen. Why do you want to hear it again? Can it be that you wish to become His disciples also?

28 And they stormed at him [they jeered, they sneered, they reviled him] and retorted, You are His disciple yourself, but we are the disciples of Moses.

29 We know for certain that God spoke with Moses, but as for this Fellow, we know nothing about where He hails from.

30 The man replied, Well, this is astonishing! Here a Man has opened my eyes, and yet you do not know where He comes from. [That is amazing!]

31 We know that God does not listen to sinners; but if anyone is Godfearing and a worshiper of Him and does His will, He listens to him.

32 Since the beginning of time it has never been heard that anyone opened the eyes of a man born blind.

33 If this Man were not from God, He would not be able to do anything like this.

34 They retorted, You were wholly born in sin [from head to foot]; and do you [presume to] teach us? So they cast him out [threw him clear outside the synagogue].

35 Jesus heard that they had put him out, and meeting him He said, Do you believe in and adhere to the Son of Man ᴾor the Son of God?

36 He answered, Who is He, Sir? Tell me, that I may believe in and adhere to Him.

37 Jesus said to him, You have seen Him; [in fact] He is talking to you right now.

38 He called out, Lord, I believe! [I rely on, I trust, I cleave to You!] And he worshiped Him.

39 Then Jesus said, I came into this world for judgment [as a Separator, in order that there may be ᵠseparation between those who believe on Me and those who reject Me], to make the sightless see and to make those who see become blind.

40 Some Pharisees who were near, hearing this remark, said to Him, Are we also blind?

41 Jesus said to them, If you were blind, you would have no sin; but because you now claim to have sight, your sin remains. [If you were blind, you would not be guilty of sin; but because you insist, We do see clear-

---

o Capitalized because of what He is, the spotless Son of God, not what the speaker may have thought He was.
p Many ancient manuscripts read "the Son of God."
q Marvin Vincent, *Word Studies.*

ly, you are unable to escape your guilt.]

CHAPTER 10

I ASSURE you, most solemnly I tell you, he who does not enter by the door into the sheepfold, but climbs up some other way (elsewhere, from some other quarter) is a thief and a robber.

2 But he who enters by the door is the shepherd of the sheep.

3 The watchman opens the door for this man, and the sheep listen to his voice *and* heed it; and he calls his own sheep by name and brings (leads) them out.

4 When he has brought his own sheep outside, he walks on before them, and the sheep follow him because they know his voice.

5 They will never [on any account] follow a stranger, but will run away from him because they do not know the voice of strangers *or* recognize their call.

6 Jesus used this parable (illustration) with them, but they did not understand what He was talking about.

7 So Jesus said again, I assure you, most solemnly I tell you, that I Myself am the Door ʳfor the sheep.

8 All others who came [as such] before Me are thieves and robbers, but the [true] sheep did not listen to *and* obey them.

9 I am the Door; anyone who enters in through Me will be saved (will live). He will come in and he will go out [freely], and will find pasture.

10 The thief comes only in order to steal and kill and destroy. I came that they may have *and* enjoy life, and have it in abundance (to the full, till it ˢoverflows).

11 I am the Good Shepherd. The Good Shepherd risks *and* lays down

His [own] life for the sheep. [Ps. 23.]

12 But the hired servant (he who merely serves for wages) who is neither the shepherd nor the owner of the sheep, when he sees the wolf coming, deserts the flock and runs away. And the wolf chases *and* snatches them and scatters [the flock].

13 Now the hireling flees because he merely serves for wages and is not himself concerned about the sheep [cares nothing for them].

14 I am the Good Shepherd; and I know *and* recognize My own, and My own know *and* recognize Me—

15 Even as [truly as] the Father knows Me and I also know the Father—and I am giving My [very own] life *and* laying it down on behalf of the sheep.

16 And I have other sheep [beside these] that are not of this fold. I must bring *and* ᵗimpel those also; and they will listen to My voice *and* heed My call, and so there will be [they will become] one flock under one Shepherd. [Ezek. 34:23.]

17 For this [reason] the Father loves Me, because I lay down My [own] life—to take it back again.

18 No one takes it away from Me. On the contrary, I lay it down voluntarily. [I put it from Myself.] I am authorized *and* have power to lay it down (to resign it) and I am authorized *and* have power to take it back again. These are the instructions (orders) which I have received [as My charge] from My Father.

19 Then a fresh division of opinion arose among the Jews because of His saying these things.

20 And many of them said, He has a demon and He is mad (insane—He raves, He rambles). Why do you listen to Him?

---

r Marvin Vincent, *Word Studies.*   s Alexander Souter, *Pocket Lexicon of the Greek New Testament.*
t G. Abbott-Smith, *Manual Greek Lexicon.*

21 Others argued, These are not the thoughts *and* the language of one possessed. Can a demon-possessed person open blind eyes?

22 After this the Feast of Dedication [of the reconsecration of the temple] was taking place at Jerusalem. It was winter,

23 And Jesus was walking in Solomon's Porch in the temple area.

24 So the Jews surrounded Him and began asking Him, How long are You going to keep us in doubt *and* suspense? If You are really the Christ (the Messiah), tell us so plainly *and* openly.

25 Jesus answered them, I have told you so, yet you do not believe Me [you do not trust Me *and* rely on Me]. The very works that I do by the power of My Father *and* in My Father's name bear witness concerning Me [they are My credentials *and* evidence in support of Me].

26 But you do not believe *and* trust *and* rely on Me because you do not belong to My fold [you are no sheep of Mine].

27 The sheep that are My own hear *and* are listening to My voice; and I know them, and they follow Me.

28 And I give them eternal life, and they shall never lose it *or* perish throughout the ages. [To all eternity they shall never by any means be destroyed.] And no one is able to snatch them out of My hand.

29 My Father, Who has given them to Me, is greater *and* mightier than all [else]; and no one is able to snatch [them] out of the Father's hand.

30 I and the Father are One.

31 Again the Jews ᵘbrought up stones to stone Him.

32 Jesus said to them, My Father has enabled Me to do many good deeds. [I have shown many acts of mercy in your presence.] For which of these do you mean to stone Me?

33 The Jews replied, We are not going to stone You for a good act, but for blasphemy, because You, a mere ᵛMan, make Yourself [out to be] God.

34 Jesus answered, Is it not written in your Law, I said, You are gods? [Ps. 82:6.]

35 So men are called gods [by the Law], men to whom God's message came—and the Scripture cannot be set aside *or* cancelled *or* broken *or* annulled—

36 [If that is true] do you say of the One Whom the Father consecrated *and* dedicated *and* set apart for Himself and sent into the world, You are blaspheming, because I said, I am the Son of God?

37 If I am not doing the works [performing the deeds] of My Father, then do not believe Me [do not adhere to Me and trust Me and rely on Me].

38 But if I do them, even though you do not believe Me *or* have faith in Me, [at least] believe the works *and* have faith in what I do, in order that you may know and understand [clearly] that the Father is in Me, and I am in the Father [One with Him].

39 They sought again to arrest Him, but He escaped from their hands.

40 He went back again across the Jordan to the locality where John was when he first baptized, and there He remained.

41 And many came to Him, and they kept saying, John did not perform a [single] sign *or* miracle, but everything John said about this Man was true.

42 And many [people] there became believers in Him. [They ad-

u Marvin Vincent, *Word Studies*.   v Capitalized because of what He is, the spotless Son of God, not what the speaker may have thought He was.

hered to *and* trusted in *and* relied on Him.]

CHAPTER 11

NOW A certain man named Lazarus was ill. He was of Bethany, the village where Mary and her sister Martha lived.

2 This Mary was the one who anointed the Lord with perfume and wiped His feet with her hair. It was her brother Lazarus who was [now] sick.

3 So the sisters sent to Him, saying, Lord, he whom You love [so well] is sick.

4 When Jesus received the message, He said, This sickness is not to end in death; but [on the contrary] it is to honor God *and* to promote His glory, that the Son of God may be glorified through (by) it.

5 Now Jesus loved Martha and her sister and Lazarus. [They were His dear friends, and He held them in loving esteem.]

6 Therefore [even] when He heard that Lazarus was sick, He still stayed two days longer in the same place where He was.

7 Then after that interval He said to His disciples, Let us go back again to Judea.

8 The disciples said to Him, Rabbi, the Jews only recently were intending *and* trying to stone You, and are You [thinking of] going back there again?

9 Jesus answered, Are there not twelve hours in the day? Anyone who walks about in the daytime does not stumble, because he sees [by] the light of this world.

10 But if anyone walks about in the night, he does stumble, because there is no light in him [the light is lacking to him].

11 He said these things, and then added, Our friend Lazarus is at rest *and* sleeping; but I am going there that I may awaken him out of his sleep.

12 The disciples answered, Lord, if he is sleeping, he will recover.

13 However, Jesus had spoken of his death, but they thought that He referred to falling into a refreshing *and* natural sleep.

14 So then Jesus told them plainly, Lazarus is dead,

15 And for your sake I am glad that I was not there; it will help you to believe (to trust and rely on Me). However, let us go to him.

16 Then Thomas, who was called the Twin, said to his fellow disciples, Let us go too, that we may die [be killed] along with Him.

17 So when Jesus arrived, He found that he [Lazarus] had already been in the tomb four days.

18 Bethany was near Jerusalem, only about two miles away,

19 And a considerable number of the Jews had gone out to see Martha and Mary to console them concerning their brother.

20 When Martha heard that Jesus was coming, she went to meet Him, while Mary remained sitting in the house.

21 Martha then said to Jesus, Master, if You had been here, my brother would not have died.

22 And even now I know that whatever You ask from God, He will grant it to You.

23 Jesus said to her, Your brother shall rise again.

24 Martha replied, I know that he will rise again in the resurrection at the last day.

25 Jesus said to her, I am [Myself] the Resurrection and the Life. Whoever believes in (adheres to, trusts in, and relies on) Me, although he may die, yet he shall live;

26 And whoever continues to live and believes in (has faith in, cleaves

to, and relies on) Me shall never [actually] die at all. Do you believe this?

27 She said to Him, Yes, Lord, I have believed [I do believe] that You are the Christ (the Messiah, the Anointed One), the Son of God, [even He] Who was to come into the world. [It is for Your coming that the world has waited.]

28 After she had said this, she went back and called her sister Mary, privately whispering to her, The Teacher is close at hand and is asking for you.

29 When she heard this, she sprang up quickly and went to Him.

30 Now Jesus had not yet entered the village, but was still at the same spot where Martha had met Him.

31 When the Jews who were sitting with her in the house and consoling her saw how hastily Mary had arisen and gone out, they followed her, supposing that she was going to the tomb to pour out her grief there.

32 When Mary came to the place where Jesus was and saw Him, she dropped down at His feet, saying to Him, Lord, if You had been here, my brother would not have died.

33 When Jesus saw her sobbing, and the Jews who came with her [also] sobbing, He was deeply moved in spirit and troubled. [He chafed in spirit and sighed and was disturbed.]

34 And He said, Where have you laid him? They said to Him, Lord, come and see.

35 Jesus wept.

36 The Jews said, See how [tenderly] He loved him!

37 But some of them said, Could not He Who opened a blind man's eyes have prevented this man from dying?

38 Now Jesus, again sighing repeatedly *and* deeply disquieted, approached the tomb. It was a cave (a hole in the rock), and a boulder lay against [the entrance to close] it.

39 Jesus said, Take away the stone. Martha, the sister of the dead man, exclaimed, But Lord, by this time he [is decaying and] throws off an offensive odor, for he has been dead four days!

40 Jesus said to her, Did I not tell you *and* ʷpromise you that if you would believe *and* rely on Me, you would see the glory of God?

41 So they took away the stone. And Jesus lifted up His eyes and said, Father, I thank You that You have heard Me.

42 Yes, I know You always hear *and* listen to Me, but I have said this on account of *und* for the benefit of the people standing around, so that they may believe that You did send Me [that You have made Me Your Messenger].

43 When He had said this, He shouted with a loud voice, Lazarus, come out!

44 And out walked the man who had been dead, his hands and feet wrapped in burial cloths (linen strips), and with a [burial] napkin bound around his face. Jesus said to them, Free him of the burial wrappings and let him go.

45 Upon seeing what Jesus had done, many of the Jews who had come with Mary believed in Him. [They trusted in Him and adhered to Him and relied on Him.]

46 But some of them went back to the Pharisees and told them what Jesus had done.

47 So the chief priests and Pharisees called a meeting of the council (the Sanhedrin) and said, What are we to do? For this Man performs many signs (evidences, miracles).

48 If we let Him alone to go on like this, everyone will believe in Him

---

ʷ Charles B. Williams, *The New Testament: A Translation.*

and adhere to Him, and the Romans will come and suppress *and* destroy *and* take away our [holy] place and our nation (ˣour temple and city and our civil organization).

49 But one of them, Caiaphas, who was the high priest that year, declared, You know nothing at all!

50 Nor do you understand *or* reason out that it is expedient *and* better for your own welfare that one man should die on behalf of the people than that the whole nation should perish (be destroyed, ruined).

51 Now he did not say this simply of his own accord [he was not self-moved]; but being the high priest that year, he prophesied that Jesus was to die for the nation, [Isa. 53:8.]

52 And not only for the nation but also for the purpose of uniting into one body the children of God who have been scattered far and wide. [Isa. 49:6.]

53 So from that day on they took counsel *and* plotted together how they might put Him to death.

54 For that reason Jesus no longer appeared publicly among the Jews, but left there and retired to the district that borders on the wilderness (the desert), to a village called Ephraim, and there He stayed with the disciples.

55 Now the Jewish Passover was at hand, and many from the country went up to Jerusalem in order that they might purify *and* consecrate themselves before the Passover.

56 So they kept looking for Jesus and questioned among themselves as they were standing about in the temple (ʸarea), What do you think? Will He not come to the Feast at all?

57 Now the chief priests and Pharisees had given orders that if anyone knew where He was, he should report it to them, so that they might arrest Him.

CHAPTER 12

SO SIX days before the Passover Feast, Jesus came to Bethany, where Lazarus was, who had died and whom He had raised from the dead.

2 So they made Him a supper; and Martha served, but Lazarus was one of those at the table with Him.

3 Mary took a pound of ointment of pure liquid nard [a rare perfume] that was very expensive, and she poured it on Jesus' feet and wiped them with her hair. And the whole house was filled with the fragrance of the perfume.

4 But Judas Iscariot, the one of His disciples who was about to betray Him, said,

5 Why was this perfume not sold for 300 denarii [a year's wages for an ordinary workman] and that [money] given to the poor (the destitute)?

6 Now he did not say this because he cared for the poor but because he was a thief; and having the bag (the money box, the purse of the Twelve), he took for himself what was put into it [pilfering the collections].

7 But Jesus said, Let her alone. It was [intended] that she should keep it for the time of My preparation for burial. [She has kept it that she might have it for the time of My ᶻembalming.]

8 You always have the poor with you, but you do not always have Me.

9 Now a great crowd of the Jews heard that He was at Bethany, and they came there, not only because of Jesus but that they also might see Lazarus, whom He had raised from the dead.

10 So the chief priests planned to put Lazarus to death also,

x Marvin Vincent, *Word Studies*.   y Richard Trench, *Synonyms of the New Testament*.

11 Because on account of him many of the Jews were going away [were withdrawing from and leaving the Judeans] and believing in *and* adhering to Jesus.

12 The next day a vast crowd of those who had come to the Passover Feast heard that Jesus was coming to Jerusalem.

13 So they took branches of palm trees and went out to meet Him. And as they went, they kept shouting, Hosanna! Blessed is He *and* praise to Him Who comes in the name of the Lord, even the King of Israel! [Ps. 118:26.]

14 And Jesus, having found a young donkey, rode upon it, [just] as it is written in the Scriptures,

15 Do not fear, O Daughter of Zion! Look! Your King is coming, sitting on a donkey's colt! [Zech. 9:9.]

16 His disciples did not understand *and* could not comprehend the meaning of these things at first; but when Jesus was glorified *and* exalted, they remembered that these things had been written about Him and had been done to Him.

17 The group that had been with Jesus when He called Lazarus out of the tomb and raised him from among the dead kept telling it [bearing witness] to others.

18 It was for this reason that the crowd went out to meet Him, because they had heard that He had performed this sign (proof, miracle).

19 Then the Pharisees said among themselves, You see how futile your efforts are *and* how you accomplish nothing. See! The whole world is running after Him!

20 Now among those who went up to worship at the Feast were some Greeks.

21 These came to Philip, who was

from Bethsaida in Galilee, and they made this request, Sir, we desire to see Jesus.

22 Philip came and told Andrew; then Andrew and Philip together [went] and told Jesus.

23 And Jesus answered them, The time has come for the Son of Man to be glorified *and* exalted.

24 I assure you, most solemnly I tell you, Unless a grain of wheat falls into the earth and dies, it remains [just one grain; it never becomes more but lives] by itself alone. But if it dies, it produces many others *and* yields a rich harvest.

25 Anyone who loves his life loses it, but anyone who hates his life in this world will keep it to life eternal. [Whoever has no love for, no concern for, no regard for his life here on earth, but despises it, preserves it, his life forever and ever.]

26 If anyone serves Me, he must continue to follow Me [zto cleave steadfastly to Me, conform wholly to My example in living and, if need be, in dying] and wherever I am, there will My servant be also. If anyone serves Me, the Father will honor him.

27 Now My soul is troubled *and* distressed, and what shall I say? Father, save Me from this hour [of trial and agony]? But it was for this very purpose that I have come to this hour [that I might undergo it].

28 [Rather, I will say,] Father, glorify (honor and extol) Your [own] name! Then there came a voice out of heaven saying, I have already glorified it, and I will glorify it again.

29 The crowd of bystanders heard the sound and said that it had thundered; others said, An angel has spoken to Him!

30 Jesus answered, This voice has

z Joseph Thayer, *A Greek-English Lexicon.*

not come for My sake, but for your sake.

31 Now the judgment (crisis) of this world is coming on [sentence is now being passed on this world]. Now the ruler (evil genius, prince) of this world shall be cast out (expelled).

32 And I, if and when I am lifted up from the earth [on the cross], will draw and attract all men [Gentiles as well as Jews] to Myself.

33 He said this to signify in what manner He would die.

34 At this the people answered Him, We have learned from the Law that the Christ is to remain forever; how then can You say, The Son of Man must be lifted up [on the cross]? Who is this Son of Man? [Ps. 110:4.]

35 So Jesus said to them, You will have the Light only a little while longer. Walk while you have the Light [keep on living by it], so that darkness may not overtake and overcome you. He who walks about in the dark does not know where he goes [he is drifting].

36 While you have the Light, believe in the Light [have faith in it, hold to it, rely on it], that you may become sons of the Light and be filled with Light. Jesus said these things, and then He went away and hid Himself from them [was lost to their view].

37 Even though He had done so many miracles before them (right before their eyes), yet they still did not trust in Him and failed to believe in Him—

38 So that what Isaiah the prophet said was fulfilled: Lord, who has believed our report and our message? And to whom has the arm (the power) of the Lord been shown (unveiled and revealed)? [Isa. 53:1.]

39 Therefore they could not believe [they were unable to believe]. For Isaiah has also said,

40 He has blinded their eyes and hardened and benumbed their [callous, degenerated] hearts [He has made their minds dull], to keep them from seeing with their eyes and understanding with their hearts and minds and repenting and turning to Me to heal them.

41 Isaiah said this because he saw His glory and spoke of Him. [Isa. 6:9, 10.]

42 And yet [in spite of all this] many even of the leading men (the authorities and the nobles) believed and trusted in Him. But because of the Pharisees they did not confess it, for fear that [if they should acknowledge Him] they would be expelled from the synagogue;

43 For they loved the approval and the praise and the glory that come from men [instead of and] more than the glory that comes from God. [They valued their credit with men more than their credit with God.]

44 But Jesus loudly declared, The one who believes in Me does not [only] believe in and trust in and rely on Me, but [in believing in Me he believes] in Him Who sent Me.

45 And whoever sees Me sees Him Who sent Me.

46 I have come as a Light into the world, so that whoever believes in Me [whoever cleaves to and trusts in and relies on Me] may not continue to live in darkness.

47 If anyone hears My teachings and fails to observe them [does not keep them, but disregards them], it is not I who judges him. For I have not come to judge and to condemn and to pass sentence and to inflict penalty on the world, but to save the world.

48 Anyone who rejects Me and persistently sets Me at naught, refusing to accept My teachings, has his judge [however]; for the [very] message that I have spoken will itself judge and convict him at the last day.

49 This is because I have never spoken on My own authority *or* of My own accord *or* as self-appointed, but the Father Who sent Me has Himself given Me orders [concerning] what to say and what to tell. [Deut. 18:18, 19.]

50 And I know that His commandment is (means) eternal life. So whatever I speak, I am saying [exactly] what My Father has told Me to say *and* in accordance with His instructions.

CHAPTER 13

[N OW] BEFORE the Passover Feast began, Jesus knew (was fully aware) that the time had come for Him to leave this world *and* return to the Father. And as He had loved those who were His own in the world, He loved them to the last *and* [a]to the highest degree.

2 So [it was] during supper, Satan having already put the thought of betraying Jesus in the heart of Judas Iscariot, Simon's son,

3 [That] Jesus, knowing (fully aware) that the Father had put everything into His hands, and that He had come from God and was [now] returning to God,

4 Got up from supper, took off His garments, and taking a [servant's] towel, He fastened it around His waist.

5 Then He poured water into the washbasin and began to wash the disciples' feet and to wipe them with the [servant's] towel with which He was girded.

6 When He came to Simon Peter, [Peter] said to Him, Lord, are my feet to be washed by You? [Is it for You to wash my feet?]

7 Jesus said to him, You do not understand now what I am doing, but you will understand later on.

8 Peter said to Him, You shall never wash my feet! Jesus answered him, Unless I wash you, you have no part with ([b]in) Me [you have no share in companionship with Me].

9 Simon Peter said to Him, Lord, [wash] not only my feet, but my hands and my head too!

10 Jesus said to him, Anyone who has bathed needs only to wash his feet, but is clean all over. And you [My disciples] are clean, but not all of you.

11 For He knew who was going to betray Him; that was the reason He said, Not all of you are clean.

12 So when He had finished washing their feet and had put on His garments and had sat down again, He said to them, Do you understand what I have done to you?

13 You call Me the Teacher (Master) and the Lord, and you are right in doing so, for that is what I am.

14 If I then, your Lord and Teacher (Master), have washed your feet, you ought [it is your duty, you are under obligation, you owe it] to wash one another's feet.

15 For I have given you this as an example, so that you should do [in your turn] what I have done to you.

16 I assure you, most solemnly I tell you, A servant is not greater than his master, and no one who is sent is superior to the one who sent him.

17 If you know these things, blessed *and* happy *and* [c]to be envied are you if you practice them [if you act accordingly and really do them].

18 I am not speaking of *and* I do not mean all of you. I know whom I have chosen; but it is that the Scripture may be fulfilled, He who eats

a Saint John Chrysostom, cited by Joseph Thayer, *A Greek-English Lexicon*.   **b** Origen (the greatest theologian of the early Greek Church); Adam Clarke, *The Holy Bible with A Commentary*; and others so interpret this passage. Notice the "in Me" emphasis in John 15, especially in verses 4-9, words spoken concerning the same subject, and on the same evening.   **c** Alexander Souter, *Pocket Lexicon*.

dMy bread *with Me* has raised up his heel against Me. [Ps. 41:9.]

19 I tell you this now before it occurs, so that when it does take place you may be persuaded *and* believe that I am He [Who I say I am—the Christ, the Anointed One, the Messiah].

20 I assure you, most solemnly I tell you, he who receives *and* welcomes *and* takes into his heart any messenger of Mine receives Me [in just that way]; and he who receives *and* welcomes *and* takes Me into his heart receives Him Who sent Me [in that same way].

21 After Jesus had said these things, He was troubled (disturbed, agitated) in spirit and said, I assure you, most solemnly I tell you, one of you will deliver Me up [one of you will be false to Me and betray Me]!

22 The disciples kept looking at one another, puzzled as to whom He could mean.

23 One of His disciples, whom Jesus loved [whom He esteemed and delighted in], was reclining [next to Him] on Jesus' bosom.

24 So Simon Peter motioned to him to ask of whom He was speaking.

25 Then leaning back against Jesus' breast, he asked Him, Lord, who is it?

26 Jesus answered, It is the one to whom I am going to give this morsel (bit) of food after I have dipped it. So when He had dipped the morsel of bread [into the dish], He gave it to Judas, Simon Iscariot's son.

27 Then after [he had taken] the bit of food, Satan entered into *and* took possession of [Judas]. Jesus said to him, What you are going to do, do emore swiftly than you seem to intend *and* fmake quick work of it.

28 But nobody reclining at the table knew why He spoke to him or what He meant by telling him this.

29 Some thought that, since Judas had the money box (the purse), Jesus was telling him, Buy what we need for the Festival, or that he should give something to the poor.

30 So after receiving the bit of bread, he went out immediately. And it was night.

31 When he had left, Jesus said, Now is the Son of Man glorified! [Now He has achieved His glory, His honor, His exaltation!] And God has been glorified through *and* in Him.

32 And if God is glorified through *and* in Him, God will also glorify Him in Himself, and He will glorify Him at once *and* not delay.

33 [Dear] little children, I am to be with you only a little longer. You will look for Me and, as I told the Jews, so I tell you now: you are not able to come where I am going.

34 I give you a new commandment: that you should love one another. Just as I have loved you, so you too should love one another.

35 By this shall all [men] know that you are My disciples, if you love one another [if you keep on showing love among yourselves].

36 Simon Peter said to Him, Lord, where are You going? Jesus answered, You are not able to follow Me now where I am going, but you shall follow Me afterwards.

37 Peter said to Him, Lord, why cannot I follow You now? I will lay down my life for You.

38 Jesus answered, Will you [really] lay down your life for Me? I assure you, most solemnly I tell you, before a rooster crows, you will deny Me [completely disown Me] three times.

d Many ancient manuscripts read "with Me."   e Joseph Thayer, *A Greek-English Lexicon.*
f Charles B. Williams, *The New Testament: A Translation.*

CHAPTER 14

DO NOT let your hearts be troubled (distressed, agitated). You believe in *and* adhere to *and* trust in *and* rely on God; believe in *and* adhere to *and* trust in *and* rely also on Me.

2 In My Father's house there are many dwelling places (homes). If it were not so, I would have told you; for I am going away to prepare a place for you.

3 And when (if) I go and make ready a place for you, I will come back again and will take you to Myself, that where I am you may be also.

4 And [to the place] where I am going, you know the way.

5 Thomas said to Him, Lord, we do not know where You are going, so how can we know the way?

6 Jesus said to him, I am the Way and the Truth and the Life; no one comes to the Father except by (through) Me.

7 If you had known Me [had learned to recognize Me], you would also have known My Father. From now on, you know Him and have seen Him.

8 Philip said to Him, Lord, show us the Father [cause us to see the Father—that is all we ask]; then we shall be satisfied.

9 Jesus replied, Have I been with all of you for so long a time, and do you not recognize *and* know Me, Philip? Anyone who has seen Me has seen the Father. How can you say then, Show us the Father?

10 Do you not believe that I am in the Father, and that the Father is in Me? What I am telling you I do not say on My own authority *and* of My own accord; but the Father Who lives continually in Me does the

(*His*) works (His own miracles, deeds of power).

11 Believe Me that I am in the Father and the Father in Me; or else believe Me for the sake of the [very] works themselves. [If you cannot trust Me, at least let these works that I do in My Father's name convince you.]

12 I assure you, most solemnly I tell you, if anyone steadfastly believes in Me, he will himself be able to do the things that I do; and he will do even greater things than these, because I go to the Father.

13 And I will do [I Myself will grant] whatever you ask in My Name [as [h]presenting all that I AM], so that the Father may be glorified *and* extolled in (through) the Son. [Exod. 3:14.]

14 [Yes] I will grant [I Myself will do for you] whatever you shall ask in My Name [as [h]presenting all that I AM].

15 If you [really] love Me, you will keep (obey) My commands.

16 And I will ask the Father, and He will give you another Comforter (Counselor, Helper, Intercessor, Advocate, Strengthener, and Standby), that He may remain with you forever—

17 The Spirit of Truth, Whom the world cannot receive (welcome, take to its heart), because it does not see Him or know *and* recognize Him. But you know *and* recognize Him, for He lives with you [constantly] and will be in you.

18 I will not leave you as orphans [comfortless, desolate, bereaved, forlorn, helpless]; I will come [back] to you.

19 Just a little while now, and the world will not see Me any more, but you will see Me; because I live, you will live also.

---

g Several ancient manuscripts read "His works."

h Hermann Cremer, *Biblico-Theological Lexicon.*

20 At that time [when that day comes] you will know [for yourselves] that I am in My Father, and you [are] in Me, and I [am] in you.

21 The person who has My commands and keeps them is the one who [really] loves Me; and whoever [really] loves Me will be loved by My Father, and I [too] will love him and will show (reveal, manifest) Myself to him. [I will let Myself be clearly seen by him and make Myself real to him.]

22 Judas, not Iscariot, asked Him, Lord, how is it that You will reveal Yourself [make Yourself real] to us and not to the world?

23 Jesus answered, If a person [really] loves Me, he will keep My word [obey My teaching]; and My Father will love him, and We will come to him and make Our home (abode, special dwelling place) with him.

24 Anyone who does not [really] love Me does not observe *and* obey My teaching. And the teaching which you hear *and* heed is not Mine, but [comes] from the Father Who sent Me.

25 I have told you these things while I am still with you.

26 But the Comforter (Counselor, Helper, Intercessor, Advocate, Strengthener, Standby), the Holy Spirit, Whom the Father will send in My name [in My place, to represent Me and act on My behalf], He will teach you all things. And He will cause you to recall (will remind you of, bring to your remembrance) everything I have told you.

27 Peace I leave with you; My [own] peace I now give *and* bequeath to you. Not as the world gives do I give to you. Do not let your hearts be troubled, neither let them be afraid. [Stop allowing yourselves to be agitated and disturbed; and do not per-

mit yourselves to be fearful and intimidated and cowardly and unsettled.]

28 You heard Me tell you, I am going away and I am coming [back] to you. If you [really] loved Me, you would have been glad, because I am going to the Father; for the Father is greater *and* mightier than I am.

29 And now I have told you [this] before it occurs, so that when it does take place you may believe *and* have faith in *and* rely on Me.

30 I will not talk with you much more, for the prince (evil genius, ruler) of the world is coming. And he has no claim on Me. [He has nothing in common with Me; there is nothing in Me that belongs to him, and he has no power over Me.]

31 But [¹Satan is coming and] I do as the Father has commanded Me, so that the world may know (be convinced) that I love the Father and that I do only what the Father has instructed Me to do. [I act in full agreement with His orders.] Rise, let us go away from here.

CHAPTER 15

I AM the True Vine, and My Father is the Vinedresser.

2 Any branch in Me that does not bear fruit [that stops bearing] He cuts away (trims off, takes away); and He cleanses *and* repeatedly prunes every branch that continues to bear fruit, to make it bear more *and* richer *and* more excellent fruit.

3 You are cleansed *and* pruned already, because of the word which I have given you [the teachings I have discussed with you].

4 Dwell in Me, and I will dwell in you. [Live in Me, and I will live in you.] Just as no branch can bear fruit of itself without abiding in (being vitally united to) the vine, neither can

i Marvin Vincent, *Word Studies*.

you bear fruit unless you abide in Me.

5 I am the Vine; you are the branches. Whoever lives in Me and I in him bears much (abundant) fruit. However, apart from Me [cut off from vital union with Me] you can do nothing.

6 If a person does not dwell in Me, he is thrown out like a [broken-off] branch, and withers; such branches are gathered up and thrown into the fire, and they are burned.

7 If you live in Me [abide vitally united to Me] and My words remain in you *and* continue to live in your hearts, ask whatever you will, and it shall be done for you.

8 When you bear (produce) much fruit, My Father is honored *and* glorified, and you show *and* prove yourselves to be true followers of Mine.

9 I have loved you, [just] as the Father has loved Me; abide in My love [¹continue in His love with Me].

10 If you keep My commandments [if you continue to obey My instructions], you will abide in My love *and* live on in it, just as I have obeyed My Father's commandments and live on in His love.

11 I have told you these things, that My joy *and* delight may be in you, and that your joy *and* gladness may be of full measure *and* complete *and* overflowing.

12 This is My commandment: that you love one another [just] as I have loved you.

13 No one has greater love [no one has shown stronger affection] than to lay down (give up) his own life for his friends.

14 You are My friends if you keep on doing the things which I command you to do.

15 I do not call you servants (slaves) any longer, for the servant does not know what his master is doing (working out). But I have called you My friends, because I have made known to you everything that I have heard from My Father. [I have revealed to you everything that I have learned from Him.]

16 You have not chosen Me, but I have chosen you and I have appointed you [I have planted you], that you might go *and* bear fruit *and* keep on bearing, and that your fruit may be lasting [that it may remain, abide], so that whatever you ask the Father in My Name [as ²presenting all that I AM], He may give it to you.

17 This is what I command you: that you love one another.

18 If the world hates you, know that it hated Me before it hated you.

19 If you belonged to the world, the world would treat you with affection *and* would love you as its own. But because you are not of the world [no longer one with it], but I have chosen (selected) you out of the world, the world hates (detests) you.

20 Remember that I told you, A servant is not greater than his master [is not superior to him]. If they persecuted Me, they will also persecute you; if they kept My word *and* obeyed My teachings, they will also keep *and* obey yours.

21 But they will do all this to you [inflict all this suffering on you] because of [your bearing] My name *and* on My account, for they do not know *or* understand the One Who sent Me.

22 If I had not come and spoken to them, they would not be guilty of sin [would be blameless]; but now they have no excuse for their sin.

23 Whoever hates Me also hates My Father.

24 If I had not done (accomplished) among them the works which no one else ever did, they would not be

guilty of sin. But [the fact is] now they have both seen [these works] and have hated both Me and My Father.

25 But [this is so] that the word written in their Law might be fulfilled, They hated Me without a cause. [Ps. 35:19; 69:4.]

26 But when the Comforter (Counselor, Helper, Advocate, Intercessor, Strengthener, Standby) comes, Whom I will send to you from the Father, the Spirit of Truth Who comes (proceeds) from the Father, He [Himself] will testify regarding Me.

27 But you also will testify and be My witnesses, because you have been with Me from the beginning.

CHAPTER 16

I HAVE told you all these things, so that you should not be offended (taken unawares and falter, or be caused to stumble and fall away). [I told you to keep you from being scandalized and repelled.]

2 They will put you out of (expel you from) the synagogues; but an hour is coming when whoever kills you will think and claim that he has offered service to God.

3 And they will do this because they have not known the Father or Me.

4 But I have told you these things now, so that when they occur you will remember that I told you of them. I did not say these things to you from the beginning, because I was with you.

5 But now I am going to Him Who sent Me, yet none of you asks Me, Where are You going?

6 But because I have said these things to you, sorrow has filled your hearts [taken complete possession of them].

7 However, I am telling you nothing but the truth when I say it is profitable (good, expedient, advantageous) for you that I go away. Because if I do not go away, the Comforter (Counselor, Helper, Advocate, Intercessor, Strengthener, Standby) will not come to you [into close fellowship with you]; but if I go away, I will send Him to you [to be in close fellowship with you].

8 And when He comes, He will convict and convince the world and bring demonstration to it about sin and about righteousness (uprightness of heart and right standing with God) and about judgment:

9 About sin, because they do not believe in Me [trust in, rely on, and adhere to Me];

10 About righteousness (uprightness of heart and right standing with God), because I go to My Father, and you will see Me no longer;

11 About judgment, because the ruler (evil genius, prince) of this world [Satan] is judged and condemned and sentence already is passed upon him.

12 I have still many things to say to you, but you are not able to bear them or to take them upon you or to grasp them now.

13 But when He, the Spirit of Truth (the Truth-giving Spirit) comes, He will guide you into all the Truth (the whole, full Truth). For He will not speak His own message [on His own authority]; but He will tell whatever He hears [from the Father; He will give the message that has been given to Him], and He will announce and declare to you the things that are to come [that will happen in the future].

14 He will honor and glorify Me, because He will take of (receive, draw upon) what is Mine and will reveal (declare, disclose, transmit) it to you.

15 Everything that the Father has is Mine. That is what I meant when I

said that He [the Spirit] will take the things that are Mine and will reveal (declare, disclose, transmit) it to you.

16 In a little while you will no longer see Me, and again after a short while you will see Me.

17 So some of His disciples questioned among themselves, What does He mean when He tells us, In a little while you will no longer see Me, and again after a short while you will see Me, and, Because I go to My Father?

18 What does He mean by a little while? We do not know or understand what He is talking about.

19 Jesus knew that they wanted to ask Him, so He said to them, Are you wondering and inquiring among yourselves what I meant when I said, In a little while you will no longer see Me, and again after a short while you will see Me?

20 I assure you, most solemnly I tell you, that you shall weep and grieve, but the world will rejoice. You will be sorrowful, but your sorrow will be turned into joy.

21 A woman, when she gives birth to a child, has grief (anguish, agony) because her time has come. But when she has delivered the child, she no longer remembers her pain (trouble, anguish) because she is so glad that a man (a child, a human being) has been born into the world.

22 So for the present you are also in sorrow (in distress and depressed); but I will see you again and [then] your hearts will rejoice, and no one can take from you your joy (gladness, delight).

23 And when that time comes, you will ask nothing of Me [you will need to ask Me no questions. I assure you, most solemnly I tell you, that My Father will grant you whatever you ask in My Name [as [k]presenting all that I AM]. [Exod. 3:14.]

24 Up to this time have not asked a [single] thing in My Name [as [k]presenting all that I AM]; but now ask and keep on asking and you will receive, so that your joy (gladness, delight) may be full and complete.

25 I have told you these things in parables (veiled language, allegories, dark sayings); the hour is now coming when I shall no longer speak to you in figures of speech, but I should tell you about the Father in plain words and openly (without reserve).

26 At that time you will ask (pray) in My Name; and I am not saying that I will ask the Father on your behalf [for it will be unnecessary].

27 For the Father Himself [tenderly] loves you because you have loved Me and have believed that I came out from the Father.

28 I came out from the Father and have come into the world; again, I am leaving the world and going to the Father.

29 His disciples said, Ah, now You are speaking plainly to us and not in parables (veiled language and figures of speech)!

30 Now we know that You are acquainted with everything and have no need to be asked questions. Because of this we believe that you [really] came from God.

31 Jesus answered them, Do you now believe? [Do you believe it at last?]

32 But take notice, the hour is coming, and it has arrived, when you will all be dispersed and scattered, every man to his own home, leaving Me alone. Yet I am not alone, because the Father is with Me.

33 I have told you these things, so that in Me you may have [perfect] peace and confidence. In the world

k Hermann Cremer, *Biblico-Theological Lexicon*.

you have tribulation *and* trials *and* distress *and* frustration; but be of good cheer [take courage; be confident, certain, undaunted]! For I have overcome the world. [I have deprived it of power to harm you and have conquered it for you.]

CHAPTER 17

WHEN JESUS had spoken these things, He lifted up His eyes to heaven and said, Father, the hour has come. Glorify *and* exalt *and* honor *and* magnify Your Son, so that Your Son may glorify *and* extol *and* honor *and* magnify You.

2 [Just as] You have granted Him power *and* authority over all flesh (all humankind), [now glorify Him] so that He may give eternal life to all whom You have given Him.

3 And this is eternal life: [it means] to know (to perceive, recognize, become acquainted with, and understand) You, the only true *and* real God, and [likewise] to know Him, Jesus [as the] Christ (the Anointed One, the Messiah), Whom You have sent.

4 I have glorified You down here on the earth by completing the work that You gave Me to do.

5 And now, Father, glorify Me along with Yourself *and* restore Me to such majesty *and* honor in Your presence as I had with You before the world existed.

6 I have manifested Your Name [I have revealed Your very Self, Your real Self] to the people whom You have given Me out of the world. They were Yours, and You gave them to Me, and they have obeyed *and* kept Your word.

7 Now [at last] they know *and* understand that all You have given Me belongs to You [is really and truly Yours].

8 For the [uttered] words that You gave Me I have given them; and they have received *and* accepted [them] and have come to know positively *and* in reality [to believe with absolute assurance] that I came forth from Your presence, and they have believed *and* are convinced that You did send Me.

9 I am praying for them. I am not praying (requesting) for the world, but for those You have given Me, for they belong to You.

10 All [things that are] Mine are Yours, and all [things that are] Yours belong to Me; and I am glorified in (through) them. [They have done Me honor; in them My glory is achieved.]

11 And [now] I am no more in the world, but these are [still] in the world, and I am coming to You. Holy Father, keep in Your Name ['in the knowledge of Yourself] those whom You have given Me, that they may be one as We [are one].

12 While I was with them, I kept *and* preserved them in Your Name ['in the knowledge and worship of You]. Those You have given Me I guarded *and* protected, and not one of them has perished *or* is lost except the son of perdition [Judas Iscariot —the one who is now doomed to destruction, destined to be lost], that the Scripture might be fulfilled. [Ps. 41:9; John 6:70.]

13 And now I am coming to You; I say these things while I am still in the world, so that My joy may be made full *and* complete *and* perfect in them [that they may experience My delight fulfilled in them, that My enjoyment may be perfected in their own souls, that they may have My gladness within them, filling their hearts].

14 I have given *and* delivered to them Your word (message) and the

---

l Albert Barnes, *Notes on the New Testament.*

world has hated them, because they are not of the world [do not belong to the world], just as I am not of the world.

15 I do not ask that You will take them out of the world, but that You will keep *and* protect them from the evil one.

16 They are not of the world (worldly, belonging to the world), [just] as I am not of the world.

17 Sanctify them [purify, consecrate, separate them for Yourself, make them holy] by the Truth; Your Word is Truth.

18 Just as You sent Me into the world, I also have sent them into the world.

19 And so for their sake *and on* their behalf I sanctify (dedicate, consecrate) Myself, that they also may be sanctified (dedicated, consecrated, made holy) in the Truth.

20 Neither for these alone do I pray [it is not for their sake only that I make this request], but also for all those who will ever come to believe in (trust in, cling to, rely on) Me through their word *and* teaching,

21 That they all may be one, [just] as You, Father, are in Me and I in You, that they also may be one in Us, so that the world may believe *and* be convinced that You have sent Me.

22 I have given to them the glory *and* honor which You have given Me, that they may be one [even] as We are one:

23 I in them and You in Me, in order that they may become one *and* perfectly united, that the world may know *and* [definitely] recognize that You sent Me and that You have loved them [even] as You have loved Me.

24 Father, I desire that they also whom You have entrusted to Me [as Your gift to Me] may be with Me

where I am, so that they may see My glory, which You have given Me [Your love gift to Me]; for You loved Me before the foundation of the world.

25 O just *and* righteous Father, although the world has not known You *and* has failed to recognize You *and* has never acknowledged You, I have known You [continually]; and these men understand *and* know that You have sent Me.

26 I have made Your Name known to them *and* revealed Your character *and* Your very ᵐSelf, and I will continue to make [You] known, that the love which You have bestowed upon Me may be in them [felt in their hearts] and that I [Myself] may be in them.

CHAPTER 18

Having SAID these things, Jesus went out with His disciples beyond (across) the winter torrent of the Kidron [in the ravine]. There was a garden there, which He and His disciples entered.

2 And Judas, who was betraying Him *and* delivering Him up, also knew the place, because Jesus had often retired there with His disciples.

3 So Judas, obtaining *and* taking charge of the band of soldiers and some guards (attendants) of the high priests and Pharisees, came there with lanterns and torches and weapons.

4 Then Jesus, knowing all that was about to befall Him, went out to them and said, Whom are you seeking? [Whom do you want?]

5 They answered Him, Jesus the Nazarene. Jesus said to them, I am He. Judas, who was betraying Him, was also standing with them.

6 When Jesus said to them, I am He, they went backwards (drew

m Joseph Thayer, *A Greek-English Lexicon.*

back, lurched backward) and fell to the ground.

7 Then again He asked them, Whom are you seeking? And they said, Jesus the Nazarene.

8 Jesus answered, I told you that I am He. So, if you want Me [if it is only I for Whom you are looking], let these men go their way.

9 Thus what He had said was fulfilled *and* verified, Of those whom You have given Me, I have not lost even one. [John 6:39; 17:12.]

10 Then Simon Peter, who had a sword, drew it and struck the high priest's servant and cut off his right ear. The servant's name was Malchus.

11 Therefore, Jesus said to Peter, Put the sword [back] into the sheath! The cup which My Father has given Me, shall I not drink it?

12 So the troops and their captain and the guards (attendants) of the Jews seized Jesus and bound Him,

13 And they brought Him first to Annas, for he was the father-in-law of Caiaphas, who was the high priest that year.

14 It was Caiaphas who had counseled the Jews that it was expedient *and* for their welfare that one man should die for (instead of, in behalf of) the people. [John 11:49, 50.]

15 Now Simon Peter and another disciple were following Jesus. And that disciple was known to the high priest, and so he entered along with Jesus into the court of the palace of the high priest;

16 But Peter was standing outside at the door. So the other disciple, who was known to the high priest, went out and spoke to the maid who kept the door and brought Peter inside.

17 Then the maid who was in charge at the door said to Peter, You

are not also one of the disciples of this [n]Man, are you? He said, I am not!

18 Now the servants and the guards (the attendants) had made a fire of coals, for it was cold, and they were standing and warming themselves. And Peter was with them, standing and warming himself.

19 Then the high priest questioned Jesus about His disciples and about His teaching.

20 Jesus answered him, I have spoken openly to the world. I have always taught in a synagogue and in the temple [area], where the Jews [habitually] congregate (assemble); and I have spoken nothing secretly.

21 Why do you ask Me? Ask those who have heard [Me] what I said to them. See! They know what I said.

22 But when He said this, one of the attendants who stood by struck Jesus, saying, Is that how [n]You answer the high priest?

23 Jesus replied, If I have said anything wrong [if I have spoken abusively, if there was evil in what I said] tell what was wrong with it. But if I spoke rightly *and* properly, why do you strike Me?

24 Then Annas sent Him bound to Caiaphas the high priest.

25 But Simon Peter [still] was standing and was warming himself. They said to him, You are not also one of His disciples, are you? He denied it and said, I am not!

26 One of the high priest's servants, a relative of the man whose ear Peter cut off, said, Did I not see you in the garden with Him?

27 And again Peter denied it. And immediately a rooster crowed.

28 Then they brought Jesus from Caiaphas into the Praetorium (judgment hall, governor's palace). And it was early. They themselves did not

---

n Capitalized because of what He is, the spotless Son of God, not what the speaker may have thought He was.

enter the Praetorium, that they might not be defiled (become ceremonially unclean), but might be fit to eat the Passover [supper].

29 So Pilate went out to them and said, What accusation do you bring against this °Man?

30 They retorted, If He were not an evildoer (criminal), we would not have handed Him over to you.

31 Pilate said to them, Take Him yourselves and judge *and* sentence *and* punish Him according to your [own] law. The Jews answered, It is not lawful for us to put anyone to death.

32 This was to fulfill the word which Jesus had spoken to show (indicate, predict) by what manner of death He was to die. [John 12:32–34.]

33 So Pilate went back again into the judgment hall and called Jesus and asked Him, Are You the King of the Jews?

34 Jesus replied, Are you saying this of yourself [on your own initiative], or have others told you about Me?

35 Pilate answered, Am I a Jew? Your [own] people *and* nation and their chief priests have delivered You to me. What have You done?

36 Jesus answered, My kingdom (kingship, royal power) belongs not to this world. If My kingdom were of this world, My followers would have been fighting to keep Me from being handed over to the Jews. But as it is, My kingdom is not from here (this world); [it has no such origin or source].

37 Pilate said to Him, Then You are a King? Jesus answered, You say it! [You speak correctly!] For I am a King. [Certainly I am a King!] This is why I was born, and for this I have come into the world, to bear witness to the Truth. Everyone who is of the Truth [who is a friend of the Truth, who belongs to the Truth] hears *and* listens to My voice.

38 Pilate said to Him, What is Truth? On saying this he went out to the Jews again and told them, I find no fault in Him.

39 But it is your custom that I release one [prisoner] for you at the Passover. So shall I release for you the King of the Jews?

40 Then they all shouted back again, Not Him [not this Man], but Barabbas! Now Barabbas was a robber.

CHAPTER 19

SO THEN Pilate took Jesus and scourged (flogged, whipped) Him.

2 And the soldiers, having twisted together a crown of thorns, put it on His head, and threw a purple cloak around Him.

3 And they kept coming to Him and saying, Hail, King of the Jews! [Good health to you! Peace to you! Long life to you, King of the Jews!] And they struck Him with the palms of their hands. [Isa. 53:3, 5, 7.]

4 Then Pilate went out again and said to them, See, I bring Him out to you, so that you may know that I find no fault (crime, cause for accusation) in Him.

5 So Jesus came out wearing the thorny crown and purple cloak, and Pilate said to them, See, [here is] the °Man!

6 When the chief priests and attendants (guards) saw Him, they cried out, Crucify Him! Crucify Him! Pilate said to them, Take Him yourselves and crucify Him, for I find no fault (crime) in Him.

7 The Jews answered him, We have a law, and according to that law He should die, because He has

---

o Capitalized because of what He is, the spotless Son of God, not what the speaker may have thought He was.

claimed *and* made Himself out to be the Son of God.

8 So, when Pilate heard this said, he was more alarmed *and* awestricken *and* afraid than before.

9 He went into the judgment hall again and said to Jesus, Where are You from? [To what world do You belong?] But Jesus did not answer him.

10 So Pilate said to Him, Will You not speak [even] to me? Do You not know that I have power (authority) to release You and I have power to crucify You?

11 Jesus answered, You would not have any power *or* authority whatsoever against (over) Me if it were not given you from above. For this reason the sin *and* guilt of the one who delivered Me over to you is greater.

12 Upon this, Pilate wanted (sought, was anxious) to release Him, but the Jews kept shrieking, If you release this Man, you are no friend of Caesar! Anybody who makes himself [out to be] a king sets himself up against Caesar [is a rebel against the emperor]!

13 Hearing this, Pilate brought Jesus out and sat down on the judgment seat at a place called the Pavement (the Mosaic Pavement, the Stone Platform)—in Hebrew, Gabbatha.

14 Now it was the day of Preparation for the Passover, and it was about the sixth hour (about twelve o'clock noon). He said to the Jews, See, [here is] your King!

15 But they shouted, Away with Him! Away with Him! Crucify Him! Pilate said to them, Crucify your King? The chief priests answered, We have no king but Caesar!

16 Then he delivered Him over to them to be crucified.

17 And they took Jesus *and* led

[Him] away; so He went out, bearing His own cross, to the spot called The Place of the Skull—in Hebrew it is called Golgotha.

18 There they crucified Him, and with Him two others—one on either side and Jesus between them. [Isa. 53:12.]

19 And Pilate also wrote a title (an inscription on a placard) and put it on the cross. And the writing was: Jesus the Nazarene, the King of the Jews.

20 And many of the Jews read this title, for the place where Jesus was crucified was near the city, and it was written in Hebrew, in Latin, [and] in Greek.

21 Then the chief priests of the Jews said to Pilate, Do not write, The King of the Jews, but, He said, I am King of the Jews.

22 Pilate replied, What I have written, I have written.

23 Then the soldiers, when they had crucified Jesus, took His garments and made four parts, one share for each soldier, and also the tunic (the long shirtlike undergarment). But the tunic was seamless, woven [in one piece] from the top throughout.

24 So they said to one another, Let us not tear it, but let us cast lots to decide whose it shall be. This was to fulfill the Scripture, They parted My garments among them, and for My clothing they cast lots. So the soldiers did these things. [Ps. 22:18.]

25 But by the cross of Jesus stood His mother, His mother's sister, Mary the [wife] of Clopas, and Mary Magdalene.

26 So Jesus, seeing His mother, and the disciple whom He loved standing near, said to His mother, [ᵖDear] woman, See, [here is] your son!

27 Then He said to the disciple,

ᵖ G. Abbott-Smith, *Manual Greek Lexicon*: "A term of respect and endearment."

See, [here is] your mother! And from that hour, the disciple took her into his own [keeping, own home].

28 After this, Jesus, knowing that all was now finished (ended), said in fulfillment of the Scripture, I thirst. [Ps. 69:21.]

29 A vessel (jar) full of sour wine (vinegar) was placed there, so they put a sponge soaked in the sour wine on [a stalk, reed of] hyssop, and held it to [His] mouth.

30 When Jesus had received the sour wine, He said, It is finished! And He bowed His head and gave up His spirit.

31 Since it was the day of Preparation, in order to prevent the bodies from hanging on the cross on the Sabbath—for that Sabbath was a very solemn *and* important one—the Jews requested Pilate to have the legs broken and the bodies taken away.

32 So the soldiers came and broke the legs of the first one, and of the other who had been crucified with Him.

33 But when they came to Jesus and they saw that He was already dead, they did not break His legs.

34 But one of the soldiers pierced His side with a spear, and immediately blood and water came (flowed) out.

35 And he who saw it (the eyewitness) gives this evidence, and his testimony is true; and he knows that he tells the truth, that you may believe also.

36 For these things took place, that the Scripture might be fulfilled (verified, carried out), Not one of His bones shall be broken; [Exod. 12:46; Num. 9:12; Ps. 34:20.]

37 And again another Scripture says, They shall look on Him Whom they have pierced. [Zech. 12:10.]

38 And after this, Joseph of Arimathea—a disciple of Jesus, but secretly for fear of the Jews—asked Pilate to let him take away the body of Jesus. And Pilate granted him permission. So he came and took away His body.

39 And Nicodemus also, who first had come to Jesus by night, came bringing a mixture of myrrh and aloes, [weighing] about a hundred pounds.

40 So they took Jesus' body and bound it in linen cloths with the spices (aromatics), as is the Jews' customary way to prepare for burial.

41 Now there was a garden in the place where He was crucified, and in the garden a new tomb, in which no one had ever [yet] been laid.

42 So there, because of the Jewish day of Preparation [and] since the tomb was near by, they laid Jesus.

CHAPTER 20

NOW ON the first day of the week, Mary Magdalene came to the tomb early, while it was still dark, and saw that the stone had been removed from (lifted out of the groove across the entrance of) the tomb.

2 So she ran and went to Simon Peter and the other disciple, whom Jesus [tenderly] loved, and said to them, They have taken away the Lord out of the tomb, and we do not know where they have laid Him!

3 Upon this, Peter and the other disciple came out and they went toward the tomb.

4 And they came running together, but the other disciple outran Peter and arrived at the tomb first.

5 And stooping down, he saw the linen cloths lying there, but he did not enter.

6 Then Simon Peter came up, following him, and went into the tomb and saw the linen cloths lying there,

7 But the burial napkin (kerchief) which had been around Jesus' head, was not lying with the other linen

cloths, but was [still] qrolled up (wrapped round and round) in a place by itself.

8 Then the other disciple, who had reached the tomb first, went in too; and he saw and was convinced *and* believed.

9 For as yet they did not know (understand) the statement of Scripture that He must rise again from the dead. [Ps. 16:10.]

10 Then the disciples went back again to their homes (lodging places).

11 But Mary remained standing outside the tomb sobbing. As she wept, she stooped down [and looked] into the tomb.

12 And she saw two angels in white sitting there, one at the head and one at the feet, where the body of Jesus had lain.

13 And they said to her, Woman, why are you sobbing? She told them, Because they have taken away my Lord, and I do not know where they have laid Him.

14 On saying this, she turned around and saw Jesus standing [there], but she did not know (recognize) that it was Jesus.

15 Jesus said to her, Woman, why are you crying [so]? For Whom are you looking? Supposing that it was the gardener, she replied, Sir, if you carried Him away from here, tell me where you have put Him and I will take Him away.

16 Jesus said to her, Mary! Turning around she said to Him in Hebrew, Rabboni!—which means Teacher *or* Master.

17 Jesus said to her, Do not cling to Me [do not hold Me], for I have not yet ascended to the Father. But go to My brethren and tell them, I am ascending to My Father and your Father, and to My God and your God.

18 Away came Mary Magdalene, bringing the disciples news (word) that she had seen the Lord and that He had said these things to her.

19 Then on that same first day of the week, when it was evening, though the disciples were behind closed doors for fear of the Jews, Jesus came and stood among them and said, Peace to you!

20 So saying, He showed them His hands and His side. And when the disciples saw the Lord, they were filled with joy (delight, exultation, ecstasy, rapture).

21 Then Jesus said to them again, Peace to you! [Just] as the Father has sent Me forth, so I am sending you.

22 And having said this, He breathed on them and said to them, Receive the Holy Spirit!

23 [Now having received the Holy Spirit, and being rled and directed by Him] if you forgive the sins of anyone, they are forgiven; if you retain the sins of anyone, they are retained.

24 But Thomas, one of the Twelve, called the Twin, was not with them when Jesus came.

25 So the other disciples kept telling him, We have seen the Lord! But he said to them, Unless I see in His hands the marks made by the nails and put my finger into the nail prints, and put my hand into His side, I will never believe [it].

26 Eight days later His disciples were again in the house, and Thomas was with them. Jesus came, though they were behind closed doors, and stood among them and said, Peace to you!

27 Then He said to Thomas, Reach out your finger here, and see My hands; and put out your hand and place [it] in My side. Do not be faithless *and* incredulous, but [stop your unbelief and] believe!

q Marvin Vincent, *Word Studies*.   r Matthew Henry, *Commentary on the Holy Bible*.

28 Thomas answered Him, My Lord and my God!

29 Jesus said to him, Because you have seen Me, *Thomas*, do you now believe (trust, have faith)? Blessed *and happy and* [s]to be envied are those who have never seen Me and yet have believed *and* adhered to *and* trusted *and* relied on Me.

30 There are also many other signs *and* miracles which Jesus performed in the presence of the disciples which are not written in this book.

31 But these are written (recorded) in order that you may believe that Jesus is the Christ (the Anointed One), the Son of God, and that through believing *and* cleaving to *and* trusting *and* relying upon Him you may have life through (in) His name [[t]through Who He is]. [Ps. 2:7, 12.]

CHAPTER 21

AFTER THIS, Jesus let Himself be seen *and* revealed [Himself] again to the disciples, at the Sea of Tiberias. And He did it in this way:

2 There were together Simon Peter, and Thomas, called the Twin, and Nathanael from Cana of Galilee, also the sons of Zebedee, and two others of His disciples.

3 Simon Peter said to them, I am going fishing! They said to him, And we are coming with you! So they went out and got into the boat, and throughout that night they caught nothing.

4 Morning was already breaking when Jesus came to the beach and stood there. However, the disciples did not know that it was Jesus.

5 So Jesus said to them, [s]Boys (children), You do not have any meat (fish), do you? [Have you caught anything to eat along with your bread?] They answered Him, No!

6 And He said to them, Cast the net on the right side of the boat and you will find [some]. So they cast the net, and now they were not able to haul it in for such a big catch (mass, quantity) of fish [was in it].

7 Then the disciple whom Jesus loved said to Peter, It is the Lord! Simon Peter, hearing him say that it was the Lord, put (girded) on his upper garment (his fisherman's coat, his outer tunic)—for he was stripped [for work]—and sprang into the sea.

8 And the other disciples came in the small boat, for they were not far from shore, only some hundred yards away, dragging the net full of fish.

9 When they got out on land (the beach), they saw a fire of coals there and fish lying on it [cooking], and bread.

10 Jesus said to them, Bring some of the fish which you have just caught.

11 So Simon Peter went aboard and hauled the net to land, full of large fish, 153 of them; and [though] there were so many of them, the net was not torn.

12 Jesus said to them, Come [and] have breakfast. But none of the disciples ventured *or* dared to ask Him, Who are You? because they [well] knew that it was the Lord.

13 Jesus came and took the bread and gave it to them, and so also [with] the fish.

14 This was now the third time that Jesus revealed Himself (appeared, was manifest) to the disciples after He had risen from the dead.

15 When they had eaten, Jesus said to Simon Peter, Simon, son of John, do you love Me more than these [others do—with reasoning, intentional, spiritual devotion, as one loves the Father]? He said to Him, Yes, Lord,

---

s Alexander Souter, *Pocket Lexicon*.   t Hermann Cremer, *Biblico-Theological Lexicon*.

You know that I love You [that I have deep, instinctive, personal affection for You, as for a close friend]. He said to him, Feed My lambs.

16 Again He said to him the second time, Simon, son of John, do you love Me [with reasoning, intentional, spiritual devotion, as one loves the Father]? He said to Him, Yes, Lord, You know that I love You [that I have a deep, instinctive, personal affection for You, as for a close friend]. He said to him, Shepherd (tend) My sheep.

17 He said to him the third time, Simon, son of John, do you love Me [with a deep, instinctive, personal affection for Me, as for a close friend]? Peter was grieved (was saddened and was hurt) that He should ask him the third time, Do you love Me? And he said to Him, Lord, You know everything; You know that I love You [that I have a deep, instinctive, personal affection for You, as for a close friend]. Jesus said to him, Feed My sheep.

18 I assure you, most solemnly I tell you, when you were young you girded yourself [put on your own belt or girdle] and you walked about wherever you pleased to go. But when you grow old you will stretch out your hands, and someone else will put a girdle around you and carry you where you do not wish to go.

19 He said this to indicate by what kind of death Peter would glorify God. And after this, He said to him, Follow Me!

20 But Peter turned and saw the disciple whom Jesus loved, following—the one who also had leaned back on His breast at the supper and had said, Lord, who is it that is going to betray You?

21 When Peter saw him, he said to Jesus, Lord, what about this man?

22 Jesus said to him, If I want him to stay (survive, live) till I come, what is that to you? [What concern is it of yours?] You follow Me!

23 So word went out among the brethren that this disciple was not going to die; yet Jesus did not say to him that he was not going to die, but, If I want him to stay (survive, live) till I come, what is that to you?

24 It is this same disciple who is bearing witness to these things and who has recorded (written) them; and we [well] know that his testimony is true.

25 And there are also many other things which Jesus did. If they should be all recorded one by one [in detail], I suppose that even the world itself could not contain (have room for) the books that would be written.

THE ACTS
OF THE APOSTLES

CHAPTER 1

IN THE former account [which I prepared], O Theophilus, I made [a continuous report] dealing with all the things which Jesus began to do and to teach [Luke 1:1–4.]

2 Until the day when He ascended, after He through the Holy Spirit had instructed and commanded the apostles (special messengers) whom He had chosen.

3 To them also He showed Himself alive after His passion (His suffering

in the garden and on the cross) by [a series of] many convincing demonstrations [unquestionable evidences and infallible proofs], appearing to them during forty days and talking [to them] about the things of the kingdom of God.

4 And while being in their comp[any] *and* eating at the table with the[m] He commanded them not to leave [Je]rusalem but to wait for what the [Fa]ther had promised, Of which, [He said] you have heard Me sp[eak] [John 14:16, 26; 15:26.]

5 For John baptized with w[ater], but not many days from now [you] shall be baptized with (uplaced, introduced into) the Holy Spirit

6 So when they were asse[mbled] they asked Him, Lord, is [it at this] time when You will reestablish the kingdom *and* restore it to Israel?

7 He said to them, It is not for you to become acquainted with *and* know *what time brings [the things and events of time and their definite periods] or fixed *years and seasons (their critical niche in time), which the Father has appointed (fixed and reserved) by His own choice *and* authority *and* personal power.

8 But you shall receive power (ability, efficiency, and might) when the Holy Spirit has come upon you, and you shall be My witnesses in Jerusalem and all Judea and Samaria and to the ends (the very bounds) of the earth.

9 And when He had said this, even as they were looking [at Him], He was caught up, and a cloud received *and* carried Him away out of their sight.

10 And while they were gazing intently into heaven as He went, behold, two men [dressed] in white robes suddenly stood beside them,

...Men of Galilee, why [...] zing into heaven? [...] Who was caught [...] up from among you [...] return in [just] the [...] ch you saw Him go

...disciples] went back [...] om the hill called Oli[vet] [...] ear Jerusalem, [only] a [...] journey (three quar[ter] [...] away.

...n they had entered [the] [...] ounted [the stairs] to the [...] here they were [indefi]ng—Peter and John and [...] Andrew; Philip and [...] Bartholomew and Mat[thew] [...] s son of Alphaeus and Si[...] ealot, and Judas [son] of [...]

14 All of these with their minds in full agreement devoted themselves steadfastly to prayer, [waiting together] with the women and Mary the mother of Jesus, and with His brothers.

15 Now on one of those days Peter arose among the brethren, the whole number of whom gathered together was about a hundred and twenty.

16 Brethren, he said, it was necessary that the Scripture be fulfilled which the Holy Spirit foretold by the lips of David, about Judas who acted as guide to those who arrested Jesus.

17 For he was counted among us and received [by divine allotment] his portion in this ministry.

18 Now this man obtained a piece of land with the [money paid him as a] reward for his treachery *and* wickedness, and falling headlong he burst open in the middle [of his body] and all his intestines poured forth.

19 And all the residents of Jerusalem became acquainted with the

u Kenneth Wuest, *Word Studies in the Greek New Testament.*   v Joseph Thayer, *A Greek-English Lexicon of the New Testament.*   w Richard Trench, *Synonyms of the New Testament.*   x James Moulton and George Milligan, *The Vocabulary of the Greek Testament.*

facts, so that they called the piece of land in their own dialect—Akeldama, that is, Field of Blood.

20 For in the book of Psalms it is written, Let his place of residence become deserted *and* gloomy, and let there be no one to live in it; and [again], Let another take his position *or* overseership. [Ps. 69:25; 109:8.]

21 So one of the [other] men who have accompanied us [apostles] during all the time that the Lord Jesus went in and out among us,

22 From the baptism of John at the outset until the day when He was taken up from among us—one of these men must join with us and become a witness to testify to His resurrection.

23 And they accordingly proposed (nominated) two men, Joseph called Barsabbas, who was surnamed Justus, and Matthias.

24 And they prayed and said, You, Lord, Who know all hearts (ʸtheir thoughts, passions, desires, appetites, purposes, and endeavors), indicate to us which one of these two You have chosen

25 To take the place in this ministry and receive the position of an apostle, from which Judas fell away *and* went astray to go [where he belonged] to his own [proper] place.

26 And they drew lots [between the two], and the lot fell on Matthias; and he was added to *and* counted with the eleven apostles (special messengers).

CHAPTER 2

AND WHEN the day of Pentecost had fully come, they were all assembled together in one place,

2 When suddenly there came a sound from heaven like the rushing of a violent tempest blast, and it filled the whole house in which they were sitting.

3 And there appeared to them tongues resembling fire, which were separated *and* distributed and which settled on each one of them.

4 And they were all filled (diffused throughout their souls) with the Holy Spirit and began to speak in other (different, foreign) languages (tongues), as the Spirit ᶻkept giving them clear *and* loud expression [in each tongue in appropriate words].

5 Now there were then residing in Jerusalem Jews, devout *and* God-fearing men from every country under heaven.

6 And when this sound was heard, the multitude came together and they were astonished *and* bewildered, because each one heard them [the apostles] speaking in his own [particular] dialect.

7 And they were beside themselves with amazement, saying, Are not all these who are talking Galileans?

8 Then how is it that we hear, each of us, in our own (particular) dialect to which we were born?

9 Parthians and Medes and Elamites and inhabitants of Mesopotamia, Judea and Cappadocia, Pontus and [the province of] Asia,

10 Phrygia and Pamphylia, Egypt and the parts of Libya about Cyrene, and the transient residents from Rome, both Jews and the proselytes [to Judaism from other religions],

11 Cretans and Arabians too—we all hear them speaking in our own native tongues [and telling of] the mighty works of God!

12 And all were beside themselves with amazement and were puzzled *and* bewildered, saying one to another, What can this mean?

13 But others made a joke of it *and* derisively said, They are simply

---

drunk *and* full of sweet [intoxicating] wine.

14 But Peter, standing with the eleven, raised his voice and addressed them: You Jews and all you residents of Jerusalem, let this be [explained] to you so that you will know *and* understand; listen closely to what I have to say.

15 For these men are not drunk, as you imagine, for it is [only] the third hour (about 9:00 a.m.) of the day;

16 But [instead] this is [the beginning of] what was spoken through the prophet Joel:

17 And it shall come to pass in the last days, God declares, that I will pour out of My Spirit upon all mankind, and your sons and your daughters shall prophesy [[a]telling forth the divine counsels] and your young men shall see visions ([b]divinely granted appearances), and your old men shall dream [[b]divinely suggested] dreams.

18 Yes, and on My menservants also and on My maidservants in those days I will pour out of My Spirit, and they shall prophesy [[c]telling forth the divine counsels *and* [b]predicting future events pertaining especially to God's kingdom];

19 And I will show wonders in the sky above and signs on the earth beneath, blood and fire and smoking vapor;

20 The sun shall be turned into darkness and the moon into blood before the obvious day of the Lord comes—that great and notable *and* conspicuous and renowned [day].

21 And it shall be that whoever shall call upon the name of the Lord [[b]invoking, adoring, and worshiping the Lord—Christ] shall be saved. [Joel 2:28–32.]

22 You men of Israel, listen to what I have to say: Jesus of Naza-

reth, a Man accredited *and* pointed out *and* shown forth *and* commended *and* attested to you by God by the mighty works and [the power of performing] wonders and signs which God worked through Him [right] in your midst, as you yourselves know—

23 This Jesus, when delivered up according to the definite *and* fixed purpose *and* settled plan and fore knowledge of God, you crucified *and* put out of the way [killing Him] by the hands of lawless *and* wicked men.

24 [But] God raised Him up, liberating Him from the pangs of death, seeing that it was not possible for Him to continue to be controlled *or* retained by it.

25 For David says in regard to Him, I saw the Lord constantly before me, for He is at my right hand that I may not be shaken *or* overthrown *or* cast down [from my secure and happy state].

26 Therefore my heart rejoiced and my tongue exulted exceedingly; moreover, my flesh also will dwell in hope [will encamp, pitch its tent, and dwell in hope in anticipation of the resurrection].

27 For You will not abandon my soul, leaving it helpless in Hades (the state of departed spirits), nor let Your Holy One know decay *or* see destruction [of the body after death].

28 You have made known to me the ways of life; You will enrapture me [diffusing My soul with joy] with *and* in Your presence. [Ps. 16:8–11.]

29 Brethren, it is permitted me to tell you confidently *and* with freedom concerning the patriarch David that he both died and was buried, and his tomb is with us to this day.

30 Being however a prophet, and

---

a G. Abbott-Smith, *Manual Greek Lexicon of the New Testament.*   b Joseph Thayer, *A Greek-English Lexicon.*   c G. Abbott-Smith, *Manual Greek Lexicon.*

knowing that God had sealed to him with an oath that He would set one of his descendants on his throne, [II Sam. 7:12–16; Ps. 132:11.]

31 He, foreseeing this, spoke [by foreknowledge] of the resurrection of the Christ (the Messiah) that He was not deserted [in death] *and* left in Hades (the state of departed spirits), nor did His body know decay *or* see destruction. [Ps. 16:10.]

32 This Jesus God raised up, and of that all we [His disciples] are witnesses.

33 Being therefore lifted high by *and* to the right hand of God, and having received from the Father *d*the promised [blessing which is the] Holy Spirit, He has made this outpouring which you yourselves both see and hear.

34 For David did not ascend into the heavens; yet he himself says, The Lord said to my Lord, Sit at My right hand *and* share My throne

35 Until I make Your enemies a footstool for Your feet. [Ps. 110:1.]

36 Therefore let the whole house of Israel recognize beyond all doubt *and* acknowledge assuredly that God has made Him both Lord and Christ (the Messiah)—this Jesus Whom you crucified.

37 Now when they heard this they were stung (cut) to the heart, and they said to Peter and the rest of the apostles (special messengers), Brethren, what shall we do?

38 And Peter answered them, Repent (change your views and purpose to accept the will of God in your inner selves instead of rejecting it) and be baptized, every one of you, in the name of Jesus Christ for the forgiveness of *and* release from your sins; and you shall receive the gift of the Holy Spirit.

39 For the promise [of the Holy Spirit] is to *and* for you and your children, and to *and* for all that are far away, [even] to *and* for as many as the Lord our God invites *and* bids to come to Himself. [Isa. 57:19; Joel 2:32.]

40 And [Peter] *e*solemnly *and* earnestly witnessed (testified) and admonished (exhorted) with much more continuous speaking *and* warned (reproved, advised, encouraged) them, saying, Be saved from this crooked (perverse, wicked, unjust) generation.

41 Therefore those who accepted *and* welcomed his message were baptized, and there were added that day about 3,000 souls.

42 And they steadfastly persevered, devoting themselves constantly to the instruction and fellowship of the apostles, to the breaking of bread [including the Lord's Supper] and prayers.

43 And a sense of awe (reverential fear) came upon every soul, and many wonders and signs were performed through the apostles (the special messengers).

44 And all who believed (who adhered to and trusted in and relied on Jesus Christ) were united and [together] they had everything in common;

45 And they sold their possessions (both their landed property and their movable goods) and distributed the price among all, according as any had need.

46 And day after day they regularly assembled in the temple with united purpose, and in their homes they broke bread [including the Lord's Supper]. They partook of their food with gladness and simplicity *and* generous hearts,

---

d Joseph Thayer, *A Greek-English Lexicon*.   e Marvin Vincent, *Word Studies*: The preposition *dia* gives this force.

47 Constantly praising God and being in favor *and* goodwill with all the people; and the Lord kept adding [to their number] daily those who were being saved [from spiritual death].

CHAPTER 3

NOW PETER and John were going up to the temple at the hour of prayer, the ninth hour (three o'clock in the afternoon),

2 [When] a certain man crippled from his birth was being carried along, who was laid each day at that gate of the temple [which is] called Beautiful, so that he might beg for charitable gifts from those who entered the temple.

3 So when he saw Peter and John about to go into the temple, he asked them to give him a gift.

4 And Peter directed his gaze intently at him, and so did John, and said, Look at us!

5 And [the man] paid attention to them, expecting that he was going to get something from them.

6 But Peter said, Silver and gold (money) I do not have; but what I do have, that I give to you: in [the ᶠuse of] the name of Jesus Christ of Nazareth, walk!

7 Then he took hold of the man's right hand with a firm grip and raised him up. And at once his feet and ankle bones became strong *and* steady,

8 And leaping forth he stood and ᵍbegan to walk, and he went into the temple with them, walking and leaping and praising God.

9 And all the people saw him walking about and praising God,

10 And they recognized him as the man who usually sat [begging] for alms at the Beautiful Gate of the temple; and they were filled with wonder and amazement (bewilderment, consternation) over what had occurred to him.

11 Now while he [still] firmly clung to Peter and John, all the people in utmost amazement ran together *and* crowded around them in the covered porch (walk) called Solomon's.

12 And Peter, seeing it, answered the people, You men of Israel, why are you so surprised *and* wondering at this? Why do you keep staring at us, as though by our [own individual] power *or* [active] piety we had made this man [able] to walk?

13 The God of Abraham and of Isaac and of Jacob, the God of our forefathers, has glorified His Servant *and* ʰSon Jesus [doing Him this honor], Whom you indeed delivered up and denied *and* rejected *and* disowned in the presence of Pilate, when he had determined to let Him go. [Exod. 3:6; Isa. 52:13.]

14 But you denied *and* rejected *and* disowned the Pure *and* Holy, the Just *and* Blameless One, and demanded [the pardon of] a murderer to be granted to you.

15 But you killed the very Source (the Author) of life, Whom God raised from the dead. To this we are witnesses.

16 And His name, through *and* by faith in His name, has made this man whom you see *and* recognize well *and* strong. [Yes] the faith which is through *and* by Him [Jesus] has given the man this perfect soundness [of body] before all of you.

17 And now, brethren, I know that you acted in ignorance [not aware of what you were doing], as did your rulers also.

18 Thus has God fulfilled what He foretold by the mouth of all the prophets, that His Christ (the Messi-

---

f Joseph Thayer, *A Greek-English Lexicon.*   g Marvin Vincent, *Word Studies.*   h The Greek word used here means both "Servant" and "Child" ("Son").

ah) should undergo ill treatment *and* be afflicted *and* suffer.

19 So repent (change your mind and purpose); turn around *and* return [to God], that your sins may be erased (blotted out, wiped clean), that times of refreshing (of recovering from the effects of heat, of [reviving with fresh air) may come from the presence of the Lord;

20 And that He may send [to you] the Christ (the Messiah), Who before was designated *and* appointed for you—even Jesus,

21 Whom heaven must receive [and retain] until the time for the complete restoration of all that God spoke by the mouth of all His holy prophets for ages past [from the most ancient time in the memory of man].

22 Thus Moses said *to the forefathers,* The Lord God will raise up for you a Prophet from among your brethren as [He raised up] me; Him you shall listen to *and* understand by hearing *and* heed in all things whatever He tells you.

23 And it shall be that every soul that does not listen to *and* understand by hearing *and* heed that Prophet shall be utterly [exterminated from among the people. [Deut. 18:15–19.]

24 Indeed, all the prophets from Samuel and those who came afterwards, as many as have spoken, also promised *and* foretold *and* proclaimed these days.

25 You are the descendants (sons) of the prophets and the heirs of the covenant which God made *and* gave to your forefathers, saying to Abraham, And in your Seed (Heir) shall all the families of the earth be blessed *and* benefited. [Gen. 22:18; Gal. 3:16.]

26 It was to you first that God sent

His Servant *and* Son *Jesus,* when He raised Him up [[provided and gave Him for us], to bless you in turning every one of you from your wickedness *and* evil ways. [Acts 2:24; 3:22.]

CHAPTER 4

AND WHILE they [Peter and John] were talking to the people, the high priests and the military commander of the temple and the Sadducees came upon them,

2 Being vexed *and* indignant through *and* through because they were teaching the people *and* proclaiming in [the case of] Jesus the resurrection from the dead.

3 So they laid hands on them (arrested them) and put them in prison until the following day, for it was already evening.

4 But many of those who heard the message believed (adhered to and trusted in and relied on Jesus as the Christ). And their number grew *and* came to about 5,000.

5 Then on the following day, their magistrates and elders and scribes were assembled in Jerusalem,

6 Including Annas the high priest and Caiaphas and John and Alexander and all others who belonged to the high priestly relationship.

7 And they set the men in their midst and repeatedly demanded, By what sort of power or by what kind of authority did [such people as] you do this [healing]?

8 Then Peter, [because he was] filled with [and controlled by] the Holy Spirit, said to them, Rulers of the people and members of the council (the Sanhedrin),

9 If we are being put on trial [here] today *and* examined concerning a good deed done to benefit a feeble (helpless) cripple, by what means

i Marvin Vincent, *Word Studies.*   j Alexander Souter, *Pocket Lexicon of the Greek New Testament.*
k Robert Jamieson, A.R. Fausset and David Brown, *A Commentary on the Old and New Testaments.*

this man has been restored to health,

10 Let it be known and understood by all of you, and by the whole house of Israel, that in the name and through the power and authority of Jesus Christ of Nazareth, Whom you crucified, [but] Whom God raised from the dead, in Him and by means of Him this man is standing here before you well and sound in body.

11 This [Jesus] is the Stone which was despised and rejected by you, the builders, but which has become the Head of the corner [the Cornerstone]. [Ps. 118:22.]

12 And there is salvation in and through no one else, for there is no other name under heaven given among men by and in which we must be saved.

13 Now when they saw the boldness and unfettered eloquence of Peter and John and perceived that they were unlearned and untrained in the schools [common men with no educational advantages], they marveled; and they recognized that they had been with Jesus.

14 And since they saw the man who had been cured standing there beside them, they could not contradict the fact or say anything in opposition.

15 But having ordered [the prisoners] to go aside out of the council [chamber], they conferred (debated) among themselves,

16 Saying, What are we to do with these men? For that an extraordinary miracle has been performed by (through) them is plain to all the residents of Jerusalem, and we cannot deny it.

17 But in order that it may not spread further among the people and the nation, let us warn and forbid them with a stern threat to speak any more to anyone in this name [or about this Person].

18 [So] they summoned them and imperatively instructed them not to converse in any way or teach at all in or about the name of Jesus.

19 But Peter and John replied to them, Whether it is right in the sight of God to listen to you and obey you rather than God, you must decide (judge).

20 But we [ourselves] cannot help telling what we have seen and heard.

21 Then when [the rulers and council members] had further threatened them, they let them go, not seeing how they could secure a conviction against them because of the people; for everybody was praising and glorifying God for what had occurred.

22 For the man on whom this sign (miracle) of healing was performed was more than forty years old.

23 After they were permitted to go, [the apostles] returned to their own [company] and told all that the chief priests and elders had said to them.

24 And when they heard it, lifted their voices together with one united mind to God and said, O Sovereign Lord, You are He Who made the heaven and the earth and the sea and everything that is in them, [Exod. 20:11; Ps. 146:6.]

25 Who by the mouth of our forefather David, Your servant and child, said through the Holy Spirit, Why did the heathen (Gentiles) become wanton and insolent and rage, and the people imagine and study and plan vain (fruitless) things [that will not succeed]?

26 The kings of the earth took their stand in array [for attack] and the rulers were assembled and combined together against the Lord and against His Anointed (Christ, the Messiah). [Ps. 2:1, 2.]

27 For in this city there actually met and plotted together against Your holy Child and Servant Jesus, Whom You consecrated by anointing, both Herod and Pontius Pilate

with the Gentiles and peoples of Israel, [Ps. 2:1, 2.]

28 To carry out all that Your hand and Your will *and* purpose had predestined (predetermined) should occur.

29 And now, Lord, observe their threats and grant to Your bond servants [full freedom] to declare Your message fearlessly,

30 While You stretch out Your hand to cure and to perform signs *and* wonders through the authority *and* by the power of the name of Your holy Child *and* Servant Jesus.

31 And when they had prayed, the place in which they were assembled was shaken; and they were all filled with the Holy Spirit, and they continued to speak the Word of God with freedom *and* boldness *and* courage.

32 Now the company of believers was of one heart and soul, and not one of them claimed that anything which he possessed was [exclusively] his own, but everything they had was in common *and* for the use of all.

33 And with great strength *and* ability *and* power the apostles delivered their testimony to the resurrection of the Lord Jesus, and great grace (loving-kindness *and* favor and goodwill) rested richly upon them all.

34 Nor was there a destitute *or* needy person among them, for as many as were owners of lands or houses proceeded to sell them, and one by one they brought (gave back) the amount received from the sales

35 And laid it at the feet of the apostles (special messengers). Then distribution was made according as anyone had need.

36 Now Joseph, a Levite and native of Cyprus who was surnamed Barnabas by the apostles, which interpreted means Son of Encouragement,

37 Sold a field which belonged to

him and brought the sum of money and laid it at the feet of the apostles.

CHAPTER 5

BUT A certain man named Ananias with his wife Sapphira sold a piece of property,

2 And with his wife's knowledge *and* connivance he kept back *and* wrongfully appropriated some of the proceeds, bringing only a part and putting it at the feet of the apostles.

3 But Peter said, Ananias, why has Satan filled your heart that you should lie to *and* attempt to deceive the Holy Spirit, and should [in violation of your promise] withdraw secretly *and* appropriate to your own use part of the price from the sale of the land?

4 As long as it remained unsold, was it not still your own? And [even] after it was sold, was not [the money] at your disposal *and* under your control? Why then, is it that you have proposed *and* purposed in your heart to do this thing? [How could you have the heart to do such a deed?] You have not [simply] lied to men [playing false and showing yourself utterly deceitful] but to God.

5 Upon hearing these words, Ananias fell down and died. And great dread and terror took possession of all who heard of it.

6 And the young men arose and wrapped up [the body] and carried it out and buried it.

7 Now after an interval of about three hours his wife came in, not having learned of what had happened.

8 And Peter said to her, Tell me, did you sell the land for so much? Yes, she said, for so much.

9 And then Peter said to her, How could you two have agreed *and* conspired together to try to deceive the Spirit of the Lord? Listen! The feet of those who have buried your husband

are at the door, and they will carry you out [also].

10 And instantly she fell down at his feet and died; and the young men entering found her dead, and they carried her out and buried her beside her husband.

11 And the whole church and all others who heard of these things were appalled [great awe and strange terror and dread seized them].

12 Now by the hands of the apostles (special messengers) numerous and startling signs and wonders were being performed among the people. And by common consent they all met together [at the temple] in the covered porch (walk) called Solomon's.

13 And none of those who were not of their number dared to join and associate with them, but the people held them in high regard and praised and made much of them.

14 More and more there were being added to the Lord those who believed [those who acknowledged Jesus as their Savior and devoted themselves to Him joined and gathered with them], crowds both of men and of women,

15 So that they [even] kept carrying out the sick into the streets and placing them on couches and sleeping pads, [in the hope] that as Peter passed by, at least his shadow might fall on some of them.

16 And the people gathered also from the towns and hamlets around Jerusalem, bringing the sick and those troubled with foul spirits, and they were all cured.

17 But the high priest rose up and all who were his supporters, that is, the party of the Sadducees, and being filled with [jealousy and indignation and rage,

18 They seized and arrested the apostles (special messengers) and put them in the public jail.

19 But during the night an angel of the Lord opened the prison doors and, leading them out, said,

20 Go, take your stand in the temple courts and declare to the people the whole doctrine concerning this Life (the eternal life which Christ revealed).

21 And when they heard this, they accordingly went into the temple about daybreak and began to teach. Now the high priest and his supporters who were with him arrived and called together the council (Sanhedrin), even all the senate of the sons of Israel, and they sent to the prison to have [the apostles] brought.

22 But when the attendants arrived there, they failed to find them in the jail; so they came back and reported,

23 We found the prison quite safely locked up and the guards were on duty outside the doors, but when we opened [it], we found no one on the inside.

24 Now when the military leader of the temple area and the chief priests heard these facts, they were much perplexed and thoroughly at a loss about them, wondering into what this might grow.

25 But some man came and reported to them, saying, Listen! The men whom you put in jail are standing [right here] in the temple and teaching the people!

26 Then the military leader went with the attendants and brought [the prisoners], but without violence, for they dreaded the people lest they be stoned by them.

27 So they brought them and set them before the council (Sanhedrin). And the high priest examined them by questioning,

28 Saying, We definitely com-

1 G. Abbott-Smith, *Manual Greek Lexicon*.

manded *and* strictly charged you not to teach in *or* about this Name; yet here you have flooded Jerusalem with your doctrine and you intend to bring this ᵐMan's blood upon us.

29 Then Peter and the apostles replied, We must obey God rather than men.

30 The God of our forefathers raised up Jesus, Whom you killed by hanging Him on a tree (cross). [Deut. 21:22, 23.]

31 God exalted Him to His right hand to be Prince *and* Leader and Savior *and* Deliverer *and* Preserver, in order to grant repentance to Israel and to bestow forgiveness *and* release from sins.

32 And we are witnesses of these things, and the Holy Spirit is also, Whom God has bestowed on those who obey Him.

33 Now when they heard this, they were cut to the heart *and* infuriated and wanted to kill the disciples.

34 But a certain Pharisee in the council (Sanhedrin) named Gamaliel, a teacher of the Law, highly esteemed by all the people, standing up, ordered that the apostles be taken outside for a little while.

35 Then he addressed them [the council, saying]: Men of Israel, take care in regard to what you propose to do concerning these men.

36 For before our time there arose Theudas, asserting himself to be a person of importance, with whom a number of men allied themselves, about 400; but he was killed and all who had listened to *and* adhered to him were scattered and brought to nothing.

37 And after this one rose up Judas the Galilean, [who led an uprising] during the time of the census, and drew away a popular following after

him; he also perished and all his adherents were scattered.

38 Now in the present case let me say to you, stand off (withdraw) from these men and let them alone. For if this doctrine *or* purpose or undertaking *or* movement is of human origin, it will fail (be overthrown and come to nothing);

39 But if it is of God, you will not be able to stop *or* overthrow *or* destroy them; you might even be found fighting against God!

40 So, convinced by him, they took his advice; and summoning the apostles, they flogged them and sternly forbade them to speak in *or* about the name of Jesus, and allowed them to go.

41 So they went out from the presence of the council (Sanhedrin), rejoicing that they were being counted worthy [dignified by the indignity] to suffer shame *and* be exposed to disgrace for [the sake of] His name.

42 Yet [in spite of the threats] they never ceased for a single day, both in the temple area and at home, to teach *and* to proclaim the good news (Gospel) of Jesus [as] the Christ (the Messiah).

CHAPTER 6

NOW ABOUT this time, when the number of the disciples was greatly increasing, complaint was made by the Hellenists (the Greek-speaking Jews) against the [native] Hebrews because their widows were being overlooked *and* neglected in the daily ministration (distribution of relief).

2 So the Twelve [apostles] convened the multitude of the disciples and said, It is not seemly *or* desirable *or* right that we should have to give up *or* neglect [preaching] the Word of

nitalized because of what He is, the spotless Son of God, not what the speakers may have thought He

God in order to attend to serving at tables and superintending the distribution of food.

3 Therefore select out from among yourselves, brethren, seven men of good and attested character and repute, full of the [Holy] Spirit and wisdom, whom we may assign to look after this business and duty.

4 But we will continue to devote ourselves steadfastly to prayer and the ministry of the Word.

5 And the suggestion pleased the whole assembly, and they selected Stephen, a man full of faith (a strong and welcome belief that Jesus is the Messiah) and full of and controlled by the Holy Spirit, and Philip, and Prochorus, and Nicanor, and Timon, and Parmenas, and Nicolaus, a proselyte (convert) from Antioch.

6 These they presented to the apostles, who after prayer laid their hands on them.

7 And the message of God kept on spreading, and the number of disciples multiplied greatly in Jerusalem; and [besides] a large number of the priests were obedient to the faith [in Jesus as the Messiah, through Whom is obtained eternal salvation in the kingdom of God].

8 Now Stephen, full of grace (divine blessing and favor) and power (strength and ability) worked great wonders and signs (miracles) among the people.

9 However, some of those who belonged to the synagogue of the Freedmen (freed Jewish slaves), as it was called, and [of the synagogues] of the Cyrenians and of the Alexandrians and of those from Cilicia and [the province of] Asia, arose [and undertook] to debate and dispute with Stephen.

10 But they were not able to resist the intelligence and the wisdom and [the inspiration of] the Spirit with which and by Whom he spoke.

11 So they [secretly] instigated and instructed men to say, We have heard this man speak, using slanderous and abusive and blasphemous language against Moses and God.

12 [Thus] they incited the people as well as the elders and the scribes, and they came upon Stephen and arrested him and took him before the council (Sanhedrin).

13 And they brought forward false witnesses who asserted, This man never stops making statements against this sacred place and the Law [of Moses];

14 For we have heard him say that this Jesus the Nazarene will tear down and destroy this place, and will alter the institutions and usages which Moses transmitted to us.

15 Then all who sat in the council (Sanhedrin), as they gazed intently at Stephen, saw that his face had the appearance of the face of an angel.

CHAPTER 7

AND THE high priest asked [Stephen], Are these charges true?

2 And he answered, Brethren and fathers, listen to me! The God of glory appeared to our forefather Abraham when he was still in Mesopotamia, before he [went to] live in Haran, [Gen. 11:31; 15:7; Ps. 29:3.]

3 And He said to him, Leave your own country and your relatives and come into the land (region) that I will point out to you. [Gen. 12:1.]

4 So then he went forth from the land of the Chaldeans and settled in Haran. And from there, after his father died, [God] transferred him to this country in which you are now dwelling. [Gen. 11:31; 12:5; 15:7.]

5 Yet He gave him no inheritable property in it, [no] not even enough ground to set his foot on; but He promised that He would give it to

Him for a [n]permanent possession and to his descendants after him, even though [as yet] he had no child. [Gen. 12:7; 17:8; Deut. 2:5.]

6 And this is [in effect] what God told him: That his descendants would be aliens (strangers) in a land belonging to other people, who would bring them into bondage and ill-treat them 400 years.

7 But I will judge the nation to whom they will be slaves, said God, and after that they will escape *and* come forth and worship Me in this [very] place. [Gen. 15:13, 14; Exod. 3:12.]

8 And [God] made with Abraham a covenant (an agreement to be religiously observed) [n]of which circumcision was the seal. And under these circumstances [Abraham] became the father of Isaac and circumcised him on the eighth day; and Isaac [did so] when he became the father of Jacob, and Jacob [when each of his sons was born], the twelve patriarchs. [Gen. 17:10–14; 21:2–4; 25:26; 29:31–35; 30:1–24; 35:16–26.]

9 And the patriarchs [Jacob's sons], boiling with envy *and* hatred *and* anger, sold Joseph into slavery in Egypt; but God was with him, [Gen. 37:11, 28; 45:4.]

10 And delivered him from all his distressing afflictions and won him goodwill *and* favor and wisdom *and* understanding in the sight of Pharaoh, king of Egypt, who made him governor over Egypt and all his house. [Gen. 39:2, 3, 21; 41:40–46; Ps. 105:21.]

11 Then there came a famine over all of Egypt and Canaan, with great distress, and our forefathers could find no fodder [for the cattle] *or* vegetable sustenance [for their households]. [Gen. 41:54, 55; 42:5.]

12 But when Jacob heard that there was grain in Egypt, he sent forth our forefathers [to go there on their] first trip. [Gen. 42:2.]

13 And on their second visit Joseph revealed himself to his brothers, and the family of Joseph became known to Pharaoh *and* his origin *and* race. [Gen. 45:1–4.]

14 And Joseph sent an invitation calling to himself Jacob his father and all his kindred, seventy-five persons in all. [Gen. 45:9, 10.]

15 And Jacob went down into Egypt, where he himself died, as did [also] our forefathers; [Deut. 10:22.]

16 And their [o]bodies [Jacob's and Joseph's] were taken back to Shechem and laid in the tomb which Abraham had purchased for a sum of [silver] money from the sons of Hamor in Shechem. [Gen. 50:13; Josh. 24:32.]

17 But as the time for the fulfillment of the promise drew near which God had made to Abraham, the [Hebrew] people increased and multiplied in Egypt,

18 Until [the time when] there arose over Egypt another *and* a different king who did not know Joseph [neither knowing his history and services nor recognizing his merits]. [Exod. 1:7, 8.]

19 He dealt treacherously with *and* defrauded our race; he abused *and* oppressed our forefathers, forcing them to expose their babies so that they might not be kept alive. [Exod. 1:7–11, 15–22.]

20 At this juncture Moses was born, and was exceedingly beautiful in God's sight. For three months he was nurtured in his father's house; [Exod. 2:2.]

21 Then when he was exposed [to perish], the daughter of Pharaoh res-

---

n Marvin Vincent, *Word Studies.*   o Stephen greatly compresses Old Testament accounts of two land purchases and two burial places (at Hebron and Shechem). See Gen. 23:17-18 and Gen. 33:19.

cued him and took him *and* reared him as her own son. [Exod. 2:5, 6, 10.]

22 So Moses was educated in all the wisdom *and* culture of the Egyptians, and he was mighty (powerful) in his speech and deeds.

23 And when he was in his fortieth year, it came into his heart to visit his kinsmen the children of Israel [ᵖto help them and to care for them].

24 And on seeing one of them being unjustly treated, he defended the oppressed man and avenged him by striking down the Egyptian *and* slaying [him].

25 He expected his brethren to understand that God was granting them deliverance by his hand [taking it for granted that they would accept him]; but they did not understand.

26 Then on the next day he ᵠsuddenly appeared to some who were quarreling *and* fighting among themselves, and he urged them to make peace *and* become reconciled, saying, Men, you are brethren; why do you abuse *and* wrong one another?

27 Whereupon the man who was abusing his neighbor pushed [Moses] aside, saying, Who appointed you a ruler (umpire) and a judge over us?

28 Do you intend to slay me as you slew the Egyptian yesterday?

29 At that reply Moses sought safety by flight and he was an exile *and* an alien in the country of Midian, where he became the father of two sons. [Exod. 2:11–15, 22; 18:3, 4.]

30 And when forty years had gone by, there appeared to him in the wilderness (desert) of Mount Sinai an angel, in the flame of a burning bramblebush.

31 When Moses saw it, he was astonished *and* marveled at the sight; but when he went close to investi-

gate, there came to him the voice of the Lord, saying,

32 I am the God of your forefathers, the God of Abraham and of Isaac and of Jacob. And Moses trembled *and* was so terrified that he did not venture to look.

33 Then the Lord said to him, Remove the sandals from your feet, for the place where you are standing is holy ground *and* worthy of veneration.

34 Because I have most assuredly seen the abuse *and* oppression of My people in Egypt and have heard their sighing *and* groaning, I have come down to rescue them. So, now come! I will send you back to Egypt [as My messenger]. [Exod. 3:1–10.]

35 It was this very Moses whom they had denied (disowned and rejected), saying, Who made you our ruler (referee) and judge? whom God sent to be a ruler and deliverer *and* redeemer, by *and* with the [protecting and helping] hand of the Angel that appeared to him in the bramblebush. [Exod. 2:14.]

36 He it was who led them forth, having worked wonders and signs in Egypt and at the Red Sea and during the forty years in the wilderness (desert). [Exod. 7:3; 14:21; Num. 14:33.]

37 It was this [very] Moses who said to the children of Israel, God will raise up for you a Prophet from among your brethren as He raised me up. [Deut. 18:15, 18.]

38 This is he who in the assembly in the wilderness (desert) was the go-between for the Angel who spoke to him on Mount Sinai and our forefathers, and he received living oracles (words that still live) to be handed down to us. [Exod. 19.]

39 [And yet] our forefathers determined not to be subject to him [refus-

---

ᵖ G. Abbott-Smith. *Manual Greek Lexicon.*　ᵠ Marvin Vincent. *Word Studies.*

ing to listen to or obey him]; but thrusting him aside they rejected him, and in their hearts yearned for and turned back to Egypt. [Num. 14:3, 4.]

40 And they said to Aaron, Make us gods who shall [be our leaders and] go before us; as for this Moses who led us forth from the land of Egypt—we have no knowledge of what has happened to him. [Exod. 32:1, 23.]

41 And they [even] made a calf in those days, and offered sacrifice to the idol and made merry and exulted in the work of their [own] hands. [Exod. 32:4, 6.]

42 But God turned [away from them] and delivered them up to worship and serve the host (stars) of heaven, as it is written in the book of the prophets: Did you [really] offer to Me slain beasts and sacrifices for forty years in the wilderness (desert), O house of Israel? [Jer. 19:13.]

43 [No!] You took up the tent (the portable temple) of Moloch and carried it [with you], and the star of the god Rephan, the images which you [yourselves] made that you might worship them; and I will remove you [carrying you away into exile] beyond Babylon. [Amos 5:25–27.]

44 Our forefathers had the tent (tabernacle) of witness in the wilderness, even as He Who directed Moses to make it had ordered, according to the pattern and model he had seen. [Exod. 25:9–40.]

45 Our forefathers in turn brought it [this tent of witness] in [with them into the land] with Joshua when they dispossessed the nations which God drove out before the face of our forefathers. [So it remained here] until the time of David, [Deut. 32:49; Josh. 3:14–17.]

46 Who found grace (favor and

spiritual blessing) in the sight of God and prayed that he might be allowed to find a dwelling place for the God of Jacob. [II Sam. 7:8–16; Ps. 132:1–5.]

47 But it was Solomon who built a house for Him. [I Kings 6.]

48 However, the Most High does not dwell in houses and temples made with hands: as the prophet says, [Isa. 66:1, 2.]

49 Heaven [is] My throne, and earth the footstool for My feet. What [kind of] house can you build for Me, says the Lord, or what is the place in which I can rest?

50 Was it not My hand that made all these things? [Isa. 66:1, 2.]

51 You stubborn and stiff-necked people, still heathen and uncircumcised in heart and ears, you are always 'actively resisting the Holy Spirit. As your forefathers [were], so you [are and so you do]! [Exod. 33:3, 5; Num. 27:14; Isa. 63:10; Jer. 6:10; 9:26.]

52 Which of the prophets did your forefathers not persecute? And they slew those who proclaimed beforehand the coming of the Righteous One, Whom you now have betrayed and murdered—

53 You who received the Law as it was ordained and set in order and delivered by angels, and [yet] you did not obey it!

54 Now upon hearing these things, they [the Jews] were cut to the heart and infuriated, and they ground their teeth against [Stephen].

55 But he, full of the Holy Spirit and controlled by Him, gazed into heaven and saw the glory (the splendor and majesty) of God, and Jesus standing at God's right hand;

56 And he said, Look! I see the heavens opened, and the Son of man standing at God's right hand!

57 But they raised a great shout

r Marvin Vincent, Word Studies.

and put their hands over their ears and rushed together upon him.

58 Then they dragged him out of the city and began to stone him, and the witnesses placed their garments at the feet of a young man named Saul. [Acts 22:20.]

59 And while they were stoning Stephen, he prayed, Lord Jesus, receive and accept and welcome my spirit!

60 And falling on his knees, he cried out loudly, Lord, fix not this sin upon them [lay it not to their charge]! And when he had said this, he fell asleep ˢ[in death].

CHAPTER 8

AND SAUL was [not only] consenting to [Stephen's] death [he was ᵗpleased and ᵘentirely approving]. On that day a great and severe persecution broke out against the church which was in Jerusalem; and they were all scattered throughout the regions of Judea and Samaria, except the apostles (special messengers).

2 [A party of] devout men ᵗwith others helped to carry out and bury Stephen and made great lamentation over him.

3 But Saul shamefully treated and laid waste the church continuously [with cruelty and violence]; and entering house after house, he dragged out men and women and committed them to prison.

4 Now those who were scattered abroad went about [through the land from place to place] preaching the glad tidings, the Word [ᵗthe doctrine concerning the attainment through Christ of salvation in the kingdom of God].

5 Philip [the deacon, not the apostle] went down to the city of Samaria and proclaimed the Christ (the Messiah) to them [the people]; [Acts 6:5.]

6 And great crowds of people with one accord listened to and heeded what was said by Philip, as they heard him and watched the miracles and wonders which he kept performing [from time to time].

7 For foul spirits came out of many who were possessed by them, screaming and shouting with a loud voice, and many who were suffering from palsy or were crippled were restored to health.

8 And there was great rejoicing in that city.

9 But there was a man named Simon, who had formerly practiced magic arts in the city to the utter amazement of the Samaritan nation, claiming that he himself was an extraordinary and distinguished person.

10 They all paid earnest attention to him, from the least to the greatest, saying, This man is that exhibition of the power of God which is called great (intense).

11 And they were attentive and made much of him, because for a long time he had amazed and bewildered and dazzled them with his skill in magic arts.

12 But when they believed the good news (the Gospel) about the kingdom of God and the name of Jesus Christ (the Messiah) as Philip preached it, they were baptized, both men and women.

13 Even Simon himself believed [he adhered to, trusted in, and relied on the teaching of Philip], and after being baptized, devoted himself constantly to him. And seeing signs and miracles of great power which were being performed, he was utterly amazed.

ˢ Hermann Cremer, Biblico-Theological Lexicon of New Testament Greek.   ᵗ Joseph Thayer, A Greek-English Lexicon.   ᵘ Alexander Souter, Pocket Lexicon.

14 Now when the apostles (special messengers) at Jerusalem heard that [the country of] Samaria had accepted *and* welcomed the Word of God, they sent Peter and John to them,

15 And they came down and prayed for them that the Samaritans might receive the Holy Spirit;

16 For He had not yet fallen upon any of them, but they had only been baptized into the name of the Lord Jesus.

17 Then [the apostles] laid their hands on them one by one, and they received the Holy Spirit.

18 However, when Simon saw that the [Holy] Spirit was imparted through the laying on of the apostles' hands, he brought money *and* offered it to them,

19 Saying, Grant me also this power *and* authority, in order that anyone on whom I place my hands may receive the Holy Spirit.

20 But Peter said to him, Destruction overtake your money and you, because you imagined you could obtain the [free] gift of God with money!

21 You have neither part nor lot in this matter, for your heart is all wrong in God's sight [it is not straightforward or right or true before God]. [Ps. 78:37.]

22 So repent of this depravity *and* wickedness of yours and pray to the Lord that, if possible, this [contriving thought *and* purpose of your heart may be removed *and* disregarded *and* forgiven you.

23 For I see that you are in the gall of bitterness and in [a bond forged by iniquity [to fetter souls]. [Isa. 58:6.]

24 And Simon answered, Pray for me [beseech the Lord, both of you], that nothing of what you have said may befall me!

25 Now when [the apostles] had borne their testimony and preached the message of the Lord, they went back to Jerusalem, proclaiming the glad tidings (Gospel) to many villages of the Samaritans [on the way].

26 But an angel of the Lord said to Philip, Rise and proceed southward *or* at midday on the road that runs from Jerusalem down to Gaza. This is the desert [route].

27 So he got up and went. And behold, an Ethiopian, a eunuch of great authority under Candace the queen of the Ethiopians, who was in charge of all her treasure, had come to Jerusalem to worship.

28 And he was [now] returning, and sitting in his chariot he was reading the book of the prophet Isaiah.

29 Then the [Holy] Spirit said to Philip, Go forward and join yourself to this chariot.

30 Accordingly Philip, running up to him, heard [the man] reading the prophet Isaiah and asked, Do you really understand what you are reading?

31 And he said, How is it possible for me to do so unless someone explains it to me *and* guides me [in the right way]? And he earnestly requested Philip to come up and sit beside him.

32 Now this was the passage of Scripture which he was reading: Like a sheep He was led to the slaughter, and as a lamb before its shearer is dumb, so He opens not His mouth.

33 In His humiliation [He was taken away by distressing *and* oppressive judgment *and* justice was denied Him [caused to cease]. Who can describe *or* relate in full [the wickedness of His contemporaries (generation)? For His life is taken from the

---

v Marvin Vincent, *Word Studies.*   w Joseph Thayer, *A Greek-English Lexicon.*   x Adam Clarke, *The Holy Bible with A Commentary.*

earth *and* ʸa bloody death inflicted upon Him. [Isa. 53:7, 8.]

34 And the eunuch said to Philip, I beg of you, tell me about whom does the prophet say this, about himself or about someone else?

35 Then Philip opened his mouth, and beginning with this portion of Scripture he announced to him the glad tidings (Gospel) of Jesus *and* about Him.

36 And as they continued along on the way, they came to some water, and the eunuch exclaimed, See, [here is] water! What is to hinder my being baptized?

37 ᶻ*And Philip said, If you believe with all your heart [if you have* ʸa *conviction, full of joyful trust, that Jesus is the Messiah and accept Him as the Author of your salvation in the kingdom of God, giving Him your obedience, then] you may. And he replied, I do believe that Jesus Christ is the Son of God.*

38 And he ordered that the chariot be stopped; and both Philip and the eunuch went down into the water, and [Philip] baptized him.

39 And when they came up out of the water, the Spirit of the Lord [ᵃsuddenly] caught away Philip; and the eunuch saw him no more, and he went on his way rejoicing.

40 But Philip was found at Azotus, and passing on he preached the good news (Gospel) to all the towns until he reached Caesarea.

CHAPTER 9

MEANWHILE SAUL, ᵃstill drawing his breath hard from threatening and murderous desire against the disciples of the Lord, went to the high priest

2 And requested of him letters to the synagogues at Damascus [author-

izing him], so that if he found any men or women belonging to the Way [of life as determined by faith in Jesus Christ], he might bring them bound [with chains] to Jerusalem.

3 Now as he traveled on, he came near to Damascus, and suddenly a light from heaven flashed around him,

4 And he fell to the ground. Then he heard a voice saying to him, Saul, Saul, why are you persecuting Me [harassing, troubling, and molesting Me]?

5 And Saul said, Who are You, Lord? And He said, I am Jesus, Whom you are persecuting. *It is dangerous and it will turn out badly for you to keep kicking against the goad [to offer vain and perilous resistance].*

6 Trembling and astonished he asked, Lord, what do You desire me to do? The Lord said to him, But arise and go into the city, and you will be told what you must do.

7 The men who were accompanying him were unable to speak [for terror], hearing the voice but seeing no one.

8 Then Saul got up from the ground, but though his eyes were opened, he could see nothing; so they led him by the hand and brought him into Damascus.

9 And he was unable to see for three days, and he neither ate nor drank [anything].

10 Now there was in Damascus a disciple named Ananias. The Lord said to him in a vision, Ananias. And he answered, Here am I, Lord.

11 And the Lord said to him, Get up and go to the street called Straight and ask at the house of Judas for a man of Tarsus named Saul, for behold, he is praying [there].

---

y Joseph Thayer, *A Greek-English Lexicon.*
a Marvin Vincent, *Word Studies.*

z Many manuscripts do not contain this verse.

12 And he has seen *in a vision* a man named Ananias enter and lay his hands on him so that he might regain his sight.

13 But Ananias answered, Lord, I have heard many people tell about this man, especially how much evil *and* what great suffering he has brought on Your saints at Jerusalem;

14 Now he is here and has authority from the high priests to put in chains all who call upon Your name.

15 But the Lord said to him, Go, for this man is a chosen instrument of Mine to bear My name before the Gentiles and kings and the descendants of Israel;

16 For I will make clear to him how much he will be afflicted *and* must endure *and* suffer for My name's sake.

17 So Ananias left and went into the house. And he laid his hands on Saul and said, Brother Saul, the Lord Jesus, Who appeared to you along the way by which you came here, has sent me that you may recover your sight and be filled with the Holy Spirit.

18 And instantly something like scales fell from [Saul's] eyes, and he recovered his sight. Then he arose and was baptized,

19 And after he took some food, he was strengthened. For several days [afterward] he remained with the disciples at Damascus.

20 And immediately in the synagogues he proclaimed Jesus, saying, He is the Son of God!

21 And all who heard him were amazed and said, Is not this the very man who harassed *and* overthrew *and* destroyed in Jerusalem those who called upon this Name? And he has come here for the express purpose of arresting them *and* bringing them in chains before the chief priests.

22 But Saul increased all the more in strength, and continued to confound *and* put to confusion the Jews who lived in Damascus by comparing *and* examining evidence *and* proving that Jesus is the Christ (the Messiah).

23 After considerable time had elapsed, the Jews conspired to put Saul out of the way by slaying him,

24 But [the knowledge of] their plot was made known to Saul. They were guarding the [city's] gates day and night to kill him,

25 But his disciples took him at night and let him down through the [city's] wall, lowering him in a basket *or* hamper.

26 And when he had arrived in Jerusalem, he tried to associate himself with the disciples; but they were all afraid of him, for they did not believe he really was a disciple.

27 However, Barnabas took him and brought him to the apostles, and he explained to them how along the way he had seen the Lord, Who spoke to him, and how at Damascus he had preached freely *and* confidently *and* courageously in the name of Jesus.

28 So he went in and out [as one] among them at Jerusalem,

29 Preaching freely *and* confidently *and* boldly in the name of the Lord. And he spoke and discussed with *and* disputed against the Hellenists (the Grecian Jews), but they were seeking to slay him.

30 And when the brethren found it out, they brought him down to Caesarea and sent him off to Tarsus [his home town].

31 So the church throughout the whole of Judea and Galilee and Samaria had peace and was edified [growing in wisdom, virtue, and piety] and walking in the respect *and* reverential fear of the Lord and in the consolation *and* exhortation of the Holy Spirit, continued to increase *and* was multiplied.

32 Now as Peter went here and there among them all, he went down also to the saints who lived at Lydda.

33 There he found a man named Aeneas, who had been bedfast for eight years and was paralyzed.

34 And Peter said to him, Aeneas, Jesus Christ (the Messiah) [now] makes you whole. Get up and make your bed! And immediately [Aeneas] stood up.

35 Then all the inhabitants of Lydda and the plain of Sharon saw [what had happened to] him and they turned to the Lord.

36 Now there was at Joppa a disciple [a woman] named [in Aramaic] Tabitha, which [in Greek] means Dorcas. She was abounding in good deeds and acts of charity.

37 About that time she fell sick and died, and when they had cleansed her, they laid [her] in an upper room.

38 Since Lydda was near Joppa [however], the disciples, hearing that Peter was there, sent two men to him begging him, Do come to us without delay.

39 So Peter [immediately] rose and accompanied them. And when he had arrived, they took him to the upper room. All the widows stood around him, crying and displaying undershirts (tunics) and [other] garments such as Dorcas was accustomed to make while she was with them.

40 But Peter put them all out [of the room] and knelt down and prayed; then turning to the body he said, Tabitha, get up! And she opened her eyes; and when she saw Peter, she raised herself and sat upright.

41 And he gave her his hand and lifted her up. Then calling in God's people and the widows, he presented her to them alive.

42 And this became known throughout all Joppa, and many came to believe on the Lord [to adhere to and trust in and rely on Him as the Christ and as their Savior].

43 And Peter remained in Joppa for considerable time with a certain Simon a tanner.

CHAPTER 10

NOW [living] at Caesarea there was a man whose name was Cornelius, a centurion (captain) of what was known as the Italian Regiment,

2 A devout man who venerated God and treated Him with reverential obedience, as did all his household; and he gave much alms to the people and prayed continually to God.

3 About the ninth hour (about 3:00 p.m.) of the day he saw clearly in a vision an angel of God entering and saying to him, Cornelius!

4 And he, gazing intently at him, became frightened and said, What is it, Lord? And the angel said to him, Your prayers and your [generous] gifts to the poor have come up [as a sacrifice] to God and have been remembered by Him.

5 And now send men to Joppa and have them call for and invite here a certain Simon whose surname is Peter;

6 He is lodging with Simon a tanner, whose house is by the seaside.

7 When the angel who spoke to him had left, Cornelius called two of his servants and a God-fearing soldier from among his own personal attendants,

8 And having rehearsed everything to them, he sent them to Joppa.

9 The next day as they were still on their way and were approaching the town, Peter went up to the roof of the house to pray, about the sixth hour (noon).

10 But he became very hungry,

and wanted something to eat; and while the meal was being prepared a trance came over him,

11 And he saw the sky opened and something like a great sheet lowered by the four corners, descending to the earth.

12 It contained all kinds of quadrupeds *and wild beasts* and creeping things of the earth and birds of the air.

13 And there came a voice to him, saying, Rise up, Peter, kill and eat.

14 But Peter said, No, by no means, Lord; for I have never eaten anything that is common *and* unhallowed or [ceremonially] unclean.

15 And the voice came to him again a second time, What God has cleansed *and* pronounced clean, do not you defile *and* profane by regarding *and* calling common *and* unhallowed or unclean.

16 This occurred three times; then immediately the sheet was taken up to heaven.

17 Now Peter was still inwardly perplexed *and* doubted as to what the vision which he had seen could mean, when [just then] behold the messengers that were sent by Cornelius, who had made inquiry for Simon's house, stopped *and* stood before the gate.

18 And they called out to inquire whether Simon who was surnamed Peter was staying there.

19 And while Peter was [b]earnestly revolving the vision in his mind *and* meditating on it, the [Holy] Spirit said to him, Behold, three men are looking for you!

20 Get up and go below and accompany them without any doubt [about its legality] *or* any discrimination *or* hesitation, for I have sent them.

21 Then Peter went down to the men and said, I am the man you seek;

what is the purpose of your coming?

22 And they said, Cornelius, a centurion (captain) who is just *and* upright *and* in right standing with God, being God-fearing *and* obedient and well spoken of by the whole Jewish nation, has been instructed by a holy angel to send for you to come to his house; and he [b]has received in answer [to prayer] a warning to listen to *and* act upon what you have to say.

23 So Peter invited them in to be his guests [for the night]. The next day he arose and went away with them, and some of the brethren from Joppa accompanied him.

24 And on the following day they entered Caesarea. Cornelius was waiting for *and* expecting them, and he had invited together his relatives and his intimate friends.

25 As Peter arrived, Cornelius met him, and falling down at his feet he made obeisance *and* paid worshipful reverence to him.

26 But Peter raised him up, saying, Get up; I myself am also a man.

27 And as [Peter] spoke with him, he entered the house and found a large group of persons assembled;

28 And he said to them, You yourselves are aware how it is not lawful *or* permissible for a Jew to keep company with or to visit *or* [even] to come near *or* to speak first to anyone of another nationality, but God has shown *and* taught me by words that I should not call any human being common *or* unhallowed or [ceremonially] unclean.

29 Therefore when I was sent for, I came without hesitation *or* objection *or* misgivings. So now I ask for what reason you sent for me.

30 And Cornelius said, This is now the fourth day since about this time I was observing the ninth hour (three o'clock in the afternoon) of prayer in

b Marvin Vincent, *Word Studies.*

my lodging place; [suddenly] a man stood before me in dazzling apparel,

31 And he said, Cornelius, your prayer has been heard *and* harkened to, and your donations to the poor have been known *and* [c]preserved before God [so that He heeds and is about to help you].

32 Send therefore to Joppa and ask for Simon who is surnamed Peter; he is staying in the house of Simon the tanner by the seaside.

33 So at once I sent for you, and you [being a Jew] have done a kind *and* [d]courteous *and* handsome thing in coming. Now then, we are all present in the sight of God to listen to all that you have been instructed by the Lord to say.

34 And Peter opened his mouth and said: Most certainly *and* thoroughly I now perceive *and* understand that God shows no partiality *and* is no respecter of persons,

35 But in every nation he who venerates *and* has a reverential fear for God, treating Him with worshipful obedience and living uprightly, is acceptable to Him *and* [e]sure of being received and welcomed [by Him].

36 You know the contents of the message which He sent to Israel, announcing the good news (Gospel) of peace by Jesus Christ, Who is Lord of all—

37 The [same] message which was proclaimed throughout all Judea, starting from Galilee after the baptism preached by John—

38 How God anointed *and* consecrated Jesus of Nazareth with the [Holy] Spirit and with strength *and* ability *and* power; how He went about doing good and, [d]in particular, curing all who were harassed *and* oppressed by [the power of] the devil, for God was with Him.

39 And we are [eye and ear] witnesses of everything that He did both in the land of the Jews and in Jerusalem. And [yet] they put Him out of the way (murdered Him) by hanging Him on a tree;

40 But God raised Him to life on the third day and caused Him to be manifest (to be plainly seen),

41 Not by all the people but to us who were chosen (designated) beforehand by God as witnesses, who ate and drank with Him after He arose from the dead.

42 And He charged us to preach to the people and to bear solemn testimony that He is the God-appointed *and* God-ordained Judge of the living and the dead.

43 To Him all the prophets testify (bear witness) that everyone who believes in Him [who adheres to, trusts in, and relies on Him, giving himself up to Him] receives forgiveness of sins through His name.

44 While Peter was still speaking these words, the Holy Spirit fell on all who were listening to the message.

45 And the believers from among the circumcised [the Jews] who came with Peter were surprised *and* amazed, because the free gift of the Holy Spirit had been bestowed *and* poured out largely even on the Gentiles.

46 For they heard them talking in [unknown] tongues (languages) and extolling *and* magnifying God. Then Peter asked,

47 Can anyone forbid *or* refuse water for baptizing these people, seeing that they have received the Holy Spirit just as we have?

48 And he ordered that they be baptized in the name of Jesus Christ

---

c Joseph Thayer, *A Greek-English Lexicon.*   d Marvin Vincent, *Word Studies.*   e *Webster's New International Dictionary* offers this phrase as a definition of "acceptable."

(the Messiah). Then they begged him to stay on there for some days.

CHAPTER 11

NOW THE apostles (special messengers) and the brethren who were throughout Judea heard [with astonishment] that the Gentiles (heathen) also had received *and* accepted *and* welcomed the Word of God [the doctrine concerning the attainment through Christ of salvation in the kingdom of God].

2 So when Peter went up to Jerusalem, the circumcision party [certain Jewish Christians] found fault with him [separating themselves from him in a hostile spirit, opposing and disputing and contending with him],

3 Saying, Why did you go to uncircumcised men and [even] eat with them?

4 But Peter began [at the beginning] and narrated *and* explained to them step by step [the whole list of events]. He said:

5 I was in the town of Joppa praying, and [falling] in a trance I saw a vision of something coming down from heaven, like a huge sheet lowered by the four corners; and it descended until it came to me.

6 Gazing intently *and* closely at it, I observed in it [a variety of] fourfooted animals and wild beasts and reptiles of the earth and birds of the air,

7 And I heard a voice saying to me, Get up, Peter; kill and eat.

8 But I said, No, by no means, Lord; for nothing common *or* unhallowed or [ceremonially] unclean has ever entered my mouth.

9 But the voice answered a second time from heaven, What God has cleansed *and* pronounced clean, do not you defile *and* profane by regard-

ing *or* calling it common *or* unhallowed or unclean.

10 This occurred three times, and then all was drawn up again into heaven.

11 And right then the three men sent to me from Caesarea arrived at the house in which we were.

12 And the [Holy] Spirit instructed me to accompany them without [the least] hesitation *or* misgivings *or* discrimination. So these six brethren accompanied me also, and we went into the man's house.

13 And he related to us how he had seen the angel in his house which stood and said to him, Send men to Joppa and bring Simon who is surnamed Peter;

14 He will give *and* explain to you a message by means of which you and all your household [as well] will be saved ['from eternal death].

15 When I began to speak, the Holy Spirit fell on them just as He did on us at the beginning. [Acts 2:1–4.]

16 Then I recalled the declaration of the Lord, how He said, John indeed baptized with water, but you shall be baptized with (ᵍbe placed in, introduced into) the Holy Spirit.

17 If then God gave to them the same Gift [equally] as He gave to us when we believed in (adhered to, trusted in, and relied on) the Lord Jesus Christ, who was I *and* what power *or* authority had I to interfere *or* hinder *or* forbid *or* withstand God?

18 When they heard this, they were quieted *and* made no further objection. And they glorified God, saying, Then God has also granted to the Gentiles repentance ʰunto [real] life [after resurrection].

19 Meanwhile those who were scattered because of the persecution that arose in connection with Ste-

---

f Hermann Cremer, *Biblico-Theological Lexicon.* Thayer, *A Greek-English Lexicon.*

g Kenneth Wuest, *Word Studies.* h Joseph

phen had traveled as far away as Phoenicia and Cyprus and Antioch, without delivering the message [concerning 'the attainment through Christ of salvation in the kingdom of God] to anyone except Jews.

20 But there were some of them, men of Cyprus and Cyrene, who on returning to Antioch spoke to the Greeks also, proclaiming [to them] the good news (the Gospel) about the Lord Jesus.

21 And the presence of the Lord was with them with power, so that a great number [learned] to believe (to adhere to and trust in and rely on the Lord) and turned *and* surrendered themselves to Him.

22 The rumors of this came to the ears of the church (assembly) in Jerusalem, and they sent Barnabas to Antioch.

23 When he arrived and saw what grace (favor) God was bestowing upon them, he was full of joy; and he continuously exhorted (warned, urged, and encouraged) them all to cleave unto *and* remain faithful to *and* devoted to the Lord with [resolute and steady] purpose of heart.

24 For he was a good man ['good in himself and also at once for the good and the advantage of other people], full of *and* controlled by the Holy Spirit and full of faith (of his 'belief that Jesus is the Messiah, through Whom we obtain eternal salvation). And a large company was added to the Lord.

25 [Barnabas] went on to Tarsus to hunt for Saul.

26 And when he had found him, he brought him back to Antioch. For a whole year they assembled together with *and* kwere guests of the church and instructed a large number of peo-ple; and in Antioch the disciples were first called Christians.

27 And during these days prophets (inspired teachers and interpreters of the divine will and purpose) came down from Jerusalem to Antioch.

28 And one of them named Agabus stood up and prophesied through the [Holy] Spirit that a great *and* severe famine would come upon the whole world. And this did occur during the reign of Claudius.

29 So the disciples resolved to send relief, each one according to his individual ability [in proportion as he had prospered], to the brethren who lived in Judea.

30 And so they did, sending [their contributions] to the elders by the hand of Barnabas and Saul.

CHAPTER 12

ABOUT THAT time Herod the king stretched forth his hands to afflict *and* oppress *and* torment some who belonged to the church (assembly).

2 And he killed James the brother of John with a sword;

3 And when he saw that it was pleasing to the Jews, he proceeded further and arrested Peter also. This was during the days of Unleavened Bread [the Passover week].

4 And when he had seized [Peter], he put him in prison and delivered him to four squads of soldiers of four each to guard him, purposing after the Passover to bring him forth to the people.

5 So Peter was kept in prison, but fervent prayer for him was persistently made to God by the church (assembly).

6 The very night before Herod was about to bring him forth, Peter was sleeping between two soldiers, fas-

i Joseph Thayer, *A Greek-English Lexicon.*
k Alternate translation.

j Hermann Cremer, *Biblico-Theological Lexicon.*

tened with two chains, and sentries before the door were guarding the prison.

7 And suddenly an angel of the Lord appeared [standing beside him], and a light shone in the place where he was. And the angel gently smote Peter on the side and awakened him, saying, Get up quickly! And the chains fell off his hands.

8 And the angel said to him, Tighten your belt and bind on your sandals. And he did so. And he said to him, Wrap your outer garment around you and follow me.

9 And [Peter] went out [along] following him, and he was not conscious that what was apparently being done by the angel was real, but thought he was seeing a vision.

10 When they had passed through the first guard and the second, they came to the iron gate which leads into the city. Of its own accord [the gate] swung open, and they went out and passed on through one street; and at once the angel left him.

11 Then Peter came to himself and said, Now I really know and am sure that the Lord has sent His angel and delivered me from the hand of Herod and from all that the Jewish people were expecting [to do to me].

12 When he, at a glance, became aware of this ['comprehending all the elements of the case], he went to the house of Mary the mother of John, whose surname was Mark, where a large number were assembled together and were praying.

13 And when he knocked at the gate of the porch, a maid named Rhoda came to answer.

14 And recognizing Peter's voice, in her joy she failed to open the gate, but ran in and told the people that Peter was standing before the porch gate.

15 They said to her, You are crazy! But she persistently and strongly and confidently affirmed that it was the truth. They said, It is his angel!

16 But meanwhile Peter continued knocking, and when they opened the gate and saw him, they were amazed.

17 But motioning to them with his hand to keep quiet and listen, he related to them how the Lord had delivered him out of the prison. And he said, Report all this to James [the Less] and to the brethren. Then he left and went to some other place.

18 Now as soon as it was day, there was no small disturbance among the soldiers over what had become of Peter.

19 And when Herod had looked for him and could not find him, he placed the guards on trial and commanded that they should be led away [to execution]. Then [Herod] went down from Judea to Caesarea and stayed on there.

20 Now [Herod] cherished bitter animosity and hostility for the people of Tyre and Sidon; and [their deputies] came to him in a united body, and having made Blastus the king's chamberlain their friend, they asked for peace, because their country was nourished by and depended on the king's [country] for food.

21 On an appointed day Herod arrayed himself in his royal robes, took his seat upon [his] throne, and addressed an oration to them.

22 And the assembled people shouted, It is the voice of a god, and not of a man!

23 And at once an angel of the Lord smote him and cut him down, because he did not give God the glory (the preeminence and kingly majesty that belong to Him as the supreme Ruler); and he was eaten by worms and died.

l Marvin Vincent. *Word Studies.*

24 But the Word of the Lord [concerning the attainment through Christ of salvation in the kingdom of God] continued to grow and spread.

25 And Barnabas and Saul came back from Jerusalem when they had completed their mission, bringing with them John whose surname was Mark. [Acts 11:28–30.]

CHAPTER 13

NOW IN the church (assembly) at Antioch there were prophets (inspired interpreters of the will and purposes of God) and teachers: Barnabas, Symeon who was called Niger [Black], Lucius of Cyrene, Manaen a member of the court of Herod the tetrarch, and Saul.

2 While they were worshiping the Lord and fasting, the Holy Spirit said, Separate now for Me Barnabas and Saul for the work to which I have called them.

3 Then after fasting and praying, they put their hands on them and sent them away.

4 So then, being sent out by the Holy Spirit, they went down to Seleucia, and from [that port] they sailed away to Cyprus.

5 When they arrived at Salamis, they preached the Word of God [concerning the attainment through Christ of salvation in the kingdom of God] in the synagogues of the Jews. And they had John [Mark] as an attendant to assist them.

6 When they had passed through the entire island of Cyprus as far as Paphos, they came upon a certain Jewish wizard or sorcerer, a false prophet named Bar-Jesus.

7 He was closely associated with the proconsul, Sergius Paulus, who was an intelligent and sensible man of sound understanding; he summoned to him Barnabas and Saul and sought to hear the Word of God [concerning salvation in the kingdom of God attained through Christ].

8 But Elymas ᵐthe wise man—for that is the translation of his name [ⁿwhich he had given himself]—opposed them, seeking to keep the proconsul from accepting the faith.

9 But Saul, who is also called Paul, filled with and controlled by the Holy Spirit, looked steadily at [Elymas]

10 And said, You master in every form of deception and recklessness, unscrupulousness, and wickedness, you son of the devil, you enemy of everything that is upright and good, will you never stop perverting and making crooked the straight paths of the Lord and plotting against His saving purposes? [Hos. 14:9.]

11 And now, behold, the hand of the Lord is upon you, and you will be blind, [so blind that you will be] unable to see the sun for a time. Instantly there fell upon him a mist and a darkness, and he groped about seeking persons who would lead him by the hand.

12 Then the proconsul believed (became a Christian) when he saw what had occurred, for he was astonished and deeply touched at the teaching concerning the Lord and from Him.

13 Now Paul and his companions sailed from Paphos and came to Perga in Pamphylia. And John [Mark] separated himself from them and went back to Jerusalem,

14 But they [themselves] came on from Perga and arrived at Antioch in Pisidia. And on the Sabbath day they went into the synagogue there and sat down.

15 After the reading of the Law and the Prophets, the leaders [of the worship] of the synagogue sent to them saying, Brethren, if you have any

m G. Abbott-Smith, *Manual Greek Lexicon*.   n Henry Alford, *The Greek New Testament, with Notes*.

word of exhortation *or* consolation *or* encouragement for the people, say it.

16 So Paul arose, and motioning with his hand said, Men of Israel and you who reverence *and* fear God, listen!

17 The God of this people Israel selected our forefathers and made this people great *and* important during their stay in the land of Egypt, and then with an uplifted arm He led them out from there. [Exod. 6:1, 6.]

18 And for about forty years °like a *fatherly nurse* He cared for them in the wilderness *and* endured their behavior. [Deut. 1:31.]

19 When He had destroyed seven nations in the land of Canaan, He gave them [the Hebrews] their land as an inheritance [distributing it to them by lot; all of which took] about 450 years. [Deut. 7:1; Josh. 14:1.]

20 After that, He gave them judges until the prophet Samuel.

21 Then they asked for a king; and God gave them Saul son of Kish, a man of the tribe of Benjamin, for forty years.

22 And when He had deposed him, He raised up David to be their king; of him He bore witness and said, I have found David son of Jesse a man after My own heart, who will do all My will *and* carry out My program fully. [I Sam. 13:14; Ps. 89:20; Isa. 44:28.]

23 Of this man's descendants God has brought to Israel a Savior [in the person of Jesus], according to His promise.

24 Before His coming John had [already] preached baptism of repentance to all the people of Israel.

25 And as John was ending his course, he asked, What *or* ᴾwho do you secretly think that I am? I am not

He [the Christ. No], but note that after me One is coming, the sandals of Whose feet I am not worthy to untie!

26 Brethren, sons of the family of Abraham, and all those others among you who reverence *and* fear God, to us has been sent the message of this salvation [the salvation obtained through Jesus Christ]. [Ps. 107:20.]

27 For those who dwell in Jerusalem and their rulers, because they did not know *or* recognize Him or understand the utterances of the prophets which are read every Sabbath, have actually fulfilled these very predictions by condemning *and* sentencing [Him].

28 And although they could find no cause deserving death with which to charge Him, yet they asked Pilate to have Him executed *and* put out of the way.

29 And when they had finished *and* fulfilled everything that was written about Him, they took Him down from the tree and laid Him in a tomb.

30 But God raised Him from the dead.

31 And for many days He appeared to those who came up with Him from Galilee to Jerusalem, and they are His witnesses to the people.

32 So now we are bringing you the good news (Gospel) that what God promised to our forefathers,

33 This He has ᑫcompletely fulfilled for us, their children, by raising up Jesus, as it is written in the second psalm, You are My Son; today I have begotten You [ʳcaused You to arise, to be born; ʳformally shown You to be the Messiah by the resurrection]. [Ps. 2:7.]

34 And as to His having raised Him from among the dead, now no more to return to [undergo] putrefaction

---

o Some ancient manuscripts so read.   p Some manuscripts so read.   q Marvin Vincent, *Word Studies.*   r Joseph Thayer, *A Greek-English Lexicon.*

and dissolution [of the grave], He spoke in this way. I will fulfill *and* give to you the holy and sure mercy *and* blessings [that were promised and assured] to David. [Isa. 55:3.]

35 For this reason He says also in another psalm, You will not allow Your Holy One to see corruption [to undergo putrefaction and dissolution of the grave]. [Ps. 16:10.]

36 For David, after he had served God's will *and* purpose *and* counsel in his own generation, fell asleep [ᵃin death] and was buried among his forefathers, and he did see corruption *and* undergo putrefaction *and* dissolution [of the grave].

37 But He Whom God raised up [to life] saw no corruption [did not experience putrefaction and dissolution of the grave].

38 So let it be clearly known *and* understood by you, brethren, that through this Man forgiveness *and* removal of sins is now proclaimed to you;

39 And that through Him everyone who believes [who ᵗacknowledges Jesus as his Savior and devotes himself to Him] is absolved (cleared and freed) from every charge from which he could not be justified *and* freed by the Law of Moses *and* given right standing with God.

40 Take care, therefore, lest there come upon you what is spoken in the prophets:

41 Look, you scoffers *and* scorners, and marvel and perish *and* vanish away; for I am doing a deed in your days, a deed which you will never have confidence in *or* believe, [even] if someone [ᵘclearly describing it in detail] declares it to you. [Hab. 1:5.]

42 As they [Paul and Barnabas] went out [of the synagogue], the peo-

ple earnestly begged that these things might be told to them [further] the next Sabbath.

43 And when the congregation of the synagogue dispersed, many of the Jews and the devout converts to Judaism followed Paul and Barnabas, who talked to them and urged them to continue [to trust themselves to and to stand fast] in the grace (the unmerited favor and blessing) of God.

44 The next Sabbath almost the entire city gathered together to hear the Word of God [concerning ᵗthe attainment through Christ of salvation in the kingdom of God].

45 But when the Jews saw the crowds, filled with envy *and* jealousy they contradicted what was said by Paul and talked abusively [reviling and slandering him].

46 And Paul and Barnabas spoke out plainly *and* boldly, saying, It was necessary that God's message [concerning ᵗsalvation through Christ] should be spoken to you first. But since you thrust it from you, you pass this judgment on yourselves that you are unworthy of eternal life *and* out of your own mouth you set to be judged. [Now] behold, we turn to the Gentiles (the heathen).

47 For so the Lord has charged us, saying, I have set you to be a light for the Gentiles (the heathen), that you may bring [eternal] salvation to the uttermost parts of the earth. [Isa. 49:6.]

48 And when the Gentiles heard this, they rejoiced and glorified (praised and gave thanks for) the Word of God; and as many as were destined (appointed and ordained) to eternal life believed (adhered to, trusted in, and relied on Jesus as the Christ and their Savior).

ˢ Hermann Cremer, *Biblico-Theological Lexicon.*   ᵗ Joseph Thayer, *A Greek-English Lexicon.*
ᵘ Marvin Vincent, *Word Studies.*

49 And so the Word of the Lord [concerning eternal salvation through Christ] scattered *and* spread throughout the whole region.

50 But the Jews stirred up the devout women of high rank and the outstanding men of the town, and instigated persecution against Paul and Barnabas and drove them out of their boundaries.

51 But [the apostles] shook off the dust from their feet against them and went to Iconium.

52 And the disciples were continually filled [throughout their souls] with joy and the Holy Spirit.

CHAPTER 14

NOW AT Iconium [also Paul and Barnabas] went into the Jewish synagogue together and spoke with such power that a great number both of Jews and of Greeks believed (became Christians);

2 But the unbelieving Jews [who rejected their message] aroused the Gentiles and embittered their minds against the brethren.

3 So [Paul and Barnabas] stayed on there for a long time, speaking freely *and* fearlessly *and* boldly in the Lord, Who continued to bear testimony to the Word of His grace, granting signs and wonders to be performed by their hands.

4 But the residents of the town were divided, some siding with the Jews and some with the apostles.

5 When there was an attempt both on the part of the Gentiles and the Jews together with their rulers, to insult *and* abuse *and* molest [Paul and Barnabas] and to stone them,

6 They, aware of the situation, made their escape to Lystra and Derbe, cities of Lycaonia, and the neighboring districts;

7 And there they continued to preach the glad tidings (Gospel).

8 Now at Lystra a man sat who found it impossible to use his feet, for he was a cripple from birth and had never walked.

9 He was listening to Paul as he talked, and [Paul] gazing intently at him and observing that he had faith to be healed,

10 Shouted at him, saying, Stand erect on your feet! And he leaped up and walked.

11 And the crowds, when they saw what Paul had done, lifted up their voices, shouting in the Lycaonian language, The gods have come down to us in human form!

12 They called Barnabas Zeus, and they called Paul, because he led in the discourse, Hermes [god of speech].

13 And the priest of Zeus, whose [temple] was at the entrance of the town, brought bulls and garlands to the [city's] gates and wanted to join the people in offering sacrifice.

14 But when the apostles Barnabas and Paul heard of it, they tore their clothing and dashed out among the crowd, shouting,

15 Men, why are you doing this? We also are [only] human beings, of nature like your own, and we bring you the good news (Gospel) that you should turn away from these foolish *and* vain things to the living God, Who made the heaven and the earth and the sea and everything that they contain. [Exod. 20:11; Ps. 146:6.]

16 In generations past He permitted all the nations to walk in their own ways;

17 Yet He did not neglect to leave some witness of Himself, for He did you good *and* [showed you] kindness and gave you rains from heaven and fruitful seasons, satisfying your hearts with nourishment and happiness;

18 Even in [the light of] these words they with difficulty prevented

the people from offering sacrifice to them.

19 But some Jews arrived there from Antioch and Iconium; and having persuaded the people *and* won them over, they stoned Paul and [afterward] dragged him out of the town, thinking that he was dead.

20 But the disciples formed a circle about him, and he got up and went back into the town; and on the morrow he went on with Barnabas to Derbe.

21 When they had preached the good news (Gospel) to that town and made disciples of many of the people, they went back to Lystra and Iconium and Antioch,

22 Establishing *and* strengthening the souls *and* the hearts of the disciples, urging *and* warning *and* encouraging them to stand firm in the faith, and [telling them] that it is through many hardships *and* tribulations we must enter the kingdom of God.

23 And when they had appointed *and* ordained elders for them in each church with prayer and fasting, they committed them to the Lord in Whom they had come to believe [being full of joyful trust that He is the Christ, the Messiah].

24 Then they went through Pisidia and arrived at Pamphylia.

25 And when they had spoken the Word in Perga [the doctrine concerning the attainment through Christ of salvation in the kingdom of God], they went down to Attalia;

26 And from there they sailed back to Antioch, where they had [first] been commended to the grace of God for the work which they had [now] completed.

27 Arriving there, they gathered the church together and declared all that God had accomplished with them and how He had opened to the Gentiles a door of faith [in Jesus as the Messiah, through Whom we obtain salvation in the kingdom of God].

28 And there they stayed no little time with the disciples.

CHAPTER 15

BUT SOME men came down from Judea and were instructing the brethren, Unless you are circumcised in accordance with the Mosaic custom, you cannot be saved. [Gen. 17:9–14.]

2 And when Paul and Barnabas had no small disagreement and discussion with them, it was decided that Paul and Barnabas and some of the others of their number should go up to Jerusalem [and confer] with the apostles (special messengers) and the elders about this matter.

3 So, being ᵛfitted out *and* sent on their way by the church, they went through both Phoenicia and Samaria telling of the conversion of the Gentiles (the heathen), and they caused great rejoicing among all the brethren.

4 When they arrived in Jerusalem, they were heartily welcomed by the church and the apostles and the elders, and they told them all that God had accomplished through them.

5 But some who believed [who ʷacknowledged Jesus as their Savior and devoted themselves to Him] belonged to the sect of the Pharisees, and they rose up and said, It is necessary to circumcise [the Gentile converts] and to charge them to obey the Law of Moses.

6 The apostles and the elders were assembled together to look into *and* consider this matter.

7 And after there had been a long debate, Peter got up and said to them, Brethren, you know that quite

---

v Henry Alford, *The Greek New Testament.* w Joseph Thayer, *A Greek-English Lexicon.*

a while ago God made a choice *or* selection from among you, that by my mouth the Gentiles should hear the message of the Gospel [concerning the ˣattainment through Christ of salvation in the kingdom of God] and believe (credit and place their confidence in it).

8 And God, Who is acquainted with *and* understands the heart, bore witness to them, giving them the Holy Spirit as He also did to us;

9 And He made no difference between us and them, but cleansed their hearts by faith (ˣby a strong and welcome conviction that Jesus is the Messiah, through Whom we obtain eternal salvation in the kingdom of God).

10 Now then, why do you try to test God by putting a yoke on the necks of the disciples, such as neither our forefathers nor we [ourselves] were able to endure?

11 But we believe that we are saved through the grace (the undeserved favor and mercy) of the Lord Jesus, just as they [are].

12 Then the whole assembly remained silent, and they listened [attentively] as Barnabas and Paul rehearsed what signs and wonders God had performed through them among the Gentiles.

13 When they had finished talking, James replied, Brethren, listen to me.

14 Simeon [Peter] has rehearsed how God first visited the Gentiles, to take out of them a people [to bear and honor] His name.

15 And with this the predictions of the prophets agree, as it is written,

16 After this I will come back, and will rebuild the house of David, which has fallen; I will rebuild its [very] ruins, and I will set it up again,

17 So that the rest of men may seek the Lord, and all the Gentiles upon whom My name has been invoked,

18 Says the Lord, Who has been making these things known from the beginning of the world. [Isa. 45:21; Jer. 12:15; Amos 9:11, 12.]

19 Therefore it is my opinion that we should not put obstacles in the way of *and* annoy *and* disturb those of the Gentiles who turn to God,

20 But we should send word to them in writing to abstain from *and* avoid anything that has been polluted by being offered to idols, and all sexual impurity, and [eating meat of animals] that have been strangled, and [tasting of] blood.

21 For from ancient generations Moses has had his preachers in every town, for he is read [aloud] every Sabbath in the synagogues.

22 Then the apostles and the elders, together with the whole church, resolved to select men from among their number and send them to Antioch with Paul and Barnabas. They chose Judas called Barsabbas, and Silas, [both] leading men among the brethren, *and* sent them.

23 With [them they sent] the following letter: The brethren, both the apostles and the elders, to the brethren who are of the Gentiles in Antioch and Syria and Cilicia, greetings:

24 As we have heard that some persons from our number have disturbed you with their teaching, unsettling your minds *and* ʸthrowing you into confusion, although we gave them no express orders *or* instructions [on the points in question],

25 It has been resolved by us in assembly to select men and send them [as messengers] to you with our beloved Barnabas and Paul,

26 Men who have hazarded their lives for the sake of our Lord Jesus Christ.

x Joseph Thayer, *A Greek-English Lexicon.*   y Marvin Vincent, *Word Studies.*

27 So we have sent Judas and Silas, who themselves will bring you the same message by word of mouth.

28 For it has seemed good to the Holy Spirit and to us not to lay upon you any greater burden than these indispensable requirements:

29 That you abstain from what has been sacrificed to idols and from [tasting] blood and from [eating the meat of animals] that have been strangled and from sexual impurity. If you keep yourselves from these things, you will do well. Farewell [be strong]!

30 So when [the messengers] were sent off, they went down to Antioch; and having assembled the congregation, they delivered the letter.

31 And when they read it, the people rejoiced at the consolation and encouragement [it brought them].

32 And Judas and Silas, who were themselves prophets (inspired interpreters of the will and purposes of God), urged and warned and consoled and encouraged the brethren with many words and strengthened them.

33 And after spending some time there, they were sent back by the brethren with [the greeting] peace to those who had sent them.

34 *However, Silas decided to stay on there.*

35 But Paul and Barnabas remained in Antioch and with many others also continued teaching and proclaiming the good news, the Word of the Lord [concerning the zattainment through Christ of eternal salvation in God's kingdom].

36 And after some time Paul said to Barnabas, Come, let us go back and again visit and help and minister to the brethren in every town where we made known the message of the Lord, and see how they are getting along.

37 Now Barnabas wanted to take with them John called Mark [his near relative].

38 But Paul did not think it best to have along with them the one who had quit and deserted them in Pamphylia and had not gone on with them to the work.

39 And there followed a sharp disagreement between them, so that they separated from each other, and Barnabas took Mark with him and sailed away to Cyprus.

40 But Paul selected Silas and set out, being commended by the brethren to the grace (the favor and mercy) of the Lord.

41 And he passed through Syria and Cilicia, establishing and strengthening the churches.

CHAPTER 16

AND [Paul] went down to Derbe and also to Lystra. A disciple named Timothy was there, the son of a Jewish woman who was a believer [she had become zconvinced that Jesus is the Messiah and the Author of eternal salvation, and yielded obedience to Him]; but [Timothy's] father was a Greek.

2 He [Timothy] had a good reputation among the brethren at Lystra and Iconium.

3 Paul desired Timothy to go with him [aas a missionary]; and he took him and circumcised him because of the Jews that were in those places, all of whom knew that his father was a Greek.

4 As they went on their way from town to town, they delivered over [to the assemblies] for their observance the regulations decided upon by the apostles and elders who were at Jerusalem.

z Joseph Thayer, *A Greek-English Lexicon.*   a Marvin Vincent, *Word Studies.*

5 So the churches were strengthened *and* made firm in the faith, and they increased in number day after day.

6 And Paul and Silas passed through the territory of Phrygia and Galatia, having been forbidden by the Holy Spirit to proclaim the Word in [the province of] Asia.

7 And when they had come opposite Mysia, they tried to go into Bithynia, but the Spirit of Jesus did not permit them.

8 So passing by Mysia, they went down to Troas.

9 [There] a vision appeared to Paul in the night: a man from Macedonia stood pleading with him and saying, Come over to Macedonia and help us!

10 And when he had seen the vision, we [including Luke] at once endeavored to go on into Macedonia, confidently inferring that God had called us to proclaim the glad tidings (Gospel) to them.

11 Therefore, setting sail from Troas, we came in a direct course to Samothrace, and the next day went on to Neapolis.

12 And from there [we came] to Philippi, which is the chief city of the district of Macedonia and a [Roman] colony. We stayed on in this place some days;

13 And on the Sabbath day we went outside the [city's] gate to the bank of the river where we supposed there was an [accustomed] place of prayer, and we sat down and addressed the women who had assembled there.

14 One of those who listened to us was a woman named Lydia, from the city of Thyatira, a dealer in fabrics dyed in purple. She was [already] a worshiper of God, and the Lord

opened her heart to pay attention to what was said by Paul.

15 And when she was baptized along with her household, she earnestly entreated us, saying, If in your opinion I am one really convinced [that Jesus is the Messiah and the Author of salvation] *and* that I will be faithful to the Lord, come to my house and stay. And she induced us [to do it].

16 As we were on our way to the place of prayer, we were met by a slave girl who was possessed by a spirit of divination [claiming to foretell future events and to discover hidden knowledge], and she brought her owners much gain by her fortunetelling.

17 She kept following Paul and [the rest of] us, shouting loudly, These men are the servants of the Most High God! They announce to you the way of salvation!

18 And she did this for many days. Then Paul, being sorely annoyed *and* worn out, turned and said to the spirit within her, I charge you in the name of Jesus Christ to come out of her! And it came out that very ᵇmoment.

19 But when her owners discovered that their hope of profit was gone, they caught hold of Paul and Silas and dragged them before the authorities in the forum (marketplace), [where trials are held].

20 And when they had brought them before the magistrates, they declared, These fellows are Jews and they are throwing our city into great confusion.

21 They encourage the practice of customs which it is unlawful for us Romans to accept or observe!

22 The crowd [also] joined in the attack upon them, and the rulers tore the clothes off of them and com-

b James Moulton and George Milligan, *The Vocabulary.*

manded that they be beaten with rods.

23 And when they had struck them with many blows, they threw them into prison, charging the jailer to keep them safely.

24 He, having received [so strict a] charge, put them into the inner prison (the dungeon) and fastened their feet in the stocks.

25 But about midnight, as Paul and Silas were praying and singing hymns of praise to God, and the [other] prisoners were listening to them,

26 Suddenly there was a great earthquake, so that the very foundations of the prison were shaken; and at once all the doors were opened and everyone's shackles were unfastened.

27 When the jailer, startled out of his sleep, saw that the prison doors were open, he drew his sword and was on the point of killing himself, because he supposed that the prisoners had escaped.

28 But Paul shouted, Do not harm yourself, for we are all here!

29 Then [the jailer] called for lights and rushed in, and trembling and terrified he fell down before Paul and Silas.

30 And he brought them out [of the dungeon] and said, Men, what is it necessary for me to do that I may be saved?

31 And they answered, Believe in the Lord Jesus *Christ* [cgive yourself up to Him, dtake yourself out of your own keeping and entrust yourself into His keeping] and you will be saved, [and this applies both to] you and your household as well.

32 And they declared the Word of the Lord [the doctrine concerning the cattainment through Christ of

eternal salvation in the kingdom of God] to him and to all who were in his house.

33 And he took them the same hour of the night and ebathed [them because of their bloody] wounds, and he was baptized immediately and all [the members of] his [household].

34 Then he took them up into his house and set food before them; and he fleaped much for joy *and* exulted with all his family that he believed in God [accepting and joyously welcoming what He had made known through Christ].

35 But when it was day, the magistrates sent policemen, saying, Release those fellows *and* let them go.

36 And the jailer repeated the words to Paul, saying, The magistrates have sent to release you *and* let you go; now therefore come out and go in peace.

37 But Paul answered them, They have beaten us openly *and* publicly, without a trial *and* uncondemned, men who are Roman citizens, and have thrown us into prison; and do they now thrust us out secretly? No, indeed! Let them come here themselves and conduct us out!

38 The police reported this message to the magistrates, and they were frightened when they heard that the prisoners were Roman citizens;

39 So they came themselves and [striving to appease them by entreaty] apologized to them. And they brought them out and asked them to leave the city.

40 So [Paul and Silas] left the prison and went to Lydia's house; and when they had seen the brethren, they warned *and* urged *and* consoled *and* encouraged them and departed.

---

c Joseph Thayer, *A Greek-English Lexicon.*   d Kenneth Wuest, *Word Studies.*   e Marvin Vincent, *Word Studies.*   f Robert Young, *Analytical Concordance to the Bible.*

CHAPTER 17

NOW AFTER [Paul and Silas] had passed through Amphipolis and Apollonia, they came to Thessalonica, where there was a synagogue of the Jews.

2 And Paul entered, as he usually did, and for three Sabbaths he reasoned *and* argued with them from the Scriptures,

3 Explaining [them] *and* [quoting passages] setting forth *and* proving that it was necessary for the Christ to suffer and to rise from the dead, and saying, This Jesus, Whom I proclaim to you, is the Christ (the Messiah).

4 And some of them [accordingly] were induced to believe and associated themselves with Paul and Silas, as did a great number of the devout Greeks and not a few of the leading women.

5 But the unbelieving Jews were aroused to jealousy, and, getting hold of some loungers (ruffians and rascals), in the marketplace they gathered together a mob, set the town in an uproar, and attacked the house of Jason, seeking to bring [Paul and Silas] out to the people.

6 But when they failed to find them, they dragged Jason and some of the brethren before the city authorities, crying, These men who have turned the world upside down have come here also,

7 And Jason has received them to his house *and* privately protected them! And they are all ignoring *and* acting contrary to the decrees of Caesar, [actually] asserting that there is another king, one Jesus!

8 And both the crowd and the city authorities, on hearing this, were irritated (stirred up and troubled).

9 And when they had taken security [bail] from Jason and the others, they let them go.

10 Now the brethren at once sent Paul and Silas away by night to Beroea; and when they arrived, they entered the synagogue of the Jews.

11 Now these [Jews] were better disposed *and* more noble than those in Thessalonica, for they were entirely ready *and* accepted *and* welcomed the message [ᵍconcerning the attainment through Christ of eternal salvation in the kingdom of God] with inclination of mind *and* eagerness, searching *and* examining the Scriptures daily to see if these things were so.

12 Many of them therefore became believers, together with not a few prominent Greeks, women as well as men.

13 But when the Jews of Thessalonica learned that the Word of God [ᵍconcerning the attainment through Christ of eternal salvation in the kingdom of God] was also preached by Paul at Beroea, they came there too, disturbing *and* inciting the masses.

14 At once the brethren sent Paul off on his way to the sea, but Silas and Timothy remained behind.

15 Those who escorted Paul brought him as far as Athens; and receiving instructions for Silas and Timothy that they should come to him as soon as possible, they departed.

16 Now while Paul was awaiting them at Athens, his spirit was grieved *and* roused to anger as he saw that the city was full of idols.

17 So he reasoned *and* argued in the synagogue with the Jews and those who worshiped there, and in the marketplace [where assemblies are held] day after day with any who chanced to be there.

18 And some also of the Epicurean and Stoic philosophers encountered

ᵍ Joseph Thayer, *A Greek-English Lexicon.*

him *and* began to engage in discussion. And some said, What is this babbler with his scrap-heap learning trying to say? Others said, He seems to be an announcer of foreign deities—because he preached Jesus and the resurrection.

19 And they took hold of him and brought him to the [h]Areopagus [Mars Hill auditorium], saying, May we know what this novel (unheard of and unprecedented) teaching is which you are openly declaring?

20 For you set forth some startling things, foreign *and* strange to our ears; we wish to know therefore just what these things mean—

21 For the Athenians, all of them, and the foreign residents *and* visitors among them spent all their leisure time in nothing except telling or hearing something newer than the last—

22 So Paul, standing in the center of the Areopagus [Mars Hill auditorium], said: Men of Athens, I perceive in every way [on every hand and with every turn I make] that you are most religious *or* very reverent to demons.

23 For as I passed along and carefully observed your objects of worship, I came also upon an altar with this inscription, To the unknown god. Now what you are already worshiping as unknown, this I set forth to you.

24 The God Who produced *and* formed the world and all things in it, being Lord of heaven and earth, does not dwell in handmade shrines.

25 Neither is He served by human hands, as though He lacked anything, for it is He Himself Who gives life and breath and all things to all [people]. [Isa. 42:5.]

26 And He made from one [common origin, one source, one blood] all nations of men to settle on the face of the earth, having definitely determined [their] allotted periods of time and the fixed boundaries of their habitation (their settlements, lands, and abodes),

27 So that they should seek God, in the hope that they might feel after Him and find Him, although He is not far from each one of us.

28 For in Him we live and move and have our being; as even some of your [own] poets have said, For we are also His offspring.

29 Since then we are God's offspring, we ought not to suppose that Deity (the Godhead) is like gold or silver or stone, [of the nature of] a representation by human art and imagination, *or* anything constructed *or* invented.

30 Such [former] ages of ignorance God, it is true, ignored *and* allowed to pass unnoticed; but now He charges all people everywhere to repent ([i]to change their minds for the better and heartily to amend their ways, with abhorrence of their past sins),

31 Because He has fixed a day when He will judge the world righteously (justly) by a Man Whom He has destined *and* appointed for that task, and He has made this credible *and* given conviction *and* assurance *and* evidence to everyone by raising Him from the dead. [Ps. 9:8; 96:13; 98:9.]

32 Now when they had heard [that there had been] a resurrection from the dead, some scoffed; but others said, We will hear you again about this matter.

33 So Paul went out from among them.

34 But some men were on his side *and* joined him and believed (became Christians); among them were Dio-

---

h Many modern interpreters note that the Areopagus may also have been a reference to the Council of the Areopagus, the supreme court of Athens, custodians of teachings that introduced new religions and foreign gods. See also Acts 17:34.　　i Joseph Thayer, *A Greek-English Lexicon*.

nysius, a judge of the Areopagus, and a woman named Damaris, and some others with them.

CHAPTER 18

AFTER THIS [Paul] departed from Athens and went to Corinth.

2 There he met a Jew named Aquila, a native of Pontus, recently arrived from Italy with Priscilla his wife, due to the fact that Claudius had issued an edict that all the Jews were to leave Rome. And [Paul] went to see them,

3 And because he was of the same occupation, he stayed with them; and they worked [together], for they were tentmakers by trade.

4 But he discoursed *and* argued in the synagogue every Sabbath and won over [both] Jews and Greeks.

5 By the time Silas and Timothy arrived from Macedonia, Paul was completely engrossed with preaching, earnestly arguing *and* testifying to the Jews that Jesus [is] the Christ.

6 But since they kept opposing *and* abusing *and* reviling him, he shook out his clothing [against them] and said to them, Your blood be upon your [own] heads! I am innocent [of it]. From now on I will go to the Gentiles (the heathen). [Acts 13:46.]

7 He then left there and went to the house of a man named Titus Justus, who worshiped God and whose house was next door to the synagogue.

8 But Crispus, the leader of the synagogue, believed [that Jesus is the Messiah and acknowledged Him with joyful trust as Savior and Lord], together with his entire household; and many of the Corinthians who listened [to Paul also] believed and were baptized.

9 And one night the Lord said to Paul in a vision, Have no fear, but speak and do not keep silent;

10 For I am with you, and no man shall assault you to harm you, for I have many people in this city. [Isa. 43:5; Jer. 1:8.]

11 So he settled down among them for a year and six months, teaching the Word of God [concerning the [j]attainment through Christ of eternal salvation in the kingdom of God].

12 But when Gallio was proconsul of Achaia (most of Greece), the Jews unitedly made an attack upon Paul and brought him before the judge's seat,

13 Declaring, This fellow is advising *and* inducing *and* inciting people to worship God in violation of the [k]Law [of Rome and of Moses].

14 But when Paul was about to open his mouth to reply, Gallio said to the Jews, If it were a matter of some misdemeanor or villainy, O Jews, I should have cause to bear with you *and* listen;

15 But since it is merely a question [of doctrine] about words and names and your own law, see to it yourselves; I decline to be a judge of such matters *and* I have no intention of trying such cases.

16 And he drove them away from the judgment seat.

17 Then they [the Greeks] all seized Sosthenes, the leader of the synagogue, and beat him right in front of the judgment seat. But Gallio paid no attention to any of this.

18 Afterward Paul remained many days longer, and then told the brethren farewell and sailed for Syria; and he was accompanied by Priscilla and Aquila. At Cenchreae he [[l]Paul] cut his hair, for he had made a vow.

j Joseph Thayer, *A Greek-English Lexicon*. not recognized by Roman law as Judaism was.   k The Jews were claiming that Paul was advocating a religion   l Some commentators (such as Marvin Vincent, *Word Studies* and Henry Alford, *The Greek New Testament*) believe Paul is the one who made the vow, while others think Aquila is meant.

19 Then they arrived in Ephesus, and [Paul] left the others there; but he himself entered the synagogue and discoursed *and* argued with the Jews.

20 When they asked him to remain for a longer time, he would not consent;

21 But when he was leaving them he said, I will return to you if God is willing, and he set sail from Ephesus.

22 When he landed at Caesarea, he went up and saluted the church [at Jerusalem], and then went down to Antioch.

23 After staying there some time, he left and went from place to place in an orderly journey through the territory of Galatia and Phrygia, establishing the disciples *and* imparting new strength to them.

24 Meanwhile, there was a Jew named Apollos, a native of Alexandria, who came to Ephesus. He was a cultured *and* eloquent man, well versed *and* mighty in the Scriptures.

25 He had been instructed in the way of the Lord, and burning with spiritual zeal, he spoke and taught diligently *and* accurately the things concerning Jesus, though he was acquainted only with the baptism of John.

26 He began to speak freely (fearlessly and boldly) in the synagogue; but when Priscilla and Aquila heard him, they took him with them and expounded to him the way of God more definitely *and* accurately.

27 And when [Apollos] wished to cross to Achaia (most of Greece), the brethren wrote to the disciples there, urging *and* encouraging them to accept *and* welcome him heartily. When he arrived, he proved a great help to those who through grace (God's unmerited favor and mercy) had believed (adhered to, trusted in, and relied on Christ as Lord and Savior).

28 For with great power he refuted the Jews in public [discussions], showing *and* proving by the Scriptures that Jesus is the Christ (the Messiah).

CHAPTER 19

WHILE APOLLOS was in Corinth, Paul went through the upper inland districts and came down to Ephesus. There he found some disciples.

2 And he asked them, Did you receive the Holy Spirit when you believed [on Jesus as the Christ]? And they said, No, we have not even heard that there is a Holy Spirit.

3 And he asked, Into what [baptism] then were you baptized? They said, Into John's baptism.

4 And Paul said, John baptized with the baptism of repentance, continually telling the people that they should believe in the One Who was to come after him, that is, in Jesus [having a conviction full of joyful trust that He is Christ, the Messiah, and being obedient to Him].

5 On hearing this they were baptized [again, this time] in the name of the Lord Jesus.

6 And as Paul laid his hands upon them, the Holy Spirit came on them; and they spoke in [foreign, unknown] tongues (languages) and prophesied.

7 There were about twelve of them in all.

8 And he went into the synagogue and for three months spoke boldly, persuading *and* arguing and pleading about the kingdom of God.

9 But when some became more and more stubborn (hardened and unbelieving), discrediting *and* reviling *and* speaking evil of the Way [of the Lord] before the congregation, he separated himself from them, taking the disciples with him, and went on holding daily discussions in the

lecture room of Tyrannus *from about ten o'clock till three*.

10 This continued for two years, so that all the inhabitants of [the province of] Asia, Jews as well as Greeks, heard the Word of the Lord [concerning the [m]attainment through Christ of eternal salvation in the kingdom of God].

11 And God did unusual *and* extraordinary miracles by the hands of Paul,

12 So that handkerchiefs *or* towels or aprons which had touched his skin were carried away *and* put upon the sick, and their diseases left them and the evil spirits came out of them.

13 Then some of the traveling Jewish exorcists (men who adjure evil spirits) also undertook to call the name of the Lord Jesus over those who had evil spirits, saying, I solemnly implore *and* charge you by the Jesus Whom Paul preaches!

14 Seven sons of a certain Jewish chief priest named Sceva were doing this.

15 But [one] evil spirit retorted, Jesus I know, and Paul I know [n]about, but who are you?

16 Then the man in whom the evil spirit dwelt leaped upon them, mastering [o]two of them, and was so violent against them that they dashed out of that house [in fear], stripped naked and wounded.

17 This became known to all who lived in Ephesus, both Jews and Greeks, and alarm *and* terror fell upon them all; and the name of the Lord Jesus was extolled *and* magnified.

18 Many also of those who were now believers came making [p]full confession *and* thoroughly exposing their [former deceptive and evil] practices.

19 And many of those who had practiced curious, magical arts collected their books and [throwing them, [p]book after book, on the pile] burned them in the sight of everybody. When they counted the value of them, they found it amounted to 50,000 pieces of silver ([p]about $9,300).

20 Thus the Word of the Lord [concerning the [m]attainment through Christ of eternal salvation in the kingdom of God] grew *and* spread *and* intensified, prevailing mightily.

21 Now after these events Paul determined in the [Holy] Spirit that he would travel through Macedonia and Achaia (most of Greece) and go to Jerusalem, saying, After I have been there, I must visit Rome also.

22 And having sent two of his assistants, Timothy and Erastus, into Macedonia, he himself stayed on in [the province of] Asia for a while.

23 But as time went on, there arose no little disturbance concerning the Way [of the Lord].

24 For a man named Demetrius, a silversmith, who made silver shrines of [the goddess] Artemis [q][Diana], brought no small income to his craftsmen.

25 These he called together, along with the workmen of similar trades, and said, Men, you are acquainted with the facts *and* understand that from this business we derive our wealth *and* livelihood.

26 Now you notice and hear that not only at Ephesus but almost all over [the province of] Asia this Paul has persuaded *and* induced people to believe his teaching and has alienated a considerable company of them, saying that gods that are made with human hands are not really gods at all.

m Joseph Thayer, *A Greek-English Lexicon*. **n** A weaker verb. **o** The best texts read "both of them." **p** Marvin Vincent, *Word Studies*. **q** Artemis is the Greek name for the Roman goddess Diana.

27 Now there is danger not merely that this trade of ours may be discredited, but also that the temple of the great goddess Artemis may come into disrepute *and* count for nothing, and that her glorious magnificence may be degraded and fall into contempt—she whom all the [province of Asia] and the wide world worship.

28 As they listened to this, they were filled with rage and they continued to shout, Great is Artemis of the Ephesians!

29 Then the city was filled with confusion; and they rushed together into the amphitheater, dragging along with them Gaius and Aristarchus, Macedonians who were fellow travelers with Paul.

30 Paul wished to go in among the crowd, but the disciples would not permit him to do it.

31 Even some of the Asiarchs (political or religious officials in Asia) who were his friends also sent to him and warned him not to risk venturing into the theater.

32 Now some shouted one thing and some another, for the gathering was in a tumult and most of them did not know why they had come together.

33 Some of the crowd called upon Alexander [to speak], since the Jews had pushed *and* urged him forward. And Alexander motioned with his hand, wishing to make a defense *and* [planning] to apologize to the people.

34 But as soon as they saw him *and* recognized that he was a Jew, a shout went up from them as the voice of one man, as for about two hours they cried, Great is Artemis of the Ephesians!

35 And when the town clerk had calmed the crowd down, he said, Men of Ephesus, what man is there who does not know that the city of the Ephesians is guardian of the temple of the great Artemis and of the sacred stone [image of her] that fell from the sky?

36 Seeing then that these things cannot be denied, you ought to be quiet (keep yourselves in check) and do nothing rashly.

37 For you have brought these men here, who are [guilty of] neither temple robberies nor blasphemous speech about our goddess.

38 Now then, if Demetrius and his fellow tradesmen who are with him have a grievance against anyone, the courts are open and proconsuls are [available]; let them bring charges against one another [legally].

39 But if you require anything further about this *or about other matters*, it must be decided *and* cleared up in the regular assembly.

40 For we are in danger of being called to render an account *and* of being accused of rioting because of [this commotion] today, there being no reason that we can offer to justify this disorder.

41 And when he had said these things, he dismissed the assembly.

CHAPTER 20

AFTER THE uproar had ceased, Paul sent for the disciples and warned *and* consoled *and* urged *and* encouraged them; then he embraced them *and* told them farewell and set forth on his journey to Macedonia.

2 Then after he had gone through those districts and had warned *and* consoled *and* urged *and* encouraged the brethren with much discourse, he came to Greece.

3 Having spent three months there, when a plot was formed against him by the Jews as he was about to set sail for Syria, he resolved to go back through Macedonia.

4 He was accompanied by Sopater the son of Pyrrhus from Beroea, and by the Thessalonians Aristarchus

and Secundus, and Gaius of Derbe and Timothy, and the Asians Tychicus and Trophimus.

5 These went on ahead and were waiting for us [including Luke] at Troas,

6 But we [ourselves] sailed from Philippi after the days of Unleavened Bread [the Passover week], and in five days we joined them at Troas, where we remained for seven days.

7 And on the first day of the week, when we were assembled together to break bread [*the Lord's Supper], Paul discoursed with them, intending to leave the next morning; and he kept on with his message until midnight.

8 Now there were numerous lights in the upper room where we were assembled,

9 And there was a young man named Eutychus sitting in the window. He was borne down with deep sleep as Paul kept on talking still longer, and [finally] completely overcome by sleep, he fell down from the third story and was picked up dead.

10 But Paul went down and bent over him and embraced him, saying, Make no ado; his life is within him.

11 When Paul had gone back upstairs and had broken bread and eaten [with them], and after he had talked confidentially *and* communed with them for a considerable time—until daybreak [in fact]—he departed.

12 They took the youth home alive, and were not a little comforted *and* cheered *and* refreshed *and* encouraged.

13 But going on ahead to the ship, the rest of us set sail for Assos, intending to take Paul aboard there, for that was what he had directed, intending himself to go by land [on foot].

14 So when he met us at Assos, we took him aboard and sailed on to Mitylene.

15 And sailing from there, we arrived the day after at a point opposite Chios; the following day we struck across to Samos, and the next day we arrived at Miletus.

16 For Paul had determined to sail on past Ephesus, lest he might have to spend time [unnecessarily] in [the province of] Asia; for he was hastening on so that he might reach Jerusalem, if at all possible, by the day of Pentecost.

17 However, from Miletus he sent to Ephesus and summoned the elders of the church [to come to him there].

18 And when they arrived he said to them: You yourselves are well acquainted with my manner of living among you from the first day that I set foot in [the province of] Asia, and how I continued afterward,

19 Serving the Lord with all humility in tears and in the midst of adversity (affliction and trials) which befell me, due to the plots of the Jews [against me];

20 How I did not shrink from telling you anything that was for your benefit and teaching you in public meetings and from house to house,

21 But constantly *and* earnestly I bore testimony both to Jews and Greeks, urging them to turn in repentance [*that is due] to God and to have faith in our Lord Jesus Christ [*that is due Him].

22 And now, you see, I am going to Jerusalem, bound by the [Holy] Spirit and obligated *and* compelled by the [convictions of my own] spirit, not knowing what will befall me there—

23 Except that the Holy Spirit clearly *and* emphatically affirms to me in city after city that imprisonment and suffering await me.

24 But *none of these things move me;* neither do I esteem my life dear to myself, if only I may finish my course *with joy* and the ministry which I have obtained from [which was entrusted to me by] the Lord Jesus, faithfully to attest to the good news (Gospel) of God's grace (His unmerited favor, spiritual blessing, and mercy).

25 And now, observe, I perceive that all of you, among whom I have gone in and out proclaiming the kingdom, will see my face no more.

26 Therefore I testify *and* protest to you on this [our parting] day that I am clean *and* innocent *and* not responsible for the blood of any of you.

27 For I never shrank *or* kept back *or* fell short from declaring to you the whole purpose *and* plan *and* counsel of God.

28 Take care *and* be on guard for yourselves and the whole flock over which the Holy Spirit has appointed you bishops and guardians, to shepherd (tend and feed and guide) the church of the Lord *or* [t]of God which He obtained for Himself [buying it and saving it for Himself] with His own blood.

29 I know that after I am gone, ferocious wolves will get in among you, not sparing the flock;

30 Even from among your own selves men will come to the front who, by saying perverse (distorted and corrupt) things, will endeavor to draw away the disciples after them [to their own party].

31 Therefore be always alert *and* on your guard, being mindful that for three years I never stopped night *or* day seriously to admonish *and* advise *and* exhort you one by one with tears.

32 And now [brethren], I commit you to God [I deposit you in His charge, entrusting you to His protection and care]. And I commend you to the Word of His grace [to the commands and counsels and promises of His unmerited favor]. It is able to build you up and to give you [your rightful] inheritance among all God's set-apart ones (those consecrated, purified, and transformed of soul).

33 I coveted no man's silver or gold or [costly] garments.

34 You yourselves know personally that these hands ministered to my own needs and those [of the persons] who were with me.

35 In everything I have pointed out to you [by example] that, by working diligently in this manner, we ought to assist the weak, being mindful of the words of the Lord Jesus, how He Himself said, It is more blessed (makes one happier and more [u]to be envied) to give than to receive.

36 Having spoken thus, he knelt down with them all and prayed.

37 And they all wept freely and threw their arms around Paul's neck and kissed him fervently *and* repeatedly,

38 Being especially distressed *and* sorrowful because he had stated that they were about to see his face no more. And they accompanied him to the ship.

CHAPTER 21

AND WHEN we had torn ourselves away from them *and* withdrawn, we set sail and made a straight run to Cos, and on the following [day came] to Rhodes and from there to Patara.

2 There we found a ship crossing over to Phoenicia; so we went aboard and sailed away.

3 After we had sighted Cyprus, leaving it on our left we sailed on to

---

t Many ancient manuscripts read "of God."   u Alexander Souter, *Pocket Lexicon.*

Syria and put in at Tyre, for there the ship was to unload her cargo.

4 And having looked up the disciples there, we remained with them for seven days. Prompted by the [Holy] Spirit, they kept telling Paul not to set foot in Jerusalem.

5 But when our time there was ended, we left and proceeded on our journey; and all of them with their wives and children accompanied us on our way till we were outside the city. There we knelt down on the beach and prayed.

6 Then when we had told one another farewell, we went on board the ship, and they returned to their own homes.

7 When we had completed the voyage from Tyre, we landed at Ptolemais, where we paid our respects to the brethren and remained with them for one day.

8 On the morrow we left there and came to Caesarea; and we went into the house of Philip the evangelist, who was one of the Seven [first deacons], and stayed with him. [Acts 6:5.]

9 And he had four maiden daughters who had the gift of prophecy.

10 While we were remaining there for some time, a prophet named Agabus came down from Judea.

11 And coming to [see] us, he took Paul's belt and with it bound his own feet and hands and said, Thus says the Holy Spirit: The Jews at Jerusalem shall bind like this the man who owns this belt, and they shall deliver him into the hands of the Gentiles (heathen).

12 When we heard this, both we and the residents of that place pleaded with him not to go up to Jerusalem.

13 Then Paul replied, What do you mean by weeping and breaking my heart like this? For I hold myself in readiness not only to be arrested and

bound *and* imprisoned at Jerusalem, but also [even] to die for the name of the Lord Jesus.

14 And when he would not yield to [our] persuading, we stopped [urging and imploring him], saying, The Lord's will be done!

15 After these days we packed our baggage and went up to Jerusalem.

16 And some of the disciples from Caesarea came with us, conducting us to the house of Mnason, a man from Cyprus, one of the disciples of long standing, with whom we were to lodge.

17 When we arrived in Jerusalem, the brethren received *and* welcomed us gladly.

18 On the next day Paul went in with us to [see] James, and all the elders of the church were present [also].

19 After saluting them, Paul gave a detailed account of the things God had done among the Gentiles through his ministry.

20 And upon hearing it, they adored *and* exalted *and* praised *and* thanked God. And they said to [Paul], You see, brother, how many thousands of believers there are among the Jews, and all of them are enthusiastic upholders of the [Mosaic] Law.

21 Now they have been informed about you that you continually teach all the Jews who live among the Gentiles to turn back from *and* forsake Moses, advising them not to circumcise their children or pay any attention to the observance of the [Mosaic] customs.

22 What then [is best that] should be done? A multitude will come together, for they will surely hear that you have arrived.

23 Therefore do just what we tell you. With us are four men who have taken a vow upon themselves.

24 Take these men and purify

yourself along with them and pay their expenses [for the temple offering], so that they may have their heads shaved. Thus everybody will know that there is no truth in what they have been told about you, but that you yourself walk in observance of the Law.

25 But with regard to the Gentiles who have believed (adhered to, trusted in, and relied on Christ), we have sent them a letter with our decision that they should keep themselves free from anything that has been sacrificed to idols and from [tasting] blood and [eating the meat of animals] which have been strangled and from all impurity *and* sexual immorality.

26 Then Paul took the [four] men with him and the following day [he went through the rites of] purifying himself along with them. And they entered the temple to give notice when the days of purification (the ending of each vow) would be fulfilled and the usual offering could be presented on behalf of each of them.

27 When the seven days were drawing to a close, some of the Jews from [the province of] Asia, who had caught sight of Paul in the temple, incited all the rabble and laid hands on him,

28 Shouting, Men of Israel, help! [Help!] This is the man who is teaching everybody everywhere against the people and the Law and this place! Moreover, he has also [actually] brought Greeks into the temple; he has desecrated *and* polluted this holy place!

29 For they had previously seen Trophimus the Ephesian in the city with Paul and they supposed that he had brought the man into the temple [into the inner court forbidden to Gentiles].

30 Then the whole city was aroused *and* thrown into confusion, and the people rushed together; they laid hands on Paul and dragged him outside the temple, and immediately the gates were closed.

31 Now while they were trying to kill him, word came to the commandant of the regular Roman garrison that the whole of Jerusalem was in a state of ferment.

32 So immediately he took soldiers and centurions and hurried down among them; and when the people saw the commandant and the troops, they stopped beating Paul.

33 Then the commandant approached and arrested Paul and ordered that he be secured with two chains. He then inquired who he was and what he had done.

34 Some in the crowd kept shouting back one thing and others something else, and since he could not ascertain the facts because of the furor, he ordered that Paul be removed to the barracks.

35 And when [Paul] came to mount the steps, he was actually being carried by the soldiers because of the violence of the mob;

36 For the mass of the people kept following them, shouting, Away with him! [Kill him!]

37 Just as Paul was about to be taken into the barracks, he asked the commandant, May I say something to you? And the man replied, Can you speak Greek?

38 Are you not then [as I supposed] the Egyptian who not long ago stirred up a rebellion and led those 4,000 men who were cutthroats out into the wilderness (desert)?

39 Paul answered, I am a Jew, from Tarsus in Cilicia, a citizen of no insignificant *or* undistinguished city. I beg you, allow me to address the people.

40 And when the man had granted him permission, Paul, standing on the steps, gestured with his hand to the people; and there was a great

hush. Then he spoke to them in the Hebrew dialect, saying:

CHAPTER 22

BRETHREN AND fathers, listen to the defense which I now make in your presence.

2 And when they heard that he addressed them in the Hebrew tongue, they were all the more quiet. And he continued,

3 I am a Jew, born in Tarsus of Cilicia but reared in this city. At the feet of Gamaliel I was educated according to the strictest care in the Law of our fathers, being ardent [even a zealot] for God, as all of you are today.

4 [Yes] I harassed (troubled, molested, and persecuted) this Way [of the Lord] to the death, putting in chains and committing to prison both men and women,

5 As the high priest and whole council of elders (Sanhedrin) can testify; for from them indeed I received letters with which I was on my way to the brethren in Damascus in order to take also those [believers] who were there, and bring them in chains to Jerusalem that they might be punished.

6 But as I was on my journey and approached Damascus, about noon a great blaze of light flashed suddenly from heaven and shone about me.

7 And I fell to the ground and heard a voice saying to me, Saul, Saul, why do you persecute Me [harass and trouble and molest Me]?

8 And I replied, Who are You, Lord? And He said to me, I am Jesus the Nazarene, Whom you are persecuting.

9 Now the men who were with me saw the light, but they did not hear

[ᵛthe sound of the uttered words of] the voice of the One Who was speaking to me [so that they could ʷunderstand it].

10 And I asked, What shall I do, Lord? And the Lord answered me, Get up and go into Damascus, and there it will be told you all that it is destined *and* appointed for you to do.

11 And since I could not see because [of the dazzlingly glorious intensity] of the brightness of that light, I was led by the hand by those who were with me, and [thus] I arrived in Damascus.

12 And one Ananias, a devout man according to the Law, well spoken of by all the Jews who resided there,

13 Came to see me, and standing by my side said to me, Brother Saul, ᵛlook up *and* receive back your sight. And in that very ˣinstant I [recovered my sight and] looking up saw him.

14 And he said, The God of our forefathers has destined *and* appointed you to come progressively to know His will [to perceive, to recognize more strongly and clearly, and to become better and more intimately acquainted with His will], and to see the Righteous One (Jesus Christ, the Messiah), and to hear a voice from His [own] mouth *and* a message from His [own] lips;

15 For you will be His witness unto all men of everything that you have seen and heard.

16 And now, why do you delay? Rise and be baptized, and ʸby calling upon His name, wash away your sins.

17 Then when I had come back to Jerusalem and was praying in the temple [ᶻenclosure], I fell into a trance (an ecstasy);

18 And I saw Him as He said to

v Joseph Thayer, *A Greek-English Lexicon.* w Marvin Vincent, *Word Studies.* x James Moulton and George Milligan, *The Vocabulary.* y Charles B. Williams, *The New Testament: A Translation in the Language of the People:* Circumstantial participle expressing manner or means. z Richard Trench, *Synonyms of the New Testament.*

me, Hurry, get quickly out of Jerusalem, because they will not receive your testimony about Me.

19 And I said, Lord, they themselves well know that throughout all the synagogues I cast into prison and flogged those who believed on (adhered to and trusted in and relied on) You.

20 And when the blood of Your witness (martyr) Stephen was shed, I also was personally standing by and consenting *and* approving and guarding the garments of those who slew him.

21 And the Lord said to me, Go, for I will send you far away unto the Gentiles (nations).

22 Up to the moment that Paul made this last statement, the people listened to him; but now they raised their voices and shouted, Away with such a fellow from the earth! He is not fit to live!

23 And as they were shouting and tossing *and* waving their garments and throwing dust into the air,

24 The commandant ordered that Paul be brought into the barracks, and that he be examined by scourging in order that [the commandant] might learn why the people cried out thus against him.

25 But when they had stretched him out with the thongs (leather straps), Paul asked the centurion who was standing by, Is it legal for you to flog a man who is a Roman citizen and uncondemned [without a trial]?

26 When the centurion heard that, he went to the commandant and said to him, What are you about to do? This man is a Roman citizen!

27 So the commandant came and said to [Paul], Tell me, are you a Roman citizen? And he said, Yes [indeed]!

28 The commandant replied, I purchased this citizenship [as a capital investment] for a big price. Paul said, But I was born [Roman]!

29 Instantly those who were about to examine *and* flog him withdrew from him; and the commandant also was frightened, for he realized that [Paul] was a Roman citizen and he had put him in chains.

30 But the next day, desiring to know the real cause for which the Jews accused him, he unbound him and ordered the chief priests and all the council (Sanhedrin) to assemble; and he brought Paul down and placed him before them.

CHAPTER 23

THEN PAUL, gazing earnestly at the council (Sanhedrin), said, Brethren, I have lived before God, doing my duty with a perfectly good conscience until this very day [a as a citizen, a true and loyal Jew].

2 At this the high priest Ananias ordered those who stood near him to strike him on the mouth.

3 Then Paul said to him, God is about to strike you, you whitewashed wall! Do you sit as a judge to try me in accordance with the Law, and yet in defiance of the Law you order me to be struck?

4 Those who stood near exclaimed, Do you rail at *and* insult the high priest of God?

5 And Paul said, I was not conscious, brethren, that he was a high priest; for the Scripture says, You shall not speak ill of a ruler of your people. [Exod. 22:28.]

6 But Paul, when he perceived that one part of them were Sadducees and the other part Pharisees, cried out to the council (Sanhedrin), Brethren, I am a Pharisee, a son of Pharisees; it is with regard to the hope and the

a Marvin Vincent, *Word Studies*.

resurrection of the dead that I am indicted *and* being judged.

7 So when he had said this, an angry dispute arose between the Pharisees and the Sadducees; and the whole [crowded] assemblage was divided [into two factions].

8 For the Sadducees hold that there is no resurrection, nor angel nor spirit, but the Pharisees declare openly *and* speak out freely, acknowledging [their belief in] them both.

9 Then a great uproar ensued, and some of the scribes of the Pharisees' party stood up and thoroughly fought the case, [contending fiercely] and declaring, We find nothing evil *or* wrong in this man. But if a spirit or an angel [really] spoke to him—? *Let us not fight against God!*

10 And when the strife became more and more tense *and* violent, the commandant, fearing that Paul would be torn in pieces by them, ordered the troops to go down and take him forcibly from among them and conduct him back into the barracks.

11 And [that same] following night the Lord stood beside Paul and said, Take courage, *Paul,* for as you have borne faithful witness concerning Me at Jerusalem, so you must also bear witness at Rome.

12 Now when daylight came, the Jews formed a plot and bound themselves by an oath *and* under a curse neither to eat nor drink till they had done away with Paul.

13 There were more than forty [men of them], who formed this conspiracy [swearing together this oath and curse].

14 And they went to the chief priests and elders, saying, We have strictly bound ourselves by an oath *and* under a curse not to taste any food until we have slain Paul.

15 So now you, along with the council (Sanhedrin), give notice to the commandant to bring [Paul] down to you, as if you were going to investigate his case more accurately. But we [ourselves] are ready to slay him before he comes near.

16 But the son of Paul's sister heard of their intended attack, and he went and got into the barracks and told Paul.

17 Then Paul, calling in one of the centurions, said, Take this young man to the commandant, for he has something to report to him.

18 So he took him and conducted him to the commandant and said, Paul the prisoner called me to him and requested me to conduct this young man to you, for he has something to report to you.

19 The commandant took him by the hand, and going aside with him, asked privately, What is it that you have to report to me?

20 And he replied, The Jews have agreed to ask you to bring Paul down to the council (Sanhedrin) tomorrow, as if [they were] intending to examine him more exactly.

21 But do not yield to their persuasion, for more than forty of their men are lying in ambush waiting for him, having bound themselves by an oath *and* under a curse neither to eat nor drink till they have killed him; and even now they are all ready, [just] waiting for your promise.

22 So the commandant sent the youth away, charging him, Do not disclose to anyone that you have given me this information.

23 Then summoning two of the centurions, he said, Have two hundred footmen ready by the third hour of the night (about 9:00 p.m.) to go as far as Caesarea, with seventy horsemen and two hundred spearmen.

24 Also provide beasts for mounts for Paul to ride, and bring him in safety to Felix the governor.

25 And he wrote a letter having this message:

26 Claudius Lysias sends greetings to His Excellency Felix the governor.

27 This man was seized [as prisoner] by the Jews, and was about to be killed by them when I came upon them with the troops and rescued him, because I learned that he is a Roman citizen.

28 And wishing to know the exact accusation which they were making against him, I brought him down before their council (Sanhedrin),

29 [Where] I found that he was charged in regard to questions of their own law, but he was accused of nothing that would call for death or [even] for imprisonment.

30 [However] when it was pointed out to me that there would be a conspiracy against the man, I sent him to you immediately, directing his accusers also to present before you their charge against him.

31 So the soldiers, in compliance with their instructions, took Paul and conducted him during the night to Antipatris.

32 And the next day they returned to the barracks, leaving the mounted men to proceed with him.

33 When these came to Caesarea and gave the letter to the governor, they also presented Paul before him.

34 Having read the letter, he asked to what province [Paul] belonged. When he discovered that he was from Cilicia [an imperial province],

35 He said, I will hear your case bfully when your accusers also have come. And he ordered that an eye be kept on him in Herod's palace (the Praetorium).

CHAPTER 24

FIVE DAYS later, the high priest Ananias came down [from Jerusalem to Caesarea] with some elders and a certain forensic advocate Tertullus [acting as spokesman and counsel]. They presented to the governor their evidence against Paul.

2 And when he was called, Tertullus began the complaint [against him] by saying: Since through you we obtain and enjoy much peace, and since by your foresight and provision wonderful reforms (amendments and improvements) are introduced and effected on behalf of this nation,

3 In every way and in every place, most excellent Felix, we accept and acknowledge this with deep appreciation and with all gratitude.

4 But not to hinder or detain you too long, I beg you in your clemency and courtesy and kindness to grant us a brief and bconcise hearing.

5 For we have found this man a perfect pest (a real plague), an agitator and source of disturbance to all the Jews throughout the world, and a ringleader of the [heretical, bdivision-producing] sect of the Nazarenes.

6 He also [even] tried to desecrate and defile the temple, but we laid hands on him cand would have sentenced him by our Law,

7 But the commandant Lysias came and took him from us with violence and force,

8 And ordered his accusers to present themselves to you. By examining and cross-questioning him yourself, you will be able to ascertain the truth from him about all these things with which we charge him.

9 The Jews also agreed and joined in the accusation, declaring that all these things were exactly so.

b Marvin Vincent, *Word Studies.*   c Many manuscripts do not contain the remainder of verse 6, all of verse 7, and the first part of verse 8.

10 And when the governor had beckoned to Paul to speak, he answered: Because I know that for many years you have been a judge over this nation, I find it easier to make my defense *and* do it cheerfully *and* with good courage.

11 As you can readily verify, it is not more than twelve days since I went up to Jerusalem to worship;

12 And neither in the temple nor in the synagogues nor in the city did they find me disputing with anybody or bringing together a seditious crowd.

13 Neither can they present argument *or* evidence to prove to you what they now bring against me.

14 But this I confess to you, however, that in accordance with the Way [of the Lord], which they call a [heretical, division-producing] sect, I worship (serve) the God of our fathers, still persuaded of the truth of *and* believing in *and* placing full confidence in everything laid down in the Law [of Moses] *or* written in the prophets;

15 Having [the same] hope in God which these themselves hold *and* look for, that there is to be a resurrection both of the righteous and the unrighteous (the just and the unjust).

16 Therefore I always exercise *and* discipline myself [mortifying my body, deadening my carnal affections, bodily appetites, and worldly desires, endeavoring in all respects] to have a clear (unshaken, blameless) conscience, void of offense toward God and toward men.

17 Now after several years I came up [to Jerusalem] to bring to my people contributions of charity and offerings.

18 While I was engaged in presenting these, they found me [occupied in the rites of purification] in the temple, without any crowd or uproar. But some Jews from [the province of] Asia [were there],

19 Who ought to be here before you and to present their charges, if they have anything against me.

20 Or else let these men themselves tell of what crime *or* wrongdoing they found me guilty when I appeared before the council (Sanhedrin),

21 Unless it be this one sentence which I cried out as I stood among them, In regard to the resurrection of the dead I am indicted *and* on trial before you this day!

22 But Felix, having a rather accurate understanding of the Way [of the Lord], put them off *and* adjourned the trial, saying, When Lysias the commandant comes down, I will determine your case more fully.

23 Then he ordered the centurion to keep [Paul] in custody, but to treat him with indulgence [giving him some liberty] and not to hinder his friends from ministering to his needs *and* serving him.

24 Some days later Felix came with his wife Drusilla, who was a Jewess; and he sent for Paul and listened to him [talk] about faith in Christ Jesus.

25 But as he continued to argue about uprightness, purity of life (the control of the passions), and the judgment to come, Felix became alarmed *and* terrified and said, Go away for the present; when I have a convenient opportunity, I will send for you.

26 At the same time he hoped to get money from Paul, for which reason he continued to send for him and was in his company *and* conversed with him often.

27 But when two years had gone by, Felix was succeeded in office by Porcius Festus; and wishing to gain favor with the Jews, Felix left Paul still a prisoner in chains.

CHAPTER 25

NOW WHEN Festus had entered into his own province, after three days he went up from Caesarea to Jerusalem.

2 And [there] the chief priests and the principal men of the Jews laid charges before him against Paul, and they kept begging *and* urging him,

3 Asking as a favor that he would have him brought to Jerusalem; [meanwhile] they were planning an ambush to slay him on the way.

4 Festus answered that Paul was in custody in Caesarea and that he himself planned to leave for there soon.

5 So, said he, let those who are in a position of authority *and* are influential among you go down with me, and if there is anything amiss *or* criminal about the man, let them so charge him.

6 So when Festus had remained among them not more than eight or ten days, he went down to Caesarea, took his seat the next day on the judgment bench, and ordered Paul to be brought before him.

7 And when he arrived, the Jews who had come down from Jerusalem stood all around him, bringing many grave accusations against him which they were not able to prove.

8 Paul declared in [his own] defense, Neither against the Law of the Jews, nor against the temple, nor against Caesar have I offended in any way.

9 But Festus, wishing to ingratiate himself with the Jews, answered Paul, Are you willing to go up to Jerusalem and there be put on trial [ᵇbefore the Jewish Sanhedrin] in my presence concerning these charges?

10 But Paul replied, I am standing before Caesar's judgment seat, where I ought to be tried. To the Jews I have done no wrong, as you know ᵈbetter [than your question implies].

11 If then I am a wrongdoer *and* a criminal and have committed anything for which I deserve to die, I do not beg off *and* seek to escape death; but if there is no ground for their accusations against me, no one can give me up *and* make a present of me [ᵉgive me up freely] to them. I appeal to Caesar.

12 Then Festus, when he had consulted with the [ᵈmen who formed his] council, answered, You have appealed to Caesar; to Caesar you shall go.

13 Now after an interval of some days, Agrippa the king and Bernice arrived at Caesarea to pay their respects to Festus [to welcome him and wish him well].

14 And while they remained there for many days, Festus acquainted the king with Paul's case, telling him, There is a man left a prisoner in chains by Felix;

15 And when I was at Jerusalem, the chief priests and the elders of the Jews informed me about him, petitioning for a judicial hearing *and* condemnation of him.

16 But I replied to them that it was not the custom of the Romans to ᵉgive up freely any man for punishment before the accused had met the accusers face to face and had opportunity to defend himself concerning the charge brought against him.

17 So when they came here together, I did not delay, but on the morrow took my place on the judgment seat and ordered that the man be brought before me.

18 [But] when the accusers stood up, they brought forward no accusation [in his case] of any such misconduct as I was expecting.

19 Instead they had some points of

d Marvin Vincent, *Word Studies*.   e G. Abbott-Smith, *Manual Greek Lexicon*.

controversy with him about their own religion *or* superstition and concerning one Jesus, Who had died but Whom Paul kept asserting [over and over] to be alive.

20 And I, being puzzled to know how to make inquiries into such questions, asked whether he would be willing to go to Jerusalem and there be tried regarding them.

21 But when Paul had appealed to have his case retained for examination *and* decision by the emperor, I ordered that he be detained until I could send him to Caesar.

22 Then Agrippa said to Festus, I also desire to hear the man myself. Tomorrow, [Festus] replied, you shall hear him.

23 So the next day Agrippa and Bernice approached with great display, and they went into the audience hall accompanied by the military commandants and the prominent citizens of the city. At the order of Festus Paul was brought in.

24 Then Festus said, King Agrippa and all the men present with us, you see this man about whom the whole Jewish people came to me *and* complained, both at Jerusalem and here, insisting *and* shouting that he ought not to live any longer.

25 But I found nothing that he had done deserving of death. Still, as he himself appealed to the emperor, I determined to send him to Rome.

26 [However] I have nothing in particular *and* definite to write to my lord concerning him. So I have brought him before all of you, and especially before you, King Agrippa, so that after [further] examination has been made, I may have something to put in writing.

27 For it seems to me senseless *and* absurd to send a prisoner and not state the accusations against him.

CHAPTER 26

THEN AGRIPPA said to Paul, You are permitted to speak on your own behalf. At that Paul stretched forth his hand and made his defense [as follows]:

2 I consider myself fortunate, King Agrippa, that it is before you that I am to make my defense today in regard to all the charges brought against me by [the] Jews,

3 [Especially] because you are so fully *and* unusually conversant with all the Jewish customs and controversies; therefore, I beg you to hear me patiently.

4 My behavior *and* manner of living from my youth up is known by all the Jews; [they are aware] that from [its] commencement my youth was spent among my own race in Jerusalem.

5 They have had knowledge of me for a long time, if they are willing to testify to it, that in accordance with the strictest sect of our religion I have lived as a Pharisee.

6 And now I stand here on trial [to be judged on the ground] of the hope of that promise made to our forefathers by God, [Acts 13:32, 33.]

7 Which hope [of the Messiah and the resurrection] our twelve tribes confidently expect to realize as they fervently worship [without ceasing] night and day. And for that hope, O king, I am accused by Jews *and* considered a criminal!

8 Why is it thought incredible by any of you that God raises the dead?

9 I myself indeed was [once] persuaded that it was my duty to do many things contrary to *and* in defiance of the name of Jesus of Nazareth.

10 And that is what I did in Jerusalem; I [not only] locked up many of the [faithful] saints (holy ones) in prison by virtue of authority received

from the chief priests, but when they were being condemned to death, I cast my vote against them.

11 And frequently I punished them in all the synagogues to make them blaspheme; and in my bitter fury against them, I harassed (troubled, molested, persecuted) *and* pursued them even to foreign cities.

12 Thus engaged I proceeded to Damascus with the authority and orders of the chief priests,

13 When on the road at midday, O king, I saw a light from heaven surpassing the brightness of the sun, flashing about me and those who were traveling with me.

14 And when we had all fallen to the ground, I heard a voice in the Hebrew tongue saying to me, Saul, Saul, why do you continue to persecute Me [to harass and trouble and molest Me]? It is dangerous *and* turns out badly for you to keep kicking against the goads [to keep offering vain and perilous resistance].

15 And I said, Who are You, Lord? And the Lord said, I am Jesus, Whom you are persecuting.

16 But arise and stand upon your feet; for I have appeared to you for this purpose, that I might appoint you to serve as [My] minister and to bear witness both to what you have seen of Me and to that in which I will appear to you,

17 ʳChoosing you out [selecting you for Myself] *and* ˢdelivering you from among this [Jewish] people and the Gentiles to whom I am sending you—[Ezek. 2:1, 3.]

18 To open their eyes that they may turn from darkness to light and from the power of Satan to God, so that they may thus receive forgiveness *and* release from their sins and a place *and* portion among those who

are consecrated *and* purified by faith in Me. [Isa. 42:7, 16.]

19 Wherefore, O King Agrippa, I was not disobedient unto the heavenly vision,

20 But made known openly first of all to those at Damascus, then at Jerusalem and throughout the whole land of Judea, and also among the Gentiles, that they should repent and turn to God, and do works *and* live lives consistent with *and* worthy of their repentance.

21 Because of these things the Jews seized me in the temple [ᵇenclosure] and tried to do away with me.

22 [But] to this day I have had the help which comes from God [as my ᵍally], and so I stand here testifying to small and great alike, asserting nothing beyond what the prophets and Moses declared would come to pass—

23 That the Christ (the Anointed One) must suffer and that He, by being the first to rise from the dead, would declare *and* show light both to the [Jewish] people and to the Gentiles.

24 And as he thus proceeded with his defense, Festus called out loudly, Paul, you are mad! Your great learning is driving you insane!

25 But Paul replied, I am not mad, most noble Festus, but I am uttering the straight, sound truth.

26 For the king understands about these things well enough, and [therefore] to him I speak with bold frankness *and* confidence. I am convinced that not one of these things has escaped his notice, for all this did not take place in a corner [in secret].

27 King Agrippa, do you believe the prophets? [Do you give credence to God's messengers and their

f Joseph Thayer, *A Greek-English Lexicon.*   g G. Abbott-Smith, *Manual Greek Lexicon.*   h Richard Trench, *Synonyms of the New Testament.*

words?] I perceive *and* know that you do believe.

28 Then Agrippa said to Paul, You think it a small task to make a Christian of me [just offhand to induce me with little ado and persuasion, at very short notice].

29 And Paul replied, Whether short or long, I would to God that not only you, but also all who are listening to me today, might become such as I am, except for these chains.

30 Then the king arose, and the governor and Bernice and all those who were seated with them;

31 And after they had gone out, they said to one another, This man is doing nothing deserving of death or [even] of imprisonment.

32 And Agrippa said to Festus, This man could have been set at liberty if he had not appealed to Caesar.

CHAPTER 27

NOW WHEN it was determined that we [including Luke] should sail for Italy, they turned Paul and some other prisoners over to a centurion of the imperial regiment named Julius.

2 And going aboard a ship from Adramyttium which was about to sail for the ports along the coast of [the province of] Asia, we put out to sea; and Aristarchus, a Macedonian from Thessalonica, accompanied us.

3 The following day we landed at Sidon, and Julius treated Paul in a loving way, with much consideration (kindness and care), permitting him to go to his friends [there] and be refreshed *and* be cared for.

4 After putting to sea from there we passed to the leeward (south side) of Cyprus [for protection], for the winds were contrary to us.

5 And when we had sailed over [the whole length] of sea which lies off Cilicia and Pamphylia, we reached Myra in Lycia.

6 There the centurion found an Alexandrian ship bound for Italy, and he transferred us to it.

7 For a number of days we made slow progress and arrived with difficulty off Cnidus; then, as the wind did not permit us to proceed, we went under the lee (shelter) of Crete off Salmone,

8 And coasting along it with difficulty, we arrived at a place called Fair Havens, near which is located the town of Lasea.

9 But as [the season was well advanced, for] much time had been lost and navigation was already dangerous, for the time for the Fast [the Day of Atonement, about the beginning of October] had already gone by, Paul warned *and* advised them,

10 Saying, Sirs, I perceive [after careful observation] that this voyage will be attended with disaster and much heavy loss, not only of the cargo and the ship but of our lives also.

11 However, the centurion paid greater attention to the pilot and to the owner of the ship than to what Paul said.

12 And as the harbor was not well situated *and* so unsuitable to winter in, the majority favored the plan of putting to sea again from there, hoping somehow to reach Phoenice, a harbor of Crete facing southwest and northwest, and winter there.

13 So when the south wind blew softly, supposing they were gaining their object, they weighed anchor and sailed along Crete, hugging the coast.

14 But soon afterward a violent wind [of the character of a typhoon], called a northeaster, came bursting down from the island.

15 And when the ship was caught and was unable to head against the

wind, we gave up and, letting her drift, were borne along.

16 We ran under the shelter of a small island called Cauda, where we managed with [much] difficulty to draw the [ship's small] boat on deck and secure it.

17 After hoisting it on board, they used supports with ropes to undergird and brace the ship; then afraid that they would be driven into the Syrtis [quicksands off the north coast of Africa], they lowered the gear (sails and ropes) and so were driven along.

18 As we were being dangerously tossed about by the violence of the storm, the next day they began to throw the freight overboard;

19 And the third day they threw out with their own hands the ship's equipment (the tackle and the furniture).

20 And when neither sun nor stars were visible for many days and no small tempest kept raging about us, all hope of our being saved was finally abandoned.

21 Then as they had eaten nothing for a long time, Paul came forward into their midst and said, Men, you should have listened to me, and should not have put to sea from Crete and brought on this disaster and harm and misery and loss.

22 But [even] now I beg you to be in good spirits and take heart, for there will be no loss of life among you but only of the ship.

23 For this [very] night there stood by my side an angel of the God to Whom I belong and Whom I serve and worship,

24 And he said, Do not be frightened, Paul! It is necessary for you to stand before Caesar; and behold, God has given you all those who are sailing with you.

25 So keep up your courage, men, for I have faith (complete confidence) in God that it will be exactly as it was told me;

26 But we shall have to be stranded on some island.

27 The fourteenth night had come and we were drifting and being driven about in the Adriatic Sea, when about midnight the sailors began to suspect that they were drawing near to some land.

28 So they took soundings and found twenty fathoms, and a little farther on they sounded again and found fifteen fathoms.

29 Then fearing that we might fall off [our course] onto rocks, they dropped four anchors from the stern and kept wishing for daybreak to come.

30 And as the sailors were trying to escape [secretly] from the ship and were lowering the small boat into the sea, pretending that they were going to lay out anchors from the bow,

31 Paul said to the centurion and the soldiers, Unless these men remain in the ship, you cannot be saved.

32 Then the soldiers cut away the ropes that held the small boat, and let it fall and drift away.

33 While they waited until it should become day, Paul entreated them all to take some food, saying, This is the fourteenth day that you have been continually in suspense and on the alert without food, having eaten nothing.

34 So I urge (warn, exhort, encourage, advise) you to take some food [for your safety]—it will give you strength; for not a hair is to perish from the head of any one of you.

35 Having said these words, he took bread and, giving thanks to God before them all, he broke it and began to eat.

36 Then they all became more cheerful and were encouraged and took food themselves.

37 All told there were 276 souls of us in the ship.

38 And after they had eaten sufficiently, [they proceeded] to lighten the ship, throwing out the wheat into the sea.

39 Now when it was day [and they saw the land], they did not recognize it, but they noticed a bay with a beach on which they [taking counsel] purposed to run the ship ashore if they possibly could.

40 So they cut the cables *and* severed the anchors and left them in the sea; at the same time unlashing the ropes that held the rudders and hoisting the foresail to the wind, they headed for the beach.

41 But striking a crosscurrent (a place open to two seas) they ran the ship aground. The prow stuck fast and remained immovable, and the stern began to break up under the violent force of the waves.

42 It was the counsel of the soldiers to kill the prisoners, lest any of them should swim to land and escape;

43 But the centurion, wishing to save Paul, prevented their carrying out their purpose. He commanded those who could swim to throw themselves overboard first and make for the shore,

44 And the rest on heavy boards or pieces of the vessel. And so it was that all escaped safely to land.

CHAPTER 28

AFTER WE were safe on the island, we knew *and* recognized that it was called Malta.

2 And the natives showed us unusual *and* remarkable kindness, for they kindled a fire and welcomed *and* received us all, since it had begun to rain and was cold.

3 Now Paul had gathered a bundle

of sticks, and he was laying them on the fire when a viper crawled out because of the heat and fastened itself on his hand.

4 When the natives saw the little animal hanging from his hand, they said to one another, Doubtless this man is a murderer, for though he has been saved from the sea, Justice [[i]the goddess of avenging] has not permitted that he should live.

5 Then [Paul simply] shook off the small creature into the fire and suffered no evil effects.

6 However, they were waiting, expecting him to swell up or suddenly drop dead; but when they had watched him a long time and saw nothing fatal *or* harmful come to him, they changed their minds and kept saying over and over that he was a god.

7 In the vicinity of that place there were estates belonging to the head man of the island, named Publius, who accepted *and* welcomed *and* entertained us with hearty hospitality for three days.

8 And it happened that the father of Publius was sick in bed with recurring attacks of fever and dysentery; and Paul went to see him, and after praying and laying his hands on him, he healed him.

9 After this had occurred, the other people on the island who had diseases also kept coming and were cured.

10 They showed us every respect *and* presented many gifts to us, honoring us with many honors; and when we sailed, they provided *and* put on [board our ship] everything we needed.

11 It was after three months' stay there that we set sail in a ship which had wintered in the island, an Alexandrian ship with the Twin Brothers

i Alexander Souter, *Pocket Lexicon*.

[Castor and Pollux] as its figurehead.

12 We landed at Syracuse and remained there three days,

13 And from there we made a circuit [following the coast] and reached Rhegium; and one day later a south wind sprang up, and the next day we arrived at Puteoli.

14 There we found some [Christian] brethren and were entreated to stay with them for seven days. And so we came to Rome.

15 And the [Christian] brethren there, having had news of us, came as far as the Forum of Appius and the Three Taverns to meet us. When Paul saw them, he thanked God and received new courage.

16 When we arrived at Rome, *the centurion delivered the prisoners to the captain of the guard, but* Paul was permitted to live by himself with the soldier who guarded him.

17 Three days after [our arrival], he called together the leading local Jews; and when they had gathered, he said to them, Brethren, though I have done nothing against the people or against the customs of our forefathers, yet I was turned over as a prisoner from Jerusalem into the hands of the Romans.

18 After they had examined me, they were ready to release me because I was innocent of any offense deserving the death penalty.

19 But when the Jews protested, I was forced to appeal to Caesar, though it was not because I had any charge to make against my nation.

20 This is the reason therefore why I have begged to see you and to talk with you, since it is because of the Hope of Israel (the Messiah) that I am bound with this chain.

21 And they answered him, We have not received any letters about you from Judea, and none of the [Jewish] brethren coming here has reported or spoken anything evil about you.

22 But we think it fitting *and* are eager to hear from you what it is that you have in mind *and* believe *and* what your opinion is, for with regard to this sect it is known to all of us that it is everywhere denounced.

23 So when they had set a day with him, they came in large numbers to his lodging. And he fully set forth *and* explained the matter to them from morning until night, testifying to the kingdom of God and trying to persuade them concerning Jesus both from the Law of Moses and from the Prophets.

24 And some were convinced *and* believed what he said, and others did not believe.

25 And as they disagreed among themselves, they began to leave, [but not before] Paul had added one statement [more]: The Holy Spirit was right in saying through Isaiah the prophet to your forefathers:

26 Go to this people and say to them, You will indeed hear *and* hear with your ears but will not understand, and you will indeed look *and* look with your eyes but will not see [not perceive, have knowledge of or become acquainted with what you look at, at all].

27 For the heart (the understanding, the soul) of this people has grown dull (stupid, hardened, and calloused), and their ears are heavy *and* hard of hearing and they have shut tight their eyes, so that they may not perceive *and* have knowledge *and* become acquainted with their eyes and hear with their ears and understand with their souls and turn [to Me and be converted], that I may heal them. [Isa. 6:9, 10.]

28 So let it be understood by you then that [this message of] the salvation of God has been sent to the Gen-

tiles, and they will listen [to it]! [Ps. 67:2.]

29 [j]*And when he had said these things, the Jews went away, arguing and disputing among themselves.*

30 After this Paul lived there for two entire years [at his own expense]

in his own rented lodging, and he welcomed all who came to him,

31 Preaching to them the kingdom of God and teaching them about the Lord Jesus Christ with boldness *and* quite openly, and without being molested *or* hindered.

THE LETTER OF PAUL TO THE

ROMANS

CHAPTER 1

FROM PAUL, a bond servant of Jesus Christ (the Messiah) called to be an apostle, (a special messenger) set apart to [preach] the Gospel (good news) of *and* from God,

2 Which He promised in advance [long ago] through His prophets in the sacred Scriptures—

3 [The Gospel] regarding His Son, Who as to the flesh (His human nature) was descended from David,

4 And [as to His divine nature] according to the Spirit of holiness was openly [k]designated the Son of God in power [in a striking, triumphant and miraculous manner] by His resurrection from the dead, even Jesus Christ our Lord (the Messiah, the Anointed One).

5 It is through Him that we have received grace (God's unmerited favor) and [our] apostleship to promote obedience to the faith *and* make disciples for His name's sake among all the nations,

6 And this includes you, called of Jesus Christ *and* invited [as you are] to belong to Him.

7 To [you then] all God's beloved ones in Rome, called to be saints *and* designated for a consecrated life:

Grace *and* spiritual blessing and peace be yours from God our Father and from the Lord Jesus Christ.

8 First, I thank my God through Jesus Christ for all of you, because [the report of] your faith is being made known to all the world *and* is [k]commended everywhere.

9 For God is my witness, Whom I serve with my [whole] spirit [rendering priestly and spiritual service] in [preaching] the Gospel *and* [telling] the good news of His Son, how incessantly I always mention you when at my prayers,

10 I keep pleading that somehow by God's will I may now at last prosper *and* come to you.

11 For I am yearning to see you, that I may impart *and* share with you some spiritual gift to strengthen *and* establish you;

12 That is, that we may be mutually strengthened *and* encouraged *and* comforted by each other's faith, both yours and mine.

13 I want you to know, brethren, that many times I have planned *and* intended to come to you, though thus far I have been hindered *and* prevented, in order that I might have some fruit (some result of my labors)

---

j Many manuscripts do not contain this verse.   k Marvin Vincent, *Word Studies in the New Testament.*

among you, as I have among the rest of the Gentiles.

14 Both to Greeks and to barbarians (to the cultured and to the uncultured), both to the wise and the foolish, I have an obligation to discharge *and* a duty to perform *and* a debt to pay.

15 So, for my part, I am willing *and* eagerly ready to preach the Gospel to you also who are in Rome.

16 For I am not ashamed of the Gospel (good news) *of Christ*, for it is God's power working unto salvation [for deliverance from eternal death] to everyone who believes *with* a personal trust *and* a confident surrender *and* firm reliance, to the Jew first and also to the Greek,

17 For in the Gospel a righteousness which God ascribes is revealed, both springing from faith and leading to faith [disclosed through the way of faith that arouses to more faith]. As it is written, The man who through faith is just *and* upright shall live *and* shall live by faith. [Hab. 2:4.]

18 For God's [holy] wrath *and* indignation are revealed from heaven against all ungodliness and unrighteousness of men, who in their wickedness repress *and* hinder the truth *and* make it inoperative.

19 For that which is known about God is evident to them *and* made plain in their inner consciousness, because God [Himself] has shown it to them.

20 For ever since the creation of the world His invisible nature *and* attributes, that is, His eternal power and divinity, have been made intelligible *and* clearly discernible in *and* through the things that have been made (His handiworks). So [men] are without excuse [altogether without

any defense or justification], [Ps. 19: 1–4.]

21 Because when they knew *and* recognized Him as God, they did not honor *and* glorify Him as God or give Him thanks. But instead they became futile *and* [l]godless in their thinking [with vain imaginings, foolish reasoning, and stupid speculations] and their senseless minds were darkened.

22 Claiming to be wise, they became fools [professing to be smart, they made simpletons of themselves].

23 And by them the glory and majesty *and* excellence of the immortal God were exchanged for *and* represented by images, resembling mortal man and birds and beasts and reptiles.

24 Therefore God gave them up in the lusts of their [own] hearts to sexual impurity, to the dishonoring of their bodies among themselves [abandoning them to the degrading power of sin],

25 Because they exchanged the truth of God for a lie and worshiped and served the creature rather than the Creator, Who is blessed forever! Amen (so be it). [Jer. 2:11.]

26 For this reason God gave them over *and* abandoned them to vile affections *and* degrading passions. For their women exchanged their natural function for an unnatural *and* abnormal one,

27 And the men also turned from natural relations with women and were set ablaze (burning out, consumed) with lust for one another—men committing shameful acts with men and suffering in their own [m]bodies and personalities the inevitable consequences *and* penalty of their

wrong-doing and going astray, which was [their] fitting retribution.

28 And so, since they did not see fit to acknowledge God or approve of Him or consider Him worth the knowing, God gave them over to a base and condemned mind to do things not proper or decent but loathsome,

29 Until they were filled (permeated and saturated) with every kind of unrighteousness, iniquity, grasping and covetous greed, and malice. [They were] full of envy and jealousy, murder, strife, deceit and treachery, ill will and cruel ways. [They were] secret backbiters and gossipers,

30 Slanderers, hateful to and hating God, full of insolence, arrogance, [and] boasting; inventors of new forms of evil, disobedient and undutiful to parents.

31 [They were] without understanding, conscienceless and faithless, heartless and loveless [and] merciless.

32 Though they are fully aware of God's righteous decree that those who do such things deserve to die, they not only do them themselves but approve and applaud others who practice them.

CHAPTER 2

THEREFORE YOU have no excuse or defense or justification, O man, whoever you are who judges and condemns another. For in posing as judge and passing sentence on another, you condemn yourself, because you who judge are habitually practicing the very same things [that you censure and denounce].

2 [But] we know that the judgment (adverse verdict, sentence) of God falls justly and in accordance with truth upon those who practice such things.

3 And do you think or imagine, O man, when you judge and condemn those who practice such things and yet do them yourself, that you will escape God's judgment and elude His sentence and adverse verdict?

4 Or are you [so blind as to] trifle with and presume upon and despise and underestimate the wealth of His kindness and forbearance and longsuffering patience? Are you unmindful or actually ignorant [of the fact] that God's kindness is intended to lead you to repent ([n]to change your mind and inner man to accept God's will)?

5 But by your callous stubbornness and impenitence of heart you are storing up wrath and indignation for yourself on the day of wrath and indignation, when God's righteous judgment (just doom) will be revealed.

6 For He will render to every man according to his works [justly, as his deeds deserve]: [Ps. 62:12.]

7 To those who by patient persistence in well-doing ([o]springing from piety) seek [unseen but sure] glory and honor and ([o]the eternal blessedness of] immortality, He will give eternal life.

8 But for those who are self-seeking and self-willed and disobedient to the Truth but responsive to wickedness, there will be indignation and wrath.

9 [And] there will be tribulation and anguish and calamity and constraint for every soul of man who [habitually] does evil, the Jew first and also the Greek (Gentile).

10 But glory and honor and [heart] peace shall be awarded to everyone who [habitually] does good, the Jew first and also the Greek (Gentile).

n Alexander Souter, *Pocket Lexicon.* o Joseph Thayer, *A Greek-English Lexicon of the New Testament.*

11 For God shows no partiality [°undue favor or unfairness; with Him one man is not different from another]. [Deut. 10:17; II Chron. 19:7.]

12 All who have sinned without the Law will also perish without [regard to] the Law, and all who have sinned under the Law will be judged and condemned by the Law.

13 For it is not merely hearing the Law [read] that makes one righteous before God, but it is the doers of the Law who will be held guiltless and acquitted and justified.

14 When Gentiles who have not the [divine] Law do instinctively what the Law requires, they are a law to themselves, since they do not have the Law.

15 They show that the essential requirements of the Law are written in their hearts and are operating there, with which their consciences (sense of right and wrong) also bear witness; and their [moral] ᵠdecisions (their arguments of reason, their condemning or approving ʳthoughts) will accuse or perhaps defend and excuse [them]

16 On that day when, as my Gospel proclaims, God by Jesus Christ will judge men in regard to ʳthe things which they conceal (their hidden thoughts). [Eccl. 12:14.]

17 But if you bear the name of Jew and rely upon the Law and pride yourselves in God and your relationship to Him,

18 And know and understand His will and discerningly approve the better things and have a sense of what is vital, because you are instructed by the Law;

19 And if you are confident that you [yourself] are a guide to the blind, a light to those who are in darkness, and [that

20 You are] a corrector of the foolish, a teacher of the childish, having in the Law the embodiment of knowledge and truth—

21 Well then, you who teach others, do you not teach yourself? While you teach against stealing, do you steal (take what does not really belong to you)?

22 You who say not to commit adultery, do you commit adultery [are you unchaste in action or in thought]? You who abhor and loathe idols, do you rob temples [do you appropriate to your own use what is consecrated to God, thus robbing the sanctuary and ˢdoing sacrilege]?

23 You who boast in the Law, do you dishonor God by breaking the Law [by stealthily infringing upon or carelessly neglecting or openly breaking it]?

24 For, as it is written, The name of God is maligned and blasphemed among the Gentiles because of you! [The words to this effect are from your own Scriptures.] [Isa. 52:5; Ezek. 36:20.]

25 Circumcision does indeed profit if you keep the Law; but if you habitually transgress the Law, your circumcision is made uncircumcision.

26 So if a man who is uncircumcised keeps the requirements of the Law, will not his uncircumcision be credited to him as [equivalent to] circumcision?

27 Then those who are physically uncircumcised but keep the Law will condemn you who, although you have the code in writing and have circumcision, break the Law.

28 For he is not a [real] Jew who is only one outwardly and publicly, nor is [true] circumcision something external and physical.

p James Moulton and George Milligan, *The Vocabulary of the Greek Testament.*   q Joseph Thayer, *A Greek-English Lexicon of the New Testament.*   r Henry Alford, *The Greek New Testament, with Notes.* s James Moulton and George Milligan, *The Vocabulary.*

29 But he is a Jew who is one inwardly, and [true] circumcision is of the heart, a spiritual and not a literal [matter]. His praise is not from men but from God.

CHAPTER 3

THEN WHAT advantage remains to the Jew? [How is he favored?] Or what is the value or benefit of circumcision?

2 Much in every way. To begin with, to the Jews were entrusted the oracles (the brief communications, the intentions, the utterances) of God. [Ps. 147:19.]

3 What if some did not believe and were without faith? Does their lack of faith and their faithlessness nullify and make ineffective and void the faithfulness of God and His fidelity [to His Word]?

4 By no means! Let God be found true though every human being is false and a liar, as it is written, That You may be justified and shown to be upright in what You say, and prevail when You are judged [by sinful men]. [Ps. 51:4.]

5 But if our unrighteousness thus establishes and exhibits the righteousness of God, what shall we say? That God is unjust and wrong to inflict His wrath upon us [Jews]? I speak in a [purely] human way.

6 By no means! Otherwise, how could God judge the world?

7 But [you say] if through my falsehood God's integrity is magnified and advertised and abounds to His glory, why am I still being judged as a sinner?

8 And why should we not do evil that good may come?—as some slanderously charge us with teaching. Such [false teaching] is justly condemned by them.

9 Well then, are we [Jews] superior and better off than they? No, not at all. We have already charged that all men, both Jews and Greeks (Gentiles), are under sin [held down by and subject to its power and control].

10 As it is written, None is righteous, just and truthful and upright and conscientious, no, not one. [Ps. 14:3.]

11 No one understands [no one intelligently discerns or comprehends]; no one seeks out God. [Ps. 14:2.]

12 All have turned aside; together they have gone wrong and have become unprofitable and worthless; no one does right, not even one!

13 Their throat is a yawning grave; they use their tongues to deceive [to mislead and to deal treacherously]. The venom of asps is beneath their lips. [Ps. 5:9; 140:3.]

14 Their mouth is full of cursing and bitterness. [Ps. 10:7.]

15 Their feet are swift to shed blood.

16 Destruction [as it dashes them to pieces] and misery mark their ways.

17 And they have no experience of the way of peace [they know nothing about peace, for a peaceful way they do not even recognize]. [Isa. 59:7, 8.]

18 There is no (reverential) fear of God before their eyes. [Ps. 36:1.]

19 Now we know that whatever the Law says, it speaks to those who are under the Law, so that [the murmurs and excuses of] every mouth may be hushed and all the world may be held accountable to God.

20 For no person will be justified (made righteous, acquitted, and judged acceptable) in His sight by observing the works prescribed by the Law. For [the real function of] the Law is to make men recognize and be conscious of sin ['not mere perception, but an acquaintance with sin

t Marvin Vincent, *Word Studies.*

...ward repentance,
...aracter].

...e righteousness of
...evealed indepen-
...her apart from the
...ually it is attested
...e Prophets,

...e righteousness of
... by believing with
...confident reliance
...e Messiah). [And
... who believe. For
...ion,

...ve sinned and are
...e honor *and* glory
...ws *and* receives.

...fied *and* made up-
...standing with God,
freely *and* gratuitously by His grace
(His unmerited favor and mercy),
through the redemption which is
[provided] in Christ Jesus,

25 Whom God put forward [be-
fore the eyes of all] as a mercy seat
and propitiation by His blood [the
cleansing and life-giving sacrifice of
atonement and reconciliation, to be
received] through faith. This was to
show God's righteousness, because
in His divine forbearance He had
passed over *and* ignored former sins
without punishment.

26 It was to demonstrate *and* prove
at the present time (*in the now season) that He Himself is righteous and
that He justifies *and* accepts as righteous him who has [true] faith in
Jesus.

27 Then what becomes of [our]
pride *and* [our] boasting? It is excluded (banished, ruled out entirely). On
what principle? [On the principle] of
doing good deeds? No, but on the
principle of faith.

28 For we hold that a man is justified *and* made upright by faith independent of *and* distinctly apart from

good deeds (works of the Law). [The
observance of the Law has nothing to
do with justification.]

29 Or is God merely [the God] of
Jews? Is He not the God of Gentiles
also? Yes, of Gentiles also,

30 Since it is one and the same God
Who will justify the circumcised by
faith [°which germinated from Abra-
ham] and the uncircumcised through
their [newly acquired] faith. [For it is
the same trusting faith in both cases,
a firmly relying faith in Jesus Christ].

31 Do we then by [this] faith make
the Law of no effect, overthrow it *or*
make it a dead letter? Certainly not!
On the contrary, we confirm *and* establish *and* uphold the Law.

CHAPTER 4

[B] UT] IF so, what shall we say
about Abraham, our forefather humanly speaking—[what did
he] find out? [How does this affect
his position, and what was gained by
him?]

2 For if Abraham was justified [°es-
tablished as just by acquittal from
guilt) by good works [that he did
then] he has grounds for boasting.
But not before God!

3 For what does the Scripture say?
Abraham believed in (trusted in)
God, and it was credited to his account as righteousness (right living
and right standing with God). [Gen.
15:6.]

4 Now to a laborer, his wages are
not counted as a favor *or* a gift, but as
an obligation (something owed to
him).

5 But to one who, not working [by
the Law], trusts (believes fully) in
Him Who justifies the ungodly, his
faith is credited to him as righteousness (the standing acceptable to
God).

u Marvin Vincent, *Word Studies.*   v Johann Bengel, *Gnomon Novi Testamenti.*   w Literal
translation.   x Hermann Cremer, *Biblico-Theological Lexicon of New Testament Greek.*

6 Thus David ʸcongratulates the man *and* pronounces a blessing on him to whom God credits righteousness apart from the works he does:

7 Blessed *and* happy *and* ʸto be envied are those whose iniquities are forgiven and whose sins are covered up *and* completely buried.

8 Blessed *and* happy *and* ʸto be envied is the person of whose sin the Lord will take no account *nor* reckon it against him. [Ps. 32:1, 2.]

9 Is this blessing (happiness) then meant only for the circumcised, or also for the uncircumcised? We say that faith was credited to Abraham as righteousness.

10 How then was it credited [to him]? Was it before or after he had been circumcised? It was not after, but before he was circumcised.

11 He received the mark of circumcision as a token *or* an evidence [and] seal of the righteousness which he had by faith while he was still uncircumcised—[faith] so that he was to be made the father of all who [truly] believe, though without circumcision, and who thus have righteousness (right standing with God) imputed to them *and* credited to their account,

12 As well as [that he be made] the father of those circumcised persons who are not merely circumcised, but also walk in the way of that faith which our father Abraham had before he was circumcised.

13 For the promise to Abraham or his posterity, that he should inherit the world, did not come through [observing the commands of] the Law but through the righteousness of faith. [Gen. 17:4–6; 22:16–18.]

14 If it is the adherents of the Law who are to be the heirs, then faith is made futile *and* empty of all meaning and the promise [of God] is made

void (is annulled and has no power).

15 For the Law results in [divine] wrath, but where there is no law there is no transgression [of it either].

16 Therefore, [inheriting] the promise is the outcome of faith *and* depends [entirely] on faith, in order that it might be given as an act of grace (unmerited favor), to make it stable *and* valid *and* guaranteed to all his descendants—not only to the devotees *and* adherents of the Law, but also to those who share the faith of Abraham, who is [thus] the father of us all.

17 As it is written, I have made you the father of many nations. [He was appointed our father] in the sight of God in Whom he believed, Who gives life to the dead and speaks of the nonexistent things that [He has foretold and promised] as if they [already] existed. [Gen. 17:5.]

18 [For Abraham, human reason for] hope being gone, hoped in faith that he should become the father of many nations, as he had been promised, So [numberless] shall your descendants be. [Gen. 15:5.]

19 He did not weaken in faith when he considered the [utter] impotence of his own body, which was as good as dead because he was about a hundred years old, or [when he considered] the barrenness of Sarah's [deadened] womb. [Gen. 17:17; 18:11.]

20 No unbelief *or* distrust made him waver (doubtingly question) concerning the promise of God, but he grew strong *and* was empowered by faith as he gave praise *and* glory to God,

21 Fully satisfied *and* assured that God was able *and* mighty to keep His word *and* to do what He had promised.

22 That is why his faith was credit-

ed to him as righteousness (right standing with God).

23 But [the words], It was credited to him, were written not for his sake alone,

24 But [they were written] for our sakes too. [Righteousness, standing acceptable to God] will be granted *and* credited to us also who believe in (trust in, adhere to, and rely on) God, Who raised Jesus our Lord from the dead,

25 Who was betrayed *and* put to death because of our misdeeds and was raised to secure our justification (our ²acquittal), [making our account balance and absolving us from all guilt before God].

CHAPTER 5

THEREFORE, SINCE we are justified (²acquitted, declared righteous, and given a right standing with God) through faith, let us [grasp the fact that we] have [the peace of reconciliation to hold and to ᵃenjoy] peace with God through our Lord Jesus Christ (the Messiah, the Anointed One).

2 Through Him also we have [our] access (entrance, introduction) by faith into this grace (state of God's favor) in which we [firmly and safely] stand. And let us rejoice *and* exult in our hope of experiencing *and* enjoying the glory of God.

3 Moreover [let us also be full of joy now!] let us exult *and* triumph in our troubles *and* rejoice in our sufferings, knowing that pressure *and* affliction *and* hardship produce patient *and* unswerving endurance.

4 And endurance (fortitude) develops maturity of ᵇcharacter (approved faith and ᶜtried integrity). And character [of this sort] produces [the hab-

it of] ᵈjoyful and confident hope of eternal salvation.

5 Such hope never disappoints *or* deludes *or* shames us, for God's love has been poured out in our hearts through the Holy Spirit Who has been given to us.

6 While we were yet in weakness [powerless to help ourselves], at the fitting time Christ died for (in behalf of) the ungodly.

7 Now it is an extraordinary thing for one to give his life even for an upright man, though perhaps for a noble *and* lovable *and* generous benefactor someone might even dare to die.

8 But God shows *and* clearly proves His [own] love for us by the fact that while we were still sinners, Christ (the Messiah, the Anointed One) died for us.

9 Therefore, since we are now justified (ᵉacquitted, made righteous, and brought into right relationship with God) by Christ's blood, how much more [certain is it that] we shall be saved by Him from the indignation *and* wrath of God.

10 For if while we were enemies we were reconciled to God through the death of His Son, it is much more [certain], now that we are reconciled, that we shall be saved (daily delivered from sin's dominion) through His [ᶜresurrection] life.

11 Not only so, but we also rejoice *and* exultingly glory in God [in His love and perfection] through our Lord Jesus Christ, through Whom we have now received *and* enjoy [our] reconciliation. [Jer. 9:24.]

12 Therefore, as sin came into the world through one man, and death as the result of sin, so death spread to all men, [ᵈno one being able to stop it

z G. Abbott-Smith, *Manual Greek Lexicon of the New Testament.*   a Literal translation: "have" or "hold," so "enjoy."   b Alexander Souter, *Pocket Lexicon.*   c Marvin Vincent, *Word Studies.*   d Joseph Thayer, *A Greek-English Lexicon.*   e G. Abbott-Smith, *Manual Greek Lexicon.*

or to escape its power] because all men sinned.

13 [To be sure] sin was in the world before ever the Law was given, but sin is not charged to men's account where there is no law [to transgress].

14 Yet death held sway from Adam to Moses [the Lawgiver], even over those who did not themselves transgress [a positive command] as Adam did. Adam was a type (prefigure) of the One Who was to come [in reverse, [the former destructive, the Latter saving]. [Gen. 5:5; 7:22; Deut. 34:5.]

15 But God's free gift is not at all to be compared to the trespass [His grace is out of all proportion to the fall of man]. For if many died through one man's falling away (his lapse, his offense), much more profusely did God's grace and the free gift [that comes] through the undeserved favor of the one Man Jesus Christ abound and overflow to and for [the benefit of] many.

16 Nor is the free gift at all to be compared to the effect of that one [man's] sin. For the sentence [following the trespass] of one [man] brought condemnation, whereas the free gift [following] many transgressions brings justification (ᵍan act of righteousness).

17 For if because of one man's trespass (lapse, offense) death reigned through that one, much more surely will those who receive [God's] overflowing grace (unmerited favor) and the free gift of righteousness [putting them into right standing with Himself] reign as kings in life through the one Man Jesus Christ (the Messiah, the Anointed One).

18 Well then, as one man's trespass [one man's false step and falling away led] to condemnation for all men, so one Man's act of righteous-

ness [leads] to acquittal and right standing with God and life for all men.

19 For just as by one man's disobedience (failing to hear, ʰheedlessness, and carelessness) the many were constituted sinners, so by one Man's obedience the many will be constituted righteous (made acceptable to God, brought into right standing with Him).

20 But then Law came in, [only] to expand and increase the trespass [making it more apparent and exciting opposition]. But where sin increased and abounded, grace (God's unmerited favor) has surpassed it and increased the more and superabounded,

21 So that, [just] as sin has reigned in death, [so] grace (His unearned and undeserved favor) might reign also through righteousness (right standing with God) which issues in eternal life through Jesus Christ (the Messiah, the Anointed One) our Lord.

CHAPTER 6

WHAT SHALL we say [to all this]? Are we to remain in sin in order that God's grace (favor and mercy) may multiply and overflow?

2 Certainly not! How can we who died to sin live in it any longer?

3 Are you ignorant of the fact that all of us who have been baptized into Christ Jesus were baptized into His death?

4 We were buried therefore with Him by the baptism into death, so that just as Christ was raised from the dead by the glorious [power] of the Father, so we too might [habitually] live and behave in newness of life.

5 For if we have become one with Him by sharing a death like His, we shall also be [one with Him in shar-

---

f Joseph Thayer, *A Greek-English Lexicon*.   g Literal translation.   h Marvin Vincent, *Word Studies*.

ing] His resurrection [by a new life lived for God].

6 We know that our old (unrenewed) self was nailed to the cross with Him in order that [our] body [which is the instrument] of sin might be made ineffective and inactive for evil, that we might no longer be the slaves of sin.

7 For when a man dies, he is freed (loosed, delivered) from [the power of] sin [among men].

8 Now if we have died with Christ, we believe that we shall also live with Him,

9 Because we know that Christ (the Anointed One), being once raised from the dead, will never die again; death no longer has power over Him.

10 For by the death He died, He died to sin [ending His relation to it] once for all; and the life that He lives, He is living to God [in unbroken fellowship with Him].

11 Even so consider yourselves also dead to sin and your relation to it broken, but alive to God [living in unbroken fellowship with Him] in Christ Jesus.

12 Let not sin therefore rule as king in your mortal (short-lived, perishable) bodies, to make you yield to its cravings and be subject to its lusts and evil passions.

13 Do not continue offering or yielding your bodily members [and ¹faculties] to sin as instruments (tools) of wickedness. But offer and yield yourselves to God as though you have been raised from the dead to [perpetual] life, and your bodily members [and ¹faculties] to God, presenting them as implements of righteousness.

14 For sin shall not [any longer] exert dominion over you, since now you are not under Law [as slaves], but under grace [as subjects of God's favor and mercy].

15 What then [are we to conclude]? Shall we sin because we live not under Law but under God's favor and mercy? Certainly not!

16 Do you not know that if you continually surrender yourselves to anyone to do his will, you are the slaves of him whom you obey, whether that be to sin, which leads to death, or to obedience which leads to righteousness (right doing and right standing with God)?

17 But thank God, though you were once slaves of sin, you have become obedient with all your heart to the standard of teaching in which you were instructed and to which you were committed.

18 And having been set free from sin, you have become the servants of righteousness (of conformity to the divine will in thought, purpose, and action).

19 I am speaking in familiar human terms because of your natural limitations. For as you yielded your bodily members [and ¹faculties] as servants to impurity and ever increasing lawlessness, so now yield your bodily members [and ¹faculties] once for all as servants to righteousness (right being and doing) [which leads] to sanctification.

20 For when you were slaves of sin, you were free in regard to righteousness.

21 But then what benefit (return) did you get from the things of which you are now ashamed? [None] for the end of those things is death.

22 But now since you have been set free from sin and have become the slaves of God, you have your

---

¹ Marvin Vincent, Word Studies: Greek mele—"Physical; though some commentators interpret it to include the mental faculties as well."

present reward in holiness and its end is eternal life.

23 For the wages which sin pays is death, but the [bountiful] free gift of God is eternal life through (in union with) Jesus Christ our Lord.

CHAPTER 7

D O YOU not know, brethren—for I am speaking to men who are acquainted with the Law—that legal claims have power over a person only for as long as he is alive?

2 For [instance] a married woman is bound by law to her husband as long as he lives; but if her husband dies, she is loosed *and* discharged from the law concerning her husband.

3 Accordingly, she will be held an adulteress if she unites herself to another man while her husband lives. But if her husband dies, the marriage law no longer is binding on her [she is free from that law]; and if she unites herself to another man, she is not an adulteress.

4 Likewise, my brethren, you have undergone death as to the Law through the [crucified] body of Christ, so that now you may belong to Another, to Him Who was raised from the dead in order that we may bear fruit for God.

5 When we were living in the flesh (mere physical lives), the sinful passions that were awakened *and* aroused up by [what] the Law [makes sin] were constantly operating in our natural powers (in our bodily organs, ^{j}in the sensitive appetites and wills of the flesh), so that we bore fruit for death.

6 But now we are discharged from the Law and have terminated all intercourse with it, having died to what once restrained *and* held us captive. So now we serve not under [obedi-

ence to] the old code of written regulations, but [under obedience to the promptings of the Spirit in newness [of life].

7 What then do we conclude? Is the Law identical with sin? Certainly not! Nevertheless, if it had not been for the Law, I should not have recognized sin *or* have known its meaning. [For instance] I would not have known about covetousness [would have had no consciousness of sin or sense of guilt] if the Law had not [repeatedly] said, You shall not covet *and* have an evil desire [for one thing and another]. [Exod. 20:17; Deut. 5:21.]

8 But sin, finding opportunity in the commandment [to express itself], got a hold on me *and* aroused *and* stimulated all kinds of forbidden desires (lust, covetousness). For without the Law sin is dead [the sense of it is inactive and a lifeless thing].

9 Once I was alive, but quite apart from *and* unconscious of the Law. But when the commandment came, sin lived again and I died (was sentenced by the Law to death). [Ps. 73:22.]

10 And the very legal ordinance which was designed *and* intended to bring life actually proved [to mean to me] death. [Lev. 18:5.]

11 For sin, seizing the opportunity *and* getting a hold on me [by taking its incentive] from the commandment, beguiled *and* entrapped *and* cheated me, and using it [as a weapon], killed me.

12 The Law therefore is holy, and [each] commandment is holy and just and good.

13 Did that which is good then prove fatal [bringing death] to me? Certainly not! It was sin, working death in me by using this good thing [as a weapon], in order that through

j Matthew Henry, *Commentary on the Holy Bible.*

the commandment sin might be shown up clearly to be sin, that the extreme malignity and immeasurable sinfulness of sin might plainly appear.

14 We know that the Law is spiritual; but I am a creature of the flesh [carnal, unspiritual], having been sold into slavery under [the control of] sin.

15 For I do not understand my own actions [I am baffled, bewildered]. I do not practice or accomplish what I wish, but I do the very thing that I loathe [kwhich my moral instinct condemns].

16 Now if I do [habitually] what is contrary to my desire, [that means that] I acknowledge and agree that the Law is good (morally excellent) and that I take sides with it.

17 However, it is no longer I who do the deed, but the sin [principle] which is at home in me and has possession of me.

18 For I know that nothing good dwells within me, that is, in my flesh. I can will what is right, but I cannot perform it. [I have the intention and urge to do what is right, but no power to carry it out.]

19 For I fail to practice the good deeds I desire to do, but the evil deeds that I do not desire to do are what I am [ever] doing.

20 Now if I do what I do not desire to do, it is no longer I doing it [it is not myself that acts], but the sin [principle] which dwells within me [lfixed and operating in my soul].

21 So I find it to be a law (rule of action of my being) that when I want to do what is right and good, evil is ever present with me and I am subject to its insistent demands.

22 For I endorse and delight in the Law of God in my inmost self [with my new nature]. [Ps. 1:2.]

23 But I discern in my bodily members [min the sensitive appetites and wills of the flesh] a different law (rule of action) at war against the law of my mind (my reason) and making me a prisoner to the law of sin that dwells in my bodily organs [min the sensitive appetites and wills of the flesh].

24 O unhappy and pitiable and wretched man that I am! Who will release and deliver me from [the shackles of] this body of death?

25 O thank God! [He will!] through Jesus Christ (the Anointed One) our Lord! So then indeed I, of myself with the mind and heart, serve the Law of God, but with the flesh the law of sin.

CHAPTER 8

THEREFORE, [there is] now no condemnation (no adjudging guilty of wrong) for those who are in Christ Jesus, who live [and] walk not after the dictates of the flesh, but after the dictates of the Spirit. [John 3:18.]

2 For the law of the Spirit of life [which is] in Christ Jesus [the law of our new being] has freed me from the law of sin and of death.

3 For God has done what the Law could not do, [its power] being weakened by the flesh [nthe entire nature of man without the Holy Spirit]. Sending His own Son in the guise of sinful flesh and as an offering for sin, [God] condemned sin in the flesh [lsubdued, overcame, odeprived it of its power over all who accept that sacrifice], [Lev. 7:37.]

4 So that the righteous and just requirement of the Law might be fully

k Frederic Godet, cited by Marvin Vincent, Word Studies.
m Matthew Henry, Commentary on the Holy Bible, Word Studies.   o Marvin Vincent, Word Studies.
l Joseph Thayer, A Greek-English Lexicon.
n Philip Melanchthon, cited by Marvin Vincent, Word Studies.

met in us who live *and* move not in the ways of the flesh but in the ways of the Spirit [our lives governed not by the standards and according to the dictates of the flesh, but controlled by the Holy Spirit].

5 For those who are according to the flesh *and* are controlled by its unholy desires set their minds on *and* ᵖpursue those things which gratify the flesh, but those who are according to the Spirit *and* are controlled by the desires of the Spirit set their minds on *and* ᵖseek those things which gratify the [Holy] Spirit.

6 Now the mind of the flesh [which is sense and reason without the Holy Spirit] is death [death that ᵖcomprises all the miseries arising from sin, both here and hereafter]. But the mind of the [Holy] Spirit is life and [soul] peace [both now and forever].

7 [That is] because the mind of the flesh [with its carnal thoughts and purposes] is hostile to God, for it does not submit itself to God's Law; indeed it cannot.

8 So then those who are living the life of the flesh [catering to the appetites and impulses of their carnal nature] cannot please *or* satisfy God, *or* be acceptable to Him.

9 But you are not living the life of the flesh, you are living the life of the Spirit, if the [Holy] Spirit of God [really] dwells within you [directs and controls you]. But if anyone does not possess the [Holy] Spirit of Christ, he is none of His [he does not belong to Christ, is not truly a child of God]. [Rom. 8:14.]

10 But if Christ lives in you, [then although] your [natural] body is dead by reason of sin *and* guilt, the spirit is alive because of [the] righteousness [that He imputes to you].

11 And if the Spirit of Him Who raised up Jesus from the dead dwells in you, [then] He Who raised up Christ *Jesus* from the dead will also restore to life your mortal (short-lived, perishable) bodies through His Spirit Who dwells in you.

12 So then, brethren, we are debtors, but not to the flesh [we are not obligated to our carnal nature], to live [a life ruled by the standards set up by the dictates] of the flesh.

13 For if you live according to [the dictates of] the flesh, you will surely die. But if through the power of the [Holy] Spirit you are [habitually] putting to death (making extinct, deadening) the [evil] deeds prompted by the body, you shall [really and genuinely] live forever.

14 For all who are led by the Spirit of God are sons of God.

15 For [the Spirit which] you have now received [is] not a spirit of slavery to put you once more in bondage to fear, but you have received the Spirit of adoption [the Spirit producing sonship] in [the bliss of] which we cry, Abba (Father)! Father!

16 The Spirit Himself [thus] testifies together with our own spirit, [assuring us] that we are children of God.

17 And if we are [His] children, then we are [His] heirs also: heirs of God and fellow heirs with Christ [sharing His inheritance with Him]; only we must share His suffering if we are to share His glory.

18 [But what of that?] For I consider that the sufferings of this present time (this present life) are not worth being compared with the glory that is about to be revealed to us *and* in us *and* ᵠfor us *and* ᵖconferred on us!

19 For [even the whole] creation (all nature) waits expectantly and longs earnestly for God's sons to be

ᵖ Joseph Thayer, *A Greek-English Lexicon in the Language of the People.*   ᵠ Charles B. Williams, *The New Testament: A Translation*

made known [waits for the revealing, the disclosing of their sonship].

20 For the creation (nature) was subjected to ʳfrailty (to futility, condemned to frustration), not because of some intentional fault on its part, but by the will of Him Who so subjected it—[yet] with the hope [Eccl. 1:2.]

21 That nature (creation) itself will be set free from its bondage to decay and corruption [and gain an entrance] into the glorious freedom of God's children.

22 We know that the whole creation [of irrational creatures] has been moaning together in the pains of labor until now. [Jer. 12:4, 11.]

23 And not only the creation, but we ourselves too, who have and enjoy the firstfruits of the [Holy] Spirit [a foretaste of the blissful things to come] groan inwardly as we wait for the redemption of our bodies [from sensuality and the grave, which will reveal] our adoption (our manifestation as God's sons).

24 For in [this] hope we were saved. But hope [the object of] which is seen is not hope. For how can one hope for what he already sees?

25 But if we hope for what is still unseen by us, we wait for it with patience and composure.

26 So too the [Holy] Spirit comes to our aid and bears us up in our weakness; for we do not know what prayer to offer nor how to offer it worthily as we ought, but the Spirit Himself goes to meet our supplication and pleads in our behalf with unspeakable yearnings and groanings too deep for utterance.

27 And He Who searches the hearts of men knows what is in the mind of the [Holy] Spirit [what His intent is], because the Spirit inter-

cedes and pleads [before God] in behalf of the saints according to and in harmony with God's will. [Ps. 139:1, 2.]

28 We are assured and know that [ˢGod being a partner in their labor] all things work together and are [fitting into a plan] for good to and for those who love God and are called according to [His] design and purpose.

29 For those whom He foreknew [of whom He was ᵗaware and ᵗloved beforehand], He also destined from the beginning [foreordaining them] to be molded into the image of His Son [and share inwardly His likeness], that He might become the firstborn among many brethren.

30 And those whom He thus foreordained, He also called; and those whom He called, He also justified (acquitted, made righteous, putting them into right standing with Himself). And those whom He justified, He also glorified [raising them to a heavenly dignity and condition or state of being].

31 What then shall we say to [all] this? If God is for us, who [can be] against us? [Who can be our foe, if God is on our side?] [Ps. 118:6.]

32 He who did not withhold or spare [even] His own Son but gave Him up for us all, will He not also with Him freely and graciously give us all [other] things?

33 Who shall bring any charge against God's elect [when it is] God Who justifies [that is, Who puts us in right relation to Himself? Who shall come forward and accuse or impeach those whom God has chosen? Will God, Who acquits us?]

34 Who is there to condemn [us]? Will Christ Jesus (the Messiah), Who died, or rather Who was raised from

r Joseph Thayer, *A Greek-English Lexicon*.   s Some manuscripts read, "God works all things with them."   t H.A.W. Meyer, cited by Marvin Vincent, *Word Studies*.   u John Murray, *The Sovereignty of God*.

the dead, Who is at the right hand of God actually pleading *as* He intercedes for us?

35 Who shall ever separate us from Christ's love? Shall suffering *and* affliction *and* tribulation? Or calamity *and* distress? Or persecution or hunger or destitution or peril or sword?

36 Even as it is written, For Thy sake we are put to death all the day long; we are regarded *and* counted as sheep for the slaughter. [Ps. 44:22.]

37 Yet amid all these things we are more than conquerors [sup]v[/sup]*and* gain a surpassing victory through Him Who loved us.

38 For I am persuaded beyond doubt (am sure) that neither death nor life, nor angels nor principalities, nor things [sup]w[/sup]impending *and* threatening nor things to come, nor powers,

39 Nor height nor depth, nor anything else in all creation will be able to separate us from the love of God which is in Christ Jesus our Lord.

CHAPTER 9

I AM speaking the truth in Christ. I am not lying; my conscience [enlightened and prompted] by the Holy Spirit bearing witness with me

2 That I have bitter grief and incessant anguish in my heart.

3 For I could wish that I myself were accursed *and* cut off and banished from Christ for the sake of my brethren *and* instead of them, my natural kinsmen *and* my fellow countrymen. [Exod. 32:32.]

4 For they are Israelites, and to them belong God's adoption [as a nation] and the glorious Presence (Shekinah). With them were the special covenants made, to them was the Law given. To them [the temple] worship was revealed and [God's

own] promises announced. [Exod. 4:22; Hos. 11:1.]

5 To them belong the patriarchs, and as far as His natural descent was concerned, from them is the Christ, Who is exalted *and* supreme over all, God, blessed forever! Amen (so let it be).

6 However, it is not as though God's Word had failed [coming to nothing]. For it is not everybody who is a descendant of Jacob (Israel) who belongs to [the true] Israel.

7 And they are not all the children of Abraham because they are by blood his descendants. No, [the promise was] Your descendants will be called *and* counted through the line of Isaac [though Abraham had an older son]. [Gen. 21:9–12.]

8 That is to say, it is not the children of the body [of Abraham] who are made God's children, but it is the offspring to whom the promise applies that shall be counted [as Abraham's true] descendants.

9 For this is what the promise said, About this time [next year] will I return and Sarah shall have a son. [Gen. 18:10.]

10 And not only that, but this too: Rebecca conceived [two sons under exactly the same circumstances] by our forefather Isaac,

11 And the children were yet unborn and had so far done nothing either good or evil. Even so, in order further to carry out God's purpose of selection (election, choice), which depends not on works *or* what men can do, but on Him Who calls [them],

12 It was said to her that the elder [son] should serve the younger [son]. [Gen. 25:21–23.]

13 As it is written, Jacob have I loved, but Esau have I hated (held in [sup]x[/sup]relative disregard in comparison

---

v Joseph Thayer, *A Greek-English Lexicon.* w Marvin Vincent, *Word Studies.* The literal translation is "standing in sight." x G. Abbott-Smith, *Manual Greek Lexicon.*

with My feeling for Jacob]. [Mal. 1:2, 3.]

14 What shall we conclude then? Is there injustice upon God's part? Certainly not!

15 For He says to Moses, I will have mercy on whom I will have mercy and I will have compassion (pity) on whom I will have compassion. [Exod. 33:19.]

16 So then [God's gift] is not a question of human will and human effort, but of God's mercy. [It depends not on one's own willingness nor on his strenuous exertion as in running a race, but on God's having mercy on him.]

17 For the Scripture says to Pharaoh, I have raised you up for this very purpose of displaying My power in [dealing with] you, so that My name may be proclaimed the whole world over.

18 So then He has mercy on whomever He wills (chooses) and He hardens (makes stubborn and unyielding the heart of) whomever He wills.

19 You will say to me, Why then does He still find fault and blame us [for sinning]? For who can resist and withstand His will?

20 But who are you, a mere man, to criticize and contradict and answer back to God? Will what is formed say to him that formed it, Why have you made me thus? [Isa. 29:16; 45:9.]

21 Has the potter no right over the clay, to make out of the same mass (lump) one vessel for beauty and distinction and honorable use, and another for menial or ignoble and dishonorable use?

22 What if God, although fully intending to show [the awfulness of] His wrath and to make known His power and authority, has tolerated with much patience the vessels (ob-

jects) of [His] anger which are ripe for destruction? [Prov. 16:4.]

23 And [what if] He thus purposes to make known and show the wealth of His glory in [dealing with] the vessels (objects) of His mercy which He has prepared beforehand for glory,

24 Even including ourselves whom He has called, not only from among the Jews but also from among the Gentiles (heathen)?

25 Just as He says in Hosea, Those who were not My people I will call My people, and her who was not beloved [I will call] My beloved. [Hos. 2:23.]

26 And it shall be that in the very place where it was said to them, You are not My people, they shall be called sons of the living God. [Hos. 1:10.]

27 And Isaiah calls out (solemnly cries aloud) over Israel: Though the number of the sons of Israel be like the sand of the sea, only the remnant (a small part of them) will be saved [⁹from perdition, condemnation, judgment]!

28 For the Lord will execute His sentence upon the earth [He will conclude and close His account with men completely and without delay], rigorously cutting it short in His justice. [Isa. 10:22, 23.]

29 It is as Isaiah predicted, If the Lord of hosts had not left us a seed [from which to propagate descendants], we [Israel] would have fared like Sodom and have been made like Gomorrah. [Isa. 1:9.]

30 What shall we say then? That Gentiles who did not follow after righteousness [who did not seek salvation by right relationship to God] have attained it by faith [a righteousness imputed by God, based on and produced by faith],

31 Whereas Israel, though ever in

pursuit of a law [for the securing] of righteousness (right standing with God), actually did not succeed in fulfilling the Law. [Isa. 51:1.]

32 For what reason? Because [they pursued it] not through faith, relying [instead] on the merit of their works [they did not depend on faith but on what they could do]. They have stumbled over the Stumbling Stone. [Isa. 8:14; 28:16.]

33 As it is written, Behold I am laying in Zion a Stone that will make men stumble, a Rock that will make them fall; but he who believes in Him [who adheres to, trusts in, and relies on Him] shall not be put to shame *nor* be disappointed in his expectations. [Isa. 28:16.]

CHAPTER 10

B RETHREN, [with all] my heart's desire *and* goodwill for [Israel], I long and pray to God that they may be saved.

2 I bear them witness that they have a [certain] zeal *and* enthusiasm for God, but it is not enlightened *and* according to [correct and vital] knowledge.

3 For being ignorant of the righteousness that God ascribes [which makes one acceptable to Him in word, thought, and deed] and seeking to establish a *righteousness (a means of salvation)* of their own, they did not obey *or* submit themselves to God's righteousness.

4 For Christ is the end of the Law [the limit at which it ceases to be, for the Law leads up to Him Who is the fulfillment of its types, and in Him the purpose which it was designed to accomplish is fulfilled. That is, the purpose of the Law is fulfilled in Him] as the means of righteousness (right relationship to God) for everyone who trusts in *and* adheres to *and* relies on Him.

5 For Moses writes that the man who [can] practice the righteousness (perfect conformity to God's will) which is based on the Law [with all its intricate demands] shall live by it. [Lev. 18:5.]

6 But the righteousness based on faith [imputed by God and bringing right relationship with Him] says, Do not say in your heart, Who will ascend into Heaven? that is, to bring Christ down;

7 Or who will descend into the abyss? that is, to bring Christ up from the dead [as if we could be saved by our own efforts]. [Deut. 30:12, 13.]

8 But what does it say? The Word (God's message in Christ) is near you, on your lips and in your heart; that is, the Word (the message, the basis and object) of faith which we preach, [Deut. 30:14.]

9 Because if you acknowledge *and* confess with your lips that Jesus is Lord and in your heart believe (adhere to, trust in, and rely on the truth) that God raised Him from the dead, you will be saved.

10 For with the heart a person believes (adheres to, trusts in, and relies on Christ) and so is justified (declared righteous, acceptable to God), and with the mouth he confesses (declares openly and speaks out freely his faith) *and* confirms [his] salvation.

11 The Scripture says, No man who believes in Him [who adheres to, relies on, and trusts in Him] will [ever] be put to shame *or* be disappointed. [Ps. 34:22; Isa. 28:16; 49:23; Jer. 17:7.]

12 [No one] for there is no distinction between Jew and Greek. The same Lord is Lord over all [of us] and He generously bestows His riches upon all who call upon Him [in faith].

13 For everyone who calls upon the name of the Lord [invoking Him as Lord] will be saved. [Joel 2:32.]

14 But how are people to call upon Him Whom they have not believed [in Whom they have no faith, on Whom they have no reliance]? And how are they to believe in Him [adhere to, trust in, and rely upon Him] of Whom they have never heard? And how are they to hear without a preacher?

15 And how can men [be expected to] preach unless they are sent? As it is written, How beautiful are the feet of those who bring glad tidings! [How welcome is the coming of those who preach the good news of His good things!] [Isa. 52:7.]

16 But they have not all heeded the Gospel; for Isaiah says, Lord, who has believed (had faith in) what he has heard from us? [Isa. 53:1.]

17 So faith comes by hearing [what is told], and what is heard comes by the preaching [of the message that came from the lips] of Christ (the Messiah Himself).

18 But I ask, Have they not heard? Indeed they have; [for the Scripture says] Their voice [that of nature bearing God's message] has gone out to all the earth, and their words to the far bounds of the world. [Ps. 19:4.]

19 Again I ask, Did Israel not understand? [Did the Jews have no warning that the Gospel was to go forth to the Gentiles, to all the earth?] First, there is Moses who says, I will make you jealous of those who are not a nation; with a foolish nation I will make you angry. [Deut. 32:21.]

20 Then Isaiah is so bold as to say, I have been found by those who did not seek Me; I have shown (revealed) Myself to those who did not [consciously] ask for Me. [Isa. 65:1.]

21 But of Israel he says, All day long I have stretched out My hands to a people unyielding *and* disobedient and self-willed [to a faultfinding, contrary, and contradicting people]. [Isa. 65:2.]

CHAPTER 11

I ASK then: Has God totally rejected *and* disowned His people? Of course not! Why, I myself am an Israelite, a descendant of Abraham, a member of the tribe of Benjamin! [I Sam. 12:22; Jer. 31:37; 33:24–26; Phil. 3:5.]

2 No, God has not rejected *and* disowned His people [whose destiny] He had marked out *and* appointed *and* foreknown from the beginning. Do you not know what the Scripture says of Elijah, how he pleads with God against Israel? [Ps. 94:14; I Kings 19.]

3 Lord, they have killed Your prophets; they have demolished Your altars, and I alone am left, and they seek my life.

4 But what is God's reply to him? I have kept for Myself seven thousand men who have not bowed the knee to Baal! [I Kings 19:18.]

5 So too at the present time there is a remnant (a small believing minority), selected (chosen) by grace (by God's unmerited favor and graciousness).

6 But if it is by grace (His unmerited favor and graciousness), it is no longer conditioned on works or anything men have done. Otherwise, grace would no longer be grace [it would be meaningless].

7 What then [shall we conclude]? Israel failed to obtain what it sought [God's favor by obedience to the Law]. Only the elect (those chosen few) obtained it, while the rest of them became callously indifferent (blinded, hardened, and made insensible to it).

8 As it is written, God gave them a spirit (an attitude) of stupor, eyes that should not see and ears that should not hear, [that has continued] down to this very day. [Deut. 29:4; Isa. 29:10.]

9 And David says, Let their table (their feasting, banqueting) become a snare and a trap, a pitfall and a [z]just retribution [[a]rebounding like a boomerang upon them]; [Ps. 69:22.]

10 Let their eyes be darkened (dimmed) so that they cannot see, and make them bend their back [stooping beneath their burden] forever. [Ps. 69:23.]

11 So I ask, Have they stumbled so as to fall [to their utter spiritual ruin, irretrievably]? By no means! But through their false step and transgression salvation [has come] to the Gentiles, so as to arouse Israel [to see and feel what they forfeited] and so to make them jealous.

12 Now if their stumbling (their lapse, their transgression) has so enriched the world [at large], and if [Israel's] failure means such riches for the Gentiles, think what an enrichment and greater advantage will follow their full reinstatement!

13 But now I am speaking to you who are Gentiles. Inasmuch then as I am an apostle to the Gentiles, I lay great stress on my ministry and magnify my office,

14 In the hope of making my fellow Jews jealous [in order to stir them up to imitate, copy, and appropriate], and thus managing to save some of them.

15 For if their rejection and exclusion from the benefits of salvation were [overruled] for the reconciliation of a world to God, what will their acceptance and admission mean? [It will be nothing short of] life from the dead!

16 Now if the first handful of dough offered as the firstfruits [Abraham and the patriarchs] is consecrated (holy), so is the whole mass [the nation of Israel]; and if the root [Abra-ham] is consecrated (holy), so are the branches. [Num. 15:19–21.]

17 But if some of the branches were broken off, while you, a wild olive shoot, were grafted in among them to share the richness [of the root and sap] of the olive tree,

18 Do not boast over the branches and pride yourself at their expense. If you do boast and feel superior, remember it is not you that support the root, but the root [that supports] you.

19 You will say then, Branches were broken (pruned) off so that I might be grafted in!

20 That is true. But they were broken (pruned) off because of their unbelief (their lack of real faith), and you are established through faith [because you do believe]. So do not become proud and conceited, but rather stand in awe and be reverently afraid.

21 For if God did not spare the natural branches [because of unbelief], neither will He spare you [if you are guilty of the same offense].

22 Then note and appreciate the gracious kindness and the severity of God: severity toward those who have fallen, but God's gracious kindness to you—provided you continue in His grace and abide in His kindness; otherwise you too will be cut off (pruned away).

23 And even those others [the fallen branches, Jews], if they do not persist in [clinging to] their unbelief, will be grafted in, for God has the power to graft them in again.

24 For if you have been cut from what is by nature a wild olive tree, and against nature grafted into a cultivated olive tree, how much easier will it be to graft these natural [branches] back on [the original parent stock of] their own olive tree.

25 Lest you be self-opinionated

---

z Marvin Vincent, *Word Studies*.   a Literal translation: "a return, a recompense."

(wise in your own conceits), I do not want you to miss this hidden truth *and* mystery, brethren: a hardening (insensibility) has [temporarily] befallen a part of Israel [to last] until the [b]full number of the ingathering of the Gentiles has come in,

26 And so all Israel will be saved. As it is written, The Deliverer will come from Zion, He will banish ungodliness from Jacob. [Isa. 59:20, 21.]

27 And this will be My covenant (My agreement) with them when I shall take away their sins. [Isa. 27:9; Jer. 31:33.]

28 From the point of view of the Gospel (good news), they [the Jews, at present] are enemies [of God], which is for your advantage *and* benefit. But from the point of view of God's choice (of election, of divine selection), they are still the beloved (dear to Him) for the sake of their forefathers.

29 For God's gifts and His call are irrevocable. [He never withdraws them when once they are given, and He does not change His mind about those to whom He gives His grace or to whom He sends His call.]

30 Just as you were once disobedient *and* rebellious toward God but now have obtained [His] mercy, through their disobedience,

31 So they also now are being disobedient [when you are receiving mercy], that they in turn may one day, through the mercy you are enjoying, also receive mercy [that they may share the mercy which has been shown to you—through you as messengers of the Gospel to them].

32 For God has consigned (penned up) all men to disobedience, only that He may have mercy on them all [alike].

33 Oh, the depth of the riches and wisdom and knowledge of God! How unfathomable (inscrutable, unsearchable) are His judgments (His decisions)! And how untraceable (mysterious, undiscoverable) are His ways (His methods, His paths)!

34 For who has known the mind of the Lord *and* who has understood His thoughts, or who has [ever] been His counselor? [Isa. 40:13, 14.]

35 Or who has first given God anything that he might be paid back *or* that he could claim a recompense?

36 For from Him and through Him and to Him are all things. [For all things originate with Him and come from Him; all things live through Him, and all things center in and tend to consummate and to end in Him.] To Him be glory forever! Amen (so be it).

CHAPTER 12

I APPEAL to you therefore, brethren, *and* beg of you in view of [all] the mercies of God, to make a decisive dedication of your bodies [presenting all your members and faculties] as a living sacrifice, holy (devoted, consecrated) and well pleasing to God, which is your reasonable (rational, intelligent) service *and* spiritual worship.

2 Do not be conformed to this world (this age), [fashioned after and adapted to its external, superficial customs], but be transformed (changed) by the [entire] renewal of your mind [by its new ideals and its new attitude], so that you may prove [for yourselves] what is the good and acceptable and perfect will of God, *even* the thing which is good and acceptable and perfect [in His sight for you].

3 For by the grace (unmerited favor of God) given to me I warn everyone among you not to estimate *and*

b Joseph Thayer, *A Greek-English Lexicon.*

think of himself more highly than he ought [not to have an exaggerated opinion of his own importance], but to rate his ability with sober judgment, each according to the degree of faith apportioned by God to him.

4 For as in one physical body we have many parts (organs, members) and all of these parts do not have the same function or use,

5 So we, numerous as we are, are one body in Christ (the Messiah) and individually we are parts one of another [mutually dependent on one another].

6 Having gifts (faculties, talents, qualities) that differ according to the grace given us, let us use them: [He whose gift is] prophecy, [let him prophesy] according to the proportion of his faith;

7 [He whose gift is] practical service, let him give himself to serving; he who teaches, to his teaching;

8 He who exhorts (encourages), to his exhortation; he who contributes, let him do it in simplicity and liberality; he who gives aid and superintends, with zeal and singleness of mind; he who does acts of mercy, with genuine cheerfulness and joyful eagerness.

9 [Let your] love be sincere (a real thing); hate what is evil [loathe all ungodliness, turn in horror from wickedness], but hold fast to that which is good.

10 Love one another with brotherly affection [as members of one family], giving precedence and showing honor to one another.

11 Never lag in zeal and in earnest endeavor; be aglow and burning with the Spirit, serving the Lord.

12 Rejoice and exult in hope; be steadfast and patient in suffering and tribulation; be constant in prayer.

13 Contribute to the needs of God's people [sharing in the necessi-

ties of the saints]; pursue the practice of hospitality.

14 Bless those who persecute you [who are cruel in their attitude toward you]; bless and do not curse them.

15 Rejoice with those who rejoice [sharing others' joy], and weep with those who weep [sharing others' grief].

16 Live in harmony with one another; do not be haughty (snobbish, high-minded, exclusive), but readily adjust yourself to [people, things] and give yourselves to humble tasks. Never overestimate yourself or be wise in your own conceits. [Prov. 3:7.]

17 Repay no one evil for evil, but take thought for what is honest and proper and noble [aiming to be above reproach] in the sight of everyone. [Prov. 20:22.]

18 If possible, as far as it depends on you, live at peace with everyone.

19 Beloved, never avenge yourselves, but leave the way open for [God's] wrath; for it is written, Vengeance is Mine, I will repay (requite), says the Lord. [Deut. 32:35.]

20 But if your enemy is hungry, feed him; if he is thirsty, give him drink; for by so doing you will heap burning coals upon his head. [Prov. 25:21, 22.]

21 Do not let yourself be overcome by evil, but overcome (master) evil with good.

CHAPTER 13

LET EVERY person be loyally subject to the governing (civil) authorities. For there is no authority except from God [by His permission, His sanction], and those that exist do so by God's appointment. [Prov. 8:15.]

2 Therefore he who resists and sets himself up against the authorities re-

sists what God has appointed *and* arranged [in divine order]. And those who resist will bring down judgment upon themselves [receiving the penalty due them].

3 For civil authorities are not a terror to [people of] good conduct, but to [those of] bad behavior. Would you have no dread of him who is in authority? Then do what is right and you will receive his approval and commendation.

4 For he is God's servant for your good. But if you do wrong, [you should dread him and] be afraid, for he does not bear *and* wear the sword for nothing. He is God's servant to execute His wrath (punishment, vengeance) on the wrongdoer.

5 Therefore one must be subject, not only to avoid God's wrath *and* escape punishment, but also as a matter of principle *and* for the sake of conscience.

6 For this same reason you pay taxes, for [the civil authorities] are official servants under God, devoting themselves to attending to this very service.

7 Render to all men their dues. [Pay] taxes to whom taxes are due, revenue to whom revenue is due, respect to whom respect is due, and honor to whom honor is due.

8 Keep out of debt *and* owe no man anything, except to love one another; for he who loves his neighbor [who practices loving others] has fulfilled the Law [relating to one's fellowmen, meeting all its requirements].

9 The commandments, You shall not commit adultery, You shall not kill, You shall not steal, You shall not covet (have an evil desire), and any other commandment, are summed up in the single command, You shall love your neighbor as [you do] yourself. [Exod. 20:13–17; Lev. 19:18.]

10 Love does no wrong to one's neighbor [it never hurts anybody].

Therefore love meets all the requirements *and* is the fulfilling of the Law.

11 Besides this you know what [a critical] hour this is, how it is high time now for you to wake up out of your sleep (rouse to reality). For salvation (final deliverance) is nearer to us now than when we first believed (adhered to, trusted in, and relied on Christ, the Messiah).

12 The night is far gone and the day is almost here. Let us then drop (fling away) the works *and* deeds of darkness and put on the [full] armor of light.

13 Let us live *and* conduct ourselves honorably *and* becomingly as in the [open light of] day, not in reveling (carousing) and drunkenness, not in immorality and debauchery (sensuality and licentiousness), not in quarreling and jealousy.

14 But clothe yourself with the Lord Jesus Christ (the Messiah) and make no provision for [indulging] the flesh [put a stop to thinking about the evil cravings of your physical nature] to [gratify its] desires (lusts).

CHAPTER 14

AS FOR the man who is a weak believer, welcome him [into your fellowship], but not to criticize his opinions *or* pass judgment on his scruples *or* perplex him with discussions.

2 One [man's faith permits him to] believe he may eat anything, while a weaker one [limits his] eating to vegetables.

3 Let not him who eats look down on *or* despise him who abstains, and let not him who abstains criticize *and* pass judgment on him who eats; for God has accepted *and* welcomed him.

4 Who are you to pass judgment on *and* censure another's household servant? It is before his own master

that he stands or falls. And he shall stand *and* be upheld, for the Master (the Lord) is mighty to support him *and* make him stand.

5 One man esteems one day as better than another, while another man esteems all days alike [sacred]. Let everyone be fully convinced (satisfied) in his own mind.

6 He who observes the day, observes it in honor of the Lord. He also who eats, eats in honor of the Lord, since he gives thanks to God; while he who abstains, abstains in honor of the Lord and gives thanks to God.

7 None of us lives to himself [but to the Lord], and none of us dies to himself [but to the Lord, for]

8 If we live, we live to the Lord, and if we die, we die to the Lord. So then, whether we live or we die, we belong to the Lord.

9 For Christ died and lived again for this very purpose, that He might be Lord both of the dead and of the living.

10 Why do you criticize *and* pass judgment on your brother? Or you, why do you look down upon *or* despise your brother? For we shall all stand before the judgment seat of God.

11 For it is written, As I live, says the Lord, every knee shall bow to Me, and every tongue shall confess to God [acknowledge Him to His honor and to His praise]. [Isa. 45:23.]

12 And so each of us shall give an account of himself [give an answer in reference to judgment] to God.

13 Then let us no more criticize *and* blame *and* pass judgment on one another, but rather decide *and* endeavor never to put a stumbling block *or* an obstacle or a hindrance in the way of a brother.

14 I know and am convinced (persuaded) as one in the Lord Jesus, that nothing is [forbidden as] essentially unclean (defiled and unholy in itself). But [none the less] it is unclean (defiled and unholy) to anyone who thinks it is unclean.

15 But if your brother is being pained *or* his feelings hurt *or* if he is being injured by what you eat, [then] you are no longer walking in love. [You have ceased to be living and conducting yourself by the standard of love toward him.] Do not let what you eat hurt *or* cause the ruin of one for whom Christ died!

16 Do not therefore let what seems good to you be considered an evil thing [by someone else]. [In other words, do not give occasion for others to criticize that which is justifiable for you.]

17 [After all] the kingdom of God is not a matter of [getting the] food and drink [one likes], but instead it is righteousness (that state which makes a person acceptable to God) and [heart] peace and joy in the Holy Spirit.

18 He who serves Christ in this way is acceptable *and* pleasing to God and is approved by men.

19 So let us then definitely aim for *and* eagerly pursue what makes for harmony and for mutual upbuilding (edification and development) of one another.

20 You must not, for the sake of food, undo *and* break down and destroy the work of God! Everything is indeed [ceremonially] clean *and* pure, but it is wrong for anyone to hurt the conscience of others *or* to make them fall by what he eats.

21 The right thing is to eat no meat or drink no wine [at all], or [do anything else] if it makes your brother stumble *or* hurts his conscience *or* offends or weakens him.

22 Your personal convictions [on such matters]—exercise [them] as in God's presence, keeping them to yourself [striving only to know the

truth and obey His will]. Blessed (happy, °to be envied) is he who has no reason to judge himself for what he approves [who does not convict himself by what he chooses to do].

23 But the man who has doubts (misgivings, an uneasy conscience) about eating, and then eats [perhaps because of you], stands condemned [before God], because he is not true to his convictions *and* he does not act from faith. For whatever does not originate *and* proceed from faith is sin [whatever is done without a conviction of its approval by God is sinful].

CHAPTER 15

WE WHO are strong [in our convictions and of robust faith] ought to bear with the failings *and* the frailties *and* the tender scruples of the weak; [we ought to help carry the doubts and qualms of others] and not to please ourselves.

2 Let each one of us make it a practice to please (make happy) his neighbor for his good *and* for his true welfare, to edify him [to strengthen him and build him up spiritually].

3 For Christ did not please Himself [gave no thought to His own interests]; but, as it is written, The reproaches *and* abuses of those who reproached *and* abused you fell on Me. [Ps. 69:9.]

4 For whatever was thus written in former days was written for our instruction, that by [our steadfast and patient] endurance and the encouragement [drawn] from the Scriptures we might hold fast to *and* cherish hope.

5 Now may the God Who gives the power of patient endurance (steadfastness) and Who supplies encouragement, grant you to live in such mutual harmony *and* such full sympathy with one another, in accord with Christ Jesus,

6 That together you may [unanimously] with united hearts *and* one voice, praise and glorify the God and Father of our Lord Jesus Christ (the Messiah).

7 Welcome *and* receive [to your hearts] one another, then, even as Christ has welcomed *and* received you, for the glory of God.

8 For I tell you that Christ (the Messiah) became a servant *and* a minister to the circumcised (the Jews) in order to show God's truthfulness *and* honesty by confirming (verifying) the promises [given] to our fathers,

9 And [also in order] that the Gentiles (nations) might glorify God for His mercy [not covenanted] to them. As it is written, Therefore I will praise You among the Gentiles and sing praises to Your name. [Ps. 18:49.]

10 Again it is said, Rejoice (exult), O Gentiles, along with His [own] people; [Deut. 32:43.]

11 And again, Praise the Lord, all you Gentiles, and let all the peoples praise Him! [Ps. 117:1.]

12 And further Isaiah says, There shall be a ᵈSprout from the Root of Jesse, He Who rises to rule over the Gentiles; in Him shall the Gentiles hope. [Isa. 11:1, 10; Rev. 5:5; 22:16.]

13 May the God of your hope so fill you with all joy and peace in believing [through the experience of your faith] that by the power of the Holy Spirit you may abound *and* be overflowing (bubbling over) with hope.

14 Personally I am satisfied about you, my brethren, that you yourselves are rich in goodness, amply filled with all [spiritual] knowledge and competent to admonish *and*

c Alexander Souter, *Pocket Lexicon.*   d G. Abbott-Smith, *Manual Greek Lexicon.*

counsel *and* instruct one another also.

15 Still on some points I have written to you the more boldly *and* unreservedly by way of reminder. [I have done so] because of the grace (the unmerited favor) bestowed on me by God

16 In making me a minister of Christ Jesus to the Gentiles. I act in the priestly service of the Gospel (the good news) of God, in order that the sacrificial offering of the Gentiles may be acceptable [to God], consecrated *and* made holy by the Holy Spirit.

17 In Christ Jesus, then, I have legitimate reason to glory (exult) in my work for God [in what through Christ Jesus I have accomplished concerning the things of God].

18 For [of course] I will not venture (presume) to speak thus of any work except what Christ has actually done through me [as an instrument in His hands] to win obedience from the Gentiles, by word and deed,

19 [Even as my preaching has been accompanied] with the power of signs and wonders, [and all of it] by the power of the Holy Spirit. [The result is] that starting from Jerusalem and as far round as Illyricum, I have fully preached the Gospel [faithfully executing, accomplishing, carrying out to the full the good news] of Christ (the Messiah) in its entirety.

20 Thus my ambition has been to preach the Gospel, not where Christ's name has already been known, lest I build on another man's foundation;

21 But [instead I would act on the principle] as it is written, They shall see who have never been told of Him, and they shall understand who have never heard [of Him]. [Isa. 52:15.]

22 This [ambition] is the reason why I have so frequently been hindered from coming to visit you.

23 But now since I have no further opportunity for work in these regions, and since I have longed for [c]enough years to come to you,

24 I hope to see you in passing [through Rome] as I go [on my intended trip] to Spain, and to be aided on my journey there by you, after I have enjoyed your company for a little while.

25 For the present, however, I am going to Jerusalem to bring aid (relief) for the saints (God's people there).

26 For it has been the good pleasure of Macedonia and Achaia to make some contribution for the poor among the saints of Jerusalem.

27 They were pleased to do it; and surely they are in debt to them, for if these Gentiles have come to share in their [the Jerusalem Jews'] spiritual blessings, then they ought also to be of service to them in material blessings.

28 When therefore I have completed this mission and have delivered to them [at Jerusalem] what has been raised, I shall go on by way of you to Spain.

29 And I know that when I do come to you, I shall come in the abundant blessing *of the Gospel* of Christ.

30 I appeal to you [I entreat you], brethren, for the sake of our Lord Jesus Christ and by the love [given by] the Spirit, to unite with me in earnest wrestling in prayer to God in my behalf.

31 [Pray] that I may be delivered (rescued) from the unbelievers in Judea and that my mission of relief to Jerusalem may be acceptable *and*

e Marvin Vincent, *Word Studies.*

graciously received by the saints (God's people there),

32 So that by God's will I may subsequently come to you with joy (with a happy heart) and be refreshed [by the interval of rest] in your company.

33 May [our] peace-giving God be with you all! Amen (so be it).

CHAPTER 16

NOW I introduce *and* commend to you our sister Phoebe, a deaconess of the church at Cenchreae,

2 That you may receive her in the Lord [with a Christian welcome], as saints (God's people) ought to receive one another. And help her in whatever matter she may require assistance from you, for she has been a helper of many including myself [shielding us from suffering].

3 Give my greetings to Prisca and Aquila, my fellow workers in Christ Jesus,

4 Who risked their lives [endangering their very necks] for my life. To them not only I but also all the churches among the Gentiles give thanks.

5 [Remember me] also to the church [that meets] in their house. Greet my beloved Epaenetus, who was a firstfruit (first convert) to Christ in Asia.

6 Greet Mary, who has worked so hard among you.

7 Remember me to Andronicus and Junias, my tribal kinsmen and once my fellow prisoners. They are men held in high esteem among the apostles, who also were in Christ before I was.

8 Remember me to Ampliatus, my beloved in the Lord.

9 Salute Urbanus, our fellow worker in Christ, and my dear Stachys.

10 Greet Apelles, that one tried *and* approved in Christ (the Messiah). Remember me to those who belong to the household of Aristobulus.

11 Greet my tribal kinsman Herodion, and those in the Lord who belong to the household of Narcissus.

12 Salute those workers in the Lord, Tryphaena and Tryphosa. Greet my dear Persis, who has worked so hard in the Lord.

13 Remember me to Rufus, eminent in the Lord, also to his mother [who has been] a mother to me as well.

14 Greet Asyncritus, Phlegon, Hermes, Patrobas, Hermas, and the brethren who are with them.

15 Greet Philologus, Julia, Nereus and his sister, and Olympas, and all the saints who are with them.

16 Greet one another with a holy (consecrated) kiss. All the churches of Christ (the Messiah) wish to be remembered to you.

17 I appeal to you, brethren, to be on your guard concerning those who create dissensions and difficulties *and* cause divisions, in opposition to the doctrine (the teaching) which you have been taught. [I warn you to turn aside from them, to] avoid them.

18 For such persons do not serve our Lord Christ but their own appetites *and* base desires, and by ingratiating and flattering speech, they beguile the hearts of the unsuspecting *and* simpleminded [people].

19 For while your loyalty *and* obedience is known to all, so that I rejoice over you, I would have you well versed *and* wise as to what is good and innocent *and* guileless as to what is evil.

20 And the God of peace will soon crush Satan under your feet. The grace of our Lord Jesus Christ (the Messiah) be with you.

21 Timothy, my fellow worker,

wishes to be remembered to you, as do Lucius and Jason and Sosipater, my tribal kinsmen.

22 I, Tertius, the writer of this letter, greet you in the Lord.

23 Gaius, who is host to me and to the whole church here, greets you. So do Erastus, the city treasurer, and our brother Quartus.

24 *The grace of our Lord Jesus Christ (the Messiah) be with you all. Amen (so be it).*

25 Now to Him Who is able to strengthen you in the faith which is in accordance with my Gospel and the preaching of (concerning) Jesus Christ (the Messiah), according to the revelation (the unveiling) of the mystery of the plan of redemption which was kept in silence *and* secret for long ages,

26 But is now disclosed and through the prophetic Scriptures is made known to all nations, according to the command of the eternal God, [to win them] to obedience to the faith,

27 To [the] only wise God be glory forevermore through Jesus Christ (the Anointed One)! Amen (so be it).

THE FIRST LETTER OF PAUL TO THE

CORINTHIANS

CHAPTER 1

PAUL, SUMMONED by the will *and* purpose of God to be an apostle (special messenger) of Christ Jesus, and our brother Sosthenes,

2 To the church (assembly) of God which is in Corinth, to those consecrated *and* purified *and* made holy in Christ Jesus, [who are] selected *and* called to be saints (God's people), together with all those who in any place call upon *and* give honor to the name of our Lord Jesus Christ, both their Lord and ours:

3 Grace (favor and spiritual blessing) be to you and [heart] peace from God our Father and the Lord Jesus Christ.

4 I thank my God at all times for you because of the grace (the favor and spiritual blessing) of God which was bestowed on you in Christ Jesus,

5 [So] that in Him in every respect you were enriched, in full power *and* readiness of speech [to speak of your faith] and complete knowledge *and* illumination [to give you full insight into its meaning].

6 In this way [our] witnessing concerning Christ (the Messiah) was so confirmed *and* established *and* made sure in you

7 That you are not [consciously] falling behind *or* lacking in any special spiritual endowment *or* Christian grace [ᶠthe reception of which is due to the power of divine grace operating in your souls by the Holy Spirit], while you wait *and* watch [constantly living in hope] for the coming of our Lord Jesus Christ *and* [His] being made visible to all.

8 And He will establish you to the end [keep you steadfast, give you strength, and guarantee your vindication; He will be your warrant against all accusation or indictment

ᶠ Joseph Thayer, *A Greek-English Lexicon of the New Testament.*

so that you will be] guiltless *and* irreproachable in the day of our Lord Jesus Christ (the Messiah).

9 God is faithful (reliable, trustworthy, and therefore ever true to His promise, and He can be depended on); by Him you were called into companionship *and* participation with His Son, Jesus Christ our Lord.

10 But I urge *and* entreat you, brethren, by the name of our Lord Jesus Christ, that all of you be in perfect harmony *and* full agreement in what you say, and that there be no dissensions *or* factions *or* divisions among you, but that you be perfectly united in your common understanding and in your opinions *and* judgments.

11 For it has been made clear to me, my brethren, by those of Chloe's household, that there are contentions *and* wrangling *and* factions among you.

12 What I mean is this, that each one of you [either] says, I belong to Paul, or I belong to Apollos, or I belong to Cephas (Peter), or I belong to Christ.

13 Is Christ (the Messiah) divided into parts? Was Paul crucified on behalf of you? Or were you baptized into the name of Paul?

14 I thank God that I did not baptize any of you except Crispus and Gaius,

15 Lest anyone should say that I baptized in my own name.

16 [Yes] I did baptize the household of Stephanas also. More than these, I do not remember that I baptized anyone.

17 For Christ (the Messiah) sent me out not to baptize but [to evangelize by] preaching the glad tidings (the Gospel), and that not with verbal eloquence, lest the cross of Christ should be deprived of force *and* emptied of its power *and* rendered vain

(fruitless, void of value, and of no effect).

18 For the story *and* message of the cross is sheer absurdity *and* folly to those who are perishing and on their way to perdition, but to us who are being saved it is the [manifestation of] the power of God.

19 For it is written, I will baffle *and* render useless *and* destroy the learning of the learned *and* the philosophy of the philosophers and the cleverness of the clever *and* the discernment of the discerning; I will frustrate *and* nullify [them] *and* bring [them] to nothing. [Isa. 29:14.]

20 Where is the wise man (the philosopher)? Where is the scribe (the scholar)? Where is the investigator (the logician, the debater) of this present time *and* age? Has not God shown up the nonsense *and* the folly of this world's wisdom?

21 For when the world with all its earthly wisdom failed to perceive *and* recognize *and* know God by means of its own philosophy, God in His wisdom was pleased through the foolishness of preaching [salvation, procured by Christ and to be had through Him], to save those who believed (who clung to and trusted in and relied on Him).

22 For while Jews [demandingly] ask for signs *and* miracles and Greeks pursue philosophy *and* wisdom,

23 We preach Christ (the Messiah) crucified, [preaching which] to the Jews is a scandal *and* an offensive stumbling block [that springs a snare or trap], and to the Gentiles it is absurd *and* utterly unphilosophical nonsense.

24 But to those who are called, whether Jew or Greek (Gentile), Christ [is] the Power of God and the Wisdom of God.

25 [This is] because the foolish thing [that has its source in] God is

wiser than men, and the weak thing [that springs] from God is stronger than men.

26 For [simply] consider your own call, brethren; not many [of you were considered to be] wise according to human estimates *and* standards, not many influential *and* powerful, not many of high *and* noble birth.

27 [No] for God selected (deliberately chose) what in the world is foolish to put the wise to shame, and what the world calls weak to put the strong to shame.

28 And God also selected (deliberately chose) what in the world is lowborn *and* insignificant and branded *and* treated with contempt, even the things that are nothing, that He might depose *and* bring to nothing the things that are,

29 So that no mortal man should [have pretense for glorying and] boast in the presence of God.

30 But it is from Him that you have your life in Christ Jesus, Whom God made our Wisdom from God, [revealed to us a knowledge of the divine plan of salvation previously hidden, manifesting itself as] our Righteousness [thus making us upright and putting us in right standing with God], and our Consecration [making us pure and holy], and our Redemption [providing our ransom from eternal penalty for sin].

31 So then, as it is written, Let him who boasts *and* proudly rejoices *and* glories, boast *and* proudly rejoice *and* glory in the Lord. [Jer. 9:24.]

CHAPTER 2

AS FOR myself, brethren, when I came to you, I did not come proclaiming to you the testimony *and* evidence or ^{g}mystery and secret of God [concerning what He has done

through Christ for the salvation of men] in lofty words of eloquence or human philosophy *and* wisdom;

2 For I resolved to know nothing (to be acquainted with nothing, to make a display of the knowledge of nothing, and to be conscious of nothing) among you except Jesus Christ (the Messiah) and Him crucified.

3 And I was in (^{h}passed into a state of) weakness and fear (dread) and great trembling [^{h}after I had come] among you.

4 And my language and my message were not set forth in persuasive (enticing and plausible) words of wisdom, but they were in demonstration of the [Holy] Spirit and power [^{i}a proof by the Spirit and power of God, operating on me and stirring in the minds of my hearers the most holy emotions and thus persuading them],

5 So that your faith might not rest in the wisdom of men (human philosophy), but in the power of God.

6 Yet when we are among the full-grown (spiritually mature Christians who are ripe in understanding), we do impart a [higher] wisdom (the knowledge of the divine plan previously hidden); but it is indeed not a wisdom of this present age *or* of this world nor of the leaders *and* rulers of this age, who are being brought to nothing *and* are doomed to pass away.

7 But rather what we are setting forth is a wisdom of God once hidden [from the human understanding] and now revealed to us by God—[that wisdom] which God devised *and* decreed before the ages for our glorification [to lift us into the glory of His presence].

8 None of the rulers of this age *or* world perceived *and* recognized *and* understood this, for if they had, they

---

g Many ancient manuscripts so read.   h Marvin Vincent, *Word Studies in the New Testament.*
i Joseph Thayer, *A Greek-English Lexicon.*

would never have crucified the Lord of glory.

9 But, on the contrary, as the Scripture says, What eye has not seen and ear has not heard and has not entered into the heart of man, [all that] God has prepared (made and keeps ready) for those who love Him [jwho hold Him in affectionate reverence, promptly obeying Him and gratefully recognizing the benefits He has bestowed]. [Isa. 64:4; 65:17.]

10 Yet to us God has unveiled and revealed them by and through His Spirit, for the [Holy] Spirit searches diligently, exploring and examining everything, even sounding the profound and bottomless things of God [the jdivine counsels and things hidden and beyond man's scrutiny].

11 For what person perceives (knows and understands) what passes through a man's thoughts except the man's own spirit within him? Just so no one discerns (comes to know and comprehend) the thoughts of God except the Spirit of God.

12 Now we have not received the spirit [that belongs to] the world, but the [Holy] Spirit Who is from God, [given to us] that we might realize and comprehend and appreciate the gifts [of divine favor and blessing so freely and lavishly] bestowed on us by God.

13 And we are setting these truths forth in words not taught by human wisdom but taught by the [Holy] Spirit, combining and interpreting spiritual truths with spiritual language [to those who possess the Holy Spirit].

14 But the natural, nonspiritual man does not accept or welcome or admit into his heart the gifts and teachings and revelations of the Spirit of God, for they are folly (meaning-

less nonsense) to him; and he is incapable of knowing them (of progressively recognizing, understanding, and becoming better acquainted with them) because they are spiritually discerned and estimated and appreciated.

15 But the spiritual man tries all things [he kexamines, investigates, inquires into, questions, and discerns all things], yet is himself to be put on trial and judged by no one [he can read the meaning of everything, but no one can properly discern or appraise or get an insight into him].

16 For who has known or understood the mind (the counsels and purposes) of the Lord so as to guide and instruct Him and give Him knowledge? But we have the mind of Christ (the Messiah) and do hold the thoughts (feelings and purposes) of His heart. [Isa. 40:13.]

CHAPTER 3

HOWEVER, BRETHREN, I could not talk to you as to spiritual [men], but as to nonspiritual [men of the flesh, in whom the carnal nature predominates], as to mere infants [in the new life] in Christ [lunable to talk yet!]

2 I fed you with milk, not solid food, for you were not yet strong enough [to be ready for it]; but even yet you are not strong enough [to be ready for it].

3 For you are still [unspiritual, having the nature] of the flesh [under the control of ordinary impulses]. For as long as [there are] envying and jealousy and wrangling and factions among you, are you not unspiritual and of the flesh, behaving yourselves after a human standard and like mere (unchanged) men?

4 For when one says, I belong to

---

j Joseph Thayer, *A Greek-English Lexicon.*   k Joseph P. Lightfoot, *Notes on the Epistles of Saint Paul.*
l Literal translation: "non-speakers."

Paul, and another, I belong to Apollos, are you not [proving yourselves] ordinary (unchanged) men?

5 What then is Apollos? What is Paul? Ministering servants [not heads of parties] through whom you believed, even as the Lord appointed to each his task:

6 I planted, Apollos watered, but God [all the while] was making it grow and [He] gave the increase.

7 So neither he who plants is anything nor he who waters, but [only] God Who makes it grow and become greater.

8 He who plants and he who waters are equal (one in aim, of the same importance and esteem), yet each shall receive his own reward (wages), according to his own labor.

9 For we are fellow workmen (joint promoters, laborers together) with and for God; you are God's [m]garden and vineyard and field under cultivation, [you are] God's building. [Isa. 61:3.]

10 According to the grace (the special endowment for my task) of God bestowed on me, like a skillful architect and master builder I laid [the] foundation, and now another [man] is building upon it. But let each [man] be careful how he builds upon it,

11 For no other foundation can anyone lay than that which is [already] laid, which is Jesus Christ (the Messiah, the Anointed One).

12 But if anyone builds upon the Foundation, whether it be with gold, silver, precious stones, wood, hay, straw,

13 The work of each [one] will become [plainly, openly] known (shown for what it is); for the day [of Christ] will disclose and declare it, because it will be revealed with fire, and the fire will test and critically

appraise the character and worth of the work each person has done.

14 If the work which any person has built on this Foundation [any product of his efforts whatever] survives [this test], he will get his reward.

15 But if any person's work is burned up [under the test], he will suffer the loss [of it all, losing his reward], though he himself will be saved, but only as [one who has passed] through fire. [Job 23:10.]

16 Do you not discern and understand that you [the whole church at Corinth] are God's temple (His sanctuary), and that God's Spirit has His permanent dwelling in you [to be at home in you, [n]collectively as a church and also individually]?

17 If anyone [o]does hurt to God's temple or corrupts it [[n]with false doctrines] or destroys it, God will [o]do hurt to him and bring him to the corruption of death and destroy him. For the temple of God is holy (sacred to Him) and that [temple] you [[n]the believing church and its individual believers] are.

18 Let no person deceive himself. If anyone among you supposes that he is wise in this age, let him become a fool [let him discard his worldly discernment and recognize himself as dull, stupid, and foolish, without true learning and scholarship], that he may become [really] wise. [Isa. 5:21.]

19 For this world's wisdom is foolishness (absurdity and stupidity) with God, for it is written, He lays hold of the wise in their [own] craftiness; [Job 5:13.]

20 And again, The Lord knows the thoughts and reasonings of the [humanly] wise and recognizes how futile they are. [Ps. 94:11.]

m Johann Bengel, *Gnomon Novi Testamenti*.
o *The Cambridge Bible for Schools and Colleges*.

n Matthew Henry, *Commentary on the Holy Bible*.

21 So let no one exult proudly concerning men [boasting of having this or that man as a leader], for all things are yours,

22 Whether Paul or Apollos or Cephas (Peter), or the universe or life or death, or the immediate *and* [p]threatening present or the [subsequent and uncertain] future—all are yours,

23 And you are Christ's, and Christ is God's.

CHAPTER 4

SO THEN, let us [apostles] be looked upon as ministering servants of Christ and stewards (trustees) of the mysteries (the secret purposes) of God.

2 Moreover, it is [essentially] required of stewards that a man should be found faithful [proving himself worthy of trust].

3 But [as for me personally] it matters very little to me that I should be put on trial by you [on this point], *and* that you or any other human tribunal should investigate *and* question *and* cross-question me. I do not even put myself on trial *and* judge myself.

4 I am not conscious of anything against myself, *and* I feel blameless; but I am not vindicated *and* acquitted before God on that account. It is the Lord [Himself] Who examines *and* judges me.

5 So do not make any hasty *or* premature judgments before the time when the Lord comes [again], for He will both bring to light the secret things that are [now hidden] in darkness and disclose *and* expose the [secret] aims (motives and purposes) of hearts. Then every man will receive his [due] commendation from God.

6 Now I have applied all this [about parties and factions] to myself and

Apollos for your sakes, brethren, so that from what I have said of us [as illustrations], you may learn [to think of men in accordance with Scripture and] not to go beyond that which is written, that none of you may be puffed up *and* inflated with pride *and* boast in favor of one [minister and teacher] against another.

7 For who separates you from the others [as a faction leader]? [Who makes you superior and sets you apart from another, giving you the preeminence?] What have you that was not given to you? If then you received it [from someone], why do you boast as if you had not received [but had gained it by your own efforts]?

8 [*q*You behave as if] you are already filled *and* think you have enough [you are full and content, feeling no need of anything more]! Already you have become rich [in spiritual gifts and graces]! [Without any counsel or instruction from us, in your conceit], you have ascended your thrones *and* come into your kingdom without including us! And would that it were true *and* that you did reign, so that we might be sharing the kingdom with you!

9 For it seems to me that God has made an exhibit of us apostles, exposing us to view last [of all, like men in a triumphal procession who are] sentenced to death [and displayed at the end of the line]. For we have become a spectacle to the world [a show in the world's amphitheater] with both men and angels [as spectators].

10 We are [looked upon as] fools on account of Christ *and* for His sake, but you are [supposedly] so amazingly wise *and* prudent in Christ! We are weak, but you are [so very] strong! You are highly es-

p Marvin Vincent, *Word Studies.*   q Henry Alford, *The Greek New Testament, with Notes.*

teemed, but we are in disrepute *and* contempt!

11 To this hour we have gone both hungry and thirsty; we [ʳhabitually] wear but one undergarment [and shiver in the cold]; we are roughly knocked about and wander around homeless.

12 And we still toil unto weariness [for our living], working hard with our own hands. When men revile us [ˢwound us with an accursed sting], we bless them. When we are persecuted, we take it patiently *and* endure it.

13 When we are slandered *and* defamed, we [try to] answer softly *and* bring comfort. We have been made and are now the rubbish *and* filth of the world [the offscouring of all things, the scum of the earth].

14 I do not write this to shame you, but to warn *and* counsel you as my beloved children.

15 After all, though you should have ten thousand teachers (guides to direct you) in Christ, yet you do not have many fathers. For I became your father in Christ Jesus through the glad tidings (the Gospel).

16 So I urge *and* implore you, be imitators of me.

17 For this very cause I sent to you Timothy, who is my beloved and trustworthy child in the Lord, who will recall to your minds my methods of proceeding *and* course of conduct *and* way of life in Christ, such as I teach everywhere in each of the churches.

18 Some of you have become conceited *and* arrogant *and* pretentious, counting on my not coming to you.

19 But I will come to you [and] shortly, if the Lord is willing, and then I will perceive *and* understand not what the talk of these puffed up *and* arrogant spirits amount to, but their force (ᵗthe moral power and excellence of soul they really possess).

20 For the kingdom of God consists of *and* is based on not talk but power (ᵘmoral power and excellence of soul).

21 Now which do you prefer? Shall I come to you with a rod of correction, or with love and in a spirit of gentleness?

CHAPTER 5

IT IS actually reported that there is sexual immorality among you, impurity of a sort that is condemned *and* does not occur even among the heathen; for a man has [his own] father's wife. [Deut. 22:30; 27:20.]

2 And you are proud *and* arrogant! And you ought rather to mourn (bow in sorrow and in shame) until the person who has done this [shameful] thing is removed from your fellowship *and* your midst!

3 As for my attitude, though I am absent [from you] in body, I am present in spirit, and I have already decided *and* passed judgment, as if actually present,

4 In the name of the Lord Jesus *Christ*, on the man who has committed such a deed. When you and my own spirit are met together with the power of our Lord Jesus,

5 You are to deliver this man over to Satan ᵛfor physical discipline [to destroy carnal lusts which prompted him to incest], that [his] spirit may [yet] be saved in the day of the Lord Jesus.

6 [About the condition of your church] your boasting is not good [indeed, it is most unseemly and entire-

r Alexander Souter, *Pocket Lexicon of the Greek New Testament.*   s Kenneth Wuest, *Word Studies in the Greek New Testament.*   t Joseph Thayer, *A Greek-English Lexicon.*   u Joseph Thayer, *A Greek-English Lexicon.*   v G. Abbott-Smith, *Manual Greek Lexicon of the New Testament.*

ly out of place]. Do you not know that [just] a little leaven will ferment the whole lump [of dough]?

7 Purge (clean out) the old leaven that you may be fresh (new) dough, still uncontaminated [as you are], for Christ, our Passover [Lamb], has been sacrificed.

8 Therefore, let us keep the feast, not with old leaven, nor with leaven of vice and malice and wickedness, but with the unleavened [bread] of purity (nobility, honor) and sincerity and [unadulterated] truth. [Exod. 12:19; 13:7; Deut. 16:3.]

9 I wrote you in my [previous] letter not to associate [closely and habitually] with unchaste (impure) people—

10 Not [meaning of course that you must] altogether shun the immoral people of this world, or the greedy graspers and cheats and thieves or idolaters, since otherwise you would need to get out of the world and human society altogether!

11 But now I write to you not to associate with anyone who bears the name of [Christian] brother if he is known to be guilty of immorality or greed, or is an idolater [whose soul is devoted to any object that usurps the place of God], or is a person with a foul tongue [railing, abusing, reviling, slandering], or is a drunkard or a swindler or a robber. [No] you must not so much as eat with such a person.

12 What [business] of mine is it and what right have I to judge outsiders? Is it not those inside [the church] upon whom you are to pass disciplinary judgment [passing censuring sentence on them as the facts require]?

13 God alone sits in judgment on those who are outside. Drive out that wicked one from among you [expel him from your church].

CHAPTER 6

DOES ANY of you dare, when he has a matter of complaint against another [brother], to go to law before unrighteous men [men neither upright nor right with God, laying it before them] instead of before the saints (the people of God)?

2 Do you not know that the saints (the believers) will [one day] judge and govern the world? And if the world [itself] is to be judged and ruled by you, are you unworthy and incompetent to try [such petty matters] of the smallest courts of justice?

3 Do you not know also that we [Christians] are to judge the [very] angels and pronounce opinion between right and wrong [for them]? How much more then [as to] matters pertaining to this world and of this life only!

4 If then you do have such cases of everyday life to decide, why do you appoint [as judges to lay them before] those who [from the standpoint] of the church count for least and are without standing?

5 I say this to move you to shame. Can it be that there really is not one man among you who [in action is governed by piety and integrity and] is wise and competent enough to decide [the private grievances, disputes, and quarrels] between members of the brotherhood,

6 But brother goes to law against brother, and that before [Gentile judges who are] unbelievers [without faith or trust in the Gospel of Christ]?

7 Why, the very fact of your having lawsuits with one another at all is a defect (a defeat, an evidence of positive moral loss for you). Why not rather let yourselves suffer wrong and be deprived of what is your due? Why not rather be cheated (defrauded and robbed)?

8 But [instead it is you] yourselves

who wrong and defraud, and that even your own brethren [by so treating them]!

9 Do you not know that the unrighteous *and* the wrongdoers will not inherit *or* have any share in the kingdom of God? Do not be deceived (misled): neither the impure *and* immoral, nor idolaters, nor adulterers, nor those who participate in homosexuality,

10 Nor cheats (swindlers and thieves), nor greedy graspers, nor drunkards, nor foulmouthed revilers *and* slanderers, nor extortioners *and* robbers will inherit *or* have any share in the kingdom of God.

11 And such some of you were [once]. But you were washed clean (purified by a complete atonement for sin and made free from the guilt of sin), and you were consecrated (set apart, hallowed), and you were justified [pronounced righteous, by trusting] in the name of the Lord Jesus Christ and in the [Holy] Spirit of our God.

12 Everything is permissible (allowable and lawful) for me; but not all things are helpful (good for me to do, expedient and profitable when considered with other things). Everything is lawful for me, but I will not become the slave of anything *or* be brought under its power.

13 Food [is intended] for the stomach and the stomach for food, but God will finally end [the functions of] both *and* bring them to nothing. The body is not intended for sexual immorality, but [is intended] for the Lord, and the Lord [is intended] for the body [ʷto save, sanctify, and raise it again].

14 And God both raised the Lord to life and will also raise us up by His power.

15 Do you not see *and* know that

your bodies are members (bodily parts) of Christ (the Messiah)? Am I therefore to take the parts of Christ and make [them] parts of a prostitute? Never! Never!

16 Or do you not know *and* realize that when a man joins himself to a prostitute, he becomes one body with her? The two, it is written, shall become one flesh. [Gen. 2:24.]

17 But the person who is united to the Lord becomes one spirit with Him.

18 Shun immorality *and* all sexual looseness [flee from impurity in thought, word, or deed]. Any other sin which a man commits is one outside the body, but he who commits sexual immorality sins against his own body.

19 Do you not know that your body is the temple (the very sanctuary) of the Holy Spirit Who lives within you, Whom you have received [as a Gift] from God? You are not your own,

20 You were bought with a price [purchased with a ˣpreciousness and paid for, ˣmade His own]. So then, honor God *and* bring glory to Him in your body.

CHAPTER 7

NOW AS to the matters of which you wrote me. It is well [and by that I mean advantageous, expedient, profitable, and wholesome] for a man not to touch a woman [to cohabit with her] *but* to remain unmarried.

2 But because of the temptation to impurity *and* to avoid immorality, let each [man] have his own wife and let each [woman] have her own husband.

3 The husband should give to his wife her conjugal rights (goodwill, kindness, and what is due her as his wife), and likewise the wife to her husband.

4 For the wife does not have [exclusive] authority *and* control over her own body, but the husband [has his rights]; likewise also the husband does not have [exclusive] authority *and* control over his body, but the wife [has her rights].

5 Do not refuse *and* deprive *and* defraud each other [of your due marital rights], except perhaps by mutual consent for a time, so that you may devote yourselves unhindered to prayer. But afterwards resume marital relations, lest Satan tempt you [to sin] through your lack of restraint of sexual desire. [Exod. 19:15.]

6 But I am saying this more as a matter of permission *and* concession, not as a command *or* regulation.

7 I wish that all men were like I myself am [in this matter of self-control]. But each has his own special gift from God, one of this kind and one of another.

8 But to the unmarried people and to the widows, I declare that it is well (good, advantageous, expedient, and wholesome) for them to remain [single] even as I do.

9 But if they have not self-control (restraint of their passions), they should marry. For it is better to marry than to be aflame [with passion and tortured continually with ungratified desire].

10 But to the married people I give charge—not I but the Lord—that the wife is not to separate from her husband.

11 But if she does [separate from and divorce him], let her remain single or else be reconciled to her husband. And [I charge] the husband [also] that he should not put away *or* divorce his wife.

12 To the rest I declare—I, not the

Lord [for Jesus did not discuss this]—that if any brother has a wife who does not believe [in Christ] and she consents to live with him, he should not leave *or* divorce her.

13 And if any woman has an unbelieving husband and he consents to live with her, she should not leave *or* divorce him.

14 For the unbelieving husband is set apart (separated, withdrawn from heathen contamination, and affiliated with the Christian people) by union with his consecrated (set-apart) wife, and the unbelieving wife is set apart *and* separated through union with her consecrated husband. Otherwise your children would be unclean (unblessed heathen, [y]outside the Christian covenant); but as it is they are [z]prepared for God [pure and clean].

15 But if the unbelieving partner [actually] leaves, let him do so; in such [cases the remaining] brother or sister is not morally bound. But God has called us to peace.

16 For, wife, how can you be sure of converting *and* saving your husband? Husband, how can you be sure of converting *and* saving your wife?

17 Only, let each one [seek to conduct himself and regulate his affairs so as to] lead the life which the Lord has allotted *and* imparted to him and to which God has invited *and* summoned him. This is my order in all the churches.

18 Was anyone at the time of his summons [from God] already circumcised? Let him not seek to remove the evidence of circumcision. Was anyone at the time [God] called him uncircumcised? Let him not be circumcised.

19 For circumcision is nothing *and* counts for nothing, neither does un-

y Robert Jamieson, A.R. Fausset and David Brown, *A Commentary on the Old and New Testaments.*
z Joseph Thayer, *A Greek-English Lexicon.*

circumcision, but [what counts is] keeping the commandments of God.

20 Everyone should remain after God calls him in the station or condition of life in which the summons found him.

21 Were you a slave when you were called? Do not let that trouble you. But if you are able to gain your freedom, avail yourself of the opportunity.

22 For he who as a slave was summoned in [to union with] the Lord is a freedman of the Lord, just so he who was free when he was called is a bond servant of Christ (the Messiah).

23 You were bought with a price [purchased with a preciousness and paid for by Christ]; then do not yield yourselves up to become [in your own estimation] slaves to men [but consider yourselves slaves to Christ].

24 So, brethren, in whatever station or state or condition of life each one was when he was called, there let him continue with and close to God.

25 Now concerning the virgins (the marriageable [a]maidens) I have no command of the Lord, but I give my opinion and advice as one who by the Lord's mercy is rendered trustworthy and faithful.

26 I think then, because of the impending distress [that is even now setting in], it is well (expedient, profitable, and wholesome) for a person to remain as he or she is.

27 Are you bound to a wife? Do not seek to be free. Are you free from a wife? Do not seek a wife.

28 But if you do marry, you do not sin [in doing so], and if a virgin marries, she does not sin [in doing so]. Yet those who marry will have physical and earthly troubles, and I would like to spare you that.

29 I mean, brethren, the appointed time has been [a]winding down and it has grown very short. From now on, let even those who have wives be as if they had none,

30 And those who weep and mourn as though they were not weeping and mourning, and those who rejoice as though they were not rejoicing, and those who buy as though they did not possess anything,

31 And those who deal with this world [[a]overusing the enjoyments of this life] as though they were not absorbed by it and as if they had no dealings with it. For the outward form of this world (the present world order) is passing away.

32 My desire is to have you free from all anxiety and distressing care. The unmarried man is anxious about the things of the Lord—how he may please the Lord;

33 But the married man is anxious about worldly matters—how he may please his wife—

34 And he is drawn in diverging directions [his interests are divided and he is distracted from his devotion to God]. And the unmarried woman or girl is concerned and anxious about the matters of the Lord, how to be wholly separated and set apart in body and spirit; but the married woman has her cares [centered] in earthly affairs—how she may please her husband.

35 Now I say this for your own welfare and profit, not to put [a halter of] restraint upon you, but to promote what is seemly and in good order and to secure your undistracted and undivided devotion to the Lord.

36 But if any man thinks that he is not acting properly toward and in regard to his virgin [that he is preparing disgrace for her or incurring reproach], in case she is passing the bloom of her youth and if there is

a Marvin Vincent, *Word Studies*.

need for it, let him do what to him seems right; he does not sin; let them marry.

37 But whoever is firmly established in his heart [strong in mind and purpose], not being forced by necessity but having control over his own will and desire, and has resolved this in his heart to keep his own virginity, he is doing well.

38 So also then, he [the father] who gives his virgin (his daughter) in marriage does well, and he [the father] who does not give [her] in marriage does better.

39 A wife is bound to her husband by law as long as he lives. If the husband dies, she is free to be married to whom she will, only [provided that he too is] in the Lord.

40 But in my opinion [a widow] is happier (more blessed and [b]to be envied) if she does not remarry. And also I think I have the Spirit of God.

CHAPTER 8

NOW ABOUT food offered to idols, of course we know that all of us possess knowledge [concerning these matters. Yet mere] knowledge causes people to be puffed up (to bear themselves loftily and be proud), but love (affection and goodwill and benevolence) edifies and builds up and encourages one to grow [to his full stature].

2 If anyone imagines that he has come to know and understand much [of divine things, without love], he does not yet perceive and recognize and understand as strongly and clearly, nor has he become as intimately acquainted with anything as he ought or as is necessary.

3 But if one loves God truly [[c]with affectionate reverence, prompt obedience, and grateful recognition of His blessing], he is known by God

[[b]recognized as worthy of His intimacy and love, and he is owned by Him].

4 In this matter, then, of eating food offered to idols, we know that an idol is nothing [has no real existence] and that there is no God but one. [Deut. 6:4.]

5 For although there may be so-called gods, whether in heaven or on earth, as indeed there are many of them, both of gods and of lords and masters,

6 Yet for us there is [only] one God, the Father, Who is the Source of all things and for Whom we [have life], and one Lord, Jesus Christ, through and by Whom are all things and through and by Whom we [ourselves exist]. [Mal. 2:10.]

7 Nevertheless, not all [believers] possess this knowledge. But some, through being all their lives until now accustomed to [thinking of] idols [as real and living], still consider the food [offered to an idol] as that sacrificed to an [actual] god; and their weak consciences become defiled and injured if they eat [it].

8 Now food [itself] will not cause our acceptance by God nor commend us to Him. Eating [food offered to idols] gives us no advantage; neither do we come short or become any worse if we do not eat [it].

9 Only be careful that this power of choice (this permission and liberty to do as you please) which is yours, does not [somehow] become a hindrance (cause of stumbling) to the weak or overscrupulous [giving them an impulse to sin].

10 For suppose someone sees you, a man having knowledge [of God, with an intelligent view of this subject and] reclining at table in an idol's temple, might he not be encouraged and emboldened [to violate his own

b Alexander Souter, Pocket Lexicon.   c Joseph Thayer, A Greek-English Lexicon.

conscientious scruples] if he is weak *and* uncertain, and eat what [to him] is for the purpose of idol worship?

11 And so by your enlightenment (your knowledge of spiritual things), this weak man is ruined (is lost and perishes)—the brother for whom Christ (the Messiah) died!

12 And when you sin against your brethren in this way, wounding *and* damaging their weak conscience, you sin against Christ.

13 Therefore, if [my eating a] food is a cause of my brother's falling *or* of hindering [his spiritual advancement], I will not eat [such] flesh forever, lest I cause my brother to be tripped up *and* fall *and* to be offended.

CHAPTER 9

AM I not an apostle (a special messenger)? Am I not free (unrestrained and exempt from any obligation)? Have I not seen Jesus our Lord? Are you [yourselves] not [the product and proof of] my workmanship in the Lord?

2 Even if I am not considered an apostle (a special messenger) by others, at least I am one to you: for you are the seal (the certificate, the living evidence) of my apostleship in the Lord [confirming and authenticating it].

3 This is my [real ground of] defense (my vindication of myself) to those who would put me on trial *and* cross-examine me.

4 Have we not the right to our food and drink [at the expense of the churches]?

5 Have we not the right also to take along with us a Christian sister as wife, as do the other apostles and the Lord's brothers and Cephas (Peter)?

6 Or is it only Barnabas and I who have no right to refrain from doing manual labor for a livelihood [in or-

der to go about the work of the ministry]?

7 [Consider this:] What soldier at any time serves at his own expense? Who plants a vineyard and does not eat any of the fruit of it? Who tends a flock and does not partake of the milk of the flock?

8 Do I say this only on human authority *and* as a man reasons? Does not the Law endorse the same principle?

9 For in the Law of Moses it is written, You shall not muzzle an ox when it is treading out the corn. Is it [only] for oxen that God cares? [Deut. 25:4.]

10 Or does He speak certainly *and* entirely for our sakes? [Assuredly] it is written for our sakes, because the plowman ought to plow in hope, and the thresher ought to thresh in expectation of partaking of the harvest.

11 If we have sown [the seed of] spiritual good among you, [is it too] much if we reap from your material benefits?

12 If others share in this rightful claim upon you, do not we [have a still better and greater claim]? However, we have never exercised this right, but we endure everything rather than put a hindrance in the way [of the spread] of the good news (the Gospel) of Christ.

13 Do you not know that those men who are employed in the services of the temple get their food from the temple? And that those who tend the altar share with the altar [in the offerings brought]? [Deut. 18:1.]

14 [On the same principle] the Lord directed that those who publish the good news (the Gospel) should live (get their maintenance) by the Gospel. [Deut. 18:1.]

15 But I have not made use of any of these privileges, nor am I writing this [to suggest] that any such provision be made for me [now]. For it

would be better for me to die than to have anyone make void *and* deprive me of my [ground for] glorifying [in this matter].

16 For if I [merely] preach the Gospel, that gives me no reason to boast, for I feel compelled of necessity to do it. Woe is me if I do not preach the glad tidings (the Gospel)!

17 For if I do this work of my own free will, then I have my pay (my reward); but if it is not of my own will, but is done reluctantly *and* under compulsion, I am [still] entrusted with a [sacred] trusteeship *and* commission.

18 What then is the [actual] reward that I get? Just this: that in my preaching the good news (the Gospel), I may offer it [absolutely] free of expense [to anybody], not taking advantage of my rights *and* privileges [as a preacher] of the Gospel.

19 For although I am free in every way from anyone's control, I have made myself a bond servant to everyone, so that I might gain the more [for Christ].

20 To the Jews I became as a Jew, that I might win Jews; to men under the Law, [I became] as one under the Law, though not myself being under the Law, that I might win those under the Law.

21 To those without (outside) law I became as one without law, not that I am without the law of God *and* lawless toward Him, but that I am [especially keeping] within *and* committed to the law of Christ, that I might win those who are without law.

22 To the weak (wanting in discernment) I have become weak (wanting in discernment) that I might win the weak *and* overscrupulous. I have [in short] become all things to all men, that I might by all means (at all costs and in any and every way) save some [by winning them to faith in Jesus Christ].

23 And I do this for the sake of the good news (the Gospel), in order that I may become a participator in it *and* share in its [blessings along with you].

24 Do you not know that in a race all the runners compete, but [only] one receives the prize? So run [your race] that you may lay hold [of the prize] *and* make it yours.

25 Now every athlete who goes into training conducts himself temperately *and* restricts himself in all things. They do it to win a wreath that will soon wither, but we [do it to receive a crown of eternal blessedness] that cannot wither.

26 Therefore I do not run uncertainly (without definite aim). I do not box like one beating the air *and* striking without an adversary.

27 But [like a boxer] I buffet my body [handle it roughly], discipline it by hardships] and subdue it, for fear that after proclaiming to others the Gospel *and* things pertaining to it, I myself should become unfit [not stand the test, be unapproved and rejected as a counterfeit].

CHAPTER 10

FOR I do not want you to be ignorant, brethren, that our forefathers were all under *and* protected by the cloud [in which God's Presence went before them], and every one of them passed [safely] through the [Red] Sea, [Exod. 13:21; 14:22, 29.]

2 And each one of them [allowed himself also] to be baptized into Moses in the cloud and in the sea [they were thus brought under obligation to the Law, to Moses, and to the covenant, consecrated and set apart to the service of God];

3 And all [of them] ate the same spiritual (supernaturally given) food, [Exod. 16:4, 35.]

4 And they all drank the same spiri-

tual (supernaturally given) drink. For they drank from a spiritual Rock which followed them [produced by the sole power of God Himself without natural instrumentality], and the Rock was Christ. [Exod. 17:6; Num. 20:11.]

5 Nevertheless, God was not pleased with the great majority of them, for they were overthrown *and* strewn down along [the ground] in the wilderness. [Num. 14:29, 30.]

6 Now these things are examples (warnings and admonitions) for us not to desire *or* crave *or* covet *or* lust after evil *and* carnal things as they did. [Num. 11:4, 34.]

7 Do not be worshipers of false gods as some of them were, as it is written, The people sat down to eat and drink [the sacrifices offered to the golden calf at Horeb] and rose to sport (to dance and give way to jesting and hilarity). [Exod. 32:4, 6.]

8 We must not gratify evil desire *and* indulge in immorality as some of them did—and twenty-three thousand [suddenly] fell *dead* in a single day! [Num. 25:1–18.]

9 We should not tempt the Lord [try His patience, become a trial to Him, critically appraise Him, and exploit His goodness] as some of them did—and were killed by poisonous serpents; [Num. 21:5, 6.]

10 Nor discontentedly complain as some of them did—and were [d]put out of the way entirely by the destroyer (death). [Num. 16:41, 49.]

11 Now these things befell them by way of a figure [as an example and warning to us]; they were written to admonish *and* fit us for right action by good instruction, we in whose days the ages have reached their climax (their consummation and concluding period).

12 Therefore let anyone who thinks he stands [who feels sure that he has a steadfast mind and is standing firm], take heed lest he fall [into sin].

13 For no temptation (no trial regarded as enticing to sin, no matter how it comes or where it leads) has overtaken you *and* laid hold on you that is not common to man [that is, no temptation or trial has come to you that is beyond human resistance and that is not [d]adjusted and [e]adapted and belonging to human experience, and such as man can bear]. But God is faithful [to His Word and to His compassionate nature], and He [can be trusted] not to let you be tempted *and* tried *and* assayed beyond your ability *and* strength of resistance *and* power to endure, but with the temptation He will [always] also provide the way out (the means of escape to [f]a landing place), that you may be capable *and* strong *and* powerful to bear up under it patiently.

14 Therefore, my dearly beloved, shun (keep clear away from, avoid by flight if need be) any sort of idolatry (of loving or venerating anything more than God).

15 I am speaking as to intelligent (sensible) men. Think over *and* make up your minds [for yourselves] about what I say. [I appeal to your reason and your discernment in these matters.]

16 The cup of blessing [of wine at the Lord's Supper] upon which we ask [God's] blessing, does it not mean [that in drinking it] we participate in *and* share a fellowship (a communion) in the blood of Christ (the Messiah)? The bread which we break, does it not mean [that in eating it] we participate in *and* share a fel-

---

d Joseph Thayer, *A Greek-English Lexicon.*   e Henry Alford, *The Greek New Testament.*   f Marvin Vincent, *Word Studies.*

lowship (a communion) in the body of Christ?

17 For we [no matter how] numerous we are, are one body, because we all partake of the one Bread [the One Whom the communion bread represents].

18 Consider those [physically] people of Israel. Are not those who eat the sacrifices partners of the altar [united in their worship of the same God]? [Lev. 7:6.]

19 What do I imply then? That food offered to idols is [intrinsically changed by the fact and amounts to] anything *or* that an idol itself is a [living] thing?

20 No, I am suggesting that what the pagans sacrifice they offer [in effect] to demons (to evil spiritual powers) and not to God [at all]. I do not want you to fellowship *and* be partners with diabolical spirits [by eating at their feasts]. [Deut. 32:17.]

21 You cannot drink the Lord's cup and the demons' cup. You cannot partake of the Lord's table and the demons' table.

22 Shall we thus provoke the Lord to jealousy *and* anger *and* indignation? Are we stronger than He [that we should defy Him]? [Deut. 32:21; Eccl. 6:10; Isa. 45:9.]

23 All things are legitimate (permissible), [and we are free to do anything we please], but not all things are helpful (expedient, profitable, and wholesome). All things are legitimate, but not all things are constructive [to character] *and* edifying [to spiritual life].

24 Let no one then seek his own good *and* advantage *and* profit, but [rather] each one of the other [let him seek the welfare of his neighbor].

25 [As to meat offered to idols] eat anything that is sold in the meat market without raising any question *or*

investigating on the grounds of conscientious scruples,

26 For the [whole] earth is the Lord's and everything that is in it. [Ps. 24:1; 50:12.]

27 In case one of the unbelievers invites you to a meal and you want to go, eat whatever is served to you without examining into its source because of conscientious scruples.

28 But if someone tells you, This has been offered in sacrifice to an idol, do not eat it, out of consideration for the person who informed you, and for conscience's sake—

29 I mean for the sake of his conscience, not yours, [do not eat it]. For why should another man's scruples apply to me *and* my liberty of action be determined by his conscience?

30 If I partake [of my food] with thankfulness, why am I accused *and* spoken evil of because of that for which I give thanks?

31 So then, whether you eat or drink, or whatever you may do, do all for the honor *and* glory of God.

32 Do not let yourselves be [hindrances by giving] an offense to the Jews or to the Greeks or to the church of God [*do not lead others into sin by your mode of life];

33 Just as I myself strive to please [to accommodate myself to the opinions, desires, and interests of others, adapting myself to] all men in everything I do, not aiming at *or* considering my own profit *and* advantage, but that of the many in order that they may be saved.

CHAPTER 11

PATTERN YOURSELVES after me [follow my example], as I imitate *and* follow Christ (the Messiah).

2 I appreciate *and* commend you because you always remember me in

g Joseph Thayer, *A Greek-English Lexicon.*

everything and keep firm possession of the traditions (the substance of my instructions), just as I have [verbally] passed them on to you.

3 But I want you to know *and* realize that Christ is the Head of every man, the head of a woman is her husband, and the Head of Christ is God.

4 Any man who prays or prophesies (teaches, refutes, reproves, admonishes, and comforts) with his head covered dishonors his Head (Christ).

5 And any woman who [publicly] prays or prophesies (teaches, refutes, reproves, admonishes, or comforts) when she is bareheaded dishonors her head (her husband); it is the same as [if her head were] shaved.

6 For if a woman will not wear [a head] covering, then she should cut off her hair too; but if it is disgraceful for a woman to have her head shorn or shaven, let her cover [her head].

7 For a man ought not to wear anything on his head [in church], for he is the image and [reflected] glory of God [ʰhis function of government reflects the majesty of the divine Rule]; but woman is [the expression of] man's glory (majesty, preeminence). [Gen. 1:26.]

8 For man was not [created] from woman, but woman from man; [Gen. 2:21–23.]

9 Neither was man created on account of *or* for the benefit of woman, but woman on account of *and* for the benefit of man. [Gen. 2:18.]

10 ⁱTherefore she should [be subject to his authority and should] have a covering on her head [as a token, a symbol, of her submission to authority, ʰthat she may show reverence as do] the angels [and not displease them].

11 Nevertheless, in [the plan of] the Lord *and* from His point of view woman is not apart from *and* independent of man, nor is man aloof from *and* independent of woman;

12 For as woman was made from man, even so man is also born of woman; and all [whether male or female go forth] from God [as their Author].

13 Consider for yourselves; is it proper *and* decent [according to your customs] for a woman to offer prayer to God [publicly] with her head uncovered?

14 Does not ʰthe native sense of propriety (experience, common sense, reason) itself teach you that for a man to wear long hair is a dishonor [humiliating and degrading] to him,

15 But if a woman has long hair, it is her ornament *and* glory? For her hair is given to her for a covering.

16 Now if anyone is disposed to be argumentative *and* contentious about this, we hold to *and* recognize no other custom [in worship] than this, nor do the churches of God generally.

17 But in what I instruct [you] next I do not commend [you], because when you meet together, it is not for the better but for the worse.

18 For in the first place, when you assemble as a congregation, I hear that there are cliques (divisions and factions) among you; and I in part believe it,

19 For doubtless there have to be factions *or* parties among you in order that they who are genuine *and* of approved fitness may become evident *and* plainly recognized among you.

20 So when you gather for your

---

h Joseph Thayer, *A Greek-English Lexicon. Commentary.*   i G.D. Kypke, cited by Adam Clarke, *The Holy Bible with A Commentary.*

meetings, it is not the supper instituted by the Lord that you eat,

21 For in eating each one [hurries] to get his own supper first [not waiting for the poor], and one goes hungry while another gets drunk.

22 What! Do you have no houses in which to eat and drink? Or do you despise the church of God *and* mean to show contempt for it, while you humiliate those who are poor (have no homes and have brought no food)? What shall I say to you? Shall I commend you in this? No, [most certainly] I will not!

23 For I received from the Lord Himself that which I passed on to you [it was given to me personally], that the Lord Jesus on the night when He was treacherously delivered up *and* while His betrayal was in progress took bread,

24 And when He had given thanks, He broke [it] and said, Take, eat. This is My body, which is broken for you. Do this to call Me [affectionately] to remembrance.

25 Similarly when supper was ended, He took the cup also, saying, This cup is the new covenant [ratified and established] in My blood. Do this, as often as you drink [it], to call Me [affectionately] to remembrance.

26 For every time you eat this bread and drink this cup, you are representing *and* signifying *and* proclaiming the fact of the Lord's death until He comes [again].

27 So then whoever eats the bread or drinks the cup of the Lord in a way that is unworthy [of Him] will be guilty of [profaning and sinning against] the body and blood of the Lord.

28 Let a man [thoroughly] examine himself, and [only when he has done] so should he eat of the bread and drink of the cup.

29 For anyone who eats and drinks without discriminating *and* recognizing with due appreciation that [it is Christ's] body, eats and drinks a sentence (a verdict of judgment) upon himself.

30 That [careless and unworthy participation] is the reason many of you are weak and sickly, and quite enough of you have fallen into the sleep of death.

31 For if we searchingly examined ourselves [detecting our shortcomings and recognizing our own condition], we should not be judged *and* penalty decreed [by the divine judgment].

32 But when we [fall short and] are judged by the Lord, we are disciplined *and* chastened, so that we may not [finally] be condemned [to eternal punishment along] with the world.

33 So then, my brothers, when you gather together to eat [the Lord's Supper], wait for one another.

34 If anyone is hungry, let him eat at home, lest you come together to bring judgment [on yourselves]. About the other matters, I will give you directions [personally] when I come.

CHAPTER 12

NOW ABOUT the spiritual gifts (the special endowments of supernatural energy), brethren, I do not want you to be misinformed.

2 You know that when you were heathen, you were led off after idols that could not speak [habitually] as impulse directed *and* whenever the occasion might arise.

3 Therefore I want you to understand that no one speaking under the power *and* influence of the [Holy] Spirit of God can [ever] say, Jesus be cursed! And no one can [really] say, Jesus is [my] Lord, except by *and* under the power *and* influence of the Holy Spirit.

4 Now there are distinctive varieties *and* distributions of endowments (gifts, [j]extraordinary powers distinguishing certain Christians, due to the power of divine grace operating in their souls by the Holy Spirit) and they vary, but the [Holy] Spirit remains the same.

5 And there are distinctive varieties of service *and* ministration, but it is the same Lord [Who is served].

6 And there are distinctive varieties of operation [of working to accomplish things], but it is the same God Who inspires *and* energizes them all in all.

7 But to each one is given the manifestation of the [Holy] Spirit [the evidence, the spiritual illumination of the Spirit] for good *and* profit.

8 To one is given in *and* through the [Holy] Spirit [the power to speak] a message of wisdom, and to another [the power to express] a word of knowledge *and* understanding according to the same [Holy] Spirit;

9 To another [[k]wonder-working] faith by the same [Holy] Spirit, to another the extraordinary powers of healing by the one Spirit;

10 To another the working of miracles, to another prophetic insight ([l]the gift of interpreting the divine will and purpose); to another the ability to discern *and* distinguish between [the utterances of true] spirits [and false ones], to another various kinds of [unknown] tongues, to another the ability to interpret [such] tongues.

11 All these [gifts, achievements, abilities] are inspired *and* brought to pass by one and the same [Holy] Spirit, Who apportions to each person individually [exactly] as He chooses.

12 For just as the body is a unity and yet has many parts, and all the parts, though many, form [only] one body, so it is with Christ (the Messiah, the Anointed One).

13 For by [[m]means of the personal agency of] one [Holy] Spirit we were all, whether Jews or Greeks, slaves or free, baptized [and [j]by baptism united together] into one body, and all made to drink of one [Holy] Spirit.

14 For the body does not consist of one limb *or* organ but of many.

15 If the foot should say, Because I am not the hand, I do not belong to the body, would it be therefore not [a part] of the body?

16 If the ear should say, Because I am not the eye, I do not belong to the body, would it be therefore not [a part] of the body?

17 If the whole body were an eye, where [would be the sense of] hearing? If the whole body were an ear, where [would be the sense of] smell?

18 But as it is, God has placed *and* arranged the limbs *and* organs in the body, each [particular one] of them, just as He wished *and* saw fit *and* with the best adaptation.

19 But if [the whole] were all a single organ, where would the body be?

20 And now there are [certainly] many limbs *and* organs, but a single body.

21 And the eye is not able to say to the hand, I have no need of you, nor again the head to the feet, I have no need of you.

22 But instead, there is [absolute] necessity for the parts of the body that are considered the more weak.

23 And those [parts] of the body which we consider rather ignoble are [the very parts] which we invest with additional honor, and our unseemly parts *and* those unsuitable for expo-

---

[j] Joseph Thayer, *A Greek-English Lexicon.*   [k] Marvin Vincent, *Word Studies.*   [l] G. Abbott-Smith, *Manual Greek Lexicon.*   [m] Kenneth Wuest, *Word Studies.*

sure arc treated with seemliness (modesty and decorum),

24 Which our more presentable parts do not require. But God has so adjusted (mingled, harmonized, and subtly proportioned the parts of) the whole body, giving the greater honor and richer endowment to the inferior parts which lack [apparent importance],

25 So that there should be no division or discord or lack of adaptation [of the parts of the body to each other], but the members all alike should have a mutual interest in and care for one another.

26 And if one member suffers, all the parts [share] the suffering; if one member is honored, all the members [share in] the enjoyment of it.

27 Now you [collectively] are Christ's body and [individually] you are members of it, each part severally and distinct [each with his own place and function].

28 So God has appointed some in the church [[n]for His own use]: first apostles (special messengers); second prophets (inspired preachers and expounders); third teachers; then wonder-workers; then those with ability to heal the sick; helpers; administrators; [speakers in] different (unknown) tongues.

29 Are all apostles (special messengers)? Are all prophets (inspired interpreters of the will and purposes of God)? Are all teachers? Do all have the power of performing miracles?

30 Do all possess extraordinary powers of healing? Do all speak with tongues? Do all interpret?

31 But earnestly desire and zealously cultivate the greatest and best gifts and graces (the higher gifts and the choicest graces). And yet I will show you a still more excellent way [one that is better by far and the highest of them all—love].

CHAPTER 13

IF I [can] speak in the tongues of men and [even] of angels, but have not love (that reasoning, intentional, spiritual devotion such [o]as is inspired by God's love for and in us), I am only a noisy gong or a clanging cymbal.

2 And if I have prophetic powers ([p]the gift of interpreting the divine will and purpose), and understand all the secret truths and mysteries and possess all knowledge, and if I have [sufficient] faith so that I can remove mountains, but have not love (God's love in me) I am nothing (a useless nobody).

3 Even if I dole out all that I have [to the poor in providing] food, and if I surrender my body to be burned or [q]in order that I may glory, but have not love (God's love in me), I gain nothing.

4 Love endures long and is patient and kind; love never is envious nor boils over with jealousy, is not boastful or vainglorious, does not display itself haughtily.

5 It is not conceited (arrogant and inflated with pride); it is not rude (unmannerly) and does not act unbecomingly. Love (God's love in us) does not insist on its own rights or its own way, for it is not self-seeking; it is not touchy or fretful or resentful; it takes no account of the evil done to it [it pays no attention to a suffered wrong].

6 It does not rejoice at injustice and unrighteousness, but rejoices when right and truth prevail.

7 Love bears up under anything and everything that comes, is ever

---

n Marvin Vincent, Word Studies.   o Alexander Souter, Pocket Lexicon.   p G. Abbott-Smith, Manual Greek Lexicon.   q Some ancient manuscripts so read.

ready to believe the best of every person, its hopes are fadeless under all circumstances, and it endures everything [without weakening].

8 Love never fails [never fades out or becomes obsolete or comes to an end]. As for prophecy ([r]the gift of interpreting the divine will and purpose), it will be fulfilled *and* pass away; as for tongues, they will be destroyed *and* cease; as for knowledge, it will pass away [it will lose its value and be superseded by truth].

9 For our knowledge is fragmentary (incomplete and imperfect), and our prophecy (our teaching) is fragmentary (incomplete and imperfect).

10 But when the complete *and* perfect (total) comes, the incomplete *and* imperfect will vanish away (become antiquated, void, and superseded).

11 When I was a child, I talked like a child, I thought like a child, I reasoned like a child; now that I have become a man, I am done with childish ways *and* have put them aside.

12 For now we are looking in a mirror that gives only a dim (blurred) reflection [of reality as [s]in a riddle or enigma], but then [when perfection comes] we shall see in reality *and* face to face! Now I know in part (imperfectly), but then I shall know *and* understand [s]fully *and* clearly, even in the same manner as I have been [s]fully *and* clearly known *and* understood [[t]by God].

13 And so faith, hope, love abide [faith—conviction and belief respecting man's relation to God and divine things; hope—joyful and confident expectation of eternal salvation; love—true affection for God and man, growing out of God's love for and in us], these three; but the greatest of these is love.

CHAPTER 14

EAGERLY PURSUE *and* seek to acquire [this] love [make it your aim, your great quest]; and earnestly desire *and* cultivate the spiritual endowments (gifts), especially that you may prophesy ([r]interpret the divine will and purpose in inspired preaching and teaching).

2 For one who speaks in an [unknown] tongue speaks not to men but to God, for no one understands *or* catches his meaning, because in the [Holy] Spirit he utters secret truths *and* hidden things [not obvious to the understanding].

3 But [on the other hand], the one who prophesies [who [r]interprets the divine will and purpose in inspired preaching and teaching] speaks to men for their upbuilding *and* constructive spiritual progress and encouragement *and* consolation.

4 He who speaks in a [strange] tongue edifies *and* improves himself, but he who prophesies [[r]interpreting the divine will and purpose and teaching with inspiration] edifies *and* improves the church *and* promotes growth [in Christian wisdom, piety, holiness, and happiness].

5 Now I wish that you might all speak in [unknown] tongues, but more especially [I want you] to prophesy (to be inspired to preach and interpret the divine will and purpose). He who prophesies [who is inspired to preach and teach] is greater (more useful and more important) than he who speaks in [unknown] tongues, unless he should interpret [what he says], so that the church may be edified *and* receive good [from it].

6 Now, brethren, if I come to you speaking in [unknown] tongues, how shall I make it to your advantage un-

r G. Abbott-Smith, *Manual Greek Lexicon.*   s Marvin Vincent, *Word Studies.*   t Matthew Henry, *Commentary on the Holy Bible.*

less I speak to you either in revelation (disclosure of God's will to man) in knowledge or in prophecy or in instruction?

7 If even inanimate musical instruments, such as the flute or the harp, do not give distinct notes, how will any-one [listening] know or understand what is played?

8 And if the war bugle gives an uncertain (indistinct) call, who will prepare for battle?

9 Just so it is with you; if you in the [unknown] tongue speak words that are not intelligible, how will anyone understand what you are saying? For you will be talking into empty space!

10 There are, I suppose, all these many [to us unknown] tongues in the world [somewhere], and none is destitute of [its own power of] expression and meaning.

11 But if I do not know the force and significance of the speech (language), I shall seem to be a foreigner to the one who speaks [to me], and the speaker who addresses [me] will seem a foreigner to me.

12 So it is with yourselves; since you are so eager and ambitious to possess spiritual endowments and manifestations of the [Holy] Spirit, [concentrate on] striving to excel and to abound [in them] in ways that will build up the church.

13 Therefore, the person who speaks in an [unknown] tongue should pray [for the power] to interpret and explain what he says.

14 For if I pray in an [unknown] tongue, my spirit [by the ᵘHoly Spirit within me] prays, but my mind is unproductive [it bears no fruit and helps nobody].

15 Then what am I to do? I will pray with my spirit [by the ᵘHoly Spirit that is within me], but I will also pray [intelligently] with my mind

and understanding; I will sing with my spirit [by the Holy Spirit that is within me], but I will sing [intelligently] with my mind and understanding also.

16 Otherwise, if you bless and render thanks with [your] spirit [ᵛthoroughly aroused by the Holy Spirit], how can anyone in the position of an outsider or he who is not gifted with [interpreting of unknown] tongues, say the Amen to your thanksgiving, since he does not know what you are saying? [I Chron. 16:36; Ps. 106:48.]

17 To be sure, you may give thanks well (nobly), but the bystander is not edified [it does him no good].

18 I thank God that I speak in [strange] tongues (languages) more than any of you or all of you put together;

19 Nevertheless, in public worship, I would rather say five words with my understanding and intelligently in order to instruct others, than ten thousand words in a [strange] tongue (language).

20 Brethren, do not be children [immature] in your thinking; continue to be babes in [matters of] evil, but in your minds be mature [men].

21 It is written in the Law, By men of strange languages and by the lips of foreigners will I speak to this people, and not even then will they listen to Me, says the Lord. [Isa. 28:11, 12.]

22 Thus [unknown] tongues are meant for a [supernatural] sign, not for believers but for unbelievers [on the point of believing], while prophecy (inspired preaching and teaching, interpreting the divine will and purpose) is not for unbelievers [on the point of believing] but for believers.

23 Therefore, if the whole church assembles and all of you speak in [unknown] tongues, and the ungifted and uninitiated or unbelievers come

u Marvin Vincent, Word Studies.   v Joseph Thayer, A Greek-English Lexicon.

in, will they not say that you are demented?

24 But if all prophesy [giving inspired testimony and interpreting the divine will and purpose] and an unbeliever or untaught outsider comes in, he is told of his sin and reproved and convicted and convinced by all, and his defects and needs are examined (estimated, determined) and he is called to account by all,

25 The secrets of his heart are laid bare; and so, falling on [his] face, he will worship God, declaring that God is among you in very truth.

26 What then, brethren, is [the right course]? When you meet together, each one has a hymn, a teaching, a disclosure of special knowledge or information, an utterance in a [strange] tongue, or an interpretation of it. [But] let everything be constructive and edifying and for the good of all.

27 If some speak in a [strange] tongue, let the number be limited to two or at the most three, and each one [taking his] turn, and let one interpret and explain [what is said].

28 But if there is no one to do the interpreting, let each of them keep still in church and talk to himself and to God.

29 So let two or three prophets speak [those inspired to preach or teach], while the rest pay attention and weigh and discern what is said.

30 But if an inspired revelation comes to another who is sitting by, then let the first one be silent.

31 For in this way you can give testimony [prophesying and thus interpreting the divine will and purpose] one by one, so that all may be instructed and all may be stimulated and encouraged;

32 For the spirits of the prophets

(the speakers in tongues) are under the speaker's control [and subject to being silenced as may be necessary].

33 For He [Who is the source of their prophesying] is not a God of confusion and disorder but of peace and order. As [is the practice] in all the churches of the saints (God's people),

34 The women should keep quiet in the churches, for they are not authorized to speak, but should take a secondary and subordinate place, just as the Law also says. [Gen. 3:16.]

35 But if there is anything they want to learn, they should ask their own husbands at home, for it is disgraceful for a woman to talk in church [*for her to usurp and exercise authority over men in the church].

36 What! Did the word of the Lord originate with you [Corinthians], or has it reached only you?

37 If anyone thinks and claims that he is a prophet [filled with and governed by the Holy Spirit of God and inspired to interpret the divine will and purpose in preaching or teaching] or has any other spiritual endowment, let him understand (recognize and acknowledge) that what I am writing to you is a command of the Lord.

38 But if anyone disregards or does not recognize [*that it is a command of the Lord], he is disregarded and not recognized [he is *one whom God knows not].

39 So [to conclude], my brethren, earnestly desire and set your hearts on prophesying (on being inspired to preach and teach and to interpret God's will and purpose), and do not forbid or hinder speaking in [unknown] tongues.

40 But all things should be done

---

w W. Robertson Nicoll, ed., *The Expositor's Greek New Testament.*   x Joseph Thayer, *A Greek-English Lexicon.*   y Marvin Vincent, *Word Studies.* Some manuscripts read: "he is not known."

with regard to decency *and* propriety and in an orderly fashion.

CHAPTER 15

AND NOW let me remind you [since it seems to have escaped you], brethren, of the Gospel (the glad tidings of salvation) which I proclaimed to you, which you welcomed *and* accepted and upon which your faith rests,

2 And by which you are saved, if you hold fast *and* keep firmly what I preached to you, unless you believed at first without effect *and* all for nothing.

3 For I passed on to you first of all what I also had received, that Christ (the Messiah, the Anointed One) died for our sins in accordance with [what] our Scriptures [foretold], [Isa. 53:5–12.]

4 That He was buried, that He arose on the third day as the Scriptures foretold, [Ps. 16:9, 10.]

5 And [also] that He appeared to Cephas (Peter), then to the Twelve.

6 Then later He showed Himself to more than five hundred brethren at one time, the majority of whom are still alive, but some have fallen asleep [in death].

7 Afterward He was seen by James, then by all the apostles (the special messengers),

8 And last of all He appeared to me also, as to one prematurely *and* born dead [²no better than an unperfected fetus among living men].

9 For I am the least [worthy] of the apostles, who am not fit *or* deserving to be called an apostle, because I once wronged *and* pursued *and* molested the church of God [oppressing it with cruelty and violence].

10 But by the grace (the unmerited favor and blessing) of God I am what I am, and His grace toward me was

not [found to be] for nothing (fruitless and without effect). In fact, I worked harder than all of them [the apostles], though it was not really I, but the grace (the unmerited favor and blessing) of God which was with me.

11 So, whether then it was I or they, this is what we preach and this is what you believed [what you adhered to, trusted in, and relied on].

12 But now if Christ (the Messiah) is preached as raised from the dead, how is it that some of you say that there is no resurrection of the dead?

13 But if there is no resurrection of the dead, then Christ has not risen;

14 And if Christ has not risen, then our preaching is in vain *it amounts to nothing* and your faith is devoid of truth *and* is fruitless (without effect, empty, imaginary, and unfounded).

15 We are even discovered to be misrepresenting God, for we testified of Him that He raised Christ, Whom He did not raise in case it is true that the dead are not raised.

16 For if the dead are not raised, then Christ has not been raised;

17 And if Christ has not been raised, your faith is mere delusion [futile, fruitless], and you are still in your sins [under the control and penalty of sin];

18 And further, those who have died in [ªspiritual fellowship and union with] Christ have perished (are lost)!

19 If we who are [abiding] in Christ have hope only in this life *and* that is all, then we are of all people most miserable *and* to be pitied.

20 But the fact is that Christ (the Messiah) has been raised from the dead, and He became the firstfruits of those who have fallen asleep [in death].

21 For since [it was] through a man

---

z Marvin Vincent, *Word Studies.*   a Joseph Thayer, *A Greek-English Lexicon.*

that death [came into the world, it is] also through a Man that the resurrection of the dead [has come].

22 For just as [because of their bunion of nature] in Adam all people die, so also [by virtue of their bunion of nature] shall all in Christ be made alive.

23 But each in his own rank *and* turn: Christ (the Messiah) [is] the firstfruits, then those who are Christ's [own at His coming or are resurrected] at His coming.

24 After that comes the end (the completion), when He delivers over the kingdom to God the Father after rendering inoperative *and* abolishing every [other] rule and every authority and power.

25 For [Christ] must be King *and* reign until He has put all [His] enemies under His feet. [Ps. 110:1.]

26 The last enemy to be subdued *and* abolished is death.

27 For He [the Father] has put all things in subjection under His [Christ's] feet. But when it says, All things are put in subjection [under Him], it is evident that He [Himself] is excepted Who does the subjecting of all things to Him. [Ps. 8:6.]

28 However, when everything is subjected to Him, then the Son Himself will also subject Himself to [the Father] Who put all things under Him, so that God may be all in all [be everything to everyone, supreme, the indwelling and controlling factor of life].

29 Otherwise, what do people mean by being [themselves] baptized in behalf of the dead? If the dead are not raised at all, why are people baptized for them?

30 [For that matter], why do I live [dangerously as I do, running such risks that I am] in peril every hour?

31 [I assure you] by the pride which I have in you in [your cfellowship and union with] Christ Jesus our Lord, that I die daily [I face death every day and die to self].

32 What do I gain if, merely from the human point of view, I fought with [wild] beasts at Ephesus? If the dead are not raised [at all], let us eat and drink, for tomorrow we will be dead. [Isa. 22:13.]

33 Do not be so deceived *and* misled! Evil companionships (communion, associations) corrupt *and* deprave good manners *and* morals *and* character.

34 Awake [dfrom your drunken stupor and return] to sober sense *and* your right minds, and sin no more. For some of you have not the knowledge of God [you are utterly and willfully and disgracefully ignorant, and continue to be so, lacking the sense of God's presence and all true knowledge of Him]. I say this to your shame.

35 But someone will say, How can the dead be raised? With what [kind of] body will they come forth?

36 You foolish man! Every time you plant seed, you sow something that does not come to life [germinating, springing up, and growing] unless it dies first.

37 Nor is the seed you sow then the body which it is going to have [later], but it is a naked kernel, perhaps of wheat or some of the rest of the grains.

38 But God gives to it the body that He plans *and* sees fit, and to each kind of seed a body of its own. [Gen. 1:11.]

39 For all flesh is not the same, but there is one kind for humans, another for beasts, another for birds, and another for fish.

b Robert Jamieson, A.R. Fausset and David Brown, *A Commentary.* c Joseph Thayer, *A Greek-English Lexicon.* d Marvin Vincent, *Word Studies.*

40 There are heavenly bodies (sun, moon, and stars) and there are earthly bodies (men, animals, and plants), but the beauty *and* glory of the heavenly bodies is of one kind, while the beauty *and* glory of earthly bodies is a different kind.

41 The sun is glorious in one way, the moon is glorious in another way, and the stars are glorious in their own [distinctive] way; for one star differs from *and* surpasses another in its beauty *and* brilliance.

42 So it is with the resurrection of the dead. [The body] that is sown is perishable *and* decays, but [the body] that is resurrected is imperishable (immune to decay, immortal). [Dan. 12:3.]

43 It is sown in dishonor *and* humiliation; it is raised in honor *and* glory. It is sown in infirmity *and* weakness; it is resurrected in strength *and* endued with power.

44 It is sown a natural (physical) body; it is raised a supernatural (a spiritual) body. [As surely as] there is a physical body, there is also a spiritual body.

45 Thus it is written, The first man Adam became a living being (an individual personality); the last Adam (Christ) became a life-giving Spirit [restoring the dead to life]. [Gen. 2:7.]

46 But it is not the spiritual life which came first, but the physical and then the spiritual.

47 The first man [was] from out of earth, made of dust (earthly-minded); the second Man [is] *the Lord* from out of heaven. [Gen. 2:7.]

48 Now those who are made of the dust are like him who was first made of the dust (earthly-minded); and as is [the Man] from heaven, so also [are

those] who are of heaven (heavenly-minded).

49 And just as we have borne the image [of the man] of dust, so shall we *and so* [e]*let us* also bear the image [of the Man] of heaven.

50 But I tell you this, brethren, flesh and blood cannot [become partakers of eternal salvation and] inherit *or* share in the kingdom of God; nor does the perishable (that which is decaying) inherit *or* share in the imperishable (the immortal).

51 Take notice! I tell you a mystery (a secret truth, an event decreed by the hidden purpose or counsel of God). We shall not all fall asleep [in death], but we shall all be changed (transformed)

52 In a moment, in the twinkling of an eye, at the [sound of the] last trumpet call. For a trumpet will sound, and the dead [in Christ] will be raised imperishable (free and immune from decay), and we shall be changed (transformed).

53 For this perishable [part of us] must put on the imperishable [nature], and this mortal [part of us, this nature that is capable of dying] must put on immortality (freedom from death).

54 And when this perishable puts on the imperishable and this that was capable of dying puts on freedom from death, then shall be fulfilled the Scripture that says, Death is swallowed up (utterly vanquished [f]forever) in *and* unto victory. [Isa. 25:8.]

55 O death, where is your victory? O death, where is your sting? [Hos. 13:14.]

56 Now sin is the sting of death, and sin exercises its power [g][upon the soul] through [g][the abuse of] the Law.

57 But thanks be to God, Who

e Many ancient manuscripts read "let us."   f Marvin Vincent, *Word Studies.*   g Joseph Thayer, *A Greek-English Lexicon.*

gives us the victory [making us conquerors] through our Lord Jesus Christ.

58 Therefore, my beloved brethren, be firm (steadfast), immovable, always abounding in the work of the Lord [always being superior, excelling, doing more than enough in the service of the Lord], knowing *and* being continually aware that your labor in the Lord is not futile [it is never wasted or to no purpose].

CHAPTER 16

NOW CONCERNING the money contributed for [the relief of] the saints (God's people): you are to do the same as I directed the churches of Galatia to do.

2 On the first [day] of each week, let each one of you [personally] put aside something and save it up as he has prospered [in proportion to what he is given], so that no collections will need to be taken after I come.

3 And when I arrive, I will send on those whom you approve *and* authorize with credentials to carry your gift [of charity] to Jerusalem.

4 If it seems worthwhile that I should go too, they will accompany me.

5 After passing through Macedonia, I will visit you, for I intend [only] to pass through Macedonia;

6 But it may be that I will stay with you [for a while], perhaps even spend the winter, so that you may bring me forward [on my journey] to wherever I may go.

7 For I am unwilling to see you right now [just] in passing, but I hope later to remain for some time with you, if the Lord permits.

8 I will remain in Ephesus [however] until Pentecost,

9 For a wide door of opportunity

for effectual [service] has opened to me [there, a great and promising one], and [there are] many adversaries.

10 When Timothy arrives, see to it that [you put him at ease, so that] he may be fearless among you, for he is [devotedly] doing the Lord's work, just as I am.

11 So [see to it that] no one despises him *or* treats him as if he were of no account *or* slights him. But send him off [cordially, speed him on his way] in peace, that he may come to me, for I am expecting him [to come along] with the other brethren.

12 As for our brother Apollos, I have urgently encouraged him to visit you with the other brethren, but it was not at all his will *or* [h]God's will that he should go now. He will come when he has opportunity.

13 Be alert *and* on your guard; stand firm in your faith ([i]your conviction respecting man's relationship to God and divine things, keeping the trust and holy fervor born of faith and a part of it). Act like men *and* be courageous; grow in strength! [Ps. 31:24.]

14 Let everything you do be done in love (true love to God and man as inspired by God's love for us).

15 Now, brethren, you know that the household of Stephanas were the first converts *and* our firstfruits in Achaia (most of Greece), and how they have consecrated *and* devoted themselves to the service of the saints (God's people).

16 I urge you to pay all deference to such leaders *and* to enlist under them *and* be subject to them, as well as to everyone who joins *and* cooperates [with you] *and* labors earnestly.

17 I am happy because Stephanas and Fortunatus and Achaicus have

---

h Although "his" may refer to Apollos, the probable reference here is to "God's will."   i Joseph Thayer, *A Greek-English Lexicon.*

come [to me], for they have made up
for your absence.

18 For they gave me 'respite from
labor *and* rested me *and* refreshed
my spirit as well as yours. Deeply
appreciate *and* thoroughly know *and*
fully recognize such men.

19 The churches of Asia send
greetings *and* best wishes. Aquila
and Prisca, together with the church
[that meets] in their house, send you
their hearty greetings in the Lord.

20 All the brethren wish to be remembered to you *and* wish you well.
Greet one another with a holy kiss.

21 I, Paul, [add this final] greeting
with my own hand.

22 If anyone does not love the
Lord [does not have a friendly affection for Him and is not kindly disposed toward Him], he shall be accursed! Our Lord will come!
(Maranatha!)

23 The grace (favor and spiritual
blessing) of our Lord Jesus *Christ* be
with you.

24 My love (that true love growing
out of sincere devotion to God) be
with you all in Christ Jesus. *Amen (so
be it)*.

THE SECOND LETTER OF PAUL TO THE
CORINTHIANS

CHAPTER 1

PAUL, AN apostle (a special messenger) of Christ Jesus by the
will of God, and Timothy [our] brother, to the church (assembly) of God
which is at Corinth, and to all the
saints (the people of God) throughout
Achaia (most of Greece):

2 Grace (favor and spiritual bless-
ing) to you and [heart] peace from
God our Father and the Lord Jesus
Christ (the Messiah, the Anointed
One).

3 Blessed be the God and Father of
our Lord Jesus Christ, the Father of
sympathy (pity and mercy) and the
God [Who is the Source] of every
comfort (consolation and encouragement),

4 Who comforts (consoles and encourages) us in every trouble (calamity and affliction), so that we may
also be able to comfort (console and

encourage) those who are in any kind
of trouble *or* distress, with the comfort (consolation and encouragement) with which we ourselves are
comforted (consoled and encouraged) by God.

5 For just as Christ's ['own] sufferings fall to our lot '[as they overflow
upon His disciples, and we share and
experience them] abundantly, so
through Christ comfort (consolation
and encouragement) is also [shared
and experienced] abundantly by us.

6 But if we are troubled (afflicted
and distressed), it is for your comfort
(consolation and encouragement)
and [for your] salvation; and if we are
comforted (consoled and encouraged), it is for your comfort (consolation and encouragement), which
works [in you when you] patiently
endure the same evils (misfortunes

j G. Abbott-Smith, *Manual Greek Lexicon*.   k Marvin Vincent, *Word Studies in the New Testament*.
l Marvin Vincent, *Word Studies*.

and calamities) that we also suffer *and* undergo.

7 And our hope for you [our joyful and confident expectation of good for you] is ever unwavering (assured and unshaken); for we know that just as you share *and* are partners in [our] sufferings *and* calamities, you also share *and* are partners in [our] comfort (consolation and encouragement).

8 For we do not want you to be uninformed, brethren, about the affliction *and* oppressing distress which befell us in [the province of] Asia, how we were so utterly and unbearably weighed down *and* crushed that we despaired even of life [itself].

9 Indeed, we felt within ourselves that we had received the [very] sentence of death, but that was to keep us from trusting in *and* depending on ourselves instead of on God Who raises the dead.

10 [For it is He] Who rescued *and* saved us from such a perilous death, and He will still rescue *and* save us; in *and* on Him we have set our hope (our joyful and confident expectation) that He will again deliver us [from danger and destruction and [m]draw us to Himself],

11 While you also cooperate by your prayers for us [helping and laboring together with us]. Thus [the lips of] many persons [turned toward God will eventually] give thanks on our behalf for the grace (the blessing of deliverance) granted us at the request of the many who have prayed.

12 It is a reason for pride *and* exultation to which our conscience testifies that we have conducted ourselves in the world [generally] and especially toward you, with devout *and* pure motives and godly sinceri-

ty, not in fleshly wisdom but by the grace of God (the unmerited favor and [n]merciful kindness by which God, exerting His holy influence upon souls, turns them to Christ, and keeps, strengthens, and increases them in Christian virtues).

13 For we write you nothing else but simply what you can read and understand [there is no double meaning to what we say], and I hope that you will become thoroughly acquainted with [o]divine things] and know *and* understand [them] accurately *and* well to the end,

14 [Just] as you have [already] partially known *and* understood *and* acknowledged us *and* recognized that you can [honestly] be proud of us, even as we [can be proud] of you on the day of our Lord Jesus.

15 It was with assurance of this that I wanted *and* planned to visit you first [of all], so that you might have a double favor *and* token of grace (goodwill).

16 [I wanted] to visit you on my way to Macedonia, and [then] to come again to you [on my return trip] from Macedonia and have you send me forward on my way to Judea.

17 Now because I changed my original plan, was I being unstable *and* capricious? Or what I plan, do I plan according to the flesh [like a worldly man], ready to say Yes, yes, [when it may mean] No, no?

18 As surely as God is trustworthy *and* faithful *and* means what He says, our speech *and* message to you have not been Yes [that might mean] No.

19 For the Son of God, Christ Jesus (the Messiah), Who has been preached among you by us, by myself, Silvanus, and Timothy, was not

---

m Joseph Thayer, *A Greek-English Lexicon of the New Testament*: Primary meaning: "to draw to one's self."
n Joseph Thayer, *A Greek-English Lexicon*.   o Joseph Thayer, *A Greek-English Lexicon of the New Testament*.

Yes and No; but in Him it is [always the divine] Yes.

20 For as many as are the promises of God, they all find their Yes [answer] in Him [Christ]. For this reason we also utter the Amen (so be it) to God through Him [in His Person and by His agency] to the glory of God.

21 But it is God Who confirms and makes us steadfast and establishes us [in joint fellowship with you in Christ, and has consecrated and anointed us [^penduing us with the gifts of the Holy Spirit];

22 [He has also appropriated and acknowledged us as His by] putting His seal upon us and giving us His [Holy] Spirit in our hearts as the security deposit and guarantee [of the fulfillment of His promise].

23 But I call upon God as my soul's witness: it was to avoid hurting you that I refrained from coming to Corinth—

24 Not that we have dominion [over you] and lord it over your faith, but [rather that we work with you as] fellow laborers [to promote] your joy, for in [your] faith (^qhas a helpful insight here in his comment on I John 2:20.in your strong and welcome conviction or belief that Jesus is the Messiah, through Whom we obtain eternal salvation in the kingdom of God) you stand firm.

CHAPTER 2

BUT I definitely made up my mind not to grieve you with another painful and distressing visit.

2 For if I cause you pain [with merited rebuke], who is there to provide me enjoyment but the [very] one whom I have grieved and made sad?

3 And I wrote the same to you so that when I came, I might not be my-

self pained by those who are the [very] ones who ought to make me glad, for I trusted in you all and felt confident that my joy would be shared by all of you.

4 For I wrote you out of great sorrow and deep distress [with mental torture and anxiety] of heart, [yes, and] with many tears, not to cause you pain but in order to make you realize the overflowing love that I continue increasingly to have for you.

5 But if someone [the one among you who committed incest] has caused [all this] grief and pain, he has caused it not to me, but in some measure, not to put it too severely, [he has distressed] all of you.

6 For such a one this censure by the majority [which he has received is] sufficient [punishment].

7 So [instead of further rebuke, now] you should rather turn and [graciously] forgive and comfort and encourage [him], to keep him from being overwhelmed by excessive sorrow and despair.

8 I therefore beg you to reinstate him in your affections and assure him of your love for him;

9 For this was my purpose in writing you, to test your attitude and see if you would stand the test, whether you are obedient and altogether agreeable [to following my orders] in everything.

10 If you forgive anyone anything, I too forgive that one; and what I have forgiven, if I have forgiven anything, has been for your sakes in the presence [and with the approval] of Christ (the Messiah),

11 To keep Satan from getting the advantage over us; for we are not ignorant of his wiles and intentions.

12 Now when I arrived at Troas [to

p Brooke F. Westcott, *The Epistles of Saint John*, has a helpful insight here in his comment on I John 2:20.
q Joseph Thayer, *A Greek-English Lexicon*.

preach] the good news (the Gospel) of Christ, a door of opportunity was opened for me in the Lord.

13 Yet my spirit could not rest (relax, get relief) because I did not find my brother Titus there. So I took leave from them *and* departed for Macedonia.

14 But thanks be to God, Who in Christ always leads us in triumph [as trophies of Christ's victory] and through us spreads *and* makes evident the fragrance of the knowledge of God everywhere,

15 For we are the sweet fragrance of Christ [which exhales] unto God, [discernible alike] among those who are being saved *and* among those who are perishing:

16 To the latter it is an aroma [wafted] from death to death [a fatal odor, the smell of doom]; to the former it is an aroma from life to life [a vital fragrance, living and fresh]. And who is qualified (fit and sufficient) for these things? [Who is able for such a ministry? We?]

17 For we are not, like so many, [like hucksters making a trade of] peddling God's Word [shortchanging and adulterating the divine message]; but like [men] of sincerity *and* the purest motive, as [commissioned and sent] by God, we speak [His message] in Christ (the Messiah), in the [very] sight *and* presence of God.

CHAPTER 3

ARE WE starting to commend ourselves again? Or we do not, like some [false teachers], need written credentials *or* letters of recommendation to you or from you, [do we]?

2 [No] you yourselves are our letter of recommendation (our credentials), written in ʳyour hearts, to be known (perceived, recognized) and read by everybody.

3 You show *and* make obvious that you are a letter from Christ delivered by us, not written with ink but with [the] Spirit of [the] living God, not on tablets of stone but on tablets of human hearts. [Exod. 24:12; 31:18; 32:15, 16; Jer. 31:33.]

4 Such is the reliance *and* confidence that we have through Christ toward *and* with reference to God.

5 Not that we are fit (qualified and sufficient in ability) of ourselves to form personal judgments *or* to claim *or* count anything as coming from us, but our power *and* ability *and* sufficiency are from God.

6 [It is He] Who has qualified us [making us to be fit and worthy and sufficient] as ministers *and* dispensers of a new covenant [of salvation through Christ], not [ministers] of the letter (of legally written code) but of the Spirit; for the code [of the Law] kills, but the [Holy] Spirit makes alive. [Jer. 31:31.]

7 Now if the dispensation of death engraved in letters on stone [the ministration of the Law], was inaugurated with such glory *and* splendor that the Israelites were not able to look steadily at the face of Moses because of its brilliance, [a glory] that was to fade *and* pass away, [Exod. 34:29–35.]

8 Why should not the dispensation of the Spirit [this spiritual ˢministry whose task it is to cause men to obtain and be governed by the Holy Spirit] be attended with much greater *and* more splendid glory?

9 For if the service that condemns [the ministration of doom] had glory, how infinitely more abounding in splendor *and* glory must be the service that makes righteous [the ministry that produces and fosters righteous living and right standing with God]!

r Many ancient manuscripts read "our."   s Joseph Thayer, *A Greek-English Lexicon*.

10 Indeed, in view of this fact, what once had splendor ['the glory of the Law in the face of Moses] has come to have no splendor at all, because of the overwhelming glory that exceeds *and* excels it ['the glory of the Gospel in the face of Jesus Christ].

11 For if that which was but passing *and* fading away came with splendor, how much more must that which remains *and* is permanent abide in glory *and* splendor!

12 Since we have such [glorious] hope (such joyful and confident expectation), we speak very freely *and* openly *and* fearlessly.

13 Nor [do we act] like Moses, who put a veil over his face so that the Israelites might not gaze upon the finish of the vanishing [splendor which had been upon it].

14 In fact, their minds were grown hard *and* calloused [they had become dull and had lost the power of understanding]; for until this present day, when the Old Testament (the old covenant) is being read, that same veil still lies [on their hearts], not being lifted [to reveal] that in Christ it is made void *and* done away.

15 Yes, down to this [very] day whenever Moses is read, a veil lies upon their minds *and* hearts.

16 But whenever a person turns [in repentance] to the Lord, the veil is stripped off *and* taken away.

17 Now the Lord is the Spirit, and where the Spirit of the Lord is, there is liberty (emancipation from bondage, freedom). [Isa. 61:1, 2.]

18 And all of us, as with unveiled face, [because we] continued to behold [in the Word of God] as in a mirror the glory of the Lord, are constantly being transfigured into His *very own* image in ever increasing splendor *and* from one degree of glory to another: [for this comes] from the Lord [Who is] the Spirit.

CHAPTER 4

THEREFORE, SINCE we do hold *and* engage in this ministry by the mercy of God [granting us favor, benefits, opportunities, and especially salvation], we do not get discouraged (spiritless and despondent with fear) *or* become faint with weariness and exhaustion.

2 We have renounced disgraceful ways (secret thoughts, feelings, desires and underhandedness, the methods and arts that men hide through shame); we refuse to deal craftily (to practice trickery and cunning) or to adulterate *or* handle dishonestly the Word of God, but we state the truth openly (clearly and candidly). And so we commend ourselves in the sight *and* presence of God to every man's conscience.

3 But even if our Gospel (the glad tidings) also be hidden (obscured and covered up with a veil that hinders the knowledge of God), it is hidden [only] to those who are perishing *and* obscured [only] to those who are spiritually dying *and* veiled [only] to those who are lost.

4 For the god of this world has blinded the unbelievers' minds [that they should not discern the truth], preventing them from seeing the illuminating light of the Gospel of the glory of Christ (the Messiah), Who is the Image *and* Likeness of God.

5 For what we preach is not ourselves but Jesus Christ as Lord, and ourselves [merely] as your servants (slaves) for Jesus' sake.

6 For God Who said, Let light shine out of darkness, has shone in our hearts so as [to beam forth] the Light for the illumination of the knowledge of the majesty *and* glory

† Marvin Vincent, *Word Studies*.

of God [as it is manifest in the Person and is revealed] in the face of *Jesus* Christ (the Messiah). [Gen. 1:3.]

7 However, we possess this precious treasure [the divine Light of the Gospel] in [frail, human] vessels of earth, that the grandeur *and* exceeding greatness of the power may be shown to be from God and not from ourselves.

8 We are hedged in (pressed) on every side [troubled and oppressed in every way], but not cramped *or* crushed; we suffer embarrassments *and* are perplexed *and* unable to find a way out, but not driven to despair;

9 We are pursued (persecuted and hard driven), but not deserted [to stand alone]; we are struck down to the ground, but never struck out *and* destroyed;

10 Always carrying about in the body the liability *and* exposure to the same putting to death that *the Lord* Jesus suffered, so that the [ᵘresurrection] life of Jesus also may be shown forth by *and* in our bodies.

11 For we who live are constantly [experiencing] being handed over to death for Jesus' sake, that the [ᵛresurrection] life of Jesus also may be evidenced through our flesh which is liable to death.

12 Thus death is actively at work in us, but [it is in order that ᵛour] life [may be actively at work] in you.

13 Yet we have the same spirit of faith as he had who wrote, I have believed, and therefore have I spoken. We too believe, and therefore we speak, [Ps. 116:10.]

14 Assured that He Who raised up the Lord Jesus will raise us up also with Jesus and bring us [along] with you into His presence.

15 For all [these] things are [taking place] for your sake, so that the more grace (divine favor and spiritual

blessing) extends to more and more people *and* multiplies through the many, the more thanksgiving may increase [and redound] to the glory of God.

16 Therefore we do not become discouraged (utterly spiritless, exhausted, and wearied out through fear). Though our outer man is [progressively] decaying *and* wasting away, yet our inner self is being [progressively] renewed day after day.

17 For our light, momentary affliction (this slight distress of the passing hour) is ever more and more abundantly preparing *and* producing *and* achieving for us an everlasting weight of glory [beyond all measure, excessively surpassing all comparisons and all calculations, a vast and transcendent glory and blessedness never to cease!],

18 Since we consider *and* look not to the things that are seen but to the things that are unseen; for the things that are visible are temporal (brief and fleeting), but the things that are invisible are deathless *and* everlasting.

CHAPTER 5

FOR WE know that if the tent which is our earthly home is destroyed (dissolved), we have from God a building, a house not made with hands, eternal in the heavens.

2 Here indeed, in this [present abode, body], we sigh *and* groan inwardly, because we yearn to be clothed over [we yearn to put on our celestial body like a garment, to be fitted out] with our heavenly dwelling,

3 So that by putting it on we may not be found naked (without a body).

4 For while we are still in this tent, we groan under the burden *and* sigh

---

u Marvin Vincent, *Word Studies.*   v Joseph Thayer, *A Greek-English Lexicon.*

deeply (weighed down, depressed, oppressed)—not that we want to put off the body (the clothing of the spirit), but rather that we would be further clothed, so that what is mortal (our dying body) may be swallowed up by life [*after the resurrection].

5 Now He Who has fashioned us [preparing and making us fit] for this very thing is God, Who also has given us the [Holy] Spirit as a guarantee [of the fulfillment of His promise].

6 So then, we are always full of good and hopeful and confident courage; we know that while we are at home in the body, we are abroad from the home with the Lord [that is promised us].

7 For we walk by faith [we *regulate our lives and conduct ourselves by our conviction or belief respecting man's relationship to God and divine things, with trust and holy fervor; thus we walk] not by sight or appearance.

8 [Yes] we have confident and hopeful courage and are pleased rather to be away from home out of the body and be at home with the Lord.

9 Therefore, whether we are at home [on earth away from Him] or away from home [and with Him], we are constantly ambitious and strive earnestly to be pleasing to Him.

10 For we must all appear and be revealed as we are before the judgment seat of Christ, so that each one may receive [his pay] according to what he has done in the body, whether good or evil [considering *what his purpose and motive have been, and what he has *achieved, been busy with, and given himself and his attention to accomplishing].

11 Therefore, being conscious of fearing the Lord with respect and reverence, we seek to win people over [to persuade them]. But *what sort of persons we are is plainly recognized and thoroughly understood by God, and I hope that it is plainly recognized and thoroughly understood also by your consciences (your inborn discernment).

12 We are not commending ourselves to you again, but we are providing you with an occasion and incentive to be [rightfully] proud of us, so that you may have a reply for those who pride themselves on surface appearances [*on the virtues they only appear to have], although their heart is devoid of them.

13 For if we are beside ourselves [mad, as some say], it is for God and concerns Him; if we are in our right mind, it is for your benefit.

14 For the love of Christ controls and urges and impels us, because we are of the opinion and conviction that [if] One died for all, then all died;

15 And He died for all, so that all those who live might live no longer to and for themselves, but to and for Him Who died and was raised again for their sake.

16 Consequently, from now on we estimate and regard no one from a [purely] human point of view [in terms of natural standards of value]. [No] even though we once did estimate Christ from a human viewpoint and as a man, yet now [we have such knowledge of Him that] we know Him no longer [in terms of the flesh].

17 Therefore if any person is [ingrafted] in Christ (the Messiah) he is a new creation (a new creature altogether); the old [previous moral and spiritual condition] has passed away. Behold, the fresh and new has come!

18 But all things are from God, Who through *Jesus* Christ reconciled

---

w Joseph Thayer, *A Greek-English Lexicon.*   x Alexander Souter, *Pocket Lexicon of the Greek New Testament.*

us to Himself [received us into favor, brought us into harmony with Himself] and gave to us the ministry of reconciliation [that by word and deed we might aim to bring others into harmony with Him].

19 It was God [personally present] in Christ, reconciling and restoring the world to favor with Himself, not counting up and holding against [men] their trespasses [but cancelling them], and committing to us the message of reconciliation (of the restoration to favor).

20 So we are Christ's ambassadors, God making His appeal as it were through us. We [as Christ's personal representatives] beg you for His sake to lay hold of the divine favor [now offered you] and be reconciled to God.

21 For our sake He made Christ [virtually] to be sin Who knew no sin, so that in and through Him we might become [ʸendued with, viewed as being in, and examples of] the righteousness of God [what we ought to be, approved and acceptable and in right relationship with Him, by His goodness].

CHAPTER 6

LABORING TOGETHER [as God's fellow workers] with Him then, we beg of you not to receive the grace of God in vain [that ᶻmerciful kindness by which God exerts His holy influence on souls and turns them to Christ, keeping and strengthening them—do not receive it to no purpose].

2 For He says, In the time of favor (of an assured welcome) I have listened to and heeded your call, and I have helped you on the day of deliverance (the day of salvation). Behold, now is truly the time for a gracious welcome and acceptance [of

you from God]; behold, now is the day of salvation! [Isa. 49:8.]

3 We put no obstruction in anybody's way [we give no offense in anything], so that no fault may be found and [our] ministry blamed and discredited.

4 But we commend ourselves in every way as [true] servants of God: through great endurance, in tribulation and suffering, in hardships and privations, in sore straits and calamities,

5 In beatings, imprisonments, riots, labors, sleepless watching, hunger;

6 By innocence and purity, knowledge and spiritual insight, longsuffering and patience, kindness, in the Holy Spirit, in unfeigned love;

7 By [speaking] the word of truth, in the power of God, with the weapons of righteousness for the right hand [to attack] and for the left hand [to defend];

8 Amid honor and dishonor; in defaming and evil report and in praise and good report. [We are branded] as deceivers (impostors), and [yet vindicated as] truthful and honest.

9 [We are treated] as unknown and ignored [by the world], and [yet we are] well-known and recognized [by God and His people]; as dying, and yet here we are alive; as chastened by suffering and [yet] not killed;

10 As grieved and mourning, yet [we are] always rejoicing; as poor [ourselves, yet] bestowing riches on many; as having nothing, and [yet in reality] possessing all things.

11 Our mouth is open to you, Corinthians [we are hiding nothing, keeping nothing back], and our heart is expanded wide [for you]! [Isa. 60:5; Ezek.33:22.]

12 There is no lack of room for you

in [our hearts], but you lack room in your own affections [for us].

13 By way of return then, do this for me—I speak as to children—open wide your hearts also [to us].

14 Do not be unequally yoked with unbelievers [do not make mismated alliances with them or come under a different yoke with them, inconsistent with your faith]. For what partnership have right living and right standing with God have with iniquity and lawlessness? Or how can light have fellowship with darkness?

15 What harmony can there be between Christ and Belial [the devil]? Or what has a believer in common with an unbeliever?

16 What agreement [can there be between] a temple of God and idols? For we are the temple of the living God; even as God said, I will dwell in and with and among them and will walk in and with and among them, and I will be their God, and they shall be My people. [Exod. 25:8; 29:45; Lev. 26:12; Jer. 31:1; Ezek. 37:27.]

17 So, come out from among [unbelievers], and separate (sever) yourselves from them, says the Lord, and touch not [any] unclean thing; then I will receive you kindly and treat you with favor, [Isa. 52:11.]

18 And I will be a Father to you, and you shall be My sons and daughters, says the Lord Almighty. [Isa. 43:6; Hos. 1:10.]

CHAPTER 7

THEREFORE, SINCE these [great] promises are ours, beloved, let us cleanse ourselves from everything that contaminates and defiles body and spirit, and bring [our] consecration to completeness in the [reverential] fear of God.

2 Do open your hearts to us again [enlarge them to take us in]. We have wronged no one, we have betrayed

or corrupted no one, we have cheated or taken advantage of no one.

3 I do not say this to reproach or condemn [you], for I have said before that you are [nested] in our hearts, [and you will remain there] together [with us], whether we die or live.

4 I have great boldness and free and fearless confidence and cheerful courage toward you; my pride in you is great. I am filled [brimful] with the comfort [of it]; with all our tribulation and in spite of it, [I am filled with comfort] I am overflowing with joy.

5 For even when we arrived in Macedonia, our bodies had no ease or rest, but we were oppressed in every way and afflicted at every turn —fighting and contentions without, dread and fears within [us].

6 But God, Who comforts and encourages and refreshes and cheers the depressed and the sinking, comforted and encouraged and refreshed and cheered us by the arrival of Titus.

7 [Yes] and not only by his coming but also by [his account of] the comfort with which he was encouraged and refreshed and cheered as to you, while he told us of your yearning affection, of how sorry you were [for me] and how eagerly you took my part, so that I rejoiced still more.

8 For even though I did grieve you with my letter, I do not regret [it now], though I did regret it; for I see that that letter did pain you, though only for a little while;

9 Yet I am glad now, not because you were pained, but because you were pained into repentance [and so turned back to God]; for you felt a grief such as God meant you to feel, so that in nothing you might suffer loss through us or harm for what we did.

10 For godly grief and the pain God is permitted to direct, produce a re-

pentance that leads *and* contributes to salvation *and* deliverance from evil, and it never brings regret; but worldly grief (the hopeless sorrow that is characteristic of the pagan world) is deadly [breeding and ending in death].

11 For [you can look back now and] observe what this same godly sorrow has done for you *and* has produced in you: what eagerness *and* earnest care to explain *and* clear yourselves [of all ªcomplicity in the condoning of incest], what indignation [at the sin], what alarm, what yearning, what zeal [to do justice to all concerned], what readiness to mete out punishment [ªto the offender]! At every point you have proved yourselves cleared *and* guiltless in the matter. [I Cor. 5.]

12 So although I did write to you [as I did], it was not for the sake *and* because of the one who did [the] wrong, nor on account of the one who suffered [the] wrong, but in order that you might realize before God [that your readiness to accept our authority revealed] how zealously you do care for us.

13 Therefore we are relieved *and* comforted *and* encouraged [at the result]. And in addition to our own [personal] consolation, we were especially delighted at the joy of Titus, because you have all set his mind at rest, soothing *and* refreshing his spirit.

14 For if I had boasted to him at all concerning you, I was not disappointed *or* put to shame, but just as everything we ever said to you was true, so our boasting [about you] to Titus has proved true also.

15 And his heart goes out to you more abundantly than ever as he recalls the submission [to his guidance] that all of you had, and the reverence

and anxiety [to meet all requirements] with which you accepted *and* welcomed him.

16 I am very happy because I now am of good courage *and* have perfect confidence in you in all things.

CHAPTER 8

WE WANT to tell you further, brethren, about the grace (the favor and spiritual blessing) of God which has been evident in the churches of Macedonia [arousing in them the desire to give alms];

2 For in the midst of an ordeal of severe tribulation, their abundance of joy and their depth of poverty [together] have overflowed in wealth of lavish generosity on their part.

3 For, as I can bear witness, [they gave] according to their ability, yes, and beyond their ability; and [they did it] voluntarily.

4 Begging us most insistently for the favor *and* the fellowship of contributing in this ministration for [the relief and support of] the saints [in Jerusalem].

5 Nor [was this gift of theirs merely the contribution] that we expected, but first they gave themselves to the Lord and to us [as His agents] by the will of God [ᵇentirely disregarding their personal interests, they gave as much as they possibly could, having put themselves at our disposal to be directed by the will of God]—

6 So much so that we have urged Titus that as he began it, he should also complete this beneficent *and* gracious contribution among you [the church at Corinth].

7 Now as you abound *and* excel *and* are at the front in everything—in faith, in expressing yourselves, in knowledge, in all zeal, and in your love for us—[see to it that you come to the front now and] abound *and*

---

a Marvin Vincent, *Word Studies*.　　**b** Joseph Thayer, *A Greek-English Lexicon*.

excel in this gracious work [of alms-giving] also.

8 I give this not as an order [to dictate to you], but to prove by [pointing out] the zeal of others, the sincerity of your [own] love also.

9 For you are becoming progressively acquainted with and recognizing more strongly and clearly the grace of our Lord Jesus Christ (His kindness, His gracious generosity, His undeserved favor and spiritual blessing), [in] that though He was [so very] rich, yet for your sakes He became [so very] poor, in order that by His poverty you might become enriched (abundantly supplied)

10 [It is then] my counsel and my opinion in this matter that I give [you when I say]: It is profitable and fitting for you [now to complete the enterprise] which more than a year ago you not only began, but were the first to wish to do anything [about contributions for the relief of the saints at Jerusalem].

11 So now finish doing it, that your [enthusiastic] readiness in desiring it may be equalled by your completion of it according to your ability and means.

12 For if the [eager] readiness to give is there, then it is acceptable and welcomed in proportion to what a person has, not according to what he does not have.

13 For it is not [intended] that other people be eased and relieved [of their responsibility] and you be burdened and suffer [unfairly];

14 But to have equality [share and share alike], your surplus over necessity at the present time going to meet their want and to equalize the difference created by it, so that [at some other time] their surplus in turn may be given to supply your want. Thus there may be equality,

15 As it is written, He who gathered much had nothing over, and he who gathered little did not lack. [Exod. 16:18.]

16 But thanks be to God Who planted the same earnest zeal and care for you in the heart of Titus.

17 For he not only welcomed and responded to our appeal, but was himself so keen in his enthusiasm and interest in you that he is going to you of his own accord.

18 But we are sending along with him that brother [Luke?] whose praise in the Gospel ministry [is spread] throughout all the churches;

19 And more than that, he has been appointed by the churches to travel as our companion in regard to this bountiful contribution which we are administering for the glory of the Lord Himself and [to show] our eager readiness [as Christians to help one another].

20 [For] we are on our guard, intending that no one should find anything for which to blame us in regard to our administration of this large contribution

21 For we take thought beforehand and aim to be honest and absolutely above suspicion, not only in the sight of the Lord but also in the sight of men.

22 Moreover, along with them we are sending our brother, whom we have often put to the test and have found him zealous (devoted and earnest) in many matters, but who is now more [eagerly] earnest than ever because of [his] absolute confidence in you.

23 As for Titus, he is my colleague and shares my work in your service; and as for the [other two] brethren, they are the [special] messengers of the churches, a credit and glory to Christ (the Messiah).

24 Show to these men, therefore, in the sight of the churches, the reality and plain truth of your love (your affection, goodwill, and benevo-

lence) and what [good reasons] I had for boasting about *and* being proud of you.

CHAPTER 9

NOW ABOUT the offering that is [to be made] for the saints (God's people in Jerusalem), it is quite superfluous that I should write you;

2 For I am well acquainted with your willingness (your readiness and your eagerness to promote it) and I have proudly told about you to the people of Macedonia, saying that Achaia (most of Greece) has been prepared since last year for this contribution; and [consequently] your enthusiasm has stimulated the majority of them.

3 Still, I am sending the brethren [on to you], lest our pride in you should be made an empty boast in this particular case, and so that you may be all ready, as I told them you would be;

4 Lest, if [any] Macedonians should come with me and find you unprepared [for this generosity], we, to say nothing of yourselves, be humiliated for our being so confident.

5 That is why I thought it necessary to urge these brethren to go to you before I do and make arrangements in advance for this bountiful, promised gift of yours, so that it may be ready, not as an extortion [wrung out of you] but as a generous *and* willing gift.

6 [Remember] this: he who sows sparingly *and* grudgingly will also reap sparingly *and* grudgingly, and he who sows generously [cthat blessings may come to someone] will also reap generously *and* with blessings.

7 Let each one [give] as he has made up his own mind *and* purposed in his heart, not reluctantly *or* sor-

rowfully or under compulsion, for God loves (He ctakes pleasure in, prizes above other things, and is unwilling to abandon or to do without) a cheerful (joyous, ''prompt to do it'') giver [whose heart is in his giving]. [Prov. 22:9.]

8 And God is able to make all grace (every favor and cearthly blessing) come to you in abundance, so that you may always *and* under all circumstances *and* whatever the need dbe self-sufficient [possessing enough to require no aid or support and furnished in abundance for every good work and charitable donation].

9 As it is written, He [the benevolent person] scatters abroad; He gives to the poor; His deeds of justice *and* goodness *and* kindness *and* benevolence will go on *and* endure forever! [Ps. 112:9.]

10 And [God] Who provides seed for the sower and bread for eating will also provide and multiply your [resources for] sowing and increase the fruits of your righteousness [cwhich manifests itself in active goodness, kindness, and charity]. [Isa. 55:10; Hos. 10:12.]

11 Thus you will be enriched in all things *and* in every way, so that you can be generous, and [your generosity as it is] administered by us will bring forth thanksgiving to God.

12 For the service that the ministering of this fund renders does not only fully supply what is lacking to the saints (God's people), but it also overflows in many [cries of] thanksgiving to God.

13 Because at [your] standing of the test of this ministry, they will glorify God for your loyalty *and* obedience to the Gospel of Christ which you confess, as well as for your generous-hearted liberality to them and to all [the other needy ones].

c Joseph Thayer, *A Greek-English Lexicon.*   d Marvin Vincent, *Word Studies.*

14 And they yearn for you while they pray for you, because of the surpassing measure of God's grace (His favor and mercy and spiritual blessing which is shown forth) in you.

15 Now thanks be to God for His Gift, [precious] beyond telling [His indescribable, inexpressible, free Gift]!

CHAPTER 10

NOW I myself, Paul, beseech you, by the gentleness and consideration of Christ [Himself; I] who [am] lowly enough [so they say] when among you face to face, but bold (fearless and outspoken) to you when [I am] absent from you!

2 I entreat you when I do come [to you] that I may not [be driven to such] boldness as I intend to show toward those few who suspect us of acting according to the flesh [on the low level of worldly motives and as if invested with only human powers].

3 For though we walk (live) in the flesh, we are not carrying on our warfare according to the flesh and using mere human weapons.

4 For the weapons of our warfare are not physical [weapons of flesh and blood], but they are mighty before God for the overthrow and destruction of strongholds,

5 [Inasmuch as we] refute arguments and theories and reasonings and every proud and lofty thing that sets itself up against the [true] knowledge of God; and we lead every thought and purpose away captive into the obedience of Christ (the Messiah, the Anointed One),

6 Being in readiness to punish every [insubordinate for his] disobedience, when your own submission and obedience [as a church] are fully secured and complete.

7 Look at [this obvious fact] which is before your eyes. If anyone is confident that he is Christ's, let him reflect and remind himself that even as he is Christ's, so too are we.

8 For even though I boast rather freely about our power and authority, which the Lord gave for your upbuilding and not for demolishing you, yet I shall not be put to shame [for exceeding the truth],

9 Neither would I seem to be overawing or frightening you with my letters;

10 For they say, His letters are weighty and impressive and forceful and telling, but his personality and bodily presence are weak, and his speech and delivery are utterly contemptible (of no account).

11 Let such people realize that what we say by letters when we are absent, [we put] also into deeds when we are present—

12 Not that we [have the audacity to] venture to class or [even to] compare ourselves with some who exalt and furnish testimonials for themselves! However, when they measure themselves with themselves and compare themselves with one another, they are without understanding and behave unwisely.

13 We, on the other hand, will not boast beyond our legitimate province and proper limit, but will keep within the limits [of our commission which] God has allotted us as our measuring line and which reaches and includes even you.

14 For we are not overstepping the limits of our province and stretching beyond our ability to reach, as though we reached not (had no legitimate mission) to you, for we were [the very first] to come even as far as to you with the good news (the Gospel) of Christ.

15 We do not boast therefore, beyond our proper limit, over other men's labors, but we have the hope and confident expectation that as

your faith continues to grow, our field among you may be greatly enlarged, still within the limits of our commission.

16 So that [we may even] preach the Gospel in lands [lying] beyond you, without making a boast of work already done in another [man's] sphere of activity [before we came on the scene].

17 However, let him who boasts and glories boast and glory in the Lord. [Jer. 9:24.]

18 For [it is] not [the man] who praises and commends himself who is approved and accepted, but [it is the person] whom the Lord accredits and commends.

CHAPTER 11

I WISH you would bear with me while I indulge in a little [socalled] foolishness. Do bear with me!

2 For I am ᵉzealous for you with a godly eagerness and a divine jealousy, for I have betrothed you to one Husband, to present you as a chaste virgin to Christ. [Hos. 2:19, 20.]

3 But [now] I am fearful, lest that even as the serpent beguiled Eve by his cunning, so your minds may be corrupted and seduced from wholehearted and sincere and pure devotion to Christ. [Gen. 3:4.]

4 For [you seem readily to endure it] if a man comes and preaches another Jesus than the One we preached, or if you receive a different spirit from the [Spirit] you [once] received or a different gospel from the one you [then] received and welcomed; you tolerate [all that] well enough!

5 Yet I consider myself as in no way inferior to these [precious] ᶠextra-super [false] apostles.

6 But even if [I am] unskilled in speaking, yet [I am] not [unskilled] in knowledge [I know what I am talking about]; we have made this evident to you in all things.

7 But did I perhaps make a mistake and do you a wrong in debasing and cheapening myself so that you might be exalted and enriched in dignity and honor and happiness by preaching God's Gospel without expense to you?

8 Other churches I have robbed by accepting [more than their share of] support for my ministry [from them in order] to serve you.

9 And when I was with you and ran short financially, I did not burden any [of you], for what I lacked was abundantly made up by the brethren who came from Macedonia. So I kept myself from being burdensome to you in any way, and will continue to keep [myself from being so].

10 As the truth of Christ is in me, this my boast [of independence] shall not be debarred (silenced or checked) in the regions of Achaia (most of Greece).

11 And why? Because I do not love you [do not have a preference for you, wish you well, and regard your welfare]? God perceives and knows that I do!

12 But what I do, I will continue to do, [for I am determined to maintain this independence] in order to cut off the claim of those who would like [to find an occasion and incentive] to claim that in their boasted [mission] they work on the same terms that we do.

13 For such men are false apostles [spurious, counterfeits], deceitful workmen, masquerading as apostles (special messengers) of Christ (the Messiah).

14 And it is no wonder, for Satan

---

e G. Abbott-Smith, *Manual Greek Lexicon of the New Testament.*   f Frederick W. Farrar, *The Life and Work of Saint Paul.*

himself masquerades as an angel of light;

15 So it is not surprising if his servants also masquerade as ministers of righteousness. [But] their end will correspond with their deeds.

16 I repeat then, let no one think I have lost my wits; but even if you do, then bear with a witless man, so that I too may boast a little.

17 What I say by way of this confident boasting, I say not with the Lord's authority [by inspiration] but, as it were, in pure witlessness!

18 [For] since many boast of worldly things and according to the flesh, I will glory (boast) also.

19 For you readily and gladly bear with the foolish, since you are so smart and wise yourselves!

20 For you endure it if a man assumes control of your souls and makes slaves of you, or devours [your substance, spends your money] and preys upon you, or deceives and takes advantage of you, or is arrogant and puts on airs, or strikes you in the face.

21 To my discredit, I must say, we have shown ourselves too weak [for you to show such tolerance of us and for us to do strong, courageous things like that to you]! But in whatever any person is bold and dares [to boast]—mind you, I am speaking in this foolish (witless) way—I also am bold and dare [to boast].

22 They are Hebrews? So am I! They are Israelites? So am I! They are descendants of Abraham? So am I!

23 Are they [ministering] servants of Christ (the Messiah)? I am talking like one beside himself, [but] I am more, with far more extensive and abundant labors, with far more imprisonments, [beaten] with countless stripes, and frequently [at the point of] death.

24 Five times I received from [the hands of] the Jews forty [lashes all] but one; [Deut. 25:3.]

25 Three times I have been beaten with rods; once I was stoned. Three times I have been aboard a ship wrecked at sea; a [whole] night and a day I have spent [adrift] on the deep;

26 Many times on journeys, [exposed to] perils from rivers, perils from bandits, perils from [my own] nation, perils from the Gentiles, perils in the city, perils in the desert places, perils in the sea, perils from those posing as believers [but destitute of Christian knowledge and piety];

27 In toil and hardship, watching often [through sleepless nights], in hunger [through thirst, frequently driven to fasting by want, in cold and exposure and lack of clothing.

28 And besides those things that are without, there is the daily [inescapable pressure] of my care and anxiety for all the churches!

29 Who is weak, and I do not feel [his] weakness? Who is made to stumble and fall and have his faith hurt, and I am not on fire [with sorrow or indignation]?

30 If I must boast, I will boast of the things that [show] my infirmity [of the things by which I am made weak and contemptible in the eyes of my opponents].

31 The God and Father of the Lord Jesus Christ knows, He Who is blessed and to be praised forevermore, that I do not lie.

32 In Damascus, the city governor acting under King Aretas guarded the city of Damascus [on purpose] to arrest me,

33 And I was [actually] let down in a [rope] basket or hamper through a window [a small door] in the wall, and I escaped through his fingers.

CHAPTER 12

TRUE, THERE is nothing to be gained by it, but [as I am obliged] to boast, I will go on to visions and revelations of the Lord.

2 I know a man in Christ who fourteen years ago—whether in the body or out of the body I do not know, God knows—was caught up to the third heaven.

3 And I know that this man—whether in the body or away from the body I do not know, God knows—

4 Was caught up into paradise, and he heard utterances beyond the power of man to put into words, which man is not permitted to utter.

5 Of this same [man's experiences] I will boast, but of myself [personally] I will not boast, except as regards my infirmities (my weaknesses).

6 Should I desire to boast, I shall not be a witless braggart, for I shall be speaking the truth. But I abstain [from it] so that no one may form a higher estimate of me than [is justified by] what he sees in me or hears from me.

7 And to keep me from being puffed up and too much elated by the exceeding greatness (preeminence) of these revelations, there was given me a thorn (ᵃa splinter) in the flesh, a messenger of Satan, to rack and buffet and harass me, to keep me from being excessively exalted. [Job. 2:6.]

8 Three times I called upon the Lord and besought [Him] about this and begged that it might depart from me;

9 But He said to me, My grace (My favor and loving-kindness and mercy) is enough for you [sufficient against any danger and enables you to bear the trouble manfully]; for My strength and power are made perfect (fulfilled and completed) and ᵇshow

themselves most effective in [your] weakness. Therefore, I will all the more gladly glory in my weaknesses and infirmities, that the strength and power of Christ (the Messiah) may rest [yes, may ᶜpitch a tent [over] and dwell] upon me!

10 So for the sake of Christ, I am well pleased and take pleasure in infirmities, insults, hardships, persecutions, perplexities and distresses; for when I am weak [ʲin human strength], then am I [truly] strong (able, powerful ʲin divine strength).

11 Now I have been [speaking like] a fool! But you forced me to it, for I ought to have been [ⁱsaved the necessity and] commended by you. For I have not fallen short one bit or proved myself at all inferior to those superlative [false] apostles [of yours], even if I am nothing (a nobody).

12 Indeed, the signs that indicate a [genuine] apostle were performed among you fully and most patiently in miracles and wonders and mighty works.

13 For in what respect were you put to a disadvantage in comparison with the rest of the churches, unless [it was for the fact] that I myself did not burden you [with my financial support]? Pardon me [for doing you] this injustice!

14 Now for the third time I am ready to come to [visit] you. And I will not burden you [financially], for it is not your [money] that I want but you; for children are not duty bound to lay up store for their parents, but parents for their children.

15 But I will most gladly spend [myself] and be utterly spent for your souls. If I love you exceedingly, am I to be loved [by you] the less?

16 But though granting that I did

g James Moulton and George Milligan, *The Vocabulary of the Greek Testament.*   h Two Greek texts so read.   i Marvin Vincent, *Word Studies.*   j Joseph Thayer, *A Greek-English Lexicon.*

not burden you [with my support, some say that] I was crafty [and that] I cheated and got the better of you with my trickery.

17 Did I [then] take advantage of you or make any money out of you through any of those [messengers] whom I sent to you?

18 [Actually] I urged Titus [to go], and I sent the brother with [him]. Did Titus overreach or take advantage of you [in anything]? Did he and I not act in the same spirit? Did we not [take the] same steps?

19 Have you been supposing [all this time] that we have been defending ourselves and apologizing to you? [It is] in the sight and the [very] presence of God [and as one] in Christ (the Messiah) that we have been speaking, dearly beloved, and all in order to build you up [spiritually].

20 For I am fearful that somehow or other I may come and find you not as I desire to find you, and that you may find me too not as you want to find me—that perhaps there may be factions (quarreling), jealousy, temper (wrath, intrigues, rivalry, divided loyalties), selfishness, whispering, gossip, arrogance (self-assertion), and disorder among you.

21 [I am fearful] that when I come again, my God may humiliate and humble me in your regard, and that I may have to sorrow over many of those who sinned before and have not repented of the impurity, sexual vice, and sensuality which they formerly practiced.

CHAPTER 13

THIS IS the third time that I am coming to you. By the testimony of two or three witnesses must any charge and every accusing statement be sustained and confirmed. [Deut. 19:15.]

2 I have already warned those who sinned formerly and all the rest also, and I warn them now again while I am absent, as I did when present on my second visit, that if I come back, I will not spare [them],

3 Since you desire and seek [perceptible] proof of the Christ Who speaks in and through me. [For He] is not weak and feeble in dealing with you, but is a mighty power within you;

4 For though He was crucified in weakness, yet He goes on living by the power of God. And though we too are weak in Him [as He was humanly weak], yet in dealing with you [we shall show ourselves] alive and strong in [fellowship with] Him by the power of God.

5 Examine and test and evaluate your own selves to see whether you are holding to your faith and showing the proper fruits of it. Test and prove yourselves [knot Christ]. Do you not yourselves realize and know [thoroughly by an ever-increasing experience] that Jesus Christ is in you?—unless you are [counterfeits] disapproved on trial and rejected!

6 But I hope you will recognize and know that we are not disapproved on trial and rejected.

7 But I pray to God that you may do nothing wrong, not in order that we [kour teaching] may appear to be approved, but that you may continue doing right, [though] we may seem to have failed and be unapproved.

8 For we can do nothing against the Truth [lnot serve any party or personal interest], but only for the Truth [mwhich is the Gospel].

9 For we are glad when we are

---

k Marvin Vincent, Word Studies. l James C. Gray and George M. Adams, Bible Commentary.
m Joseph Thayer, A Greek-English Lexicon.

weak (ᵏunapproved) and you are really strong. And this we also pray for, your all-round strengthening and perfecting of soul.

10 So I write these things while I am absent from you, that when I come to you, I may not have to deal sharply in my use of the authority which the Lord has given me [to be employed, however] for building [you] up and not for tearing [you] down.

11 Finally, brethren, farewell (rejoice)! Be strengthened (perfected, completed, made what you ought to be); be encouraged and consoled and comforted; be of the same [agree-

able] mind one with another; live in peace, and [then] the God of love [Who is the Source of affection, goodwill, love, and benevolence toward men] and the Author and Promoter of peace will be with you.

12 Greet one another with a consecrated kiss.

13 All the saints (the people of God here) salute you.

14 The grace (favor and spiritual blessing) of the Lord Jesus Christ and the love of God and the presence and fellowship (the communion and sharing together, and participation) in the Holy Spirit be with you all. Amen (so be it).

THE LETTER OF PAUL TO THE
GALATIANS

CHAPTER 1

PAUL, AN apostle—[special messenger appointed and commissioned and sent out] not from [any body of] men nor by or through ⁿany man, but by and through Jesus Christ (the Messiah) and God the Father, Who raised Him from among the dead—

2 And all the brethren who are with me, to the churches of Galatia:

3 Grace and spiritual blessing be to you and [soul] peace from God the Father and our Lord Jesus Christ (the Messiah),

4 Who gave (yielded) Himself up [ⁿto atone] for our sins [and ᵒto save and sanctify us], in order to rescue and deliver us from this present wicked age and world order, in ac-

cordance with the will and purpose and plan of our God and Father—

5 To Him [be ascribed all] the glory through all the ages of the ages and the eternities of the eternities! Amen (so be it).

6 I am surprised and astonished that you are so quickly ᵖturning renegade and deserting Him Who invited and called you ⁿby the grace (unmerited favor) of Christ (the Messiah) [and that you are transferring your allegiance to] a different [even an opposition] gospel.

7 Not that there is [or could be] any other [genuine Gospel], but there are [obviously] some who are troubling and disturbing and bewildering you [ⁿwith a different kind of teaching which they offer as a gospel] and

n Marvin Vincent, *Word Studies in the New Testament*. o Marvin Vincent, *Word Studies in the New Testament*. p Joseph P. Lightfoot, *Notes on the Epistles of Saint Paul*.

want to pervert *and* distort the Gospel of Christ (the Messiah) [into something which it absolutely is not].

8 But even if we or an angel from heaven should preach to you a gospel contrary to *and* different from that which we preached to you, let him be accursed (anathema, devoted to destruction, doomed to eternal punishment)!

9 As we said before, so I now say again, If anyone is preaching to you a gospel different from *or* contrary to that which you received [from us], let him be accursed (anathema, devoted to destruction, doomed to eternal punishment)!

10 Now, am I trying to win the favor of men, or of God? Do I seek to please men? If I were still seeking popularity with men, I should not be a bond servant of Christ (the Messiah).

11 For I want you to know, brethren, that the Gospel which was proclaimed *and* made known by me is not man's gospel [a human invention, according to or patterned after any human standard].

12 For indeed I did not receive it from man, nor was I taught it, but [it came to me] through a [direct] revelation [given] by Jesus Christ (the Messiah).

13 You have heard of my earlier career *and* former manner of life in the Jewish religion (Judaism), how I persecuted *and* abused the church of God furiously *and* extensively, and [with fanatical zeal did my best] to make havoc of it *and* destroy it.

14 And [you have heard how] I outstripped many of the men of my own generation among the people of my race in [my advancement in study and observance of the laws of] Judaism, so extremely enthusiastic *and* zealous I was for the traditions of my ancestors.

15 But when He, Who had chosen *and* set me apart [even] before I was born and had called me by His grace (His undeserved favor and blessing), saw fit *and* was pleased [Isa. 49:1; Jer. 1:5.]

16 To reveal (unveil, disclose) His Son within me so that I might proclaim Him among the Gentiles (the non-Jewish world) as the glad tidings (Gospel), immediately I did not confer with flesh and blood [did not consult or counsel with any frail human being or communicate with anyone].

17 Nor did I [even] go up to Jerusalem to those who were apostles (special messengers of Christ) before I was, but I went away *and* retired into Arabia, and afterward I came back again to Damascus.

18 Then three years later, I did go up to Jerusalem to become [personally] acquainted with Cephas (Peter), and remained with him for fifteen days.

19 But I did not see any of the other apostles (the special messengers of Christ) except James the brother of our Lord.

20 Now [note carefully what I am telling you, for it is the truth], I write this as if I were standing before the bar of God; I do not lie.

21 Then I went into the districts (countries, regions) of Syria and Cilicia.

22 And so far I was still unknown by sight to the churches of Christ in Judea [the country surrounding Jerusalem].

23 They were only hearing it said, He who used to persecute us is now proclaiming the very faith he once reviled *and* which he set out to ruin *and* tried [with all his might] to destroy.

24 And they glorified God [as the Author and Source of what had taken place] in me.

CHAPTER 2

THEN AFTER [an interval] of fourteen years I again went up to Jerusalem. [This time I went] with Barnabas, taking Titus along with [me] also.

2 I went because it was specially *and* divinely revealed to me that I should go, and I put before them the Gospel [declaring to them that] which I preach among the Gentiles. However, [I presented the matter] privately before those of repute, [for I wanted to make certain, by thus at first confining my communication to this private conference] that I was not running or had not run in vain [guarding against being discredited either in what I was planning to do or had already done].

3 But [all went well!] even Titus, who was with me, was not compelled [as some had anticipated] to be circumcised, although he was a Greek.

4 [My precaution was] because of false brethren who had been secretly smuggled in [to the Christian brotherhood]; they had slipped in to spy on our liberty *and* the freedom which we have in Christ Jesus, that they might again bring us into bondage [under the Law of Moses].

5 To them we did not yield submission even for a moment, that the truth of the Gospel might continue to be [preserved] for you [in its purity].

6 Moreover, [no new requirements were made] by those who were reputed to be something—though what was their individual position *and* whether they really were of importance or not makes no difference to me; God is not impressed with the positions that men hold *and* He is not partial *and* recognizes no external distinctions—those [I say] who were of repute imposed no new requirements upon me [had nothing to add to

my Gospel, and from them I received no new suggestions]. [Deut. 10:17.]

7 But on the contrary, when they [really] saw that I had been entrusted [to carry] the Gospel to the uncircumcised [Gentiles, just as definitely] as Peter had been entrusted [to proclaim] the Gospel to the circumcised [Jews, they were agreeable];

8 For He Who motivated *and* fitted Peter *and* worked effectively through him for the mission to the circumcised, motivated *and* fitted me *and* worked through me also for [the mission to] the Gentiles.

9 And when they knew (perceived, recognized, understood, and acknowledged) the grace (God's unmerited favor and spiritual blessing) that had been bestowed upon me, James and Cephas (Peter) and John, who were reputed to be pillars of the Jerusalem church, gave to me and Barnabas the right hand of fellowship, with the understanding that we should go to the Gentiles and they to the circumcised (Jews).

10 They only [made one stipulation], that we were to remember the poor, which very thing I was also eager to do.

11 But when Cephas (Peter) came to Antioch, I protested *and* opposed him to his face [concerning his conduct there], for he was blameable *and* stood condemned.

12 For up to the time that certain persons came from James, he ate his meals with the Gentile [converts]; but when the men [from Jerusalem] arrived, he withdrew *and* held himself aloof from the Gentiles and [ate] separately [for fear of those of the circumcision [party].

13 And the rest of the Jews along with him also concealed their true convictions *and* acted insincerely, with the result that even Barnabas was carried away by their hypocrisy

(by their example of insincerity and pretense).

14 But as soon as I saw that they were not straightforward *and* were not living up to the truth of the Gospel, I said to Cephas (Peter) before everybody present, If you, though born a Jew, can live [as you have been living] like a Gentile and not like a Jew, how do you dare now to urge *and* practically force the Gentiles to [comply with the ritual of Judaism and] live like Jews?

15 [I went on to say] Although we ourselves (you and I) are Jews by birth and not Gentile (heathen) sinners,

16 Yet we know that a man is justified *or* reckoned righteous *and* in right standing with God, not by works of the Law but [only] through faith *and* [absolute] reliance on *and* adherence to *and* trust in Jesus Christ (the Messiah, the Anointed One). [Therefore] even we [ourselves] have believed on Christ Jesus, in order to be justified by faith in Christ and not by works of the Law [for we cannot be justified by any observance of the ritual of the Law given by Moses], because by keeping legal rituals *and* by works no human being can ever be justified (declared righteous and put in right standing with God). [Ps. 143:2.]

17 But if, in our desire *and* endeavor to be justified in Christ (to be declared righteous and put in right standing with God wholly and solely through Christ), we have shown ourselves sinners also *and* convicted of sin, does that make Christ a minister (a party and contributor) to our sin? Banish the thought! (Of course not!)

18 For if I [or any others who have taught] that the observance of the Law of Moses is not essential to being justified by God, should now by word or practice teach or intimate that it is essential to] build up again what I tore down, I prove myself a transgressor.

19 For I through the Law [under the operation of the curse of the Law] have [in Christ's death for me] myself died to the Law *and* all the Law's demands upon me, so that I may [henceforth] live to *and* for God.

20 I have been crucified with Christ [in Him I have shared His crucifixion]; it is no longer I who live, but Christ (the Messiah) lives in me; and the life I now live in the body I live by faith in (by adherence to *and* reliance on *and* [complete] trust in) the Son of God, Who loved me and gave Himself up for me.

21 [Therefore, I do not treat God's gracious gift as something of minor importance and defeat its very purpose]; I do not set aside *and* invalidate *and* frustrate *and* nullify the grace (unmerited favor) of God. For if justification (righteousness, acquittal from guilt) comes through [observing the ritual of] the Law, then Christ (the Messiah) died groundlessly *and* to no purpose *and* in vain. [His death was then wholly superfluous.]

CHAPTER 3

O YOU poor *and* silly *and* thoughtless *and* unreflecting *and* senseless Galatians! Who has fascinated *or* bewitched *or* cast a spell over you, unto whom—right before your very eyes—Jesus Christ (the Messiah) was openly *and* graphically set forth *and* portrayed as crucified?

2 Let me ask you this one question: Did you receive the [Holy] Spirit as the result of obeying the Law *and* doing its works, or was it by hearing [the message of the Gospel] and believing [it]? [Was it from observing a law of rituals or from a message of faith?]

3 Are you so foolish *and* so sense-

less *and* so silly? Having begun [your new life spiritually] with the [Holy] Spirit, are you now reaching perfection [by dependence] on the flesh?

4 Have you suffered so many things *and* experienced so much all for nothing (to no purpose)—if it really is to no purpose *and* in vain?

5 Then does He Who supplies you with His marvelous [Holy] Spirit and works powerfully *and* miraculously among you, do so on [the grounds of your doing] what the Law demands, or because of your believing in *and* adhering to *and* trusting in *and* relying on the message that you heard?

6 Thus Abraham believed in *and* adhered to *and* trusted in *and* relied on God, and it was reckoned *and* placed to his account *and* credited as righteousness [as conformity to the divine will in purpose, thought, and action]. [Gen. 15:6.]

7 Know *and* understand that it is [really] the people [who live] by faith who are [the true] sons of Abraham.

8 And the Scripture, foreseeing that God would justify (declare righteous, put in right standing with Himself) the Gentiles in consequence of faith, proclaimed the Gospel [foretelling the glad tidings of a Savior long beforehand] to Abraham in the promise, saying, In you shall all the nations [of the earth] be blessed. [Gen. 12:3.]

9 So then, those who are people of faith are blessed *and* made happy *and* favored by God [as partners in fellowship] with the believing *and* trusting Abraham.

10 And all who depend on the Law [who are seeking to be justified by obedience to the Law of rituals] are under a curse *and* doomed to disappointment *and* destruction, for it is written in the Scriptures, Cursed (accursed, devoted to destruction, doomed to eternal punishment) be

everyone who does not continue to abide (live and remain) by all the precepts *and* commands written in the Book of the Law and to practice them. [Deut. 27:26.]

11 Now it is evident that no person is justified (declared righteous and brought into right standing with God) through the Law; for the Scripture says, The man in right standing with God (the just, the righteous) shall live by *and* out of faith, *and* he who through *and* by faith is declared righteous *and* in right standing with God shall live. [Hab. 2:4.]

12 But the Law does not rest on faith (does not require faith, has nothing to do with faith), for it itself says, He who does them [the things prescribed by the Law] shall live by them [not by faith]. [Lev. 18:5.]

13 Christ purchased our freedom [redeeming us] from the curse (doom) of the Law [and its condemnation] by [Himself] becoming a curse for us, for it is written [in the Scriptures], Cursed is everyone who hangs on a tree (is crucified); [Deut. 21:23.]

14 To the end that through [their receiving] Christ Jesus, the blessing [promised] to Abraham might come upon the Gentiles, so that we through faith might [all] receive [the realization of] the promise of the [Holy] Spirit.

15 To speak in terms of human relations, brethren, [if] even a man makes a last will and testament [a merely human covenant], no one sets it aside *or* makes it void *or* adds to it when once it has been drawn up *and* signed (ratified, confirmed).

16 Now the promises (covenants, agreements) were decreed *and* made to Abraham and his Seed (his Offspring, his Heir). He [God] does not say, And to seeds (descendants, heirs), as if referring to many persons; but, And to your Seed (your

Descendant, your Heir), obviously referring to one individual, Who is [none other than] Christ (the Messiah). [Gen. 13:15; 17:8.]

17 This is my argument: The Law, which began 430 years after the covenant [concerning the coming Messiah], does not and cannot annul the covenant previously established (ratified) by God, so as to abolish the promise and make it void. [Exod. 12:40.]

18 For if the inheritance [of the promise depends on observing] the Law [as these false teachers would like you to believe], it no longer [depends] on the promise; however, God gave it to Abraham [as a free gift solely] by virtue of His promise.

19 What then was the purpose of the Law? It was added [later on, after the promise, to disclose and expose to men their guilt] because of transgressions and [to make men more conscious of the sinfulness] of sin; and it was intended to be in effect until the Seed (the Descendant, the Heir) should come, to and concerning Whom the promise had been made. And it [the Law] was arranged and ordained and appointed through the instrumentality of angels [and was given] by the hand (in the person) of a go-between [Moses, an intermediary person between God and man].

20 Now a go-between (intermediary) has to do with and implies more than one party [there can be no mediator with just one person]. Yet God is [only] one Person [and He was the sole party in giving that promise to Abraham. But the Law was a contract between two, God and Israel; its validity was dependent on both].

21 Is the Law then contrary and opposed to the promises of God? Of course not! For if a Law had been given which could confer [spiritual] life, then righteousness and right standing with God would certainly have come by Law.

22 But the Scriptures [picture all mankind as sinners] shut up and imprisoned by sin, so that [the inheritance, blessing] which was promised through faith in Jesus Christ (the Messiah) might be given (released, delivered, and committed) to [all] those who believe [who adhere to and trust in and rely on Him].

23 Now before the faith came, we were perpetually guarded under the Law, kept in custody in preparation for the faith that was destined to be revealed (unveiled, disclosed),

24 So that the Law served [to us Jews] as our trainer [our guardian, our guide to Christ, to lead us] until Christ [came], that we might be justified (declared righteous, put in right standing with God) by and through faith.

25 But now that the faith has come, we are no longer under a trainer [the guardian of our childhood].

26 For in Christ Jesus you are all sons of God through faith.

27 For as many [of you] as were baptized into Christ [into a spiritual union and communion with Christ, the Anointed One, the Messiah] have put on (clothed yourselves with) Christ.

28 There is [now no distinction] neither Jew nor Greek, there is neither slave nor free, there is not male 'and female; for you are all one in Christ Jesus.

29 And if you belong to Christ [are in Him Who is Abraham's Seed], then you are Abraham's offspring and [spiritual] heirs according to promise.

q Marvin Vincent, *Word Studies*.   r Literal translation.

CHAPTER 4

NOW WHAT I mean is that as long as the inheritor (heir) is a child and under age, he does not differ from a slave, although he is the master of all the estate;

2 But he is under guardians and administrators *or* trustees until the date fixed by his father.

3 So we [Jewish Christians] also, when we were minors, were kept like slaves under [the rules of the Hebrew ritual and subject to] the elementary teachings of a system of external observations *and* regulations.

4 But when the proper time had fully come, God sent His Son, born of a woman, born subject to [the regulations of] the Law,

5 To purchase the freedom of (to ransom, to redeem, to [s]atone for) those who were subject to the Law, that we might be adopted *and* have sonship conferred upon us [be recognized as God's sons].

6 And because you [really] are [His] sons, God has sent the [[t]Holy] Spirit of His Son into our hearts, crying, Abba (Father)! Father!

7 Therefore, you are no longer a slave (bond servant) but a son; and if a son, then [it follows that you are] an heir [u]by the aid of God, *through Christ.*

8 But at that previous time, when you had not come to be acquainted with *and* understand *and* know the true God, you [Gentiles] were in bondage to gods who by their very nature could not be gods at all [gods that really did not exist].

9 Now, however, that you have come to be acquainted with *and* understand *and* know [the true] God, or rather to be understood *and* known by God, how can you turn back again to the weak and beggarly *and* worthless elementary things [[u]of all religions before Christ came], whose slaves you once more want to become?

10 You observe [particular] days and months and seasons and years!

11 I am alarmed [about you] lest I have labored among *and* over you to no purpose *and* in vain.

12 Brethren, I beg of you, become as I am [free from the bondage of Jewish ritualism and ordinances], for I also have become as you are [[1]a Gentile]. You did me no wrong [[1]in the days when I first came to you; do not do it now].

13 On the contrary, you know that it was on account of a bodily ailment that [I remained and] preached the Gospel to you the first time.

14 And [yet] although my physical condition was [such] a trial to you, you did not regard it with contempt, or scorn *and* loathe *and* reject me; but you received me as an angel of God, [even] as Christ Jesus [Himself]!

15 What has become of that blessed enjoyment *and* satisfaction *and* self-congratulation that once was yours [in what I taught you and in your regard for me]? For I bear you witness that you would have torn out your own eyes and have given them to me [to replace mine], if that were possible.

16 Have I then become your enemy by telling the truth to you *and* dealing sincerely with you?

17 These men [the Judaizing teachers] are zealously trying to dazzle you [paying court to you, making much of you], but their purpose is not honorable *or* worthy *or* for any good. What they want to do is to isolate you [from us who oppose them], so that

---

s *Webster's New International Dictionary* offers this as a definition of "redeem."   t Marvin Vincent, *Word Studies*.   u Joseph Thayer, *A Greek-English Lexicon of the New Testament*.

they may win you over to their side *and* get you to court their favor.

18 It is always a fine thing [of course] to be zealously sought after [as you are, provided that it is] for a good purpose *and* done ᵛby reason of purity of heart and life, and not just when I am present with you!

19 My little children, for whom I am again suffering birth pangs until Christ is completely *and* permanently formed (molded) within you!

20 Would that I were with you now and could coax you vocally, for I am fearful *and* perplexed about you.

21 Tell me, you who are bent on being under the Law, will you listen to what the Law [really] says?

22 For it is written that Abraham had two sons, one by the bondmaid and one by the free woman. [Gen. 16:15; 21:2, 9.]

23 But whereas the child of the slave woman was born according to the flesh *and* had an ordinary birth, the son of the free woman was born in fulfillment of the promise.

24 Now all this is an allegory; these [two women] represent two covenants. One covenant originated from Mount Sinai [where the Law was given] and bears [children destined] for slavery; this is Hagar.

25 Now Hagar is (stands for) Mount Sinai in Arabia and she corresponds to *and* belongs in the same category with the present Jerusalem, for she is in bondage together with her children.

26 But the Jerusalem above [ˣthe Messianic kingdom of Christ] is free and she is our mother.

27 For it is written in the Scriptures, Rejoice, O barren woman, who has not given birth to children; break forth into a joyful shout, you who are not feeling birth pangs, for the desolate woman has many more children than she who has a husband. [Isa. 54:1.]

28 But we, brethren, are children [ʷnot by physical descent, as was Ishmael, but] like Isaac, born ʷin virtue of promise.

29 Yet [just] as at that time the child [of ordinary birth] born according to the flesh, despised *and* persecuted him [who was born remarkably] according to [the promise and the working of] the [Holy] Spirit, so it is now also. [Gen. 21:9.]

30 But what does the Scripture say? Cast out *and* send away the slave woman and her son, for never shall the son of the slave woman be heir *and* share the inheritance with the son of the free woman. [Gen. 21:10.]

31 So, brethren, we [who are born again] are not children of a slave woman [ˣthe natural], but of the free [ˣthe supernatural].

CHAPTER 5

IN [this] freedom Christ has made us free [completely liberated us]; stand fast then, and do not be hampered *and* held ensnared *and* submit again to a yoke of slavery [which you have once put off].

2 Notice, it is I, Paul, who tells you that if you receive circumcision, Christ will be of no profit (advantage, avail) to you [ʸfor if you distrust Him, you can gain nothing from Him].

3 I once more protest *and* testify to every man who receives circumcision that he is under obligation *and* bound to practice the whole of the Law *and* its ordinances.

4 If you seek to be justified *and* declared righteous *and* to be given a right standing with God through the Law, you are brought to nothing *and*

v Joseph Thayer, *A Greek-English Lexicon*.   w Marvin Vincent, *Word Studies*.   x Joseph S. Exell, ed., *The Biblical Illustrator*.   y John Chrysostom, one of the Doctors of the Greek Church.

so separated (severed) from Christ. You have fallen away from grace (from God's gracious favor and unmerited blessing).

5 For we, [not relying on the Law but] through the [Holy] Spirit's [help], by faith anticipate *and* wait for the blessing *and* good for which our righteousness *and* right standing with God [our ᶻconformity to His will in purpose, thought, and action, causes us] to hope.

6 For [if we are] in Christ Jesus, neither circumcision nor uncircumcision counts for anything, but only faith activated *and* energized *and* expressed *and* working through love.

7 You were running the race nobly. Who has interfered in (hindered and stopped you from) your heeding *and* following the Truth?

8 This [evil] persuasion is not from Him Who called you [Who invited you to freedom in Christ].

9 A little leaven [a slight inclination to error, or a few false teachers] leavens the whole lump [it perverts the whole conception of faith or misleads the whole church].

10 This [for my part] I have confidence [toward you] in the Lord that you will take no contrary view of the matter *but* will come to think with me. But he who is unsettling you, whoever he is, will have to bear the penalty.

11 But, brethren, if I still preach circumcision [as some accuse me of doing, as necessary to salvation], why am I still suffering persecution? In that case the cross has ceased to be a stumbling block *and* is made meaningless (done away).

12 I wish those who unsettle *and* confuse you would [ᵃgo all the way and] cut themselves off!

13 For you, brethren, were [indeed] called to freedom; only [do not let your] freedom be an incentive to

your flesh *and* an opportunity *or* excuse [for ᵃselfishness], but through love you should serve one another.

14 For the whole Law [concerning human relationships] is ᵃcomplied with in the one precept, You shall love your neighbor as [you do] yourself. [Lev. 19:18.]

15 But if you bite and devour one another [in partisan strife], be careful that you [and your whole fellowship] are not consumed by one another.

16 But I say, walk *and* live [habitually] in the [Holy] Spirit [responsive to *and* controlled *and* guided by the Spirit]; then you will certainly not gratify the cravings *and* desires of the flesh [of human nature without God].

17 For the desires of the flesh are opposed to the [Holy] Spirit, and the [desires of the] Spirit are opposed to the flesh (godless human nature); for these are antagonistic to each other [continually withstanding and in conflict with each other], so that you are not free *but* are prevented from doing what you desire to do.

18 But if you are guided (led) by the [Holy] Spirit, you are not subject to the Law.

19 Now the doings (practices) of the flesh are clear (obvious): they are immorality, impurity, indecency,

20 Idolatry, sorcery, enmity, strife, jealousy, anger (ill temper), selfishness, divisions (dissensions), party spirit (factions, sects with peculiar opinions, heresies),

21 Envy, drunkenness, carousing, and the like. I warn you beforehand, just as I did previously, that those who do such things shall not inherit the kingdom of God.

22 But the fruit of the [Holy] Spirit [the work which His presence within accomplishes] is love, joy (gladness), peace, patience (an even temper, for-

z G. Abbott-Smith, *Manual Greek Lexicon of the New Testament.*   a Marvin Vincent, *Word Studies.*

bearance), kindness, goodness (benevolence), faithfulness,

23 Gentleness (meekness, humility), self-control (self-restraint, continence). Against such things there is no law [ᵇthat can bring a charge].

24 And those who belong to Christ Jesus, the Messiah, have crucified the flesh (the godless human nature) with its passions and appetites *and* desires.

25 If we live by the [Holy] Spirit, let us also walk by the Spirit. [If by the [Holy] Spirit ᶜwe have our life in God, let us go forward ᵇwalking in line, our conduct controlled by the Spirit.]

26 Let us not become vainglorious *and* self-conceited, competitive *and* challenging *and* provoking *and* irritating to one another, envying *and* being jealous of one another.

CHAPTER 6

B RETHREN, IF any person is overtaken in misconduct *or* sin of any sort, you who are spiritual [who are responsive to and controlled by the Spirit] should set him right *and* restore *and* reinstate him, without any sense of superiority *and* with all gentleness, keeping an attentive eye on yourself, lest you should be tempted also.

2 Bear (endure, carry) one another's burdens *and* ᵈtroublesome moral faults, and in this way fulfill *and* observe perfectly the law of Christ (the Messiah) and complete ᵇwhat is lacking [in your obedience to it].

3 For if any person thinks himself to be somebody [too important to condescend to shoulder another's load] when he is nobody [of superiority except in his own estimation],

he deceives *and* deludes *and* cheats himself.

4 But let every person carefully scrutinize *and* examine *and* test his own conduct *and* his own work. He can then have the personal satisfaction *and* joy of doing something commendable [ᵇin itself alone] without [resorting to] boastful comparison with his neighbor.

5 For every person will have to bear ᵈ[be equal to understanding and calmly receive] his own [ᵉlittle] load ᵈ[of oppressive faults].

6 Let him who receives instruction in the Word [of God] share all good things with his teacher [contributing to his support].

7 Do not be deceived *and* deluded *and* misled; God will not allow Himself to be sneered at [scorned, disdained or mocked ᵇby mere pretensions or professions, or by His precepts being set aside.] [He inevitably deludes himself who attempts to delude God.] For whatever a man sows, that *and* ᵇthat only is what he will reap.

8 For he who sows to his own flesh (lower nature, sensuality) will from the flesh reap decay *and* ruin *and* destruction, but he who sows to the Spirit will from the Spirit reap eternal life.

9 And let us not lose heart *and* grow weary *and* faint in acting nobly *and* doing right, for in due time *and* at the appointed season we shall reap, if we do not loosen *and* relax our courage *and* faint.

10 So then, as occasion *and* opportunity open up to us, let us do good [ᵇmorally] to all people [not only ᵇbeing useful or profitable to them, but also doing what is for their spiritual good and advantage]. Be mindful to be a blessing, especially to those of

b Marvin Vincent, *Word Studies*.   c Adam Clarke, *The Holy Bible with A Commentary*.   d Joseph Thayer, *A Greek-English Lexicon*.   e Diminutive (indicating small size) form of the Greek word.
f Matthew Henry, *Commentary on the Holy Bible*.

the household of faith [those who belong to God's family with you, the believers].

11 See with what large letters I am writing with my own hand. [*Mark carefully these closing words of mine.]

12 Those who want to make a good impression *and* a fine show in the flesh would try to compel you to receive circumcision, simply so that they may escape being persecuted for allegiance to the cross of Christ (the Messiah, the Anointed One).

13 For even the circumcised [Jews] themselves do not [really] keep the Law, but they want to have you circumcised in order that they may glory in your flesh (your subjection to external rites).

14 But far be it from me to glory [in anything or anyone] except in the cross of our Lord Jesus Christ (the Messiah) through Whom the world has been crucified to me, and I to the world!

15 For neither is circumcision [now] of any importance, nor uncircumcision, but [only] a new creation [the result of a new birth and a new nature in Christ Jesus, the Messiah].

16 Peace and mercy be upon all who walk by this rule [who discipline themselves and regulate their lives by this principle], even upon the [true] Israel of God! [Ps. 125:5.]

17 From now on let no person trouble me [by *making it necessary for me to vindicate my apostolic authority and the divine truth of my Gospel, for I bear on my body the [brand] marks of the Lord Jesus [the wounds, scars, and other outward evidence of persecutions—these testify to His ownership of me]!

18 The grace (spiritual favor, blessing) of our Lord Jesus Christ (the Anointed One, the Messiah) be with your spirit, brethren. Amen (so be it).

THE LETTER OF PAUL TO THE
EPHESIANS

CHAPTER 1

PAUL, AN apostle (special messenger) of Christ Jesus (the Messiah), by the divine will (the purpose and the choice of God) to the saints (the consecrated, set-apart ones) *at Ephesus who are also faithful *and* loyal *and* steadfast in Christ Jesus:

2 May grace (God's unmerited favor) and spiritual peace [which means peace with God and harmony, unity, and undisturbedness] be yours from God our Father and from the Lord Jesus Christ.

3 May blessing (praise, laudation, and eulogy) be to the God and Father of our Lord Jesus Christ (the Messiah) Who has blessed us *in Christ* with every spiritual (given by the Holy Spirit) blessing in the heavenly realm!

4 Even as [in His love] He chose us [actually picked us out for Himself as His own] in Christ before the foundation of the world, that we should be

g Marvin Vincent, *Word Studies.*   h Some manuscripts do not contain "at Ephesus."

holy (consecrated and set apart for Him) and blameless in His sight, *even* above reproach, before Him in love.

5 For He foreordained us (destined us, planned in love for us) to be adopted (revealed) as His own children through Jesus Christ, in accordance with the purpose of His will [because it pleased Him and was His kind intent];

6 [So that we might be] to the praise *and* the commendation of His glorious grace (favor and mercy) which He so freely bestowed on us in the Beloved.

7 In Him we have redemption (deliverance and salvation) through His blood, the remission (forgiveness) of our offenses (shortcomings and trespasses) in accordance with the riches *and* the generosity of His gracious favor,

8 Which He lavished upon us in every kind of wisdom and understanding (practical insight and prudence),

9 Making known to us the mystery (secret) of His will (of His plan, of His purpose). [And it is this:] In accordance with His good pleasure (His merciful intention) which He had previously purposed *and* set forth in 'Him,

10 [He planned] for the maturity of the times *and* the climax of the ages to unify all things *and* head them up *and* consummate them in Christ, [both] things in heaven and things on the earth.

11 In Him we also were made [God's] heritage (portion) *and* we obtained an inheritance; for we had been foreordained (chosen and appointed beforehand) in accordance with His purpose, Who works out everything in agreement with the counsel *and* design of His [own] will,

12 So that we who first hoped in Christ [who first put our confidence in Him have been destined and appointed to] live for the praise of His glory!

13 In Him you also who have heard the Word of Truth, the glad tidings (Gospel) of your salvation, and have believed in *and* adhered to *and* relied on Him, were stamped with the seal of the long-promised Holy Spirit.

14 That [Spirit] is the guarantee of our inheritance [the firstfruits, the pledge and foretaste, the down payment on our heritage], in anticipation of its full redemption *and* our acquiring [complete] possession of it, to the praise of His glory.

15 For this reason, because I have heard of your faith in the Lord Jesus and your love toward all the saints (the people of God),

16 I do not cease to give thanks for you, making mention of you in my prayers.

17 [For I always pray to] the God of our Lord Jesus Christ, the Father of glory, that He may grant you a spirit of wisdom and revelation [of insight into mysteries and secrets] in the [deep and intimate] knowledge of Him,

18 By having the eyes of your heart flooded with light, so that you can know *and* understand the hope to which He has called you and how rich is His glorious inheritance in the saints (His set-apart ones);

19 And [so that you can know and understand] what is the immeasurable *and* unlimited *and* surpassing greatness of His power in *and* for us who believe, as demonstrated in the working of His mighty strength,

20 Which He exerted in Christ

---

i Marvin Vincent, *Word Studies in the New Testament.* mean "in Himself, " while others see it as "in Christ."

j Some commentators interpret "in Him" to

when He raised Him from the dead and seated Him at His [own] right hand in the heavenly [places],

21 Far above all rule and authority and power and dominion and every name that is named [above every title that can be conferred], not only in this age *and* in this world, but also in the age *and* the world which are to come.

22 And He has put all things under His feet and has appointed Him the universal and supreme Head of the church [a headship exercised throughout the church], [Ps. 8:6.]

23 Which is His body, the fullness of Him Who fills all in all [for in that body lives the full measure of Him Who makes everything complete, and Who fills everything everywhere with Himself].

CHAPTER 2

AND YOU [He made alive], when you were dead (slain) by [your] trespasses and sins

2 In which at one time you walked [habitually]. You were following the course *and* fashion of this world [were under the sway of the tendency of this present age], following the prince of the power of the air. [You were obedient to and under the control of] the [demon] spirit that still constantly works in the sons of disobedience [the careless, the rebellious, and the unbelieving, who go against the purposes of God].

3 Among these we as well as you once lived *and* conducted ourselves in the passions of our flesh [our behavior governed by our corrupt and sensual nature], obeying the impulses of the flesh and the thoughts of the mind [our cravings dictated by our senses and our dark imaginings]. We were then by nature children of

[God's] wrath *and* heirs of [His] indignation, like the rest of mankind.

4 But God—so rich in His mercy! Because of *and* in order to satisfy the great *and* wonderful *and* intense love with which He loved us,

5 Even when we were dead (slain) by [our own] shortcomings *and* trespasses, He made us alive together in fellowship *and* in union with Christ; [He gave us the very life of Christ Himself, the same new life with which He quickened Him, for] it is by grace (His favor and mercy which you did not deserve) that you are saved (*k*delivered from judgment and made partakers of Christ's salvation).

6 And He raised us up together with Him and made us sit down together [giving us *l*joint seating with Him] in the heavenly sphere [by virtue of our being] in Christ Jesus (the Messiah, the Anointed One).

7 He did this that He might clearly demonstrate through the ages to come the immeasurable (limitless, surpassing) riches of His free grace (His unmerited favor) in [His] kindness *and* goodness of heart toward us in Christ Jesus.

8 For it is by free grace (God's unmerited favor) that you are saved (*m*delivered from judgment *and* made partakers of Christ's salvation) through [your] faith. And this [salvation] is not of yourselves [of your own doing, it came not through your own striving], but it is the gift of God;

9 Not because of works [not the fulfillment of the Law's demands], lest any man should boast. [It is not the result of what anyone can possibly do, so no one can pride himself in it or take glory to himself.]

10 For we are God's [own] handi-

k Joseph Thayer, *A Greek-English Lexicon of the New Testament.* New Testament. m Joseph Thayer, *A Greek-English Lexicon.* l H.A.W. Meyer, *Commentary on the New Testament.*

work (His workmanship), [n]recreated in Christ Jesus, [born anew] that we may do those good works which God predestined (planned beforehand) for us [taking paths which He prepared ahead of time], that we should walk in them [living the good life which He prearranged and made ready for us to live].

11 Therefore, remember that at one time you were Gentiles (heathens) in the flesh, called Uncircumcision by those who called themselves Circumcision, [Itself a [o]mere mark] in the flesh made by human hands.

12 [Remember] that you were at that time separated (living apart) from Christ [excluded from all part in Him], utterly estranged *and* outlawed from the rights of Israel as a nation, and strangers with no share in the sacred compacts of the [Messianic] promise [with no knowledge of or right in God's agreements, His covenants]. And you had no hope (no promise); you were in the world without God.

13 But now in Christ Jesus, you who once were [so] far away, through (by, in) the blood of Christ have been brought near.

14 For He is [Himself] our peace (our bond of unity and harmony). He has made us both [Jew and Gentile] one [body], and has broken down (destroyed, abolished) the hostile dividing wall between us,

15 By abolishing in His [own crucified] flesh the enmity [caused by] the Law with its decrees and ordinances [which He annulled]; that He from the two might create in Himself one new man [one new quality of humanity out of the two], so making peace.

16 And [He designed] to reconcile to God both [Jew and Gentile, united] in a single body by means of His cross, thereby killing the mutual enmity *and* bringing the feud to an end.

17 And He came and preached the glad tidings of peace to you who were afar off and [peace] to those who were near. [Isa. 57:19.]

18 For it is through Him that we both [whether far off or near] now have an introduction (access) by one [Holy] Spirit to the Father [so that we are able to approach Him].

19 Therefore you are no longer outsiders (exiles, migrants, and aliens, excluded from the rights of citizens), but you now share citizenship with the saints (God's own people, consecrated and set apart for Himself); and you belong to God's [own] household.

20 You are built upon the foundation of the apostles and prophets with Christ Jesus Himself the chief Cornerstone.

21 In Him the whole structure is joined (bound, welded) together harmoniously, and it continues to rise (grow, increase) into a holy temple in the Lord [a sanctuary dedicated, consecrated, and sacred to the presence of the Lord].

22 In Him [and in fellowship with one another] you yourselves also are being built up [into this structure] with the rest, to form a fixed abode (dwelling place) of God in (by, through) the Spirit.

CHAPTER 3

FOR THIS reason [[p]because I preached that you are thus built up together], I, Paul, [am] the prisoner of Jesus the Christ [p]for the sake *and* on behalf of you Gentiles—

2 Assuming that you have heard of

n Arthur S. Way, *Way's Epistles: The Letters of St. Paul to Seven Churches and Three Friends.*   o Arthur S. Way, *The Letters of St. Paul to Seven Churches and Three Friends.*   p Matthew Henry, *Commentary on the Holy Bible*: The Jews persecuted and imprisoned Paul because he was an apostle to the Gentiles and preached the Gospel to them.

the stewardship of God's grace (His unmerited favor) that was entrusted to me [to dispense to you] for your benefit,

3 [And] that the mystery (secret) was made known to me and I was allowed to comprehend it by direct revelation, as I already briefly wrote you.

4 When you read this you can understand my insight into the mystery of Christ.

5 [This mystery] was never disclosed to human beings in past generations as it has now been revealed to His holy apostles (consecrated messengers) and prophets by the [Holy] Spirit.

6 [It is this:] that the Gentiles are now to be fellow heirs [with the Jews], members of the same body and joint partakers [sharing] in the same divine promise in Christ through [their acceptance of] the glad tidings (the Gospel).

7 Of this [Gospel] I was made a minister according to the gift of God's free grace (undeserved favor) which was bestowed on me by the exercise (the working in all its effectiveness) of His power.

8 To me, though I am the very least of all the saints (God's consecrated people), this grace (favor, privilege) was granted and graciously entrusted: to proclaim to the Gentiles the unending (boundless, fathomless, incalculable, and exhaustless) riches of Christ [wealth which no human being could have searched out],

9 Also to enlighten all men and make plain to them what is the plan [regarding the Gentiles and providing for the salvation of all men] of the mystery kept hidden through the ages and concealed until now in [the mind of] God Who created all things by Christ Jesus.

10 [The purpose is] that through the church the ᵍcomplicated, many-sided wisdom of God in all its infinite variety and innumerable aspects might now be made known to the angelic rulers and authorities (principalities and powers) in the heavenly sphere.

11 This is in accordance with the terms of the eternal and timeless purpose which He has realized and carried into effect in [the person of] Christ Jesus our Lord,

12 In Whom, because of our faith in Him, we dare to have the boldness (courage and confidence) of free access (an unreserved approach to God with freedom and without fear).

13 So I ask you not to lose heart [not to faint or become despondent through fear] at what I am suffering in your behalf. [Rather glory in it] for it is an honor to you.

14 For this reason [ʳseeing the greatness of this plan by which you are built together in Christ], I bow my knees before the Father of our Lord Jesus Christ,

15 For Whom every family in heaven and on earth is named [that Father from Whom all fatherhood takes its title and derives its name].

16 May He grant you out of the rich treasury of His glory to be strengthened and reinforced with mighty power in the inner man by the [Holy] Spirit [Himself indwelling your innermost being and personality].

17 May Christ through your faith [actually] dwell (settle down, abide, make His permanent home) in your hearts! May you be rooted deep in love and founded securely on love,

18 That you may have the power

---

q *Webster's New International Dictionary* offers this as a definition of "manifold" (the *King James Version's* rendering of the Greek *polupoikilos*).   r Many manuscripts consider that Paul here resumes the thread of verse 1.

and be strong to apprehend *and* grasp with all the saints [God's devoted people, the experience of that love] what is the breadth and length and height and depth [of it];

19 [That you may really come] to know [practically, [s]through experience for yourselves] the love of Christ, which far surpasses [s]mere knowledge [without experience]; that you may be filled [through all your being] [u]unto all the fullness of God [may have the richest measure of the divine Presence, and [t]become a body wholly filled and flooded with God Himself]!

20 Now to Him Who, by (in consequence of) the [action of His] power that is at work within us, is able to [carry out His purpose and] do superabundantly, far over *and* above all that we [dare] ask or think [infinitely beyond our highest prayers, desires, thoughts, hopes, or dreams]—

21 To Him be glory in the church and in Christ Jesus throughout all generations forever and ever. Amen (so be it).

CHAPTER 4

I THEREFORE, the prisoner for the Lord, appeal to *and* beg you to walk (lead a life) worthy of the [divine] calling to which you have been called [with behavior that is a credit to the summons to God's service,

2 Living as becomes you] with complete lowliness of mind (humility) and meekness (unselfishness, gentleness, mildness), with patience, bearing with one another *and* making allowances because you love one another.

3 Be eager *and* strive earnestly to guard *and* keep the harmony and

oneness of [and produced by] the Spirit in the binding power of peace.

4 [There is] one body and one Spirit—just as there is also one hope [that belongs] to the calling you received—

5 [There is] one Lord, one faith, one baptism,

6 One God and Father of [us] all, Who is above all [Sovereign over all], pervading all and [living] in [us] all.

7 Yet grace (God's unmerited favor) was given to each of us individually [not indiscriminately, but in different ways] in proportion to the measure of Christ's [rich and bounteous] gift.

8 Therefore it is said, When He ascended on high, He led captivity captive [He led a train of [u]vanquished foes] and He bestowed gifts on men. [Ps. 68:18.]

9 [But He ascended?] Now what can this, He ascended, mean but that He had previously descended from [the heights of] heaven into [the depths], the lower parts of the earth?

10 He Who descended is the [very] same as He Who also has ascended high above all the heavens, that He [His presence] might fill all things (the whole universe, from the lowest to the highest).

11 And His gifts were [varied; He Himself appointed and gave men to us] some to be apostles (special messengers), some prophets (inspired preachers and expounders), some evangelists (preachers of the Gospel, traveling missionaries), some pastors (shepherds of His flock) and teachers.

12 His intention was the perfecting *and* the full equipping of the saints (His consecrated people), [that they should do] the work of ministering

---

s Marvin Vincent, *Word Studies*.   t Joseph Thayer, *A Greek-English Lexicon*.   u Matthew Henry, *Commentary on the Holy Bible*: "He conquered those who had conquered us—such as sin, the devil, and death."

toward building up Christ's body (the church),

13 [That it might develop] until we all attain oneness in the faith and in the comprehension of the [ᵛfull and accurate] knowledge of the Son of God, that [we might arrive] at really mature manhood (the completeness of personality which is nothing less than the standard height of Christ's own perfection), the measure of the stature of the fullness of the Christ *and* the completeness found in Him.

14 So then, we may no longer be children, tossed [like ships] to and fro between chance gusts of teaching *and* wavering with every changing wind of doctrine, [the prey of] the cunning *and* cleverness of ᵂunscrupulous men, [gamblers engaged] in every shifting form of trickery in inventing errors to mislead.

15 Rather, let our lives lovingly ᵛexpress truth [in all things, speaking truly, dealing truly, living truly]. Enfolded in love, let us grow up in every way *and* in all things into Him Who is the Head, [even] Christ (the Messiah, the Anointed One).

16 For because of Him the whole body (the church, in all its various parts), closely joined and firmly knit together by the joints *and* ligaments with which it is supplied, when each part [with power adapted to its need] is working properly [in all its functions], grows to full maturity, building itself up in love.

17 So this I say and solemnly testify in [the name of] the Lord [as in His presence], that you must no longer live as the heathen (the Gentiles) do in their perverseness [in the folly, vanity, and emptiness of their souls and the futility] of their minds.

18 Their ᵛmoral understanding is darkened *and* their reasoning is beclouded. [They are] alienated (estranged, self-banished) from the life of God [with no share in it; this is] because of the ignorance (the want of knowledge and perception, the willful blindness) that is ᵛdeep-seated in them, due to their hardness of heart [to the insensitiveness of their moral nature].

19 In their spiritual apathy they have become callous *and* past feeling *and* reckless and have abandoned themselves [a prey] to unbridled sensuality, eager *and* greedy to indulge in every form of impurity [that their depraved desires may suggest and demand].

20 But you did not so learn Christ!

21 Assuming that you have really heard Him *and* been taught by Him, as [all] Truth is in Jesus [embodied and personified in Him],

22 Strip yourselves of your former nature [put off and discard your old unrenewed self] which characterized your previous manner of life and becomes corrupt through lusts *and* desires that spring from delusion;

23 And be constantly renewed in the spirit of your mind [having a fresh mental and spiritual attitude],

24 And put on the new nature (the regenerate self) created in God's image, [Godlike] in true righteousness and holiness.

25 Therefore, rejecting all falsity *and* being done now with it, let everyone express the truth with his neighbor, for we are all parts of one body *and* members one of another. [Zech. 8:16.]

26 When angry, do not sin; do not ever let your wrath (your exasperation, your fury or indignation) last until the sun goes down.

27 Leave no [such] room *or* foothold for the devil [give no opportunity to him].

28 Let the thief steal no more, but

ᵛ Marvin Vincent, *Word Studies*.   ᵂ Literal translation: "dice-playing."

rather let him be industrious, making an honest living with his own hands, so that he may be able to give to those in need.

29 Let no foul *or* polluting language, *nor* evil word *nor* unwholesome *or* worthless talk [ever] come out of your mouth, but only such [speech] as is good *and* beneficial to the spiritual progress of others, as is fitting to the need *and* the occasion, that it may be a blessing *and* give grace (God's favor) to those who hear it.

30 And do not grieve the Holy Spirit of God [do not offend or vex or sadden Him], by Whom you were sealed (marked, branded as God's own, secured) for the day of redemption (of final deliverance through Christ from evil and the consequences of sin).

31 Let all bitterness and indignation *and* wrath (passion, rage, bad temper) and resentment (anger, animosity) and quarreling (brawling, clamor, contention) and slander (evil-speaking, abusive or blasphemous language) be banished from you, with all malice (spite, ill will, or baseness of any kind).

32 And become useful *and* helpful *and* kind to one another, tenderhearted (compassionate, understanding, loving-hearted), forgiving one another [readily and freely], as God in Christ forgave you.

CHAPTER 5

THEREFORE BE imitators of God [copy Him *and* follow His example], as well-beloved children [imitate their father].

2 And walk in love, [esteeming and delighting in one another] as Christ loved us and gave Himself up for us, a ˣslain offering and sacrifice to God [for you, so that it became] a sweet fragrance. [Ezek. 20:41.]

3 But immorality (sexual vice) and all impurity [ʸof lustful, rich, wasteful living] or greediness must not even be named among you, as is fitting *and* proper among saints (God's consecrated people).

4 Let there be no filthiness (obscenity, indecency) nor foolish *and* sinful (silly and corrupt) talk, nor coarse jesting, which are not fitting *or* becoming; but instead voice your thankfulness [to God].

5 For be sure of this: that no person practicing sexual vice or impurity in thought or in life, or one who is covetous [who has lustful desire for the property of others and is greedy for gain]—for he [in effect] is an idolater—has any inheritance in the kingdom of Christ and of God.

6 Let no one delude *and* deceive you with empty excuses *and* groundless arguments [for these sins], for through these things the wrath of God comes upon the sons of rebellion *and* disobedience.

7 So do not associate *or* be sharers with them.

8 For once you were darkness, but now you are light in the Lord; walk as children of Light [lead the lives of those native-born to the Light].

9 For the fruit (the effect, the product) of the Light *or* ᶻthe Spirit [consists] in every form of kindly goodness, uprightness of heart, and trueness of life.

10 And try to learn [in your experience] what is pleasing to the Lord [let your lives be constant proofs of what is most acceptable to Him].

11 Take no part in *and* have no fellowship with the fruitless deeds *and* enterprises of darkness, but instead [let your lives be so in contrast

x Marvin Vincent, *Word Studies*. y Joseph Thayer, *A Greek-English Lexicon*. z Some ancient manuscripts so read.

as to] ᵃexpose and reprove and convict them.

12 For it is a shame even to speak of or mention the things that [such people] practice in secret.

13 But when anything is exposed and reproved by the light, it is made visible and clear; and where everything is visible and clear there is light.

14 Therefore He says, Awake, O sleeper, and arise from the dead, and Christ shall shine (make day dawn) upon you and give you light. [Isa. 26:19; 60:1, 2.]

15 Look carefully then how you walk! Live purposefully and worthily and accurately, not as the unwise and witless, but as wise (sensible, intelligent people),

16 Making the very most of the time [buying up each opportunity], because the days are evil.

17 Therefore do not be vague and thoughtless and foolish, but understanding and firmly grasping what the will of the Lord is.

18 And do not get drunk with wine, for that is debauchery; but ever be filled and stimulated with the [Holy] Spirit. [Prov. 23:20.]

19 Speak out to one another in psalms and hymns and spiritual songs, offering praise with voices [ᵇand instruments] and making melody with all your heart to the Lord,

20 At all times and for everything giving thanks in the name of our Lord Jesus Christ to God the Father,

21 Be subject to one another out of reverence for Christ (the Messiah, the Anointed One).

22 Wives, be subject (be submissive and adapt yourselves) to your own husbands as [a service] to the Lord.

23 For the husband is head of the wife as Christ is the Head of the church, Himself the Savior of [His] body.

24 As the church is subject to Christ, so let wives also be subject in everything to their husbands.

25 Husbands, love your wives, as Christ loved the church and gave Himself up for her,

26 So that He might sanctify her, having cleansed her by the washing of water with the Word,

27 That He might present the church to Himself in glorious splendor, without spot or wrinkle or any such things [that she might be holy and faultless].

28 Even so husbands should love their wives as [being in a sense] their own bodies. He who loves his own wife loves himself.

29 For no man ever hated his own flesh, but nourishes and carefully protects and cherishes it; as Christ does the church,

30 Because we are members (parts) of His body.

31 For this reason a man shall leave his father and his mother and shall be joined to his wife, and the two shall become one flesh. [Gen. 2:24.]

32 This mystery is very great, but I speak concerning [the relation of] Christ and the church.

33 However, let each man of you [without exception] love his wife as [being in a sense] his very own self; and let the wife see that she respects and reverences her husband [ᶜthat she notices him, regards him, honors him, prefers him, venerates, and esteems him; and ᶜthat she defers to him, praises him, and loves and admires him exceedingly]. [I Pet. 3:2.]

a Joseph Thayer, A Greek-English Lexicon.　　b George R. Berry, Greek-English New Testament Lexicon.
c Webster's New International Dictionary offers this as a list of English words with the same (or nearly the same) essential meaning as "respect" and "reverence." The latter ("reverence") includes the concept of "adore" in the sense not applied to deity.

CHAPTER 6

CHILDREN, OBEY your parents in the Lord [as His representatives], for this is just and right.

2 Honor (esteem and value as precious) your father and your mother —this is the first commandment with a promise—[Exod. 20:12.]

3 That all may be well with you and that you may live long on the earth.

4 Fathers, do not irritate *and* provoke your children to anger [do not exasperate them to resentment], but rear them [tenderly] in the training *and* discipline and the counsel *and* admonition of the Lord.

5 Servants (slaves), be obedient to those who are your physical masters, having respect for them and eager concern to please them, in singleness of motive *and* with all your heart, as [service] to Christ [Himself]—

6 Not in the way of eye-service [as if they were watching you] and only to please men, but as servants (slaves) of Christ, doing the will of God heartily *and* with your whole soul,

7 Rendering service readily with goodwill, as to the Lord and not to men,

8 Knowing that for whatever good anyone does, he will receive his reward from the Lord, whether he is slave or free.

9 You masters, act on the same [principle] toward them and give up threatening *and* using violent *and* abusive words, knowing that He Who is both their Master and yours is in heaven, and that there is no respect of persons (no partiality) with Him.

10 In conclusion, be strong in the Lord [be empowered through your union with Him]; draw your strength from Him [that strength which His boundless might provides].

11 Put on God's whole armor [the armor of a heavy-armed soldier which God supplies], that you may be able successfully to stand up against [all] the strategies *and* the deceits of the devil.

12 For we are not wrestling with flesh and blood [contending only with physical opponents], but against the despotisms, against the powers, against [the master spirits who are] the world rulers of this present darkness, against the spirit forces of wickedness in the heavenly (supernatural) sphere.

13 Therefore put on God's complete armor, that you may be able to resist *and* stand your ground on the evil day [of danger], and, having done all [the crisis demands], to stand [firmly in your place].

14 Stand therefore [hold your ground], having tightened the belt of truth around your loins and having put on the breastplate of integrity *and* of moral rectitude *and* right standing with God,

15 And having shod your feet in preparation [to face the enemy with the [d]firm-footed stability, the promptness, and the readiness [e]produced by the good news] of the Gospel of peace. [Isa. 52:7.]

16 Lift up over all the [covering] shield of [d]saving faith, upon which you can quench all the flaming missiles of the wicked [one].

17 And take the helmet of salvation and the sword that the Spirit [f]wields, which is the Word of God.

18 Pray at all times (on every occasion, in every season) in the Spirit, with all [manner of] prayer and entreaty. To that end keep alert and watch with strong purpose *and* per-

---

d Marvin Vincent, *Word Studies.*   e Joseph Thayer, *A Greek-English Lexicon.*   f Charles B. Williams, *The New Testament: A Translation in the Language of the People:* Subjective genitive—a type of genitive of possession. Thus here the Spirit is the subject or agent of the verbal action.

severance, interceding in behalf of all the saints (God's consecrated people).

19 And [pray] also for me, that [freedom of] utterance may be given me, that I may open my mouth to proclaim boldly the mystery of the good news (the Gospel),

20 For which I am an ambassador in a coupling chain [in prison. Pray] that I may declare it boldly *and* courageously, as I ought to do.

21 Now that you may know how I am and what I am doing, Tychicus, the beloved brother and faithful minister in the Lord [and His service], will tell you everything.

22 I have sent him to you for this very purpose, that you may know how we are and that he may [g]console *and* cheer *and* encourage *and* strengthen your hearts.

23 Peace be to the brethren, and love joined with faith, from God the Father and the Lord Jesus Christ (the Messiah, the Anointed One).

24 Grace (God's undeserved favor) be with all who love our Lord Jesus Christ with undying *and* incorruptible [love]. *Amen (so let it be).*

THE LETTER OF PAUL TO THE
PHILIPPIANS

CHAPTER 1

PAUL AND Timothy, bond servants of Christ Jesus (the Messiah), to all the saints (God's consecrated people) in Christ Jesus who are at Philippi, with the bishops (overseers) and deacons (assistants):

2 Grace (favor and blessing) to you and [heart] peace from God our Father and the Lord Jesus Christ (the Messiah).

3 I thank my God in all my remembrance of you.

4 In every prayer of mine I always make my entreaty *and* petition for you all with joy (delight).

5 [I thank my God] for your fellowship (your [h]sympathetic cooperation and contributions and partnership) in advancing the good news (the Gospel) from the first day [you heard it] until now.

6 And I am convinced *and* sure of this very thing, that He Who began a good work in you will continue until the day of Jesus Christ [right up to the time of His return], developing [that good work] *and* perfecting *and* bringing it to full completion in you.

7 It is right *and* appropriate for me to have this confidence *and* feel this way about you all, because [i]you have me in your heart *and* I hold you in my heart as partakers *and* sharers, one *and* all with me, of grace (God's unmerited favor and spiritual blessing). [This is true] both when I am shut up in prison and when I am out in the defense and confirmation of the good news (the Gospel).

8 For God is my witness how I long for *and* [j]pursue you all with love, in the tender mercy of Christ Jesus [Himself]!

9 And this I pray: that your love may abound yet more and more *and*

---

g Joseph Thayer, *A Greek-English Lexicon.* h Marvin Vincent, *Word Studies in the New Testament.*
i Alternate translation. j Joseph Thayer, *A Greek-English Lexicon of the New Testament.*

extend to its fullest development in knowledge and all keen insight [that your love may ^k display itself in greater depth of acquaintance and more comprehensive discernment],

10 So that you may surely learn to sense what is vital, *and* approve *and* prize what is excellent *and* of real value [recognizing the highest and the best, and distinguishing the moral differences], and that you may be untainted *and* pure and unerring *and* blameless [so that with hearts sincere and certain and unsullied, you may approach] the day of Christ [not stumbling *nor* causing others to stumble].

11 May you abound in *and* be filled with the fruits of righteousness [of right standing with God and right doing] which come through Jesus Christ (the Anointed One), to the honor and praise of God [^l that His glory may be both manifested and recognized].

12 Now I want you to know *and* continue to rest assured, brethren, that what [has happened] to me [this imprisonment] has actually only served to advance *and* give a renewed impetus to the [spreading of the] good news (the Gospel).

13 So much is this a fact that throughout the whole imperial guard and to all the rest [here] my imprisonment has become generally known to be in Christ [that I am a prisoner in His service and for Him].

14 And [also] most of the brethren have derived fresh confidence in the Lord because of my chains and are much more bold to speak *and* publish fearlessly the Word of God [acting with more freedom and indifference to the consequences].

15 Some, it is true, [actually] preach Christ (the Messiah) [for no

better reason than] out of envy and rivalry (party spirit), but others are doing so out of a loyal spirit *and* goodwill.

16 ^m The latter [proclaim Christ] out of love, because they recognize *and* know that I am [providentially] put here for the defense of the good news (the Gospel).

17 ^m But the former preach Christ out of a party spirit, insincerely [out of no pure motive], but thinking to annoy me], supposing they are making my bondage more bitter *and* my chains more galling.

18 But what does it matter, so long as either way, whether in pretense [for personal ends] or in all honesty [for the furtherance of the Truth], Christ is being proclaimed? And in that I [now] rejoice, yes, and I shall rejoice [hereafter] also.

19 For I am well assured *and* indeed know that through your prayers and a ^k bountiful supply of the Spirit of Jesus Christ (the Messiah) this will turn out for my preservation (for the spiritual health and ^k welfare of my own soul and avail toward the saving work of the Gospel).

20 This is in keeping with my own eager desire *and* persistent expectation *and* hope, that I shall not disgrace myself *nor* be put to shame in anything; but that with the utmost freedom of speech *and* unfailing courage, now as always heretofore, Christ (the Messiah) will be magnified *and* get glory and praise in this body of mine *and* be boldly exalted in my person, whether through (by) life or through (by) death.

21 For me to live is Christ [His life in me], and to die is gain [the gain of the glory of eternity].

22 If, however, it is to be life in the flesh *and* I am to live on here, that

---

k Marvin Vincent, *Word Studies.*   l Marvin Vincent, *Word Studies in the New Testament.*   m The order of verses 16 and 17 is that of the most ancient manuscripts; the *King James Version* has them reversed.

means fruitful service for me; so I can say nothing as to my personal preference [I cannot choose].

23 But I am hard pressed between the two. My yearning desire is to depart (to be free of this world, to set forth) and be with Christ, for that is far, far better;

24 But to remain in my body is more needful and essential for your sake.

25 Since I am convinced of this, I know that I shall remain and stay by you all, to promote your progress and joy in believing,

26 So that in me you may have abundant cause for exultation and glorying in Christ Jesus, through my coming to you again.

27 Only be sure as citizens so to conduct yourselves [that] your manner of life [will be] worthy of the good news (the Gospel) of Christ, so that whether I [do] come and see you or am absent, I may hear this of you: that you are standing firm in united spirit and purpose, striving side by side and contending with a single mind for the faith of the glad tidings (the Gospel).

28 And do not [for a moment] be frightened or intimidated in anything by your opponents and adversaries, for such [constancy and fearlessness] will be a clear sign (proof and seal) to them of [their impending] destruction, but [a sure token and evidence] of your deliverance and salvation, and that from God.

29 For you have been granted [the privilege] for Christ's sake not only to believe in (adhere to, rely on, and trust in) Him, but also to suffer in His behalf.

30 So you are engaged in the same conflict which you saw me [wage] and which you now hear to be mine [still].

CHAPTER 2

SO BY whatever [appeal to you there is in our mutual dwelling in Christ, by whatever] strengthening and consoling and encouraging [our relationship] in Him [affords], by whatever persuasive [n]incentive there is in love, by whatever participation in the [Holy] Spirit [we share], and by whatever depth of affection and compassionate sympathy,

2 Fill up and complete my joy by living in harmony and being of the same mind and one in purpose, having the same love, being in full accord and of one harmonious mind and intention.

3 Do nothing from factional motives [through contentiousness, strife, selfishness, or for unworthy ends] or prompted by conceit and empty arrogance. Instead, in the true spirit of humility (lowliness of mind) let each regard the others as better than and superior to himself [thinking more highly of one another than you do of yourselves].

4 Let each of you esteem and look upon and be concerned for not [merely] his own interests, but also each for the interests of others.

5 Let this same attitude and purpose and [humble] mind be in you which was in Christ Jesus: [Let Him be your example in humility:]

6 Who, although being essentially one with God and in the form of God [[o]possessing the fullness of the attributes which make God God], did not [p]think this equality with God was a thing to be eagerly grasped [p]or retained,

7 But stripped Himself [of all privileges and [q]rightful dignity], so as to

assume the guise of a servant (slave), in that He became like men *and* was born a human being.

8 And after He had appeared in human form, He abased *and* humbled Himself [still further] and carried His obedience to the extreme of death, even the death of the cross!

9 Therefore [because He stooped so low] God has highly exalted Him and has [r]freely bestowed on Him the name that is above every name,

10 That in (at) the name of Jesus every knee [s]should (must) bow, in heaven and on earth and under the earth,

11 And every tongue [[r]frankly and openly] confess *and* acknowledge that Jesus Christ is Lord, to the glory of God the Father.

12 Therefore, my dear ones, as you have always obeyed [my suggestions], so now, not only [with the enthusiasm you would show] in my presence but much more because I am absent, work out (cultivate, carry out to the goal, and fully complete) your own salvation with reverence *and* awe and trembling (self-distrust, [r]with serious caution, tenderness of conscience, watchfulness against temptation, timidly shrinking from whatever might offend God and discredit the name of Christ),

13 [Not in your own strength] for it is God Who is all the while [r]effectually at work in you [energizing and creating in you the power and desire), both to will and to work for His good pleasure *and* satisfaction *and* [t]delight.

14 Do all things without grumbling *and* faultfinding *and* complaining [[r]against God] and [r]questioning *and* doubting [among yourselves],

15 That you may show yourselves to be blameless *and* guileless, innocent *and* uncontaminated, children of God without blemish (faultless, unrebukable) in the midst of a crooked *and* wicked generation [spiritually perverted and perverse], among whom you are seen as bright lights (stars or beacons shining out clearly) in the [dark] world,

16 Holding out [to it] *and* offering [to all men] the Word of Life, so that in the day of Christ I may have something of which exultantly to rejoice *and* glory in that I did not run my race in vain or spend my labor to no purpose.

17 Even if [my lifeblood] must be poured out as a libation on the sacrificial offering of your faith [to God], still I am glad [to do it] and [u]congratulate you all on [your share in] it.

18 And you also in like manner be glad and [v]congratulate me on [my share in] it.

19 But I hope *and* trust in the Lord Jesus soon to send Timothy to you, so that I may also be encouraged *and* cheered by learning news of you.

20 For I have no one like him [no one of so kindred a spirit] who will be so genuinely interested in your welfare *and* devoted to your interests.

21 For the others all seek [to advance] their own interests, not those of Jesus Christ (the Messiah).

22 But Timothy's tested worth you know, how as a son with his father he has toiled with me zealously in [serving and helping to advance] the good news (the Gospel).

23 I hope therefore to send him promptly, just as soon as I know how my case is going to turn out.

24 But [really] I am confident *and*

r Marvin Vincent, *Word Studies.*   s "Should" is the past tense of "shall," implying authority or compulsion.   t Alexander Souter, *Pocket Lexicon of the Greek New Testament.*   u Joseph P. Lightfoot, *Saint Paul's Epistle to the Philippians* and James Moulton and George Milligan, *The Vocabulary of the Greek Testament.*   v Joseph P. Lightfoot, *Saint Paul's Epistle to the Philippians* and James Moulton and George Milligan, *The Vocabulary of the Greek Testament.*

fully trusting in the Lord that shortly I myself shall come to you also.

25 However, I thought it necessary to send Epaphroditus [back] to you. [He has been] my brother and companion in labor and my fellow soldier, as well as [having come as] your special messenger (apostle) and minister to my need.

26 For he has been [homesick] longing for you all and has been distressed because you had heard that he was ill.

27 He certainly was ill [too], near to death. But God had compassion on him, and not only on him but also on me, lest I should have sorrow [over him] ʷcoming upon sorrow.

28 So I have sent him the more willingly and eagerly, that you may be gladdened at seeing him again, and that I may be the less disquieted.

29 Welcome him [home] then in the Lord with all joy, and honor and highly appreciate men like him,

30 For it was through working for Christ that he came so near death, risking his [very] life to complete the deficiencies in your service to me [which distance prevented you yourselves from rendering].

CHAPTER 3

FOR THE rest, my brethren, delight yourselves in the Lord and continue to rejoice that you are in Him. To keep writing to you [over and over] of the same things is not irksome to me, and it is [a precaution] for your safety.

2 Look out for those dogs [Judaizers, legalists], look out for those mischief-makers, look out for those who mutilate the flesh.

3 For we [Christians] are the true circumcision, who worship God in spirit and by the Spirit of God and exult and glory and pride ourselves in Jesus Christ, and put no confidence or dependence [on what we are] in the flesh and on outward privileges and physical advantages and external appearances—

4 Though for myself I have [at least grounds] to rely on the flesh. If any other man considers that he has or seems to have reason to rely on the flesh and his physical and outward advantages, I have still more!

5 Circumcised when I was eight days old, of the race of Israel, of the tribe of Benjamin, a Hebrew [and the son] of Hebrews; as to the observance of the Law I was of [the party of] the Pharisees.

6 As to my zeal, I was a persecutor of the church, and by the Law's standard of righteousness (supposed justice, uprightness, and right standing with God) I was proven to be blameless and no fault was found with me.

7 But whatever former things I had that might have been gains to me, I have come to consider as [ˣone combined] loss for Christ's sake.

8 Yes, furthermore, I count everything as loss compared to the possession of the priceless privilege (the overwhelming preciousness, the surpassing worth, and supreme advantage) of knowing Christ Jesus my Lord and of progressively becoming more deeply and intimately acquainted with Him [of perceiving and recognizing and understanding Him more fully and clearly]. For His sake I have lost everything and consider it all to be mere rubbish (refuse, dregs), in order that I may win (gain) Christ (the Anointed One),

9 And that I may [actually] be found and known as in Him, not having any [self-achieved] righteousness that can be called my own, based on

---

ʷ Marvin Vincent, *Word Studies.*   ˣ Marvin Vincent, *Word Studies:* His "gains" are plural, but they are all counted as one combined "loss" (singular).

my obedience to the Law's demands (ritualistic uprightness and supposed right standing with God thus acquired), but possessing that [genuine righteousness] which comes through faith in Christ (the Anointed One), the [truly] right standing with God, which comes from God by [saving] faith.

10 [For my determined purpose is] that I may know Him [that I may progressively become more deeply and intimately acquainted with Him, perceiving and recognizing and understanding the wonders of His Person more strongly and more clearly], and that I may in that same way come to know the power outflowing from His resurrection [ʸwhich it exerts over believers], and that I may so share His sufferings as to be continually transformed [in spirit into His likeness even] to His death, [in the hope]

11 That if possible I may attain to the [ᶻspiritual and moral] resurrection [that lifts me] out from among the dead [even while in the body].

12 Not that I have now attained [this ideal], or have already been made perfect, but I press on to lay hold of (grasp) and make my own, that for which Christ Jesus (the Messiah) has laid hold of me and made me His own.

13 I do not consider, brethren, that I have captured and made it my own [yet]; but one thing I do [it is my one aspiration]: forgetting what lies behind and straining forward to what lies ahead,

14 I press on toward the goal to win the [supreme and heavenly] prize to which God in Christ Jesus is calling us upward.

15 So let those [of us] who are spiritually mature and full-grown have

this mind and hold these convictions; and if in any respect you have a different attitude of mind, God will make that clear to you also.

16 Only let us hold true to what we have already attained and walk and order our lives by that.

17 Brethren, together follow my example and observe those who live after the pattern we have set for you.

18 For there are many, of whom I have often told you and now tell you even with tears, who walk (live) as enemies of the cross of Christ (the Anointed One).

19 They are doomed and their ᵃfate is eternal misery (perdition); their god is their stomach (their appetites, their sensuality) and they glory in their shame, ᵃsiding with earthly things and being of their party.

20 But we are citizens of the state (commonwealth, homeland) which is in heaven, and from it also we ʸearnestly and patiently await [the coming of] the Lord Jesus Christ (the Messiah) [as] Savior,

21 Who will ʸtransform and fashion anew the body of our humiliation to conform to and be like the body of His glory and majesty, by exerting that power which enables Him even to subject everything to Himself.

CHAPTER 4

THEREFORE, MY brethren, whom I love and yearn to see, my delight and crown (wreath of victory), thus stand firm in the Lord, my beloved.

2 I entreat and advise Euodia and I entreat and advise Syntyche to agree and to work in harmony in the Lord.

3 And I exhort you too, [my] genuine yokefellow, help these [two women to keep on cooperating], for

y Marvin Vincent, *Word Studies*.   z Charles B. Williams, *The New Testament: A Translation in the Language of the People*: A spiritual, moral resurrection—not the final, physical one, which will be the climax. a Joseph Thayer, *A Greek-English Lexicon*.

they have toiled along with me in [the spreading of] the good news (the Gospel), as have Clement and the rest of my fellow workers whose names are in the Book of Life.

4 Rejoice in the Lord always [delight, gladden yourselves in Him]; again I say, Rejoice! [Ps. 37:4.]

5 Let all men know and perceive and recognize your unselfishness (your considerateness, your forbearing spirit). The Lord is near [He is ᵇcoming soon].

6 Do not fret or have any anxiety about anything, but in every circumstance and in everything, by prayer and petition (ᵇdefinite requests), with thanksgiving, continue to make your wants known to God.

7 And God's peace [shall be yours, that ᵇtranquil state of a soul assured of its salvation through Christ, and so fearing nothing from God and being content with its earthly lot of whatever sort that is, that peace] which transcends all understanding shall ᶜgarrison and mount guard over your hearts and minds in Christ Jesus.

8 For the rest, brethren, whatever is true, whatever is worthy of reverence and is honorable and seemly, whatever is just, whatever is pure, whatever is lovely and lovable, whatever is kind and winsome and gracious, if there is any virtue and excellence, if there is anything worthy of praise, think on and weigh and take account of these things [fix your minds on them].

9 Practice what you have learned and received and heard and seen in me, and model your way of living on it, and the God of peace (of ᵈuntroubled, undisturbed well-being) will be with you.

10 I was made very happy in the Lord that now you have revived your interest in my welfare after so long a time; you were indeed thinking of me, but you had no opportunity to show it.

11 Not that I am implying that I was in any personal want, for I have learned how to be ᵉcontent (satisfied to the point where I am not disturbed or disquieted) in whatever state I am.

12 I know how to be abased and live humbly in straitened circumstances, and I know also how to enjoy plenty and live in abundance. I have learned in any and all circumstances the secret of facing every situation, whether well-fed or going hungry, having a sufficiency and enough to spare or going without and being in want.

13 I have strength for all things in Christ Who empowers me [I am ready for anything and equal to anything through Him Who ᶠinfuses inner strength into me; I am ᵍself-sufficient in Christ's sufficiency].

14 But it was right and commendable and noble of you to contribute for my needs and to share my difficulties with me.

15 And you Philippians yourselves well know that in the early days of the Gospel ministry, when I left Macedonia, no church (assembly) entered into partnership with me and opened up [a debit and credit] account in giving and receiving except you only.

16 For even in Thessalonica you sent [me contributions] for my needs, not only once but a second time.

17 Not that I seek or am eager for [your] gift, but I do seek and am eager for the fruit which increases to your credit [the harvest of blessing

---

b Joseph Thayer, *A Greek-English Lexicon.*   c William Gurnall, cited by Marvin Vincent, *Word Studies.*
d Hermann Cremer, *Biblico-Theological Lexicon of New Testament Greek.*   e Literal translation: "self-sufficient."   f Marvin Vincent, *Word Studies.*   g Note that in Phil. 4:11, the Greek *autarkas,* translated "content," is literally "self-sufficient."

that is accumulating to your account].

18 But I have [your full payment] and more; I have everything I need *and* am amply supplied, now that I have received from Epaphroditus the gifts you sent me. [They are the] fragrant odor of an offering *and* sacrifice which God welcomes *and in* which He delights.

19 And my God will liberally supply ([h]fill to the full) your every need according to His riches in glory in Christ Jesus.

20 To our God and Father be glory

forever and ever (through the endless eternities of the eternities). *Amen (so be it)*.

21 Remember me to every saint (every born-again believer) in Christ Jesus. The brethren (my [i]associates) who are with me greet you.

22 All the saints (God's consecrated ones here) wish to be remembered to you, especially those of Caesar's household.

23 The grace (spiritual favor and blessing) of the Lord Jesus Christ (the Anointed One) be with your spirit. *Amen (so be it)*.

THE LETTER OF PAUL TO THE

COLOSSIANS

CHAPTER 1

PAUL, AN apostle (special messenger) of Christ Jesus (the Messiah), by the will of God, and Timothy [our] brother,

2 To the saints (the consecrated people of God) and [j]believing *and* faithful brethren in Christ who are at Colossae: Grace (spiritual favor and blessing) to you and [heart] peace from God our Father.

3 We [k]continually give thanks to God the Father of our Lord Jesus Christ (the Messiah), as we are praying for you,

4 For we have heard of your faith in Christ Jesus ['the leaning of your entire human personality on Him in absolute trust and confidence in His power, wisdom, and goodness] and of the love which you [have and

show] for all the saints (God's consecrated ones),

5 Because of the hope [of experiencing what is] laid up ([j]reserved and waiting) for you in heaven. Of this [hope] you heard in the past in the message of the truth of the Gospel,

6 Which has come to you. Indeed, in the whole world [that Gospel] is bearing fruit *and* still is growing [[j]by its own inherent power], even as it has done among yourselves ever since the day you first heard and came to know *and* understand the grace of God in truth. [You came to know the grace or undeserved favor of God in reality, deeply and clearly and thoroughly, becoming accurately and intimately acquainted with it.]

7 You so learned it from Epaphras, our beloved fellow servant. He is a faithful minister of Christ in our stead

---

h Joseph Thayer, *A Greek-English Lexicon.*   i Alexander Souter, *Pocket Lexicon.*   j Marvin
Vincent, *Word Studies in the New Testament.*   k Marvin Vincent, *Word Studies in the New Testament:*
''Continually'' belongs with ''give thanks,'' not elsewhere.   l Alexander Souter, *Pocket Lexicon of the
Greek New Testament.*

and as our representative *and* [m]*yours*.

8 Also he has informed us of your love in the [Holy] Spirit.

9 For this reason we also, from the day we heard of it, have not ceased to pray *and* make [[n]special] request for you, [asking] that you may be filled with the [n]full (deep and clear) knowledge of His will in all spiritual wisdom [[o]in comprehensive insight into the ways and purposes of God] and in understanding *and* discernment of spiritual things—

10 That you may walk (live and conduct yourselves) in a manner worthy of the Lord, fully pleasing to Him *and* [p]desiring to please Him in all things, bearing fruit in every good work and steadily growing *and* increasing in *and* by the knowledge of God [with fuller, deeper, and clearer insight, [q]acquaintance, and recognition].

11 [We pray] that you may be invigorated *and* strengthened with all power according to the might of His glory, [to exercise] every kind of endurance and patience (perseverance and forbearance) with joy,

12 Giving thanks to the Father, Who has qualified *and* made us fit to share the [r]portion which is the inheritance of the saints (God's holy people) in the Light.

13 [The Father] has delivered *and* [s]drawn us to Himself out of the control *and* the dominion of darkness and has transferred us into the kingdom of the Son [t]of His love,

14 In Whom we have our redemption *through His blood*, [which means] the forgiveness of our sins.

15 [Now] He is the [u]exact likeness of the unseen God [the visible representation of the invisible]; He is the Firstborn of all creation.

16 For it was in Him that all things were created, in heaven and on earth, things seen and things unseen, whether thrones, dominions, rulers, or authorities; all things were created *and* exist through Him [by His service, intervention] and in *and* for Him.

17 And He Himself existed before all things, and in Him all things consist (cohere, are held together). [Prov. 8:22–31.]

18 He also is the Head of [His] body, the church; seeing He is the Beginning, the Firstborn from among the dead, so that He alone in everything *and* in every respect might occupy the chief place [stand first and be preeminent].

19 For it has pleased [the Father] that all the divine fullness (the sum total of the divine perfection, powers, and attributes) should dwell in Him [r]permanently.

20 And God purposed that through ([s]by the service, the intervention of) Him [the Son] all things should be completely reconciled [r]back to Himself, whether on earth or in heaven, as through Him, [the Father] made peace by means of the blood of His cross.

21 And although you at one time were estranged *and* alienated from Him and were of hostile attitude of mind in your wicked activities,

22 Yet now has [Christ, the Messiah] reconciled [you to God] in the body of His flesh through death, in order to present you holy and faultless and irreproachable in His [the Father's] presence.

23 [And this He will do] provided

m Many ancient manuscripts read "yours." **n** Marvin Vincent, *Word Studies in the New Testament*. **o** Alexander Souter, *Pocket Lexicon*. **p** Joseph Thayer, *A Greek-English Lexicon of the New Testament*. **q** G. Abbott-Smith, *Manual Greek Lexicon of the New Testament*. **r** Marvin Vincent, *Word Studies*. **s** Joseph Thayer, *A Greek-English Lexicon*. **t** Literal translation. **u** Charles B. Williams, *The New Testament: A Translation in the Language of the People*: Strong terms—thus translated "exact likeness."

that you continue to ᵛstay with *and* in the faith [in Christ], well-grounded and settled *and* steadfast, not shifting *or* moving away from the hope [which rests on and is inspired by] the glad tidings (the Gospel), which you heard and which has been preached ʷ[as being designed for and offered without restrictions] to every person under heaven, and of which [Gospel] I, Paul, became a minister.

24 [Even] now I rejoice in ᵛthe midst of my sufferings on your behalf. And in my own person I am making up whatever is still lacking *and* remains to be completed [ᵛon our part] of Christ's afflictions, for the sake of His body, which is the church.

25 In it I became a minister in accordance with the divine ᵛstewardship which was entrusted to me for you [as its object and for your benefit], to make the Word of God fully known [among you]—

26 The mystery of which was hidden for ages and generations [ˣfrom angels and men], but is now revealed to His holy people (the saints),

27 To whom God was pleased to make known how great for the Gentiles are the riches of the glory of this mystery, which is Christ within *and* among you, the Hope of [realizing the] glory.

28 Him we preach *and* proclaim, warning *and* admonishing everyone and instructing everyone in all wisdom (ʸcomprehensive insight into the ways and purposes of God), that we may present every person mature (full-grown, fully initiated, complete, and perfect) in Christ (the Anointed One).

29 For this I labor [ᵛunto weariness], striving with all the ˢsuperhuman energy which He so mightily enkindles *and* works within me.

CHAPTER 2

FOR I want you to know how great is my solicitude for you [how severe an inward struggle I am engaged in for you] and for those [believers] at Laodicea, and for all who [ᵛlike yourselves] have never seen my face *and* known me personally.

2 [For my concern is] that their hearts may be ᵛbraced (comforted, cheered, and encouraged) as they are knit together in love, that they may come to have all the abounding wealth *and* blessings of assured conviction of understanding, and that they may become progressively ᶻmore intimately acquainted with *and* may know more definitely *and* accurately *and* thoroughly that mystic secret of God, [which is] Christ (the Anointed One).

3 In Him all the treasures of [divine] wisdom (ʸcomprehensive insight into the ways and purposes of God) and [all the riches of spiritual] knowledge *and* enlightenment are stored up *and* lie hidden.

4 I say this in order that no one may mislead *and* delude you by plausible *and* persuasive *and* attractive arguments *and* beguiling speech.

5 For though I am away from you in body, yet I am with you in spirit, delighted at the sight of your [standing shoulder to shoulder in such] orderly array and the firmness *and* the solid front *and* steadfastness of your faith in Christ [that ʸleaning of the entire human personality on Him in absolute trust and confidence in His power, wisdom, and goodness].

6 As you have therefore received Christ, [even] Jesus the Lord, [so]

---

v Marvin Vincent, *Word Studies*. w Adam Clarke, *The Holy Bible with A Commentary*. x Johann Bengel, *Gnomom Novi Testamenti* and Henry Alford, *The Greek New Testament*. y Alexander Souter, *Pocket Lexicon*. z Richard Trench, *Synonyms of the New Testament*.

walk (regulate your lives and conduct yourselves) in union with *and* conformity to Him.

7 Have the roots [of your being] firmly *and* deeply planted [in Him, fixed and founded in Him], being continually built up in Him, becoming increasingly more confirmed *and* established in the faith, just as you were taught, and abounding *and* overflowing in it with thanksgiving.

8 See to it that no one carries you off as spoil *or* makes you yourselves captive by his so-called philosophy *and* intellectualism and vain deceit (idle fancies and plain nonsense), following human tradition (men's ideas of the material rather than the spiritual world), just crude notions following the rudimentary *and* elemental teachings of the universe and disregarding [the teachings of] Christ (the Messiah).

9 For in Him the whole fullness of Deity (the Godhead) continues to dwell in bodily form [giving complete expression of the divine nature].

10 And you [a]are in Him, made full *and* having come to fullness of life [in Christ you too are filled with the Godhead—Father, Son and Holy Spirit—and reach full spiritual stature]. And He is the Head of all rule and authority [of every angelic principality and power].

11 In Him also you were circumcised with a circumcision not made with hands, but in a [spiritual] circumcision [performed by] Christ by stripping off the body of the flesh (the whole corrupt, carnal nature with its passions and lusts).

12 [Thus [b]you were circumcised when] you were buried with Him in [your] baptism, in which you were also raised with Him [a]to a new life] through [your] faith in the working of

God [a]as displayed] when He raised Him up from the dead.

13 And you who were dead in trespasses and in the uncircumcision of your flesh (your sensuality, your sinful carnal nature), [God] brought to life together with [Christ], having [freely] forgiven us all our transgressions,

14 Having cancelled *and* blotted out *and* wiped away the handwriting of the note (bond) with its legal decrees *and* demands which was in force *and* stood against us (hostile to us). This [note with its regulations, decrees, and demands] He set aside *and* cleared [a]completely out of our way by nailing it to [His] cross.

15 [God] disarmed the principalities and powers that were ranged against us and made a bold display *and* public example of them, in triumphing over them in Him *and* in it [the cross].

16 Therefore let no one sit in judgment on you in matters of food and drink, or with regard to a feast day or a New Moon or a Sabbath.

17 Such [things] are only the shadow of things that are to come, *and* they have only a symbolic value. But the reality (the substance, the solid fact of what is foreshadowed, the body of it) belongs to Christ.

18 Let no one defraud you by acting as an umpire *and* declaring you unworthy *and* disqualifying you for the prize, insisting on self-abasement and worship of angels, taking his stand on visions [he claims] he has seen, vainly puffed up by his sensuous notions *and* inflated by his unspiritual thoughts *and* fleshly conceit,

19 And not holding fast to the Head, from Whom the entire body, supplied and knit together by means

---

a Marvin Vincent, *Word Studies.*   b Marvin Vincent, *Word Studies*: "The aorist tense puts the burial as contemporaneous with the circumcision."

of its joints and ligaments, grows with a growth that is from God.

20 If then you have died with Christ to material ways of looking at things *and* have escaped from the world's crude *and* elemental notions *and* teachings of externalism, why do you live as if you still belong to the world? [Why do you still submit to rules *and* regulations?—such as]

21 Do not handle [this], Do not taste [that], Do not even touch [them],

22 Referring to things all of which perish with being used. To do this is to follow human precepts and doctrines. [Isa. 29:13.]

23 Such [practices] have indeed the outward appearance [that popularly passes] for wisdom, in promoting self-imposed rigor of devotion *and* delight in self-humiliation *and* severity of discipline of the body, but they are of no value in checking the indulgence of the flesh (the lower nature). [Instead, they do not honor God but serve only to indulge the flesh.]

CHAPTER 3

IF THEN you have been raised with Christ [to a new life, thus sharing His resurrection from the dead], aim at *and* seek the [rich, eternal treasures] that are above, where Christ is, seated at the right hand of God. [Ps. 110:1.]

2 And set your minds *and* keep them set on what is above (the higher things), not on the things that are on the earth.

3 For [as far as this world is concerned] you have died, and your [new, real] life is hidden with Christ in God.

4 When Christ, Who is our life, appears, then you also will appear with Him in [the splendor of His] glory.

5 So kill (deaden, ^cdeprive of power) the evil desire lurking in your members [those animal impulses and all that is earthly in you that is employed in sin]: sexual vice, impurity, sensual appetites, unholy desires, and all greed *and* covetousness, for that is idolatry (the deifying of self and other created things instead of God).

6 It is on account of these [very sins] that the [holy] anger of God is ever coming upon the sons of disobedience (those who are obstinately opposed to the divine will),

7 Among whom you also once walked, when you were living in *and* addicted to [such practices].

8 But now put away *and* rid yourselves [completely] of all these things: anger, rage, bad feeling toward others, curses *and* slander, and foulmouthed abuse *and* shameful utterances from your lips!

9 Do not lie to one another, for you have stripped off the old (unregenerate) self with its evil practices,

10 And have clothed yourselves with the new [spiritual self], which is [ever in the process of being] renewed *and* remolded into [fuller and more perfect ^dknowledge upon] knowledge after the image (the likeness) of Him Who created it. [Gen. 1:26.]

11 [In this new creation all distinctions vanish.] There ^eis no room for *and* there can be neither Greek nor Jew, circumcised nor uncircumcised, [nor difference between nations whether alien] barbarians or Scythians [^ewho are the most savage of all], nor slave or free man; but

---

c Joseph Thayer, *A Greek-English Lexicon.*   d Literal translation.   e Marvin Vincent, *Word Studies.*
f James C. Gray and George M. Adams, *Bible Commentary.*

Christ is all and in all [¹everything and everywhere, to all men, without distinction of person].

12 Clothe yourselves therefore, as God's own chosen ones (His own picked representatives), [who are] purified *and* holy and well-beloved [by God Himself, by putting on behavior marked by] tenderhearted pity *and* mercy, kind feeling, a lowly opinion of yourselves, gentle ways, [and] patience [which is tireless and long-suffering, and has the power to endure whatever comes, with good temper].

13 Be gentle *and* forbearing with one another and, if one has a difference (a grievance or complaint) against another, readily pardoning each other; even as the Lord has [freely] forgiven you, so must you also [forgive].

14 And above all these [put on] love *and* enfold yourselves with the bond of perfectness [which binds everything together completely in ideal harmony].

15 And let the peace (soul harmony which comes) from Christ rule (act as umpire continually) in your hearts [deciding and settling with finality all questions that arise in your minds, in that peaceful state] to which as [members of Christ's] one body you were also called [to live]. And be thankful (appreciative), [giving praise to God always].

16 Let the word [spoken by] Christ (the Messiah) have its home [in your hearts and minds] *and* dwell in you in [all its] richness, as you teach and admonish *and* train one another in all insight *and* intelligence *and* wisdom [in spiritual things, and as you sing] psalms and hymns and spiritual songs, making melody to God with [His] grace in your hearts.

17 And whatever you do [no matter what it is] in word or deed, do everything in the name of the Lord Jesus *and* in [dependence upon] His Person, giving praise to God the Father through Him.

18 Wives, be subject to your husbands [subordinate and adapt yourselves to them], as is right *and* fitting *and* your proper duty in the Lord.

19 Husbands, love your wives [be affectionate and sympathetic with them] and do not be harsh *or* bitter *or* resentful toward them.

20 Children, obey your parents in everything, for this is pleasing to the Lord.

21 Fathers, do not provoke *or* irritate *or* fret your children [do not be hard on them or harass them], lest they become discouraged *and* sullen *and* morose *and* feel inferior *and* frustrated. [Do not break their spirit.]

22 Servants, obey in everything those who are your earthly masters, not only when their eyes are on you as pleasers of men, but in simplicity of purpose [with all your heart] because of your reverence for the Lord *and* as a sincere expression of your devotion to Him.

23 Whatever may be your task, work at it heartily (from the soul), as [something done] for the Lord and not for men,

24 Knowing [with all certainty] that it is from the Lord [and not from men] that you will receive the inheritance which is your [real] reward. [The One Whom] you are actually serving [is] the Lord Christ (the Messiah).

25 For he who deals wrongfully will [reap the fruit of his folly and] be punished for his wrongdoing. And [with God] there is no partiality [no matter what a person's position may be, whether he is the slave or the master].

CHAPTER 4

M ASTERS, [on your part] deal with your slaves justly and fairly, knowing that also you have a Master in heaven. [Lev. 25:43, 53.]

2 Be earnest and unwearied and steadfast in your prayer [life], being [both] alert and intent in [your praying] with thanksgiving.

3 And at the same time pray for us also, that God may open a door to us for the Word (the Gospel), to proclaim the mystery concerning Christ (the Messiah) on account of which I am in prison;

4 That I may proclaim it fully and make it clear [speak boldly and unfold that mystery], as is my duty.

5 Behave yourselves wisely [living prudently and with discretion] in your relations with those of the outside world (the non-Christians), making the very most of the time and seizing (buying up) the opportunity.

6 Let your speech at all times be gracious (pleasant and winsome), seasoned [as it were] with salt, [so that you may never be at a loss] to know how you ought to answer anyone [who puts a question to you].

7 Tychicus will give you full information about my affairs; [he is] a much-loved brother and faithful ministering assistant and fellow servant [with us] in the Lord.

8 I have sent him to you for this very purpose, that you may know how we are faring and that he may comfort and cheer and encourage your hearts.

9 And with [him is] Onesimus, [our] faithful and beloved brother, who is [one] of yourselves. They will let you know everything that has taken place here [in Rome].

10 Aristarchus my fellow prisoner wishes to be remembered to you, as does Mark the relative of Barnabas. You received instructions concerning him; if he comes to you give him a [ᵍhearty] welcome.

11 And [greetings also from] Jesus, who is called Justus. These [Hebrew Christians] alone of the circumcision are among my fellow workers for [the extension of] God's kingdom, and they have proved a relief and a comfort to me.

12 Epaphras, who is one of yourselves, a servant of Christ Jesus, sends you greetings. [He is] always striving for you earnestly in his prayers, [pleading] that you may [as persons of ripe character and clear conviction] stand firm and mature [in spiritual growth], convinced and fully assured in ʰeverything willed by God.

13 For I bear him testimony that he has labored hard in your behalf and for [the believers] in Laodicea and those in Hierapolis.

14 Luke the beloved physician and Demas salute you.

15 Give my greetings to the brethren at Laodicea, and to Nympha and the assembly (the church) which meets in her house.

16 And when this epistle has been read before you, [see] that it is read also in the assembly (the church) of the Laodiceans, and also [see] that you yourselves in turn read the [letter that comes to you] from Laodicea.

17 And say to Archippus, See that you discharge carefully [the duties of] the ministry and fulfill the stewardship which you have received in the Lord.

18 I, Paul, [add this final] greeting, writing with my own hand. Remem-

---

g Charles B. Williams, *The New Testament: A Translation*: A very strong verb—thus translated "give him a hearty welcome." h Marvin Vincent, *Word Studies*.

ber I am still in prison *and* in chains. May grace (God's unmerited favor and blessing) be with you! *Amen (so be it).*

THE FIRST LETTER OF PAUL TO THE
THESSALONIANS

CHAPTER 1

PAUL, SILVANUS (Silas), and Timothy, to the assembly (church) of the Thessalonians in God the Father and the Lord Jesus Christ (the Messiah): Grace (spiritual blessing and divine favor) to you and [heart] peace.

2 We are ever giving thanks to God for all of you, continually mentioning [you when engaged] in our prayers,

3 Recalling unceasingly before our God and Father your work energized by faith and service motivated by love and unwavering hope in [the return of] our Lord Jesus Christ (the Messiah). [I Thess. 1:10.]

4 [O] brethren beloved by God, we recognize *and* know that He has selected (chosen) you;

5 For our [preaching of the] glad tidings (the Gospel) came to you not only in word, but also in [its own inherent] power and in the Holy Spirit and with great conviction *and* absolute certainty [on our part]. You know what kind of men we proved [ourselves] to be among you for your good.

6 And you [set yourselves to] become imitators of us and [through us] of the Lord Himself, for you welcomed our message in [spite of] much persecution, with joy [inspired] by the Holy Spirit;

7 So that you [thus] became a pattern to all the believers (those who adhere to, trust in, and rely on Christ Jesus) in Macedonia and Achaia (most of Greece).

8 For not only has the Word concerning *and* from the Lord resounded forth from you unmistakably in Macedonia and Achaia, but everywhere the report has gone forth of your faith in God [of your ⁱleaning of your whole personality on Him in complete trust and confidence in His power, wisdom, and goodness]. So we [find that we] never need to tell people anything [further about it].

9 For they themselves volunteer testimony concerning us, telling what an entrance we had among you, and how you turned to God from [your] idols to serve a God Who is alive and true *and* genuine,

10 And [how you] look forward to *and* await the coming of His Son from heaven, Whom He raised from the dead—Jesus, Who personally rescues *and* ʲdelivers us out of *and* from the wrath [bringing punishment] which is coming [upon the impenitent] *and* ʲdraws us to Himself [ᵏinvesting us with all the privileges and rewards of the new life in Christ, the Messiah].

---

i Alexander Souter, *Pocket Lexicon of the Greek New Testament.*   j Literal translation of the verb "to deliver."   k Marvin Vincent, *Word Studies in the New Testament.*

CHAPTER 2

FOR YOU yourselves know, brethren, that our coming among you was not useless *and* fruitless.

2 But though we had already suffered and been outrageously treated at Philippi, as you know, yet in [the strength of] our God we summoned courage to proclaim to you unfalteringly the good news (the Gospel) with earnest contention *and* much conflict *and* great opposition.

3 For our appeal [in preaching] does not [originate] from delusion *or* error *or* impure purpose *or* motive, nor in fraud *or* deceit.

4 But just as we have been approved by God to be entrusted with the glad tidings (the Gospel), so we speak not to please men but to please God, Who tests our hearts [[1]expecting them to be approved].

5 For as you well know, we never resorted either to words of flattery or to any cloak to conceal greedy motives *or* pretexts for gain, [as] God is our witness.

6 Nor did we seek to extract praise *and* honor *and* glory from men, either from you or from anyone else, though we might have asserted our authority [stood on our dignity and claimed honor] as apostles (special missionaries) of Christ (the Messiah).

7 But we behaved gently when we were among you, like a devoted mother nursing *and* cherishing her own children.

8 So, being thus tenderly *and* affectionately desirous of you, we continued to share with you not only God's good news (the Gospel) but also our own lives as well, for you had become so very dear to us.

9 For you recall our hard toil and struggles, brethren. We worked night and day [and plied our trade] in order not to be a burden to any of you [for our support] while we proclaimed the glad tidings (the Gospel) of God to you.

10 You are witnesses, [yes] and God [also], how unworldly and upright and blameless was our behavior toward you believers [who adhered to and trusted in and relied on our Lord Jesus Christ].

11 For you know how, as a father [dealing with] his children, we used to exhort each of you personally, stimulating *and* encouraging and charging you

12 To live lives worthy of God, Who calls you into His own kingdom and the glorious blessedness [[m]into which true believers will enter after Christ's return].

13 And we also [especially] thank God continually for this, that when you received the message of God [which you heard] from us, you welcomed it not as the word of [mere] men, but as it truly is, the Word of God, which is effectually at work in you who believe [[n]exercising its superhuman power in those who adhere to and trust in and rely on it].

14 For you, brethren, became imitators of the assemblies (churches) of God in Christ Jesus which are in Judea, for you too have suffered the same kind of treatment from your own fellow countrymen as they did [who were persecuted at the hands] of the Jews,

15 Who killed both the Lord Jesus and the prophets, and harassed *and* drove us out, and continue to make themselves hateful *and* offensive to God and to show themselves foes of all men,

16 Forbidding *and* hindering us from speaking to the Gentiles (the na-

l G. Abbott-Smith, *Manual Greek Lexicon of the New Testament.* m Joseph Thayer, *A Greek-English Lexicon of the New Testament.* n Marvin Vincent, *Word Studies.*

tions) that they may be saved. So as always they fill up [to the brim the measure of] their sins. But God's wrath has come upon them at last [completely and forever]! [Gen. 15:16.]

17 But since we were bereft of you, brethren, for a little while in person, [of course] not in heart, we endeavored the more eagerly and with great longing to see you face to face.

18 Because it was our will to come to you. [I mean that] I, Paul, again and again [wanted to come], but Satan hindered and impeded us.

19 For what is our hope or happiness or our victor's wreath of exultant triumph when we stand in the presence of our Lord Jesus at His coming? Is it not you?

20 For you are [indeed] our glory and our joy!

CHAPTER 3

THEREFORE, WHEN [the suspense of separation and our yearning for some personal communication from you] became intolerable, we consented to being left behind alone at Athens.

2 And we sent Timothy, our brother and God's servant in [spreading] the good news (the Gospel) of Christ, to strengthen and establish and to exhort and comfort and encourage you in your faith,

3 That no one [of you] should be disturbed and beguiled and led astray by these afflictions and difficulties [to which I have referred]. For you yourselves know that this is [unavoidable in our position, and must be recognized as] our appointed lot.

4 For even when we were with you, [you know] we warned you plainly beforehand that we were to be pressed with difficulties and made

to suffer affliction, just as to your own knowledge it has [since] happened.

5 That is the reason that, when I could bear [the suspense] no longer, I sent that I might learn [how you were standing the strain, and the endurance of] your faith, [for I was fearful] lest somehow the tempter had tempted you and our toil [among you should prove to] be fruitless and to no purpose.

6 But now that Timothy has just come back to us from [his visit to] you and has brought us the good news of [the steadfastness of] your faith and [the warmth of your] love, and [reported] how kindly you cherish a constant and affectionate remembrance of us [and that you are] longing to see us as we [are to see] you,

7 Brethren, for this reason, in [spite of all] our stress and crushing difficulties we have been filled with comfort and cheer about you [because of] your faith (°the leaning of your whole personality on God in complete trust and confidence).

8 Because now we [really] live, if you stand [firm] in the Lord.

9 For what [adequate] thanksgiving can we render to God for you for all the gladness and delight which we enjoy for your sakes before our God?

10 [And we] continue to pray especially and with most intense earnestness night and day that we may see you face to face and mend and make good whatever may be imperfect and lacking in your faith.

11 Now may our God and Father Himself and our Lord Jesus Christ (the Messiah) guide our steps to you.

12 And may the Lord make you to increase and excel and overflow in love for one another and for all people, just as we also do for you,

13 So that He may strengthen *and* confirm *and* establish your hearts faultlessly pure *and* unblamable in holiness in the sight of our God and Father, at the coming of our Lord Jesus *Christ (the Messiah)* with all His saints (the [p]holy and glorified people of God)! *Amen, (so be it)!*

CHAPTER 4

FURTHERMORE, [p]BRETH-REN, we beg and admonish you in [virtue of our union with] the Lord Jesus, that [you follow the instructions which] you learned from us about how you ought to walk so as to please *and* gratify God, as indeed you are doing, [and] that you do so even more and more abundantly [attaining yet greater perfection in living this life].

2 For you know what charges *and* precepts we gave you [[q]on the authority and by the inspiration of] the Lord Jesus.

3 For this is the will of God, that you should be consecrated (separated and set apart for pure and holy living): that you should abstain *and* shrink from all sexual vice,

4 That each one of you should know how to [r]possess (control, manage) his own [s]body in consecration (purity, separated from things profane) and honor,

5 Not [to be used] in the passion of lust like the heathen, who are ignorant of the true God *and* have no knowledge of His will,

6 That no man transgress and overreach his brother *and* defraud him in this matter *or* defraud his brother in business. For the Lord is an avenger in all these things, as we have already warned you solemnly *and* [q]told you plainly.

7 For God has not called us to impurity but to consecration [to dedicate ourselves to the most thorough purity].

8 Therefore whoever disregards (sets aside and rejects this) disregards not man but God, Whose [very] Spirit [Whom] He gives to you is holy (chaste, pure).

9 But concerning brotherly love [for all other Christians], you have no need to have anyone write you, for you yourselves have been [personally] taught by God to love one another.

10 And indeed you already are [extending and displaying your love] to all the brethren throughout Macedonia. But we beseech *and* earnestly exhort you, brethren, that you [q]excel [in this matter] more and more,

11 To make it your ambition *and* definitely endeavor to live quietly *and* peacefully, to mind your own affairs, and to work with your hands, as we charged you,

12 So that you may bear yourselves becomingly and be correct *and* honorable *and* command the respect of the outside world, being dependent on nobody [self-supporting] *and* having need of nothing.

13 Now also we would not have you ignorant, brethren, about those who fall asleep ['in death], that you may not grieve [for them] as the rest do who have no hope [beyond the grave].

14 For since we believe that Jesus died and rose again, even so God will also bring with Him through Jesus

---

p Marvin Vincent, *Word Studies.* Standard Version and others so read. reading "body" is supported by most lexicons, and by such translations as Ronald Knox, *The Holy Bible: A Translation from the Latin Vulgate*; J.B. Phillips, *New Testament in Modern English*; and Arthur S. Way, *Way's Epistles: The Letters of St. Paul to Seven Churches and Three Friends.*   q G. Abbott-Smith, *Manual Greek Lexicon.*   r *The American* s Some of the early versions of the Bible read "vessel" here. The   t Hermann Cremer, *Biblico-Theological Lexicon of New Testament Greek.*

those who have fallen asleep [*in death].

15 For this we declare to you by the Lord's [own] word, that we who are alive and remain until the coming of the Lord shall in no way precede [into His presence] *or* have any advantage at all over those who have previously fallen asleep [in Him *in death].

16 For the Lord Himself will descend from heaven with a loud cry of summons, with the shout of an archangel, and with the blast of the trumpet of God. And those who have departed this life in Christ will rise first.

17 Then we, the living ones who remain [on the earth], shall simultaneously be caught up along with [the resurrected dead] in the clouds to meet the Lord in the air; and so always (through the eternity of the eternities) we shall be with the Lord!

18 Therefore comfort *and* encourage one another with these words.

CHAPTER 5

BUT AS to the suitable times and the precise seasons *and* dates, brethren, you have no necessity for anything being written to you.

2 For you yourselves know perfectly well that the day of the [return of the] Lord will come [as unexpectedly and suddenly] as a thief in the night.

3 When people are saying, All is well and secure, *and,* There is peace and safety, then in a moment unforeseen destruction (ruin and death) will come upon them as suddenly as labor pains come upon a woman with child; and they shall by no means escape, for there will be no escape.

4 But you are not in [given up to the power of] darkness, brethren, for that day to overtake you by surprise like a thief.

5 For you are all sons of light and sons of the day; we do not belong either to the night or to darkness.

6 Accordingly then, let us not sleep, as the rest do, but let us keep wide awake (alert, watchful, cautious, and on our guard) and let us be sober (calm, collected, and circumspect).

7 For those who sleep, sleep at night, and those who are drunk, get drunk at night.

8 But we belong to the day; therefore, let us be sober and put on the breastplate (corslet) of faith and love and for a helmet the hope of salvation.

9 For God has not appointed us to [incur His] wrath [He did not select us to condemn us], but [that we might] obtain [His] salvation through our Lord Jesus Christ (the Messiah)

10 Who died for us so that whether we are still alive or are dead [at Christ's appearing], we might live together with Him *and* share His life.

11 Therefore encourage (admonish, exhort) one another and edify (strengthen and build up) one another, just as you are doing.

12 Now also we beseech you, brethren, get to know those who labor among you [recognize them for what they are, acknowledge and appreciate and respect them all]—your leaders who are over you in the Lord and those who warn *and* kindly reprove *and* exhort you.

13 And hold them in very high and most affectionate esteem in [intelligent and sympathetic] appreciation of their work. Be at peace among yourselves.

14 And we earnestly beseech you, brethren, admonish (warn and seriously advise) those who are out of line [the loafers, the disorderly, and the unruly]; encourage the timid *and*

u Hermann Cremer, *Biblico-Theological Lexicon of New Testament Greek.*

fainthearted, help *and* give your support to the weak souls, [and] be very patient with everybody [always keeping your temper]. [Isa. 35:4.]

15 See that none of you repays another with evil for evil, but always aim to show kindness *and* seek to do good to one another and to everybody.

16 Be happy [in your faith] *and* rejoice *and* be glad-hearted continually (always);

17 Be unceasing in prayer [praying perseveringly];

18 Thank [God] in everything [no matter what the circumstances may be, be thankful and give thanks], for this is the will of God for you [who are] in Christ Jesus [the Revealer and Mediator of that will].

19 Do not quench (suppress or subdue) the [Holy] Spirit;

20 Do not spurn the gifts *and* utterances of the prophets [do not depreciate prophetic revelations nor despise inspired instruction or exhortation or warning].

21 But test *and* prove all things [until you can recognize] what is good; [to that] hold fast.

22 Abstain from evil [shrink from it and keep aloof from it] in whatever form *or* whatever kind it may be.

23 And may the God of peace Himself sanctify you through and through [separate you from profane things, make you pure and wholly consecrated to God]; and may your spirit and soul and body be preserved sound *and* complete [and found] blameless at the coming of our Lord Jesus Christ (the Messiah).

24 Faithful is He Who is calling you [to Himself] *and* utterly trustworthy, and He will also do it [fulfill His call by hallowing and keeping you].

25 Brethren, pray for us.

26 Greet all the brethren with a sacred kiss.

27 I solemnly charge you [in the name of] the Lord to have this letter read before all the brethren.

28 The grace (the unmerited favor and blessings) of our Lord Jesus Christ (the Messiah) be with you all. *Amen, (so be it).*

THE SECOND LETTER OF PAUL TO THE

THESSALONIANS

CHAPTER 1

PAUL, SILVANUS (Silas), and Timothy, to the church (assembly) of the Thessalonians in God our Father and the Lord Jesus Christ (the Messiah, the Anointed One):

2 Grace (unmerited favor) be to you and [heart] peace from God the Father and the Lord Jesus Christ (the Messiah, the Anointed One).

3 We ought *and* indeed are obligated [as those in debt] to give thanks always to God for you, brethren, as is fitting, because your faith is growing exceedingly and the love of every one of you each toward the others is increasing *and* abounds.

4 And this is a cause of our mentioning you with pride among the churches (assemblies) of God for your steadfastness (your unflinching endurance and patience) and your

firm faith in the midst of all the persecutions and crushing distresses and afflictions under which you are holding up.

5 This is positive proof of the just and right judgment of God to the end that you may be deemed deserving of His kingdom [a plain token of His fair verdict which designs that you should be made and counted worthy of the kingdom of God], for the sake of which you are also suffering.

6 [It is a fair decision] since it is a righteous thing with God to repay with distress and affliction those who distress and afflict you,

7 And to [*recompense] you who are so distressed and afflicted [by granting you] relief and rest along with us [your fellow sufferers] when the Lord Jesus is revealed from heaven with His mighty angels in a flame of fire,

8 To deal out retribution (chastisement and vengeance) upon those who do not know or perceive or become acquainted with God, and [upon those] who ignore and refuse to obey the Gospel of our Lord Jesus Christ.

9 Such people will pay the penalty and suffer the punishment of everlasting ruin (destruction and perdition) and eternal exclusion and banishment from the presence of the Lord and from the glory of His power,

10 When He comes to be glorified in His saints [on that day He will be made more glorious in His consecrated people], and [He will] be marveled at and admired [in His glory reflected] in all who have believed [who have adhered to, trusted in, and relied on Him], because our witnessing among you was confidently accepted

and believed [and confirmed in your lives].

11 With this in view we constantly pray for you, that our God may deem and count you worthy of [your] calling and [His] every gracious purpose of goodness, and with power may complete in [your] every particular work of faith (faith which is that ᵂleaning of the whole human personality on God in absolute trust and confidence in His power, wisdom, and goodness).

12 Thus may the name of our Lord Jesus *Christ* be glorified and become more glorious through and in you, and may you [also be glorified] in Him according to the grace (favor and blessing) of our God and the Lord Jesus Christ (the Messiah, the Anointed One).

CHAPTER 2

B UT RELATIVE to the coming of our Lord Jesus Christ (the Messiah) and our gathering together to [meet] Him, we beg you, brethren,

2 Not to allow your minds to be quickly unsettled or disturbed or kept excited or alarmed, whether it be by some [pretended] revelation of [the] Spirit or by word or by letter [alleged to be] from us, to the effect that the day of the Lord has [already] arrived and is here.

3 Let no one deceive or beguile you in any way, for that day will not come except the ˣapostasy comes first [unless the predicted great ˣfalling away of those who have professed to be Christians has come], and the man of lawlessness (sin) is revealed, who is the son of doom (of perdition), [Dan. 7:25; 8:25; I Tim. 4:1.]

4 Who opposes and exalts himself

---

v Robert Jamieson, A.R. Fausset and David Brown, *A Commentary on the Old and New Testaments.*
w Alexander Souter, *Pocket Lexicon of the Greek New Testament.* x A possible rendering of the Greek *apostasia* is "departure [of the church]."

so proudly *and* insolently against *and* over all that is called God or that is worshiped, [even to his actually] taking his seat in the temple of God, proclaiming that he himself is God. [Ezek. 28:2; Dan. 11:36, 37.]

5 Do you not recollect that when I was still with you, I told you these things?

6 And now you know what is restraining him [from being revealed at this time]; it is so that he may be manifested (revealed) in his own [appointed] time.

7 For the mystery of lawlessness (that hidden principle of rebellion against constituted authority) is already at work in the world, [but it is] restrained only until [y]he who restrains is taken out of the way.

8 And then the lawless one (the antichrist) will be revealed and the Lord Jesus will slay him with the breath of His mouth and bring him to an end by His appearing at His coming. [Isa. 11:4.]

9 The coming [of the lawless one, the antichrist] is through the activity *and* working of Satan and will be attended by great power and with all sorts of [pretended] miracles and signs *and* delusive marvels—[all of them] lying wonders—

10 And by unlimited seduction to evil and with all wicked deception for those who are perishing (going to perdition) because they did not welcome the Truth *but* refused to love it that they might be saved.

11 Therefore God sends upon them a misleading influence, a working of error *and* a strong delusion to make them believe what is false,

12 In order that all may be judged *and* condemned who did not believe in [who refused to adhere to, trust in,

and rely on] the Truth, but [instead] took pleasure in unrighteousness.

13 But we, brethren beloved by the Lord, ought *and* are obligated [as those who are in debt] to give thanks always to God for you, because God chose you from the beginning [z]*as His firstfruits (first converts)* for salvation through the sanctifying work of the [Holy] Spirit and [your] belief in (adherence to, trust in, and reliance on) the Truth.

14 [It was] to this end that He called you through our Gospel, so that you may obtain *and* share in the glory of our Lord Jesus Christ (the Messiah).

15 So then, brethren, stand firm and hold fast to the traditions *and* instructions which you were taught by us, whether by our word of mouth or by letter.

16 Now may our Lord Jesus Christ Himself and God our Father, Who loved us and gave us everlasting consolation *and* encouragement and well-founded hope through [His] grace (unmerited favor),

17 Comfort *and* encourage your hearts and strengthen them [make them steadfast and keep them unswerving] in every good work and word.

CHAPTER 3

FURTHERMORE, BRETHREN, do pray for us, that the Word of the Lord may speed on (spread rapidly and run its course) and be glorified (extolled) *and* triumph, even as [it has done] with you,

2 And that we may be delivered from perverse (improper, unrighteous) and wicked (actively malicious) men, for not everybody has faith *and* is held by it.

3 Yet the Lord is faithful, and He will strengthen [you] *and* set you on a firm foundation and guard you from the evil [one].

4 And we have confidence in the Lord concerning you, that you are doing and will continue to do the things which we suggest *and* with which we charge you.

5 May the Lord direct your hearts into [realizing and showing] the love of God and into the steadfastness *and* patience of Christ *and* [a]in waiting for His return.

6 Now we charge you, brethren, in the name *and* on the authority of our Lord Jesus Christ (the Messiah) that you withdraw *and* keep away from every brother (fellow believer) who is slack in the performance of duty *and* is disorderly, living as a shirker *and* not walking in accord with the traditions *and* instructions that you have received from us.

7 For you yourselves know how it is necessary to imitate our example, for we were not disorderly *or* shirking of duty when we were with you [we were not idle].

8 Nor did we eat anyone's bread without paying for it, but with toil and struggle we worked night and day, that we might not be a burden *or* impose on any of you [for our support].

9 [It was] not because we do not have a right [to such support], but [we wished] to make ourselves an example for you to follow.

10 For while we were yet with you, we gave you this rule *and* charge: If anyone will not work, neither let him eat.

11 Indeed, we hear that some among you are disorderly [that they are passing their lives in idleness, neglectful of duty], being busy with other people's affairs instead of their own and doing no work.

12 Now we charge and exhort such persons [as [b]ministers in Him exhorting those] in the Lord Jesus Christ (the Messiah) that they work in quietness and earn their own food *and* other necessities.

13 And as for you, brethren, do not become weary *or* lose heart in doing right [but continue in well-doing without weakening].

14 But if anyone [in the church] refuses to obey what we say in this letter, take note of that person and do not associate with him, so that he may be ashamed.

15 Do not regard him as an enemy, but simply admonish *and* warn him as [being still] a brother.

16 Now may the Lord of peace Himself grant you His peace (the peace of His kingdom) at all times and in all ways [under all circumstances and conditions, whatever comes]. The Lord [be] with you all.

17 I, Paul, write you this final greeting with my own hand. This is the mark *and* sign [that it is not a forgery] in every letter of mine. It is the way I write [my handwriting and signature].

18 The grace (spiritual blessing and favor) of our Lord Jesus Christ (the Messiah) be with you all. *Amen (so be it).*

---

a Joseph Thayer, *A Greek-English Lexicon of the New Testament.*   b Robert Jamieson, A.R. Fausset and David Brown, *A Commentary.*

THE FIRST LETTER OF PAUL TO
TIMOTHY

CHAPTER 1

PAUL, AN apostle (special messenger) of Christ Jesus by appointment *and* command of God our Savior *and* of Christ Jesus (the Messiah), our Hope,

2 To Timothy, my true son in the faith: Grace (spiritual blessing and favor), mercy, and [heart] peace [be yours] from God the Father and Christ Jesus our Lord.

3 As I urged you when I was on my way to Macedonia, stay on where you are at Ephesus in order that you may warn *and* admonish *and* charge certain individuals not to teach any different doctrine,

4 Nor to give importance to *or* occupy themselves with legends (fables, myths) and endless genealogies, which foster *and* promote useless speculations *and* questionings rather than acceptance in faith of God's administration *and* the divine training that is in faith (*in that leaning of the entire human personality on God in absolute trust and confidence)—

5 Whereas the object *and* purpose of our instruction *and* charge is love, which springs from a pure heart and a good (clear) conscience and sincere (unfeigned) faith.

6 But certain individuals have missed the mark on this very matter [and] have wandered away into vain arguments *and* discussions *and* purposeless talk.

7 They are ambitious to be doctors

of the Law (teachers of the Mosaic ritual), but they have no understanding either of the words *and* terms they use *or* of the subjects about which they make [such] dogmatic assertions.

8 Now we recognize *and* know that the Law is good if anyone uses it lawfully [for the purpose for which it was designed],

9 Knowing *and* understanding this: that the Law is not enacted for the righteous (the upright and just, who are in right standing with God), but for the lawless and unruly, for the ungodly and sinful, for the irreverent and profane, for those who strike *and* beat *and* [even] murder fathers and strike *and* beat *and* [even] murder mothers, for manslayers,

10 [For] impure *and* immoral persons, those who abuse themselves with men, kidnapers, liars, perjurers —and whatever else is opposed to wholesome teaching *and* sound doctrine

11 As laid down by the glorious Gospel of the blessed God, with which I have been entrusted.

12 I give thanks to Him Who has granted me [the needed] strength *and* made me able [for this], Christ Jesus our Lord, because He has judged *and* counted me faithful *and* trustworthy, appointing me to [this stewardship of] the ministry.

13 Though I formerly blasphemed and persecuted and was shamefully *and* outrageously *and* aggressively

a Alexander Souter, *Pocket Lexicon of the Greek New Testament.*

insulting [to Him], nevertheless, I obtained mercy because I had acted out of ignorance in unbelief.

14 And the grace (unmerited favor and blessing) of our Lord [actually] flowed out superabundantly *and* beyond measure for me, accompanied by faith and love that are [to be realized] in Christ Jesus.

15 The saying is sure *and* true and worthy of full *and* universal acceptance, that Christ Jesus (the Messiah) came into the world to save sinners, of whom I am foremost.

16 But I obtained mercy for the reason that in me, as the foremost [of sinners], Jesus Christ might show forth and display all His perfect long-suffering *and* patience for an example to [encourage] those who would thereafter believe on Him for [the gaining of] eternal life.

17 Now to the King of eternity, incorruptible *and* immortal, invisible, the only God, be honor and glory forever and ever (to the ages of ages). Amen (so be it).

18 This charge *and* admonition I commit in trust to you, Timothy, my son, [b]in accordance with prophetic intimations which I formerly received concerning you, so that inspired *and* aided by them you may wage the good warfare,

19 Holding fast to faith ([c]that leaning of the entire human personality on God in absolute trust and confidence) and having a good (clear) conscience. By rejecting *and* thrusting from them [their conscience], some individuals have made shipwreck of their faith.

20 Among them are Hymenaeus and Alexander, whom I have delivered to Satan in order that they may be disciplined [by punishment and learn] not to blaspheme.

CHAPTER 2

FIRST OF all, then, I admonish *and* urge that petitions, prayers, intercessions, and thanksgivings be offered on behalf of all men,

2 For kings and all who are in positions of authority *or* high responsibility, that [outwardly] we may pass a quiet *and* undisturbed life [and inwardly] a peaceable one in all godliness *and* reverence and seriousness in every way.

3 For such [praying] is good *and* right, and [it is] pleasing *and* acceptable to God our Savior,

4 Who wishes all men to be saved and [increasingly] to perceive *and* recognize *and* discern *and* know precisely *and* correctly the [divine] Truth.

5 For there [is only] one God, and [only] one Mediator between God and men, the Man Christ Jesus,

6 Who gave Himself as a ransom for all [people, a fact that was] attested to at the right *and* proper time.

7 And of this matter I was appointed a preacher and an apostle (special messenger)—I am speaking the truth *in Christ*, I do not falsify [when I say this]—a teacher of the Gentiles in [the realm of] faith and truth.

8 I desire therefore that in every place men should pray, without anger *or* quarreling *or* resentment or doubt [in their minds], lifting up holy hands.

9 Also [I desire] that women should adorn themselves modestly *and* appropriately and sensibly in seemly apparel, not with [elaborate] hair arrangement or gold or pearls or expensive clothing,

10 But by doing good deeds (deeds in themselves good and for the good and advantage of those contacted by them), as befits women who profess

b Marvin Vincent, *Word Studies in the New Testament*.   c Alexander Souter, *Pocket Lexicon*.

reverential fear for and devotion to God.

11 Let a woman learn in quietness, in entire submissiveness.

12 I allow no woman to teach or to have authority over men; she is to remain in quietness and keep silence [in religious assemblies].

13 For Adam was first formed, then Eve; [Gen. 2:7, 21, 22.]

14 And it was not Adam who was deceived, but [the] woman who was deceived and deluded and fell into transgression. [Gen. 3:1–6.]

15 Nevertheless [the sentence put upon women of pain in motherhood does not hinder their souls' salvation, and] they will be saved [eternally] if they continue in faith and love and holiness with self-control, [saved indeed] [d]through the Childbearing or by the birth of the divine Child.

CHAPTER 3

THE SAYING is true and irrefutable: If any man [eagerly] seeks the office of bishop (superintendent, overseer), he desires an excellent task (work).

2 Now a bishop (superintendent, overseer) must give no grounds for accusation but must be above reproach, the husband of one wife, circumspect and temperate and self-controlled; [he must be] sensible and well behaved and dignified and lead an orderly (disciplined) life; [he must be] hospitable [showing love for and being a friend to the believers, especially strangers or foreigners, and be] a capable and qualified teacher,

3 Not given to wine, not combative but gentle and considerate, not quarrelsome but forbearing and peaceable, and not a lover of money [insatiable for wealth and ready to obtain it by questionable means].

4 He must rule his own household

well, keeping his children under control, with true dignity, commanding their respect in every way and keeping them respectful.

5 For if a man does not know how to rule his own household, how is he to take care of the church of God?

6 He must not be a new convert, or he may [develop a beclouded and stupid state of mind] as the result of pride [be blinded by conceit, and] fall into the condemnation that the devil [once] did. [Isa. 14:12–14.]

7 Furthermore, he must have a good reputation and be well thought of by those outside [the church], lest he become involved in slander and incur reproach and fall into the devil's trap.

8 In like manner the deacons [must be] worthy of respect, not shifty and double-talkers but sincere in what they say, not given to much wine, not greedy for base gain [craving wealth and resorting to ignoble and dishonest methods of getting it].

9 They must possess the mystic secret of the faith [Christian truth as hidden from ungodly men] with a clear conscience.

10 And let them also be tried and investigated and proved first; then, if they turn out to be above reproach, let them serve [as deacons].

11 [e][The] women likewise must be worthy of respect and serious, not gossipers, but temperate and self-controlled, [thoroughly] trustworthy in all things.

12 Let deacons be the husbands of but one wife, and let them manage [their] children and their own households well.

13 For those who perform well as deacons acquire a good standing for themselves and also gain much confidence and freedom and boldness in

---

d Marvin Vincent, Word Studies. See also Gal. 4:4.   e Either their wives or the deaconesses, or both.

the faith which is [founded on and centers] in Christ Jesus.

14 Although I hope to come to you before long, I am writing these instructions to you so that,

15 If I am detained, you may know how people ought to conduct themselves in the household of God, which is the church of the living God, the pillar and stay (the prop and support) of the Truth.

16 And great *and* important *and* weighty, we confess, is the hidden truth (the mystic secret) of godliness. He [God] was made visible in human flesh, justified *and* vindicated in the [Holy] Spirit, was seen by angels, preached among the nations, believed on in the world, [and] taken up in glory.

CHAPTER 4

BUT THE [Holy] Spirit distinctly *and* expressly declares that in latter times some will turn away from the faith, giving attention to deluding *and* seducing spirits and doctrines that demons teach,

2 Through the hypocrisy *and* pretensions of liars whose consciences are seared (cauterized),

3 Who forbid people to marry and [teach them] to abstain from [certain kinds of] foods which God created to be received with thanksgiving by those who believe *and* have [an increasingly clear] knowledge of the truth.

4 For everything God has created is good, and nothing is to be thrown away *or* refused if it is received with thanksgiving.

5 For it is hallowed *and* consecrated by the Word of God and by prayer.

6 If you lay all these instructions before the brethren, you will be a worthy steward *and* a good minister

of Christ Jesus, ever nourishing your own self on the truths of the faith and of the good [Christian] instruction which you have closely followed.

7 But refuse *and* avoid irreverent legends (profane and impure and godless fictions, mere grandmothers' tales) and silly myths, *and* express your disapproval of them. Train yourself toward godliness (piety), [keeping yourself spiritually fit].

8 For physical training is of some value (useful for a little), but godliness (spiritual training) is useful *and* of value in everything *and* in every way, for it holds promise for the present life and also for the life which is to come.

9 This saying is reliable *and* worthy of complete acceptance by everybody.

10 With a view to this we toil and strive, [yes and] ᵍ*suffer reproach*, because we have [fixed our] hope on the living God, Who is the Savior (Preserver, Maintainer, Deliverer) of all men, especially of those who believe (trust in, rely on, and adhere to Him).

11 Continue to command these things and to teach them.

12 Let no one despise *or* think less of you because of your youth, but be an example (pattern) for the believers in speech, in conduct, in love, in faith, and in purity.

13 Till I come, devote yourself to [public and private] reading, to exhortation (preaching and personal appeals), and to teaching *and* instilling doctrine.

14 Do not neglect the gift which is in you, [that special inward endowment] which was directly imparted to you [by the Holy Spirit] by prophetic utterance when the elders laid their hands upon you [at your ordination].

15 Practice *and* cultivate *and* med-

---

f Some manuscripts read "God."   g Some manuscripts so read.

itate upon these duties; throw yourself wholly into them [as your ministry], so that your progress may be evident to everybody.

16 Look well to yourself [to your own personality] and to [your] teaching; persevere in these things [hold to them], for by so doing you will save both yourself and those who hear you.

CHAPTER 5

DO NOT sharply censure *or* rebuke an older man, but entreat *and* plead with him as [you would with] a father. Treat younger men like brothers;

2 [Treat] older women like mothers [and] younger women like sisters, in all purity.

3 [Always] treat with great consideration *and* give aid to those who are truly widowed (solitary and without support).

4 But if a widow has children or grandchildren, see to it that these are first made to understand that it is their religious duty [to defray their natural obligation to those] at home, and make return to their parents *or* grandparents [for all their care by contributing to their maintenance], for this is acceptable in the sight of God.

5 Now [a woman] who is a real widow and is left entirely alone *and* desolate has fixed her hope on God and perseveres in supplications and prayers night and day,

6 Whereas she who lives in pleasure *and* self-gratification [giving herself up to luxury and self-indulgence] is dead even while she [still] lives.

7 Charge [the people] thus, so that they may be without reproach *and* blameless.

8 If anyone fails to provide for his relatives, and especially for those of his own family, he has disowned the faith [by failing to accompany it with fruits] and is worse than an unbeliever [who performs his obligation in these matters].

9 Let no one be put on the roll of widows [who are to receive church support] who is under sixty years of age or who has been the wife of more than one man;

10 And she must have a reputation for good deeds, as one who has brought up children, who has practiced hospitality to strangers [of the brotherhood], washed the feet of the saints, helped to relieve the distressed, [and] devoted herself diligently to doing good in every way.

11 But refuse [to enroll on this list the] younger widows, for when they become restive *and* their natural desires grow strong, they withdraw themselves against Christ [and] wish to marry [again].

12 And so they incur condemnation for having set aside *and* slighted their previous pledge.

13 Moreover, as they go about from house to house, they learn to be idlers, and not only idlers, but gossips and busybodies, saying what they should not say *and* talking of things they should not mention.

14 So I would have younger [widows] marry, bear children, guide the household, [and] not give opponents of the faith occasion for slander or reproach.

15 For already some [widows] have turned aside after Satan.

16 If any believing woman *or* believing man has [relatives or persons in the household who are] widows, let him relieve them; let the church not be burdened [with them], so that it may [be free to] assist those who are truly widows (those who are all alone and are dependent).

17 Let the elders who perform the duties of their office well be consid-

ered doubly worthy of honor [and of adequate hfinancial support], especially those who labor faithfully in preaching and teaching.

18 For the Scripture says, You shall not muzzle an ox when it is treading out the grain, and again, The laborer is worthy of his hire. [Deut. 25:4; Luke 10:7.]

19 Listen to no accusation [presented before a judge] against an elder unless it is confirmed by the testimony of two or three witnesses. [Deut. 19:15.]

20 As for those who are guilty and persist in sin, rebuke and admonish them in the presence of all, so that the rest may be warned and stand in wholesome awe and fear.

21 I solemnly charge you in the presence of God and of Christ Jesus and of the chosen angels that you guard and keep [these rules] without personal prejudice or favor, doing nothing from partiality.

22 Do not be in a hurry in the laying on of hands [giving the sanction of the church too hastily in reinstating expelled offenders or in ordination in questionable cases], nor share or participate in another man's sins; keep yourself pure.

23 Drink water no longer exclusively, but use a little wine for the sake of your stomach and your frequent illnesses.

24 The sins of some men are conspicuous (openly evident to all eyes), going before them to the judgment [seat] and proclaiming their sentence in advance; but the sins of others appear later [following the offender to the bar of judgment and coming into view there].

25 So also, good deeds are evident and conspicuous, and even when they are not, they cannot remain hidden [indefinitely].

CHAPTER 6

LET ALL who are under the yoke as bond servants esteem their own [personal] masters worthy of honor and fullest respect, so that the name of God and the teaching [about Him] may not be brought into disrepute and blasphemed.

2 Let those who have believing masters not be disrespectful or scornful [to them] on the grounds that they are brothers [in Christ]; rather, they should serve [them all the better] because those who benefit by their kindly service are believers and beloved. Teach and urge these duties.

3 But if anyone teaches otherwise and does not hassent to the sound and wholesome messages of our Lord Jesus Christ (the Messiah) and the teaching which is in agreement with godliness (piety toward God),

4 He is puffed up with pride and stupefied with conceit, [although he is] woefully ignorant. He has a imorbid fondness for controversy and disputes and strife about words, which result in (produce) envy and jealousy, quarrels and dissension, abuse and insults and slander, and base suspicions,

5 And protracted wrangling and wearing discussion and perpetual friction among men who are corrupted in mind and bereft of the truth, who imagine that godliness or righteousness is a hsource of profit [a moneymaking business, a means of livelihood]. From such withdraw.

6 [And it is, indeed, a source of immense profit, for] godliness accompanied with contentment (that contentment which is a sense of hinward sufficiency) is great and abundant gain.

7 For we brought nothing into the

h Marvin Vincent, Word Studies.   i Joseph Thayer, A Greek-English Lexicon of the New Testament.

world, and *obviously* we cannot take anything out of the world;

8 But if we have food and clothing, with these we shall be content (satisfied).

9 But those who crave to be rich fall into temptation and a snare and into many foolish (useless, godless) and hurtful desires that plunge men into ruin *and* destruction and miserable perishing.

10 For the love of money is a root of all evils; it is through this craving that some have been led astray *and* have wandered from the faith and pierced themselves through with many ¹acute [mental] pangs.

11 But as for you, O man of God, flee from all these things; aim at *and* pursue righteousness (right standing with God and true goodness), godliness (which is the loving fear of God and being Christlike), faith, love, steadfastness (patience), and gentleness of heart.

12 Fight the good fight of the faith; lay hold of the eternal life to which you were summoned and [for which] you confessed the good confession [of faith] before many witnesses.

13 In the presence of God, Who preserves alive all living things, and of Christ Jesus, Who in His testimony before Pontius Pilate made the good confession, I [solemnly] charge you

14 To keep all His precepts unsullied *and* flawless, irreproachable, until the appearing of our Lord Jesus Christ (the Anointed One),

15 Which [appearing] will be shown forth in His own proper time by the blessed, only Sovereign (Ruler), the King of kings and the Lord of lords,

16 Who alone has immortality [in the sense of exemption from every kind of death] and lives in unapproachable light, Whom no man has ever seen or can see. Unto Him be honor and everlasting power *and* dominion. Amen (so be it).

17 As for the rich in this world, charge them not to be proud *and* arrogant *and* contemptuous of others, nor to set their hopes on uncertain riches, but on God, Who richly *and* ceaselessly provides us with everything for [our] enjoyment.

18 [Charge them] to do good, to be rich in good works, to be liberal *and* generous of heart, ready to share [with others],

19 In this way laying up for themselves [the riches that endure forever as] a good foundation for the future, so that they may grasp that which is life indeed.

20 O Timothy, guard *and* keep the deposit entrusted [to you]! Turn away from the irreverent babble *and* godless chatter, with the vain *and* empty *and* worldly phrases, and the subtleties *and* the contradictions in what is falsely called knowledge *and* spiritual illumination.

21 [For] by making such profession some have erred (missed the mark) as regards the faith. Grace (divine favor and blessing) be with you all! *Amen (so be it).*

THE SECOND LETTER OF PAUL TO

TIMOTHY

CHAPTER 1

PAUL, AN apostle (special messenger) of Christ Jesus by the will of God, according to the promise of life that is in Christ Jesus,

2 To Timothy, [my] beloved child: Grace (favor and spiritual blessing), mercy, and [heart] peace from God the Father and Christ Jesus our Lord!

3 I thank God Whom I worship with a pure conscience, [a]in the spirit of my fathers, when without ceasing I remember you night and day in my prayers,

4 And when, as I recall your tears, I yearn to see you so that I may be filled with joy.

5 I am calling up memories of your sincere *and* unqualified faith, the [b]leaning of your entire personality on God in Christ in absolute trust and confidence in His power, wisdom, and goodness), [a faith] that first lived permanently in [the heart of] your grandmother Lois and your mother Eunice and now, I am [fully] persuaded, [dwells] in you also.

6 That is why I would remind you to stir up (rekindle the embers of, fan the flame of, and keep burning) the [gracious] gift of God, [the inner fire] that is in you by means of the laying on of my hands [[a]with those of the elders at your ordination].

7 For God did not give us a spirit of timidity (of cowardice, of craven and cringing and fawning fear), but [He has given us a spirit] of power and of love and of calm *and* well-balanced mind *and* discipline *and* self-control.

8 Do not blush *or* be ashamed then, to testify *to and* for our Lord, nor of me, a prisoner for His sake, but [[a]with me] take your share of the suffering [to which the preaching] of the Gospel [may expose you, and do it] in the power of God.

9 [For it is He] Who delivered *and* saved us and called us with a calling in itself holy *and* leading to holiness [to a life of consecration, a vocation of holiness]; [He did it] not because of anything of merit that we have done, but because of *and* to further His own purpose and grace (unmerited favor) which was given us in Christ Jesus before the world began [eternal ages ago].

10 [It is that purpose and grace] which He now has made known *and* has fully disclosed *and* made real [to us] through the appearing of our Savior Christ Jesus, Who annulled death *and* made it of no effect and brought life and immortality (immunity from eternal death) to light through the Gospel.

11 For [the proclaiming of] this [Gospel] I was appointed a herald (preacher) and an apostle (special messenger) and a teacher *of the Gentiles.*

12 And this is why I am suffering as I do. Still I am not ashamed, for I know (perceive, have knowledge of,

---

a Marvin Vincent, *Word Studies in the New Testament.*
Greek New Testament.

b Alexander Souter, *Pocket Lexicon of the Greek New Testament.*

and am acquainted with) Him Whom I have believed (adhered to and trusted in and relied on), and I am [positively] persuaded that He is able to guard *and* keep that which has been entrusted to me *and* which ᶜI have committed [to Him] until that day.

13 Hold fast *and* follow the pattern of wholesome *and* sound teaching which you have heard from me, in [all] the faith and love which are [for us] in Christ Jesus.

14 Guard *and* keep [with the greatest care] the precious *and* excellently adapted [Truth] which has been entrusted [to you], by the [help of the] Holy Spirit Who makes His home in us.

15 You already know that all who are in Asia turned away *and* forsook me, Phygelus and Hermogenes among them.

16 May the Lord grant [His] mercy to the family of Onesiphorus, for he often showed me kindness *and* ministered to my needs [comforting and reviving and bracing me like fresh air]! He was not ashamed of my chains *and* imprisonment [for Christ's sake].

17 No, rather when he reached Rome, he searched diligently *and* eagerly for me and found me.

18 May the Lord grant to him that he may find mercy from the Lord on that [great] day! And you know how many things he did for me *and* what a help he was at Ephesus [you know better than I can tell you].

CHAPTER 2

SO YOU, my son, be strong (strengthened inwardly) in the grace (spiritual blessing) that is [to be found only] in Christ Jesus.

2 And the [instructions] which you have heard from me along with many witnesses, transmit *and* entrust [as a deposit] to reliable *and* faithful men who will be competent *and* qualified to teach others also.

3 Take [with me] your share of the hardships *and* suffering [which you are called to endure] as a good (first-class) soldier of Christ Jesus.

4 No soldier when in service gets entangled in the enterprises of [civilian] life; his aim is to satisfy *and* please the one who enlisted him.

5 And if anyone enters competitive games, he is not crowned unless he competes lawfully (fairly, according to the rules laid down).

6 [It is] the hard-working farmer [who labors to produce] who must be the first partaker of the fruits.

7 Think over these things I am saying [understand them and grasp their application], for the Lord will grant you full insight *and* understanding in everything.

8 Constantly keep in mind Jesus Christ (the Messiah) [as] risen from the dead, [as the prophesied King] descended from David, according to the good news (the Gospel) that I preach. [Ps. 16:10.]

9 For that [Gospel] I am suffering affliction *and* even wearing chains like a criminal. But the Word of God is not chained *or* imprisoned!

10 Therefore I [am ready to] persevere *and* stand my ground with patience *and* endure everything for the sake of the elect [God's chosen], so that they too may obtain [the] salvation which is in Christ Jesus, with [the reward of] eternal glory.

11 The saying is sure *and* worthy of confidence: If we have died with Him, we shall also live with Him.

12 If we endure, we shall also reign with Him. If we deny *and* disown *and* reject Him, He will also deny *and* disown *and* reject us.

13 If we are faithless [do not be-

ᶜ Alternate translation.

lieve and are untrue to Him], He remains true (faithful to His Word and His righteous character), for He cannot deny Himself.

14 Remind [the people] of these facts and [solemnly] charge them in the presence of the Lord to avoid petty controversy over words, which does no good but upsets and undermines the faith of the hearers.

15 Study and be eager and do your utmost to present yourself to God approved (tested by trial), a workman who has no cause to be ashamed, correctly analyzing and accurately dividing [rightly handling and skillfully teaching] the Word of Truth.

16 But avoid all empty (vain, useless, idle) talk, for it will lead people into more and more ungodliness.

17 And their teaching [will devour; it] will eat its way like cancer or spread like gangrene. So it is with Hymenaeus and Philetus,

18 Who have missed the mark and swerved from the truth by arguing that the resurrection has already taken place. They are undermining the faith of some.

19 But the firm foundation of (laid by) God stands, sure and unshaken, bearing this seal (inscription): The Lord knows those who are His, and, Let everyone who names [himself by] the name of the Lord give up all iniquity and stand aloof from it. [Num. 16:5; Isa. 26:13.]

20 But in a great house there are not only vessels of gold and silver, but also [utensils] of wood and earthenware, and some for honorable and noble [use] and some for menial and ignoble [use].

21 So whoever cleanses himself [from what is ignoble and unclean, who separates himself from contact with contaminating and corrupting influences] will [then himself] be a vessel set apart and useful for honorable and noble purposes, consecrated and profitable to the Master, fit and ready for any good work.

22 Shun youthful lusts and flee from them, and aim at and pursue righteousness (all that is virtuous and good, right living, conformity to the will of God in thought, word, and deed); [and aim at and pursue] faith, love, [and] peace (harmony and concord with others) in fellowship with all [Christians], who call upon the Lord out of a pure heart.

23 But refuse (shut your mind against, have nothing to do with) trifling (ill-informed, unedifying, stupid) controversies over ignorant questionings, for you know that they foster strife and breed quarrels.

24 And the servant of the Lord must not be quarrelsome (fighting and contending). Instead, he must be kindly to everyone and mild-tempered [preserving the bond of peace]; he must be a skilled and suitable teacher, patient and forbearing and willing to suffer wrong.

25 He must correct his opponents with courtesy and gentleness, in the hope that God may grant that they will repent and come to know the Truth [that they will perceive and recognize and become accurately acquainted with and acknowledge it],

26 And that they may come to their senses [and] escape out of the snare of the devil, having been held captive by him, [henceforth] to do His [God's] will.

CHAPTER 3

BUT UNDERSTAND this, that in the last days will come (set in) perilous times of great stress and trouble [hard to deal with and hard to bear].

2 For people will be lovers of self and [utterly] self-centered, lovers of money and aroused by an inordinate [greedy] desire for wealth, proud and

arrogant *and* contemptuous boasters. They will be abusive (blasphemous, scoffing), disobedient to parents, ungrateful, unholy *and* profane.

3 [They will be] without natural [human] affection (callous and inhuman), relentless (admitting of no truce or appeasement); [they will be] slanderers (false accusers, troublemakers), intemperate *and* loose in morals *and* conduct, uncontrolled *and* fierce, haters of good.

4 [They will be] treacherous [betrayers], rash, [and] inflated with self-conceit. [They will be] lovers of sensual pleasures *and* vain amusements more than *and* rather than lovers of God.

5 For [although] they hold a form of piety (true religion), they deny *and* reject *and* are strangers to the power of it [their conduct belies the genuineness of their profession]. Avoid [all] such people [turn away from them].

6 For among them are those who worm their way into homes and captivate silly *and* weak-natured *and* spiritually dwarfed women, loaded down with [the burden of their] sins [and easily] swayed *and* led away by various evil desires *and* seductive impulses.

7 [These weak women will listen to anybody who will teach them]; they are forever inquiring *and* getting information, but are never able to arrive at a recognition *and* knowledge of the Truth.

8 Now just as ᵈJannes and Jambres were hostile to *and* resisted Moses, so these men also are hostile to *and* oppose the Truth. They have depraved *and* distorted minds, and are reprobate *and* counterfeit *and* to be rejected as far as the faith is concerned. [Exod. 7:11.]

9 But they will not get very far, for their rash folly will become obvious to everybody, as was that of those [magicians mentioned].

10 Now you have closely observed *and* diligently followed my teaching, conduct, purpose in life, faith, patience, love, steadfastness,

11 Persecutions, sufferings—such as occurred to me at Antioch, at Iconium, and at Lystra, persecutions I endured, but out of them all the Lord delivered me.

12 Indeed all who delight in piety *and* are determined to live a devoted *and* godly life in Christ Jesus will meet with persecution [will be made to suffer because of their religious stand].

13 But wicked men and imposters will go on from bad to worse, deceiving *and* leading astray others and being deceived *and* led astray themselves.

14 But as for you, continue to hold to the things that you have learned and of which you are convinced, knowing from whom you learned [them],

15 And how from your childhood you have had a knowledge of *and* been acquainted with the sacred Writings, which are able to instruct you *and* give you the understanding for salvation which comes through faith in Christ Jesus [through the ᵉleaning of the entire human personality on God in Christ Jesus in absolute trust and confidence in His power, wisdom, and goodness].

16 Every Scripture is God-breathed (given by His inspiration) and profitable for instruction, for reproof *and* conviction of sin, for correction of error *and* discipline in obedience, [and] for training in righteousness (in holy living, in

---

d Neither of these men is mentioned in the Old Testament, but according to Jewish tradition they were the Egyptian court magicians who opposed Moses.   e Alexander Souter, *Pocket Lexicon.*

conformity to God's will in thought, purpose, and action).

17 So that the man of God may be complete *and* proficient, well fitted *and* thoroughly equipped for every good work.

CHAPTER 4

I CHARGE [you] in the presence of God and of Christ Jesus, Who is to judge the living and the dead, and by (in the light of) His coming and His kingdom:

2 Herald *and* preach the Word! Keep your sense of urgency [stand by, be at hand and ready], whether the opportunity seems to be favorable or unfavorable. [Whether it is convenient or inconvenient, whether it is welcome or unwelcome, you as preacher of the Word are to show people in what way their lives are wrong.] And convince them, rebuking *and* correcting, warning *and* urging *and* encouraging them, being unflagging *and* inexhaustible in patience and teaching.

3 For the time is coming when [people] will not tolerate (endure) sound *and* wholesome instruction, but, having ears itching [for something pleasing and gratifying], they will gather to themselves one teacher after another to a considerable number, chosen to satisfy their own liking *and* to foster the errors they hold,

4 And will turn aside from hearing the truth and wander off into myths *and* man-made fictions.

5 As for you, be calm *and* cool *and* steady, accept *and* suffer unflinchingly every hardship, do the work of an evangelist, fully perform all the duties of your ministry.

6 For I am already about to be sacrificed [my life is about to be poured out as a drink offering]; the time of my [spirit's] release [from the body] is at hand *and* I will soon go free.

7 I have fought the good (worthy, honorable, and noble) fight, I have finished the race, I have kept (firmly held) the faith.

8 [As to what remains] henceforth there is laid up for me the [victor's] crown of righteousness [for being right with God and doing right], which the Lord, the righteous Judge, will award to me *and* recompense me on that [great] day—and not to me only, but also to all those who have loved *and* yearned for *and* welcomed His appearing (His return).

9 Make every effort to come to me soon.

10 For Demas has deserted me for love of this present world and has gone to Thessalonica; Crescens [has gone] to Galatia, Titus to Dalmatia.

11 Luke alone is with me. Get Mark and bring him with you, for he is very helpful to me for the ministry.

12 Tychicus I have sent to Ephesus.

13 [When] you come, bring the cloak that I left at Troas with Carpus, also the books, especially the parchments.

14 Alexander the coppersmith did me great wrongs. The Lord will pay him back for his actions.

15 Beware of him yourself, for he opposed *and* resisted our message very strongly *and* exceedingly.

16 At my first trial no one acted in my defense [as my advocate] *or* took my part *or* [even] stood with me, but all forsook me. May it not be charged against them!

17 But the Lord stood by me and strengthened me, so that through me the [Gospel] message might be fully proclaimed and all the Gentiles might hear it. So I was delivered out of the jaws of the lion.

18 [And indeed] the Lord will cer-

tainly deliver *and* [draw me to Himself] from every assault of evil. He will preserve *and* bring me safe unto His heavenly kingdom. To Him be the glory forever and ever. Amen (so be it).

19 Give my greetings to Prisca and Aquila and to the household of Onesiphorus.

20 Erastus stayed on at Corinth, but Trophimus I left ill at Miletus.

21 Do hasten *and* try your best to come to me before winter. Eubulus wishes to be remembered to you, as do Pudens and Linus and Claudia and all the brethren.

22 The Lord *Jesus Christ* be with your spirit. Grace (God's favor and blessing) be with you. *Amen (so be it)*.

THE LETTER OF PAUL TO
TITUS

CHAPTER 1

PAUL, A bond servant of God and an apostle (a special messenger) of Jesus Christ (the Messiah) to stimulate *and* promote the faith of God's chosen ones and to lead them on to accurate discernment *and* recognition of *and* acquaintance with the Truth which belongs to *and* harmonizes with *and* tends to godliness,

2 [Resting] in the hope of eternal life, [life] which the ever truthful God Who cannot deceive promised before the world *or* the ages of time began.

3 And [now] in His own appointed time He has made manifest (made known) His Word *and* revealed it as His message through the preaching entrusted to me by command of God our Savior;

4 To Titus, my true child according to a common (general) faith: Grace (favor and spiritual blessing) and [heart] peace from God the Father and *the Lord* Christ Jesus our Savior.

5 For this reason I left you [behind] in Crete, that you might set right what was defective *and* finish what was left undone, and that you might appoint elders *and* set them over the churches (assemblies) in every city as I directed you.

6 [These elders should be] men who are of unquestionable integrity *and* are irreproachable, the husband of [but] one wife, whose children are [well trained and are] believers, not open to the accusation of being loose in morals *and* conduct or unruly *and* disorderly.

7 For the bishop (an overseer) as God's steward must be blameless, not self-willed *or* arrogant *or* presumptuous; he must not be quick-tempered or given to drink *or* pugnacious (brawling, violent); he must not be grasping *and* greedy for filthy lucre (financial gain);

8 But he must be hospitable (loving and a friend to believers, especially to strangers and foreigners); [he must be] a lover of goodness [of good people and good things], sober-minded (sensible, discreet), upright *and* fair-minded, a devout man *and* religious-

---

f Joseph Thayer, *A Greek-English Lexicon of the New Testament*: A primary meaning of the Greek *ruomai*: "draw to one's self."

ly correct, temperate *and* keeping himself in hand.

9 He must hold fast to the sure *and* trustworthy Word of God as he was taught it, so that he may be able both to give stimulating instruction *and* encouragement in sound (wholesome) doctrine and to refute *and* convict those who contradict *and* oppose it [showing the wayward their error].

10 For there are many disorderly *and* unruly men who are idle (vain, empty) *and* misleading talkers and self-deceivers *and* deceivers of others. [This is true] especially of those of the circumcision party [who have come over from Judaism].

11 Their mouths must be stopped, for they are mentally distressing *and* subverting whole families by teaching what they ought not to teach, for the purpose of getting base advantage *and* disreputable gain.

12 One of their [very] number, a prophet of their own, said, Cretans are always liars, hurtful beasts, idle *and* lazy gluttons.

13 And this account of them is [really] true. Because it is [true], rebuke them sharply [deal sternly, even severely with them], so that they may be sound in the faith *and* free from error,

14 [And may show their soundness by] ceasing to give attention to Jewish myths *and* fables or to rules [laid down] by [mere] men who reject *and* turn their backs on the Truth.

15 To the pure [in heart and conscience] all things are pure, but to the defiled *and* corrupt and unbelieving nothing is pure; their very minds and consciences are defiled *and* polluted.

16 They profess to know God [to recognize, perceive, and be acquainted with Him], but deny *and*

disown *and* renounce Him by what they do; they are detestable *and* loathsome, unbelieving *and* disobedient *and* disloyal *and* rebellious, and [they are] unfit *and* worthless for good work (deed or enterprise) of any kind.

CHAPTER 2

BUT [as for] you, teach what is fitting *and* becoming to sound (wholesome) doctrine [the character and right living that identify true Christians].

2 Urge the older men to be temperate, venerable (serious), sensible, self-controlled, and sound in the faith, in the love, and in the steadfastness *and* patience [of Christ].

3 Bid the older women similarly to be reverent *and* devout in their deportment as becomes those engaged in sacred service, not slanderers or slaves to drink. They are to give good counsel *and* be teachers of what is right *and* noble,

4 So that they will wisely train the young women to be [g]sane and sober of mind (temperate, disciplined) and to love their husbands and their children,

5 To be self-controlled, chaste, homemakers, good-natured (kindhearted), adapting *and* subordinating themselves to their husbands, that the word of God may not be exposed to reproach (blasphemed or discredited).

6 In a similar way, urge the younger men to be self-restrained *and* to behave prudently [taking life seriously].

7 And show your own self in all respects to be a pattern *and* a model of good deeds *and* works, teaching what is unadulterated, showing gravity [having the strictest regard

---

g Marvin Vincent, *Word Studies in the New Testament*: The Greek verb here translated "train" means "to make sane or sober of mind, to moderate, to discipline."

for truth and purity of motive], with dignity *and* seriousness.

8 And let your instruction be sound *and* fit *and* wise *and* wholesome, vigorous *and* irrefutable *and* above censure, so that the opponent may be put to shame, finding nothing discrediting *or* evil to say about us.

9 [Tell] bond servants to be submissive to their masters, to be pleasing *and* give satisfaction in every way. [Warn them] not to talk back *or* contradict,

10 Nor to steal by taking things of small value, but to prove themselves truly loyal *and* entirely reliable *and* faithful throughout, so that in everything they may be an ornament *and* do credit to the teaching [which is] from *and* about God our Savior.

11 For the grace of God (His unmerited favor and blessing) has come forward (appeared) for the deliverance from sin and the eternal salvation for all mankind.

12 It has trained us to reject *and* renounce all ungodliness (irreligion) and worldly (passionate) desires, to live discreet (temperate, self-controlled), upright, devout (spiritually whole) lives in this present world,

13 Awaiting *and* looking for the [fulfillment, the realization of our] blessed hope, even the glorious appearing of our great God and Savior Christ Jesus (the Messiah, the Anointed One),

14 Who gave Himself on our behalf that He might redeem us (purchase our freedom) from all iniquity and purify for Himself a people [to be peculiarly His own, people who are] eager *and* enthusiastic about [living a life that is good and filled with] beneficial deeds. [Deut. 14:2; Ps. 130:8; Ezek. 37:23.]

15 Tell [them all] these things. Urge (advise, encourage, warn) and

rebuke with full authority. Let no one despise *or* disregard *or* think little of you [conduct yourself and your teaching so as to command respect].

CHAPTER 3

REMIND PEOPLE to be submissive to [their] magistrates and authorities, to be obedient, to be prepared *and* willing to do any upright *and* honorable work,

2 To slander *or* abuse *or* speak evil of no one, to avoid being contentious, to be forbearing (yielding, gentle, and conciliatory), and to show unqualified courtesy toward everybody.

3 For we also were once thoughtless *and* senseless, obstinate *and* disobedient, deluded *and* misled; [we too were once] slaves to all sorts of cravings *and* pleasures, wasting our days in malice and jealousy *and* envy, hateful (hated, detestable) and hating one another.

4 But when the goodness and loving-kindness of God our Savior to man [as man] appeared,

5 He saved us, not because of any works of righteousness that we had done, but because of His own pity *and* mercy, by [the] cleansing [bath] of the new birth (regeneration) and renewing of the Holy Spirit,

6 Which He poured out [so] richly upon us through Jesus Christ our Savior,

7 [And He did it in order] that we might be justified by His grace (by His favor, wholly undeserved), [that we might be acknowledged and counted as conformed to the divine will in purpose, thought, and action], and that we might become heirs of eternal life according to [our] hope.

8 This message is most trustworthy, and concerning these things I want you to insist steadfastly, so that

h Arthur S. Way, *Way's Epistles: The Letters of St. Paul to Seven Churches and Three Friends.*

those who have believed in (trusted in, relied on) God may be careful to apply themselves to honorable occupations *and* to doing good, for such things are [not only] excellent *and* right [in themselves], but [they are] good *and* profitable for the people.

9 But avoid stupid *and* foolish controversies and genealogies and dissensions and wrangling about the Law, for they are unprofitable and futile.

10 [As for] a man who is factious [a heretical sectarian and cause of divisions], after admonishing him a first and second time, reject [him from your fellowship and have nothing more to do with him],

11 Well aware that such a person has utterly changed (is perverted and corrupted); he goes on sinning [though he] is convicted of guilt *and* self-condemned.

12 When I send Artemas or [perhaps] Tychicus to you, lose no time *but* make every effort to come to me at Nicopolis, for I have decided to spend the winter there.

13 Do your utmost to speed Zenas the lawyer and Apollos on their way; see that they want for (lack) nothing.

14 And let our own [people really] learn to apply themselves to good deeds (to honest labor and honorable employment), so that they may be able to meet necessary demands 'whenever the occasion may require and not be living idle *and* uncultivated *and* unfruitful lives.

15 All who are with me wish to be remembered to you. Greet those who love us in the faith. Grace (God's favor and blessing) be with you all. *Amen (so be it).*

THE LETTER OF PAUL TO

PHILEMON

PAUL, A prisoner [for the sake] of Christ Jesus (the Messiah), and our brother Timothy, to Philemon our dearly beloved sharer with us in our work,

2 And to Apphia our sister and Archippus our fellow soldier [in the Christian warfare], and to the church [assembly that meets] in your house:

3 Grace (spiritual blessing and favor) be to all of you and [heart] peace from God our Father and the Lord Jesus Christ (the Messiah).

4 I give thanks to my God for you always when I mention you in my prayers,

5 Because I continue to hear of your love and of your loyal faith which you have toward the Lord Jesus and [which you show] toward all the saints (God's consecrated people).

6 [And I pray] that the participation in *and* sharing of your faith may produce *and* promote full recognition *and* appreciation *and* understanding *and* precise knowledge of every good [thing] that is ours in [our identification with] Christ *Jesus* [and unto His glory].

7 For I have derived great joy and comfort *and* encouragement from

i Marvin Vincent, *Word Studies.*

your love, because the hearts of the saints [who are your fellow Christians] have been cheered *and* refreshed through you, [my] brother.

8 Therefore, though I have abundant boldness in Christ to charge you to do what is fitting *and* required *and* your duty to do,

9 Yet for love's sake I prefer to appeal to you just for what I am—I, Paul, an ambassador [of Christ Jesus] *and* an old man and now a prisoner for His sake also—

10 I appeal to you for my [own spiritual] child, Onesimus [meaning profitable], whom I have begotten [in the faith] while a captive in these chains.

11 Once he was unprofitable to you, but now he is indeed profitable to you as well as to me.

12 I am sending him back to you in ʲhis own person, [and it is like sending] my very heart.

13 I would have chosen to keep him with me, in order that he might minister to my needs in your stead during my imprisonment for the Gospel's sake.

14 But it has been my wish to do nothing about it without first consulting you *and* getting your consent, in order that your benevolence might not seem to be the result of compulsion *or* of pressure but might be voluntary [on your part].

15 Perhaps it was for this reason that he was separated [from you] for a while, that you might have him back as yours forever,

16 Not as a slave any longer but as [something] more than a slave, as a brother [Christian], especially dear to me but how much more to you, both in the flesh [as a servant] and in the Lord [as a fellow believer].

17 If then you consider me a partner *and* a ʲcomrade in fellowship, welcome *and* receive him as you would [welcome and receive] me.

18 And if he has done you any wrong in any way or owes anything [to you], charge that to my account.

19 I, Paul, write it with my own hand, I promise to repay it [in full] —and that is to say nothing [of the fact] that you owe me your very self!

20 Yes, brother, let me have some profit from you in the Lord. Cheer *and* refresh my heart in Christ.

21 I write to you [perfectly] confident of your obedient compliance, knowing that you will do even more than I ask.

22 At the same time prepare a guest room [in expectation of extending your hospitality] to me, for I am hoping through your prayers to be granted [the gracious privilege of coming] to you.

23 Greetings to you from Epaphras, my fellow prisoner here in [the cause of] Christ Jesus (the Messiah),

24 And [from] Mark, Aristarchus, Demas, and Luke, my fellow workers.

25 The grace (blessing and favor) of the Lord Jesus Christ (the Messiah) be with your spirit. *Amen (so be it).*

ʲ Marvin Vincent, *Word Studies in the New Testament.*

THE LETTER TO THE
HEBREWS

CHAPTER 1

IN MANY separate revelations [*each of which set forth a portion of the Truth] and in different ways God spoke of old to [our] forefathers in *and* by the prophets.

2 [But] in bthe last of these days He has spoken to us in [the person of a] Son, Whom He appointed Heir *and* lawful Owner of all things, also by *and* through Whom He created the worlds *and* the reaches of space *and* the ages of time [He made, produced, built, operated, and arranged them in order].

3 He is the sole expression of the glory of God [the Light-being, the cout-raying or radiance of the divine], and He is the perfect imprint *and* very image of [God's] nature, upholding *and* maintaining *and* guiding *and* propelling the universe by His mighty word of power. When He had *by offering Himself* accomplished *our* cleansing of sins *and* riddance of guilt, He sat down at the right hand of the divine Majesty on high,

4 [Taking a place and rank by which] He Himself became as much superior to angels as the glorious Name (title) which He has inherited is different from *and* more excellent than theirs.

5 For to which of the angels did [God] ever say, You are My Son, today I have begotten You [established You in an official Sonship relation, with kingly dignity]? And again, I will be to Him a Father, and He will be to Me a Son? [II Sam. 7:14; Ps. 2:7.]

6 Moreover, when He brings the firstborn Son dagain into the habitable world, He says, Let all the angels of God worship Him.

7 Referring to the angels He says, [God] Who makes His angels winds and His ministering servants flames of fire; [Ps. 104:4.]

8 But as to the Son, He says to Him, Your throne, O God, is forever and ever [to the ages of the ages], and the scepter of Your kingdom is a scepter of absolute righteousness (of justice and straightforwardness).

9 You have loved righteousness [You have delighted in integrity, virtue, and uprightness in purpose, thought, and action] and You have hated lawlessness (injustice and iniquity). Therefore God, [even] Your God (eGodhead), has anointed You with the oil of exultant joy and gladness above *and* beyond Your companions. [Ps. 45:6, 7.]

10 And [further], You, Lord, did lay the foundation of the earth in the beginning, and the heavens are the works of Your hands.

11 They will perish, but You remain *and* continue permanently; they will all grow old *and* wear out like a garment.

a Marvin Vincent, *Word Studies in the New Testament. Notes.*   c Literal translation.   d Henry Alford, *The Greek New Testament, with Notes* and W. Robertson Nicoll, ed., *The Expositor's Greek New Testament.*   b Henry Alford, *The Greek New Testament, with Notes.*   e Arthur S. Way, *Way's Epistles: The Letters of St. Paul to Seven Churches and Three Friends.*

12 Like a mantle [thrown about one's self] You will roll them up, and they will be changed and replaced by others. But You remain the same, and Your years will never end nor come to failure. [Ps. 102:25–27.]

13 Besides, to which of the angels has He ever said, Sit at My right hand [associated with Me in My royal dignity] till I make your enemies a stool for your feet? [Ps. 110:1.]

14 Are not the angels all ministering spirits (servants) sent out in the service [of God for the assistance] of those who are to inherit salvation?

CHAPTER 2

SINCE ALL this is true, we ought to pay much closer attention than ever to the truths that we have heard, lest in any way we drift past [them] and slip away.

2 For if the message given through angels [the Law spoken by them to Moses] was authentic and proved sure, and every violation and disobedience received an appropriate (just and adequate) penalty,

3 How shall we escape [appropriate retribution] if we neglect and refuse to pay attention to such a great salvation [as is now offered to us, letting it drift past us forever]? For it was declared at first by the Lord [Himself], and it was confirmed to us and proved to be real and genuine by those who personally heard [Him speak].

4 [Besides this evidence] it was also established and plainly endorsed by God, Who showed His approval of it by signs and wonders and various miraculous manifestations of [His] power and by imparting the gifts of the Holy Spirit [to the believers] according to His own will.

5 For it was not to angels that God subjected the habitable world of the future, of which we are speaking.

6 It has been solemnly and earnestly said in a certain place, What is man that You are mindful of him, or the son of man that You graciously and helpfully care for and visit and look after him?

7 For some little time You have ranked him lower than and inferior to the angels; You have crowned him with glory and honor and set him over the works of Your hands, [Ps. 8:4–6.]

8 For You have put everything in subjection under his feet. Now in putting everything in subjection to man, He left nothing outside [of man's] control. But at present we do not yet see all things subjected to him [man].

9 But we are able to see Jesus, Who was ranked lower than the angels for a little while, crowned with glory and honor because of His having suffered death, in order that by the grace (unmerited favor) of God [to us sinners] He might experience death for every individual person.

10 For it was an act worthy [of God] and fitting [to the divine nature] that He, for Whose sake and by Whom all things have their existence, in bringing many sons into glory, should make the Pioneer of their salvation perfect [should bring to maturity the human experience necessary to be perfectly equipped for His office as High Priest] through suffering.

11 For both He Who sanctifies [making men holy] and those who are sanctified all have one [Father]. For this reason He is not ashamed to call them brethren;

12 For He says, I will declare Your [the Father's] name to My brethren; in the midst of the [worshiping] congregation I will sing hymns of praise to You. [Ps. 22:22.]

13 And again He says, My trust and assured reliance and confident

hope shall be fixed in Him. And yet again, Here I am, I and the children whom God has given Me. [Isa. 8:17, 18.]

14 Since, therefore, [these His] children share in flesh and blood [in the physical nature of human beings], He [Himself] in a similar manner partook of the same [nature], that by [going through] death He might bring to nought *and* make of no effect him who had the power of death— that is, the devil—

15 And also that He might deliver *and* completely set free all those who through the [haunting] fear of death were held in bondage throughout the whole course of their lives.

16 For, as we all know, He [Christ] did not take hold of angels [[f]the fallen angels, to give them a helping and delivering hand], but He did take hold of [[f]the fallen] descendants of Abraham [to reach out to them a helping and delivering hand]. [Isa. 41:8, 9.]

17 So it is evident that it was essential that He be made like His brethren in every respect, in order that He might become a merciful (sympathetic) and faithful High Priest in the things related to God, to make atonement *and* propitiation for the people's sins.

18 For because He Himself [in His humanity] has suffered in being tempted (tested and tried), He is able [immediately] [g]to run to the cry of (assist, relieve) those who are being tempted *and* tested *and* tried [and who therefore are being exposed to suffering].

CHAPTER 3

SO THEN, brethren, consecrated *and* set apart for God, who share in the heavenly calling, [thoughtfully and attentively] consider Jesus, the Apostle and High Priest Whom we confessed [as ours when we embraced the Christian faith].

2 [See how] faithful He was to Him Who appointed Him [Apostle and High Priest], as Moses was also faithful in the whole house [of God]. [Num. 12:7.]

3 Yet Jesus has been considered worthy of much greater honor *and* glory than Moses, just as the builder of a house has more honor than the house [itself].

4 For [of course] every house is built *and* furnished by someone, but the Builder of all things *and* the Furnisher [of the entire equipment of all things] is God.

5 And Moses certainly was faithful in the administration of all God's house [but it was only] as a ministering servant. [In his entire ministry he was but] a testimony to the things which were to be spoken [the revelations to be given afterward in Christ]. [Num. 12:7.]

6 But Christ (the Messiah) was faithful over His [own Father's] house as a Son [and Master of it]. And it is we who are [now members] of this house, if we hold *fast and firm to the end* our joyful *and* exultant confidence and sense of triumph in our hope [in Christ].

7 Therefore, as the Holy Spirit says: Today, if you will hear His voice,

8 Do not harden your hearts, as [happened] in the rebellion [of Israel] *and* their provocation *and* [h]embitterment [of Me] in the day of testing in the wilderness,

9 Where your fathers tried [My patience] *and* tested [My forbearance]

---

and [f]found I stood their test, and they saw My works for forty years.

10 And so I was provoked (displeased and sorely grieved) with that generation, and said, They always err *and* are led astray in their hearts, and they have not perceived *or* recognized My ways *and* become progressively better *and* more experimentally *and* intimately acquainted with them.

11 Accordingly, I swore in My wrath *and* indignation, They shall not enter into My rest. [Ps. 95:7–11.]

12 [Therefore beware] brethren, take care, lest there be in any one of you a wicked, unbelieving heart [which refuses to cleave to, trust in, and rely on Him], leading you to turn away *and* desert *or* stand aloof from the living God.

13 But instead warn (admonish, urge, and encourage) one another every day, as long as it is called Today, that none of you may be hardened [into settled rebellion] by the deceitfulness of sin [by the fraudulence, the stratagem, the trickery which the delusive glamor of his sin may play on him].

14 For we [i]have become fellows with Christ (the Messiah) *and* share in all He has for us, if only we hold our first newborn confidence *and* original assured expectation [in virtue of which we are believers] firm *and* unshaken to the end.

15 Then while it is [still] called Today, if you would hear His voice *and* when you hear it, do not harden your hearts as in the rebellion [in the desert, when the people provoked and irritated and embittered God against them]. [Ps. 95:7, 8.]

16 For who were they who heard *and* yet were rebellious *and* provoked [Him]? Was it not all those who came out of Egypt led by Moses?

17 And with whom was He irritated *and* provoked *and* grieved for forty years? Was it not with those who sinned, whose [j]dismembered bodies were strewn *and* left in the desert?

18 And to whom did He swear that they should not enter His rest, but to those who disobeyed [who had not listened to His word and who refused to be compliant or be persuaded]?

19 So we see that they were not able to enter [into His rest], because of their unwillingness to adhere to *and* trust in *and* rely on God [unbelief had shut them out]. [Num. 14:1–35.]

CHAPTER 4

THEREFORE, WHILE the promise of entering His rest still holds *and* is offered [today], let us be afraid [[j]to distrust it], lest any of you should [j]think he has come too late *and* has come short of [reaching] it.

2 For indeed we have had the glad tidings [Gospel of God] proclaimed to us just as truly as they [the Israelites of old did when the good news of deliverance from bondage came to them]; but the message they heard did not benefit them, because it was not mixed with faith (with [k]the leaning of the entire personality on God in absolute trust and confidence in His power, wisdom, and goodness) by those who heard it; [l]*neither were they united in faith with the ones [Joshua and Caleb] who heard (did believe).*

3 For we who have believed (adhered to and trusted in and relied on God) do enter that rest, [j]in accordance with His declaration that those [who did not believe] should not enter when He said, As I swore in My wrath, They shall not enter My rest;

i Charles B. Williams, *The New Testament: A Translation in the Language of the People.*   j Marvin Vincent, *Word Studies.*   k Alexander Souter, *Pocket Lexicon.*   l Many manuscripts so read.

and this He said although [His] works had been completed *and* prepared [and waiting for all who would believe] from the foundation of the world. [Ps. 95:11.]

4 For in a certain place He has said this about the seventh day: And God rested on the seventh day from all His works. [Gen. 2:2.]

5 And [they forfeited their part in it, for] in this [passage] He said, They shall not enter My rest. [Ps. 95:11.]

6 Seeing then that the promise remains over [from past times] for some to enter that rest, and that those who formerly were given the good news about it *and* the opportunity, failed to appropriate it *and* did not enter because of disobedience,

7 Again He sets a definite day, [a new] Today, [and gives another opportunity of securing that rest] saying through David after so long a time in the words already quoted, Today, if you would hear His voice *and* when you hear it, do not harden your hearts. [Ps. 95:7, 8.]

8 [This mention of a rest was not a reference to their entering into Canaan.] For if Joshua had given them rest, He [God] would not speak afterward about another day.

9 So then, there is still awaiting a full *and* complete Sabbath-rest reserved for the [true] people of God;

10 For he who has once entered [God's] rest also has ceased from [the weariness and pain] of human labors, just as God rested from those labors [m]peculiarly His own. [Gen. 2:2.]

11 Let us therefore be zealous *and* exert ourselves *and* strive diligently to enter that rest [of God, to know and experience it for ourselves], that no one may fall *or* perish by the same kind of unbelief *and* disobedience

[into which those in the wilderness fell].

12 For the Word that God speaks is alive and full of power [making it active, operative, energizing, and effective]; it is sharper than any two-edged sword, penetrating to the dividing line of the [n]breath of life (soul) and [the immortal] spirit, and of joints and marrow [of the deepest parts of our nature], exposing *and* sifting *and* analyzing *and* judging the very thoughts and purposes of the heart.

13 And not a creature exists that is concealed from His sight, but all things are open *and* exposed, naked *and* defenseless to the eyes of Him with Whom we have to do.

14 Inasmuch then as we have a great High Priest Who has [already] ascended *and* passed through the heavens, Jesus the Son of God, let us hold fast our confession [of faith in Him].

15 For we do not have a High Priest Who is unable to understand *and* sympathize *and* have a shared feeling with our weaknesses *and* infirmities *and* liability to the assaults of temptation, but One Who has been tempted in every respect as we are, yet without sinning.

16 Let us then fearlessly *and* confidently *and* boldly draw near to the throne of grace (the throne of God's unmerited favor to us sinners), that we may receive mercy [for our failures] and find grace to help in good time for every need [appropriate help and well-timed help, coming just when we need it].

CHAPTER 5

FOR EVERY high priest chosen from among men is appointed to act on behalf of men in things relating

m Marvin Vincent, *Word Studies*. **n** Joseph Thayer, *A Greek-English Lexicon of the New Testament*.

to God, to offer both gifts and sacrifices for sins.

2 He is able to exercise gentleness *and* forbearance toward the ignorant and erring, since he himself also is liable to moral weakness *and* physical infirmity.

3 And because of this he is obliged to offer sacrifice for his own sins, as well as for those of the people.

4 Besides, one does not appropriate for himself the honor [of being high priest], but he is called by God *and* receives it of Him, just as Aaron did.

5 So too Christ (the Messiah) did not exalt Himself to be made a high priest, but was appointed *and* exalted by Him Who said to Him, You are My Son; today I have begotten You; [Ps. 2:7.]

6 As He says also in another place, You are a Priest [appointed] forever after the order (with [o]the rank) of Melchizedek. [Ps. 110:4.]

7 In the days of His flesh [Jesus] offered up definite, special petitions [for that which He not only wanted [p]but needed] and supplications with strong crying and tears to Him Who was [always] able to save Him [out] from death, and He was heard because of His reverence toward God [His godly fear, His piety, [q]in that He shrank from the horrors of separation from the bright presence of the Father].

8 Although He was a Son, He learned [active, special] obedience through what He suffered,

9 And, [His completed experience] making Him perfectly [equipped], He became the Author *and* Source of eternal salvation to all those who give heed *and* obey Him, [Isa. 45:17.]

10 Being [r]designated *and* recognized *and* saluted by God as High Priest after the order (with [o]the rank) of Melchizedek. [Ps. 110.4.]

11 Concerning this we have much to say which is hard to explain, since you have become dull in your [spiritual] hearing *and* sluggish [even [p]slothful in achieving spiritual insight].

12 For even though by this time you ought to be teaching others, you actually need someone to teach you over again the very first principles of God's Word. You have come to need milk, not solid food.

13 For everyone who continues to feed on milk is obviously inexperienced *and* unskilled in the doctrine of righteousness (of conformity to the divine will in purpose, thought, and action), for he is a mere infant [not able to talk yet]!

14 But solid food is for full-grown men, for those whose senses *and* mental faculties are trained by practice to discriminate *and* distinguish between what is morally good *and* noble and what is evil *and* contrary either to divine or human law.

CHAPTER 6

THEREFORE LET us go on and get past the elementary stage in the teachings *and* doctrine of Christ (the Messiah), advancing steadily toward the completeness *and* perfection that belong to spiritual maturity. Let us not again be laying the foundation of repentance *and* abandonment of dead works (dead formalism) and of the faith [by which you turned] to God,

2 With teachings about purifying, the laying on of hands, the resurrection from the dead, and eternal judgment *and* punishment. [These are all

o Joseph Thayer, *A Greek-English Lexicon*. p G. Abbott-Smith, *Manual Greek Lexicon of the New Testament*. q Robert Jamieson, A.R. Fausset and David Brown, *A Commentary on the Old and New Testaments*. r Alexander Souter, *Pocket Lexicon*.

matters of which you should have been fully aware long, long ago.]

3 If indeed God permits, we will [now] proceed [to advanced teaching].

4 For it is impossible [to restore and bring again to repentance] those who have been once for all enlightened, who have consciously tasted the heavenly gift and have become sharers of the Holy Spirit,

5 And have felt how good the Word of God is and the mighty powers of the age *and* world to come,

6 If they then deviate from the faith *and* turn away from their allegiance —[it is impossible]—to bring them back to repentance, for (because, while, as long as) they nail upon the cross the Son of God afresh [as far as they are concerned] and are holding [Him] up to contempt *and* shame *and* public disgrace.

7 For the soil which has drunk the rain that repeatedly falls upon it and produces vegetation useful to those for whose benefit it is cultivated partakes of a blessing from God.

8 But if [that same soil] persistently bears thorns and thistles, it is considered worthless and near to being cursed, whose end is to be burned. [Gen. 3:17, 18.]

9 Even though we speak this way, yet in your case, beloved, we are now firmly convinced of better things that are near to salvation *and* accompany it.

10 For God is not unrighteous to forget *or* overlook your labor and the love which you have shown for His name's sake in ministering to the needs of the saints (His own consecrated people), as you still do.

11 But we do ['strongly and earnestly] desire for each of you to show the same diligence *and* sincerity [all the way through] in realizing *and* en-

joying the full assurance *and* development of [your] hope until the end,

12 In order that you may not grow disinterested *and* become [spiritual] sluggards, but imitators, behaving as do those who through faith ('by their leaning of the entire personality on God in Christ in absolute trust and confidence in His power, wisdom, and goodness) and by practice of patient endurance *and* waiting are [now] inheriting the promises.

13 For when God made [His] promise to Abraham, He swore by Himself, since He had no one greater by whom to swear,

14 Saying, Blessing I certainly will bless you and multiplying I will multiply you. [Gen. 22:16, 17.]

15 And so it was that he [Abraham], having waited long *and* endured patiently, realized *and* obtained [in the birth of Isaac as a pledge of what was to come] what God had promised him.

16 Men indeed swear by a greater [than themselves], and with them in all disputes the oath taken for confirmation is final [ending strife].

17 Accordingly God also, in His desire to show more convincingly *and* beyond doubt to those who were to inherit the promise the unchangeableness of His purpose *and* plan, intervened (mediated) with an oath.

18 This was so that, by two unchangeable things [His promise and His oath] in which it is impossible for God ever to prove false *or* deceive us, we who have fled [to Him] for refuge might have mighty indwelling strength *and* strong encouragement to grasp *and* hold fast the hope appointed for us *and* set before [us].

19 [Now] we have this [hope] as a sure and steadfast anchor of the soul [it cannot slip and it cannot 'break down under whoever steps out upon

---

s Marvin Vincent, *Word Studies*.   t Alexander Souter, *Pocket Lexicon*.

it—a hope] that reaches ᵘfarther *and* enters into [the very certainty of the Presence] within the veil, [Lev. 16:2.]

20 Where Jesus has entered in for us [in advance], a Forerunner having become a High Priest forever after the order (with ᵛthe rank) of Melchizedek. [Ps. 110:4.]

CHAPTER 7

FOR THIS Melchizedek, king of Salem [and] priest of the Most High God, met Abraham as he returned from the slaughter of the kings and blessed him,

2 And Abraham gave to him a tenth portion of all [the spoil]. He is primarily, as his name when translated indicates, king of righteousness, and then he is also king of Salem, which means king of peace.

3 Without [record of] father or mother or ancestral line, neither with beginning of days nor ending of life, but, resembling the Son of God, he continues to be a priest without interruption *and* without successor.

4 Now observe *and* consider how great [a personage] this was to whom even Abraham the patriarch gave a tenth [the topmost or the pick of the heap] of the spoils.

5 And it is true that those descendants of Levi who are charged with the priestly office are commanded in the Law to take tithes from the people —which means, from their brethren —though these have descended from Abraham.

6 But this person who has not their Levitical ancestry received tithes from Abraham [himself] and blessed him who possessed the promises [of God].

7 Yet it is beyond all contradiction that it is the lesser person who is blessed by the greater one.

8 Furthermore, here [in the Levitical priesthood] tithes are received by men who are subject to death; while there [in the case of Melchizedek], they are received by one of whom it is testified that he lives [perpetually].

9 A person might even say that Levi [the father of the priestly tribe] himself, who received tithes (the tenth), paid tithes through Abraham,

10 For he was still in the loins of his forefather [Abraham] when Melchizedek met him [Abraham].

11 Now if perfection (a perfect fellowship between God and the worshiper) had been attainable by the Levitical priesthood—for under it the people were given the Law—why was it further necessary that there should arise another *and* different kind of Priest, one after the order of Melchizedek, rather than one appointed after the order *and* rank of Aaron?

12 For when there is a change in the priesthood, there is of necessity an alteration of the law [concerning the priesthood] as well.

13 For the One of Whom these things are said belonged [not to the priestly line but] to another tribe, no member of which has officiated at the altar.

14 For it is obvious that our Lord sprang from the tribe of Judah, and Moses mentioned nothing about priests in connection with that tribe.

15 And this becomes more plainly evident when another Priest arises Who bears the likeness of Melchizedek, [Ps. 110:4.]

16 Who has been constituted a Priest, not on the basis of a bodily legal requirement [an externally imposed command concerning His physical ancestry], but on the basis of the power of an endless *and* indestructible Life.

u Marvin Vincent, *Word Studies.*   v Joseph Thayer, *A Greek-English Lexicon.*

17 For it is witnessed of Him, You are a Priest forever after the order (with the rank) of Melchizedek. [Ps. 110:4.]

18 So a previous physical regulation *and* command is cancelled because of its weakness *and* ineffectiveness *and* uselessness—

19 For the Law never made anything perfect—but instead a better hope is introduced through which we [now] come close to God.

20 And it was not without the taking of an oath [that Christ was made Priest].

21 For those who formerly became priests received their office without its being confirmed by the taking of an oath by God, but this One was designated *and* addressed *and* saluted with an oath, The Lord has sworn and will not regret it *or* change His mind, You are a Priest forever *according to the order of Melchizedek.* [Ps. 110:4.]

22 In keeping with [the oath's greater strength and force], Jesus has become the Guarantee of a better (stronger) agreement [a more excellent and more advantageous covenant].

23 [Again, the former successive line of priests] was made up of many, because they were each prevented by death from continuing [perpetually in office];

24 But He holds His priesthood unchangeably, because He lives on forever.

25 Therefore He is able also to save to the uttermost (completely, perfectly, finally, and for all time and eternity) those who come to God through Him, since He is always living to make petition to God *and* intercede with Him *and* intervene for them.

26 [Here is] the High Priest [perfectly adapted] to our needs, as was fitting—holy, blameless, unstained

by sin, separated from sinners, and exalted higher than the heavens.

27 He has no day by day necessity, as [do each of these other] high priests, to offer sacrifice first of all for his own [personal] sins and then for those of the people, because He [met all the requirements] once for all when He brought Himself [as a sacrifice] which He offered up.

28 For the Law sets up men in their weakness [frail, sinful, dying human beings] as high priests, but the word of [God's] oath, which [was spoken later] after the institution of the Law, [chooses and appoints as priest One Whose appointment is complete and permanent], a Son Who has been made perfect forever. [Ps. 110:4.]

CHAPTER 8

NOW THE main point of what we have to say is this: We have such a High Priest, One Who is seated at the right hand of the majestic [God] in heaven, [Ps. 110:1.]

2 As officiating Priest, a Minister in the holy places *and* in the true tabernacle which is erected not by man but by the Lord.

3 For every high priest is appointed to offer up gifts and sacrifices; so it is essential for this [High Priest] to have some offering to make also.

4 If then He were still living on earth, He would not be a priest at all, for there are [already priests] who offer the gifts in accordance with the Law.

5 [But these offer] service [merely] as a pattern and as a foreshadowing of [what has its true existence and reality in] the heavenly sanctuary. For when Moses was about to erect the tabernacle, he was warned by God, saying, See to it that you make it all [exactly] according to the copy (the model) which was shown to you on the mountain. [Exod. 25:40.]

6 But as it now is, He [Christ] has acquired a [priestly] ministry which is as much superior *and* more excellent [than the old] as the covenant (the agreement) of which He is the Mediator (the Arbiter, Agent) is superior *and* more excellent, [because] it is enacted *and* rests upon more important (sublimer, higher, and nobler) promises.

7 For if that first covenant had been without defect, there would have been no room for another one *or* an attempt to institute another one.

8 However, He finds fault with them [showing its inadequacy] when He says, Behold, the days will come, says the Lord, when I will make *and* ratify a new covenant *or* agreement with the house of Israel and with the house of Judah.

9 It will not be like the covenant that I made with their forefathers on the day when I grasped them by the hand to help *and* relieve them *and* to lead them out from the land of Egypt, for they did not abide in My agreement with them, and so I withdrew My favor *and* disregarded them, says the Lord.

10 For this is the covenant that I will make with the house of Israel after those days, says the Lord: I will imprint My laws upon their minds, even upon their innermost thoughts *and* understanding, and engrave them upon their hearts; and I will be their God, and they shall be My people.

11 And it will nevermore be necessary for each one to teach his neighbor and his fellow citizen or each one his brother, saying, Know (perceive, have knowledge of, and get acquainted by experience with) the Lord, for all will know Me, from the smallest to the greatest of them.

12 For I will be merciful *and* gracious toward their sins and I will remember their deeds of unrighteousness no more. [Jer. 31:31–34.]

13 When God speaks of a new [covenant *or* agreement], He makes the first one obsolete (out of use). And what is obsolete (out of use and annulled because of age) is ripe for disappearance *and* to be dispensed with altogether.

CHAPTER 9

NOW EVEN the first covenant had its own rules *and* regulations for divine worship, and it had a sanctuary [but one] of this world. [Exod. 25:10–40.]

2 For a tabernacle (tent) was erected, in the outer division *or* compartment of which were the lampstand and the table with [its loaves of] the showbread set forth. [This portion] is called the Holy Place. [Lev. 24:5, 6.]

3 But [inside] beyond the second curtain *or* veil, [there stood another] tabernacle [division] known as the Holy of Holies. [Exod. 26:31–33.]

4 It had the golden *altar of incense and the ark (chest) of the covenant, covered over with wrought gold. This [ark] contained a golden jar which held the manna and the rod of Aaron that sprouted and the [two stone] slabs of the covenant [bearing the Ten Commandments]. [Exod. 16:32–34; 30:1–6; Num. 17:8–10.]

5 Above [the ark] and overshadowing the mercy seat were the representations of the cherubim [winged creatures which were the symbols] of glory. We cannot now go into detail about these things.

6 These arrangements having thus been made, the priests enter [habitually] into the outer division of the tab-

---

w Henry Alford, *The Greek New Testament, with Notes*: Not kept permanently in the Holy of Holies, but taken in on the Day of Atonement.

ernacle in performance of their ritual acts of worship.

7 But into the second [division of the tabernacle] none but the high priest goes, and he only once a year, and never without taking a sacrifice of blood with him, which he offers for himself and for the errors *and* sins of ignorance *and* thoughtlessness which the people have committed. [Lev. 16:15.]

8 By this the Holy Spirit points out that the way into the [true Holy of] Holies is not yet thrown open as long as the former [the outer portion of the] tabernacle remains a recognized institution *and* is still standing,

9 Seeing that that first [outer portion of the] tabernacle was a parable (a visible symbol or type or picture of the present age). In it gifts and sacrifices are offered, and yet are incapable of perfecting the conscience *or* of cleansing *and* renewing the inner man of the worshiper.

10 For [the ceremonies] deal only with clean and unclean meats and drinks and different washings, [mere] external rules *and* regulations for the body imposed to tide the worshipers over until the time of setting things straight [of reformation, of the complete new order when Christ, the Messiah], shall establish the reality of what these things foreshadow—a better covenant].

11 But [that appointed time came] when Christ (the Messiah) appeared as a High Priest of the better things that have come *and* are to come. [Then] through the greater and more perfect tabernacle not made with [human] hands, that is, not a part of this material creation,

12 He went once for all into the [Holy of] Holies [of heaven], not by virtue of the blood of goats and calves [by which to make reconcilia-

tion between God and man], but His own blood, having found *and* secured a complete redemption (an everlasting release for us).

13 For if [the mere] sprinkling of unholy *and* defiled persons with blood of goats and bulls and with the ashes of a burnt heifer is sufficient for the purification of the body, [Lev. 16:6, 16; Num. 19:9, 17, 18.]

14 How much more surely shall the blood of Christ, Who [x] by virtue of [His] eternal Spirit [His own preexistent [y] divine personality] has offered Himself as an unblemished sacrifice to God, purify our consciences from dead works *and* lifeless observances to serve the [ever] living God?

15 [Christ, the Messiah] is therefore the Negotiator *and* Mediator of an [entirely] new agreement (testament, covenant), so that those who are called *and* offered it may receive the fulfillment of the promised everlasting inheritance—since a death has taken place which rescues *and* delivers *and* redeems them from the transgressions committed under the [old] first agreement.

16 For where there is a [last] will *and* testament involved, the death of the one who made it must be established,

17 For a will *and* testament is valid and takes effect only at death, since it has no force *or* legal power as long as the one who made it is alive.

18 So even the [old] first covenant (God's will) was not inaugurated *and* ratified *and* put in force without the shedding of blood.

19 For when every command of the Law had been read out by Moses to all the people, he took the blood of slain calves and goats, together with water and scarlet wool and with a bunch of hyssop and sprinkled both the Book (the roll of the Law and

x Marvin Vincent, *Word Studies*.   y Henry Alford, cited by Kenneth Wuest, *Word Studies*.

covenant) itself and all the people,

20 Saying these words: This is the blood that seals *and* ratifies the agreement (the testament, the covenant) which God commanded [me to deliver to] you. [Exod. 24:6-8.]

21 And in the same way he sprinkled with the blood both the tabernacle and all the [sacred] vessels *and* appliances used in [divine] worship.

22 [In fact] under the Law almost everything is purified by means of blood, and without the shedding of blood there is neither release from sin *and* its guilt *nor* the remission of the due *and* merited punishment for sins.

23 By such means, therefore, it was necessary for the [earthly] copies of the heavenly things to be purified, but the actual heavenly things themselves [required far] better *and* nobler sacrifices than these.

24 For Christ (the Messiah) has not entered into a sanctuary made with [human] hands, only a copy *and* pattern *and* type of the true one, but [He has entered] into heaven itself, now to appear in the [very] presence of God on our behalf.

25 Nor did He [enter into the heavenly sanctuary to] offer Himself regularly again and again, as the high priest enters the [Holy of] Holies every year with blood not his own.

26 For then would He often have had to suffer [over and over again] since the foundation of the world. But as it now is, He has once for all at the consummation *and* close of the ages appeared to put away *and* abolish sin by His sacrifice [of Himself].

27 And just as it is appointed for [all] men once to die, and after that the [certain] judgment,

28 Even so it is that Christ, having been offered to take upon Himself *and* bear as a burden the sins of many

once *and* ²once for all, will appear a second time, not to carry any burden of sin *nor* to deal with sin, but to bring to full salvation those who are [eagerly, constantly, and patiently] waiting for *and* expecting Him.

CHAPTER 10

FOR SINCE the Law has merely a rude outline (foreshadowing) of the good things to come—instead of fully expressing those things—it can never by offering the same sacrifices continually year after year make perfect those who approach [its altars].

2 For if it were otherwise, would [these sacrifices] not have stopped being offered? Since the worshipers had ²once for all been cleansed, they would no longer have any guilt *or* consciousness of sin.

3 But [as it is] these sacrifices annually bring a fresh remembrance of sins [to be atoned for],

4 Because the blood of bulls and goats is powerless to take sins away.

5 Hence, when He [Christ] entered into the world, He said, Sacrifices and offerings You have not desired, but instead You have made ready a body for Me [to offer];

6 In burnt offerings and sin offerings You have taken no delight.

7 Then I said, Behold, here I am, coming to do Your will, O God—[to fulfill] what is written of Me in the volume of the Book. [Ps. 40:6-8.]

8 When He said just before, You have neither desired, nor have You taken delight in sacrifices and offerings and burnt offerings and sin offerings—all of which are offered according to the Law—

9 He then went on to say, Behold, [here] I am, coming to do Your will. Thus He does away with *and* annuls the first (former) order [as a means of expiating sin] so that He might

---

z G. Abbott-Smith, *Manual Greek Lexicon*.

inaugurate *and* establish the second (latter) order. [Ps. 40:6-8.]

10 And in accordance with this will [of God], we have been made holy (consecrated and sanctified) through the offering made once for all of the body of Jesus Christ (the Anointed One).

11 Furthermore, every [human] priest stands [at his altar of service] ministering daily, offering the same sacrifices over and over again, which never are able to strip [from every side of us] the sins [that envelop us] *and* take them away—

12 Whereas this One [Christ], after He had offered a single sacrifice for our sins [that shall avail] for all time, sat down at the right hand of God,

13 Then to wait until His enemies should be made a stool beneath His feet. [Ps. 110:1.]

14 For by a single offering He has forever completely cleansed *and* perfected those who are consecrated *and* made holy.

15 And also the Holy Spirit adds His testimony to us [in confirmation of this]. For having said,

16 This is the agreement (testament, covenant) that I will set up *and* conclude with them after those days, says the Lord: I will imprint My laws upon their hearts, and I will inscribe them on their minds (on their inmost thoughts and understanding),

17 He then goes on to say, And their sins and their lawbreaking I will remember no more. [Jer. 31:33, 34.]

18 Now where there is absolute remission (forgiveness and cancellation of the penalty) of these [sins and lawbreaking], there is no longer any offering made to atone for sin.

19 Therefore, brethren, since we have full freedom *and* confidence to enter into the [Holy of] Holies [by the

power and virtue] in the blood of Jesus,

20 By this fresh (new) and living way which He initiated *and* dedicated *and* opened for us through the separating curtain (veil of the Holy of Holies), that is, through His flesh,

21 And since we have [such] a great *and* wonderful *and* noble Priest [Who rules] over the house of God,

22 Let us all come forward *and* draw near with true (honest and sincere) hearts in unqualified assurance *and* absolute conviction engendered by faith (by [a]that leaning of the entire human personality on God in absolute trust and confidence in His power, wisdom, and goodness), having our hearts sprinkled *and* purified from a guilty (evil) conscience and our bodies cleansed with pure water.

23 So let us seize *and* hold fast *and* retain without wavering the [b]hope we cherish *and* confess *and* our acknowledgement of it, for He Who promised is reliable (sure) *and* faithful to His word.

24 And let us consider *and* give [c]attentive, continuous care to watching over one another, studying how we may stir up (stimulate and incite) to love *and* helpful deeds *and* noble activities,

25 Not forsaking *or* neglecting to assemble together [as believers], as is the habit of some people, but admonishing (warning, urging, and encouraging) one another, and all the more faithfully as you see the day approaching.

26 For if we go on deliberately *and* willingly sinning after once acquiring the knowledge of the Truth, there is no longer any sacrifice left to atone for [our] sins [no further offering to which to look forward],

27 [There is nothing left for us

---

a Alexander Souter, *Pocket Lexicon*.   b William Tyndale, *The Tyndale Bible*. Miles Coverdale, *The Coverdale Bible*, and others.   c Marvin Vincent, *Word Studies*.

then] but a kind of awful *and* fearful prospect *and* expectation of divine judgment *and* the fury of burning wrath *and* indignation which will consume those who put themselves in opposition [to God]. [Isa. 26:11.]

28 Any person who has violated *and* [thus] rejected *and* set at naught the Law of Moses is put to death without pity *or* mercy on the evidence of two *and* three witnesses. [Deut. 17:2–6.]

29 How much worse (sterner and heavier) punishment do you suppose he will be judged to deserve who has spurned *and* [thus] trampled underfoot the Son of God, and who has considered the covenant blood by which he was consecrated common *and* unhallowed, thus profaning it *and* insulting *and* outraging the [Holy] Spirit [Who imparts] grace (the unmerited favor and blessing of God)? [Exod. 24:8.]

30 For we know Him Who said, Vengeance is Mine [retribution and the meting out of full justice rest with Me]; I will repay [I will exact the compensation], *says the Lord.* And again, The Lord will judge *and* determine *and* solve *and* settle the cause *and* the cases of His people. [Deut. 32:35, 36.]

31 It is a fearful (formidable and terrible) thing to incur the divine penalties *and* be cast into the hands of the living God!

32 But be ever mindful of the days gone by in which, after you were first spiritually enlightened, you endured a great *and* painful struggle,

33 Sometimes being yourselves a gazingstock, publicly exposed to insults *and* abuse *and* distress, and sometimes claiming fellowship *and* making common cause with others who were so treated.

34 For you did sympathize *and* suffer along with those who were imprisoned, and you bore cheerfully the plundering of your belongings *and* the confiscation of your property, in the knowledge *and* consciousness that you yourselves had a better and lasting possession.

35 Do not, therefore, fling away your fearless confidence, for it carries a great *and* glorious compensation of reward.

36 For you have need of steadfast patience *and* endurance, so that you may perform *and* fully accomplish the will of God, and thus receive *and* dcarry away [and enjoy to the full] what is promised.

37 For still a little while (a very little while), and the Coming One will come and He will not delay.

38 But the just shall live by faith [My righteous servant shall live eby his conviction respecting man's relationship to God and divine things, and holy fervor born of faith and conjoined with it]; and if he draws back *and* shrinks in fear, My soul has no delight *or* pleasure in him. [Hab. 2:3, 4.]

39 But our way is not that of those who draw back to eternal misery (perdition) and are utterly destroyed, but we are of those who believe [who cleave to and trust in and rely on God through Jesus Christ, the Messiah] *and* by faith preserve the soul.

CHAPTER 11

NOW FAITH is the assurance (the confirmation, fthe title deed) of the things [we] hope for, being the proof of things [we] do not see *and* the conviction of their reality [faith perceiving as real fact what is not revealed to the senses].

2 For by [faith—etrust and holy fer-

---

d Marvin Vincent, *Word Studies.*   **e** Joseph Thayer, *A Greek-English Lexicon.*   **f** James Moulton and George Milligan, *The Vocabulary of the Greek Testament.*

vor born of faith] the men of old had divine testimony borne to them and obtained a good report.

3 By faith we understand that the worlds [during the successive ages] were framed [fashioned, put in order, and equipped for their intended purpose] by the word of God, so that what we see was not made out of things which are visible.

4 [Prompted, actuated] by faith Abel brought God a better and more acceptable sacrifice than Cain, because of which it was testified of him that he was righteous [that he was upright and in right standing with God]; and God bore witness to him by accepting and acknowledging his gifts. And though he died, yet [through the incident] he is still speaking. [Gen. 4:3-10.]

5 Because of faith Enoch was caught up and transferred to heaven, so that he did not have a glimpse of death; and he was not found, because God had translated him. For even before he was taken to heaven, he received testimony [still on record] that he had pleased and been satisfactory to God. [Gen. 5:21-24.]

6 But without faith it is impossible to please and be satisfactory to Him. For whoever would come near to God must [necessarily] believe that God exists and that He is the rewarder of those who earnestly and diligently seek Him [out].

7 [Prompted] by faith Noah, being forewarned by God concerning events of which as yet there was no visible sign, took heed and diligently and reverently constructed and prepared an ark for the deliverance of his own family. By this [his faith which relied on God] he passed judgment and sentence on the world's unbelief and became an heir and possessor of righteousness (ᵍthat rela-

tion of being right into which God puts the person who has faith). [Gen. 6.13-22.]

8 [Urged on] by faith Abraham, when he was called, obeyed and went forth to a place which he was destined to receive as an inheritance; and he went, although he did not know or trouble his mind about where he was to go.

9 [Prompted] by faith he dwelt as a temporary resident in the land which was designated in the promise [of God, though he was like a stranger] in a strange country, living in tents with Isaac and Jacob, fellow heirs with him of the same promise. [Gen. 12:1-8.]

10 For he was [waiting expectantly and confidently] looking forward to the city which has fixed and firm foundations, whose Architect and Builder is God.

11 Because of faith also Sarah herself received physical power to conceive a child, even when she was long past the age for it, because she considered [God] Who had given her the promise to be reliable and trustworthy and true to His word. [Gen. 17:19; 18:11-14; 21:2.]

12 So from one man, though he was physically as good as dead, there have sprung descendants whose number is as the stars of heaven and as countless as the innumerable sands on the seashore. [Gen. 15:5, 6; 22:17; 32:12.]

13 These people all died controlled and sustained by their faith, but not having received the tangible fulfillment of [God's] promises, only having seen it and greeted it from a great distance by faith, and all the while acknowledging and confessing that they were strangers and temporary residents and exiles upon the earth. [Gen. 23:4; Ps. 39:12.]

ᵍ Joseph Thayer, *A Greek-English Lexicon.*

14 Now those people who talk as they did show plainly that they are in search of a fatherland (their own country).

15 If they had been thinking with [homesick] remembrance of that country from which they were emigrants, they would have found constant opportunity to return to it.

16 But the truth is that they were yearning for *and* aspiring to a better *and* more desirable country, that is, a heavenly [one]. For that reason God is not ashamed to be called their God [even to be surnamed their God—the God of Abraham, Isaac, and Jacob], for He has prepared a city for them. [Exod. 3:6, 15; 4:5.]

17 By faith Abraham, when he was put to the test [while the testing of his faith was [h]still in progress], [h]had already brought Isaac for an offering; he who had gladly received *and* welcomed [God's] promises was ready to sacrifice his only son, [Gen. 22:1–10.]

18 Of whom it was said, Through Isaac shall your descendants be reckoned. [Gen. 21:12.]

19 For he reasoned that God was able to raise [him] up even from among the dead. Indeed in the sense that Isaac was figuratively dead [potentially sacrificed], he did [actually] receive him back from the dead.

20 [With eyes of] faith Isaac, looking far into the future, invoked blessings upon Jacob and Esau. [Gen. 27:27–29, 39, 40.]

21 [Prompted] by faith Jacob, when he was dying, blessed each of Joseph's sons and bowed in prayer over the top of his staff. [Gen. 48.]

22 [Actuated] by faith Joseph, when nearing the end of his life, referred to [the promise of God for] the departure of the Israelites out of Egypt and gave instructions concerning the burial of his own bones. [Gen. 50:24, 25; Exod. 13:19.]

23 [Prompted] by faith Moses, after his birth, was kept concealed for three months by his parents, because they saw how comely the child was; and they were not overawed *and* terrified by the king's decree. [Exod. 1:22; 2:2.]

24 [Aroused] by faith Moses, when he had grown to maturity *and* [i]become great, refused to be called the son of Pharaoh's daughter, [Exod. 2:10, 15.]

25 Because he preferred to share the oppression [suffer the hardships] *and* bear the shame of the people of God rather than to have the fleeting enjoyment of a sinful life.

26 He considered the contempt *and* abuse *and* shame [borne for] the Christ (the Messiah Who was to come) to be greater wealth than all the treasures of Egypt, for he looked forward *and* away to the reward (recompense).

27 [Motivated] by faith he left Egypt behind him, being unawed *and* undismayed by the wrath of the king; for he never flinched *but* held staunchly to his purpose *and* endured steadfastly as one who gazed on Him Who is invisible. [Exod. 2:15.]

28 By faith (simple trust and confidence in God) he instituted *and* carried out the Passover and the sprinkling of the blood [on the doorposts], so that the destroyer of the firstborn (the angel) might not touch those [of the children of Israel]. [Exod. 12:21–30.]

29 [Urged on] by faith the people crossed the Red Sea as [though] on dry land, but when the Egyptians tried to do the same thing they were swallowed up [by the sea]. [Exod. 14:21–31.]

h Marvin Vincent, *Word Studies*.   i Literal translation.

30 Because of faith the walls of Jericho fell down after they had been encompassed for seven days [by the Israelites]. [Josh. 6:12–21.]

31 [Prompted] by faith Rahab the prostitute was not destroyed along with those who refused to believe and obey, because she had received the spies in peace [without enmity]. [Josh. 2:1–21; 6:22–25.]

32 And what shall I say further? For time would fail me to tell of Gideon, Barak, Samson, Jephthah, of David and Samuel and the prophets, [Judg. 4:1–5, 31; 6:1–8, 35; 11:1–12, 15; 13:1–16, 31; I Sam. 1–30; II Sam. 1–24; I Kings 1–2; Acts 3:24.]

33 Who by [the help of] faith subdued kingdoms, administered justice, obtained promised blessings, closed the mouths of lions, [Dan. 6.]

34 Extinguished the power of raging fire, escaped the devourings of the sword, out of frailty and weakness won strength and became stalwart, even mighty and resistless in battle, routing alien hosts. [Dan. 3.]

35 [Some] women received again their dead by a resurrection. Others were tortured 'to death with clubs, refusing to accept release [offered on the terms of denying their faith], so that they might be resurrected to a better life. [I Kings 17:17–24; II Kings 4:25–37.]

36 Others had to suffer the trial of mocking and scourging and even chains and imprisonment.

37 They were stoned to death; they were lured with tempting offers [to renounce their faith]; they were sawn asunder; they were slaughtered by the sword; [while they were alive] they had to go about wrapped in the skins of sheep and goats, utterly destitute, oppressed, cruelly treated—

38 [Men] of whom the world was not worthy—roaming over the desolate places and the mountains, and [living] in caves and caverns and holes of the earth.

39 And all of these, though they won divine approval by [means of] their faith, did not receive the fulfillment of what was promised,

40 Because God had us in mind and had something better and greater in view for us, so that they [these heroes and heroines of faith] should not come to perfection apart from us [before we could join them].

CHAPTER 12

THEREFORE THEN, since we are surrounded by so great a cloud of witnesses [who have borne testimony to the Truth], let us strip off and throw aside every encumbrance (unnecessary weight) and that sin which so readily (deftly and cleverly) clings to and entangles us, and let us run with patient endurance and steady and active persistence the appointed course of the race that is set before us,

2 Looking away [from all that will distract] to Jesus, Who is the Leader and the Source of our faith [giving the first incentive for our belief] and is also its Finisher [bringing it to maturity and perfection]. He, for the joy [of obtaining the prize] that was set before Him, endured the cross, despising and ignoring the shame, and is now seated at the right hand of the throne of God. [Ps. 110:1.]

3 Just think of Him Who endured from sinners such grievous opposition and bitter hostility against Himself [reckon up and consider it all in comparison with your trials], so that you may not grow weary or exhausted, losing heart and relaxing and fainting in your minds.

4 You have not yet struggled and fought agonizingly against sin, nor

have you yet resisted and withstood to the point of pouring out your [own] blood.

5 And have you [completely] forgotten the divine word of appeal and encouragement in which you are reasoned with and addressed as sons? My son, do not think lightly or scorn to submit to the correction and discipline of the Lord, nor lose courage and give up and faint when you are reproved or corrected by Him;

6 For the Lord corrects and disciplines everyone whom He loves, and He punishes, even scourges, every son whom He accepts and welcomes to His heart and cherishes.

7 You must submit to and endure [correction] for discipline; God is dealing with you as with sons. For what son is there whom his father does not [thus] train and correct and discipline?

8 Now if you are exempt from correction and left without discipline in which all [of God's children] share, then you are illegitimate offspring and not true sons [at all]. [Prov. 3:11, 12.]

9 Moreover, we have had earthly fathers who disciplined us and we yielded [to them] and respected [them for training us]. Shall we not much more cheerfully submit to the Father of spirits and so [truly] live?

10 For [our earthly fathers] disciplined us for only a short period of time and chastised us as seemed proper and good to them; but He disciplines us for our certain good, that we may become sharers in His own holiness.

11 For the time being no discipline brings joy, but seems grievous and painful; but afterwards it yields a peaceable fruit of righteousness to those who have been trained by it [a harvest of fruit which consists in righteousness—in conformity to God's will in purpose, thought, and action, resulting in right living and right standing with God].

12 So then, brace up and reinvigorate and set right your slackened and weakened and drooping hands and strengthen your feeble and palsied and tottering knees, [Isa. 35:3.]

13 And cut through and make firm and plain and smooth, straight paths for your feet [yes, make them safe and upright and happy paths that go in the right direction], so that the lame and halting [limbs] may not be put out of joint, but rather may be cured.

14 Strive to live in peace with everybody and pursue that consecration and holiness without which no one will [ever] see the Lord.

15 Exercise foresight and be on the watch to look [after one another], to see that no one falls back from and fails to secure God's grace (His unmerited favor and spiritual blessing), in order that no root of resentment (rancor, bitterness, or hatred) shoots forth and causes trouble and bitter torment, and the many become contaminated and defiled by it—

16 That no one may become guilty of sexual vice, or become a profane (godless and sacrilegious) person as Esau did, who sold his own birthright for a single meal. [Gen. 25:29-34.]

17 For you understand that later on, when he wanted [to regain title to] his inheritance of the blessing, he was rejected (disqualified and set aside), for he could find no opportunity to repair by repentance [what he had done, no chance to recall the choice he had made], although he sought for it carefully with [bitter] tears. [Gen. 27:30-40.]

18 For you have not come [as did the Israelites in the wilderness] to a [material] mountain that can be touched, [a mountain] that is ablaze with fire, and to gloom and darkness and a raging storm,

19 And to the blast of a trumpet and a voice whose words make the listeners beg that nothing more be said to them. [Exod. 19:12–22; 20:18–21; Deut. 4:11, 12; 5:22–27.]

20 For they could not bear the command that was given: If even a wild animal touches the mountain, it shall be stoned to death. [Exod. 19:12, 13.]

21 In fact, so awful *and* terrifying was the [phenomenal] sight that Moses said, I am terrified (aghast and trembling with fear). [Deut. 9:19.]

22 But rather, you have come to Mount Zion, even to the city of the living God, the heavenly Jerusalem, and to countless multitudes of angels in festal gathering,

23 And to the church (assembly) of the Firstborn who are registered [as citizens] in heaven, and to the God Who is Judge of all, and to the spirits of the righteous (the redeemed in heaven) who have been made perfect,

24 And to Jesus, the Mediator (Go-between, Agent) of a new covenant, and to the sprinkled blood which speaks [of mercy], a better *and* nobler *and* more gracious message than the blood of Abel [which cried out for vengeance]. [Gen. 4:10.]

25 So see to it that you do not reject Him *or* refuse to listen to *and* heed Him Who is speaking [to you now]. For if they [the Israelites] did not escape when they refused to listen *and* heed Him Who warned *and* divinely instructed them [here] on earth [revealing with heavenly warnings His will], how much less shall we escape if we reject *and* turn our backs on Him Who cautions *and* admonishes [us] from heaven?

26 Then [at Mount Sinai] His voice shook the earth, but now He has given a promise: Yet once more I will shake *and* make tremble not only the earth but also the [starry] heavens. [Hag. 2:6.]

27 Now this expression, Yet once more, indicates the final removal *and* transformation of all [that can be] shaken—that is, of that which has been created—in order that what cannot be shaken may remain *and* continue. [Ps. 102:26.]

28 Let us therefore, receiving a kingdom that is firm *and* stable *and* cannot be shaken, offer to God pleasing service *and* acceptable worship, with modesty *and* pious care *and* godly fear *and* awe;

29 For our God [is indeed] a consuming fire. [Deut. 4:24.]

CHAPTER 13

LET LOVE for your fellow believers continue *and* be a fixed practice with you [never let it fail].

2 Do not forget *or* neglect *or* refuse to extend hospitality to strangers [in the brotherhood—being friendly, cordial, and gracious, sharing the comforts of your home and doing your part generously], for through it some have entertained angels without knowing it. [Gen. 18:1–8; 19:1–3.]

3 Remember those who are in prison as if you were their fellow prisoner, and those who are ill-treated, since you also are liable to bodily sufferings.

4 Let marriage be held in honor (esteemed worthy, precious, of great price, and especially dear) in all things. And thus let the marriage bed be undefiled (kept undishonored); for God will judge *and* punish the unchaste [all guilty of sexual vice] and adulterous.

5 Let your ᵏcharacter *or* moral disposition be free from love of money

k Marvin Vincent, *Word Studies*.

[including greed, avarice, lust, and craving for earthly possessions] and be satisfied with your present [circumstances and with what you have]; for He [God] [l]Himself has said, I will not in any way fail you *nor* [l]give you up *nor* leave you without support. [I will] not, [m][I will] not, [I will] not in any degree leave you helpless *nor* forsake *nor* [m]let [you] down ([l]relax My hold on you)! [[n]Assuredly not!] [Josh. 1:5.]

6 So we take comfort *and* are encouraged *and* confidently *and* boldly say, The Lord is my Helper; I will not be seized with alarm [I will not fear *or* dread *or* be terrified]. What can man do to me? [Ps. 27:1;118:6.]

7 Remember your leaders *and* superiors in authority [for it was they] who brought to you the Word of God. Observe attentively *and* consider their manner of living (the outcome of their well-spent lives) and imitate their faith ([o]their conviction that God exists and is the Creator and Ruler of all things, the Provider and Bestower of eternal salvation through Christ, and their [n]leaning of the entire human personality on God in absolute trust and confidence in His power, wisdom, and goodness).

8 Jesus Christ (the Messiah) is [always] the same, yesterday, today, [yes] and forever (to the ages).

9 Do not be carried about by different *and* varied and alien teachings; for it is good for the heart to be established *and* ennobled *and* strengthened by means of grace (God's favor and spiritual blessing) and not [to be devoted to] foods [rules of diet and ritualistic meals], which bring no [spiritual] benefit *or* profit to those who observe them.

10 We have an altar from which those who serve *and* [l]worship in the tabernacle have no right to eat.

11 For when the blood of animals is brought into the sanctuary by the high priest as a sacrifice for sin, the victims' bodies are burned outside the limits of the camp. [Lev. 16:27.]

12 Therefore Jesus also suffered *and* died outside the [city's] gate in order that He might purify *and* consecrate the people through [the shedding of] His own blood *and* set them apart as holy [for God].

13 Let us then go forth [from all that would prevent us] to Him outside the camp [at Calvary], bearing the contempt *and* abuse *and* shame with Him. [Lev. 16:27.]

14 For here we have no permanent city, but we are looking for the one which is to come.

15 Through Him, therefore, let us constantly *and* at all times offer up to God a sacrifice of praise, which is the fruit of lips that thankfully acknowledge *and* confess *and* glorify His name. [Lev. 7:12; Isa. 57:19; Hos. 14:2.]

16 Do not forget *or* neglect to do kindness *and* good, to be generous *and* distribute *and* contribute to the needy [of the church [o]as embodiment and proof of fellowship], for such sacrifices are pleasing to God.

17 Obey your spiritual leaders and submit to them [continually recognizing their authority over you], for they are constantly keeping watch over your souls *and* guarding your spiritual welfare, as men who will have to render an account [of their trust]. [Do your part to] let them do this with gladness and not with sighing *and* groaning, for that would not be profitable to you [either].

18 Keep praying for us, for we are convinced that we have a good

(clear) conscience, that we want to walk uprightly *and* live a noble life, acting honorably *and in* complete honesty in all things.

19 And I beg of you [to pray for us] the more earnestly, in order that I may be restored to you the sooner.

20 Now may the God of peace [Who is the Author and the Giver of peace], Who brought again from among the dead our Lord Jesus, that great Shepherd of the sheep, by the blood [that sealed, ratified] the everlasting agreement (covenant, testament), [Isa. 55:3; 63:11; Ezek. 37:26; Zech. 9:11.]

21 Strengthen (complete, perfect) *and* make you what you ought to be *and* equip you with everything good that you may carry out His will; [while He Himself] works in you *and* accomplishes that which is pleasing in His sight, through Jesus Christ (the Messiah); to Whom be the glory forever and ever (to the ages of the ages). Amen (so be it).

22 I call on you, brethren, to listen patiently *and* bear with this message of exhortation *and* admonition *and* encouragement, for I have written to you briefly.

23 Notice that our brother Timothy has been released [from prison]. If he comes here soon, I will see you along with him.

24 Give our greetings to all of your spiritual leaders and to all of the saints (God's consecrated believers). The Italian Christians send you their greetings [also].

25 Grace (God's favor and spiritual blessing) be with you all. *Amen (so be it).*

THE LETTER OF
JAMES

CHAPTER 1

JAMES, A servant of God and of the Lord Jesus Christ, to the twelve tribes scattered abroad [among the Gentiles in the dispersion]: Greetings (ᵖrejoice)!

2 Consider it wholly joyful, my brethren, whenever you are enveloped in *or* encounter trials of any sort *or* fall into various temptations.

3 Be assured *and* understand that the trial *and* proving of your faith bring out endurance *and* steadfastness *and* patience.

4 But let endurance *and* steadfastness *and* patience have full play and do a thorough work, so that you may be [people] perfectly and fully developed [with no defects], lacking in nothing.

5 If any of you is deficient in wisdom, let him ask of ᵖthe giving God [Who gives] to everyone liberally *and* ungrudgingly, without reproaching *or* faultfinding, and it will be given him.

6 Only it must be in faith that he asks with no wavering (no hesitating, no doubting). For the one who wavers (hesitates, doubts) is like the billowing surge out at sea that is blown hither *and* thither and tossed by the wind.

ᵖ Literal translation.

7 For truly, let not such a person imagine that he will receive anything [he asks for] from the Lord,

8 [For being as he is] a man of two minds (hesitating, dubious, irresolute), [he is] unstable and unreliable and uncertain about everything [he thinks, feels, decides].

9 Let the brother in humble circumstances glory in his elevation [as a Christian, called to the true riches and to be an heir of God],

10 And the rich [person ought to glory] in being humbled [by being shown his human frailty], because like the flower of the grass he will pass away.

11 For the sun comes up with a scorching heat and parches the grass; its flower falls off and its beauty fades away. Even so will the rich man wither and die in the midst of his pursuits. [Isa. 40:6, 7.]

12 Blessed (happy, ᑫto be envied) is the man who is patient under trial and stands up under temptation, for when he has stood the test and been approved, he will receive [the victor's] crown of life which God has promised to those who love Him.

13 Let no one say when he is tempted, I am tempted from God; for God is incapable of being tempted by [what is] evil and He Himself tempts no one.

14 But every person is tempted when he is drawn away, enticed and baited by his own evil desire (lust, passions).

15 Then the evil desire, when it has conceived, gives birth to sin, and sin, when it is fully matured, brings forth death.

16 Do not be misled, my beloved brethren.

17 Every good gift and every perfect (ʳfree, large, full) gift is from above; it comes down from the Father of all [that gives] light, in [the shining of] Whom there can be no variation [rising or setting] or shadow cast by His turning [as in an eclipse].

18 And it was of His own [free] will that He gave us birth [as sons] by [His] Word of Truth, so that we should be a kind of firstfruits of His creatures [a sample of what He created to be consecrated to Himself].

19 Understand [this], my beloved brethren. Let every man be quick to hear [a ready listener], slow to speak, slow to take offense and to get angry.

20 For man's anger does not promote the righteousness God [wishes and requires].

21 So get rid of all uncleanness and the rampant outgrowth of wickedness, and in a humble (gentle, modest) spirit receive and welcome the Word which implanted and rooted [in your hearts] contains the power to save your souls.

22 But be doers of the Word [obey the message], and not merely listeners to it, betraying yourselves [into deception by reasoning contrary to the Truth].

23 For if anyone only listens to the Word without obeying it and being a doer of it, he is like a man who looks carefully at his [own] natural face in a mirror;

24 For he thoughtfully observes himself, and then goes off and promptly forgets what he was like.

25 But he who looks carefully into the faultless law, the [law] of liberty, and is faithful to it and perseveres in looking into it, being not a heedless listener who forgets but an active doer [who obeys], he shall be blessed in his doing (his life of obedience).

26 If anyone thinks himself to be

---

q Alexander Souter, *Pocket Lexicon of the Greek New Testament.*   r Marvin Vincent, *Word Studies in the New Testament.*

religious (piously observant of the external duties of his faith) and does not bridle his tongue but deludes his own heart, this person's religious service is worthless (futile, barren).

27 External [religious worship [[re]ligion as it is expressed in outward acts] that is pure and unblemished in the sight of God the Father is this: to visit and help and care for the orphans and widows in their affliction and need, and to keep oneself unspotted and uncontaminated from the world.

CHAPTER 2

MY BRETHREN, pay no servile regard to people [show no prejudice, no partiality]. Do not [attempt to] hold and practice the faith of our Lord Jesus Christ [the Lord] of glory [together with snobbery]!

2 For if a person comes into your congregation whose hands are adorned with gold rings and who is wearing splendid apparel, and also a poor [man] in shabby clothes comes in,

3 And you pay special attention to the one who wears the splendid clothes and say to him, Sit here in this preferable seat! while you tell the poor [man], Stand there! or, Sit there on the floor at my feet!

4 Are you not discriminating among your own and becoming critics and judges with wrong motives?

5 Listen, my beloved brethren: Has not God chosen those who are poor in the eyes of the world to be rich in faith and in their position as believers and to inherit the kingdom which He has promised to those who love Him?

6 But you [in contrast] have insulted (humiliated, dishonored, and

shown your contempt for) the poor. Is it not the rich who domineer over you? Is it not they who drag you into the law courts?

7 Is it not they who slander and blaspheme that precious name by which you are distinguished and called [the name of Christ invoked in baptism]?

8 If indeed you [really] fulfill the royal Law in accordance with the Scripture, You shall love your neighbor as [you love] yourself, you do well. [Lev. 19:18.]

9 But if you show servile regard (prejudice, favoritism) for people, you commit sin and are rebuked and convicted by the Law as violators and offenders.

10 For whosoever keeps the Law [as a] whole but stumbles and offends in one [single instance] has become guilty of [breaking] all of it.

11 For He Who said, You shall not commit adultery, also said, You shall not kill. If you do not commit adultery but do kill, you have become guilty of transgressing the [whole] Law. [Exod. 20:13, 14; Deut. 5:17, 18.]

12 So speak and so act as [people should] who are to be judged under the law of liberty [the moral instruction given by Christ, especially about love].

13 For to him who has shown no mercy the judgment [will be] merciless, but mercy [full of glad confidence] exults victoriously over judgment.

14 What is the use (profit), my brethren, for anyone to profess to have faith if he has no [good] works [to show for it]? Can [such] faith save [his soul]?

15 If a brother or sister is poorly clad and lacks food for each day,

---

s Robert Jamieson, A.R. Fausset and David Brown, *A Commentary on the Old and New Testaments:* "Religion in its rise interests us about **ourselves**; in its progress, about our **fellow creatures**; in its highest stage, about the honor of **God**."   t G. Abbott-Smith, *Manual Greek Lexicon of the New Testament.*

16 And one of you says to him, Good-bye! Keep [yourself] warm and well fed, without giving him the necessities for the body, what good does that do?

17 So also faith, if it does not have works (deeds and actions of obedience to back it up), by itself is destitute of power (inoperative, dead).

18 But someone will say [to you then], You [say you] have faith, and I have [good] works. Now you show me your [alleged] faith apart from any [good] works [if you can], and I by [good] works [of obedience] will show you my faith.

19 You believe that God is one; you do well. So do the demons believe and shudder [in terror and horror such as "make a man's hair stand on end and contract the surface of his skin]!

20 Are you willing to be shown [proof], you foolish (unproductive, spiritually deficient) fellow, that faith apart from [good] works is inactive and ineffective and worthless?

21 Was not our forefather Abraham [shown to be] justified (made acceptable to God) by [his] works when he brought to the altar as an offering his [own] son Isaac? [Gen. 22:1–14.]

22 You see that [his] faith was co-operating with his works, and [his] faith was completed and reached its supreme expression [when he implemented it] by [good] works.

23 And [so] the Scripture was fulfilled that says, Abraham believed in (adhered to, trusted in, and relied on) God, and this was accounted to him as righteousness (as conformity to God's will in thought and deed), and he was called God's friend. [Gen. 15:6; II Chron. 20:7; Isa. 41:8.]

24 You see that a man is justified (pronounced righteous before God)

through what he does and not alone through faith [through works of obedience as well as by what he believes].

25 So also with Rahab the harlot —was she not shown to be justified (pronounced righteous before God) by [good] deeds when she took in the scouts (spies) and sent them away by a different route? [Josh. 2:1–21.]

26 For as the human body apart from the spirit is lifeless, so faith apart from [its] works of obedience is also dead.

CHAPTER 3

NOT MANY [of you] should become teachers ("self-constituted censors and reprovers of others), my brethren, for you know that we [teachers] will be judged by a higher standard and with greater severity [than other people; thus we assume the greater accountability and the more condemnation].

2 For we all often stumble and fall and offend in many things. And if anyone does not offend in speech [never says the wrong things], he is a fully developed character and a perfect man, able to control his whole body and to curb his entire nature.

3 If we set bits in the horses' mouths to make them obey us, we can turn their whole bodies about.

4 Likewise, look at the ships: though they are so great and are driven by rough winds, they are steered by a very small rudder wherever the impulse of the helmsman determines.

5 Even so the tongue is a little member, and it can boast of great things. See how much wood or how great a forest a tiny spark can set ablaze!

6 And the tongue is a fire. [The tongue is a] world of wickedness set

u Marvin Vincent, *Word Studies.* v John Calvin, cited by Robert Jamieson, A.R. Fausset and David Brown, *A Commentary.*

among our members, contaminating *and* depraving the whole body and setting on fire the wheel of birth (the cycle of man's nature), being itself ignited by hell (Gehenna).

7 For every kind of beast and bird, of reptile and sea animal, can be tamed and has been tamed by human genius (nature).

8 But the human tongue can be tamed by no man. It is a restless (undisciplined, irreconcilable) evil, full of deadly poison.

9 With it we bless the Lord and Father, and with it we curse men who were made in God's likeness!

10 Out of the same mouth come forth blessing and cursing. These things, my brethren, ought not to be so.

11 Does a fountain send forth [simultaneously] from the same opening fresh water and bitter?

12 Can a fig tree, my brethren, bear olives, or a grapevine figs? Neither can a salt spring furnish fresh water.

13 Who is there among you who is wise and intelligent? Then let him by his noble living show forth his [good] works with the [unobtrusive] humility [which is the proper attribute] of true wisdom.

14 But if you have bitter jealousy (envy) and contention (rivalry, selfish ambition) in your hearts, do not pride yourselves on it and thus be in defiance of *and* false to the Truth.

15 This [superficial] wisdom is not such as comes down from above, but is earthly, unspiritual (animal), even devilish (demoniacal).

16 For wherever there is jealousy (envy) and contention (rivalry and selfish ambition), there will also be confusion (unrest, disharmony, rebellion) and all sorts of evil *and* vile practices.

17 But the wisdom from above is first of all pure (undefiled); then it is peace-loving, courteous (consider-

ate, gentle). [It is willing to] yield to reason, full of compassion and good fruits; it is wholehearted *and* straightforward, impartial *and* unfeigned (free from doubts, wavering, and insincerity).

18 And the harvest of righteousness (of conformity to God's will in thought and deed) is [the fruit of the seed] sown in peace by those who work for *and* make peace [in themselves and in others, that peace which means concord, agreement, and harmony between individuals, with undisturbedness, in a peaceful mind free from fears and agitating passions and moral conflicts].

CHAPTER 4

WHAT LEADS to strife (discord and feuds) *and* how do conflicts (quarrels and fightings) originate among you? Do they not arise from your sensual desires that are ever warring in your bodily members?

2 You are jealous *and* covet [what others have] and your desires go unfulfilled; [so] you become murderers. [To hate is to murder as far as your hearts are concerned.] You burn with envy *and* anger and are not able to obtain [the gratification, the contentment, and the happiness that you seek], so you fight and war. You do not have, because you do not ask. [I John 5:15.]

3 [Or] you do ask [God for them] and yet fail to receive, because you ask with wrong purpose and evil, selfish motives. Your intention is [when you get what you desire] to spend it in sensual pleasures.

4 You [are like] unfaithful wives [having illicit love affairs with the world and breaking your marriage vow to God]! Do you not know that being the world's friend is being God's enemy? So whoever chooses

to be a friend of the world takes his stand as an enemy of God.

5 Or do you suppose that the Scripture is speaking to no purpose that says, The Spirit Whom He has caused to dwell in us yearns over us *and* He yearns for the Spirit [to be welcome] with a jealous love? [Jer. 3:14; Hos. 2:19ff.]

6 But He gives us more and more grace ("power of the Holy Spirit, to meet this evil tendency and all others fully). That is why He says, God sets Himself against the proud and haughty, but gives grace [continually] to the lowly (those who are humble enough to receive it). [Prov. 3:34.]

7 So be subject to God. Resist the devil [stand firm against him], and he will flee from you.

8 Come close to God and He will come close to you. [Recognize that you are] sinners, get your soiled hands clean; [realize that you have been disloyal] wavering individuals with divided interests, and purify your hearts [of your spiritual adultery].

9 [As you draw near to God] be deeply penitent and grieve, even weep [over your disloyalty]. Let your laughter be turned to grief and your mirth to dejection *and* heartfelt shame [for your sins].

10 Humble yourselves [feeling very insignificant] in the presence of the Lord, and He will lift you up and make your lives significant.

11 [My] brethren, do not speak evil about or accuse one another. He that maligns a brother or judges his brother is maligning *and* criticizing the Law *and* judging the Law. But if you judge the Law, you are not a practicer of the Law but a censor *and* judge [of it].

12 One only is the Lawgiver *and* Judge Who is able to save and to destroy [the One Who has the absolute power of life and death]. [But you] who are you that [you presume to] pass judgment on your neighbor?

13 Come now, you who say, Today or tomorrow we will go into such *and* such a city and spend a year there and carry on our business and make money.

14 Yet you do not know [the least thing] about what may happen tomorrow. What is the nature of your life? You are [really] but a wisp of vapor (a puff of smoke, a mist) that is visible for a little while and then disappears [into thin air].

15 You ought instead to say, If the Lord is willing, we shall live and we shall do this or that [thing].

16 But as it is, you boast [falsely] in your presumption *and* your self-conceit. All such boasting is wrong.

17 So any person who knows what is right to do but does not do it, to him it is sin.

CHAPTER 5

COME NOW, you rich [people], weep aloud and lament over the miseries (the woes) that are surely coming upon you.

2 Your abundant wealth has rotted *and* is ruined, and your [many] garments have become moth-eaten.

3 Your gold and silver are completely rusted through, and their rust will be testimony against you and it will devour your flesh as if it were fire. You have heaped together treasure for the last days.

4 [But] look! [Here are] the wages that you have withheld by fraud from the laborers who have reaped your fields, crying out [for vengeance]; and the cries of the harvesters have come to the ears of the Lord of hosts.

5 [Here] on earth you have aban-

doned yourselves to soft (prodigal) living and to [the pleasures of] self-indulgence *and* self-gratification. You have fattened your hearts in a day of slaughter.

6 You have condemned and have murdered the righteous (innocent man), [while] he offers no resistance to you.

7 So be patient, brethren, [as you wait] till the coming of the Lord. See how the farmer waits expectantly for the precious harvest from the land. [See how] he keeps up his patient [vigil] over it until it receives the early and late rains.

8 So you also must be patient. Establish your hearts [strengthen and confirm them in the final certainty], for the coming of the Lord is very near.

9 Do not complain, brethren, against one another, so that you [yourselves] may not be judged. Look! The Judge is [already] standing at the very door.

10 [As] an example of suffering and ill-treatment together with patience, brethren, take the prophets who spoke in the name of the Lord [as His messengers].

11 You know how we call those blessed (happy) who were steadfast [who endured]. You have heard of the endurance of Job, and you have seen the Lord's [purpose and how He richly blessed him in the] end, inasmuch as the Lord is full of pity *and* compassion *and* tenderness and mercy. [Job 1:21, 22; 42:10; Ps. 111:4.]

12 But above all [things], my brethren, do not swear, either by heaven or by earth or by any other oath; but let your yes be [a simple] yes, and your no be [a simple] no, so that you

may not sin *and* fall under condemnation.

13 Is anyone among you afflicted (ill-treated, suffering evil)? He should pray. Is anyone glad at heart? He should sing praise [to God].

14 Is anyone among you sick? He should call in the church elders (the spiritual guides). And they should pray over him, anointing him with oil in the Lord's name.

15 And the prayer [that is] of faith will save him who is sick, and the Lord will restore him; and if he has committed sins, he will be forgiven.

16 Confess to one another therefore your faults (your slips, your false steps, your offenses, your sins) and pray [also] for one another, that you may be healed *and* restored [to a spiritual tone of mind and heart]. The earnest (heartfelt, continued) prayer of a righteous man makes tremendous power available [dynamic in its working].

17 Elijah was a human being with a nature such as we have [with feelings, affections, and a constitution like ours]; and he prayed earnestly for it not to rain, and no rain fell on the earth for three years and six months. [I Kings 17:1.]

18 And [then] he prayed again and the heavens supplied rain and the land produced its crops [as usual]. [I Kings 18:42–45.]

19 [My] brethren, if anyone among you strays from the Truth *and* falls into error and another [person] brings him back [to God],

20 Let the [latter] one be sure that whoever turns a sinner from his evil course will save [that one's] soul from death and will cover a multitude of sins [*procure the pardon of the many sins committed by the convert].

---

x Adam Clarke, *The Holy Bible with A Commentary* and many other translators.

THE FIRST LETTER OF

PETER

CHAPTER 1

PETER, AN apostle (a special messenger) of Jesus Christ, [writing] to the elect exiles of the dispersion scattered (sowed) abroad in Pontus, Galatia, Cappadocia, Asia, and Bithynia,

2 Who were chosen *and* foreknown by God the Father and consecrated (sanctified, made holy) by the Spirit to be obedient to Jesus Christ (the Messiah) and to be sprinkled with [His] blood: May grace (spiritual blessing) and peace be given you in increasing abundance [that spiritual peace to be realized in and through Christt, bfreedom from fears, agitating passions, and moral conflicts].

3 Praised (honored, blessed) be the God and Father of our Lord Jesus Christ (the Messiah)! By His boundless mercy we have been born again to an ever-living hope through the resurrection of Jesus Christ from the dead,

4 [Born anew] into an inheritance which is beyond the reach of change *and* decay [imperishable], unsullied and unfading, reserved in heaven for you,

5 Who are being guarded (garrisoned) by God's power through [your] faith [till you fully inherit that cfinal] salvation that is ready to be revealed [for you] in the last time.

6 [You should] be exceedingly glad on this account, though now for a little while you may be distressed by trials *and* suffer temptations,

7 So that [the genuineness] of your faith may be tested, [your faith] which is infinitely more precious than the perishable gold which is tested *and* purified by fire. [This proving of your faith is intended] to redound to [your] praise and glory and honor when Jesus Christ (the Messiah, the Anointed One) is revealed.

8 Without having seen Him, you love Him; though you do not [even] now see Him, you believe in Him and exult *and* thrill with inexpressible and glorious (triumphant, heavenly) joy.

9 [At the same time] you receive the result (outcome, consummation) of your faith, the salvation of your souls.

10 The prophets, who prophesied of the grace (divine blessing) which was intended for you, searched and inquired earnestly about this salvation.

11 They sought [to find out] to whom or when this was to come which the Spirit of Christ working within them was indicating when He predicted the sufferings of Christ and the glories that should follow [them].

12 It was then disclosed to them that the services they were rendering were not meant for themselves *and* their period of time, but for you. [It is these very] things which have now

---

a Hermann Cremer, *Biblico-Theological Lexicon of New Testament Greek.*   b *Webster's New International Dictionary* offers this as a definition of "peace."   c Charles B. Williams, *The New Testament: A Translation in the Language of the People.*

already been made known plainly to you by those who preached the good news (the Gospel) to you by the [same] Holy Spirit sent from heaven. Into these things [the very] angels long to look!

13 So brace up your minds; be sober (circumspect, morally alert); set your hope wholly and unchangeably on the grace (divine favor) that is coming to you when Jesus Christ (the Messiah) is revealed.

14 [Live] as children of obedience [to God]; do not conform yourselves to the evil desires [that governed you] in your former ignorance [when you did not know the requirements of the Gospel].

15 But as the One Who called you is holy, you yourselves also be holy in all your conduct and manner of living.

16 For it is written, You shall be holy, for I am holy. [Lev. 11:44, 45.]

17 And if you call upon Him as [your] Father Who judges each one impartially according to what he does, [then] you should conduct yourselves with true reverence throughout the time of your temporary residence [on the earth, whether long or short].

18 You must know (recognize) that you were redeemed (ransomed) from the useless (fruitless) way of living inherited by tradition from [your] forefathers, not with corruptible things [such as] silver and gold,

19 But [you were purchased] with the precious blood of Christ (the Messiah), like that of a [sacrificial] lamb without blemish or spot.

20 It is true that He was chosen and foreordained (destined and foreknown for it) before the foundation of the world, but He was brought out to public view (made manifest) in

these last days (at the end of the times) for the sake of you.

21 Through Him you believe in (adhere to, rely on) God, Who raised Him up from the dead and gave Him honor and glory, so that your faith and hope are [centered and rest] in God.

22 Since by your obedience to the Truth through the [Holy] Spirit you have purified your hearts for the sincere affection of the brethren, [see that you] love one another fervently from a pure heart.

23 You have been regenerated (born again), not from a mortal ᵈorigin (ᵉseed, sperm), but from one that is immortal by the ever living and lasting Word of God.

24 For all flesh (mankind) is like grass, and all its glory (honor) like [the] flower of grass. The grass withers and the flower drops off,

25 But the Word of the Lord (ᶠdivine instruction, the Gospel) endures forever. And this Word is the good news which was preached to you. [Isa. 40:6–9.]

CHAPTER 2

SO BE done with every trace of wickedness (depravity, malignity) and all deceit and insincerity (pretense, hypocrisy) and grudges (envy, jealousy) and slander and evil speaking of every kind.

2 Like newborn babies you should crave (thirst for, earnestly desire) the pure (unadulterated) spiritual milk, that by it you may be nurtured and grow unto [completed] salvation,

3 Since you have [already] tasted the goodness and kindness of the Lord. [Ps. 34:8.]

4 Come to Him [then, to that] Living Stone which men ᵍtried and threw

---

d Joseph Thayer, A Greek-English Lexicon of the New Testament.   e G. Abbott-Smith, Manual Greek Lexicon of the New Testament.   f Joseph Thayer, A Greek-English Lexicon.   g Marvin Vincent, Word Studies in the New Testament.

away, but which is chosen [and] precious in God's sight. [Ps. 118:22; Isa. 28:16.]

5 [Come] and, like living stones, be yourselves built [into] a spiritual house, for a holy [dedicated, consecrated] priesthood, to offer up [those] spiritual sacrifices [that are] acceptable *and* pleasing to God through Jesus Christ.

6 For thus it stands in Scripture: Behold, I am laying in Zion a chosen ([h]honored), precious chief Cornerstone, and he who believes in Him [who adheres to, trusts in, and relies on Him] shall never be [i]disappointed *or* put to shame. [Isa. 28:16.]

7 To you then who believe (who adhere to, trust in, and rely on Him) is the preciousness; but for those who disbelieve [it is true], The [very] Stone which the builders rejected has become the main Cornerstone, [Ps. 118:22.]

8 And, A Stone that will cause stumbling and a Rock that will give [men] offense; they stumble because they disobey *and* disbelieve [God's] Word, as those [who reject Him] were destined (appointed) to do.

9 But you are a chosen race, a royal priesthood, a dedicated nation, [God's] own [j]purchased, special people, that you may set forth the wonderful deeds *and* display the virtues *and* perfections of Him Who called you out of darkness into His marvelous light. [Exod. 19:5, 6.]

10 Once you were not a people [at all], but now you are God's people; once you were unpitied, but now you are pitied *and* have received mercy. [Hos. 2:23.]

11 Beloved, I implore you as aliens and strangers *and* exiles [in this world] to abstain from the sensual urges (the evil desires, the passions of the flesh, your lower nature) that wage war against the soul.

12 Conduct yourselves properly (honorably, righteously) among the Gentiles, so that, although they may slander you as evildoers, [yet] they may by witnessing your good deeds [come to] glorify God in the day of inspection [[k]when God shall look upon you wanderers as a pastor or shepherd looks over his flock].

13 Be submissive to every human institution *and* authority for the sake of the Lord, whether it be to the emperor as supreme,

14 Or to governors as sent by him to bring vengeance (punishment, justice) to those who do wrong and to encourage those who do good service.

15 For it is God's will *and* intention that by doing right [your good and honest lives] should silence (muzzle, gag) the ignorant charges *and* ill-informed criticisms of foolish persons.

16 [Live] as free people, [yet] without employing your freedom as a pretext for wickedness; but [live at all times] as servants of God.

17 Show respect for all men [treat them honorably]. Love the brotherhood (the Christian fraternity of which Christ is the Head). Reverence God. Honor the emperor.

18 [You who are] household servants, be submissive to your masters with all [proper] respect, not only to those who are kind and considerate *and* reasonable, but also to those who are surly (overbearing, unjust, and crooked).

19 For one is regarded favorably (is approved, acceptable, and thankworthy) if, as in the sight of God, he endures the pain of unjust suffering.

20 [After all] what [l]kind of glory [is there in it] if, when you do wrong and

h Marvin Vincent, *Word Studies in the New Testament.*   i Joseph Thayer, *A Greek-English Lexicon.*   j John Wycliffe, *The Wycliffe Bible.*   k J. Rawson Lumby, cited by *Speaker's Commentary.*   l Literal translation.

are punished for it, you take it patiently? But if you bear patiently with suffering [which results] when you do right *and* that is undeserved, it is acceptable *and* pleasing to God.

21 For even to this were you called [it is inseparable from your vocation]. For Christ also suffered for you, leaving you [His personal] example, so that you should follow in His footsteps.

22 He was guilty of no sin, neither was deceit (guile) ever found on His lips. [Isa. 53:9.]

23 When He was reviled *and* insulted, He did not revile *or* offer insult in return; [when] He was abused *and* suffered, He made no threats [of vengeance]; but he trusted [Himself and everything] to Him Who judges fairly.

24 He personally bore our sins in His [own] body on the tree m[as on an altar and offered Himself on it], that we might die (cease to exist) to sin and live to righteousness. By His wounds you have been healed.

25 For you were going astray like [so many] sheep, but now you have come back to the Shepherd and Guardian (nthe Bishop) of your souls. [Isa. 53:5, 6.]

CHAPTER 3

IN LIKE manner, you married women, be submissive to your own husbands [subordinate yourselves as being secondary to and dependent on them, and adapt yourselves to them], so that even if any do not obey the Word [of God], they may be won over not by discussion but by the [godly] lives of their wives,

2 When they observe the pure *and* modest way in which you conduct yourselves, together with your °reverence [for your husband; you are to feel for him all that reverence includes: to respect, defer to, revere him—to honor, esteem, appreciate, prize, and, in the human sense, to adore him, that is, to admire, praise, be devoted to, deeply love, and enjoy your husband].

3 Let not yours be the [merely] external adorning with [elaborate] °interweaving *and* knotting of the hair, the wearing of jewelry, or changes of clothes;

4 But let it be the inward adorning *and* beauty of the hidden person of the heart, with the incorruptible *and* unfading charm of a gentle and peaceful spirit, which [is not anxious or wrought up, but] is very precious in the sight of God.

5 For it was thus that the pious women of old who hoped in God were [accustomed] to beautify themselves and were submissive to their husbands [adapting themselves to them as themselves secondary and dependent upon them].

6 It was thus that Sarah obeyed Abraham [following his guidance and acknowledging his headship over her by] calling him lord (master, leader, authority). And you are now her true daughters if you do right and let nothing terrify you [not giving way to hysterical fears or letting anxieties unnerve you].

7 In the same way you married men should live considerately with [your wives], with an mintelligent recognition [of the marriage relation], honoring the woman as [physically] the weaker, but [realizing that you] are joint heirs of the grace (God's unmerited favor) of life, in order that your prayers may not be hindered *and* cut off. [Otherwise you cannot pray effectively.]

m Marvin Vincent, *Word Studies.*   n Literal translation.   o Joseph Thayer, *A Greek-English Lexicon.*

8 Finally, all [of you] should be of one *and* the same mind [united in spirit], sympathizing [with one another], loving [each other] as brethren [of one household], compassionate *and* courteous (tenderhearted and humble).

9 Never return evil for evil or insult for insult (scolding, tongue-lashing, berating), but on the contrary blessing [praying for their welfare, happiness, and protection, and truly pitying and loving them]. For *know that* to this you have been called, that you may yourselves inherit a blessing [from God—that you may obtain a blessing as heirs, bringing welfare and happiness and protection].

10 For let him who wants to enjoy life and see good days [good—whether apparent or not] keep his tongue free from evil and his lips from guile (treachery, deceit).

11 Let him turn away from wickedness *and* shun it, and let him do right. Let him search for peace (harmony; undisturbedness from fears, agitating passions, and moral conflicts) and seek it eagerly. [Do not merely desire peaceful relations with God, with your fellowmen, and with yourself, but pursue, go after them!]

12 For the eyes of the Lord are upon the righteous (those who are upright and in right standing with God), and His ears are attentive to their prayer. But the face of the Lord is against those who practice evil [to oppose them, to frustrate, and defeat them]. [Ps. 34:12–16.]

13 Now who is there to hurt you if you are *p*zealous followers of that which is good?

14 But even in case you should suffer for the sake of righteousness, [you are] blessed (happy, to be envied). Do not dread *or* be afraid of their threats, nor be disturbed [by their opposition].

15 But in your hearts set Christ apart as holy [and acknowledge Him] as Lord. Always be ready to give a logical defense to anyone who asks you to account for the hope that is in you, but do it courteously and respectfully. [Isa. 8:12, 13.]

16 [And see to it that] your conscience is entirely clear (*q*unimpaired), so that, when you are falsely accused as evildoers, those who threaten you abusively *and* revile your right behavior in Christ may come to be ashamed [of slandering your good lives].

17 For [it is] better to suffer [unjustly] for doing right, if that should be God's will, than to suffer [justly] for doing wrong.

18 For Christ [the Messiah Himself] died for sins once *r*for all, the Righteous for the unrighteous (the Just for the unjust, the Innocent for the guilty), that He might bring us to God. In His human body He was put to death, but He was made alive in the spirit,

19 In which He went and preached to the spirits in prison,

20 [The souls of those] who long before in the days of Noah had been disobedient, when God's patience waited during the building of the ark in which a few [people], actually eight in number, were saved through water. [Gen. 6–8.]

21 And baptism, which is a figure [of their deliverance], does now also save you [from inward questionings and fears], not by the removing of outward body filth [bathing], but by [providing you with] the answer of a good and clear conscience (inward cleanness and peace) before God [because you are demonstrating what

p Best manuscripts read "zealous." q Marvin Vincent, *Word Studies.* r Joseph Thayer, *A Greek-English Lexicon.*

you believe to be yours] through the resurrection of Jesus Christ.

22 [And He] has now entered into heaven and is at the right hand of God, with [all] angels and authorities and powers made subservient to Him.

CHAPTER 4

SO, SINCE Christ suffered in the flesh *for us, for you*, arm yourselves with the same thought *and* [purpose [patiently to suffer rather than fail to please God]. For whoever has suffered in the flesh [having [the mind of Christ] is done with [intentional] sin [has stopped pleasing himself and the world, and pleases God],

2 So that he can no longer spend the rest of his natural life living by [his] human appetites *and* desires, but [he lives] for what God wills.

3 For the time that is past already suffices for doing what the Gentiles like to do—living [as you have done] in shameless, insolent wantonness, in lustful desires, drunkenness, reveling, drinking bouts *and* abominable, lawless idolatries.

4 They are astonished *and* think it very queer that you do not now run hand in hand with them in the same excesses of dissipation, and they abuse [you].

5 But they will have to give an account to Him Who is ready to judge *and* pass sentence on the living and the dead.

6 For this is why the good news (the Gospel) was preached ['in their lifetime] even to the dead, that though judged in fleshly bodies as men are, they might live in the spirit as God does.

7 But the end *and* culmination of all things has now come near; keep

sound minded *and* self-restrained and alert therefore for [the practice of] prayer.

8 Above all things have intense *and* unfailing love for one another, for love covers a multitude of sins [forgives and "disregards the offenses of others]. [Prov. 10:12.]

9 Practice hospitality to one another (those of the household of faith). [Be hospitable, be a lover of strangers, with brotherly affection for the unknown guests, the foreigners, the poor, and all others who come your way who are of Christ's body.] And [in each instance] do it ungrudgingly (cordially and graciously), without complaining but as representing Him).

10 As each of you has received a gift (a particular spiritual talent, a gracious divine endowment), employ it for one another as [befits] good trustees of God's many-sided grace [faithful stewards of the "extremely diverse powers and gifts granted to Christians by unmerited favor].

11 Whoever speaks, [let him do it as one who utters] oracles of God; whoever renders service, [let him do it] as with the strength which God furnishes "abundantly, so that in all things God may be glorified through Jesus Christ (the Messiah). To Him be the glory and dominion forever and ever (through endless ages). Amen (so be it).

12 Beloved, do not be amazed *and* bewildered at the fiery ordeal which is taking place to test your quality, as though something strange (unusual and alien to you and your position) were befalling you.

13 But insofar as you are sharing Christ's sufferings, rejoice, so that when His glory [full of radiance and

s Some ancient manuscripts read "for us," while some "for you."   t G. Abbott-Smith, *Manual Greek Lexicon*.   u *The Cambridge Bible for Schools and Colleges*.   v Most commentators interpret this preaching to be a past event, done not after these people had died, but while they were still alive.   w Joseph Thayer, *A Greek-English Lexicon*.

splendor] is revealed, you may also rejoice with triumph [exultantly].

14 If you are censured *and* suffer abuse [because you bear] the name of Christ, blessed [are you—happy, fortunate, ˣto be envied, ʸwith life joy, and satisfaction in God's favor and salvation, regardless of your outward condition], because the Spirit of glory, the Spirit of God, is resting upon you. *On their part He is blasphemed, but on your part He is glorified.* [Isa. 11:2.]

15 But let none of you suffer as a murderer or a thief or any sort of criminal, or as a mischief-maker (a meddler) in the affairs of others [infringing on their rights].

16 But if [one is ill-treated and suffers] as a Christian [which he is contemptuously called], let him not be ashamed, but give glory to God that he is [deemed worthy to suffer] in this name.

17 For the time [has arrived] for judgment to begin with the household of God; and if it begins with us, what will [be] the end of those who do not respect *or* believe *or* obey the good news (the Gospel) of God?

18 And if the righteous are barely saved, what will become of the godless and wicked? [Prov. 11:31.]

19 Therefore, those who are ill-treated *and* suffer in accordance with God's will must do right and commit their souls [in charge as a deposit] to the One Who created [them] and will never fail [them].

CHAPTER 5

I WARN *and* counsel the elders among you (the pastors and spiritual guides of the church) as a fellow elder and as an eyewitness [called to

testify] of the sufferings of Christ, as well as a sharer in the glory (the honor and splendor) that is to be revealed (disclosed, unfolded):

2 Tend (nurture, guard, guide, and fold) the flock of God that is [your responsibility], not by coercion *or* constraint, but willingly; not dishonorably motivated by the advantages *and* profits [belonging to the office], but eagerly and cheerfully;

3 Not domineering [as arrogant, dictatorial, and overbearing persons] over those in your charge, but being examples (patterns and models of Christian living) to the flock (the congregation).

4 And [then] when the Chief Shepherd is revealed, you will win the ᶻconqueror's crown of glory.

5 Likewise, you who are younger *and* of lesser rank, be subject to the elders (the ministers and spiritual guides of the church)—[giving them due respect and yielding to their counsel]. Clothe (apron) yourselves, all of you, with humility [as the garb of a servant, ªso that its covering cannot possibly be stripped from you, with freedom from pride and arrogance] toward one another. For God sets Himself against the proud (the insolent, the overbearing, the disdainful, the presumptuous, the boastful) [and He opposes, frustrates, and defeats them], but gives grace (favor, blessing) to the humble. [Prov. 3:34.]

6 Therefore humble yourselves [demote, lower yourselves in your own estimation] under the mighty hand of God, that in due time He may exalt you,

7 Casting the ᵇwhole of your care [all your anxieties, all your worries,

---

x Alexander Souter, *Pocket Lexicon of the Greek New Testament.*   y Hermann Cremer, *Biblico-Theological Lexicon.*   z Marvin Vincent, *Word Studies*: When Paul uses the word translated "crown," he typically has the conqueror's crown in mind, using the imagery of the winner of an athletic contest. (see I Cor. 9:25). Peter seems to have this same imagery in mind as a symbol of the heavenly reward.   a Johann Bengel, *Gnomon Novi Testamenti.*   b Marvin Vincent, *Word Studies.*

all your concerns, ^conce and for all] on Him, for He cares for you affectionately *and* cares about you ^cwatchfully. [Ps. 55:22.]

8 Be well balanced (temperate, sober of mind), be vigilant *and* cautious at all times; for that enemy of yours, the devil, roams around like a lion roaring [^cin fierce hunger], seeking someone to seize upon *and* devour.

9 Withstand him; be firm in faith [against his onset—rooted, established, strong, immovable, and determined], knowing that the same (^cidentical) sufferings are appointed to your brotherhood (the whole body of Christians) throughout the world.

10 And after you have suffered a little while, the God of all grace [Who imparts all blessing and favor], Who has called you to His [own] eternal glory in Christ *Jesus*, will Himself complete *and* make you what you ought to be, establish *and* ground you securely, and strengthen, and settle you.

11 To Him be the dominion (power, authority, rule) forever and ever. Amen (so be it).

12 By Silvanus, a true (loyal, consistent, incorruptible) brother, as I consider him, I have written briefly to you, to counsel *and* urge *and* stimulate [you] and to declare [to you] that this is the true [account of the] grace (the undeserved favor) of God. Be steadfast *and* persevere in it.

13 She [your sister church here] in Babylon, [who is] elect (chosen) with [yourselves], sends you greetings, and [so does] my son (disciple) Mark.

14 Salute one another with a kiss of love [the symbol of mutual affection]. To all of you that are in Christ *Jesus* (the Messiah), may there be peace (^devery kind of peace and blessing, especially peace with God, and ^ffreedom from fears, agitating passions, and moral conflicts). *Amen (so be it)*.

THE SECOND LETTER OF
PETER

CHAPTER 1

SIMON PETER, a servant and apostle (special messenger) of Jesus Christ, to those who have received (obtained an equal privilege of) like precious faith with ourselves in *and* through the righteousness of our God and Savior Jesus Christ:

2 May grace (God's favor) and peace (which is ^fperfect well-being, all necessary good, all spiritual prosperity, and ^efreedom from fears and agitating passions and moral conflicts) be multiplied to you in [the full, personal, ^gprecise, and correct] knowledge of God and of Jesus our Lord.

3 For His divine power has bestowed upon us all things that [are requisite and suited] to life and godliness, through the [^hfull, personal] knowledge of Him Who called us by

c Marvin Vincent, *Word Studies*. d Joseph Thayer, *A Greek-English Lexicon*. e Webster's New International Dictionary offers this as a definition of "peace." f Matthew Henry, *Commentary on the Holy Bible*. g Joseph Thayer, *A Greek-English Lexicon of the New Testament*. h Marvin Vincent, *Word Studies in the New Testament*.

and to His own glory and excellence (virtue).

4 By means of these He has bestowed on us His precious and exceedingly great promises, so that through them you may escape [by flight] from the moral decay (rottenness and corruption) that is in the world because of covetousness (lust and greed), and become sharers (partakers) of the divine nature.

5 For this very reason, [i]adding your diligence [to the divine promises], employ every effort in [exercising your faith to develop virtue (excellence, resolution, Christian energy), and in [exercising] virtue [develop] knowledge (intelligence),

6 And in [exercising] knowledge [develop] self-control, and in [exercising] self-control [develop] steadfastness (patience, endurance), and in [exercising] steadfastness [develop] godliness (piety),

7 And in [exercising] godliness [develop] brotherly affection, and in [exercising] brotherly affection [develop] Christian love.

8 For as these qualities are yours and increasingly abound in you, they will keep [you] from being idle or unfruitful unto the [j]full personal] knowledge of our Lord Jesus Christ (the Messiah, the Anointed One).

9 For whoever lacks these qualities is blind, [j]spiritually] shortsighted, [k]seeing only what is near to him, and has become oblivious [to the fact] that he was cleansed from his old sins.

10 Because of this, brethren, be all the more solicitous *and* eager to make sure (to ratify, to strengthen, to make steadfast) your calling and election; for if you do this, you will never stumble *or* fall.

11 Thus there will be richly *and*

abundantly provided for you entry into the eternal kingdom of our Lord and Savior Jesus Christ.

12 So I intend always to remind you about these things, although indeed you know them and are firm in the truth that [you] now [hold].

13 I think it right, as long as I am in this tabernacle (tent, body), to stir you up by way of remembrance,

14 Since I know that the laying aside of this body of mine will come speedily, as our Lord Jesus Christ made clear to me.

15 Moreover, I will diligently endeavor [to see to it] that [even] after my departure (decease) you may be able at all times to call these things to mind.

16 For we were not following cleverly devised stories when we made known to you the power and coming of our Lord Jesus Christ (the Messiah), but we were eyewitnesses of His majesty (grandeur, authority of sovereign power).

17 For when He was invested with honor and glory from God the Father and a voice was borne to Him by the [splendid] Majestic Glory [in the bright cloud that overshadowed Him, saying], This is My beloved Son in Whom I am well pleased *and* delight,

18 We [actually] heard this voice borne out of heaven, for we were together with Him on the holy mountain.

19 And we have the prophetic word [made] firmer still. You will do well to pay close attention to it as to a lamp shining in a dismal (squalid and dark) place, until the day breaks through [the gloom] and the Morning Star rises ([l]comes into being) in your hearts.

20 [Yet] first [you must] under-

---

i Marvin Vincent, *Word Studies in the New Testament*.   j Marvin Vincent, *Word Studies*.   k Joseph P. Rotherham, *The Emphasized Bible*.   l G. Abbott-Smith, *Manual Greek Lexicon of the New Testament*.

stand this, that no prophecy of Scripture is [a matter] of any personal *or* private *or* special interpretation (loosening, solving).

21 For no prophecy ever originated because some man willed it [to do so—it never came by human impulse], but men spoke from God who were borne along (moved and impelled) by the Holy Spirit.

CHAPTER 2

BUT ALSO [in those days] there arose false prophets among the people, just as there will be false teachers among yourselves, who will subtly and stealthily introduce heretical doctrines (destructive heresies), even denying *and* disowning the Master Who bought them, bringing upon themselves swift destruction.

2 And many will follow their immoral ways *and* lascivious doings; because of them the true Way will be maligned *and* defamed.

3 And in their covetousness (lust, greed) they will exploit you with false (cunning) arguments. From of old the sentence [of condemnation] for them has not been idle; their destruction (eternal misery) has not been asleep.

4 For God did not [even] spare angels that sinned, but cast them into hell, delivering them to be kept there in pits of gloom till the judgment *and* their doom.

5 And He spared not the ancient world, but preserved Noah, a preacher of righteousness, with seven other persons, when He brought a flood upon the world of ungodly [people]. [Gen. 6–8; I Peter 3:20.]

6 And He condemned to ruin *and* extinction the cities of Sodom and Gomorrah, reducing them to ashes [and thus] set them forth as an example to those who would be ungodly; [Gen. 19:24.]

7 And He rescued righteous Lot, greatly worn out *and* distressed by the wanton ways of the ungodly *and* lawless— [Gen. 19:16, 29.]

8 For that just man, living [there] among them, tortured his righteous soul every day with what he saw and heard of [their] unlawful and wicked deeds—

9 Now if [all these things are true, then be sure] the Lord knows how to rescue the godly out of temptations *and* trials, and how to keep the ungodly under chastisement until the day of judgment *and* doom,

10 And particularly those who walk after the flesh and indulge in the lust of polluting passion and scorn *and* despise authority. Presumptuous [and] daring [self-willed and self-loving creatures]! They scoff at *and* revile dignitaries (glorious ones) without trembling,

11 Whereas [even] angels, though superior in might and power, do not bring a defaming charge against them before the Lord.

12 But these [people]! Like unreasoning beasts, mere creatures of instinct, born [only] to be captured and destroyed, railing at things of which they are ignorant, they shall utterly perish in their [own] corruption [in their destroying they shall surely be destroyed],

13 Being destined to receive [punishment as] the reward of [their] unrighteousness [suffering wrong as the hire for their wrongdoing]. They count it a delight to revel in the daytime [living luxuriously and delicately]. They are blots and blemishes, reveling in their ᵐdeceptions *and* carousing together [even] as they feast with you.

14 They have eyes full of harlotry, insatiable for sin. They beguile *and* bait *and* lure away unstable souls.

---

m Some ancient manuscripts read "love feasts."

Their hearts are trained in covetousness (lust, greed), [they are] children of a curse [[n]exposed to cursing]!

15 Forsaking the straight road they have gone astray; they have followed the way of Balaam [the son] of Beor, who loved the reward of wickedness. [Num. 22:5, 7.]

16 But he was rebuked for his own transgression when a dumb beast of burden spoke with human voice and checked the prophet's madness. [Num. 22:21–31.]

17 These are springs without water and mists driven along before a tempest, for whom is reserved *forever* the gloom of darkness.

18 For uttering loud boasts of folly, they beguile *and* lure with lustful desires of the flesh those who are barely escaping from them who are wrongdoers.

19 They promise them liberty, when they themselves are the slaves of depravity *and* defilement—for by whatever anyone is made inferior *or* worse *or* is overcome, to that [person or thing] he is enslaved.

20 For if, after they have escaped the pollutions of the world through [the full, personal] knowledge of our Lord and Savior Jesus Christ, they again become entangled in them and are overcome, their last condition is worse [for them] than the first.

21 For never to have obtained a [full, personal] knowledge of the way of righteousness would have been better for them than, having obtained [such knowledge], to turn back from the holy commandment which was [verbally] delivered to them.

22 There has befallen them the thing spoken of in the true proverb, The dog turns back to his own vomit, and, The sow is washed only to wallow again in the mire. [Prov. 26:11.]

n Joseph Thayer, *A Greek-English Lexicon.*

CHAPTER 3

BELOVED, I am now writing you this second letter. In [both of] them I have stirred up your unsullied (sincere) mind by way of remembrance,

2 That you should recall the predictions of the holy (consecrated, dedicated) prophets and the commandment of the Lord and Savior [given] through your apostles (His special messengers).

3 To begin with, you must know *and* understand this, that scoffers (mockers) will come in the last days with scoffing, [people who] walk after their own fleshly desires

4 And say, Where is the promise of His coming? For since the forefathers fell asleep, all things have continued exactly as they did from the beginning of creation.

5 For they willfully overlook *and* forget this [fact], that the heavens [came into] existence long ago by the word of God, and the earth also which was formed out of water and by means of water,

6 Through which the world that then [existed] was deluged with water and perished. [Gen. 1:6–8; 7:11.]

7 But by the same word the present heavens and earth have been stored up (reserved) for fire, being kept until the day of judgment and destruction of the ungodly people.

8 Nevertheless, do not let this one fact escape you, beloved, that with the Lord one day is as a thousand years and a thousand years as one day. [Ps. 90:4.]

9 The Lord does not delay *and* is not tardy *or* slow about what He promises, according to some people's conception of slowness, but He is long-suffering (extraordinarily patient) toward you, not desiring that

any should perish, but that all should turn to repentance.

10 But the day of the Lord will come like a thief, and then the heavens will vanish (pass away) with a thunderous crash, and the [°material] elements [of the universe] will be dissolved with fire, and the earth and the works that are upon it will be burned up.

11 Since all these things are thus Pin the process of being dissolved, what kind of person ought [each of] you to be [in the meanwhile] in consecrated *and* holy behavior and devout *and* godly qualities,

12 While you wait and earnestly long for (expect and hasten) the coming of the day of God by reason of which the flaming heavens will be dissolved, and the [°material] elements [of the universe] will flare *and* melt with fire? [Isa. 34:4.]

13 But we look for new heavens and a new earth according to His promise, in which righteousness (uprightness, freedom from sin, and right standing with God) is to abide. [Isa. 65:17; 66:22.]

14 So, beloved, since you are expecting these things, be eager to be found by Him [at His coming] without spot or blemish and at peace [in serene confidence, qfree from fears and agitating passions and moral conflicts].

15 And consider that the long-suffering of our Lord [rHis slowness in avenging wrongs and judging the world] is salvation (rthat which is conducive to the soul's safety), even as our beloved brother Paul also wrote to you according to the spiritual insight given him,

16 Speaking of this as he does in all of his letters. There are some things in those [epistles of Paul] that are difficult to understand, which the ignorant and unstable twist *and* misconstrue to their own rutter destruction, just as [they] distort and misinterpret the rest of the Scriptures.

17 Let me warn you therefore, beloved, that knowing these things beforehand, you should be on your guard, lest you be carried away by the error of lawless *and* wicked [persons and] fall from your own [present] firm condition [your own steadfastness of mind].

18 But grow in grace (undeserved favor, spiritual strength) and srecognition *and* knowledge *and* understanding of our Lord and Savior Jesus Christ (the Messiah). To Him [be] glory (honor, majesty, and splendor) both now and to the day of eternity. Amen (so be it)!

---

o G. Abbott-Smith, *Manual Greek Lexicon.*   p Marvin Vincent, *Word Studies.*   q *Webster's New International Dictionary* offers this as a definition of "peace."   r Joseph Thayer, *A Greek-English Lexicon.*   s Hermann Cremer, *Biblico-Theological Lexicon of New Testament Greek.*

THE FIRST LETTER OF

JOHN

CHAPTER 1

[WE ARE writing] about the Word of Life [*in] Hım Who existed from the beginning, Whom we have heard, Whom we have seen with our [own] eyes, Whom we have gazed upon [for ourselves] and have touched with our [own] hands.

2 And the Life [*an aspect of His being] was revealed (made manifest, demonstrated), and we saw [as eye-witnesses] and are testifying to and declare to you the Life, the eternal Life [*in Him] Who already existed with the Father and Who [actually] was made visible (was revealed) to us [His followers].

3 What we have seen and [ourselves] heard, we are also telling you, so that you too may *realize and enjoy fellowship as partners and partakers with us. And [this] fellowship that we have [which is a *distinguishing mark of Christians] is with the Father and with His Son Jesus Christ (the Messiah).

4 And we are now writing these things to you so that our joy [in seeing you included] may be full [and *your joy may be complete].

5 And this is the message [the message of *promise] which we have heard from Him and now are reporting to you: God is Light, and there is no darkness in Him at all [*no, not in any way].

6 [So] if we say we are partakers together *and* enjoy fellowship with Him when we live *and* move *and* are walking about in darkness, we are [both] speaking falsely and do not live *and* practice the Truth [which the Gospel presents].

7 But if we [really] are living *and* walking in the Light, as He [Himself] is in the Light, we have [true, unbroken] fellowship with one another, and the blood of Jesus *Christ* His Son cleanses (removes) us from all sin *and* guilt [keeps us cleansed from sin in all its forms and manifestations].

8 If we say we have no sin [refusing to admit that we are sinners], we delude *and* lead ourselves astray, and the Truth [which the Gospel presents] is not in us [does not dwell in our hearts].

9 If we [freely] admit that we have sinned *and* confess our sins, He is faithful and just (true to His own nature and promises) and will forgive our sins [dismiss our lawlessness] and [continuously] cleanse us from all unrighteousness [everything not in conformity to His will in purpose, thought, and action].

10 If we say (claim) we have not sinned, we contradict His Word *and* make Him out to be false *and* a liar, and His Word is not in us [the divine message of the Gospel is not in our hearts].

<hr>

a Marvin Vincent, *Word Studies in the New Testament.*　　b Many ancient manuscripts read "your joy."
c Literal translation.

CHAPTER 2

MY LITTLE children, I write you these things so that you may not violate God's law and sin. But if anyone should sin, we have an Advocate (One Who will intercede for us) with the Father—[it is] Jesus Christ [the all] righteous [upright, just, Who conforms to the Father's will in every purpose, thought, and action].

2 And He [dthat same Jesus Himself] is the propitiation (the atoning sacrifice) for our sins, and not for ours alone but also for [the sins of] the whole world.

3 And this is how we may discern [ddaily, by experience] that we are coming to know Him [to perceive, recognize, understand, and become better acquainted with Him]: if we keep (bear in mind, observe, practice) His teachings (precepts, commandments).

4 Whoever says, I know Him [I perceive, recognize, understand, and am acquainted with Him] but fails to keep and obey His commandments (teachings) is a liar, and the Truth [eof the Gospel] is not in him.

5 But he who keeps (treasures) His Word [who bears in mind His precepts, who observes His message in its entirety], truly in him has the love of and for God been perfected (completed, reached maturity). By this we may perceive (know, recognize, and be sure) that we are in Him:

6 Whoever says he abides in Him ought [as da personal debt] to walk and conduct himself in the same way in which He walked and conducted Himself.

7 Beloved, I am writing you no new commandment, but an old commandment which you have had from the beginning; the old commandment is the message which you have heard [the edoctrine of salvation through Christ].

8 Yet I am writing you a new commandment, which is true (is realized) in Him and in you, because the darkness (dmoral blindness) is clearing away and the true Light (dthe revelation of God in Christ) is already shining.

9 Whoever says he is in the Light and [yet] hates his brother [Christian, eborn-again child of God his Father] is in darkness even until now.

10 Whoever loves his brother [believer] abides (lives) in the Light, and in It or in him there is no occasion for stumbling or cause for error or sin.

11 But he who hates (detests, despises) his brother [ein Christ] is in darkness and walking (living) in the dark; he is straying and does not perceive or know where he is going, because the darkness has blinded his eyes.

12 I am writing to you, little children, because for His name's sake your sins are forgiven [pardoned through His name and on account of confessing His name].

13 I am writing to you, fathers, because you have come to know (recognize, be aware of, and understand) Him Who [has existed] from the beginning. I am writing to you, young men, because you have been victorious over the wicked [one]. I write to you, fboys (lads), because you have come to know (recognize and be aware) of the Father.

14 I write to you, fathers, because you have come to know (recognize, be conscious of, and understand) Him Who [has existed] from the beginning. I write to you, young men, because you are strong and vigorous, and the Word of God is [always] abiding in you (in your hearts), and

---

d Marvin Vincent, *Word Studies*.   e Joseph Thayer, *A Greek-English Lexicon of the New Testament*.
f G. Abbott-Smith, *Manual Greek Lexicon of the New Testament*.

you have been victorious over the wicked one.

15 Do not love *or* cherish the world or the things that are in the world. If anyone loves the world, love for the Father is not in him.

16 For all that is in the world—the lust of the flesh [craving for sensual gratification] and the lust of the eyes [greedy longings of the mind] and the pride of life [assurance in one's own resources or in the stability of earthly things]—these do not come from the Father but are from the world [itself].

17 And the world passes away *and* disappears, and with it the forbidden cravings (the passionate desires, the lust) of it; but he who does the will of God and carries out His purposes in his life abides (remains) forever.

18 ᵍBoys (lads), it is the last time (hour, the end of this age). And as you have heard that the antichrist [he who will oppose Christ in the guise of Christ] is coming, even now many antichrists have arisen, which confirms our belief that it is the final (the end) time.

19 They went out from our number, but they did not [really] belong to us; for if they had been of us, they would have remained with us. But [they withdrew] that it might be plain that they all are not of us.

20 But you have been anointed by [you hold a sacred appointment from, you have been given an unction from] the Holy One, and you all know [the Truth].

21 I write to you not because you are ignorant *and* do not perceive *and* know the Truth, but because you do perceive *and* know it, and [know positively] that nothing false (no deception, no lie) is of the Truth.

22 Who is [such a] liar as he who denies that Jesus is the Christ (the Messiah)? He is the antichrist (the antagonist of Christ), who [ʰhabitually] denies *and* refuses to acknowledge the Father and the Son.

23 No one who [ʰhabitually] denies (disowns) the Son ʰeven has the Father. *Whoever confesses (acknowledges and has) the Son has the Father also.*

24 As for you, keep in your hearts what you have heard from the beginning. If what you heard from the first dwells *and* remains in you, then you will dwell in the Son and in the Father [always].

25 And this is what He Himself has promised us—the life, the eternal [life].

26 I write this to you with reference to those who would deceive you [seduce and lead you astray].

27 But as for you, the anointing (the sacred appointment, the unction) which you received from Him abides [ⁱpermanently] in you; [so] then you have no need that anyone should instruct you. But just as His anointing teaches you concerning everything and is true and is no falsehood, so you must abide in (live in, never depart from) Him [being ⁱrooted in Him, knit to Him], just as [His anointing] has taught you [to do].

28 And now, little children, abide (live, remain ⁱpermanently) in Him, so that when He is made visible, we may have *and* enjoy perfect confidence (boldness, assurance) and not be ashamed *and* shrink from Him at His coming.

29 If you know (perceive and are sure) that He [Christ] is [absolutely] righteous [conforming to the Father's will in purpose, thought, and action], you may also know (be sure) that everyone who does righteously [and is therefore in like manner con-

g G. Abbott-Smith, *Manual Greek Lexicon of the New Testament.*   **h** Marvin Vincent, *Word Studies.*
i Joseph Thayer, *A Greek-English Lexicon.*

formed to the divine will] is born (begotten) of Him [[j]God].

CHAPTER 3

SEE WHAT [[k]an incredible] quality of love the Father has given (shown, bestowed on) us, that we should [be permitted to] be named and called and counted the children of God! And so we are! The reason that the world does not know (recognize, acknowledge) us is that it does not know (recognize, acknowledge) Him.

2 Beloved, we are [even here and] now God's children; it is not yet disclosed (made clear) what we shall be [hereafter], but we know that when He comes and is manifested, we shall [[j]as God's children] resemble and be like Him, for we shall see Him [[j]just as He [really] is.

3 And everyone who has this hope [resting] on Him cleanses (purifies) himself just as He is pure (chaste, undefiled, guiltless).

4 Everyone who commits (practices) sin is guilty of lawlessness; for [that is what] sin is, lawlessness [the breaking, violating of God's law by transgression or neglect—being unrestrained and unregulated by His commands and His will].

5 You know that He appeared in visible form and became Man to take away [upon Himself] sins, and in Him there is no sin [[k]essentially and forever].

6 No one who abides in Him [who lives and remains [k]in communion with and in obedience to Him—deliberately, knowingly, and [k]habitually] commits (practices) sin. No one who [habitually] sins has either seen or known Him [recognized, perceived, or understood Him, or has had an experiential acquaintance with Him].

7 [m]Boys (lads), let no one deceive and lead you astray. He who practices righteousness [who is upright, conforming to the divine will in purpose, thought, and action, living a consistently conscientious life] is righteous, even as He is righteous.

8 [But] he who commits sin [who practices evildoing] is of the devil [takes his character from the evil one], for the devil has sinned (violated the divine law) from the beginning. The reason the Son of God was made manifest (visible) was to undo (destroy, loosen, and dissolve) the works the devil [has done].

9 No one born (begotten) of God [deliberately, knowingly, and [k]habitually] practices sin, for God's nature abides in him [His principle of life, the divine sperm, remains permanently within him]; and he cannot practice sinning because he is born (begotten) of God.

10 By this it is made clear who take their nature from God and are His children and who take their nature from the devil and are his children: no one who does not practice righteousness [who does not conform to God's will in purpose, thought, and action] is of God; neither is anyone who does not love his brother (his fellow [n]believer in Christ).

11 For this is the message (the announcement) which you have heard from the first, that we should love one another,

12 [And] not be like Cain who [took his nature and got his motivation] from the evil one and slew his brother. And why did he slay him? Because his deeds (activities, works) were wicked and malicious and his brother's were righteous (virtuous).

---

j Brooke F. Westcott, *The Epistles of Saint John*: When John thinks of God in relation to men, he never thinks of Him apart from Christ.   k Marvin Vincent, *Word Studies*.   l Robert Jamieson, A.R. Fausset and David Brown, *A Commentary on the Old and New Testaments*.   m G. Abbott-Smith, *Manual Greek Lexicon*.   n Joseph Thayer, *A Greek-English Lexicon*.

13 Do not be surprised *and* wonder, brethren, that the world detests *and* pursues you with hatred.

14 We know that we have passed over out of death into Life by the fact that we love the brethren (our fellow Christians). He who does not love abides (remains, is °held and kept continually) in [spiritual] death.

15 Anyone who hates (abominates, detests) his brother [in Christ] is [at heart] a murderer, and you know that no murderer has eternal life abiding (°persevering) within him.

16 By this we come to know (progressively to recognize, to perceive, to understand) the [essential] love: that He laid down His [own] life for us; and we ought to lay [our] lives down for [those who are our] brothers [°in Him].

17 But if anyone has this world's goods (resources for sustaining life) and sees his brother *and* °fellow believer in need, yet closes his heart of compassion against him, how can the love of God live *and* remain in him?

18 Little children, let us not love [merely] in theory *or* in speech but in deed and in truth (in practice and in sincerity).

19 By this we shall come to know (perceive, recognize, and understand) that we are of the Truth, and can reassure (quiet, conciliate, and pacify) our hearts in His presence,

20 Whenever our hearts in [ᵖtormenting] self-accusation make us feel guilty *and* condemn us. [For ᵖwe are in God's hands.]; For He is above *and* greater than our consciences (our hearts), and He knows (perceives and understands) everything [nothing is hidden from Him].

21 And, beloved, if our consciences (our hearts) do not accuse us [if they do not make us feel guilty

and condemn us], we have confidence (complete assurance and boldness) before God,

22 And we receive from Him whatever we ask, because we [ᵖwatchfully] obey His orders [observe His suggestions and injunctions, follow His plan for us] *and* [ᵖhabitually] practice what is pleasing to Him.

23 And this is His order (His command, His injunction): that we should believe in (put our faith and trust in and adhere to and rely on) the name of His Son Jesus Christ (the Messiah), and that we should love one another, just as He has commanded us.

24 All who keep His commandments [who obey His orders and follow His plan, live and continue to live, to stay and] abide in Him, and He in them. [ᵠThey let Christ be a home to them and they are the home of Christ.] And by this we know *and* understand *and* have the proof that He [really] lives *and* makes His home in us: by the [Holy] Spirit Whom He has given us.

CHAPTER 4

B ELOVED, DO not put faith in every spirit, but prove (test) the spirits to discover whether they proceed from God; for many false prophets have gone forth into the world.

2 By this you may know (perceive and recognize) the Spirit of God: every spirit which acknowledges *and* confesses [the fact] that Jesus Christ (the Messiah) [actually] has become man *and* has come in the flesh is of God [has God for its source];

3 And every spirit which does not acknowledge *and* confess *that* Jesus *Christ has come in the flesh* [but would ʳannul, destroy, ˢsever, disu-

o Joseph Thayer, *A Greek-English Lexicon.*   p Marvin Vincent, *Word Studies.*   q Bede, a translator
of portions of the Bible from the Latin into Old English.   r An ancient reading.   s *The Latin Vulgate.*

nite Him] is not of God [does not proceed from Him]. This ['non-confession] is the [spirit] of the antichrist, [of] which you heard that it was coming, and now it is already in the world.

4 Little children, you are of God [you belong to Him] and have [already] defeated *and* overcome them [the agents of the antichrist], because He Who lives in you is greater (mightier) than he who is in the world.

5 They proceed from the world *and* are of the world; therefore it is out of the world [its 'whole economy morally considered] that they speak, and the world listens (pays attention) to them.

6 We are [children] of God. Whoever is learning to know God [progressively to perceive, recognize, and understand God by observation and experience, and to 'get an ever-clearer knowledge of Him] listens to us; and he who is not of God does not listen *or* pay attention to us. By this we know (recognize) the Spirit of Truth and the spirit of error.

7 Beloved, let us love one another, for love is (springs) from God; and he who loves [his fellowmen] is begotten (born) of God and is coming [progressively] to know *and* understand God [to perceive and recognize and get a better and clearer knowledge of Him].

8 He who does not love has not become acquainted with God [does not and never did know Him], for God is love.

9 In this the love of God was made manifest (displayed) where we are concerned: in that God sent His Son, the only begotten *or* "unique [Son], into the world so that we might live through Him.

10 In this is love: not that we loved God, but that He loved us and sent His Son to be the propitiation (the atoning sacrifice) for our sins.

11 Beloved, if God loved us so [very much], we also ought to love one another.

12 No man has at any time [yet] seen God. But if we love one another, God abides (lives and remains) in us and His love (that love which is essentially His) is brought to completion (to its full maturity, runs its full course, is perfected) in us!

13 By this we come to know (perceive, recognize, and understand) that we abide (live and remain) in Him and He in us: because He has given (imparted) to us of His [Holy] Spirit.

14 And [besides] we ourselves have seen (have deliberately and steadfastly contemplated) and bear witness that the Father has sent the Son [as the] Savior of the world.

15 Anyone who confesses (acknowledges, owns) that Jesus is the Son of God, God abides (lives, makes His home) in him and he [abides, lives, makes his home] in God.

16 And we know (understand, recognize, are conscious of, by observation and by experience) and believe (adhere to and put faith in and rely on) the love God cherishes for us. God is love, and he who dwells *and* continues in love dwells *and* continues in God, and God dwells *and* continues in him.

17 In this [union and communion with Him] love is brought to completion *and* attains perfection with us, that we may have confidence for the day of judgment [with assurance and boldness to face Him], because as He is, so are we in this world.

---

t Marvin Vincent, *Word Studies.*   u James Moulton and George Milligan, *The Vocabulary of the Greek Testament.*

18 There is no fear in love [dread does not exist], but full-grown (complete, perfect) love 'turns fear out of doors and expels every trace of terror! For fear ʷbrings with it the thought of punishment, and [so] he who is afraid has not reached the full maturity of love [is not yet grown into love's complete perfection].

19 We love *Him*, because He first loved us.

20 If anyone says, I love God, and hates (detests, abominates) his brother [ʷin Christ], he is a liar; for he who does not love his brother, whom he has seen, cannot love God, Whom he has not seen.

21 And this command (charge, order, injunction) we have from Him: that he who loves God shall love his brother [ʷbeliever] also.

CHAPTER 5

EVERYONE WHO believes (adheres to, trusts, and relies on the fact) that Jesus is the Christ (the Messiah) is a born-again child of God; and everyone who loves the Father also loves the one born of Him (His offspring).

2 By this we come to know (recognize and understand) that we love the children of God: when we love God and obey His commands (orders, charges)—[when we keep His ordinances and are mindful of His precepts and His teaching].

3 For the [true] love of God is this: that we do His commands [keep His ordinances and are mindful of His precepts and teaching]. And these orders of His are not irksome (burdensome, oppressive, or grievous).

4 For whatever is born of God is victorious over the world; and this is the victory that conquers the world, even our faith.

5 Who is it that is victorious over [that conquers] the world but he who believes that Jesus is the Son of God [who adheres to, trusts in, and relies on that fact]?

6 This is He Who came by (with) water and blood [ᵈHis baptism and His death], Jesus Christ (the Messiah)—not by (in) the water only, but by (in) the water and the blood. And it is the [Holy] Spirit Who bears witness, because the [Holy] Spirit is the Truth.

7 So there are three witnesses ˣin heaven: the Father, the Word and the Holy Spirit, and these three are One;

8 and there are three witnesses on the earth: the Spirit, the water, and the blood; and these three agree [are in unison; their testimony coincides].

9 If we accept [as we do] the testimony of men [if we are willing to take human authority], the testimony of God is greater (of stronger authority), for this is the testimony of God, even the witness which He has borne regarding His Son.

10 He who believes in the Son of God [who adheres to, trusts in, and relies on Him] has the testimony [possesses this divine attestation] within himself. He who does not believe God [in this way] has made Him out to be *and* represented Him as a liar, because he has not believed (put his faith in, adhered to, and relied on) the evidence (the testimony) that God has borne regarding His Son.

11 And this is that testimony (that evidence): God gave us eternal life, and this life is in His Son.

12 He who possesses the Son has that life; he who does not possess the Son of God does not have that life.

13 I write this to you who believe in (adhere to, trust in, and rely on)

---

v Marvin Vincent, *Word Studies*.   w Joseph Thayer, *A Greek-English Lexicon*.   x The italicized section is found only in late manuscripts.

the name of the Son of God [in the peculiar services and blessings conferred by Him on men], so that you may know [with settled and absolute knowledge] that you [already] have life, ᶻyes, eternal life.

14 And this is the confidence (the assurance, the privilege of boldness) which we have in Him: [we are sure] that if we ask anything (make any request) according to His will (in agreement with His own plan), He listens to and hears us.

15 And if (since) we [positively] know that He listens to us in whatever we ask, we also know [with settled and absolute knowledge] that we have [granted us as our present possessions] the requests made of Him.

16 If anyone sees his brother [believer] committing a sin that does not [lead] to death (the extinguishing of life), he will pray and [God] will give him life [yes, He will grant life to all those whose sin is not one leading to death]. There is a sin [that leads] to death: I do not say that one should pray for that.

17 All wrongdoing is sin, and there is sin which does not [involve] death [that may be repented of and forgiven].

18 We know [absolutely] that anyone born of God does not [deliberately and knowingly] practice committing sin, but the One Who was begotten of God carefully watches over and protects him [Christ's divine presence within him preserves him against the evil], and the wicked one does not lay hold (get a grip) on him or touch [him].

19 We know [positively] that we are of God, and the whole world [around us] is under the power of the evil one.

20 And we [have seen and] know [positively] that the Son of God has [actually] come to this world and has given us understanding and insight [progressively] to perceive (recognize) and come to know better and more clearly Him Who is true; and we are in Him Who is true—in His Son Jesus Christ (the Messiah). This [Man] is the true God and Life eternal.

21 Little children, keep yourselves from idols (false gods)—[from anything and everything that would occupy the place in your heart due to God, from any sort of substitute for Him that would take first place in your life]. Amen (so let it be).

THE SECOND LETTER OF

JOHN

THE ELDERLY elder [of the church addresses this letter] to the elect (chosen) lady (Cyria) and her children, whom I truly love—and not only I but also all who are [progressively] learning to recognize and know and understand the Truth—

2 Because of the Truth which lives and stays on in our hearts and will be with us forever:

3 Grace (spiritual blessing), mercy, and [soul] peace will be with us, from God the Father and from Jesus Christ (the Messiah), the Father's Son, in all sincerity (truth) and love.

y Joseph Thayer, A Greek-English Lexicon.   z Brooke F. Westcott, cited by Speaker's Commentary.

4 I was greatly delighted to find some of your children walking (living) in [the] Truth, just as we have been commanded by the Father [Himself].

5 And now I beg you, lady (Cyria), not as if I were issuing a new charge (injunction or command), but [simply recalling to your mind] the one we have had from the beginning, that we love one another.

6 And what this love consists in is this: that we live *and* walk in accordance with *and* guided by His commandments (His orders, ordinances, precepts, teaching). This is the commandment, as you have heard from the beginning, that you continue to walk in love [guided by it and following it].

7 For many imposters (seducers, deceivers, and false leaders) have gone out into the world, men who will not acknowledge (confess, admit) the coming of Jesus Christ (the Messiah) in bodily form. Such a one is the imposter (the seducer, the deceiver, the false leader, the antagonist of Christ) and the antichrist.

8 Look to yourselves (take care) that you may not lose (throw away or destroy) all that we *and* you have labored for, but that you may [persevere until you] win *and* receive back a perfect reward [in full].

9 Anyone who runs on ahead [of God] and does not abide in the doctrine of Christ [who is not content with what He taught] does not have God; but he who continues to live in the doctrine (teaching) of Christ [does have God], he has both the Father and the Son.

10 If anyone comes to you and does not bring this doctrine [is disloyal to what Jesus Christ taught], do not receive him [do not accept him, do not welcome or admit him] into [your] house or bid him Godspeed *or* give him any encouragement.

11 For he who wishes him success [who encourages him, wishing him Godspeed] is a partaker in his evil doings.

12 I have many things to write to you, but I prefer not to do so with paper and ink; I hope to come to see you and talk with you face to face, so that our joy may be complete.

13 The children of your elect (chosen) sister wish to be remembered to you. *Amen (so be it).*

THE THIRD LETTER OF
JOHN

THE ELDERLY elder [of the church addresses this letter] to the beloved (esteemed) Gaius, whom I truly love.

2 Beloved, I pray that you may prosper in every way and [that your body] may keep well, even as [I know] your soul keeps well *and* prospers.

3 In fact, I greatly rejoiced when [some of] the brethren from time to time arrived and spoke [so highly] of the sincerity *and* fidelity of your life, as indeed you do live in the Truth [the whole Gospel presents].

4 I have no greater joy than this, to hear that my [spiritual] children are living their lives in the Truth.

5 Beloved, it is a fine *and* faithful work that you are doing when you give any service to the [Christian] brethren, and [especially when they are] strangers.

6 They have testified before the church of your love *and* friendship. You will do well to forward them on their journey [and you will please do so] in a way worthy of God's [service].

7 For these [traveling missionaries] have gone out for the Name's sake (for His sake) and are accepting nothing from the Gentiles (the heathen, the non-Israelites).

8 So we ourselves ought to support such people [to welcome and provide for them], in order that we may be fellow workers in the Truth (the whole Gospel) *and* cooperate with its teachers.

9 I have written briefly to the church; but Diotrephes, who likes to take the lead among them *and* put himself first, does not acknowledge my authority *and* refuses to accept my suggestions *or* to listen to me.

10 So when I arrive, I will call attention to what he is doing, his boiling over *and* casting malicious reflections upon us with insinuating language. And not satisfied with that, he refuses to receive *and* welcome the [missionary] brethren himself, and also interferes with *and* forbids those who would welcome them, and tries to expel (excommunicate) them from the church.

11 Beloved, do not imitate evil, but imitate good. He who does good is of God; he who does evil has not seen (discerned or experienced) God [has enjoyed no vision of Him and does not know Him at all].

12 Demetrius has warm commendation from everyone—and from the Truth itself; we add our testimony also, and you know that our testimony is true.

13 I had much [to say to you when I began] to write, but I prefer not to put it down with pen (a reed) and ink;

14 I hope to see you soon, and we will talk together face to face.

15 Peace be to you! (Good-bye!) The friends here send you greetings. Remember me to the friends there [to every one of them personally] by name.

THE LETTER OF
JUDE

JUDE, A servant of Jesus Christ (the Messiah), and brother of James, [writes this letter] to those who are called (chosen), dearly loved by God the Father *and separated (set apart)* and kept for Jesus Christ:

2 May mercy, [soul] peace, and love be multiplied to you.

3 Beloved, my whole concern was to write to you in regard to our common salvation. [But] I found it necessary *and* was impelled to write you and urgently appeal to *and* exhort [you] to contend for the faith which was once for all ªhanded down to the saints [the faith which is that sum of

ª G. Abbott-Smith, *Manual Greek Lexicon of the New Testament.*

Christian belief which was delivered [a]verbally to the holy people of God].

4 For certain men have crept in stealthily [[b]gaining entrance secretly by a side door]. Their doom was predicted long ago, ungodly (impious, profane) persons who pervert the grace (the spiritual blessing and favor) of our God into lawlessness and wantonness and immorality, and disown and deny our sole Master and Lord, Jesus Christ (the Messiah, the Anointed One).

5 Now I want to remind you, though you were fully informed once for all, that though the Lord [at one time] delivered a people out of the land of Egypt, He subsequently destroyed those [of them] who did not believe [who refused to adhere to, trust in, and rely upon Him].

6 And angels who did not keep (care for, guard, and hold to) their own first place of power but abandoned their proper dwelling place—these He has reserved in custody in eternal chains (bonds) under the thick gloom of utter darkness until the judgment and doom of the great day.

7 [The wicked are sentenced to suffer] just as Sodom and Gomorrah and the adjacent towns—which likewise gave themselves over to impurity and indulged in unnatural vice and sensual perversity—are laid out [in plain sight] as an exhibit of perpetual punishment [to warn] of everlasting fire. [Gen. 19.]

8 Nevertheless in like manner, these dreamers also corrupt the body, scorn and reject authority and government, and revile and libel and scoff at [heavenly] glories (the glorious ones).

9 But when [even] the archangel Michael, contending with the devil, judicially argued (disputed) about the body of Moses, he dared not [presume to] bring an abusive condemnation against him, but [simply] said, The Lord rebuke you! [Zech. 3:2.]

10 But these men revile (scoff and sneer at) anything they do not happen to be acquainted with and do not understand; and whatever they do understand physically [that which they know by mere instinct], like irrational beasts—by these they corrupt themselves and are destroyed (perish).

11 Woe to them! For they have run riotously in the way of Cain, and have abandoned themselves for the sake of gain [it offers them, following] the error of Balaam, and have perished in rebellion [like that] of Korah! [Gen. 4:3–8; Num. 16; 22–24.]

12 These are hidden reefs (elements of danger) in your love feasts, where they boldly feast sumptuously [carousing together in your midst], without scruples providing for themselves [alone]. They are clouds without water, swept along by the winds; trees, without fruit at the late autumn gathering time—twice (doubly) dead, [lifeless and] plucked up by the roots;

13 Wild waves of the sea, flinging up the foam of their own shame and disgrace; wandering stars, for whom the gloom of eternal darkness has been reserved forever.

14 It was of these people, moreover, that Enoch in the seventh [generation] from Adam prophesied when he said, Behold, the Lord comes with His myriads of holy ones (ten thousands of His saints)

15 To execute judgment upon all and to convict all the impious (unho-

---

a G. Abbott-Smith, *Manual Greek Lexicon of the New Testament*.   b The use of this verb paints this kind of picture.

ly ones) of all their ungodly deeds which they have committed [in such an] ungodly [way], and of all the severe (abusive, jarring) things which ungodly sinners have spoken against Him.

16 These are inveterate murmurers (grumblers) who complain [of their lot in life], going after their own desires [controlled by their passions]; their talk is boastful *and* arrogant, [and they claim to] admire men's persons *and* pay people flattering compliments to gain advantage.

17 But you must remember, beloved, the predictions which were made by the apostles (the special messengers) of our Lord Jesus Christ (the Messiah, the Anointed One).

18 They told you beforehand, In the last days (in the end time) there will be scoffers [who seek to gratify their own unholy desires], following after their own ungodly passions.

19 It is these who are [agitators] setting up distinctions *and* causing divisions—merely sensual [creatures, carnal, worldly-minded people], devoid of the [Holy] Spirit *and* destitute of any higher spiritual life.

20 But you, beloved, build yourselves up [founded] on your most holy faith [᪼make progress, rise like an edifice higher and higher], praying in the Holy Spirit;

21 Guard *and* keep yourselves in the love of God; expect *and* patiently wait for the mercy of our Lord Jesus Christ (the Messiah)—[which will bring you] unto life eternal.

22 And *refute [so as to] convict* some who dispute with you, *and* on some have mercy who waver *and* doubt.

23 [Strive to] save others, snatching [them] out of [the] fire; on others take pity [but] with fear, loathing even the garment spotted by the flesh *and* polluted by their sensuality. [Zech. 3:2–4.]

24 Now to Him Who is able to keep you without stumbling *or* slipping *or* falling, and to present [you] unblemished (blameless and faultless) before the presence of His glory in triumphant joy *and* exultation [with unspeakable, ecstatic delight]—

25 To the one only God, our Savior through Jesus Christ our Lord, be glory (splendor), majesty, might *and* dominion, and power *and* authority, before all time and now and forever (unto all the ages of eternity). Amen (so be it).

THE REVELATION

TO JOHN

CHAPTER 1

[T HIS IS] the revelation of Jesus Christ [His unveiling of the divine mysteries]. God gave it to Him to disclose *and* make known to His bond servants certain things which must shortly *and* speedily come to pass ᪷in their entirety. And He sent and communicated it through His angel (messenger) to His bond servant John,

2 Who has testified to *and* vouched

c Joseph Thayer, *A Greek-English Lexicon of the New Testament.*   d Marvin Vincent, *Word Studies in the New Testament.*

for all that he saw [°in his visions], the word of God and the testimony of Jesus Christ.

3 Blessed (happy, ᶠto be envied) is the man who reads aloud [in the assemblies] the word of this prophecy; and blessed (happy, ᶠto be envied) are those who hear [it read] and who keep themselves true to the things which are written in it [heeding them and laying them to heart], for the time [for them to be fulfilled] is near.

4 John to the seven assemblies (churches) that are in Asia: May grace (God's unmerited favor) be granted to you and spiritual peace (ᵍthe peace of Christ's kingdom) from Him Who is and Who was and Who is to come, and from the seven Spirits [ᵇthe sevenfold Holy Spirit] before His throne, [Isa. 11:2.]

5 And from Jesus Christ the faithful *and* trustworthy Witness, the Firstborn of the dead [first to be brought back to life] and the Prince (Ruler) of the kings of the earth. To Him Who ⁱever loves us and has ⁱonce [for all] loosed *and* freed us from our sins by His own blood, [Ps. 89:27.]

6 And formed us into a kingdom (a royal race), priests to His God and Father—to Him be the glory and the power *and* the majesty and the dominion throughout the ages *and* forever and ever. Amen (so be it). [Exod. 19:6; Isa. 61:6.]

7 Behold, He is coming with the clouds, and every eye will see Him, even those who pierced Him; and all the tribes of the earth shall gaze upon Him *and* beat their breasts *and* mourn *and* lament over Him. Even

so [must it be]. Amen (so be it). [Dan. 7:13; Zech. 12:10.]

8 I am the Alpha and the Omega, *the Beginning and the End*, says the Lord God, He Who is and Who was and Who is to come, the Almighty (the Ruler of all). [Isa. 9:6.]

9 I, John, your brother and companion (sharer and participator) with you in the tribulation and kingdom and patient endurance [which are] in Jesus *Christ*, was on the isle called Patmos, [banished] on account of [my witnessing to] the Word of God and the testimony (the proof, the evidence) for Jesus *Christ*.

10 I was in the Spirit [rapt in His power] on the Lord's Day, and I heard behind me a great voice like the calling of a ʲwar trumpet,

11 Saying, *I am the Alpha and the Omega, the First and the Last.* Write promptly what you see (your vision) in a book and send it to the seven churches *which are in Asia*—to Ephesus and to Smyrna and to Pergamum and to Thyatira and to Sardis and to Philadelphia and to Laodicea.

12 Then I turned to see [whose was] the voice that was speaking to me, and on turning I saw seven golden lampstands,

13 And in the midst of the lampstands [One] like a Son of Man, clothed with a robe which reached to His feet and with a girdle of gold about His breast. [Dan. 7:13; 10:5.]

14 His head and His hair were white like white wool, [as white] as snow, and His eyes [flashed] like a flame of fire. [Dan. 7:9.]

15 His feet glowed like burnished (bright) bronze as it is refined in a furnace, and His voice was like the

---

e Marvin Vincent, *Word Studies in the New Testament.*   f Alexander Souter, *Pocket Lexicon of the Greek New Testament.*   g G. Abbott-Smith, *Manual Greek Lexicon of the New Testament.*   h Richard of St. Victor, cited by Richard Trench, *Synonyms of the New Testament.*   i Charles B. Williams, *The New Testament: A Translation in the Language of the People:* "ever" and "once" captures the idea of ongoing and completed action contained within the Greek present and aorist (past) verb tenses used here.   j Marvin Vincent, *Word Studies.*

sound of many waters. [Dan. 10:6.]

16 In His right hand He held seven stars, and from His mouth there came forth a sharp two-edged sword, and His face was like the sun shining in full power at midday. [Exod. 34:29.]

17 When I saw Him, I fell at His feet as if dead. But He laid His right hand on me and said, Do not be afraid! I am the First and the Last, [Isa. 44:6.]

18 And the Ever-living One [I am living in the eternity of the eternities]. I died, but see, I am alive forevermore; and I possess the keys of death and Hades (the realm of the dead).

19 Write therefore the things you see, what they are [and signify] and what is to take place hereafter.

20 As to the hidden meaning (the mystery) of the seven stars which you saw on My right hand and the seven lampstands of gold: the seven stars are the seven angels (messengers) of the seven assemblies (churches) and the seven lampstands are the seven churches.

CHAPTER 2

TO THE angel (messenger) of the assembly (church) in Ephesus write: These are the words of Him Who holds the seven stars [which are the messengers of the seven churches] in His right hand, Who goes about among the seven golden lampstands [which are the seven churches]:

2 I know your industry and activities, laborious toil and trouble, and your patient endurance, and how you cannot tolerate wicked [men] and have tested and critically appraised those who call [themselves] apostles (special messengers of Christ) and yet are not, and have found them to be impostors and liars.

3 I know you are enduring patiently and are bearing up for My name's sake, and you have not fainted or become exhausted or grown weary.

4 But I have this [one charge to make] against you: that you have left (abandoned) the love that you had at first [you have deserted Me, your first love].

5 Remember then from what heights you have fallen. Repent (change the inner man to meet God's will) and do the works you did previously [when first you knew the Lord], or else I will visit you and remove your lampstand from its place, unless you change your mind and repent.

6 Yet you have this [in your favor and to your credit]: you hate the works of the Nicolaitans [what they are doing as corrupters of the people], which I Myself also detest.

7 He who is able to hear, let him listen to and give heed to what the Spirit says to the assemblies (churches). To him who overcomes (is victorious), I will grant to eat [of the fruit] of the tree of life, which is in the paradise of God. [Gen. 2:9; 3:24.]

8 And to the angel (messenger) of the assembly (church) in Smyrna write: These are the words of the First and the Last, Who died and came to life again: [Isa. 44:6.]

9 I know your affliction and distress and pressing trouble and your poverty—but you are rich! and how you are abused and reviled and slandered by those who say they are Jews and are not, but are a synagogue of Satan.

10 Fear nothing that you are about to suffer. [Dismiss your dread and your fears!] Behold, the devil is indeed about to throw some of you into prison, that you may be tested and proved and critically appraised, and for ten days you will have affliction. Be loyally faithful unto death [even if

you must die for it], and I will give you the crown of life. [Rev. 3:10, 11.]

11 He who is able to hear, let him listen to *and* heed what the Spirit says to the assemblies (churches). He who overcomes (is victorious) shall in no way be injured by the second death.

12 Then to the angel (messenger) of the assembly (church) in Pergamum write: These are the words of Him Who has *and* wields the sharp two-edged sword:

13 I know where you live— a place where Satan sits enthroned. [Yet] you are clinging to *and* holding fast My name, and you did not deny My faith, even in the days of Antipas, My witness, My faithful one, who was killed (martyred) in your midst— where Satan dwells.

14 Nevertheless, I have a few things against you: you have some people there who are clinging to the teaching of Balaam, who taught Balak to set a trap *and* a stumbling block before the sons of Israel, [to entice them] to eat food that had been sacrificed to idols and to practice lewdness [giving themselves up to sexual vice]. [Num. 25:1, 2; 31:16.]

15 You also have some who in a similar way are clinging to the teaching of the Nicolaitans [those corrupters of the people], *which thing I hate.*

16 Repent [then]! Or else I will come to you quickly and fight against them with the sword of My mouth.

17 He who is able to hear, let him listen to *and* heed what the Spirit says to the assemblies (churches). To him who overcomes (conquers), I will give to eat of the manna that is hidden, and I will give him a white stone with a new name engraved on the stone, which no one knows *or* understands except he who receives it. [Ps. 78:24; Isa. 62:2.]

18 And to the angel (messenger) of the assembly (church) in Thyatira write: These are the words of the Son of God, Who has eyes that flash like a flame of fire, *and* Whose feet glow like bright *and* burnished *and* white-hot bronze: [Dan. 10:6.]

19 I know your record *and* what you are doing, your love and faith and service and patient endurance, and that your recent works are more numerous *and* greater than your first ones.

20 But I have this against you: that you tolerate the woman Jezebel, who calls herself a prophetess [claiming to be inspired], and who is teaching and leading astray my servants *and* beguiling them into practicing sexual vice and eating food sacrificed to idols. [I Kings 16:31; II Kings 9:22, 30.]

21 I gave her time to repent, but she has no desire to repent of her immorality [symbolic of idolatry] *and* refuses to do so.

22 Take note: I will throw her on a bed [[k]of anguish], and those who commit adultery with her [her paramours] I will bring down to [l]pressing distress and severe affliction, unless they turn away their minds from conduct [such as] hers *and* repent of [m]*their* doings.

23 And I will strike her children (her proper followers) dead [thoroughly exterminating them]. And all the assemblies (churches) shall recognize *and* understand that I am He Who searches minds (the thoughts, feelings, and purposes) and the [inmost] hearts, and I will give to each of you [the reward for what you have done] as your work deserves. [Ps. 62:12; Jer. 17:10.]

24 But to the rest of you in Thyatira, who do not hold this teaching, who have not explored *and* known

---

k Marvin Vincent, *Word Studies.*   l Literal translation.   m Many ancient manuscripts so read.

the depths of Satan, as they say—I tell you that I do not lay upon you any other [fresh] burden:

25 Only hold fast to what you have until I come.

26 And he who overcomes (is victorious) and who obeys My commands to the [very] end [doing the works that please Me], I will give him authority *and* power over the nations;

27 And he shall rule them with a sceptre (rod) of iron, as when earthen pots are broken in pieces, and [his power over them shall be] like that which I Myself have received from My Father; [Ps. 2:8, 9.]

28 And I will give him the Morning Star.

29 He who is able to hear, let him listen to *and* heed what the [Holy] Spirit says to the assemblies (churches).

CHAPTER 3

AND TO the angel (messenger) of the assembly (church) in Sardis write: These are the words of Him Who has the seven Spirits of God [ⁿthe sevenfold Holy Spirit] and the seven stars: I know your record *and* what you are doing; you are supposed to be alive, but [in reality] you are dead.

2 Rouse yourselves *and* keep awake, and strengthen *and* invigorate what remains and is on the point of dying; for I have not found a thing that you have done [any work of yours] meeting the requirements of My God *or* perfect in His sight.

3 So call to mind the lessons you received and heard; continually lay them to heart *and* obey them, and repent. In case you will not rouse yourselves *and* keep awake and

watch, I will come upon you like a thief, and you will not know *or* suspect at what hour I will come.

4 Yet you still have a few [persons'] names in Sardis who have not soiled their clothes, and they shall walk with Me in white, because they are worthy *and* deserving.

5 Thus shall he who conquers (is victorious) be clad in white garments, and I will not erase *or* blot out his name from the Book of Life; I will acknowledge him [as Mine] *and* I will confess his name openly before My Father and before His angels. [Ps. 69:28; Dan. 12:1.]

6 He who is able to hear, let him listen to *and* heed what the [Holy] Spirit says to the assemblies (churches).

7 And to the angel (messenger) of the assembly (church) in Philadelphia write: These are the words of the Holy One, the True One, He Who has the key of David, Who opens and no one shall shut, Who shuts and no one shall open: [Isa. 22:22.]

8 I know your [record of] works *and* what you are doing. See! I have set before you a door wide open which no one is able to shut; I know that you have but little power, and yet you have kept My Word *and* guarded My message and have not renounced *or* denied My name.

9 Take note! I will make those of the synagogue of Satan who say they are Jews and are not, but lie—behold, I will make them come and bow down before your feet and learn *and* acknowledge that I have loved you. [Isa. 43:4; 49:23; 60:14.]

10 Because you have guarded *and* kept My word of patient endurance [have held fast the ᵒlesson of My patience with the ᵉexpectant endurance that I give you], I also will keep you

n Richard of St. Victor, cited by Richard Trench, *Synonyms of the New Testament*. o Joseph Thayer, *A Greek-English Lexicon of the New Testament*: The Greek, which we translate "of patient endurance," paints a picture of "a patient, steadfast waiting" for someone or something.

[safe] from the hour of trial (testing) which is coming on the whole world to try those who dwell upon the earth.

11 I am coming quickly; hold fast what you have, so that no one may rob you *and* deprive you of your crown.

12 He who overcomes (is victorious), I will make him a pillar in the sanctuary of My God; he shall never be put out of it *or* go out of it, and I will write on him the name of My God and the name of the city of My God, the new Jerusalem, which descends from My God out of heaven, and My own new name. [Isa. 62:2; Ezek. 48:35.]

13 He who can hear, let him listen to *and* heed what the Spirit says to the assemblies (churches).

14 And to the angel (messenger) of the assembly (church) in Laodicea write: These are the words of the Amen, the trusty *and* faithful and true Witness, the Origin *and* Beginning *and* Author of God's creation: [Isa. 55:4; Prov. 8:22.]

15 I know your [record of] works *and* what you are doing; you are neither cold nor hot. Would that you were cold or hot!

16 So, because you are lukewarm and neither cold nor hot, I will spew you out of My mouth!

17 For you say, I am rich; I have prospered *and* grown wealthy, and I am in need of nothing; and you do not realize *and* understand that you are wretched, pitiable, poor, blind, and naked. [Hos. 12:8.]

18 Therefore I counsel you to purchase from Me gold refined *and* tested by fire, that you may be [truly] wealthy, and white clothes to clothe you and to keep the shame of your nudity from being seen, and salve to put on your eyes, that you may see.

19 Those whom I [dearly and tenderly] love, I tell their faults and convict *and* convince *and* reprove and chasten [I discipline and instruct them]. So be enthusiastic *and* in earnest *and* burning with zeal and repent [changing your mind and attitude]. [Prov. 3:12.]

20 Behold, I stand at the door and knock; if anyone hears *and* listens to *and* heeds My voice and opens the door, I will come in to him and will eat with him, and he [will eat] with Me.

21 He who overcomes (is victorious), I will grant him to sit beside Me on My throne, as I Myself overcame (was victorious) and sat down beside My Father on His throne.

22 He who is able to hear, let him listen to *and* heed what the [Holy] Spirit says to the assemblies (churches).

CHAPTER 4

AFTER THIS I looked, and behold, a door standing open in heaven! And the first voice which I had heard addressing me like [the calling of] a [p]war trumpet said, Come up here, and I will show you what must take place in the future.

2 At once I came under the [Holy] Spirit's power, and behold, a throne stood in heaven, with One seated on the throne! [Ezek. 1:26.]

3 And He Who sat there appeared like [the crystalline brightness of] jasper and [the fiery] sardius, and encircling the throne there was a halo that looked like [a rainbow of] emerald. [Ezek. 1:28.]

4 Twenty-four other thrones surrounded the throne, and seated on these thrones were twenty-four elders ([q]the members of the heavenly Sanhedrin), arrayed in white cloth-

p Marvin Vincent, *Word Studies*.   q George R. Berry, *Greek-English New Testament Lexicon*.

ing, with crowns of gold upon their heads.

5 Out from the throne came flashes of lightning and rumblings and peals of thunder, and in front of the throne seven blazing torches burned, which are the seven Spirits of God [ᵣthe sevenfold Holy Spirit];

6 And in front of the throne there was also what looked like a transparent glassy sea, as if of crystal. And around the throne, in the center at each side of the throne, were four living creatures (beings) who were full of eyes in front and behind [with intelligence as to what is before and at the rear of them]. [Ezek. 1:5, 18.]

7 The first living creature (being) was like a lion, the second living creature like an ox, the third living creature had the face of a man, and the fourth living creature [was] like a flying eagle. [Ezek. 1:10.]

8 And the four living creatures, individually having six wings, were full of eyes all over and within [underneath their wings]; and day and night they never stop saying, Holy, holy, holy is the Lord God Almighty (Omnipotent), Who was and Who is and Who is to come. [Isa. 6:1–3.]

9 And whenever the living creatures offer glory and honor and thanksgiving to Him Who sits on the throne, Who lives forever and ever (through the eternities of the eternities), [Ps. 47:8.]

10 The twenty-four elders (ˢthe members of the heavenly Sanhedrin) fall prostrate before Him Who is sitting on the throne, and they worship Him Who lives forever and ever; and they throw down their crowns before the throne, crying out,

11 Worthy are You, our Lord and God, to receive the glory and the honor and dominion, for You created all things; by Your will they were [brought into being] and were created. [Ps. 19:1.]

CHAPTER 5

AND I saw lying on the ᵗopen hand of Him Who was seated on the throne a scroll (book) written within and on the back, closed *and* sealed with seven seals. [Isa. 29:11; Ezek. 2:9, 10; Dan. 12:4.]

2 And I saw a strong angel announcing in a loud voice, Who is worthy to open the scroll? And [who is entitled and deserves and is morally fit] to break its seals?

3 And no one in heaven or on earth or under the earth [in the realm of the dead, Hades] was able to open the scroll or to take a [single] look at its contents.

4 And I wept audibly *and* bitterly because no one was found fit to open the scroll or to inspect it.

5 Then one of the elders [ˢof the heavenly Sanhedrin] said to me, Stop weeping! See, the Lion of the tribe of Judah, the ᵘRoot (Source) of David, has won (has overcome and conquered)! He can open the scroll and break its seven seals! [Gen. 49:9, 10; Isa. 11:1, 10; Rev. 22:16.]

6 And there between the throne and the four living creatures (beings) and among the elders [ˢof the heavenly Sanhedrin] I saw a Lamb standing, as though it had been slain, with seven horns and with seven eyes, which are the seven Spirits of God [ᵣthe sevenfold Holy Spirit] Who have been sent [on duty far and wide] into all the earth. [Isa. 53:7; Zech. 3:8, 9; 4:10.]

7 He then went and took the scroll from the right hand of Him Who sat on the throne.

---

r Richard of St. Victor, cited by Richard Trench, *Synonyms of the New Testament.* s George R. Berry, *Greek-English New Testament Lexicon.* t Marvin Vincent, *Word Studies.* u Rev. 22:16.

8 And when He had taken the scroll, the four living creatures and the twenty-four elders ['of the heavenly Sanhedrin] prostrated themselves before the Lamb. Each was holding a harp (lute or guitar), and they had golden bowls full of incense (fragrant spices and gums for burning), which are the prayers of God's people (the saints).

9 And [now] they sing a new song, saying, You are worthy to take the scroll and to break the seals that are on it, for You were slain (sacrificed), and with Your blood You purchased men unto God from every tribe and language and people and nation. [Ps. 33:3.]

10 And You have made them a kingdom (royal race) and priests to our God, and they shall reign [as kings] over the earth! [Exod. 19:6; Isa. 61:6.]

11 Then I looked, and I heard the voices of many angels on every side of the throne and of the living creatures and the elders ['of the heavenly Sanhedrin], and they numbered ten thousand times ten thousand and thousands of thousands, [Dan. 7:10.]

12 Saying in a loud voice, Deserving is the Lamb, Who was sacrificed, to receive all the power and riches and wisdom and might and honor and majesty (glory, splendor) and blessing!

13 And I heard every created thing in heaven and on earth and under the earth [in Hades, the place of departed spirits] and on the sea and all that is in it, crying out together, To Him Who is seated on the throne and to the Lamb be ascribed the blessing and the honor and the majesty (glory, splendor) and the power (might and dominion) forever and ever (through the eternities of the eternities)! [Dan. 7:13, 14.]

14 Then the four living creatures (beings) said, Amen (so be it)! And the elders ['of the heavenly Sanhedrin] prostrated themselves and worshiped *Him Who lives forever and ever.*

CHAPTER 6

THEN I saw as the Lamb broke open one of the seven seals, and as if in a voice of thunder I heard one of the four living creatures call out, Come!

2 And I looked, and saw there a white horse whose rider carried a bow. And a crown was given him, and he rode forth conquering and to conquer. [Ps. 45:4, 5; Zech. 1:8; 6:1–3.]

3 And when He broke the second seal, I heard the second living creature call out, Come!

4 And another horse came out, flaming red. And its rider was empowered to take the peace from the earth, so that men slaughtered one another; and he was given a huge sword.

5 When He broke open the third seal, I heard the third living creature call out, Come *and look*! And I saw, and behold, a black horse, and in his hand the rider had a pair of scales (a balance).

6 And I heard what seemed to be a voice from the midst of the four living creatures, saying, A quart of wheat for a denarius [a whole day's wages], and three quarts of barley for a denarius; but do not harm the oil and the wine! [II Kings 6:25.]

7 When the Lamb broke open the fourth seal, I heard the fourth living creature call out, Come!

8 So I looked, and behold, an ashy

v George R. Berry, *Greek-English New Testament Lexicon.*

pale horse [*black and blue as if made so by bruising], and its rider's name was Death, and Hades (the realm of the dead) followed him closely. And they were given authority *and* power over a fourth part of the earth to kill with the sword and with famine and with plague (pestilence, disease) and with wild beasts of the earth. [Ezek. 5:12; Hos. 13:14.]

9 When the Lamb broke open the fifth seal, I saw at the foot of the altar the souls of those whose lives had been sacrificed for [adhering to] the Word of God and for the testimony they had borne.

10 They cried in a loud voice, O [Sovereign] Lord, holy and true, how long now before You will sit in judgment and avenge our blood upon those who dwell on the earth? [Gen. 4:10; Ps. 79:5; Zech. 1:12.]

11 Then they were each given a *x*long *and* flowing *and* festive white robe and told to rest *and* wait patiently a little while longer, until the number should be complete of their fellow servants and their brethren who were to be killed as they themselves had been.

12 When He [the Lamb] broke open the sixth seal, I looked, and there was a great earthquake; and the sun grew black as sackcloth of hair, [the full disc of] the moon became like blood. [Joel 2:10, 31.]

13 And the stars of the sky dropped to the earth like a fig tree shedding its unripe fruit out of season when shaken by a strong wind. [Isa. 34:4.]

14 And the *y*sky rolled up like a scroll *and* vanished, and every mountain and island was dislodged from its place.

15 Then the kings of the earth and their noblemen and their magnates and their military chiefs and the wealthy and the strong and [everyone, whether] slave or free hid themselves in the caves and among the rocks of the mountains, [Isa. 2:10.]

16 And they called to the mountains and the rocks, Fall on (before) us and hide us from the face of Him Who sits on the throne and from the *x*deep-seated indignation *and* wrath of the Lamb. [Isa. 2:19–21; Hos. 10:8.]

17 For the great day of His wrath (vengeance, retribution, indignation) has come, and who is able to stand before it? [Joel 2:11; Mal. 3:2.]

CHAPTER 7

AFTER THIS I saw four angels stationed at the four corners of the earth, *x*firmly holding back the four winds of the earth so that no wind should blow on the earth or sea or upon any tree. [Zech. 6:5.]

2 Then I saw a second angel coming up from the east (the rising of the sun) and carrying the seal of the living God. And with a loud voice he called out to the four angels who had been given authority *and* power to injure earth and sea,

3 Saying, Harm neither the earth nor the sea nor the trees, until we have sealed the bond servants of our God upon their foreheads. [Ezek. 9:4.]

4 And [then] I heard how many were sealed (marked) out of every tribe of the sons of Israel: there were 144,000.

5 Twelve thousand were sealed (marked) out of the tribe of Judah, 12,000 of the tribe of Reuben, 12,000 of the tribe of Gad,

6 Twelve thousand of the tribe of Asher, 12,000 of the tribe of Naphtali, 12,000 of the tribe of Manasseh,

w A description of the livid, ashen, discolored appearance of the dead; it symbolizes death and pestilence.
x Marvin Vincent, *Word Studies.*   y James Moulton and George Milligan, *The Vocabulary of the Greek Testament.*

7 Twelve thousand of the tribe of Simeon, 12,000 of the tribe of Levi, 12,000 of the tribe of Issachar,

8 Twelve thousand of the tribe of Zebulun, 12,000 of the tribe of Joseph, 12,000 of the tribe of Benjamin.

9 After this I looked and a vast host appeared which no one could count, [gathered out] of every nation, from all tribes and peoples and languages. These stood before the throne and before the Lamb; they were attired in white robes, with palm branches in their hands.

10 In loud voice they cried, saying, [Our] salvation is due to our God, Who is seated on the throne, and to the Lamb [to Them we owe our deliverance]!

11 And all the angels were standing round the throne and round the elders [²of the heavenly Sanhedrin] and the four living creatures, and they fell prostrate before the throne and worshiped God.

12 Amen! (So be it!) they cried. Blessing and glory and majesty and splendor and wisdom and thanks and honor and power and might [be ascribed] to our God to the ages and ages (forever and ever, throughout the eternities of the eternities)! Amen! (So be it!)

13 Then, addressing me, one of the elders [²of the heavenly Sanhedrin] said, Who are these [people] clothed in the long white robes? And from where have they come?

14 I replied, Sir, you know. And he said to me, These are they who have come out of the great tribulation (persecution), and have washed their robes and made them white in the blood of the Lamb. [Gen. 49:11; Dan. 12:1.]

15 For this reason they are [now] before the [very] throne of God and serve Him day and night in His sanc-

tuary (temple); and He Who is sitting upon the throne will protect and spread His tabernacle over and shelter them with His presence.

16 They shall hunger no more, neither thirst any more; neither shall the sun smite them, nor any ²scorching heat. [Isa. 49:10; Ps. 121:6.]

17 For the Lamb Who is in the midst of the throne will be their Shepherd, and He will guide them to the springs of the waters of life; and God will wipe away every tear from their eyes. [Ps. 23:2; Isa. 25:8; Ezek. 34:23.]

CHAPTER 8

WHEN HE [the Lamb] broke open the seventh seal, there was silence for about half an hour in heaven.

2 Then I saw the seven angels who stand before God, and to them were given seven trumpets.

3 And another angel came and stood over the altar. He had a golden censer, and he was given very much incense (fragrant spices and gums which exhale perfume when burned), that he might mingle it with the prayers of all the people of God (the saints) upon the golden altar before the throne. [Ps. 141:2.]

4 And the smoke of the incense (the perfume) arose in the presence of God, with the prayers of the people of God (the saints), from the hand of the angel.

5 So the angel took the censer and filled it with fire from the altar and cast it upon the earth. Then there followed peals of thunder and loud rumblings and blasts and noises, and flashes of lightning and an earthquake. [Lev. 16:12; Ezek. 10:2.]

6 Then the seven angels who had the seven trumpets prepared to sound them.

² George R. Berry, Greek-English New Testament Lexicon.

7 The first angel blew [his] trumpet, and there was a storm of hail and fire mingled with blood cast upon the earth. And a third part of the earth was burned up and a third of the trees was burned up and all the green grass was burned up. [Exod. 9:23–25.]

8 The second angel blew [his] trumpet, and something resembling a great mountain, blazing with fire, was hurled into the sea. [Jer. 51:25.]

9 And a third of the sea was turned to blood, a third of the living creatures in the sea perished, and a third of the ships were destroyed.

10 The third angel blew [his] trumpet, and a huge star fell from heaven, burning like a torch, and it dropped on a third of the rivers and on the springs of water—

11 And the name of the star is Wormwood. A third part of the waters was changed into wormwood, and many people died from using the water, because it had become bitter.

12 Then the fourth angel blew [his] trumpet, and a third of the sun was smitten, and a third of the moon, and a third of the stars, so that [the light of] a third of them was darkened, and a third of the daylight [itself] was withdrawn, and likewise a third [of the light] of the night was kept from shining.

13 Then I [looked and I] saw a solitary eagle flying in midheaven, and as it flew I heard it crying with a loud voice, Woe, woe, woe to those who dwell on the earth, because of the rest of the trumpet blasts which the three angels are about to sound!

CHAPTER 9

THEN THE fifth angel blew [his] trumpet, and I saw a star that had fallen from the sky to the earth; and to the angel was given the key [a]of the shaft of the Abyss (the bottomless pit).

2 He opened the [a]long shaft of the Abyss (the bottomless pit), and smoke like the smoke of a huge furnace puffed out of the [a]long shaft, so that the sun and the atmosphere were darkened by the smoke from the long shaft. [Gen. 19:28; Exod. 19:18; Joel 2:10.]

3 Then out of the smoke locusts came forth on the earth, and such power was granted them as the power the earth's scorpions have. [Exod. 10: 12–15.]

4 They were told not to injure the herbage of the earth nor any green thing nor any tree, but only [to attack] such human beings as do not have the seal (mark) of God on their foreheads. [Ezek. 9:4.]

5 They were not permitted to kill them, but to torment (distress, vex) them for five months; and the pain caused them was like the torture of a scorpion when it stings a person.

6 And in those days people will seek death and will not find it; and they will yearn to die, but death evades *and* flees from them. [Job 3:21.]

7 The locusts resembled horses equipped for battle. On their heads was something like golden crowns. Their faces resembled the faces of people. [Joel 2:4.]

8 They had hair like the hair of women, and their teeth were like lions' teeth. [Joel 1:6.]

9 Their breastplates (scales) resembled breastplates made of iron, and the [whirring] noise made by their wings was like the roar of a vast number of horse-drawn chariots going at full speed into battle. [Joel 2:5.]

10 They have tails like scorpions, and they have stings, and in their tails

a Marvin Vincent, *Word Studies.*

lies their ability to hurt men for [the] five months.

11 Over them as king they have the angel of the Abyss (of the bottomless pit). In Hebrew his name is Abaddon [destruction], but in Greek he is called Apollyon [destroyer].

12 The first woe (calamity) has passed; behold, two others are yet to follow.

13 Then the sixth angel blew [his] trumpet, and from the four horns of the golden altar which stands before God I heard a solitary voice,

14 Saying to the sixth angel who had the trumpet, Liberate the four angels who are bound at the great river Euphrates.

15 So the four angels who had been in readiness for that hour in the appointed day, month, and year were liberated to destroy a third of mankind.

16 The number of their troops of cavalry was twice ten thousand times ten thousand (200,000,000); I heard what their number was.

17 And in [my] vision the horses and their riders appeared to me like this: the riders wore breastplates the color of fiery red and sapphire blue and sulphur (brimstone) yellow. The heads of the horses looked like lions' heads, and from their mouths there poured fire and smoke and sulphur (brimstone).

18 A third of mankind was killed by these three plagues—by the fire and the smoke and the sulphur (brimstone) that poured from the mouths of the horses.

19 For the power of the horses to do harm is in their mouths and also in their tails. Their tails are like serpents, for they have heads, and it is by means of them that they wound people.

20 And the rest of humanity who were not killed by these plagues even then did not repent of [the worship of] the works of their [own] hands, so as to cease paying homage to the demons and idols of gold and silver and bronze and stone and wood, which can neither see nor hear nor move. [Ps. 115:4–7; 135:15–17; Isa. 17:8.]

21 And they did not repent of their murders or their practice of magic (sorceries) or their sexual vice or their thefts.

CHAPTER 10

THEN I saw another mighty angel coming down from heaven, robed in a cloud, with a [halo like a] rainbow over his head; his face was like the sun, and his feet (legs) were like columns of fire.

2 He had a little book (scroll) open in his hand. He set his right foot on the sea and his left foot on the land,

3 And he shouted with a loud voice like the roaring of a lion; and when he had shouted, the seven thunders gave voice *and* uttered their message in distinct words.

4 And when the seven thunders had spoken (sounded), I was going to write [it down], but I heard a voice from heaven saying, Seal up what the seven thunders have said! Do not write it down!

5 Then the [mighty] angel whom I had seen stationed on sea and land raised his right hand to heaven (the [b]sky), [Deut. 32:40; Dan. 12:6, 7.]

6 And swore in the name of (by) Him Who lives forever and ever, Who created the heavens ([b]sky) and all they contain, and the earth and all that it contains, and the sea and all that it contains. [He swore] that no more time should intervene *and* there should be no more waiting *or* delay,

7 But that when the days come

b G. Abbott-Smith, *Manual Greek Lexicon.*

when the trumpet call of the seventh angel is about to be sounded, then God's mystery (His secret design, His hidden purpose), as He had announced the glad tidings to His servants the prophets, should be fulfilled (accomplished, completed). [Dan. 12:6, 7.]

8 Then the voice that I heard from heaven spoke again to me, saying, Go and take the little book (scroll) which is open on the hand of the angel who is standing on the sea and on the land.

9 So I went up to the angel and asked him to give me the little book. And he said to me, Take it and eat it. It will embitter your stomach, though in your mouth it will be as sweet as honey. [Ezek. 2:8, 9; 3:1–3.]

10 So I took the little book from the angel's hand and ate *and* swallowed it; it was as sweet as honey in my mouth, but once I had swallowed it, my stomach was embittered.

11 Then they said to me, You are to make a fresh prophecy concerning many peoples *and* races and nations and languages and kings. [Jer. 1:10.]

CHAPTER 11

A REED [as a measuring rod] was then given to me, [shaped] like a staff, and I was told: Rise up and measure the sanctuary of God and the altar [of incense], and [number] those who worship there. [Ezek. 40:3.]

2 But leave out of your measuring the court outside the sanctuary of God; omit that, for it is given over to the Gentiles (the nations), and they will trample the holy city underfoot for 42 months (three and one-half years). [Isa. 63:18; Zech. 12:3.]

3 And I will grant the power of prophecy to My two witnesses for

1,260 (42 months; three and one-half years), dressed in sackcloth.

4 These [witnesses] are the two olive trees and the two lampstands which stand before the Lord of the earth. [Zech. 4:3, 11–14.]

5 And if anyone attempts to injure them, fire pours from their mouth and consumes their enemies; if anyone should attempt to harm them, thus he is doomed to be slain. [II Kings 1:10; Jer. 5:14.]

6 These [two witnesses] have power to shut up the sky, so that no rain may fall during the days of their prophesying (their ᶜprediction of events relating to Christ's kingdom and its speedy triumph); and they also have power to turn the waters into blood and to smite *and* scourge the earth with all manner of plagues as often as they choose. [Exod. 7:17, 19; I Kings 17:1.]

7 But when they have finished their testimony *and* their evidence is all in, the beast (monster) that comes up out of the Abyss (bottomless pit) will wage war on them, and conquer them and kill them. [Dan. 7:3, 7, 21.]

8 And their dead bodies [will lie exposed] in the open street (ᵈa public square) of the great city which is in a spiritual sense called [by the mystical and allegorical names of] Sodom and Egypt, where also their Lord was crucified. [Isa. 1:9.]

9 For three and a half days men from the races and tribes and languages and nations will gaze at their dead bodies and will not allow them to be put in a tomb.

10 And those who dwell on the earth will gloat *and* exult over them *and* rejoice exceedingly, taking their ease and sending presents [in congratulation] to one another, because these two prophets had been such a

---

c Joseph Thayer, *A Greek-English Lexicon.*   d Alexander Souter, *Pocket Lexicon.*

vexation *and* trouble *and* torment to all the dwellers on the earth.

11 But after three and a half days, by God's gift the breath of life again entered into them, and they rose up on their feet, and great dread and terror fell on those who watched them. [Ezek. 37:5, 10.]

12 Then [the two witnesses] heard a strong voice from heaven calling to them, Come up here! And before the very eyes of their enemies they ascended into heaven in a cloud. [II Kings 2:11.]

13 And at that [very] hour there was a tremendous earthquake and one tenth of the city was destroyed (fell); seven thousand people perished in the earthquake, and those who remained were filled with dread *and* terror *and* were awe-struck, and they glorified the God of heaven.

14 The second woe (calamity) has passed; now the third woe is speedily to come.

15 The seventh angel then blew [his] trumpet, and there were mighty voices in heaven, shouting, The dominion (kingdom, sovereignty, rule) of the world has now come into the possession and become the kingdom of our Lord and of His Christ (the Messiah), and He shall reign forever and ever (for the eternities of the eternities)! [Ps. 22:28; Dan. 7:13, 14, 27.]

16 Then the twenty-four elders [of ^ethe heavenly Sanhedrin], who sit on their thrones before God, prostrated themselves before Him and worshiped,

17 Exclaiming, To You we give thanks, Lord God Omnipotent, [the One] Who is and [ever] was, for assuming the high sovereignty *and* the great power that are Yours and for beginning to reign.

18 And the heathen (the nations) raged, but Your wrath (retribution, indignation) came, the time when the dead will be judged and Your servants the prophets and saints rewarded—and those who revere (fear) Your name, both low and high *and* small and great—and [the time] for destroying the corrupters of the earth. [Ps. 2:1.]

19 Then the sanctuary of God in heaven was thrown open, and the ark of His covenant was seen standing inside in His sanctuary; and there were flashes of lightning, loud rumblings (blasts, mutterings), peals of thunder, an earthquake, and a terrific hailstorm. [I Kings 8:1–6.]

CHAPTER 12

AND A great sign (wonder) [warning of future events of ominous significance] appeared in heaven: a woman clothed with the sun, with the moon under her feet, and with a crownlike garland (tiara) of twelve stars on her head.

2 She was pregnant and she cried out in her birth pangs, in the anguish of her delivery.

3 Then another ominous sign (wonder) was seen in heaven: Behold, a huge, fiery-red dragon, with seven heads and ten horns, and seven kingly crowns (diadems) upon his heads. [Dan. 7:7.]

4 His tail swept [across the sky] *and* dragged down a third of the stars and flung them to the earth. And the dragon stationed himself in front of the woman who was about to be delivered, so that he might devour her child as soon as she brought it forth. [Dan. 8:10.]

5 And she brought forth a male Child, One Who is destined to shepherd (rule) all the nations with an iron staff (scepter), and her Child was

caught up to God and to His throne. [Ps. 2:8, 9; 110:1, 2.]

6 And the woman [herself] fled into the desert (wilderness), where she has a retreat prepared [for her] by God, in which she is to be fed *and* kept safe for 1,260 days (42 months; three and one-half years).

7 Then war broke out in heaven; Michael and his angels went forth to battle with the dragon, and the dragon and his angels fought.

8 But they were defeated, and there was no room found for them in heaven any longer.

9 And the huge dragon was cast down *and* out—that age-old serpent, who is called the Devil and Satan, he who is the seducer (deceiver) of all humanity the world over; he was forced out *and* down to the earth, and his angels were flung out along with him. [Gen. 3:1, 14, 15; Zech. 3:1.]

10 Then I heard a strong (loud) voice in heaven, saying, Now it has come—the salvation and the power and the kingdom (the dominion, the reign) of our God, and the power (the sovereignty, the authority) of His Christ (the Messiah); for the accuser of our brethren, he who keeps bringing before our God charges against them day and night, has been cast out! [Job 1:9–11.]

11 And they have overcome (conquered) him by means of the blood of the Lamb and by the utterance of their testimony, for they did not love *and* cling to life even when faced with death [holding their lives cheap till they had to die for their witnessing].

12 Therefore be glad (exult), O heavens and you that dwell in them! But woe to you, O earth and sea, for the devil has come down to you in fierce anger (fury), because he

knows that he has [only] a short time [left]! [Isa. 44:23; 49:13.]

13 And when the dragon saw that he was cast down to the earth, he went in pursuit of the woman who had given birth to the male Child.

14 But the woman was supplied with the two wings of a giant eagle, so that she might fly from the presence of the serpent into the desert (wilderness), to the retreat where she is to be kept safe *and* fed for a time, and times, and half a time (three and one-half years, or 1,260 days). [Dan. 7:25; 12:7.]

15 Then out of his mouth the serpent spouted forth water like a flood after the woman, that she might be carried off with the torrent.

16 But the earth came to the rescue of the woman, and the ground opened its mouth and swallowed up the stream of water which the dragon had spouted from his mouth.

17 So then the dragon was furious (enraged) at the woman, and he went away to wage war on the remainder of her descendants—[on those] who obey God's commandments and who have the testimony of Jesus *Christ* [and adhere to it and ⁿbear witness to Him].

CHAPTER 13

[AS] ᵍI stood on the sandy beach, I saw a beast coming up out of the sea with ten horns and seven heads. On his horns he had ten royal crowns (diadems) and blasphemous titles (names) on his heads.

2 And the beast that I saw resembled a leopard, but his feet were like those of a bear and his mouth was like that of a lion. And to him the dragon gave his [own] might *and* power and his [own] throne and great dominion.

---

f Charles B. Williams, *The New Testament: A Translation in the Language of the People.*   g Many ancient manuscripts read "he."

3 And one of his heads seemed to have a deadly wound. But his death stroke was healed; and the whole earth went after the beast in amazement and admiration.

4 They fell down and paid homage to the dragon, because he had bestowed on the beast all his dominion and authority; they also praised and worshiped the beast, exclaiming, Who is a match for the beast, and, Who can make war against him?

5 And the beast was given the power of speech, uttering boastful and blasphemous words, and he was given freedom to exert his authority and to exercise his will during forty-two months (three and a half years), [Dan. 7:8.]

6 And he opened his mouth to speak slanders against God, blaspheming His name and His abode, [even vilifying] those who live in heaven.

7 He was further permitted to wage war on God's holy people (the saints) and to overcome them. And power was given him to extend his authority over every tribe and people and tongue and nation, [Dan. 7:21, 25.]

8 And all the inhabitants of the earth will fall down in adoration and pay him homage, everyone whose name has not been recorded in the Book of Life of the Lamb that was slain [in sacrifice] [b]from the foundation of the world.

9 If anyone is able to hear, let him listen:

10 Whoever leads into captivity will himself go into captivity; if anyone slays with the sword, with the sword must he be slain. Herein is [the call for] the patience and the faith and fidelity of the saints (God's people). [Jer. 15:2.]

11 Then I saw another beast rising up out of the land [itself]; he had two horns like a lamb, and he spoke (roared) like a dragon.

12 He exerts all the power and right of control of the former beast in his presence, and causes the earth and those who dwell upon it to exalt and deify the first beast, whose deadly wound was healed, and to worship him.

13 He performs great signs (startling miracles), even making fire fall from the sky to the earth in men's sight.

14 And because of the signs (miracles) which he is allowed to perform in the presence of the [first] beast, he deceives those who inhabit the earth, commanding them to erect a statue (an image) in the likeness of the beast who was wounded by the [small] sword and still lived. [Deut. 13:1–5.]

15 And he is permitted [also] to impart the breath of life into the beast's image, so that the statue of the beast could actually talk and cause to be put to death those who would not bow down and worship the image of the beast. [Dan. 3:5.]

16 Also he compels all [alike], both small and great, both the rich and the poor, both free and slave, to be marked with an inscription [[i]stamped] on their right hands or on their foreheads,

17 So that no one will have power to buy or sell unless he bears the stamp (mark, inscription), [that is] the name of the beast or the number of his name.

18 Here is [room for] discernment [a call for the wisdom [i]of interpretation]. Let anyone who has intelligence (penetration and insight enough) calculate the number of the beast, for it is a human number [the

---

h Alternate translation: "recorded from the foundation of the world in the Book of Life of the Lamb that was slain [in sacrifice]."   i Joseph Thayer, *A Greek-English Lexicon.*

number of a certain man]; his number
is 666.

CHAPTER 14

THEN I looked, and behold, the
Lamb stood on Mount Zion, and
with Him 144,000 [men] who had His
name and His Father's name inscribed on their foreheads.

2 And I heard a voice from heaven
like the sound of great waters and
like the rumbling of mighty thunder;
the voice I heard [seemed like the
music] of harpists ʲaccompanying
themselves on their harps.

3 And they sang a new song before
the throne [of God] and before the
four living creatures and before the
elders [of ᵏthe heavenly Sanhedrin].
No one could learn [to sing] that song
except the 144,000 who had been ransomed (purchased, redeemed) from
the earth.

4 These are they who have not defiled themselves by relations with
women, for they are [ˡpure as] virgins. These are they who follow the
Lamb wherever He goes. These are
they who have been ransomed (purchased, redeemed) from among men
as the firstfruits for God and the
Lamb.

5 No lie was found to be upon their
lips, for they are blameless (spotless,
untainted, without blemish) *before
the throne of God.*

6 Then I saw another angel flying
in midair, with an eternal Gospel
(good news) to tell to the inhabitants
of the earth, to every race and tribe
and language and people.

7 And he cried with a mighty voice,
Revere God and give Him glory (hon-
or and praise in worship), for the
hour of His judgment has arrived.
Fall down before Him; pay Him

homage *and* adoration *and* worship
Him Who created heaven and earth,
the sea and the springs (fountains) of
water.

8 Then another angel, a second,
followed, declaring, Fallen, fallen is
Babylon the great! She who made all
nations drink of the [maddening]
wine of her passionate unchastity
[ᵐidolatry]. [Isa. 21:9.]

9 Then another angel, a third, followed them, saying with a mighty
voice, Whoever pays homage to the
beast and his statue and permits the
[beast's] stamp (mark, inscription) to
be put on his forehead or on his hand,

10 He too shall [have to] drink of
the wine of God's indignation *and*
wrath, poured undiluted into the cup
of His anger; and he shall be tormented with fire and brimstone in the
presence of the holy angels and in the
presence of the Lamb. [Gen. 19:24.]

11 And the smoke of their torment
ascends forever and ever; and they
have no respite (no pause, no inter-
mission, no rest, no peace) day or
night—these who pay homage to the
beast and to his image and whoever
receives the stamp of his name upon
him. [Isa. 34:10.]

12 Here [comes in a call for] the
steadfastness of the saints [the patience, the endurance of the people
of God], those who [habitually] keep
God's commandments and [their]
faith in Jesus.

13 Then I heard further [ᵐperceiv-
ing the distinct words of] a voice
from heaven, saying, Write this:
Blessed (happy, ⁿto be envied) are
the dead from now on who die in the
Lord! Yes, blessed (happy, ⁿto be envied indeed), says the Spirit, [in] that
they may rest from their labors, for
their works (deeds) do follow (attend, accompany) them!

j Marvin Vincent, *Word Studies.*   k George R. Berry, *Greek-English New Testament Lexicon.*
l Charles B. Williams, *The New Testament: A Translation.*   m Joseph Thayer, *A Greek-English Lexicon.*
n Alexander Souter, *Pocket Lexicon.*

14 Again I looked, and behold, [I saw] a white cloud, and sitting on the cloud °One resembling a Son of Man, with a crown of gold on His head and a sharp scythe (sickle) in His hand. [Dan. 7:13.]

15 And another angel came out of the temple sanctuary, calling with a mighty voice to Him Who was sitting upon the cloud, Put in Your scythe and reap, for the hour has arrived to gather the harvest, for the earth's crop is fully ripened. [Joel 3:13.]

16 So He Who was sitting upon the cloud swung His scythe (sickle) on the earth, and the earth's crop was harvested.

17 Then another angel came out of the temple [sanctuary] in heaven, and he also carried a sharp scythe (sickle).

18 And another angel came forth from the altar, [the angel] who has authority and power over fire, and he called with a loud cry to him who had the sharp scythe (sickle), Put forth your scythe and reap the fruitage of the vine of the earth, for its grapes are entirely ripe.

19 So the angel swung his scythe on the earth and stripped the grapes and gathered the vintage from the vines of the earth and cast it into the huge winepress of God's indignation and wrath.

20 And [the grapes in] the winepress were trodden outside the city, and blood poured from the winepress, [reaching] as high as horses' bridles, for a distance of 1,600 stadia (about 200 miles). [Joel 3:13.]

CHAPTER 15

THEN I saw another wonder (sign, token, symbol) in heaven, great and marvelous [warning of events of ominous significance]: There were seven angels bringing seven plagues (afflictions, calamities), which are the last, for with them God's wrath (indignation) is completely expressed [reaches its climax and is ended]. [Lev. 26:21.]

2 Then I saw what seemed to be a glassy sea blended with fire, and those who had come off victorious from the beast and from his statue and from the number corresponding to his name were standing beside the glassy sea, with harps of God in their hands.

3 And they sang the song of Moses the servant of God and the song of the Lamb, saying, Mighty and marvelous are Your works, O Lord God the Omnipotent! Righteous (just) and true are Your ways, O Sovereign of the ages (King of the ᵖnations)! [Exod. 15:1; Ps. 145:17.]

4 Who shall not reverence and glorify Your name, O Lord [giving You honor and praise in worship]? For You only are holy. All the nations shall come and pay homage and adoration to You, for Your just judgments (Your righteous sentences and deeds) have been made known and displayed. [Ps. 86:9, 10; Jer. 10:7.]

5 After this I looked and the sanctuary of the tent of the testimony in heaven was thrown open,

6 And there came out of the temple sanctuary the seven angels bringing the seven plagues (afflictions, calamities). They were arrayed in pure gleaming linen, and around their breasts they wore golden girdles.

7 And one of the four living creatures [then] gave the seven angels seven golden bowls full of the wrath and indignation of God, Who lives forever and ever (in the eternities of the eternities).

o There is no consensus of opinion concerning the figure resembling a "son of man." Thus the capitals are tentatively presented as a possible interpretation. Many commentators question whether this refers to Christ.
p Many manuscripts read "nations."

8 And the sanctuary was filled with smoke from the glory (the radiance, the splendor) of God and from His might *and* power, and no one was able to go into the sanctuary until the seven plagues (afflictions, calamities) of the seven angels were ended. [I Kings 8:10; Isa. 6:4; Ezek. 44:4.]

CHAPTER 16

THEN I heard a mighty voice from the temple sanctuary saying to the seven angels, Go and empty out on the earth the seven bowls of God's wrath *and* indignation. [Ps. 69:24; Isa. 66:6.]

2 So the first [angel] went and emptied his bowl on the earth, and foul and painful ulcers (sores) came on the people who were marked with the stamp of the beast and who did homage to his image. [Exod. 9:10, 11; Deut. 28:35.]

3 The second [angel] emptied his bowl into the sea, and it turned into blood like that of a corpse [thick, corrupt, ill-smelling, and disgusting], and every living thing that was in the sea perished.

4 Then the third [angel] emptied out his bowl into the rivers and the springs of water, and they turned into (became) blood. [Exod. 7:17–21.]

5 And I also heard the angel of the waters say, Righteous (just) are You in these Your decisions *and* judgments, You Who are and were, O Holy One!

6 Because they have poured out the blood of Your people (the saints) and the prophets, and You have given them blood to drink. Such is their due [they deserve it]! [Ps. 79:3.]

7 And [from] the altar I heard [the] cry, Yes, Lord God the Omnipotent, Your judgments (sentences, decisions) are true and just *and* righteous! [Ps. 119:137.]

8 Then the fourth [angel] emptied out his bowl upon the sun, and it was permitted to burn (scorch) humanity with [fierce, glowing] heat (fire).

9 People were severely burned (scorched) by the fiery heat, and they reviled *and* blasphemed the name of God, Who has control of these plagues, and they did not repent of their sins [felt no regret, contrition, and compunction for their waywardness, refusing to amend their ways] to give Him glory.

10 Then the fifth [angel] emptied his bowl on the throne of the beast, and his kingdom was [plunged] in darkness; and people gnawed their tongues for the torment [of their excruciating distress and severe pain] [Exod. 10:21.]

11 And blasphemed the God of heaven because of their anguish and their ulcers (sores), and they did not deplore their wicked deeds *or* repent [for what they had done].

12 Then the sixth [angel] emptied his bowl on the mighty river Euphrates, and its water was dried up to make ready a road for [the coming of] the kings of the east (from the rising sun). [Isa. 11:15, 16.]

13 And I saw three loathsome spirits like frogs, [leaping] from the mouth of the dragon and from the mouth of the beast and from the mouth of the false prophet. [Exod. 8:3; I Kings 22:21–23.]

14 For really they are the spirits of demons that perform signs (wonders, miracles). And they go forth to the rulers *and* leaders all over the world, to gather them together for war on the great day of God the Almighty,

15 Behold, I am going to come like a thief! Blessed (happy, qto be envied) is he who stays awake (alert) and who guards his clothes, so that

___

q Alexander Souter. *Pocket Lexicon.*

he may not be naked and [have the shame of being] seen exposed!

16 And they gathered them together at the place which in Hebrew is called Armageddon. [II Kings 9:27.]

17 Then the seventh [angel] emptied out his bowl into the air, and a mighty voice came out of the sanctuary *of heaven* from the throne [of God], saying, It is done! [It is all over, it is all accomplished, it has come!] [Isa. 66:6.]

18 And there followed lightning flashes, loud rumblings, peals of thunder, and a tremendous earthquake; nothing like it has ever occurred since men dwelt on the earth, so severe *and* far-reaching was that earthquake. [Exod. 19:16; Dan. 12:1.]

19 The mighty city was broken into three parts, and the cities of the nations fell. And God kept in mind mighty Babylon, to make her drain the cup of His furious wrath *and* indignation.

20 And every island fled and no mountains could be found.

21 And great (excessively oppressive) hailstones, as heavy as a talent [between fifty and sixty pounds], of immense size, fell from the sky on the people; and men blasphemed God for the plague of the hail, so very great was [the torture] of that plague. [Exod. 9:23.]

CHAPTER 17

ONE OF the seven angels who had the seven bowls then came and spoke to me, saying, Come with me! I will show you the doom (sentence, judgment) of the great harlot (idolatress) who is seated on many waters, [Jer. 51:13.]

2 [She] with whom the rulers of the earth have joined in prostitution (idolatry) and with the wine of whose immorality (idolatry) the inhabitants of the earth have become intoxicated. [Jer. 25:15, 16.]

3 And [the angel] bore me away [rapt] in the Spirit into a desert (wilderness), and I saw a woman seated on a scarlet beast that was all covered with blasphemous titles (names), and he had seven heads and ten horns.

4 The woman was robed in purple and scarlet and bedecked with gold, precious stones, and pearls, [and she was] holding in her hand a golden cup full of the accursed offenses and the filth of her lewdness *and* vice. [Jer. 51:7.]

5 And on her forehead there was inscribed a name of mystery [with a secret symbolic meaning]: Babylon the great, the mother of prostitutes (idolatresses) and of the filth *and* atrocities *and* abominations of the earth.

6 I also saw that the woman was drunk, [drunk] with the blood of the saints (God's people) and the blood of the martyrs [who witnessed] for Jesus. And when I saw her, I was utterly amazed *and* wondered greatly.

7 But the angel said to me, Why do you wonder? I will explain to you the [secret symbolic meaning of the] mystery of the woman, as well as of the beast having the seven heads and ten horns that carries her.

8 The beast that you saw [once] was, but [now] is no more, and he is going to come up out of the Abyss (the bottomless pit) and proceed to go to perdition. And the inhabitants of the earth whose names have not been recorded in the Book of Life from the foundation of the world will be astonished when they look at the beast, because he [once] was, but [now] is no more, and he is [yet] to come. [Dan. 7:3.]

9 This calls for a mind [to consider that is packed] with wisdom *and* in-

telligence [it is something for a particular mode of thinking and judging of thoughts, feelings, and purposes]. The seven heads are seven hills upon which the woman is sitting;

10 And they are also seven kings, five of whom have fallen, one still exists [and is reigning]; the other [the seventh] has not yet appeared, and when he does arrive, he must stay [but] a brief time.

11 And as for the beast that [once] was, but now is no more, he [himself] is an eighth ruler (king, head), but he is of the seven *and* belongs to them, and he goes to perdition.

12 Also the ten horns that you observed are ten rulers (kings) who have as yet received no royal dominion, but together they are to receive power *and* authority as rulers for a single hour, along with the beast. [Dan. 7:20–24.]

13 These have one common policy (opinion, purpose), and they deliver their power and authority to the beast.

14 They will wage war against the Lamb, and the Lamb will triumph over them; for He is Lord of lords and King of kings—and those with Him *and* on His side are chosen and called [elected] and loyal *and* faithful followers. [Dan. 2:47.]

15 And [the angel further] said to me, The waters that you observed, where the harlot is seated, are races and multitudes and nations and dialects (languages).

16 And the ten horns that you saw, they and the beast will [be the very ones to] hate the harlot (the idolatrous woman); they will make her cheerless (bereaved, desolate), and they will strip her and eat up her flesh and utterly consume her with fire.

17 For God has put it into their hearts to carry out His own purpose by acting in harmony in surrendering their royal power *and* authority to

the beast, until the prophetic words (intentions and promises) of God shall be fulfilled.

18 And the woman that you saw is herself the great city which dominates *and* controls the rulers *and* the leaders of the earth.

CHAPTER 18

THEN I saw another angel descending from heaven, possessing great authority, and the earth was illuminated with his radiance *and* splendor.

2 And he shouted with a mighty voice, She is fallen! Mighty Babylon is fallen! She has become a resort *and* dwelling place for demons, a dungeon haunted by every loathsome spirit, an abode for every filthy and detestable bird.

3 For all nations have drunk the wine of her passionate unchastity, and the rulers *and* leaders of the earth have joined with her in committing fornication (idolatry), and the businessmen of the earth have become rich with the wealth of her excessive luxury *and* wantonness. [Jer. 25:15, 27.]

4 I then heard another voice from heaven saying, Come out from her, my people, so that you may not share in her sins, neither participate in her plagues. [Isa. 48:20; Jer. 50:8.]

5 For her iniquities (her crimes and transgressions) are piled up as high as heaven, and God has remembered her wickedness *and* [her] crimes [and calls them up for settlement]. [Jer. 51:9.]

6 Repay to her what she herself has paid [to others] and double [her doom] in accordance with what she has done. Mix a double portion for her in the cup she mixed [for others]. [Ps. 137:8.]

7 To the degree that she glorified herself and reveled in her wanton-

ness [living deliciously and luxuriously], to that measure impose on her torment *and* anguish and tears *and* mourning. Since in her heart she boasts, I am not a widow; as a queen [on a throne] I sit, and I shall never see suffering *or* experience sorrow —[Isa. 47:8, 9.]

8 So shall her plagues (afflictions, calamities) come thick upon her in a single day, pestilence and anguish *and* sorrow and famine; and she shall be utterly consumed (burned up with fire), for mighty is the Lord God Who judges her.

9 And the rulers *and* leaders of the earth who joined her in her immorality (idolatry) and luxuriated with her will weep *and* beat their breasts and lament over her when they see the smoke of her conflagration. [Ezek. 26:16, 17.]

10 They will stand a long way off, in terror of her torment, and they will cry, Woe *and* alas, the great city, the mighty city, Babylon! In one single hour how your doom (judgment) has overtaken you!

11 And earth's businessmen will weep *and* grieve over her because no one buys their freight (cargo) any more. [Ezek. 27:36.]

12 Their merchandise is of gold, silver, precious stones, and pearls; of fine linen, purple, silk, and scarlet [stuffs]; all kinds of scented wood, all sorts of articles of ivory, all varieties of objects of costly woods, bronze, iron, and marble; [Ezek. 27:12, 13, 22.]

13 Of cinnamon, spices, incense, ointment *and* perfume, and frankincense, of wine and olive oil, fine flour and wheat; of cattle and sheep, horses and conveyances; and of slaves (the bodies) and souls of men!

14 The ripe fruits *and* delicacies for which your soul longed have gone from you, and all your luxuries *and* dainties, your elegance *and* splendor

are lost to you, never again to be recovered *or* experienced!

15 The dealers who handled these articles, who grew wealthy through their business with her, will stand a long way off, in terror of her doom *and* torment, weeping and grieving aloud, and saying,

16 Alas, alas for the great city that was robed in fine linen, in purple and scarlet, bedecked *and* glittering with gold, with precious stones, and with pearls! [Ezek. 27:31, 36.]

17 Because in one [single] hour all the vast wealth has been destroyed (wiped out). And all ship captains *and* pilots, navigators and all who live by seafaring, the crews and all who ply their trade on the sea, stood a long way off, [Isa. 23:14; Ezek. 27:26–30.]

18 And exclaimed as they watched the smoke of her burning, What city could be compared to the great city!

19 And they threw dust on their heads as they wept and grieved, exclaiming, Woe *and* alas, for the great city, where all who had ships on the sea grew rich [through her extravagance] from her great wealth! In one single hour she has been destroyed *and* has become a desert! [Ezek. 27:30–34.]

20 Rejoice (celebrate) over her, O heaven! O saints (people of God) and apostles and prophets, because God has executed vengeance for you upon her! [Isa. 44:23; Jer. 51:48.]

21 Then a single powerful angel took up a boulder like a great millstone and flung it into the sea, crying, With such violence shall Babylon the great city be hurled down to destruction and shall never again be found. [Jer. 51:63, 64; Ezek. 26:21.]

22 And the sound of harpists and minstrels and flute players and trumpeters shall never again be heard in you, and no skilled artisan of any craft shall ever again be found in you,

and the sound of the millstone shall never again be heard in you. [Isa. 24:8; Ezek. 26:13.]

23 And never again shall the light of a lamp shine in you, and the voice of bridegroom and bride shall never be heard in you again; for your businessmen were the great and prominent men of the earth, and by your magic spells and poisonous charm all nations were led astray (seduced and deluded).

24 And in her was found the blood of prophets and of saints, and of all those who have been slain (slaughtered) on earth. [Jer. 51:49.]

CHAPTER 19

AFTER THIS I heard what sounded like a mighty shout of a great crowd in heaven, exclaiming, Hallelujah (praise the Lord)! Salvation and glory (splendor and majesty) and power (dominion and authority) [belong] to our God!

2 Because His judgments (His condemnation and punishment, His sentences of doom) are true and sound and just and upright. He has judged (convicted, pronounced sentence, and doomed) the great and notorious harlot (idolatress) who corrupted and demoralized and poisoned the earth with her lewdness and adultery (idolatry). And He has avenged (visited on her the penalty for) the blood of His servants at her hand. [Deut. 32:43.]

3 And again they shouted, Hallelujah (praise the Lord)! The smoke of her [burning] shall continue to ascend forever and ever (through the eternities of the eternities). [Isa. 34:10.]

4 Then the twenty-four elders [of 'the heavenly Sanhedrin] and the four living creatures fell prostrate and worshiped [paying divine honors to] God, Who sits on the throne, saying, Amen! Hallelujah (praise the Lord)!

5 Then from the throne there came a voice, saying, Praise our God, all you servants of His, you who reverence Him, both small and great! [Ps. 115:13.]

6 After that I heard what sounded like the shout of a vast throng, like the boom of many pounding waves, and like the roar of terrific and mighty peals of thunder, exclaiming, Hallelujah (praise the Lord)! For now the Lord our God the Omnipotent (the All-Ruler) reigns!

7 Let us rejoice and shout for joy [exulting and triumphant]! Let us celebrate and ascribe to Him glory and honor, for the marriage of the Lamb [at last] has come, and His bride has prepared herself. [Ps. 118:24.]

8 She has been permitted to dress in fine (radiant) linen, dazzling and white—for the fine linen is (signifies, represents) the righteousness (the upright, just, and godly living, deeds, and conduct, and right standing with God) of the saints (God's holy people).

9 Then [the angel] said to me, Write this down: Blessed (happy, 'to be envied) are those who are summoned (invited, called) to the marriage supper of the Lamb. And he said to me [further], These are the true words (the genuine and exact declarations) of God.

10 Then I fell prostrate at his feet to worship (to pay divine honors) to him, but he [restrained me] and said, Refrain! [You must not do that!] I am [only] another servant with you and your brethren who have [accepted and hold] the testimony borne by Jesus. Worship God! For the substance (essence) of the truth revealed by Jesus is the spirit of all prophecy

r George R. Berry, *Greek-English New Testament Lexicon.*   s Alexander Souter, *Pocket Lexicon.*

[the vital breath, the inspiration of all inspired preaching and interpretation of the divine will and purpose, including both mine and yours].

11 After that I saw heaven opened, and behold, a white horse [appeared]! The One Who was riding it is called Faithful (Trustworthy, Loyal, Incorruptible, Steady) and True, and He passes judgment and wages war in righteousness (holiness, justice, and uprightness). [Ezek. 1:1.]

12 His eyes [blaze] like a flame of fire, and on His head are many kingly crowns (diadems); and He has a title (name) inscribed which He alone knows *or* can understand. [Dan. 10:6.]

13 He is dressed in a robe dyed by ⁱdipping in blood, and the title by which He is called is The Word of God.

14 And the troops of heaven, clothed in fine linen, dazzling and clean, followed Him on white horses.

15 From His mouth goes forth a sharp sword with which He can smite (afflict, strike) the nations; and He will shepherd *and* control them with a staff (scepter, rod) of iron. He will tread the winepress of the fierceness of the wrath *and* indignation of God the All-Ruler (the Almighty, the Omnipotent). [Ps. 2:9.]

16 And on His garment (robe) and on His thigh He has a name (title) inscribed, KING OF KINGS AND LORD OF LORDS. [Deut. 10:17; Dan. 2:47.]

17 Then I saw a single angel stationed in the sun's ᵘlight, and with a mighty voice he shouted to all the birds that fly across the sky, Come, gather yourselves together for the great supper of God, [Ezek. 39:4, 17–20.]

18 That you may feast on the flesh of rulers, the flesh of generals *and* captains, the flesh of powerful *and*

mighty men, the flesh of horses and their riders, and the flesh of all humanity, both free and slave, both small and great!

19 Then I saw the beast and the rulers *and* leaders of the earth with their troops mustered to go into battle *and* make war against Him Who is mounted on the horse and against His troops.

20 And the beast was seized *and* overpowered, and with him the false prophet who in his presence had worked wonders *and* performed miracles by which he led astray those who had accepted *or* permitted to be placed upon them the stamp (mark) of the beast and those who paid homage *and* gave divine honors to his statue. Both of them were hurled alive into the fiery lake that burns *and* blazes with brimstone.

21 And the rest were killed with the sword that issues from the mouth of Him Who is mounted on the horse, and all the birds fed ravenously *and* glutted themselves with their flesh.

CHAPTER 20

THEN I saw an angel descending from heaven; he was holding the key of the Abyss (the bottomless pit) and a great chain was in his hand.

2 And he gripped *and* overpowered the dragon, that old serpent [of primeval times], who is the devil and Satan, and [securely] bound him for a thousand years.

3 Then he hurled him into the Abyss (the bottomless pit) and closed it and sealed it above him, so that he should no longer lead astray *and* deceive *and* seduce the nations until the thousand years were at an end. After that he must be liberated for a short time.

4 Then I saw thrones, and sitting on them were those to whom authori-

---

t Some ancient manuscripts read "sprinkled with blood."   u Joseph Thayer, *A Greek-English Lexicon.*

ty to act as judges *and* to pass sentence was entrusted. Also I saw the souls of those who had been slain with axes [beheaded] for their witnessing to Jesus and [for preaching and testifying] for the Word of God, and who had refused to pay homage to the beast or his statue and had not accepted his mark *or* permitted it to be stamped on their foreheads or on their hands. And they lived again and ruled with Christ (the Messiah) a thousand years. [Dan. 7:9, 22, 27.]

5 The remainder of the dead were not restored to life again until the thousand years were completed. This is the first resurrection.

6 Blessed (happy, ʷto be envied) and holy (spiritually whole, of unimpaired innocence and proved virtue) is the person who takes part (shares) in the first resurrection! Over them the second death exerts no power *or* authority, but they shall be ministers of God and of Christ (the Messiah), and they shall rule along with Him a thousand years.

7 And when the thousand years are completed, Satan will be released from his place of confinement,

8 And he will go forth to deceive *and* seduce *and* lead astray the nations which are in the four quarters of the earth—Gog and Magog—to muster them for war; their number is like the sand of the sea. [Ezek. 38:2, 9, 15, 22.]

9 And they swarmed up over the broad plain of the earth and encircled the fortress (camp) of God's people (the saints) and the beloved city; but fire descended from heaven and consumed them. [II Kings 1:10–12; Ezek. 38:2, 22.]

10 Then the devil who had led them astray [deceiving and seducing them] was hurled into the fiery lake of burn-

ing brimstone, where the beast and false prophet were; and they will be tormented day and night forever and ever (through the ages of the ages).

11 Then I saw a great white throne and the One Who was seated upon it, from Whose presence *and* from the sight of Whose face earth and sky fled away, and no place was found for them.

12 I [also] saw the dead, great and small; they stood before the throne, and books were opened. Then another book was opened, which is [the Book] of Life. And the dead were judged (sentenced) by what they had done [ʷtheir whole way of feeling and acting, their aims and endeavors] in accordance with what was recorded in the books.

13 And the sea delivered up the dead who were in it, death and Hades (ˣthe state of death or disembodied existence) surrendered the dead in them, and all were tried *and* their cases determined by what they had done [according to their motives, aims, and works].

14 Then death and Hades (ˣthe state of death or disembodied existence) were thrown into the lake of fire. This is the second death, the lake of fire.

15 And if anyone's [name] was not found recorded in the Book of Life, he was hurled into the lake of fire.

CHAPTER 21

THEN I saw a new ʷsky(heaven) and a new earth, for the former ʷsky and the former earth had passed away (vanished), and there no longer existed any sea. [Isa. 65:17; 66:22.]

2 And I saw the holy city, the new Jerusalem, descending out of heaven from God, all arrayed like a bride

v Alexander Souter, *Pocket Lexicon.*   w Joseph Thayer, *A Greek-English Lexicon.*   x James Orr et al., eds., *The International Standard Bible Encyclopedia.*

beautified *and* adorned for her husband;

3 Then I heard a mighty voice from the throne *and* I perceived its distinct words, saying, See! the abode of God is with men, and He will live (encamp, tent) among them; and they shall be His people, and God shall personally be with them and be their God. [Ezek. 37:27.]

4 God will wipe away every tear from their eyes; and death shall be no more, neither shall there be anguish (sorrow and mourning) nor grief nor pain any more, for the old conditions *and* the former order of things have passed away. [Isa. 25:8; 35:10.]

5 And He Who is seated on the throne said, See! I make all things new. Also He said, Record this, for these sayings are faithful (accurate, incorruptible, and trustworthy) and true (genuine). [Isa. 43:19.]

6 And He [further] said to me, It is done! I am the Alpha and the Omega, the Beginning and the End. To the thirsty I [Myself] will give water without price from the fountain (springs) of the water of Life. [Isa. 55:1.]

7 He who is victorious shall inherit all these things, and I will be God to him and he shall be My son.

8 But as for the cowards *and* the ignoble *and* the contemptible *and* the cravenly lacking in courage *and* the cowardly submissive, and as for the unbelieving and faithless, and as for the depraved and defiled with abominations, and as for murderers and the lewd *and* adulterous and the practicers of magic arts and the idolaters (those who give supreme devotion to anyone or anything other than God) and all liars (those who knowingly convey untruth by word or deed)— [all of these shall have] their part in the lake that blazes with fire and brimstone. This is the second death. [Isa. 30:33.]

9 Then one of the seven angels who had the seven bowls filled with the seven final plagues (afflictions, calamities) came and spoke to me. He said, Come with me! I will show you the bride, the Lamb's wife.

10 Then in the Spirit He conveyed me away to a vast and lofty mountain and exhibited to me the holy (hallowed, consecrated) city of Jerusalem descending out of heaven from God, [Ezek. 40:2.]

11 Clothed in God's glory [in all its splendor and radiance]. The luster of it resembled a rare *and* most precious jewel, like jasper, shining clear as crystal.

12 It had a massive and high wall with twelve [large] gates, and at the gates [there were stationed] twelve angels, and [on the gates] the names of the twelve tribes of the sons of Israel were written: [Exod. 28:21; Ezek 48:30 35.]

13 On the east side three gates, on the north side three gates, on the south side three gates, and on the west side three gates.

14 And the wall of the city had twelve foundation [stones], and on them the twelve names of the twelve apostles of the Lamb.

15 And he who spoke to me had a golden measuring reed (rod) to measure the city and its gates and its wall. [Ezek. 40:5.]

16 The city lies in a square, its length being the same as its width. And he measured the city with his reed—12,000 stadia (about 1,500 miles); its length and width and height are the same.

17 He measured its wall also—144 cubits (about 72 yards) by a man's measure [³of a cubit from his elbow

to his third fingertip], which is [the measure] of the angel.

18 The wall was built of jasper, while the city [itself was of] pure gold, clear and transparent like glass.

19 The foundation [stones] of the wall of the city were ornamented with all of the precious stones. The first foundation [stone] was jasper, the second sapphire, the third chalcedony (or white agate), the fourth emerald. [Isa. 54:11, 12.]

20 The fifth onyx, the sixth sardius, the seventh chrysolite, the eighth beryl, the ninth topaz, the tenth chrysoprase, the eleventh jacinth, the twelfth amethyst.

21 And the twelve gates were twelve pearls, each separate gate being built of one solid pearl. And the main street (the broadway) of the city was of gold as pure *and* translucent as glass.

22 I saw no temple in the city, for the Lord God Omnipotent [Himself] and the Lamb [Himself] are its temple.

23 And the city has no need of the sun nor of the moon to give light to it, for the splendor *and* radiance (glory) of God illuminate it, and the Lamb is its lamp. [Isa. 24:23; 60:1, 19.]

24 The nations shall walk by its light and the rulers *and* leaders of the earth shall bring into it their glory.

25 And its gates shall never be closed by day, and there shall be no night there. [Isa. 60:11.]

26 They shall bring the glory (the splendor and majesty) and the honor of the nations into it.

27 But nothing that defiles *or* profanes *or* is ²unwashed shall ever enter it, nor anyone who commits abominations (unclean, detestable, morally repugnant things) or practices falsehood, but only those whose names

are recorded in the Lamb's Book of Life.

CHAPTER 22

THEN HE showed me the river whose waters give life, sparkling like crystal, flowing out from the throne of God and of the Lamb

2 Through the middle of the broadway of the city; also, on either side of the river was the tree of life with its twelve varieties of fruit, yielding each month its fresh crop; and the leaves of the tree were for the healing *and* the restoration of the nations. [Gen. 2:9.]

3 There shall no longer exist there anything that is accursed (detestable, foul, offensive, impure, hateful, or horrible). But the throne of God and of the Lamb shall be in it, and His servants shall worship Him [pay divine honors to Him and do Him holy service]. [Zech. 14:21.]

4 They shall see His face, and His name shall be on their foreheads. [Ps. 17:15.]

5 And there shall be no more night; they have no need for lamplight or sunlight, for the Lord God will illuminate them *and* be their light, and they shall reign [as kings] forever and ever (through the eternities of the eternities).

6 And he [of the seven angels further] said to me, These statements are reliable (worthy of confidence) and genuine (true). And the Lord, the God of the spirits of the prophets, has sent His messenger (angel) to make known *and* exhibit to His servants what must soon come to pass.

7 And behold, I am coming speedily. Blessed (happy and ²to be envied) is he who observes *and* lays to heart *and* keeps the truths of the prophecy (the predictions, consolations, and

---

z Alexander Souter. *Pocket Lexicon.*

warnings) contained in this [little] book.

8 And I, John, am he who heard and witnessed these things. And when I heard and saw them, I fell prostrate before the feet of the messenger (angel) who showed them to me, to worship him.

9 But he said to me, Refrain! [You must not do that!] I am [only] a fellow servant along with yourself and with your brethren the prophets and with those who are mindful of *and* practice [the truths contained in] the messages of this book. Worship God!

10 And he [further] told me, Do not seal up the words of the prophecy of this book *and* make no secret of them, for the time ᵃwhen things are brought to a crisis *and* the period of their fulfillment is near.

11 He who is unrighteous (unjust, wicked), let him be unrighteous still; and he who is filthy (vile, impure), let him be filthy still; and he who is righteous (just, upright, in right standing with God), let him do right still; and he who is holy, let him be holy still. [Dan. 12:10.]

12 Behold, I am coming soon, and I shall bring My wages *and* rewards with Me, to repay *and* render to each one just what his own actions *and* his own work merit. [Isa. 40:10; Jer. 17:10.]

13 I am the Alpha and the Omega, the First and the Last (the Before all and the End of all). [Isa. 44:6; 48:12.]

14 Blessed (happy and ᵇto be envied) are those who cleanse their garments, that they may have the authority *and* right to [approach] the tree of life and to enter through the gates into the city. [Gen. 2:9; 3:22, 24.]

15 [But] without are the dogs and those who practice sorceries (magic arts) and impurity [the lewd, adulterers] and the murderers and idolaters and everyone who loves and deals in falsehood (untruth, error, deception, cheating).

16 I, Jesus, have sent My messenger (angel) to you to witness *and* to give you assurance of these things for the churches (assemblies). I am the Root (the Source) and the Offspring of David, the radiant *and* brilliant Morning Star. [Isa. 11:1, 10.]

17 The [Holy] Spirit and the bride (the church, the true Christians) say, Come! And let him who is listening say, Come! And let everyone come who is thirsty [who is painfully conscious of his need ᵃof those things by which the soul is refreshed, supported, and strengthened]; and whoever [earnestly] desires to do it, let him come, take, appropriate, *and* drink the water of Life without cost. [Isa. 55:1.]

18 I [personally solemnly] warn everyone who listens to the statements of the prophecy [the ᵃpredictions and the consolations and admonitions pertaining to them] in this book: If anyone shall add anything to them, God will add *and* lay upon him the plagues (the afflictions and the calamities) that are recorded *and* described in this book.

19 And if anyone cancels *or* takes away from the statements of the book of this prophecy [these ᵃpredictions relating to Christ's kingdom and its speedy triumph, together with the consolations and admonitions or warnings pertaining to them], God will cancel *and* take away from him his share in the tree of life and in the city of holiness (purity and hallowedness), which are described *and* promised in this book.

20 He Who gives this warning *and* affirms *and* testifies to these things

a Joseph Thayer, *A Greek-English Lexicon.*   **b** Alexander Souter, *Pocket Lexicon.*

says, Yes (it is true). [Surely] I am coming quickly (swiftly, speedily). Amen (so let it be)! Yes, come, Lord Jesus!

21 The grace (blessing and favor) of the Lord Jesus *Christ (the Messiah)* be ᶜwith all the saints (God's holy people, ᵈthose set apart for God, to be, as it were, exclusively His). Amen (so let it be)!

---

c Some manuscripts have "be with all," while others have "be with the saints."   d Joseph Thayer, *A Greek-English Lexicon.*

BIBLIOGRAPHY

This bibliography has been developed as a companion to the footnotes of
The Amplified New Testament. Just a quick glance at the sources indexed will
reveal the thousands of hours of research that went into the making of The
Amplified New Testament.

The bibliography is broken down into several categories: Bible Versions;
Greek Testaments; Word Studies and Lexical Aids; Commentaries; Other
Reference Works; General Resources. In addition, there is a section entitled
"Persons Cited," with a brief description of the individual's background.

In spite of rigorous efforts to recover information about the sources used,
the bibliographic material will be incomplete in some cases. However, there is
enough in the bibliography to make it a useful tool for understanding the
footnotes.

BIBLE VERSIONS

The American Standard Version. New York: Thomas Nelson & Sons, 1901.
Bede, translated portions of the Bible from Latin into Old English. A.D. 735.
The Cambridge Bible for Schools and Colleges. 49 vols. 1878-1952.
Coverdale, Miles, trans. *The Coverdale Bible*. 1535.
Darby, John, trans. *The Bible, a New Translation*. N.T., 1871; O.T., 1890.
Jerome, trans. *The Latin Vulgate*. 4th century A.D.
The King James Version. 1611.
Knox, Ronald, trans. *The Holy Bible: A Translation from the Latin Vulgate*. New York: Sheed &
    Ward, N.T., 1944; O.T., 1948-50.
Lamsa, George M., trans. *The Holy Bible from ancient Eastern manuscripts*. Philadelphia: A.J.
    Holman Co., N.T., 1940.
The Old Testament Translated from The Septuagint. 2 vols. London: Skeffington & Son, 1904.
Phillips, J.B., trans. *New Testament in Modern English: Letters to Young Churches; a translation of
    the New Testament Epistles*. New York: Macmillan, 1951.
Rotherham, Joseph B., trans. *The Emphasized Bible*. New York: Fleming H. Revell Company, N.T.,
    1872; O.T., 1902.
Tyndale, William, trans. *The Tyndale Bible* (first printing of a New Testament into English). 1526.
Verkuyl, Gerrit, trans. *The Berkeley Version in Modern English*. Grand Rapids: Zondervan Publishing
    House, N.T., 1945; O.T., 1953.
Way, Arthur S., trans. *Way's Epistles: The Letters of St. Paul to Seven Churches and Three Friends*.
    London: Macmillan, 1901 (revised 1906, Hebrews added).
Wesley, John, trans. *The New Testament*. London: Epworth Press, 1755.
Williams, Charles B., trans. *The New Testament: A Translation in the Language of the People*.
    Chicago: Moody Press, 1950.
Wycliffe, John, trans. *The Wycliffe Bible* (first translation of the Bible into English). 1380.

GREEK TESTAMENTS

Alford, Henry. *The Greek New Testament, with Notes*. 5 vols. London: Rivingtons, 1857-1861.
Bengel, Johann. *Gnomon Novi Testamenti*. 3 vols. Edinburgh: T.& T. Clark, 1877.
Nicoll, W. Robertson, ed. *The Expositor's Greek New Testament*. 5 vols. London: Hodder &
    Stoughton, 1897-1910.

WORD STUDIES AND LEXICAL AIDS

Abbott-Smith, G. *Manual Greek Lexicon of the New Testament*. Edinburgh: T.& T. Clark, 1937.

Berry, George Ricker. *Greek-English New Testament Lexicon*. Grand Rapids: Zondervan Publishing House, 1966.

Cremer, Hermann. *Biblico-Theological Lexicon of New Testament Greek*. Edinburgh: T. & T. Clark, 1895.

Hickie, W.J. *Greek-English Lexicon to the New Testament*. New York: Macmillan, 1921.

Kennedy, H.A.A. *Sources of New Testament Greek*.

Moulton, James Hope, and George Milligan. *The Vocabulary of the Greek Testament*. London: Hodder & Stoughton, 1952.

Robertson, Archibald Thomas. *Word Pictures in the New Testament*. New York: R.R. Smith Inc., 1930-1933.

Schmidt, J.H. Heinrich. *Synonymik der Griechischen Sprache*. 1886.

Souter, Alexander. *Pocket Lexicon of the Greek New Testament*. London: Oxford University Press, 1916.

Thayer, Joseph Henry. *A Greek-English Lexicon of the New Testament*. New York: American Book Co., 1889.

Trench, Richard C. *Synonyms of the New Testament*. New York: Blakeman & Mason, 1859.

Vincent, Marvin. *Word Studies in the New Testament*. 4 vols. New York: C. Scribner's Sons, 1887-1900.

Wuest, Kenneth. *Word Studies in the Greek New Testament*. Multivolume: *Mark in the Greek New Testament; Golden Nuggets from the Greek New Testament; Treasures from the Greek New Testament; Bypaths in the Greek New Testament; Untranslatable Riches from the Greek New Testament; Hebrews in the Greek New Testament*. Grand Rapids: Wm. B. Eerdmans Co., 1966.

Young, Robert. *Analytical Concordance to the Bible*. New York: American Book Co., 1881.

COMMENTARIES

Barnes, Albert. *Notes on the New Testament*. 12 vols. Grand Rapids: Baker Book House, 1949-1957.

Clarke, Adam. *The Holy Bible with A Commentary and Critical Notes*. 6 vols. New York: G. Lane & C.B. Tippett, 1837-1847.

Gray, James C., and George M. Adams. *Bible Commentary*. 5 vols. Grand Rapids: Zondervan Publishing House, n.d.

Henry, Matthew. *Commentary on the Holy Bible*. Philadelphia: Lippincott, 1856.

Jamieson, Robert, A.R. Fausset, and David Brown. *A Commentary, Critical, Experimental and Practical, on the Old and New Testaments*. 6 vols. Grand Rapids: Wm. B. Eerdmans Co., 1935.

Lightfoot, Joseph P. *Notes on the Epistles of Saint Paul*. London: Macmillan, 1869.

_____. *Saint Paul's Epistle to the Philippians*. London: Macmillan, 1908.

_____. *Saint Paul's Epistle to the Colossians and Philemon*. London: Macmillan, 1886.

Meyer, H.A.W. *Commentary on the New Testament*. 11 vols. Edinburgh: T. & T. Clark, 1883-1884.

Speaker's Commentary. 10 vols. London: J. Murray, 1871-1881.

Swete, Henry Barclay. *The Gospel According to Saint Mark*. London: Macmillian, 1898.

Trench, Richard C. *Notes on the Miracles of our Lord*. London: Parker, 1862.

_____. *Studies in the Gospels*. 1867.

Westcott, Brooke Foss. *The Epistles of Saint John*. Grand Rapids: Wm. B. Eerdmans, 1955.

OTHER REFERENCE WORKS

Davis, John D. *A Dictionary of the Bible*. Philadelphia: Westminster, 1936.

Exell, Joseph S., ed. *The Biblical Illustrator*. 28 vols. Grand Rapids: Baker Book House, 1956.

Orr, James et al., eds. *The International Standard Bible Encyclopedia*. 5 vols. Chicago: The Howard Severance Company, 1930.

Webster, Noah. *New International Dictionary of the English Language*. Springfield: G. & C. Merriam Company, 1961.

GENERAL RESOURCES

Farrar, Frederick W. *The Life and Work of Saint Paul*. 2 vols. New York: E.P. Dutton and company, 1889.

Lamsa, George M. *Gospel Light: comments on the teachings of Jesus from Aramaic and unchanged Eastern customs*. Philadelphia: A.J. Holman Co, 1936.

Murray, John. *The Sovereignty of God*. Grand Rapids: Zondervan Publishing House, 1940.

Warfield, B.B. *Biblical Doctrines*. London: Oxford University Press, 1929.

PERSONS CITED

Aristotle, 4th century B.C. Greek philosopher.

Bengel, Johann, Lutheran minister and theologian (1687-1752).

Calvin, John, 16th century Protestant Reformer (1509-1564).

Clark, George Whitefield, Scripture harmonist (1831-1911).

Chrysostom, John, 4th century Doctor of the Greek Church.

Doddridge, Philip, British Nonconformist minister, educator, author, and hymn writer (1702-1751).

Godet, Frederic L., Swiss Reformed theologian and exegete (1812-1900).

Gould, Ezra Palmer, Professor of New Testament literature (1841-1900).

Gurnall, William, British theologian and Bible commentator (1617-1679).

Kypke, G.D., Bible scholar (1724-1779).

Lumby, J. Rawson, Church historian and Bible commentator (1831-1895).

Luther, Martin, leader of the German Reformation (1483-1546).

Macknight, James, Church of Scotland minister and Bible translator (1721-1800).

Melanchthon, Philip, German Reformer, theologian, and educator (1497-1560).

Meyer, H.A.W., German Protestant minister and New Testament scholar (1800-1873).

Origen, 3rd century theologian of the early Greek Church.

Richard of St. Victor, 12th century scholar and mystic.

Schmidt, J.H. Heinrich, German classical language scholar (1834-??).

Taylor, Jeremy, Anglican bishop and writer (1613-1667).

Westcott, Brooke F., New Testament scholar (1825-1901).